AA Lifestyle Guides in association with Moat Hou

are giving away 30 wee for

in 6 free prize draws

5 winners will be drawn every 2 months; on the last day of:

- December 1997
- February 1998
- April 1998
- June 1998
- August 1998
- October 1998

Choose your "Views of Britain" weekend break from a selection of over 50 properties in the Moat House Hotels group, a number of which enjoy water-front locations.

Moat House Hotels offer the highest standards of service and hospitality to ensure that your stay is one to remember. Selected hotels offer Club Moativation health and fitness clubs, where facilities include swimming pool, jacuzzi, sauna, solarium and fully equipped gym. At a few you'll even find a golf course!

For more information on Moat House Hotels or for your free copy of their "Views of Britain" weekend breaks brochure, call **0541 556 556** quoting "AA Lifestyle Guides".

MOAT HOUSE HOTELS

HOW TO ENTER

Just complete (in capitals, please) and send off this card or, alternatively, send your name and address on a **stamped** postcard to the address overleaf (no purchase required). Entries limited to one per household and to residents of the UK and Republic of Ireland. This card will require a stamp if posted in the Republic of Ireland.

MR/MRS/MISS/MS/OTHER, PLEASE STATE: ____________________

NAME: ____________________

ADDRESS: ____________________

POSTCODE: ____________________

TEL.NOS: ____________________

Are you an AA Member ? Yes/No

Have you bought this or any other AA Lifestyle Guide before? Yes/No

If yes, please indicate the year of the last edition you bought:

The AA Hotel Guide	19____	AA Camping and Caravanning (Europe)	19____
AA Best Restaurants	19____	AA Hotels in France	19____
AA Bed and Breakfast Guide	19____	AA Bed & Breakfast in France	19____
AA Camping & Caravanning (Britain & Ireland)	19____	AA Best Pubs & Inns	19____

If you do not wish to receive further information or special offers from

AA Publishing ☐ Moat House Hotels ☐ please tick the box

BPI98

Terms and Conditions

1. Five winners will be drawn for each of six prize draws to take place on 31 December 1997, 28 February, 30 April, 30 June, 31 August, 31 October 1998.

2. Closing date for receipt of entries is midday on the relevant draw date. Final close date for receipt of entries is 31 October 1998.

3. Entries received after any draw date except the final one will go forward into the next available draw. Entries will be placed in one draw only. Only one entry per household accepted.

4. Winners will be notified by post within 14 days of the relevant draw date. Prizes will be valid for 3 months from the relevant draw date. Prizes are not transferable and there will be no cash alternative.

5. Each prize consists of a two night Views of Britain weekend break at a Moat House Hotel. The prize includes two nights' accommodation and full breakfast for two people sharing a twin or double bedded room. The prize does not include dinner, lunch or additional expenses such as drinks or travelling expenses Any additional expenses will be charged as taken and payable on departure.

6. All hotel accommodation, services and facilities are provided by Moat House Hotels and AA Publishing is not party to your agreement with Moat House Hotels in this regard.

7. The prize draw is open to anyone resident in the UK or the Republic of Ireland over the age of 18 other than employees of the Automobile Association or Moat House Hotels, their subsidiary companies, their families or agents

8. For a list of winners, please send a stamped, self-addressed envelope to AA Lifestyle Guide winners, Publishing Admin, Fanum House, Basing View, Basingstoke, Hants RG21 4EA.

9. If this card is posted in the Republic of Ireland it must have a stamp.

BUSINESS REPLY SERVICE
Licence No BZ 343

PLEASE NOTE: Requires a stamp if posted in Republic of Ireland

2

AA Lifestyle Guide Prize Draw

AA PUBLISHING
FANUM HOUSE
BASING VIEW
BASINGSTOKE
HANTS RG21 4EA

AA

Best Pubs & Inns 1998

The Globe, Linslade, Bedfordshire, page 91

Produced by AA Publishing

Maps prepared by the Cartographic Department of
The Automobile Association

Assistant Editors: Lin Hutton, Jim Barker

Cover photograph by Andy Williams Photo Library.
Feature photography:, The Glenelg Inn p310, Harvey & Son Ltd p12, King & Barnes Ltd p10, p12, Pictures Colour Library p152, p152/3, p226/7, Traquair House Brewery p331 Wadworth & Co Ltd p11, p12/13.

Editorial contributors: Jim Barker, Christopher Blackford, Bernadette Faurie, Sarah Hudson, Julia Hynard

Head of Advertisement Sales
Christopher Heard: Tel 0990 448866 Direct line 01256 491544

Advertisement Production
Karen Weeks: Tel 0990 448866 Direct line 01256 491545

Typeset by Avonset, Midsomer Norton, Nr Bath

Printed and bound by Jarrolds Book Printing, Norfolk.

The contents of this book are believed correct at the time of printing. Nevertheless, the Publisher cannot be held responsible for any errors or omissions or for changes in the details given in this guide or for the consequences of any reliance on the information provided in the same. Although every effort has been made to ensure accuracy we always welcome any information from readers to assistin such efforts and to keep the book up to date.

A CIP catalogue record for this book is available from the British Library

Published by AA Publishing, which is a trading name of Automobile Association Developments Limited whose registered office is Norfolk House, Priestley Road, Basingstoke, Hampshire RG24 9NY, Registered number 1878835.

ISBN 0 7495 1583 X Softback AA Ref 59909
ISBN 0 7495 1768 9 Hardback AA Ref 10132

Contents

BREWED WITH PURE HONEY
WAGGLE DANCE
TRADITIONAL HONEY BEER
5% vol
STRONG, SMOOTH AND DELICIOUS

How to Use this Guide

SYMBOLS AND ABBREVIATIONS

- Accommodation
- Atmosphere
- Children welcome
- Credit cards taken
- Dogs welcome
- Garden
- Horses and their riders welcome
- Quiet location
- Telephone number
- Vegetarian food available
- Walkers welcome

BLUE TINT PANEL
Blue tint panel indicates a waterside location

YELLOW TINT PANEL
Yellow tint panel indicates a village restaurant, bistro or an establishment that serves food but is not a public house.

Establishment name/Symbols (*see above*)	**Any Pub**
Town name	*ANY TOWN*
Map reference	*Map 3 F7*
Address & post code	**Any Road GU27 0HZ**
Telephone number	**01798 422870**
Description	Very much a dining pub, this popular venue is renowned for its warm welcome and hearty range of good-value and well-cooked meals. Good quality meat, fish, game plus vegetarian dishes vary according to season; puds are always good. 2 comfortable bedrooms. Speedy service with a smile. Principal Beers: Otter, Wadworth 6X, Adnams, Royal Oak
Directions	**Directions** 3m E of Any Town
Brewery name or Free House	**Brakspear**
Opening times	**Open** 11–3 6–11 (Sun 10.30pm)
Times when food is served	**Bar food** 12–2 7–9.30 Av main course £5
Av. cost of meal	**Restaurant** 12–2 7–9.30 Av 3 course à la carte £15.75 Av 4 course fixed price £8.50
Room tariff	**Accommodation** s £18 d £30
Credit cards accepted. *See opposite*	

REGIONS
Entries are located in one of six regions:

- **West Country •**
- **South & South East England •**
- **Central England & East Anglia •**
- **Wales & The Marches •**
- **Northern England •**
- **Scotland •**

COUNTIES
Counties are listed alphabetically within each Region.

PLACE NAMES
Place names are listed alphabetically within each County. Please note that there have recently been many county changes, particularly in Scotland and Wales, and entries are listed in their new counties.

MAP REFERENCE
The reference number denotes the map page number in the atlas section at the back of the book and the National Grid reference

TELEPHONE NUMBERS
Telephone numbers may be changed during the currency of this Guide in some areas. In case of difficulty check with the operator or Directory Enquiries.

Explanation of the symbols

ATMOSPHERE
Expect to find a selection of such features as antique furniture, old beams, open fires or perhaps a thatched roof.

CHILDREN WELCOME
This symbol indicates that the pub welcomes children, usually in certain areas only, some specify well behaved children only. There may be a children's play area in the garden, but check beforehand. If you have very young children ask about provisions like high chairs or cots if you are staying overnight. Alcohol cannot be bought or drunk until the age of 18.

DOGS WELCOME
Well behaved dogs on leads are permitted at the Manager's discretion. Please note that dogs may only be allowed in specific areas.

GARDEN
A garden is available for customers' use in good weather. There may be a children's play area or other facilities.

HORSES AND THEIR RIDERS WELCOME
There is room in the car park or other designated area for horses and their riders whilst they are taking refreshment. Horses should not be left be unattended by a competent handler.

QUIET LOCATION
The establishment is considered by the proprietor to be in a quiet and peaceful location

VEGETARIAN FOOD AVAILABLE
Vegetarian meals are always available.

WALKERS WELCOME
Although walkers are welcome, their muddy boots may not be and these should be left where indicated by the proprietor.

WATERFRONT LOCATION
All establishments highlighted by a blue tint panel are next to water. This could be the sea or a lake, loch, canal or river.

BREWERY
Brewery indicates the name of the Brewery the pub is 'tied' to. The extent of the 'tie' depends on whether the pub is managed by employees of the Brewery or leased to a tenant. Tenants generally have more freedom to buy drinks, including beer, from other sources.

FREE HOUSE
Free House indicates that the pub is independently owned and run and in theory can buy drinks from any brewery.

VILLAGE RESTAURANT
Where there is no brewery or free house listed, then the establishment will be a restaurant or bistro and highlighted by a yellow tint panel.

DIRECTIONS
Directions are given wherever they have been supplied by the proprietor.

OPEN
Open indicates the hours when the establishment is open and closed. Times when food is available may be different (see below).

BAR FOOD
Bar Food indicates the times when bar food is available, and the average price of a main course as supplied by the proprietor.

RESTAURANT
Restaurant indicates the times when restaurant food is available. The average cost of a 3 or 4 course à la carte meal and a 3 or 4 course fixed price menu are shown as supplied by the proprietor.

ACCOMMODATION
Accommodation prices indicate the lowest single room and double room prices per night. En suite bedrooms or adjacent private bathrooms may be available; breakfast may be included in the price, so guests should check when making a reservation. Circumstances and prices may vary during the currency of the Guide.

CREDIT CARDS TAKEN
The major credit cards such as Visa and Master Card are taken where C is shown at the end of each entry. Telephone first to check if you wish to use other cards or charge cards.

WHAT'S IN A NAME?

In the Middle Ages, when few people could read, the law required inns to have names and signs that were instantly recognisable. Faced with this problem, inn-keepers drew on the ready-made collection of heraldic badges and crests, often choosing those of the family on whose estate the inn was built. Many of the heraldic badges themselves derived from medieval Bestiaries - illustrated books of real and imaginary beasts - or from Christian symbolism. This is where we get most of our commonest signs - all those Dragons, Lions, Eagles, Griffins, Unicorns, Harts, Boars, Dolphins, Falcons, Bulls, Swans, Stags, and Talbots (a family name, normally represented by the talbot, a breed of hound), not to mention Mermaids, Stars, Suns, Feathers, Roses, Bells, and Fleur-de-Lis.

Not only great families had badges; medieval guilds, too, had their "logos". The Lamb and Flag represented the Merchants Tailors, the Elephant and Castle, the Cutlers, and the Three Tuns, the Vintners Companies. Down the centuries, as travel became easier and inns multiplied, heraldry continued to provide signs, hence the Miners Arms, Masons Arms, Blockmakers Arms, Brickmakers Arms and so forth. Though such signs are common, they are never commonplace, but full of hidden meanings. Some originally religious signs such like the George and Dragon are still self-explanatory, but others are more enigmatic. The Lamb and Flag seems an odd combination until you know it is the Agnus Dei, the Lamb of God (Jesus Christ) carrying the banner which in Christian art symbolizes His victory over death. And though the Three Crowns in some places may have commemorated the accession of James I, who united England, Wales and Scotland, earlier it symbolized the Three Wise Men of the Nativity story, venerated by pilgrims from all over Europe as the Three Kings of Cologne, where their reputed heads are still preserved as relics in the cathedral.

More unusual than heraldic signs but still fairly widespread are pubs whose names and signboards refer to legends, ballads, songs, nursery rhymes and popular sayings, for example the John Barleycorn, the Green Man, the Dun Cow, the Man in the Moon (in places changed to Man on the Moon after Neil Armstrong's moon landing in 1969), the Cat and Fiddle, the Bird in Hand and the Live and Let Live. Here too belong traditional jokes and satires, such as the Eel's Foot, the Dew Drop (or more obviously Dew Drop Inn), the First and Last, the Hit or Miss, the Triple Plea, the Case is Altered, the Trusty Servant, the Five Alls, the Load of Mischief, the Honest Lawyer and the Silent Woman.

Pubs called the Case is Altered get their name from a phrase first used by the lawyer Edmund Plowden (1518-85) which became a common saying, applied to all sorts of changes. Different stories are told to explain the name wherever it occurs. Pubs called the Load of Mischief or The Mischief are probably imitations of The Man with the Load of Mischief, an ale-house in Oxford Street, London, for which William Hogarth painted the sign. This showed a man carrying a drunken wife on his shoulders, to which she is attached by the chain of wedlock.

Most fascinating for the "pub-spotter" are the often unique pub names which refer to local history or tradition. The Never Turn Back, opened in 1957 next to the old lifeboat shed at Caister-on-Sea, Norfolk, commemorates the night of 13 November 1901, when during a rescue attempt in heavy seas, the lifeboat *Beauchamp* capsized and nine of her crew were lost. When, at the inquest, someone said the lifeboat should not have persisted under such conditions, James Haylett, the former coxswain, who lost his sons that night and dragged his grandson and son-in-law from the surf, replied: "Caister lifeboatmen never turn back".

Less to do with fact than fiction is The Wicked Lady, a free house on Nomansland, a large tract of

common south of Wheathampstead, Hertfordshire. The sign shows a highwaywoman normally identified as Lady Katherine Ferrers, said to have lived in the 18th century at the mansion of Markyate Cell, southwest of Luton. She led a double life, creeping out at night by a secret stairway dressed in men's clothes and a mask, and galloping off on her black horse to rob travellers on the Holyhead road. Her career came to a full stop when she was shot at Nomansland and subsequently found lying dead outside the door to the hidden stair. Her fame was spread far beyond Hertfordshire when she was portrayed by the glamorous "bad girl" of British cinema, Margaret Lockwood, co-starring with James Mason in the utterly romantic black-and-white film The Wicked Lady (1945).

Among pubs whose names have this kind of local reference and repay closer inspection are Turpin's Cave, near Loughton, Essex; the King Coel, Colchester, Essex; the Devil in the Boot, Winslow, Bucks; Rattlebone Inn, Sherston, Wiltshire; the Cuckoo Bush, Gotham, Nottinghamshire; the Widow's Son, Bow, London; the Cauld Lad, Hylton, Tyne and Wear; the Lincoln Imp, Lincoln; the Blind Beggar, Bethnal Green, London; the Whiffler, Norwich; the Devil's Stone, Shebbear, Devon; the Great Stone, Northfield, Birmingham; the Bladud Arms, Bath; the Flying Monk, Malmesbury, Gloucestershire; Tucker's Grave, Radstock, Somerset; and the Pandora, Restronguet Creek, Cornwall. Even seemingly obvious pub names are not always what they seem. The signboards of the Flying Dutchman at Queenborough, Kent and Oulton Broad, Suffolk, show the spectral ship which haunts the Cape of Good Hope and inspired Wagner's opera. However, other pubs of the same name elsewhere carry the famous racehorse, the Flying Dutchman, winner of the Derby in 1849 - in view of other pubs named after racehorses, a more likely reason for one to take this name. Anyone who had never been there might think the White Horse of Burnham Green, Hertfordshire, was just another example of a sign in common use since the 15th century. But here the sign shows a headless horse eerily prancing by moonlight - for this is no ordinary White Horse but a phantom that can be heard at night galloping down nearby White Horse Lane. Again, though the poetic name of the Rose Revived (in Kent and elsewhere), originally referred to the Restoration of Charles II in 1660, at Newbridge, Oxfordshire, the pub is said to have been "revived" by a landlord named Rose.

Local associations are what makes changing pub signs a tricky business. Signboard painters have long given free rein to their imaginations, as at the World's End, King's Road, London, one of several pubs so-called because they originally stood on the edge of a town or parish. Its sign was repainted to show a galleon shooting the waterfall at the world's end, a myth that mariners believed in

before they knew the world was round. This was a witty and successful re-interpretation, but sometimes in repainting a unique local connection is lost. Although the sign of the Wild Man originally referred to the heraldic "woodwose" or wild man of the woods, in two places it acquired special significance. Norwich Wild Man and St Albans Wild Boy are both connected with Peter the Wild Boy, found in 1725 in a forest near Hanover. King George I had Peter brought to the English court, but later sent him to be looked after by a farmer at Haxter End, near Berkhampstead. Hertfordshire. In 1751, Peter wandered off and fetched up in Norwich, where he was imprisoned in the Bridewell as a vagrant. This was nearly the end of the story, for the Bridewell caught fire, and Peter, too simple to save himself, had to be rescued. He was returned to Hertfordshire, where eventually he died and was buried at Northchurch under a headstone marked "Peter the Wild Boy 1785". Strangers to Norwich would never have guessed at the Wild Man's connection with Peter from its last-but one sign, a literal interpretation of the name as a feather-wearing savage. However, the present sign shows Rudyard Kipling's wild boy, Mowgli - a step in the right direction towards its local meaning.

Some odd combinations have arisen from the amalgamation of two signs: the Spyglass and Kettle, Wigmore, Kent, is the result of the amalgamation by the Phoenix Brewery in 1946 of the Lord Nelson (famous for the "spyglass" or telescope to which he turned his blind eye) and the Steam Engine ("kettle") once being applied to iron vessels of any kind. Though the modern trend is to imitate this kind of sign and use "humorous" combinations - "Slug and Lettuce", "Wig and Dickle", "Bull and Spectacles", and so on - uniqueness, aptness and poetry are not dead when it comes to pubs changing signboards: with the oilmen to Yarmouth came "The Rising Flame" (formerly "The Station Stores"), while at Kidlington the former "Railway Inn", in commemoration of Frank Wise, chairman of the parish council and vice-chairman of Oxfordshire County Council, became "The Wise Alderman".

Jennifer Westwood

THE BREWING PROCESS

Andrew Hepworth, Head Brewer, King & Barnes Ltd

The chances are that you've bought this Guide because you enjoy beer, whether it be as cool refreshment after a long walk or as the accompaniment to a pub meal. But how much do you know about the process behind the pint? What, for example, does 'sparging' involve, what is a 'mash tun', and where does the sturgeon fish fit in? In this feature we explore how beer goes from the basic ingredients of malt, hops, yeast and water, to the finished pint standing before you on the bar.

Horses and dray outside King & Barnes Brewery, Horsham, West Sussex

Delivery of malt barley (Wadworth)

Hops are added to the wort in the copper (Wadworth)

THE BASIC INGREDIENTS

MALT is the basic ingredient of beer and is often known as the soul of beer. Malt is partially germinated barley and gives beer its body, sweetness and some of its fruitiness. The barley is steeped in water to induce germination and after a few days rootlets begin to sprout, which makes the starches in the grain soluble. The process is swiftly halted by the kilning process: the roasting kills the growth, enhances the flavour and enriches the colour.

HOPS are the flower of the hop bine, which is part of the nettle and cannabis family, and were introduced in the 16th century for their preservative and seasoning properties. These flavours help produce the aromatic bitter flavour special to British beers, so each brewer carefully selects the variety of hops he uses as each gives a different taste and aroma - some are herby, others are peppery or may have citrus undertones.

WATER in the trade is called the 'liquor'. The water used in the brewing process has to suit the type of beer being produced and certain waters have mineral compositions that suit different styles of beer.

YEAST Each strain of yeast imparts its own subtle characteristics to the beer and turns beer into an alcoholic drink. Brewers guard and preserve their own strain zealously as it may have characterised their beers for many years.

Above: The mash tun (Harveys)

Right: Checking the gravity of the fermentation (King & Barnes)

HOW BEER IS MADE

The brewing process is a batch rather than a continuous process, and is often completed in a day using predetermined quantities of raw materials, although fermentation and maturation takes longer.

Milling and Mashing

Malt is freshly crushed for each brewing requirement, producing what is known as the grist. The brewing process starts with the mash, where the grist is carefully mixed with hot water to produce the mash at a critical temperature of 145°F to 150°F. This stands in the mash tun for approximately one hour to allow the enzymes that are naturally present in the malt to convert the starches to sugars. Sparging is then carried out, where hot water is passed through the mash to draw off all the soluble malt extract. The exhausted spent grains are then sold as cattle feed.

The Copper and Hop-Back

The wort or sweet liquid drawn off from the mash tun is run into the copper where special invert sugar and hops are added. The hops impart their special delicate bitter flavour to the wort. The mixture is boiled for about an hour. The enhanced wort is then drawn off by casting the copper into the hop-back, which is a large vessel that acts principally as a sieve. The spent hops are useful to gardeners as a fertiliser.

Right: Cooper at work making barrels (Wadworth)

Below: Stacking barrels (Wadworth)

Fermentation

The temperature of the wort is dramatically lowered from just below boiling point to 60°F before passing into the fermenting vessel. At this point each brew is carefully gauged for volume and original gravity.

Modern breweries use stainless steel fermenters whilst traditional producers still use high-sided oak vessels lined with copper. The fermentation is started by the introduction of live yeast to the wort in the fermenting vessels. The yeast will multiply approximately fourfold over the next three days. The yeast feeds on the sugars in the wort, producing alcohol and carbon dioxide. When the yeast is tired and clumps together, primary fermentation is complete and the beer is run out into conditioning casks.

HOW BEER IS SERVED

Cask Conditioned Beers

Draught beers acquire their natural condition in the cask and are racked directly into the cask from the conditioning casks. Small amounts of finings (from the sturgeon fish) are added to draw the yeast to the bottom of the cask. Bitter has additional choice hops added to further enhance the flavour. Other brews such as Mild have additional sugar primings added. When the cask is finally set up on its stillage in the cellars of pubs, the finings and yeast precipitate out, leaving the beer clear and bright, ready to drink. Cask beer has its own natural gas and so can be served by gravity or by a simple handpump. Cask beer is a living substance and must be drunk within about three days or it may spoil.

Keg Beers

Keg and nitrokeg beers are not fined but pasteurised and filtered to kill off and remove any yeast still present and so prevent further fermentation. Keg beer is pressurised and inert and is pumped up to the bar for serving by gas. It is often chilled and has a long shelf life, making it very profitable.

Bottle Conditioned Beers

Bottled beers are treated similarly to keg beers, but gain their condition in the bottle where they may be further hopped and primed for approximately a further two weeks of maturation. The finished bottled product is usually crystal clear and fully flavoured with a long shelf life.

Horses and dray outside Wadworth's Brewery, Devizes, Wiltshire

Quick Reference Lists

BAR GAMES

The following offer one or more bar games: darts, bar billiards, pool, dominoes, shove ha'penny, cards, cribbage. Please note: these may be available on set nights only.

WEST COUNTRY

BRISTOL
Highbury Vaults, BRISTOL

CORNWALL & ISLES OF SCILLY
Rising Sun, ALTARNUN
St Mabyn Inn, BODMIN
Wellington Hotel, BOSCASTLE
Maltsters Arms, CHAPEL AMBLE
Trengilly Wartha Inn, CONSTANTINE
Borough Arms, DUNMERE
King of Prussia, FOWEY
Ship Inn, FOWEY
Halzephron Inn, GUNWALLOE
Ferryboat Inn, HELFORD PASSAGE
Blue Anchor Inn, HELSTON
Halfway House Inn, KINGSAND
Lamorna Wink, LAMORNA
Crown Inn, LANLIVERY
Eliot Arms (Square & Compass), LAUNCESTON
Ship Inn, LERRYN
Royal Oak Inn, LOSTWITHIEL
White Hart, LUDGVAN
Carpenters Arms, METHERELL
Miners Arms, MITHIAN
Jubilee Inn, PELYNT
Roseland Inn, PHILLEIGH
Ship Inn, PORTHLEVEN
Basset Arms, PORTREATH
Driftwood Spars Hotel, ST AGNES
Star Inn, ST JUST (near Land's End)
Falcon Inn, ST MAWGAN
Mill House Inn, TREBARWITH
Port William, TREBARWITH
New Inn, TRESCO
New Inn, VERYAN
Hawkins Arms, ZELAH

DEVON
Watermans Arms, ASHPRINGTON
Ship Inn, AXMOUTH
Sloop Inn, BANTHAM
Anchor Inn, BEER
Old Plough Inn, BERE FERRERS
Normandy Arms, BLACKAWTON
Masons Arms, BRANSCOMBE
Drake Manor Inn, BUCKLAND MONACHORUM
Old Thatch Inn, CHERITON BISHOP
Hunters Lodge Inn, CORNWORTHY
New Inn, CREDITON
Anchor Inn, DAWLISH
Drewe Arms, DREWSTEIGNTON
Turf Hotel, EXMINSTER
Church House Inn, HARBERTON
Mildmay Colours Inn, HOLBETON
Church House Inn, HOLNE
Otter Inn, HONITON
Elephant's Nest Inn, HORNDON
Royal Inn, HORSEBRIDGE
Church House Inn, KINGSBRIDGE
Masons Arms Inn, KNOWSTONE
Manor Inn, LOWER ASHTON
Cleave, LUSTLEIGH
Rising Sun Hotel, LYNMOUTH
Royal Oak Inn, MEAVY
Crown and Sceptre, NEWTON ST CYRES
Ring of Bells Inn, NORTH BOVEY
Castle Inn & Hotel, OKEHAMPTON
Peter Tavy Inn, PETER TAVY
Warren House Inn, POSTBRIDGE
Tower Inn, SLAPTON
Millbrook Inn, SOUTH POOL
Oxenham Arms, SOUTH ZEAL
Tom Cobley Tavern, SPREYTON
Village Inn, THURLESTONE
Yarcombe Inn, YARCOMBE

DORSET
Shave Cross Inn, BRIDPORT
Gaggle of Geese, BUCKLAND NEWTON
Royal Oak, CERNE ABBAS
Fox Inn, CORSCOMBE
Fleur-de-Lys, CRANBORNE
Sailors Return, EAST CHALDON
Cock & Bottle, EAST MORDEN
Kings Arms Inn, GILLINGHAM
Three Elms, NORTH WOOTTON
Thimble Inn, PIDDLEHINTON
Pulpit Inn, PORTLAND
Crown Inn, PUNCKNOWLE
White Hart, SHERBORNE
Skippers Inn, SHERBORNE
Bankes Arms Hotel, STUDLAND
Langton Arms, TARRANT MONKTON
Wise Man Inn, WEST STAFFORD

GLOUCESTERSHIRE
Amberley Inn Hotel, AMBERLEY
Village Pub, BARNSLEY
Bear Inn, BISLEY
Kings Head Inn, BLEDINGTON
Brockweir Country Inn, BROCKWEIR
Gumstool Inn, CALCOT
Hare & Hounds, CHEDWORTH
Seven Tuns, CHEDWORTH
Eight Bells Inn, CHIPPING CAMPDEN
Wyndham Arms, CLEARWELL
Colesbourne Inn, COLESBOURNE
New Inn, COLN ST ALDWYNS
Wild Duck, EWEN
Fossebridge Inn, FOSSEBRIDGE
Harvest Home, GREET

Bull Inn, HINTON
Hunters Hall, KINGSCOTE
Trout Inn, LECHLADE
Rose & Crown Inn, NYMPSFIELD
Butcher's Arms, OAKRIDGE LYNCH
Anchor Inn, OLDBURY-ON-SEVERN
Greyhound, SIDDINGTON
Coach and Horses, STOW-ON-THE-WOLD
Ram Inn, STROUD
Trouble House Inn, TETBURY
Compass Inn, TORMARTON

SOMERSET
Ring o'Bells, ASHCOTT
Square & Compass, ASHILL
New Inn, BLAGDON
White Horse Inn, BRADFORD-ON-TONE
Ashcott Inn, BRIDGWATER
Hornsbury Mill, CHARD
Crown Inn, CHURCHILL
Wheatsheaf, COMBE HAY
Carew Arms, CROWCOMBE
Exmoor House Hotel, DUNSTER
Anchor Inn, EXEBRIDGE
Horse & Groom, FROME
Who'd a Thought It Inn, GLASTONBURY
Ilchester Arms, ILCHESTER
New Inn, ILMINSTER
Hood Arms, KILVE
Kingsdon Inn, KINGSDON
Martlet Inn, LANGFORD BUDVILLE
Three Horseshoes, LANGLEY MARSH
Royal Oak Inn, LUXBOROUGH
Talbot Inn, MELLS
Cottage Inn, NETHER STOWEY
George at Nunney, NUNNEY
Ship Inn, PORLOCK
New Inn, PRIDDY
Full Moon at Rudge, RUDGE
Riverside Inn, SALTFORD
Sparkford Inn, SPARKFORD
Greyhound Inn, STAPLE FITZPAINE
Rose & Crown, STOKE ST GREGORY
Rock Inn, WATERROW
Crossways Inn, WEST HUNTSPILL
Rest and Be Thankful Inn, WHEDDON CROSS

WILTSHIRE
Green Dragon, ALDERBURY
Red Lion Inn, AXFORD
Barford Inn, BARFORD ST MARTIN
Waggon & Horses, BECKHAMPTON
Quarrymans Arms, BOX
Canal Tavern, BRADFORD ON AVON
Three Crowns, BRINKWORTH
Crown at Tolldown, CHIPPENHAM
Methuen Arms Hotel, CORSHAM
Royal Oak Inn, CORSLEY HEATH
Fox & Hounds, DEVIZES
Fox and Hounds, EAST KNOYLE
Beckford Arms, FONTHILL GIFFORD
Angel Inn, HEYTESBURY
Lamb at Hindon, HINDON
Bath Arms, HORNINGSHAM
Bridge Inn, HORTON
Red Lion Inn, KILMINGTON
Red Lion Inn, LACOCK
George Inn, LACOCK
Hop Pole Inn, LIMPLEY STOKE
Wheatsheaf, LOWER WOODFORD
Smoking Dog, MALMESBURY
Tipsy Miller, MARTEN
Woodbridge Inn, NORTH NEWNTON
Radnor Arms, NUNTON
French Horn, PEWSEY
Silver Plough, PITTON
George and Dragon, ROWDE
Kings Arms Hotel, SALISBURY
Bell Inn, SEEND
Rattlebone Inn, SHERSTON
Pelican Inn, STAPLEFORD
King John Inn, TOLLARD ROYAL
Shepherd's Rest, WANBOROUGH
Woodfalls Inn, WOODFALLS

SOUTH & SOUTH-EAST ENGLAND

BERKSHIRE
Sun in the Wood, ASHMORE GREEN
Uncle Tom's Cabin, COOKHAM DEAN
Horns, CRAZIES HILL
Bunk Inn, CURRIDGE
Palmer Arms, DORNEY
Pot Kiln, FRILSHAM
Swan Inn, GREAT SHEFFORD
Queen Victoria, HARE HATCH
Rising Sun, HURLEY
Wheelwrights Arms, HURST
Swan Inn, INKPEN
Fishermans Cottage, READING
Bull Inn, STANFORD DINGLEY
Rose & Crown, WINKFIELD
Winterbourne Arms, WINTERBOURNE

BUCKINGHAMSHIRE
Lions of Bledlow, BLEDLOW
Peacock, BOLTER END
Wheatsheaf, BUCKINGHAM
Swan, CHESHAM
Chester Arms, CHICHELEY
Full Moon, CHOLESBURY
Dinton Hermit, FORD
Old Red Lion, GREAT BRICKHILL
George Inn, GREAT MISSENDEN
Crooked Billet, KINGSWOOD
White Lion, MARSWORTH
Red Lion, PRINCES RISBOROUGH
George and Dragon Hotel, WEST WYCOMBE

HAMPSHIRE
Bull Inn, BENTLEY
Five Bells, BURITON
White Hart, CHARTER ALLEY
Red Lion Inn, CLANVILLE
Queen Inn, DUMMER
Ye Olde George Inn, EAST MEON
Star Inn, EAST TYTHERLEY
Cricketers Inn, EASTON
Sussex Brewery, EMSWORTH
Compasses Inn, FORDINGBRIDGE

Crooked Billet, HOOK
Yew Tree Inn, LOWER WIELD
Waggon & Horses, LYMINGTON
Fox, NORTH WALTHAM
Red Lion, OVERTON
Ship Inn, OWSLEBURY
Wine Vaults, PORTSMOUTH & SOUTHSEA
Rose & Thistle, ROCKBOURNE
Castle Inn, ROWLANDS CASTLE
Hatchet Inn, SHERFIELD ENGLISH
George Inn, ST MARY BOURNE
Harrow Inn, STEEP
Tichborne Arms, TICHBORNE
Hen & Chicken Inn, UPPER FROYLE
White Lion, WHERWELL
Red House Inn, WHITCHURCH
Cartwheel Inn, WHITSBURY
Game Keeper, WOODLANDS

KENT
Three Chimneys, BIDDENDEN
Brickmakers Arms, BOROUGH GREEN
Golden Eagle, BURHAM
Castle Inn, CHIDDINGSTONE
White Horse, CHILHAM
Gate Inn, CHISLET
Black Bull, CLIFFE
Carpenters Arms, EASTLING
Shipwrights Arms, FAVERSHAM
Chafford Arms, FORDCOMBE
Peacock, IDEN GREEN
George & Dragon, IGHTHAM
Bull Inn, LINTON
Alma, PAINTERS FORSTAL
Dering Arms, PLUCKLEY
Crown Inn, ROYAL TUNBRIDGE WELLS
Hare on Langton Green, ROYAL TUNBRIDGE WELLS
Rose and Crown, SELLING
Chequers Inn, SMARDEN
George and Dragon, SPELDHURST

LONDON POSTAL DISTRICTS
Crocker's Folly, LONDON NW8
Chelsea Ram, LONDON SW10

OXFORDSHIRE
Boars Head, ARDINGTON
Marston Inn, BANBURY
Roebuck Inn, BANBURY
Bottle & Glass, BINFIELD HEATH
Fox Inn, BIX
Inn for All Seasons, BURFORD
Chequers, CHIPPING NORTON
Vine Inn, CUMNOR
White Horse Inn, DUNS TEW
White Hart, FYFIELD
Falkland Arms, GREAT TEW
Golden Ball, HENLEY-ON-THAMES
Gate Hangs High, HOOK NORTON
Mill & Old Swan, MINSTER LOVELL
Nut Tree, MURCOTT
Bear, NORTH MORETON
Roebuck Inn, NORTH NEWINGTON
Crown, NUFFIELD
Anchor, OXFORD
Bell, SHENINGTON
Shaven Crown Hotel, SHIPTON-UNDER-WYCHWOOD
Crown Inn, SOUTH MORETON
Star Inn, SPARSHOLT
Abingdon Arms, THAME
Chequers, WESTON-ON-THE-GREEN
Killingworth Castle Inn, WOOTTON

SURREY
Jolly Farmer Inn, BRAMLEY
Crown Inn, CHIDDINGFOLD
Plough Inn, COLDHARBOUR
Woolpack, ELSTEAD
Windmill Inn, EWHURST
White Horse, HASCOMBE
Running Horses, MICKLEHAM
Six Bells, NEWDIGATE
Royal Oak, PIRBRIGHT
White Hart, WITLEY

SUSSEX, EAST
Rose Cottage Inn, ALCISTON
Anchor Inn, BARCOMBE
Cricketers Arms, BERWICK
Blackboys Inn, BLACKBOYS
Greys, BRIGHTON
Six Bells, CHIDDINGLY
White Dog Inn, EWHURST GREEN
Golden Galleon, EXCEAT
Griffin Inn, FLETCHING
Black Peter's Bar at Brambletye Hotel, FOREST ROW
Anchor Inn, HARTFIELD
Juggs, KINGSTON NEAR LEWES
Plough & Harrow, LITLINGTON
Middle House, MAYFIELD
Star Inn, OLD HEATHFIELD
Plough, UPPER DICKER
Warbill in Tun Inn, WARBLETON
Ram Inn, WEST FIRLE
Dorset Arms WITHYHAM

SUSSEX, WEST
Fountain Inn, ASHURST
Ye Olde Six Bells, BILLINGSHURST
Coach & Horses, COMPTON
George Inn, EARTHAM
Red Lion, FERNHURST
Anglesey Arms, HALNAKER
Half Moon Inn, KIRDFORD
Jeremy's at the Crabtree, LOWER BEEDING
Noah's Ark, LURGASHALL
Elsted Inn, MIDHURST
Black Rabbit, OFFHAM
Gribble Inn, OVING
Halfway Bridge Inn, PETWORTH
Chequers Inn, ROWHOOK
Star Inn, RUSPER
White Hart, SOUTH HARTING
Ship Inn, SOUTH HARTING
White Hart, STOPHAM

White Horse Inn, SUTTON
Horse Guards Inn, TILLINGTON
Greets Inn, WARNHAM

WIGHT, ISLE OF
Crab & Lobster Inn, BEMBRIDGE
Bonchurch Inn, BONCHURCH
Clarendon Hotel & Wight Mouse Inn, CHALE
Red Lion, FRESHWATER
Buddle Inn, NITON
Seaview Hotel, SEAVIEW

CENTRAL ENGLAND & EAST ANGLIA

BEDFORDSHIRE
Tudor Oaks Lodge, ASTWICK
Ye Olde Plough, BOLNHURST
Cock, BROOM
White Horse, EATON BRAY
Bell, ODELL
Swan Inn, RADWELL

CAMBRIDGESHIRE
Free Press, CAMBRIDGE
Cambridge Blue, CAMBRIDGE
Black Horse, DRY DRAYTON
Leeds Arms, ELTISLEY
Red Lion, ELY
Ancient Shepherds, FEN DITTON
King William IV, FENSTANTON
Black Bull, GODMANCHESTER
Woodmans, Cottage GOREFIELD
Pheasant, GREAT CHISHILL
Pear Tree, HILDERSHAM
Plough & Fleece, HORNINGSEA
Queen's Head, NEWTON
Kings, REACH
Bell Inn, STILTON

ESSEX
Axe & Compasses, ARKESDEN
Bell Inn, CASTLE HEDINGHAM
Sun Hotel, DEDHAM
Crown, ELSENHAM
Sun Inn, FEERING
Green Man, GOSFIELD
Du Cane Arms, GREAT BRAXTED
Cock & Bell Inn, HIGH EASTER
Crooked Billet, LEIGH-ON-SEA
Flitch of Bacon, LITTLE DUNMOW
Ferry Boat Inn, NORTH FAMBRIDGE
Cricketers Arms, RICKLING GREEN
Hoop, STOCK
Cap & Feathers Inn, TILLINGHAM
Bell, WENDENS AMBO
Mitre, WICKHAM BISHOPS
Black Buoy Inn, WIVENHOE

HERTFORDSHIRE
Jolly Waggoner, ARDELEY
Fox & Hounds, BARLEY
Sword in Hand, BUNTINGFORD
Royal Oak, CHIPPERFIELD
Bricklayers Arms, FLAUNDEN
Green Dragon, FLAUNDEN
Lytton Arms, KNEBWORTH
Nags Head, LITTLE HADHAM
Jolly Waggoners, MUCH HADHAM
Sow & Pigs, WARE
Rising Sun, WESTON

LEICESTERSHIRE
Bewicke Arms, HALLATON
Rose & Crown, HOSE
Cap & Stocking, KEGWORTH
Welford Place LEICESTER
Swan in The Rushes, LOUGHBOROUGH
Black Horse, MARKET BOSWORTH
Queens Head Inn, MARKET HARBOROUGH
Nevill Arms, MEDBOURNE
Swan Inn, MOUNTSORREL
Crown Inn, OLD DALBY
Peacock Inn, REDMILE
White Swan, SILEBY
Old Brewery, SOMERBY
Bakers Arms, THORPE LANGTON
Black Horse Inn, WALCOTE

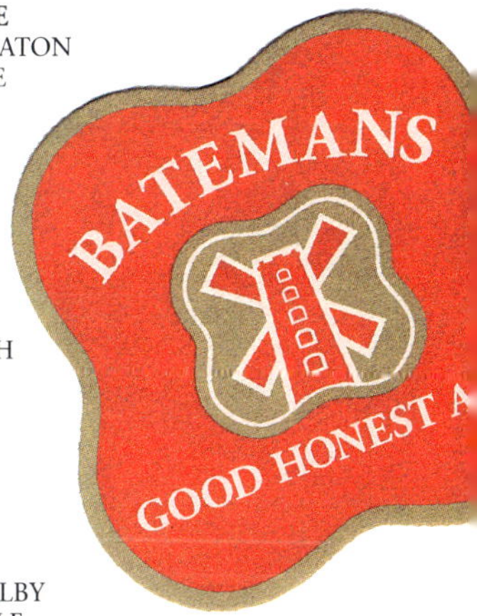

LINCOLNSHIRE
Ye Olde Red Lion, BICKER
Wishing Well Inn, BOURNE
Woodhouse Inn, CORBY GLEN
Kings Head, FREISTON
Beehive Inn, GRANTHAM
George & Dragon, HAGWORTHINGHAM
Nags Head, HECKINGTON
Thorold Arms, MARSTON
Kings Head, NAVENBY
Red Lion Inn, PARTNEY
Red Lion Inn, RAITHBY
Nickerson Arms, ROTHWELL
Bridge Inn, SAXILBY
Ship Inn, SPALDING
New Inn, SPRINGTHORPE
White Hart Inn, TETFORD
Rutland Arms, WOOLSTHORPE

NORFOLK
Chequers Inn, BINHAM
Buckinghamshire Arms, BLICKLING
Old Garden House, BRESSINGHAM
Hoste Arms, BURNHAM MARKET
Lord Nelson, BURNHAM THORPE
George & Dragon Hotel, CLEY NEXT THE SEA
Boar Inn, GREAT RYBURGH
Hill House, HAPPISBURGH
Hare and Hounds, HEMPSTEAD
Kings Head, HETHERSETT
Crown Hotel, MUNDFORD
Ribs of Beef, NORWICH
Stiffkey Red Lion, STIFFKEY
Darbys Freehouse, SWANTON MORLEY
Chequers Inn, THOMPSON
Toft Lion, TOFT MONKS
Red Lion Inn ,UPPER SHERINGHAM
Three Horseshoes, WARHAM ALL SAINTS

Fishermans Return, WINTERTON-ON-SEA
Fur & Feather, WOODBASTWICK

NORTHAMPTONSHIRE
Olde Coach House Inn, ASHBY ST LEDGERS
Bulls Head, CLIPSTON
Falcon Inn, FOTHERINGHAY
White Hart, GRAFTON REGIS
White Swan, HARRINGWORTH
Overstone Arms, KETTERING
Lamb, LITTLE HARROWDEN
Mill at Oundle, OUNDLE
Boat Inn, STOKE BRUERNE
Benefield Wheatsheaf Hotel, UPPER BENEFIELD
King's Head, WADENHOE
Shoulder of Mutton Inn, WELFORD

RUTLAND
Monckton Arms Hotel, GLASTON
Blue Ball, OAKHAM
Cuckoo Inn, WING

SUFFOLK
Mill Inn, ALDEBURGH
Six Bells Inn, BARDWELL
Swan House Restaurant, BECCLES
Queens Head, BRANDESTON
Three Horseshoes, COCKFIELD
Trowel & Hammer Inn, COTTON
Ship Inn, DUNWICH
Eels Foot Inn, EASTBRIDGE
Queens Head, ERWARTON
Dobermann Inn, FRAMSDEN
Marquis of Cornwallis, HADLEIGH
Lion, HONEY TYE
Angel Hotel, LAVENHAM
Kings Head, LAXFIELD
Star Inn, LIDGATE
Wilford Bridge, MELTON
White Hart, NAYLAND
Jolly Sailor Inn ORFORD
Brewers Arms, RATTLESDEN
Hamblyn House Hotel, RICKINGHALL
White Horse Inn, RISBY
Old Mill House, SAXTEAD GREEN
Crown Hotel, SOUTHWOLD
Bell Inn, WALBERSWICK

WARWICKSHIRE
Plough Inn, EATHORPE
Castle Inn, EDGEHILL
Red Lion, LONG COMPTON
Harvester, LONG ITCHINGTON
George Hotel, LOWER BRAILES
Rose and Crown, RATLEY
Blue Boar, TEMPLE GRAFTON
Four Alls, WELFORD-ON-AVON
Royal Oak, WHATCOTE
Mary Arden Inn, WILMCOTE

WEST MIDLANDS
Vine, WEST BROMWICH
Barley Mow, WOLVERHAMPTON

WALES & THE MARCHES

ANGLESEY, ISLE OF
Ye Olde Bulls Head Inn, BEAUMARIS

BRIDGEND
Prince of Wales Inn, KENFIG

CAERPHILLY
Courthouse, CAERPHILLY

CARMARTHENSHIRE
Black Lion, ABERGORLECH
Golden Grove Arms, LLANARTHNE
Castle Brewery, LLANDEILO

CONWY
Cobdens Hotel, CAPEL CURIG
Lion Inn Hotel, GWYTHERIN
Hawk & Buckle Inn, LLANNEFYDD

DENBIGHSHIRE
Druid Inn, LLANFERRES
Cerrigllwydion Arms, LLANYNYS

FLINTSHIRE
White Horse Inn, CILCAIN
Britannia Inn, HALKYN

GWYNEDD
Penhelig Arms Hotel, ABERDYFI
Halfway House, BONTDDU
Pen-Y-Gwryd, LLANBERIS
Sun Inn, LLANENGAN
Grapes Hotel, MAENTWROG
George III Hotel, PENMAENPOOL
Ship, PORTHMADOG
Lion Hotel, TUDWEILIOG

HEREFORD & WORCESTER
Riverside Inn, AYMESTREY
Little Pack Horse, BEWDLEY
Fleece Inn, BRETFORTON
Cottage of Content, CAREY
Robin Hood, CASTLEMORTON
Pandy Inn, DORSTONE
Green Man Inn, FOWNHOPE
Bunch of Carrots, HAMPTON BISHOP
Crown, HOWLE HILL
Talbot at Knightwick, KNIGHTWICK
Talbot, LEDBURY
Three Horseshoes Inn, LITTLE COWARNE
Farmers Arms, MALVERN
Slip Tavern, MUCH MARCLE
New Inn, PEMBRIDGE
Bell Inn, PENSAX
New Inn, ST OWEN'S CROSS
Carpenters Arms, WALTERSTONE
Ye Olde Salutation Inn, WEOBLEY
Rhydspence Inn, WHITNEY-ON-WYE
Sun Inn, WINFORTON
Crown Inn, WOOLHOPE
Anchor Inn, WYRE PIDDLE

HEREFORDSHIRE
Butchers Arms, WOOLHOPE

MONMOUTHSHIRE
Clytha Arms, ABERGAVENNY
Black Bear Inn, BETTWS-NEWYDD
Castle View Hotel, CHEPSTOW
Greyhound Inn, LLANTRISANT
Red Hart Inn, LLANVAPLEY
Boat Inn, PENALLT
Carpenters Arm, SHIRENEWTON
Tredegar Arms, SHIRENEWTON
Halfway House Inn, TAL-Y-COED
Lion Inn, TRELLECK
Fountain Inn, TRELLECK GRANGE

PEMBROKESHIRE
New Inn, AMROTH
Galleon Inn, BROAD HAVEN
Carew Inn, CAREW
Pendre Inn, CILGERRAN
Dial Inn, LAMPHEY
Stanley Arms, LANDSHIPPING
Harp Inn, LETTERSTON
Trewern Arms, NEVERN
Sloop Inn, PORTHGAIN
Tates at Tafarn Newydd, ROSEBUSH
Armstrong Arms, STACKPOLE
Wolfe Inn, WOLF'S CASTLE

POWYS
Lion Hotel, BERRIEW
Aleppo Merchant Inn, CARNO
Elan Valley Hotel, ELAN VILLAGE
Llanerch Inn, LLANDRINDOD WELLS
Red Lion Inn, LLANFIHANGEL-NANT-MELAN
Cain Valley Hotel, LLANFYLLIN
Griffin Inn, LLYSWEN
Dolbrodmaeth Inn, MACHYNLLETH
Severn Arms Hotel, PENYBONT
Star Inn, TALYBONT-ON-USK

SHROPSHIRE
Lion O'Morfe, BRIDGNORTH
Red Lion Inn, LLANFAIR WATERDINE
Unicorn Inn, LUDLOW
New Inn, MADELEY
Stables Inn, MINSTERLEY
Acton Arms, MORVILLE
George & Dragon, MUCH WENLOCK
Longville Arms, MUCH WENLOCK
Crown, MUNSLOW
Hundred House Hotel & Country Inn, NORTON
Bottle & Glass Inn, PICKLESCOTT
Boathouse Inn, SHREWSBURY
Willey Moor Lock Tavern, WHITCHURCH

SWANSEA
King Arthur Hotel, REYNOLDSTON

VALE OF GLAMORGAN
Blue Anchor Inn, EAST ABERTHAW
Six Bells Inn, PENMARK
Bush Inn, ST HILARY

WREXHAM
Hanmer Arms Village Hotel, HANMER

NORTHERN ENGLAND

CHESHIRE
White Lion Inn, BARTHOMLEY
Church House Inn, BOLLINGTON
Jolly Thresher, BROOMEDGE
Copper Mine, BROXTON
Combermere Arms, BURLEYDAM
Pheasant Inn, BURWARDSLEY
Shrewsbury Arms, LITTLE BUDWORTH
Ye Olde Parkgate Inn, OVER PEOVER
Dog Inn, OVER PEOVER
Bulls Head, SMALLWOOD
Blue Bell Inn, TUSHINGHAM CUM GRINDLEY
Cat & Fiddle, WILDBOARCLOUGH
Swan, WYBUNBURY

CO DURHAM
Morritt Arms Hotel, BARNARD CASTLE
McOrville Inn, ELWICK
Dun Cow Inn, SEDGEFIELD

CUMBRIA
Drunken Duck Inn, AMBLESIDE
Royal Oak Inn, APPLEBY-IN-WESTMORLAND
Punchbowl Inn, ASKHAM
Barbon Inn, BARBON
Wheatsheaf Hotel, BEETHAM
Bridge Hotel, BUTTERMERE
Bay Horse Hotel, CANAL FOOT
Pheasant Inn, CASTERTON
Sun Inn, DENT
Royal Hotel, DOCKRAY
Britannia Inn, ELTERWATER
Bower House Inn, ESKDALE
King George IV Inn, ESKDALE
Travellers Rest Inn, GRASMERE
Rusland Pool, HAVERTHWAITE
Queens Head Hotel, HAWKSHEAD
Blue Bell Hotel, HEVERSHAM
Snooty Fox Tavern, KIRKBY LONSDALE
Sun Inn, KIRKBY LONSDALE
Whoop Hall Inn, KIRKBY LONSDALE
Joiners Arms, LAZONBY
Three Shires Inn, LITTLE LANGDALE
Shepherds Inn, MELMERBY
Tower Banks, NEAR SAWREY
Screes Hotel, NETHER WASDALE
Outgate Inn, OUTGATE
Fat Lamb Country Inn, RAVENSTONEDALE
Newfield Inn, SEATHWAITE
Kings Head, THIRLSPOT
Queens Head Hotel, TROUTBECK
Mortal Man Hotel, TROUTBECK
Royal Oak, ULVERSTON
Wasdale Head Inn, WASDALE HEAD

DERBYSHIRE
White Horse Inn, ALFRETON
Green Man, ASHBOURNE
Lathkil Hotel, BAKEWELL
Druid Inn, BIRCHOVER

Ye Olde Gate Inne, BRASSINGTON
Ye Olde Cheshire Cheese Inn, CASTLETON
Abbey, DARLEY ABBEY
Brunswick Inn, DERBY
Miners Arms, EYAM
Royal Hotel, HAYFIELD
Red Lion Inn, HOGNASTON
Cheshire Cheese Inn, HOPE
Packhorse Inn, LITTLE LONGSTONE
Grouse & Claret, ROWSLEY
Old Crown, SHARDLOW
Chequers Inn, STANTON BY DALE
George Hotel, TIDESWELL
Bluebell Inn, TISSINGTON

LANCASHIRE
Black Dog, BELMONT
Owd Nell's Tavern, BILSBORROW
Stork Hotel, GALGATE
Farmers Arms, HESKIN GREEN
Farmhouse Tavern, LANCASTER
Kettledrum Inn & Restaurant, MERECLOUGH
White Bull, RIBCHESTER
Fishermans Retreat, SHUTTLEWORTH
Hark to Bounty Inn, SLAIDBURN
Grapes Hotel, WREA GREEN

MANCHESTER, GREATER
Station, ASHTON-UNDER-LYNE
Woodstock Tavern, DIDSBURY
White Hart Inn, OLDHAM

MERSEYSIDE
Fox and Hounds, BARNSTON

NORTHUMBERLAND
Allenheads Inn, ALLENHEADS
Masons Arms, ALNWICK
Victoria Hotel, BAMBURGH
Rob Roy, BERWICK-UPON-TWEED
Lord Crewe Arms, BLANCHLAND
Manor House Inn, CARTERWAY HEADS
Percy Arms Hotel, CHATTON
Cottage Inn, DUNSTAN
Black Bull, ETAL
Queens Head Inn, GREAT WHITTINGTON
Dipton Mill Inn, HEXHAM
Ship, LOW NEWTON BY THE SEA
Black Bull, MATFEN
Cook and Barker Inn, NEWTON ON THE MOOR
Wallace Arms, ROWFOOT
Olde Ship Hotel, SEAHOUSES
Warenford Lodge, WARENFORD

NOTTINGHAMSHIRE
Victoria Hotel, BEESTON
Robin Hood Inn, ELKESLEY
Square & Compass, NORMANTON ON TRENT
Lincolnshire Poacher, NOTTINGHAM
King William, SCAFTWORTH
Star Inn, WEST LEAKE

STAFFORDSHIRE
Crown Inn, ABBOTS BROMLEY
Black Lion Inn, BUTTERTON
Junction Country Inn & Restaurant, NORBURY JUNCTION
Horseshoe Inn, TATENHILL
Crown, YOXALL

YORKSHIRE, EAST RIDING OF
White Horse Inn, BEVERLEY
Seabirds Inn, FLAMBOROUGH
Wolds Inn, HUGGATE
Minerva Hotel, HULL
Gold Cup Inn, LOW CATTON
Wellington Inn, LUND
Star Inn, NORTH DALTON
Half Moon Inn, SKIDBY

YORKSHIRE, NORTH
Ship Inn, ACASTER MALBIS
Craven Arms, APPLETREEWICK
Kings Arms Hotel, ASKRIGG
Rose & Crown Hotel, BAINBRIDGE
Malt Shovel Inn, BREARTON
Buck Inn, BUCKDEN
Red Lion, BURNSALL
Foresters Arms, CARLTON
New Inn, CLAPHAM
Fauconberg Arms, COXWOLD
Royal Oak Inn, DACRE BANKS
Duke of Wellington Inn, DANBY
Horseshoe Hotel, EGTON BRIDGE
Tempest Arms, ELSLACK
General Tarleton Inn, FERRENSBY
Mallyan Spout, GOATHLAND
Star Inn, HAROME
Board Hotel, HAWES
George Inn, HUBBERHOLME
Racehorses Hotel, KETTLEWELL
George & Dragon Hotel, KIRKBYMOORSIDE
Lion Inn, KIRKBYMOORSIDE
Stone Trough Inn, KIRKHAM
Fountaine Inn, LINTON
Farmers Arms, MUKER
Three Tuns Inn, OSMOTHERLEY
Sportsmans Arms, PATELEY BRIDGE
White Swan, PICKERING
Nags Head Country Inn, PICKHILL
Yorke Arms, RAMSGILL
Milburn Arms Hotel, ROSEDALE ABBEY
White Horse Farm Hotel, ROSEDALE ABBEY
Hare Inn, SCAWTON
Golden Lion Hotel, SETTLE
Royal Oak Hotel, SETTLE
Fox & Hounds Country Inn, SINNINGTON
Bay Horse Inn, TERRINGTON
Buck Inn, THORNTON WATLASS
Old Hall Inn, THRESHFIELD
Fox & Hounds, WEST BURTON
Plough Inn, WIGGLESWORTH

YORKSHIRE, WEST
Rock Inn Hotel, HALIFAX
Old White Lion Hotel, HAWORTH
Chequers Inn, LEDSHAM
Will's O' Nat's, MELTHAM
Spite, NEWALL

SCOTLAND

ABERDEEN CITY
Prince of Wales, ABERDEEN

ABERDEENSHIRE
Gordon Arms Hotel, KINCARDINE O'NEIL
Old Mill Inn, MARYCULTER
Lairhillock Inn, NETHERLEY
Redgarth, OLDMELDRUM
Marine Hotel, STONEHAVEN

ANGUS
Glenisla Hotel, GLENISLA

ARGYLL & BUTE
Ardentinny Hotel, ARDENTINNY
Galley of Lorne Inn, ARDFERN
Tigh an Truish Inn, CLACHAN-SEIL
Barn, OBAN
Tayvallich Inn, TAYVALLICH

AYRSHIRE, SOUTH
Wheatsheaf Inn, SYMINGTON

DUMFRIES & GALLOWAY
Steam Packet Inn, ISLE OF WHITHORN
Royal Hotel, KIRKCUDBRIGHT
Creebridge House Hotel, MINNIGAFF
Black Bull Inn, MOFFAT

DUNDEE CITY
Fisherman's Tavern, BROUGHTY FERRY

EDINBURGH, CITY OF
Hawes Inn, SOUTH QUEENSFERRY

FALKIRK
Castlecary House Hotel, CASTLECARY

FIFE
Dreel Tavern, ANSTRUTHER
Ship Inn, ELIE
Crusoe Hotel, LOWER LARGO
Cabin, ST MONANS

GLASGOW, CITY OF
Rab Ha's, GLASGOW

HIGHLAND
Altnaharra Hotel, ALTNAHARRA
Applecross Inn, APPLECROSS
Ardvasar Hotel, ARDVASAR
Old Bridge Inn, AVIEMORE
Cawdor Tavern, CAWDOR
Achilty Hotel, CONTIN
Mallin House Hotel, DORNOCH
Inchbae Lodge Hotel, GARVE
Glenelg Inn, GLENELG
Hotel Eilean Iarmain, ISLE ORNSAY
Creag-nan-Darach Hotel, PLOCKTON
Argyll Hotel, ULLAPOOL

MORAY
Gordon Arms Hotel, FOCHABERS

PERTH & KINROSS
Ailean Chraggan Hotel, ABERFELDY
Almondbank Inn, ALMONDBANK
Nivingston House, CLEISH
Lomond Country Inn, KINNESSWOOD
Muirs Inn, KINROSS
Moulin Hotel, MOULIN

RENFREWSHIRE
Fox & Hounds, HOUSTON

SCOTTISH BORDERS
Traquair Arms Hotel, INNERLEITHEN
Pheasant, JEDBURGH
Burts Hotel, MELROSE
Tibbie Shiels Inn, SELKIRK
Wheatsheaf Hotel, SWINTON
Tushielaw Inn, TUSHIELAW INN
Crook Inn, TWEEDSMUIR

STIRLING
Kirkhouse Inn, STRATHBLANE

WESTERN ISLES
Polochar Inn, LOCHBOISDALE

CHILDREN NOT WELCOME

Over 1,200 establishments welcome children (see symbol). We list those who do **NOT** welcome children:

WEST COUNTRY

CORNWALL & ISLES OF SCILLY
Earl of St Vincent, EGLOSHAYLE
Bush Inn, MORWENSTOW
Ship Inn, PORTHLEVEN
New Inn, VERYAN

DEVON
Old Thatch Inn, CHERITON BISHOP
Cherub Inn, DARTMOUTH
Nobody Inn, DODDISCOMBSLEIGH
Barn Owl Inn, KINGSKERSWELL
Manor Inn, LOWER ASHTON
Warren House Inn, POSTBRIDGE
Rising Sun Hotel, LYNMOUTH

SOMERSET
Old Green Tree, BATH
Walnut Tree, WEST CAMEL
Royal Oak Inn, WITHYPOOL

WILTSHIRE
Three Horseshoes Inn, BURBAGE
Kings Arms Hotel, MELKSHAM
Rattlebone Inn, SHERSTON
King John Inn, TOLLARD ROYAL

SOUTH & SOUTH-EAST ENGLAND

BERKSHIRE
Hinds Head, ALDERMASTON
Rising Sun, HURLEY
White Hart Inn, NEWBURY
Royal Oak Hotel, YATTENDON

BUCKINGHAMSHIRE
Greyhound, BEACONSFIELD
Five Arrows Hotel, WADDESDON

HAMPSHIRE
Red Lion Inn, BOLDRE
Queen Inn, DUMMER
Chestnut Horse, EASTON
Harrow Inn, STEEP
Wykeham Arms, WINCHESTER

KENT
Golden Eagle, BURHAM
White Horse, CHILHAM
Griffins Head, CHILLENDEN

GREATER LONDON
Crown, KESTON

LONDON
Lansdowne, NW1
Queens, NW1
Crocker's Folly, NW8
Orange Brewery, SW1
Chelsea Ram, SW10
O'Neills, SW5

OXFORDSHIRE
Marston Inn, BANBURY
Fox Inn, BIX
Angel, BURFORD
Chequers, CHIPPING NORTON
George, DORCHESTER-ON-THAMES
Crown Inn, PISHILL
Crooked Billet, STOKE ROW

SURREY
Plough, BLACKBROOK
Three Horseshoes, THURSLEY
Brickmakers Arms, WINDLESHAM

SUSSEX, EAST
Dorset Arms, WITHYHAM

SUSSEX, WEST
Avins Bridge, ARDINGLY
Fountain Inn, ASHURST
George & Dragon, BURPHAM
White Horse, CHILGROVE
Hunters Moon Inn, COPTHORNE
Halfway Bridge Inn, PETWORTH
Ship Inn, SOUTH HARTING

CENTRAL ENGLAND & EAST ANGLIA

BEDFORDSHIRE
Swan Inn, RADWELL
Black Horse, WOBURN

CAMBRIDGESHIRE
Black Horse, DRY DRAYTON
John Barleycorn, DUXFORD,
Leeds Arms, ELTISLEY,
Ancient Shepherds, FEN DITTON,
Pheasant, GREAT CHISHILL,
Pear Tree, HILDERSHAM,
Red Lion, HINXTON,
Plough & Fleece, HORNINGSEA,
New Sun Inn, KIMBOLTON,

ESSEX
Axe & Compasses, ARKESDEN
Bell Inn & Hill House, HORNDON ON THE HILL
Bell, WENDENS AMBO

HERTFORDSHIRE
Bricklayers Arms, FLAUNDEN
Green Dragon, FLAUNDEN
George & Dragon, WATTON-AT-STONE

LEICESTERSHIRE
Nag's Head, CASTLE DONINGTON
Black Horse, MARKET BOSWORTH
Swan Inn, MOUNTSORREL
Bakers Arms, THORPE LANGTON

LINCOLNSHIRE
Welby Arms, ALLINGTON
Beehive Inn, GRANTHAM
Abbey Lodge Inn, WOODHALL SPA

NORFOLK
Chequers Inn, BINHAM
Ship, BRANDON CREEK
Nelson Head, HORSEY

NORTHAMPTONSHIRE
Red Lion Inn, CRICK
Tollemache Arms, HARRINGTON
Countryman, STAVERTON
Star Inn, SULGRAVE

SUFFOLK
Mill Inn, ALDEBURGH
Swan House Restaurant, BECCLES
Jolly Sailor Inn, ORFORD
Nutshell, BURY ST EDMUNDS
Dobermann Inn, FRAMSDEN
Ship Inn, LEVINGTON
Crown Inn, SNAPE
Angel Inn, STOKE-BY-NAYLAND

WARWICKSHIRE
Fleur De Lys, LOWSONFORD
Dirty Duck, STRATFORD-UPON-AVON

WEST MIDLANDS
Bulls Head, BARSTON

WALES & THE MARCHES

CONWY
Queens Head, LLANDUDNO JUNCTION
Hawk & Buckle Inn, LLANNEFYDD

FLINTSHIRE
White Horse Inn, CILCAIN

PEMBROKESHIRE
Georges Restaurant/Café Bar, HAVERFORDWEST

HEREFORD & WORCESTER
Ancient Camp Inn, RUCKHALL
Ye Olde Salutation Inn, WEOBLEY

SHROPSHIRE
Red Lion Inn, LLANFAIR WATERDINE

NORTHERN ENGLAND

CHESHIRE
Ye Olde Parkgate Inn, OVER PEOVER

CUMBRIA
New Inn, BLENCOGO
Bay Horse Hotel, CANAL FOOT
Cavendish, CARTMEL
Joiners Arms, LAZONBY
Outgate Inn, OUTGATE

DERBYSHIRE
Aitch's Wine Bar & Bistro, BAKEWELL
Chequers Inn, STANTON BY DALE

GREATER MANCHESTER
Egerton Arms, BAMFORD

NOTTINGHAMSHIRE
Ye Olde Trip to Jerusalem, NOTTINGHAM

YORKSHIRE
Friar's Head, AKEBAR
Bell, DRIFFIELD
Harewood Arms Hotel, HAREWOOD
White Hart, POOL
Milburn Arms Hotel, ROSEDALE ABBEY

SCOTLAND

ABERDEEN CITY
Prince of Wales, ABERDEEN

HIGHLAND
Altnaharra Hotel, ALTNAHARRA
Dores Inn, DORES

ARGYLL & BUTE
Cairnbaan Hotel, CAIRNBAAN

CITY OF GLASGOW
The Buttery, GLASGOW

VILLAGE RESTAURANTS

Village restaurants are also highlighted in the guide by a yellow panel

WEST COUNTRY

CORNWALL & THE ISLES OF SCILLY
Yard Bistro, HELSTON
Broomer's Restaurant, ST MAWES
Cornish Range, MOUSEHOLE
Ward's Brasserie, PENZANCE
Tregain Restaurant, PORTLOE

DEVON
62 The Bank, BARNSTAPLE

GLOUCESTERSHIRE
The Three Choirs, NEWENT

SOUTH & SOUTH-EAST ENGLAND

HAMPSHIRE
Grapevine Bistro, ODIHAM
The Terracotta Room, SHEDFIELD

KENT
Sankey's Cellar, TUNBRIDGE WELLS

SUSSEX, WEST
Avins Bridge, ARDINGLY
Burdocks Restaurant, BILLINGSHURST

CENTRAL ENGLAND & EAST ANGLIA

LEICESTERSHIRE
Softley's Restaurant, MARKET BOSWORTH

LINCOLNSHIRE
Brandy Wharf, WADDINGHAM

OXFORDSHIRE
The Nosebag, OXFORD

WALES & THE MARCHES

PEMBROKESHIRE
The Georges Restaurant, HAVERFORDWEST

HEREFORD & WORCESTER
Cider House, PEMBRIDGE

SHROPSHIRE
Henry's Restaurant, SHREWSBURY

NORTHERN ENGLAND

CUMBRIA
Yew Tree Restaurant, SEATOLLER

DERBYSHIRE
Aitch's Wine Bar, BAKEWELL

MERSEYSIDE
Everyman Bistro, LIVERPOOL

NORTHUMBERLAND
Canty's Brig, BERWICK-UPON-TWEED

YORKSHIRE
West Riding Refreshment Rooms, DEWSBURY
Olive Tree, RODLEY
Betty's Café Tea Rooms, YORK

SCOTLAND

ARGYL & BUTE
The Barn, OBAN

PERTH & KINROSS
Tullybannocher Farm Food Bar, COMRIE

FIFE
Kind Kyttock's Kitchen, FALKLAND

MULL, ISLE OF
The Old Byre, DERVAIG

WATERFRONT ESTABLISHMENTS

Waterfront establishments are also highlighted in the Guide by a blue panel.

WEST COUNTRY

CORNWALL & ISLES OF SCILLY
Borough Arms, DUNMERE
King of Prussia, FOWEY
Ship Inn, FOWEY
Halzephron Inn, GUNWALLOE
Gweek Inn, GWEEK
Shipwright Arms, HELFORD
Ferryboat Inn, HELFORD PASSAGE
Halfway House Inn, KINGSAND
Pandora Inn, MYLOR BRIDGE
Rising Sun Inn, MEVAGISSEY
Rashleigh Inn, PAR
Port Gaverne Hotel, PORT GAVERNE
Ship Inn, PORTHLEVEN
Basset Arms, PORTREATH
Broomers Restaurant, ST MAWES
Port William, TREBARWITH

DEVON
Watermans Arms, ASHPRINGTON
Anchor Inn, BEER
Old Plough Inn, BERE FERRERS
Masons Arms, BRANSCOMBE
Dartbridge Inn, BUCKFASTLEIGH
New Inn, CREDITON
Anchor Inn, DAWLISH
Turf Hotel, EXMINSTER
Otter Inn, HONITON
Elephant's Nest Inn, HORNDON
Royal Inn, HORSEBRIDGE
Rising Sun Hotel, LYNMOUTH
Crown and Sceptre, NEWTON ST CYRES
China House, PLYMOUTH
Millbrook Inn, SOUTH POOL
Rising Sun Inn, UMBERLEIGH

DORSET
Fox Inn, CORSCOMBE
Thimble Inn, PIDDLEHINTON
Pulpit Inn, PORTLAND
Bankes Arms Hotel, STUDLAND
Fishermans Haunt Hotel, WINKTON

GLOUCESTERSHIRE
Crown of Crucis, AMPNEY CRUCIS
Kings Head Inn BLEDINGTON
Brockweir Country Inn, BROCKWEIR
Fossebridge Inn FOSSEBRIDGE
Trout Inn, LECHLADE
Anchor Inn, OLDBURY-ON-SEVERN
Horse & Groom Inn, UPPER ODDINGTON

SOMERSET
George Inn, BATHAMPTON
New Inn, BLAGDON
White Horse Inn, BRADFORD-ON-TONE
The Hornsbury Mill, CHARD
Wheatsheaf, COMBE HAY
Exmoor House Hotel, DUNSTER
Anchor Inn, EXEBRIDGE
Crown Inn, EXFORD
The Inn, FRESHFORD
Royal Oak Inn, LUXBOROUGH
The George, NUNNEY
Riverside Inn, SALTFORD
Greyhound Inn, STAPLE FITZPAINE
Rock Inn,WATERROW
Crossways Inn, WEST HUNTSPILL

WILTSHIRE
Red Lion Inn, AXFORD
Canal Tavern. BRADFORD ON AVON
White Hart, FORD
The Lamb, HINDON
Bridge Inn, HORTON
Wheatsheaf, LOWER WOODFORD
Woodbridge Inn, NORTH NEWNTON
Pelican Inn, STAPLEFORD
Prince Leopold, UPTON LOVELL

SOUTH & SOUTH-EAST ENGLAND

BERKSHIRE
Swan Inn, GREAT SHEFFORD
Dundas Arms, KINTBURY
Fishermans Cottage, READING
Winterbourne Arms, WINTERBOURNE

BUCKINGHAMSHIRE
White Lion, MARSWORTH

KENT
Black Bull, CLIFFE
Shipwrights Arms, FAVERSHAM
Albion Tavern, FAVERSHAM
Fordwich Arms, FORDWICH

HAMPSHIRE
Bull Inn, BENTLEY
Ye Olde George Inn, EAST MEON
Crooked Billet, HOOK
Waggon & Horses, LYMINGTON
Bosuns Chair, LYMINGTON
Mayfly, Testcombe, STOCKBRIDGE
Vine Inn, STOCKBRIDGE
Red House Inn, WHITCHURCH

ISLE OF WIGHT
Crab & Lobster Inn, BEMBRIDGE
Clarendon Hotel & Wight Mouse Inn, CHALE
Red Lion, FRESHWATER
Seaview Hotel, SEAVIEW
Spyglass Inn, VENTNOR

GREATER LONDON
The Crown, KESTON
Turning Point, UXBRIDGE

LONDON
Crocker's Folly, NW8
Mayflower Inn, SE16

SUSSEX, EAST
Anchor Inn, BARCOMBE
Golden Galleon, EXCEAT

SUSSEX, WEST
Bridge Inn, AMBERLEY
Black Rabbit, OFFHAM
Halfway Bridge Inn, PETWORTH
White Hart, STOPHAM

SURREY
The Volunteer, ABINGER
Royal Oak, PIRBRIGHT

OXFORDSHIRE
Trout Inn, LOWER WOLVERCOTE
Mill & Old Swan, MINSTER LOVELL
Beetle & Wedge Hotel, MOULSFORD
The Anchor, OXFORD
The Fish, SUTTON COURTENAY

CENTRAL ENGLAND & EAST ANGLIA

BEDFORDSHIRE
Ye Olde Plough, BOLNHURST
Globe Inn, LINSLADE
The Bell, ODELL

ESSEX
Axe & Compasses, ARKESDEN
Ye Olde White Harte Hotel, BURNHAM-ON-CROUCH
White Hart, GREAT YELDHAM
Crooked Billet, LEIGH-ON-SEA
Ferry Boat Inn, NORTH FAMBRIDGE
Black Buoy Inn, WIVENHOE

SUFFOLK
Mill Inn, ALDEBURGH
Swan House Restaurant, BECCLES
Peacock Inn, CHELSWORTH
Ship Inn, DUNWICH
Dobermann Inn , FRAMSDEN
Marquis of Cornwallis, HADLEIGH
Red Lion, ICKLINGHAM
Bell Inn, KERSEY
Kings Head, LAXFIELD
Ship Inn, LEVINGTON
White Hart, NAYLAND
Jolly Sailor Inn, ORFORD
Crown Hotel, SOUTHWOLD
St Peter's Hall, ST PETER SOUTH ELMHAM
Bell Inn, WALBERSWICK

LEICESTERSHIRE
Bewicke Arms, HALLATON
Swan Inn, MOUNTSORREL
Nevill Arms, MEDBOURNE

LINCOLNSHIRE
Bridge Inn, SAXILBY
Ship Inn, SPALDING
St Peter's Inn, STAMFORD
Brandy Wharf Cider Centre, WADDINGHAM
Rutland Arms, WOOLSTHORPE

NORFOLK
Kings Head, BAWBURGH
Ship, BRANDON CREEK
George & Dragon Hotel,
CLEY NEXT THE SEA
Hill House, HAPPISBURGH
Ribs of Beef, NORWICH

NORTHAMPTONSHIRE
Navigation Inn, COSGROVE
White Hart, GRAFTON REGIS
White Swan, HARRINGWORTH
The Mill, OUNDLE
Boat Inn, STOKE BRUERNE
King's Head, WADENHOE
Shoulder of Mutton Inn, WELFORD

CAMBRIDGESHIRE
Old Ferryboat Inn, HOLYWELL
Old Bridge Hotel, HUNTINGDON
Charters Café Bar, PETERBOROUGH
Anchor Inn, SUTTON

WARWICKSHIRE
Old Mill Hotel, BAGINTON
Fleur De Lys, LOWSONFORD
Bell Inn, MONKS KIRBY
Four Alls, WELFORD-ON-AVON
The Pheasant, WITHYBROOK

WEST MIDLANDS
Rose and Castle, COVENTRY
Little Dry Dock, NETHERTON

RUTLAND
White Horse Inn, EMPINGHAM

WALES & THE MARCHES

CARMARTHENSHIRE
Black Lion, ABERGORLECH

CONWY
Cobdens Hotel, CAPEL CURIG

MONMOUTHSHIRE
Llanwenarth Arms Hotel, ABERGAVENNY
Castle View Hotel, CHEPSTOW
Boat Inn, PENALLT
Fountain Inn, TRELLECK GRANGE

PEMBROKESHIRE
New Inn, AMROTH
Galleon Inn, BROAD HAVEN
Carew Inn, CAREW
The Georges Restaurant/Cafe Bar, HAVERFORDWEST
Trewern Arms, NEVERN
Ferry Inn, PEMBROKE DOCK
Sloop Inn, PORTHGAIN
Wolfe Inn, WOLF'S CASTLE

SHROPSHIRE
Woodbridge Inn, COALPORT
Crown at Hopton, HOPTON WAFERS
Red Lion Inn, LLANFAIR WATERDINE
Unicorn Inn, LUDLOW
Boathouse Inn, SHREWSBURY
Willey Moor Lock Tavern, WHITCHURCH

HEREFORD & WORCESTER
Riverside Inn, AYMESTREY
Fox & Hounds Inn & Restaurant, BREDON
Bunch of Carrots, HAMPTON BISHOP
The Talbot, KNIGHTWICK
New Inn, PEMBRIDGE
Ancient Camp Inn, RUCKHALL
Rhydspence Inn, WHITNEY-ON-WYE
Anchor Inn, WYRE PIDDLE

POWYS
Gliffaes Country House Hotel, CRICKHOWELL
Elan Valley Hotel, ELAN
Griffin Inn, LLYSWEN
Dolbrodmaeth Inn, MACHYNLLETH
Star Inn, TALYBONT-ON-USK

CAERPHILLY
The Courthouse, CAERPHILLY

DENBIGHSHIRE
Britannia Inn, LLANGOLLEN

GLAMORGAN
Blue Anchor Inn EAST ABERTHAW

GWYNEDD
The Pen-Y-Gwryd, LLANBERIS
George III Hotel, PENMAENPOOL

NORTHERN ENGLAND

CHESHIRE
Ferry Tavern, PENKETH
Bears Paw Hotel, WARMINGHAM
Ship Inn, WINCLE

CUMBRIA
Dukes Head Hotel, ARMATHWAITE
The Pheasant, BASSENTHWAITE LAKE
Bridge Hotel, BUTTERMERE
Bay Horse Hotel, CANAL FOOT
The Rusland Pool, HAVERTHWAITE
Fat Lamb Inn, RAVENSTONEDALE
Royal Oak, ULVERSTON
Wasdale Head Inn, WASDALE HEAD

DERBYSHIRE
Mowsal Head Hotel, BAKEWELL
The Abbey, DARLEY ABBEY
Red Lion Inn, HOGNASTON
Grouse & Claret, ROWSLEY
Clock Warehouse, SHARDLOW

CO DURHAM
Morritt Arms Hotel, BARNARD CASTLE

GREATER MANCHESTER
Egerton Arms, BAMFORD
Diggle Hotel, DIGGLE

Dukes 92, MANCHESTER
Mash & Air, MANCHESTER
White Lion, MANCHESTER

LANCASHIRE
Owd Nell's Tavern, BILSBORROW
Fishermans Retreat, SHUTTLEWORTH
Inn At Whitewell, WHITEWELL

NORTHUMBERLAND
Victoria Hotel, BAMBURGH
Canty's Brig Bar/ Bistro, BERWICK-UPON-TWEED
Rob Roy, BERWICK-UPON-TWEED
Angel Inn, CORBRIDGE
Black Bull, ETAL
General Havelock Inn, HAYDON BRIDGE
Dipton Mill Inn, HEXHAM
The Ship, LOW NEWTON BY THE SEA
Black Bull, MATFEN

NOTTINGHAMSHIRE
Martins Arms Inn, COLSTON BASSETT
King William, SCAFTWORTH

STAFFORDSHIRE
Black Lion Inn, BUTTERTON
The Junction Inn, NORBURY JUNCTION

YORKSHIRE
Ship Inn, ACASTER MALBIS
Red Lion, BURNSALL
Foresters Arms, CARLTON
Royal Oak Inn, DACRE BANKS
Duke of Wellington Inn, DANBY
Horseshoe Hotel, EGTON BRIDGE
Tempest Arms, ELSLACK
The Bell, DRIFFIELD
Seabirds Inn, FLAMBOROUGH
George Inn, HUBBERHOLME
Minerva Hotel, HULL
Racehorses Hotel, KETTLEWELL
Fountaine Inn, LINTON
Gold Cup Inn, LOW CATTON
Sportsmans Arms, PATELEY BRIDGE
Yorke Arms, RAMSGILL
Old Bridge Inn, RIPPONDEN
Olive Tree, RODLEY
New Inn, CLAPHAM

SCOTLAND

ABERDEENSHIRE
Old Mill Inn, MARYCULTER
Marine Hotel, STONEHAVEN

ARGYLL & BUTE
Ardentinny Hotel, ARDENTINNY
Galley of Lorne Inn, ARDFERN
Cairnbaan Hotel & Restaurant, CAIRNBAAN
Tigh an Truish Inn, CLACHAN-SEIL
Old Byre Heritage Centre, DERVAIG
Coylet Inn, DUNOON
Scottish Salmon Centre, KILNINVER
Polfearn Hotel, TAYNUILT
Tayvallich Inn, TAYVALLICH

CITY OF EDINBURGH
Bridge Inn, RATHO
Hawes Inn, SOUTH QUEENSFERRY

DUMFRIES & GALLOWAY
Steam Packet Inn, ISLE OF WHITHORN
Criffel Inn, NEW ABBEY

FALKIRK
Castlecary House Hotel, CASTLECARY

FIFE
Ship Inn, ELIE
Hoffmans, KIRKCALDY
Crusoe Hotel, LOWER LARGO
The Cabin, ST MONANS

HIGHLAND
Altnaharra Hotel, ALTNAHARRA
Applecross Inn, APPLECROSS
Ardvasar Hotel, ARDVASAR
Old Bridge Inn, AVIEMORE
Dalrachney Lodge Hotel, CARRBRIDGE
Dores Inn, DORES
Lock Inn, FORT AUGUSTUS
Inchbae Lodge Hotel, GARVE
Glenelg Inn, GLENELG
Hotel Eilean Iarmain, ISLE ORNSAY
Kylesku Hotel, KYLESKU
Creag-nan-Darach Hotel, PLOCKTON
Ceilidh Place, ULLAPOOL

MORAY
Gordon Arms Hotel, FOCHABERS

PERTH & KINROSS
Almondbank Inn, ALMONDBANK
Tullybannocher Farm Food Bar, COMRIE
Tormaukin Hotel, GLENDEVON

RENFREWSHIRE
Fox & Hounds, HOUSTON

SCOTTISH BORDERS
Tibbie Shiels Inn, SELKIRK
Tushielaw Inn, TUSHIELAW
Crook Inn, TWEEDSMUIR

STIRLING
Byre Inn, BRIG O'TURK

WESTERN ISLES
Polochar Inn, LOCHBOISDALE

West Country

In the heart of old maritime England, many little ports nestling in the rugged coastline still retain that buccaneering spirit. Ancient landscapes and rich farmland are peppered with secluded villages, country towns, historic sites and outstanding beaches.

• Bristol • Cornwall & Isles of Scilly •
• Devon • Dorset • Gloucestershire •
• Somerset • Wiltshire •

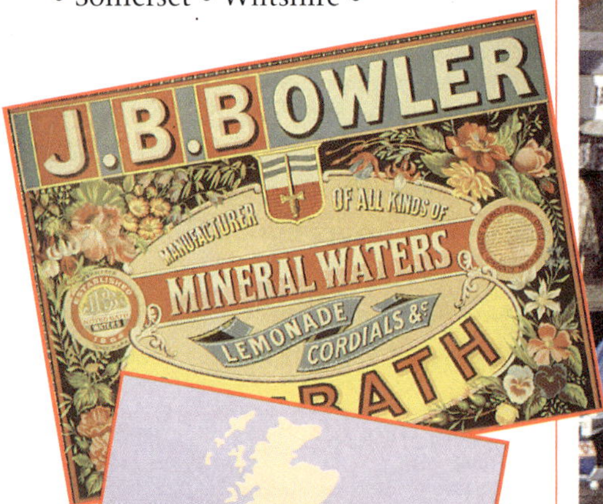

BRISTOL Bristol

Highbury Vaults

BRISTOL Map 03 ST57

164 St Michaels Hill, Cotham BS2 8DE

☎ 01179 733203

Named after the original owner who came from London's Highbury in 1840, this popular hostelry features snug corners and old Victorian prints. Local customers seek out the convivial fruit machine-free atmosphere and menu, featuring casseroles, curry and home-made puddings which change daily. Principal beers: Smiles, Brains SA.

Directions Take main road to Cotham from inner ring dual carriageway

Smiles

Open 12-11 (Sun 12-10.30)

Bar food 12-2 5.30-8.30 Av main course £2.90

Cornwall & Isles of Scilly

ALTARNUN Cornwall & Isles of Scilly

The Rising Sun

ALTARNUN Map 02 SX28

PL15 7SN ☎ 01566 86636

Granite roughcast and hung slate 16th-century inn with timber and slate floor in the bar area. Situated at the edge of Bodmin Moor. Bar snacks available, alongside main dishes which include moussaka, home-made steak pie, vegetable chilli, and cannelloni. Principal beers: Brakspears, Guinness, Stella, Heineken.

Directions Off A30 S of Launceston

Free House

Open 11-3 5.30-11

Bar food 12-2.30 6.30-9.30 Av main course £4.95

BODMIN Cornwall & Isles of Scilly

St Mabyn Inn

BODMIN Map 02 SX06

PL30 3BA ☎ 01208 841266

This quaint country village inn takes its name from St Mabena, who once stayed here. The character applies to the food too with the lunchtime menu broadening to include specials such as monkfish medallions with a dry vermouth sauce or breast of Barbary duck for supper. Principal beers: Sharp's Bass, John Smith,Miller Pils, Kronenberg 1664.

Free House

Open 11.30-3 6-11

Bar food 12-2 Av main course £10

Restaurant 6.30-9

BOSCASTLE Cornwall & Isles of Scilly

The Wellington Hotel

BOSCASTLE Map 02 SX09

The Harbour PL35 0AQ

☎ 01840 250202

Thomas Hardy, Edward VII and Guy Gibson VC all stayed at this 16th-century coaching inn. Set in National Trust countryside, this fascinating, haunted hotel has open fires and old beams. The Long Bar offers traditional pub food like scampi, sandwiches and steaks, and La Belle Alliance restaurant has French and English cuisine. There is live music on Fridays. Principal beers: Flowers IPA, St Austell HSD, Bass, Worthington.

Directions A30 onto A395, then A39, R onto B3314, R onto B3266

Free House

Open 11-3 5.30-11

Bar food 12-2.30 6-9.30 Av main course £4.25

Restaurant 7-9.30 Av 3 course à la carte £19.75 Av 3 course fixed price £18.50

Accommodation s£17 d£48

CHAPEL AMBLE Cornwall & Isles of Scilly

The Maltsters Arms

CHAPEL AMBLE Map 02 SW97

PL27 6EV ☎ 01208 812473

Enhanced by flower tubs, this 300 year old inn, a bargees' port of call in the days when the river was navigable, is the only pub in this pretty village. Fresh fish, the speciality, varies daily, but could include whole sea bass or sardines in garlic butter. Principal beers: Sharps Coaster,Maltsters, London Pride.

Directions From Wadebridge take B3314.Village on R

Free House

Open 11-2.30 6-11 (Sun 12-2.30,7-10.30)

Bar food 12-2 6-10 Av main course £5

Restaurant 12-2 6-10 Av 3 course à la carte £17

CONSTANTINE Cornwall & Isles of Scilly

Trengilly Wartha Inn

CONSTANTINE Map 02 SW72

Nancenoy TR11 5RP ☎ 01326 340332

A traditional inn offering food, drink and accommodation set in six acres of gardens and meadows in a peaceful valley close to the Helford River. Seafood is a speciality, and other options might be salsiccia - spicy Italian sausages - or stir-fried smoked duck with mange-tout and ginger. Principal beers: Sharps Coaster, Dartmoor Best.

Directions SW of Falmouth

Free House

Open 11-3 6.30-11

Bar food 12-2.30 6.30-9.30 Av main course £6.50

Restaurant 7.30-9.30 Av 3 course fixed price £21.50

Accommodation s£42 d£48

DUNMERE Cornwall & Isles of Scilly

The Borough Arms

DUNMERE Map 02 SX06

PL31 2RD ☎ 01208 73118

Situated on a well used holiday route to the North Coast, this pub is a busy food house, serving good home-cooked fare including steaks, daily fresh fish, carvery specials and vegetarian options. The pub is near the River Camel and the car park has exit points for the Camel Trail. Principal beers: Worthingtons, Boddingtons, Whitbread, T Greenalls.

Directions From A30 take A389 to Wadebridge, pub about a mile out of Bodmin

Greenalls

Open 11-11.20

Bar food 12-2.30 6.30-9.30 Av main course £5

Restaurant 12-2.30 6.30-9.30 Av 3 course à la carte £12 Av 2 course fixed price £5.95

EGLOSHAYLE Cornwall & Isles of Scilly

The Earl of St Vincent

EGLOSHAYLE Map 02 SX07

PL27 6HT ☎ 01208 814807

Dating from the Middle Ages, with colourful floral displays and a collection of old clocks, the Earl of St Vincent is named after Sir John Jervis, the Earl of St Vincent and Nelson's superior officer. There is a comprehensive menu with specialities like tournedos Rossini, chicken in leek and Stilton sauce, and fresh fish. Principal beers: Tinners, Hicks Special, Duchy, Carlsberg.

St Austell Brewery

Open 11-3 6.30-11

FOWEY Cornwall & Isles of Scilly

King of Prussia

FOWEY Map 02 SX15

Town Quay PL23 1AT

☎ 01726 832450

Name derived from a roguish privateer called John Carter who went by the nickname *The King of Prussia*. The pub enjoys fine views of the River Fowey. Specials vary from week to week. Main menu features home-made dishes like seafood lasagne, fish and pasta bake, and tomato and vegetable tagliatelle. Principal beers: St Austell Cask Ales, Carlsberg Lagers, Guinness, Murphys.

St Austell Brewery

Open 11-11 (Sun 12-10.30)

Bar food 12-2.30 6.30-9 Av main course £5

Restaurant 12-2.30 6.30-9 Av 3 course à la carte £8 Av 3 course fixed price £8

Accommodation d£46

The Ship Inn
FOWEY Map 02 SX15
Trafalgar Square PL23 1AZ
☎ 01726 832230
Fowey is regarded as one of the prettiest villages on the south coast, and this 16th-century inn, visited both by Cromwell and Sir Francis Drake, has been an integral part of its history. Deep fried jalopenos, battered calamari, spinach and feta goujons, and Hick's special sausages may be on the menu. Principal beers: St Austell Ales.
Directions From A30,take B3269 & A390.
St Austell Brewery
Open 11-11
Bar food 12-2.30 6-9 Av main course £4.75
Accommodation s£18.50 d£37

GUNWALLOE Cornwall & Isles of Scilly

The Halzephron Inn
GUNWALLOE Map 02 SW62
TR12 7QB ☎ 01326 240406
Although the name Halzephron comes from the old Cornish for 'Cliffs of Hell', visitors to this pub on the unspoilt Lizard peninsula should get a welcoming reception. The menu may include grilled goats cheese on garlic bread, Mr. Kearsley's crab salad platter, or the speciality, Halzephron chicken. Principal beers: Sharp's Own, Dartmoor Best, Guinness.
Directions 3m S of Helston on A3083, R to Gunwalloe. then thru village inn is on L overlooking Mount's Bay.
Free House
Open 11-2.30 6.30-11 (Sun 7-10.30)
Bar food 12-2 7-9.30 Av main course £7
Restaurant 12-2 7-9.30 Av 3 course à la carte £19 Av 3 course fixed price £9.50
Accommodation s£35 d£56

GWEEK Cornwall & Isles of Scilly

The Gweek Inn
GWEEK Map 02 SW71
TR12 6TU ☎ 01326 221502
Situated at the mouth of the River Helford, this old country pub has low-beamed ceilings, a restaurant in a converted barn, and an outside salad and sandwich bar in good weather. Today's menu may include pork Suisse, lamb Arabesque, devilled seafood rosti, or a variety of griddled steaks. Principal beers: Flowers IPA, Boddingtons, Speckled Hen, Bass.
Directions 2m E of Helston near Seal Sanctuary
Greenalls
Open 12-3 6.30-11
Bar food 12-2.15 6.30-9 Av main course £5
Restaurant 12-2.15 7-11 Av 3 course à la carte £16 Av 2 course fixed price £10

HELFORD Cornwall & Isles of Scilly

Shipwright Arms
HELFORD Map 02 SW72
TR12 6JX ☎ 01326 231235
Small thatched pub overlooking the River Helford. Snacks and starters range from monkfish, scallop and bacon kebab, to beef and Guinness pie. Other dishes include scallops Mornay, lamb and chicken curries, sirloin steak, and chicken or turkey with sweet pepper. Principal beers: Castle Eden, Flowers IPA.
Directions A390 thru Truro then A39 to Mabe Burnthouse, A394 to Helston, A3083 to Carminowe, E to Helford
Free House
Open 11-2.30 6-11
Bar food 12-2 7-9 Av main course £5.50
Restaurant 12-2 7-9 Av 3 course à la carte £11

HELFORD PASSAGE Cornwall & Isles of Scilly

Ferryboat Inn
HELFORD PASSAGE Map 02 SW72
TR11 5LB ☎ 01326 250625
Named after the ferry which has linked Helford and Helford Passage since the 16th century, this pub caters well for vegetarians with dishes such as spinach and Feta goujons or deep-fried Brie with redcurrant jelly. Others might try grilled plaice, Cornish pork

sausages or lemon sole. Principal beers: St Austell Real Ales, XXXX Mild, Tinners ale, Hicks HSD Special.
Directions Exit M5 onto A30 into Cornwall
St Austell Brewery
Open 11-11
Bar food 12-2.30 6.30-9 Av main course £4
Restaurant 12-2.30 6.30-9

HELSTON Cornwall & Isles of Scilly

Blue Anchor Inn
HELSTON Map 02 SW62
59 Coinagehall St TR13 8EX
☎ 01326 562821
There are only four original inns brewing their own beer in Great Britain and this is one of them. The name comes from the days when Helston was a port - before it silted up. Traditional home-made dishes are served, such as sausage and mash, beef and ale pie, and bubble and squeak. Principal beers: Spingo.
Directions Helston off the A30 towards Penzance
Free House
Open 11-11 (Sun 12-10.30)
Bar food 12-4 Av main course £3

Yard Bistro
HELSTON Map 02 SW62
Trelowarren, Mawgan TR12 6AF
☎ 01326 221595
A converted carriage house amid acres of woodland countryside, this charming bistro is on the banks of the Helford and Gweek rivers. The menu includes such inventiveness as fresh local crab with tomato syllabub and roasted beetroot dressing, and souffléd saffron bread pudding with chestnut ice cream. Enjoy it all to the accompaniment of live jazz. Principal beers: Carlsberg Export.
Directions Off B3293, 3m SE of Helston
Free House
Open 11-2 7-9

KINGSAND Cornwall & Isles of Scilly

The Halfway House Inn
KINGSAND Map 02 SX45
Fore St PL10 1NA ☎ 01752 822279
Only a few yards from the beach, this traditional Cornish pub is located in a picturesque fishing village. Obviously the menu is very fish-oriented, but also features dishes such as venison with port and wild mushroom, parma ham, and quail wrapped in bacon. Principal beers: Bass, Boddingtons, Flowers, IPA.
Free House
Open 12-3.30 7-11
Bar food 12-2 7-9.30 Av main course £4.75
Restaurant 12-2 7-9.30 Av 3 course à la carte £15 Av 3 course fixed price £14.75
Accommodation s£22 d£44

LAMORNA Cornwall & Isles of Scilly

Lamorna Wink
LAMORNA Map 02 SW42
TR19 6XH ☎ 01736 731566
The Lamorna Wink was one of the 'Kiddleywinks' created by the 1830 Beer Act which allowed any householder to get a licence to sell beer. The 'Winks' in more remote areas sold smuggled liquor, giving the name a different meaning! Sandwiches, ploughmans and quiche are the traditional fare. Principal beers: Marstons Pedigree, Worthington Draught, Boddingtons, Stella.
Directions 4m along B3315 towards Lands End, then 1/2m into turning on L
Greenalls
Open 11-11
Bar food 11-2.30 6-9 Av main course £3.50

LANLIVERY Cornwall & Isles of Scilly

The Crown Inn
LANLIVERY Map 02 SX05
PL30 5BT ☎ 01208 872707
12th-century longhouse building with flag slate floors and a priest hole in the chimney. Wide selection of bar snacks, supplemented by seafood dishes such as salmon steak en papillote. The roast duckling is served with honey and almond sauce, and the pork with apricots, raisins and red wine sauce. Principal beers: Sharps, Bass, Carling, Tennants.
Directions From Bodmin take A30 S,follow signs 'Lanhydrock',L at mini r'about.3m take A390, Lanlivery 2nd R
Free House
Open 11-3 6-11

contd.

Bar food 12-2.15 7-9.30 Av main course £5.75
Restaurant 12-2.15 7-9.30 Av 3 course à la carte £11.50
Accommodation s£25 d£40

LAUNCESTON Cornwall & Isles of Scilly

Eliot Arms (Square & Compass)
LAUNCESTON Map 02 SX38
Tregadillett PL15 7EU ☎ 01566 772051
The dual naming of this 14th century pub housing a collection of clocks, snuffs and ephemera, is based in the lore of freemasonry. Offering honest, home-made food the menu's mouthwatering fresh fish selection is a feature. Principal beers: Old Speckled Hen, Wadworth 6X, Flowers Original, Pedigree.
Directions Turn of A30 for Tregadillett, Bodmin side of Launceston
Free House
Open 11-2.30 6-11
Bar food 12-2 7-9.30 Av main course £7.50
Restaurant 12-2 7-9.30
Accommodation s£22 d£38

LERRYN Cornwall & Isles of Scilly

Ship Inn
LERRYN Map 02 SX15
PL22 0PT ☎ 01208 872374
Oak-panelled walls and slate-flagged floors are features of this 17th-century inn, which is situated in the centre of a lovely riverside village, surrounded by wood and farmland. Home-cooked country food is served, including pies, fresh local fish, steaks, vegetarian dishes and bar snacks. Principal beers: Bass, Doom Bar, London Pride, Wadworths 6X.
Directions From Bodmin take B3269 to Lostwithiel then south to Lerryn
Free House
Open 11.30-3 6-11
Bar food 12-2 7-9 Av main course £5
Restaurant 12-2 7-9 Av 3 course à la carte £9
Accommodation s£20 d£20

AA members can call AA Hotel Booking Service on 0990 050505 to book at AA recognised hotels and B & Bs in the UK and Ireland, or through our Internet site: http://www.theaa.co.uk/hotels

LOSTWITHIEL Cornwall & Isles of Scilly

Royal Oak Inn
LOSTWITHIEL Map 02 SX15
Duke St PL22 1AH ☎ 01208 872552
This 13th century free house situated in the old capital of Cornwall has an underground tunnel reputed to lead to Restormel Castle. The inn, which retains its original character, is a popular local meeting place. Local produce features with daily specials ranging from Mrs Hines' game pie to fresh lemon sole. Principal beers: Bass, London Pride, Pedigree, Sharps.
Free House
Open 11-11
Bar food 12-2 6.30-9.30
Restaurant 12-2 6.30-9.30

LUDGVAN Cornwall & Isles of Scilly

White Hart
LUDGVAN Map 02 SW53
Churchtown TR20 8EY ☎ 01736 740574
Early 14th-century pub with splendid views across St. Michael's Mount and Bay. The specials board typically features New Zealand green lipped mussels, cider braised pork, and toad in the hole. Also on offer are home-made pasta dishes, steak grills, and home-made treacle tart and carrot cake. Principal beers: Marstons Pedigree, Flowers.
Directions From A30 take B3309 at Crowlas
Greenalls
Open 11-2.30 6-11
Bar food 12-2 7-9 Av main course £4.75
Restaurant 12-2 7-9

METHERELL Cornwall & Isles of Scilly

Carpenters Arms
METHERELL Map 02 SX46
PL17 8BJ ☎ 01579 350242
Originally built to house workers building the Cotehele House and estate, this inn dates from the 15th century and retains much of its historic charm. Basket meals, baguettes, and a choice of main courses are served at lunch, while the dinner menu offers steaks, tasty fish dishes and vegetarian options. Principal beers: St Austell, Sharps.
Directions S of A390 between Tavistock & Callington
Free House
Open 11-3 5-11

Bar food 12.30-2.30 Av main course £6
Restaurant 12.30-2.30 7-10 Av 3 course à la carte £11.50
Accommodation s£45 d£40

MEVAGISSEY Cornwall & Isles of Scilly

Rising Sun Inn
MEVAGISSEY Map 02 SX04
Portmellon Cove PL26 6PL
☎ 01726 843235
A 17th-century smugglers inn situated right next to the beach in a superb cove with a slipway for launching boats. The menu offers light meals including local crab and Cornish pasty; burgers and baked potatoes for children, and main courses such as sirloin steak or fresh pan-fried cod. Principal beers: Wadworth 6X, Marstons Pedigree, Boddingtons.
Free House
Open 11.30-3 6-11
Bar food 12-2 6.30-9 Av main course £4.50
Restaurant 12-2 6.30-9 Av 3 course à la carte £10
Accommodation s£26.95 d£43.90

MITHIAN Cornwall & Isles of Scilly

Miners Arms
MITHIAN Map 02 SW75
TR5 0QU ☎ 01872 552375
Decorative ceilings are a feature of this old pub, one of which incorporates the date 1577. There was once a secret passage leading to the manor house, used by monks in difficult times. Food includes steak and kidney pie, curry of the day and scampi and chips. Principal beers: Pedigree, Bass.
Directions From A30 take B3277 to St Agnes. Take 1st R to Mithian
Greenalls
Open 12-3 6-11.30
Bar food 12-2.30 6.30-9.30 Av main course £7

MORWENSTOW Cornwall & Isles of Scilly

The Bush Inn
MORWENSTOW Map 02 SS21
EX23 9SR ☎ 01288 331242
Once the haunt of smugglers and wreckers, this 13th-century pub has low beamed ceilings, plenty of brass and copper ware and lovely old wooden furniture. The food on offer includes home-made soups and stews, crab and smoked mackerel in season, Cornish pasties, ploughman's and sandwiches. Principal beers: HSD, Worthington, Guinness.
Free House
Open 12-3 7-11

MOUSEHOLE Cornwall & Isles of Scilly

Cornish Range
MOUSEHOLE Map 02 SW42
6 Chapel St TR19 6SB
☎ 01736 731488
The building dates from the turn of the century and was originally a pilchard press, processing pilchards caught in the harbour. The name comes from the beautiful old black leaded range in the restaurant. The dishes are cosmopolitan in style, specialising in fish and shellfish, all cooked to order.
Directions On Coast road from Penzance toward Newlyn
Restaurant 12-2 7-9 Av 3 course à la carte £15

MYLOR BRIDGE Cornwall & Isles of Scilly

Pandora Inn
MYLOR BRIDGE Map 02 SW83
Restronguet Creek TR11 5ST
☎ 01326 372678
The inn was re-named in memory of the Pandora, the ill-fated ship sent to capture the Bounty mutineers, whose captain bought the inn on his retirement. It actually dates from the 13th century and is beautifully located

contd.

on the Carnon River. Seafood is the speciality of the menus. Principal beers: Bass, St Austells, HSD, Trelawney's Pride.
Directions North of Falmouth off the A39
St Austell Brewery
Open 11-11 (Sun 12-10.30)
Bar food 12-2.30 6.30-9.30 Av main course £5
Restaurant 7-9.45 Av 3 course à la carte £20 Av 3 course fixed price £16.50

PAR Cornwall & Isles of Scilly

The Rashleigh Inn
PAR Map 02 SX05
PL24 2TL ☎ 01726 813991
In a beautiful, unique beach setting, this listed building furnished with antiques and pictures takes it name from the family which owns the Menabilly estate, famed as Daphne du Maurier's inspiration for Manderley. From the extensive French influenced menu, try Fowey sea trout or canard à la bière. Principal beers: Draught Bass, Burtons, Dartmoor Best.
Directions off the A3082 outside Fowey
Free House
Open 11-2.30 6-11
Bar food 11.30-2.15 6-10 Av main course £6
Restaurant 7-11

PELYNT Cornwall & Isles of Scilly

Jubilee Inn
PELYNT Map 02 SX25
PL13 2JZ ☎ 01503 220312
Beamed ceilings, log fires and antique furniture are features of this 16th-century inn, situated in a quiet village surrounded by beautiful countryside. Seafood fresh from nearby Looe is a speciality of the restaurant carte, and good value home-made fare is served in the bar. Principal beers: Bass, Trelawneys Pride, Tetley, Carlsberg.
Directions A38 from Plymouth, thru Liskeard L onto A390, to E Taphouse, L onto B3359 to Pelynt
Free House
Open 11-11
Bar food 11.30-2.30 6-9 Av main course £5
Restaurant 11.30-2.30 6-9 Av 3 course à la carte £15
Accommodation s£36 d£59

PENZANCE Cornwall & Isles of Scilly

The Turks Head Inn
PENZANCE Map 02 SW43
Chapel St TR18 4AF ☎ 01736 363093
Principal beers: Boddingtons, Bass, Wadworth 6X, Ringwood.
Directions town centre
Greenalls
Open 11-3 5.30-11
Bar food 11-2.30 6-10 Av main course £4.50
Restaurant 11-2.30 6-10

Ward's Brasserie
PENZANCE Map 02 SW43
12-13 Chapel St TR18 4AW
☎ 01736 363540
There's a relaxed bistro atmosphere at Ward's which offers a range of snacks and light meals like marinated mackerel with gooseberry sauce. Dinner menu dishes range from sauté of rabbit with cider and cream, to duck marinated in honey and ginger on a spiced apple glaze. Vegetarian options are also available. Principal beers: Holsten, Becks, Budweiser, Carlsberg.
Open 9.30-5 7-9.30
Restaurant 12-2 7-9.30 Av 3 course à la carte £17

PHILLEIGH Cornwall & Isles of Scilly

The Roseland Inn
PHILLEIGH Map 02 SW83
TR2 5NB ☎ 01872 580254
A characterful establishment with a friendly, family atmosphere where the art of talking still prevails, the inn's name is believed to be unique. Sample Philleigh Angels, fresh local scallops sautéed with smoked bacon and garlic butter, one of the home made dishes on a colourful menu. Principal beers: Sharps, Greenalls, Bass, Old Speckled Hen.
Free House
Open 11.30-3 6.30-11 (Sun 12-3, 7-10.30)
Bar food 12-2.15 7-9 Av main course £4.95
Restaurant 12-2.15 7-9 Av 3 course à la carte £10

PILLATON Cornwall & Isles of Scilly

The Weary Friar Inn
PILLATON Map 02 SX36
PL12 6QS ☎ 01579 350238
For eight long centuries the Weary Friar has provided food, drink and accommodation for travellers and locals alike. It is reputed to have housed the monks who built three of the local churches. The bar offers a choice of hearty dishes and there is a modern English menu in the restaurant. Principal beers: Plymouth Pride, Dartmoor Best, Abbots Ale, Tetley.

Directions 2m W of A388 between Launceston & Saltash
Free House
Open 11.30-3 6.30-11.20
Bar food 12-2 7-9.30 Av main course £5.99
Restaurant 7-9 Av 3 course à la carte £15 Av 3 course fixed price £15
Accommodation s£30 d£45

PORT GAVERNE Cornwall & Isles of Scilly

Port Gaverne Hotel
PORT GAVERNE Map 02 SX08
PL29 3SQ ☎ 01208 880244
It's a different world at this 16th-century inn, located in a little cove on the north Cornish coast. Bar food includes sandwiches, basket meals, and dishes such as Cornish fish pie, while the restaurant might offer local scallops, and rack of Cornish lamb with rosemary and garlic. Principal beers: Sharps.
Free House
Open Normal licensing hours
Restaurant 12-2 7-9

PORTHLEVEN Cornwall & Isles of Scilly

The Ship Inn
PORTHLEVEN Map 02 SW62
TR13 9JS ☎ 01326 57284
Emphatically a 'real pub', this 17th-century smugglers' haunt, overlooking the harbour, is very atmospheric, and has been the star of several advertisements. Menu options range from filled 'crusties', ploughman's and baked potatoes to three course meals, with dishes such as vegetable curry, fish pie and steak and kidney pudding. Principal beers: Sharps, Abbot, Ushers, Fullers.
Free House
Open 11.30-3 7-11
Bar food 12-2 7-9

PORTLOE Cornwall & Isles of Scilly

Tregain Restaurant
PORTLOE Map 02 SW93
The Post Office TR2 5QU
☎ 01872 501252
The tiny unspoilt fishing village of Portloe is the location for this tea room and licensed restaurant which is also the local post office, shop and information centre. Fresh local seafood dominates a menu which may also include lemon chicken breast with cider, lamb fillet with cherry sauce, or pizza with salad. Principal beers: Ruddles, Becks, Guinness, Local Cider.
Directions From A390 between St Austell/Truro.Take A3078. Follow signs for St Mawes.Turn L after Esso Garage for Portloe
Open 9-11
Restaurant 11.30-5.15 7-11 Av 3 course à la carte £20
Accommodation s£19 d£38

PORTREATH Cornwall & Isles of Scilly

Basset Arms
PORTREATH Map 02 SW64
Tregea Ter TR16 4NG
☎ 01209 842077
A low ceilinged stone pub, built to serve ship builders in the early 19th century. There are many old photos of the harbour and the village when it was a working tin port. The menu offers doorstep sandwiches, fisherman's pie, steaks, and chicken tikka masala, supplemented by daily specials. Principal beers: Tetley, Bass, Carlsberg.
Directions Follow Portreath signs from A30 after passing Redruth
Free House
Open 11-3 6-11
Bar food 12-2 6.30-9.30 Av main course £5.15
Restaurant 7-9.30 Av 3 course à la carte £12.50

ST AGNES Cornwall & Isles of Scilly

Driftwood Spars Hotel
ST AGNES Map 02 SW75
Trevaunance Cove TR5 0RT
☎ 01872 552428 553323
Head for magnificent Trevaunance Cove to find this nautically influenced, history steeped Hotel. The upper deck bar was once known as the only watering hole in the village high enough for the legendary giant to stand up in. Bar fare features hearty pasties to Mexican nachos with steak and fish specials in the restaurant. Principal beers: Tetleys, Carlsberg, Bass, Caffreys.
Directions A30 onto B3285, thru St Agnes, down steep hill, L at Peterville Inn, onto rd signed Travaunance Cove
Free House
Open 11-11 (Fri-Sat 11-12)
Bar food 12-2.30 6.30-9.30 Av main course £6
Restaurant 7-9.30 Av 3 course à la carte £18
Accommodation s£29 d£58

ST EWE Cornwall & Isles of Scilly

Crown Inn
ST EWE Map 02 SW94
PL26 6EY ☎ 01726 843322
16th-century inn with flagstone floors, original beams and an old roasting spit in the fireplace. The menu may include smoked salmon, gammon steak, lamb cutlets, or lemon sole. Local fresh crab is something of a speciality in season and is used in sandwiches, jacket potatoes and salad. Principal beers: St Austell, Hicks Special Draught, Tinners Ale, Carlsberg.
Directions From St Austell take B3273.At Tregiskey x-rds turn R.St Ewe is signposted on R
St Austell Brewery
Open 11-3 6-11
Bar food 12.30-2 7-9.30
Restaurant 12.30-2 7-9.30

ST JUST (NEAR LAND'S END) Cornwall & Isles of Scilly

Star Inn
ST JUST (NEAR LAND'S END) Map 02 SW33
TR19 7LL ☎ 01736 788767
Small Cornish coastal pub offering a range of soups, filled jacket potatoes and sandwiches. Home-made dishes feature local seafood, especially crab. For vegetarians there is a vegetable curry. And the home-made desserts include hot syrup pudding with cream and ice cream. Principal beers: Hicks Special Draught, Tinners Ale, Trelawneys Pride, XXXX Mild.
St Austell Brewery
Open 11-11 (Sun 12-10.30)
Bar food 12-2 6.30-8.30
Accommodation s£15 d£15

ST MAWES Cornwall & Isles of Scilly

Broomers Restaurant
ST MAWES Map 02 SW83
14 Marine Pde TR2 5DW
☎ 01326 270440
The restaurant is set by the water's edge overlooking St Mawes Bay and the Fal Estuary. Tables are laid out in the courtyard, lit at night, where there

are parasols, hanging baskets and a trellis of climbing flowers. The Anglo-European bistro food includes plenty of local seafood.
Open 10.30-5 7-9.30
Restaurant 12-2.30 7-9.30

ST MAWGAN Cornwall & Isles of Scilly

The Falcon Inn
ST MAWGAN Map 02 SW86
TR8 4EP ☎ 01637 860225
A 16th-century inn enjoying a lovely village location in the Vale of Lanherne. There's a warm welcome, and old beams and log fires add to the atmosphere. Wholesome home-made fare includes crab soup, vegetable curry, steaks, fresh cod in herb batter, and spotted dick with custard. Principal beers: Hicks Special draught, Trelawneys Pride, Carlsberg.

Directions From A30 8m W of Bodmin, follow signs to Newquay RAF St Mawgan,after 2m turn R into village
St Austell Brewery
Open 11-3 6-11
Bar food 12-2 6.30-9.30 Av main course £5.50
Restaurant 12-2 6.30-9.30 Av 3 course à la carte £15
Accommodation s£15 d£40

TREBARWITH Cornwall & Isles of Scilly

Mill House Inn
TREBARWITH Map 02 SX08
PL34 0HD ☎ 01840 770200 770932
Converted to an inn in 1945, this 16th-century mill house is set in the beautiful Trebarwith Valley, surrounded by trees and just a few minutes from the beach. Fresh local fish is a feature of the menu, which might include monkfish stir-fry, chilli con carne, and tomato and aubergine bake. Principal beers: Tinners, Bass, Cornish Gold, Sharps Own.
Directions From A39(Wadebridge/Bude rd)take B3314,then B3263 signed Tintagel
Free House
Open 11-11
Bar food 7.30-10 Av main course £5
Restaurant 7.30-10 Av 3 course à la carte £12
Accommodation s£23 d£36

The Port William
TREBARWITH Map 02 SX08
Trebarwith Strand Pl34 0HB
☎ 01840 770230
Enjoying one of the best situations in Cornwall, this 350-year-old inn overlooks the sea, beach and cliffs at Trebarwith Strand. Naturally, it has smuggling connections, with a tunnel accessible at the rear of the building. There are daily home-cooked dishes, fresh fish and vegetarian specialities. Principal beers: St Austell Ales, Flowers, Boddingtons.
Directions Off B3263 between Camelford & Tintagel
Free House
Bar food 12-2.30 6-9.30 Av main course £6
Restaurant 12-2.30 6-9.30 Av 3 course à la carte £15
Accommodation s£35 d£50

TRESCO Cornwall & Isles of Scilly

The New Inn
TRESCO Map 02
New Grimsby TR24 0QQ
☎ 01720 422844
The bar at the New Inn is made of drift wood from a jettisoned cargo. The bistro menu offers stone baked pizzas, salads and popular hot dishes, such as steak or battered cod. Typical restaurant dishes are salmon mousse, and escalopes of chicken with rice noodles, beansprouts and oriental sauce. Principal beers: Trelawney Pride, Castle Eden, Fuggles Imperial, Flowers.
Free House
Open 11-11
Bar food 12-2 7-9 Av main course £6.80
Accommodation d£52

TRURO Cornwall & Isles of Scilly

Old Ale House
TRURO Map 02 SW84

7 Quay St TR1 2HD ☎ 01872 271122
Up to 14 real ales are available on a daily changing basis at this traditional ale house. Other features are the sawdust and free monkey nuts. Skillet meals are a speciality, as are huge hands of hot bread, and dishes such as chicken tikka, oriental beef and cashew nut paella. Principal beers: Sharps, Bass, Speckled Hen, Flowers.
Directions A30, Truro City centre
Greenalls
Open 11-10.50 (Sun 12-3, 7-10.20)
Bar food 12-2.30 6-8 Av main course £5.95

VERYAN Cornwall & Isles of Scilly

The New Inn
VERYAN Map 02 SW93

TR2 5QA ☎ 01872 501362
Based upon two 16th-century cottages, the New Inn is in the heart of the Roseland District, and is only one mile from the English Channel. A typical menu includes wing of skate, lamb Rousseau, baked snails, a variety of homemade pizzas, and duck and kumquats. Principal beers: HSD & Tinners Ale.
Directions Off A3078 towards Portloe
St Austell Brewery
Open 11.30-3 6-11
Bar food 12-2 7-9 Av main course £7
Accommodation s£15.50 d£31

WENDRON Cornwall & Isles of Scilly

The Wendron New Inn
WENDRON Map 02 SW63

TR13 0EA ☎ 01326 572683
In fact over two centuries old, this village inn lies next to the church and offers lovely rural views. A collection of Shire brasses, assembled from local farms over 21 years, decorates both bars. Wide choice using local produce: trout, asparagus, clotted cream from the adjacent farm. Principal beers: Bass, Boddingtons, Tetleys.
Directions Off A30 at Redruth, take B3297 to Helston, Wendron 2m before Helston, pub next to church
Greenalls
Open 11.30-3 7-11
Bar food 11.30-2 7-9.30 Av main course £5
Restaurant 11.30-2 7-9.30 Av 3 course à la carte £15
Accommodation s£21 d£37.50

ZELAH Cornwall & Isles of Scilly

Hawkins Arms
ZELAH Map 02 SW85

TR4 9HU ☎ 01872 540339
A 16th-century coaching inn, set in the recently bypassed village of Zelah, hopes to solve drink driving problems by brewing its own ginger beer, which was taken from a recipe in a 1940 W.I. book. Menu may include vegetable lasagne, Cantonese-style prawn, or a 16oz 'Desperate Dan' steak.
Directions half mile off A30 between Truro & Newquay
Free House
Open 11-3 6-11
Bar food 12-2 6-9.30 Av main course £6
Accommodation s£14 d£30

Devon

ASHPRINGTON Devon

Durant Arms
ASHPRINGTON Map 03 SX85

TQ9 7UP ☎ 01803 732240
Situated in a village untouched by the passing of time, this 17th century former estate managers' house offers a warm welcome. Choose your cooked-to-order dish such as chicken suprême with asparagus, or lemon sole in mushroom and tarragon sauce in the elegant ambience of the central bar. Principal beers: Flowers Original, IPA, Wadworth 6X, Boddingtons.
Directions Leave A38 at Totnes Jct, proceed to Dartington & Totnes, at 1st set of traffic lights R for Knightsbridge on A381, after 1m L for Ashprington
Free House
Open 11.30-2.30 6-11
Bar food 11-2.30 6-11 Av main course £5.95
Restaurant 11-2.30 6-11 Av 3 course à la carte £12.50
Accommodation s£30 d£20

The Watermans Arms
ASHPRINGTON Map 03 SX85

Bow Bridge TQ9 7EG
☎ 01803 732214
This historic inn enjoys a glorious riverside location at the head of Bow

Creek. It has been a smithy, brewhouse and even a prison during the Napoleonic wars, and was once the haunt of the notorious pressgangs. Dishes range from popular pasta to traditional steak and kidney pie. Principal beers: Palmers, Dartmoor, Bass, Caffreys.
Directions Take A381 south from Totnes.After 1m turn left to village.Pub 2m
Free House
Open 11-11
Bar food 12-2.30 6.30-9.30 Av main course £5.95
Restaurant 12-2.30 6.30-9.30
Accommodation d£40

AXMOUTH Devon

The Ship Inn
AXMOUTH Map 03 SY29
EX12 4AF ☎ 01297 21838
Centrally located in Axmouth village, 1 mile from the sea, the Ship houses a large collection of dolls, a Guinness museum, and a centre for rescued birds and animals. Steak, kidney and Guinness pie, cheese and lentil bake, pheasant, mackerel, or baked plaice fillet may be on today's menu. Principal beers: Draught Bass, Flowers IPA, Guinness.

Directions 1m S of A3052 between Lyme Regis & Exeter
Greenalls
Open 11-2.30 6-11
Bar food 12-2.30 7.30-9 Av main course £4.50
Restaurant 12-2.30 7.30-9

BANTHAM Devon

Sloop Inn
BANTHAM Map 03 SX64
TQ7 3AJ ☎ 01548 560489 560215
Part 16th-century village inn attached to thatched former fishermen's cottages once owned by a notorious local smuggler. Within easy reach of the Avon Estuary. Main meals include smoked haddock with creamy spinach sauce, roast pheasant, and pork loin with cider and French mustard sauce. Plus Mediterranean hot pot for vegetarians. Principal beers: Blackawton Bitter, Ushers Best, Draught Beers.
Free House
Open 11-2.30 6-11 (7pm on Sundays)
Bar food 12-2 7-10 Av main course £7
Restaurant 12-2 7-10 Av 3 course à la carte £12
Accommodation d£55

BARNSTAPLE Devon

62 The Bank
BARNSTAPLE Map 02 SS53
62 Boutport St EX31 1HG
☎ 01271 24446
Built as a Spanish merchant's house with spectacular vaulting ceilings dating from 1620, from the turn of the century until the early 70s, the property housed a branch of the Westminster bank. Tex-Mex, burgers, classic pasta and salad dishes can be enjoyed in this lively setting retaining the original bank features. Principal beers: Draught Grolsch, Caffreys, Murphys.
Directions A361 from M5, pub in town centre
Open 10-10.30
Restaurant 12-3 6-10.30 Av 3 course à la carte £14
Accommodation s£44 d£63

BEER Devon

The Anchor Inn
BEER Map 03 SY28
Fore St EX12 3ET ☎ 01297 20386
A cosy local freehouse, overlooking the beach, the boats and the whole of Lyme Bay, the Anchor has a busy restaurant with an international menu specialising in seafood. Typical dishes include lobster thermidor, seafood

contd.

paella, and spicy coated fillet of pollock. Principal beers: Otter Ale, Otter Bitter, Wadworths 6X, Boddingtons.

Directions From A3052 between Seaton & Sidmouth take B3174
Free House
Open 11-2.30 5.30-11 (Summer & w/e 11-11)
Bar food 12-2 7-9.30 Av main course £5
Restaurant 12-2 7-9.30 Av 3 course à la carte £15.75 Av 4 course fixed price £8.50
Accommodation s£26 d£39

BERE FERRERS Devon

Old Plough Inn
BERE FERRERS Map 02 SX46
PL20 7JL ☎ 01822 840358
Relax at this unspoilt, traditional inn decorated with pictures and bric-a-brac, set in a farming village on the tidal River Tavy. Both bar and quiet, intimate restaurant offer the same range including home cooked specials and fresh fish, perhaps bass steak with dill or stuffed mussels. Principal beers: IPA, 6X, Bass, Dartmoor Pride.
Directions A386 from Plymouth, A390 from Tavistock
Free House
Open 12-3 7-11
Bar food 12-3 7-11 Av main course £6
Restaurant 12-3 7-12 Av 3 course à la carte £12

AA members can call AA Hotel Booking Service on 0990 050505 to book at AA recognised hotels and B & Bs in the UK and Ireland, or through our Internet site: http://www.theaa.co.uk/hotels

BLACKAWTON Devon

Normandy Arms
BLACKAWTON Map 03 SX85
Chapel St TQ9 7BN ☎ 01803 712316
Venture off the beaten track to find this 15th century inn in a peaceful backwater. Named in honour of the Normandy Landings, for which training exercises took place on nearby Slapton Beach, follow the signpost 'forces tavern' to sample traditional English dishes like Devonish pork and tipsy cake. Principal beers: Blackawton Bitter, Draught Bass.
Directions A381 from Totnes, L onto A3122, 1st R to Blackawton after Kingsbridge turning
Free House
Open 12-2.30 7-11
Bar food 12-1.45 7-9 Av main course £4
Restaurant 12-1.45 7-9 Av 3 course à la carte £10
Accommodation s£25 d£40

BRANSCOMBE Devon

The Masons Arms
BRANSCOMBE Map 03 SY18
EX12 3DJ ☎ 01297 680300
Find real Devon fare on the daily changing menu at this partially thatched 14th century inn. Set in a charming coastal village, it was once the haunt of smugglers. Taste home made asparagus soup or crab cakes using locally caught Branscombe crab. Principal beers: Carlsberg, Stella, Dartmoor, Bass.
Directions A375 from Honiton, off A3052 between Sidmouth and Seaton
Free House
Open 11-11
Bar food 12-2.15 7-9.15 Av main course £6
Restaurant 12-2 7-9 Av 3 course à la carte £17.50 Av 3 course fixed price £17.50
Accommodation s£22 d£44

BUCKFASTLEIGH Devon

Dartbridge Inn
BUCKFASTLEIGH Map 03 SX76
Totnes Rd TQ11 0YR
☎ 01364 642214
Situated on the banks of the River Dart, this inn is famous for its award winning floral displays. The menu contains a wide selection of poultry

and veal dishes, like honey roast duckling with peaches and champagne, plus steak specialities, including venison haunch steak with black cherry and port wine sauce. Principal beers: Worthington Smooth, John Smiths, 6X, Butcombe.
Directions Off A38
Free House
Open 11.30-2.30 6.30-11
Bar food 12-2 6.30-9.30 Av main course £5.95
Restaurant 12-2 6.30-9.30 Av 3 course à la carte £15
Accommodation s£37.50 d£55

BUCKLAND MONACHORUM Devon

Drake Manor Inn
BUCKLAND MONACHORUM Map 02 SX46
The Village PL20 7NA ☎ 01822 853892
Largely 16th century, but with some 12th century bits, the inn was built by the masons who built the church. It is known for its award-winning floral displays and its collection, now approaching 100, of single malt whiskies. The menu offers pies, grills, fisherman's platter and vegetable cassoulet. Principal beers: Ushers Best, John Smiths, Ushers Ales.
Directions Off A386 near Yelverton
Ushers
Open 11.30-2.30 6.30-11
Restaurant 12-2 7-10 Av 3 course à la carte £12

CHERITON BISHOP Devon

The Old Thatch Inn
CHERITON BISHOP Map 03 SX79
EX6 6HJ ☎ 01647 24204
The emphasis is on home- cooking with a difference at this 17th century listed inn which tastefully combines old world charm with 20th century comfort. Thatcher's pie, turkey cooked in a rich sauce with cheese and breadcrumb crust, is one hearty choice. Principal beers: Cotleigh Tawny, Wadsworth 6X, Tanglefoot.
Directions Take A30 from M5, about 10m then turning on L signed Cheriton Bishop
Free House
Open 12-3 6.30-11
Bar food 12-2.15 6.30-9.30 Av main course £6.75
Accommodation s£33.50 d£43

CLYST HYDON Devon

The Five Bells Inn
CLYST HYDON Map 03 ST00
EX15 2NT ☎ 01884 277288
All four owners are interested in antiques, so there are many interesting pieces at this thatched 16th-century longhouse. Fresh local produce is used wherever possible, including fish and game in season. Dishes include marinated pigeon breast, monkfish poached with prawns and dill, and treacle tart. Principal beers: Wadworth 6X, Dartmoor Bitter, Cotleigh Tawny.
Directions B3181 3m out of Cullompton, L to Clyst Hydon but R just before village for pub
Free House
Open 11.30-2.30 6.30-11 (Sun 12-3, 7-10.30)
Bar food 12-2.30 7-11 Av main course £6
Restaurant 12-2.30 7-10.30 Av 3 course à la carte £20

CORNWORTHY Devon

Hunters Lodge Inn
CORNWORTHY Map 03 SX85
TQ9 7ES ☎ 01803 732204
17th-century village Free House near the ruins of Cornworthy Priory. An interesting selection of home-made soups is available, such as broccoli and Stilton, tomato and roasted red peppers, and watercress. Main dishes include seafood mix grill, pan fried lamb in redcurrant sauce, and nut Wellington for vegetarians. Principal beers: Blackawton 44, Ansells Mild, Ushers Best, Beamish.
Directions Off A381 S of Totnes
Free House

contd.

Open 11.30-3 6.30-11
Bar food 12-2 7-10 Av main course £5.95
Restaurant 12-2 7-10 Av 3 course à la carte £15 Av 3 course fixed price £6.75

CREDITON Devon

The New Inn

CREDITON Map 03 SS80

Coleford EX17 5BZ ☎ 01363 84242

Haunted by Sebastian, a mischievous ghost with a penchant for knocking things off walls, this charming 13th century thatched inn's garden features a running brook. Fare from the black board menu is all home made using local produce such as fillet of brill with lemon, cream and butter sauce or Dorset mussels. Principal beers: Wadworth 6X, Otter Ale, Badger, Bitburger.

Free House
Open 12-2.30 6-11
Bar food 12-2 7-10 Av main course £5.95
Restaurant 12-2 7-10 Av 3 course à la carte £15
Accommodation s£38 d£52

DARTINGTON Devon

Cott Inn

DARTINGTON Map 03 SX76

TQ9 6HE ☎ 01803 863777

A real picture postcard of a place, reputed to be the second oldest licensed inn - and to have the longest thatch - in the country. Food is traditional, with an emphasis on fish, with dishes such as fillets of gurnard with local mussels and a sweet tomato and dill sauce. Principal beers: Otter Best, Butcombe Bitter, Draught Bass.

Directions On A384 between Totnes & Buckfastleigh
Free House
Open 11-2.30 5.30-11
Bar food 12-2.15 6-9.30 Av main course £7
Restaurant 12-2.15 6-9.30 Av 3 course à la carte £17.50
Accommodation s£40 d£50

AA members can call AA Hotel Booking Service on 0990 050505 to book at AA recognised hotels and B & Bs in the UK and Ireland, or through our Internet site: http://www.theaa.co.uk/hotels

DARTMOUTH Devon

The Cherub Inn

DARTMOUTH Map 03 SX85

13 Higher St TQ6 9RB ☎ 01803 832571

Dartmouth's oldest building, dating from about 1380. Starters include Cherub smokie, which is fillet of smoked haddock with turmeric, white wine and cheese. Among the main seafood dishes are poached salmon with orange butter sauce, and poached fillet of John Dory with Pernod and chive cream sauce. Principal beers: Wadsworth 6X, Old Speckled Hen, Flowers Original, Carlsberg lager.

Free House
Open 11-3, 6-11 (Sunday 10.30 closing) (Summer all day opening)
Bar food 12-2 7-10 Av main course £4.95
Restaurant 12-2 7-9.30 Av 3 course à la carte £20

DAWLISH Devon

The Anchor Inn

DAWLISH Map 03 SX97

Cockwood, Starcross EX6 8RA
☎ 01626 890203 891203

Specialising in fresh local fish and an impressive array of shellfish, this harbourside inn welcomes visiting boats. Reputedly over 400 years old and originally opened as a Seaman's mission, The Anchor was a haven for sailors and smugglers and is haunted by a friendly ghost and his dog. Principal beers: Whitbread Ales, Bass.

Directions Off A379 between Dawlish & Starcross
Heavitree
Open 11-11 (Sun 12-10.30)
Bar food 12-3 6.30-10 Av main course £5
Restaurant 12-3 6.30-10 Av 3 course à la carte £20

DODDISCOMBSLEIGH Devon

The Nobody Inn

DODDISCOMBSLEIGH Map 03 SX88

EX6 7PS ☎ 01647 252394

16th-century inn close to a 13th-century manor house and a short drive from Dartmoor and the coast. The restaurant menu ranges from snails Bourguignonne, and braised lamb sweetbreads in white wine sauce, to fillet of beef with tarragon

sauce, and roast duck with an orange Curaçao sauce. Principal beers: Nobodys Best Bitter, Bass, Grolsch, Carlsberg and 2 Guest Beers.
Directions From A38 follow signs for Dunchideock and Diddiscombleigh
Free House
Open 12-2.30 6-11 (7-11 in winter)
Bar food 12-2.30 7-11
Restaurant 7.30-12mid Av 3 course à la carte £13
Accommodation s£23 d£48

DREWSTEIGNTON Devon

The Drewe Arms
DREWSTEIGNTON Map 03 SX79
The Square EX6 6GQ ☎ 01647 281224
Unspoilt country inn which describes itself as 'The Time Warp Pub' and hosts a jazz club every Friday. A typical meal may include scallop parcels or duck liver parfait for starters, and baked fillet of pork, chicken Credo, or venison and beef Balmoral as main courses. Principal beers: Flowers IPA, Wadsworth 6X, Marstons Pedigree, Old Speckled Hen.
Directions Leave A30 for Carhampton at Woodleigh jct, follow signs for Castle Drogo
Whitbread
Open 11-2.30 6-11 (Sun 12-3, 7-10.30)
Bar food 12-2.30 7-10 Av main course £5
Restaurant 7-10 Av 3 course à la carte £20
Accommodation s£35 d£50

EXMINSTER Devon

Turf Hotel
EXMINSTER Map 03 SX98
Turf Lock EX6 8EE ☎ 01392 833128
Built in 1820 at the end of the oldest shipping canal in the country, this pub is surrounded by water and cannot be reached by car - only by foot, boat or bike. Good home-made pub grub is served, including soup, toasties and burgers, plus chilli, nut roast and lasagne. Principal beers: Dartmoor Best, Tetley Smooth Flow, Kilkenny, Marstons Pedigree.
Directions Off A379 turn L at end of Exminster by-pass/over rail bridge. Park by canal(pub is 0.75m on foot)
Free House
Open 11-11
Accommodation s£25 d£50

HARBERTON Devon

The Church House Inn
HARBERTON Map 03 SX75
TQ9 7SF ☎ 01803 863707
Originally built in the 12th century to house masons working on the nearby church, this picturesque village inn is just outside Totnes. Typical specials menu includes crêpes Florentine au gratin, pheasant in red wine, mushroom and Stilton sauce, and a selection of Portuguese and Madeira style dishes. Principal beers: Courage Best, Bass.
Directions 2 1/2m outside Totnes on the A381
Free House
Open 12-3 6-11.20
Bar food 12-3 7-11
Restaurant 12-3 7-11
Accommodation d£15

HAYTOR VALE Devon

The Rock Inn
HAYTOR VALE Map 03 SX77
TQ13 9XP ☎ 01364 661305
Venture off the beaten track to discover this old world coaching inn nestling in a rural hamlet on the edge of Dartmoor. Accompanied by a comprehensive wine list, the menu might feature a salad of warm scallops followed by a 'Coachman' steak topped with Stilton and a port wine sauce. Principal beers: Royal Oak, Dartmoor.
Directions L at Bovey Tracey onto B3387
Free House
Bar food 11-3 7-10 Av main course £10
Accommodation s£45 d£51

HOLBETON Devon

Mildmay Colours Inn
HOLBETON Map 03 SX65
PL8 1NA ☎ 01752 830248
Originally a manor house, built in 1671, the pub was renamed after the late Anthony Mildmay, a keen jockey. The racing theme is taken up in the menu, which has a good choice of popular dishes. The pub has its own brewery, so you can taste the beer and see it made. Principal beers: Mildmay Colours, Old Horsewhip, Kilkenny, Guinness.
Directions S from Exeter on A38, ex at Nat Shire Horse Centre, S past Ugborough & Ermington R onto A379. After 1 1/2m turn L.
Free House
Open 11-3 6-11 (Sun 12-3, 7-10.30)
Bar food 12-2 6-9.30 Av main course £6
Restaurant 12-2 7-9.30 Av 3 course à la carte £12
Accommodation s£20 d£20

HOLNE Devon Map 03 SX76

Church House Inn
HOLNE Map 03 SX76
TQ13 7SJ ☎ 01364 631208
Head for the village centre to find this 14th-century inn with a cosy bar. Once a resting place for pilgrims, Oliver Cromwell reputedly stayed while visiting troops during the Battle of Totnes. Local growers and suppliers ensure the freshest ingredients for home-cooked English and French regional dishes. Principal beers: Dartmoor Best, Butcombe Bitter, Speckled Hen.
Directions Turn off A38 at Buckfast, take road signed for Two Bridges and Princetown, Holne is on the way
Free House
Open 11.30-3 6.30-11
Bar food 12-2.15 7-9.15 Av main course £5.95
Restaurant 12.15-1.45 7-8.30 Av 3 course à la carte £17
Accommodation s£22.50 d£19.50

HONITON Devon

The Otter Inn
HONITON Map 03 ST10
Weston EX14 0NZ ☎ 01404 42594
A 14th-century inn, full of character, with spit roasts over the log fire on a Thursday in colder weather. Home cooked dishes are served with fresh vegetables, ranging from sandwiches and jacket potatoes to sausage and mash or sirloin steak, plus fresh fish specials. Principal beers: Boddingtons, Bass, Hardy Country, Worthington.
Directions Just off A30 W of Honiton
Free House
Open 11-3 6-11
Bar food 12-2 7-10 Av main course £6.85
Restaurant 12-2 7-10

HORNDON Devon

The Elephant's Nest Inn
HORNDON Map 02 SX58
PL19 9NQ ☎ 01822 810273
Originally 16th-century miners' cottages, and a farm, this friendly local retains its old world atmosphere. The name comes from a former landlord, who was very large and never moved from his stool. Food is offered from blackboard menus, including game pie, Tavy trout, and lamb Vindaloo. Principal beers: Boddingtons BB, Palmers IPA, St Austells HSD.
Directions Off A386 N of Tavistock
Free House
Open 11.30-2.30 6.30-11
Bar food 11.30-2.30 6.30-11

HORSEBRIDGE Devon

The Royal Inn
HORSEBRIDGE Map 02 SX47
PL19 8PJ ☎ 01822 870214
In the 15th century this pub close to the River Tamar was a nunnery, but since 1981 it has housed the smallest brewery in Devon, producing three ales which are only available here. Pub food may include gammon steak, chicken curry, mushroom Stroganoff, or pears poached in red wine. Principal beers: Tamar, Right Royal, Heller, Bass.
Directions South of B3362 Launceston/Tavistock road
Free House
Open 12-3 7-11 (Sun 7-10.30)
Bar food 12-2 7-9 Av main course £4.25

KINGSBRIDGE Devon

Church House Inn

KINGSBRIDGE Map 03 SX47

Churchstow TQ7 3QW ☎ 01548 852237

Rebuilt in the 15th century, this historic roadside inn originated as a rest house for Cistercian monks two centuries before that, hence the name. The accent is on unpretentious home cooking with a choice of succulent hot roasts available in the Friars Carvery. Principal beers: Bass, Worthington, Caffreys.

Directions On A379 1 1/2m W of Kingsbridge

Free House

Open 11-2.30 6-11

Bar food 12-1.30 6.30-9 Av main course £4.75

Restaurant 12-1.30 6.30-9 Av 3 course à la carte £9.50 Av 2 course fixed price £8.65

KINGSKERSWELL Devon

Barn Owl Inn

KINGSKERSWELL Map 03 SX86

Aller Mills TQ12 5AN ☎ 01803 872130

Period features at this 16th-century former farmhouse include beams, inglenook fireplaces, flagged floors, a black leaded range, oak panelling and ornate plaster work. The menu offers grills, jacket potatoes, cold platters, and traditional dishes such as liver and onions, plus 'specials' including game and seafood. Principal beers: Dartmoor Best, Burton, Marstons Pedigree, Carlsberg.

Free House

Open 11.30-2.30 6.30-11

Bar food 11.45-2 6.30-10 Av main course £8.50

Restaurant 7-9.30 Av 3 course à la carte £17.75 Av 2 course fixed price £14.75

Accommodation s£40 d£60

KINGSTEIGNTON Devon

Old Rydon Inn

KINGSTEIGNTON Map 03 SX87

Rydon Rd TQ12 3QG ☎ 01626 54626

Pass a residential area to discover this atmospheric, listed former farmhouse, featuring a convivial dual level conservatory , walled garden and warm welcome. Blackboard and à la carte fare mixes local produce, herbs, spices and a liberal dash of flair for nasi goreng, Provençale fish soup or Gressingham duck. Principal beers: Bass, Wadworths 6X, Worthington Best, Draught Guinness.

Directions From A380 take B3193 into Kingsteignton

Free House

Open 11-2.45 6-11

Bar food 12-2.30 7-10 Av main course £6.20

Restaurant 7-12 Av 3 course à la carte £20.85 Av 2 course fixed price £11

KINGSTON Devon

The Dolphin Inn

KINGSTON Map 03 SX64

TQ7 4QE ☎ 01548 810314

Watch your head on the low beams at this 16th-century stone-built inn. All the food is home cooked using locally grown produce, freshly caught fish and seasonal meats. There's a choice of vegetarian meals, dishes from the charcoal grill and a favourite fisherman's pie. Principal beers: Ushers Founders, Ushers Four Seasons Bitter, Courage Best, Fosters.

Ushers

Open 12-3 7-10.30

Bar food 12-2 6-10 Av main course £6

Accommodation s£37.50 d£49.50

KNOWSTONE Devon

Masons Arms Inn

KNOWSTONE Map 03 SS82

EX36 4RY ☎ 01398 341231 341582

Dating from the 13th century, this thatched inn is situated in a conservation village of mainly stone cob and thatch cottages. Bar food includes a curry of the day and a number of other specials. Examples from the dinner menu are roast cod with puy lentils and sticky toffee pudding. Principal beers: Dorset Best Bitter, Tawny Bitter.

contd.

Directions M5 J27 Off A361 between Tiverton & S Molton
Free House
Open 11-3 6-11
Bar food 12-2 7-9.30 Av main course £4.25
Restaurant 12.30-2 7-9 Av 3 course à la carte £14.50 Av 3 course fixed price £14.50
Accommodation d£21

LOWER ASHTON Devon

Manor Inn

LOWER ASHTON Map 03 SX88
EX6 7QL ☎ 01647 252304
Surrounded by fields and woodland overlooking the Teign Valley, this country freehouse is close to a river and offers stabling facilities for riders. Typical menu includes steak and kidney pie, lamb goulash, tuna and prawn bake, and a selection of steaks from the grill. Principal beers: Teignworthy, Wadworth 6X, Theakston XB, Bateman XXXB.
Directions A38, Teign Valley turning, follow signs for B3193, pub 5m on R
Free House
Open 12-2.30 6-11
Bar food 12-1.30 7-9.30 Av main course £5.50

LUSTLEIGH Devon

The Cleave

LUSTLEIGH Map 03 SX78
TQ13 9TJ ☎ 01647 277223
A 15th-century thatched inn, with a large inglenook fireplace inside and a pretty cottage garden outside, situated on the edge of Dartmoor National Park. Food is prepared to order, and dishes range from ploughman's and salads to traditional roasts (including nut roast), sirloin steak, pizza and chilli. Principal beers: Flowers Original, Bass, 6X, Guinness.
Directions Off A382 between Newton Abbot and Moretonhampstead
Heavitree
Open 11-11
Bar food 12-2.30 6.30-9 Av main course £5.50

AA members can call AA Hotel Booking Service on 0990 050505 to book at AA recognised hotels and B & Bs in the UK and Ireland, or through our Internet site: http://www.theaa.co.uk/hotels

LYNMOUTH Devon

Rising Sun Hotel

LYNMOUTH Map 03 SS74
Harbourside EX35 6EQ
☎ 01598 753223
Local fish and game are the specialities at this thatched 14th-century smugglers inn, overlooking the picturesque harbour. Dishes include salmon en croute stuffed with spinach and Brie on a light Champagne sauce, and medallions of Exmoor venison with pear and blackberry compôte on a Madeira and game sauce. Principal beers: Ruddles County, Exmoor Gold, Theakstons XB.

Directions From M5 J29 to Minehead A39 to Lynmouth
Free House
Open 11-2.30 6.30-11 (Sun 12-3, 7-10.30)
Bar food 12-2 Av main course £6
Restaurant 7-9 Av 3 course à la carte £25
Accommodation s£49.50 d£79

MEAVY Devon

The Royal Oak Inn

MEAVY Map 02 SX56
PL20 6PJ ☎ 01822 852944
Monks used to brew their wine and beer at this 15th-century former church house, situated next to St Peter's church. Fish pie, lasagne and chicken tikka masala are among the mainly home-made dishes, alongside pasties and ploughman's; and there are popular puds such as spotted dick with custard. Principal beers: Courage, Whitbread.
Directions Off A386 between Tavistock & Plymouth
Free House

Open 11.30-3 6.30-11 (Sun 12-3,7-10.30)
Bar food 11.30-2.15 6.30-9.30 Av main course £4.95

MORETONHAMPSTEAD Devon

White Hart Hotel
MORETONHAMPSTEAD Map 03 SX78
The Square TQ13 8NF ☎ 01647 440406
Golf enthusiasts should note that this 18th-century inn on the edge of Dartmoor is within 30 miles of 20 golf courses. A varied menu may include Tavistock trout citronique, Aylesbury duckling Bigarade, or darne of Teign salmon Chambourcy. The home-made Dartmoor applecake was a favourite of Edward VII. Principal beers: Jail Ale, Bass, Dartmoor IPA.
Directions A38 to A382 Bovey Tracey bypass, 8m to Morehamptonstead
Free House
Open 11-11
Bar food 12-2.30 6-9 Av main course £4.75
Restaurant 7-8.30 Av 3 course à la carte £17.95 Av 3 course fixed price £17.95
Accommodation s£43 d£65

NEWTON ST CYRES Devon

Crown and Sceptre
NEWTON ST CYRES Map 03 SX89
EX5 5DA ☎ 01392 851278
Thirty years ago this 16th-century inn was destroyed in a chip-pan fire. It was rebuilt in traditional style, and there was another complete refurbishment in 1996. A selection of home-cooked starters and entrées is offered on the blackboard menus each day, using fresh local meat, fish and cheese. Principal beers: Bass, Boddingtons, 6X, Stella Artois.
Directions 2m NW of Exeter on A377
Free House
Open 11.30-2.30 6-11.30
Bar food 12-2 6-9
Restaurant 12-2 6-9 Av 3 course à la carte £12
Accommodation d£40

NORTH BOVEY Devon

Ring of Bells Inn
NORTH BOVEY Map 03 SX78
TQ13 8RB ☎ 01647 440375
Originally built to house the masons constructing the church, this 13th-century thatched inn offers a welcoming atmosphere with good local gossip. The food ranges from snacks to full meals, with dishes such as oven baked local trout and pork Devonshire, with cider, apple and cream sauce. Principal beers: Butcombe Best Bitter, Wadworth 6X, Teignworthy 'Reel' Ale.
Free House
Bar food 12-2 6.30-9 Av main course £6
Restaurant 12-2 6.30-9
Accommodation s£20 d£30

OKEHAMPTON Devon

Castle Inn & Hotel
OKEHAMPTON Map 02 SX59
Lydford EX20 4BH
☎ 01822 820242 820241
Low lamp-lit beams, antique settles and polished slate floors characterise this 16th-century freehouse. There is an emphasis on home cooking, with fresh fish, oriental and vegetarian dishes featuring. The choice is good, from roasted red pepper roulade to Dartmoor pie (venison and dried fruit with vegetables). Principal beers: Blackawton Bitter, London Pride.

Directions Off A386 S of Okehampton
Free House
Open 11-3.30 6-11
Bar food 12-2.30 6.30-9.30 Av main course £5.90
Restaurant 7-9.30 Av 3 course à la carte £17 Av 4 course fixed price £15.95

PETER TAVY Devon

The Peter Tavy Inn
PETER TAVY Map 02 SX57
PL19 9NN ☎ 01822 810348
Once a smithy and miners' cottages, this 15th-century moorland inn has plenty of character with beams, slate floors and log fires. Home-style pub food is served in

contd.

the bar - rabbit pie and seafood lasagne - while the evening menu offers Barbary duck with fresh mango sauce, and monkfish Provençale. Principal beers: Jail Ale, Exmoor Gold, Dartmoor Best, Bass.
Directions Off A386 NE of Tavistock
Free House
Open 11.30-2.30 6.30-11
Bar food 12-2 7-9.30 Av main course £4.95
Restaurant 7-9.30 Av 3 course à la carte £12.50

PLYMOUTH Devon

The China House
PLYMOUTH Map 02 SX45
Marrowbone Slip, Sutton Harbour PL4 0DW ☎ 01752 260930
Waterfront pub, built around 1650 and formerly used as a naval storehouse. Restaurant menu offers snacks and light meals which range from chicken satay with peanut sauce, to baked salmon with dill and horseradish mustard and, for vegetarians, nut and broccoli rice cakes with mustard and herb sauce. Principal beers: Dartmoor Best, Tetleys, Marston Pedigree, Lowenbrau.
Directions A38 to Plymouth centre, follow Exeter St to Sutton Rd, follow signs for Queen Anns Battery
Allied Domecq
Open 11-11 (Sun 12-10.30)
Bar food 12-10/11 Av main course £4.95
Restaurant 12-10/11

POSTBRIDGE Devon

Warren House Inn
POSTBRIDGE Map 03 SX67
PL20 6TA ☎ 01822 880208
Rustic, beamed and decorated with granite and wood, the fire at this former tin miners' inn, the third highest in England, has burned continuously since 1845. Moorland views are breathtaking in this isolated spot. Enjoy home-cooked lunchtime snacks or, in the evening, Warrener's pie and toffee apple pud. Principal beers: Bishops Tipple, Hicks Special Draught, Butcombe Bitter, Tanglefoot.
Directions Take B3212 thru Morehamptonstead and on for 5m
Free House
Open 10-3 6-11 (Summer 10-11)
Bar food 12-2.30 6-9.30 Av main course £6

PRINCETOWN Devon

Plume of Feathers Inn
PRINCETOWN Map 02 SX57
The Square PL20 6QG ☎ 01822 890240
Good value food to suit all tastes from a local butcher's burger to three courses culminating in 'death by white chocolate' is offered at this welcoming inn which is part of the Duchy of Cornwall estate, hence the name. Children, horse riders, all are warmly welcomed. Principal beers: St Austell, Bass.
Free House

ROCKBEARE Devon

Jack in the Green Inn
ROCKBEARE Map 03 SV09
London Rd EX5 2EE ☎ 01404 822240
5 miles from the centre of Exeter this inn has connections with the ancient British pagan legend of the Green Man, as well as a bookable skittle alley. A meal here may include roast pheasant, venison stew with dumplings, salmon and dill fishcakes, or pan-fried lambs liver with bacon and lentils. Principal beers: Bass, Cotleigh Tawny, Teignworthy Real Ale.
Directions 5m E of Exeter on A30
Free House
Open 11-3 6-11
Bar food 12-2 6.30-10 Av main course £5.25
Restaurant 12-2 6.30-10 Av 3 course fixed price £14.95

SLAPTON Devon

The Tower Inn
SLAPTON Map 03 SX84
TQ7 2PN ☎ 01548 580216
Originally cottages built for workers who constructed the monastic collegiate next door, this 14th-century inn stands in the shadow of its bell tower. Traditional pub grub is served in the bar, while the restaurant offers speciality pasta dishes, grills, vegetarian options and home-made puddings. Principal beers: Dartmoor Best, Exmoor Ale, Tanglefoot, Bishops Tipple.
Directions Off A379 south of Dartmouth
Free House
Open 12-3.30 6-12
Bar food 12-2.30 6-9.30 Av main course £4
Restaurant 12-2.30 6-9.30 Av 3 course à la carte £12
Accommodation s£20 d£20

SOUTH POOL Devon

Millbrook Inn
SOUTH POOL Map 03 SX74
TQ7 2RW ☎ 01548 531581
Watch the ducks on the stream from the terrace of this cosy old beamed pub. Boats from nearby Salcombe moor at a pontoon in the creek, 2 minutes walk from the pub. Naturally seafood features on the daily specials board: fresh crab and avocado, halibut au poivre, seafood pasta. Principal beers: Bass, Ruddles, 6X, Murphys.
Directions Take A379 from Kingsbridge to Frogmore then E
Free House
Open 11-3 5.30-11 (winter 11.45-2.30, 6.30-11)
Bar food 12-2 7-9 Av main course £4

SOUTH ZEAL Devon

Oxenham Arms
SOUTH ZEAL Map 03 SX69
EX20 2JT ☎ 01837 840244
First licensed in 1477, the inn is believed to have been built by monks in the late 12th century. It is in a village setting overlooking the beacon on Dartmoor. There is traditional bar food and a set-price dinner, which might offer prawn cocktail, coq au vin and lemon meringue pie. Principal beers: Princetown Dartmoor, Princetown Jail Ale, Kronenbourg, Carlsberg.
Directions Off A30 between Exeter & Okehampton
Free House
Open 11.30-2.30 6-11
Bar food 12-2.30 7-9.30 Av main course £4.95
Restaurant 12-2 7.30-9 Av 3 course à la carte £15 Av 3 course fixed price £15
Accommodation s£40 d£50

SPREYTON Devon

The Tom Cobley Tavern
SPREYTON Map 03 SX69
EX17 5AL ☎ 01647 231314
According to legend this is the very pub that 'Old Uncle Tom Cobley and all' set off from in 1882. There are also panoramic views of Dartmoor. A meal may include spinach pancakes with garlic mushrooms, duck and cherry pie, casseroled pheasant in red wine sauce, or autumn vegetable pie. Principal beers: Cotleigh Tawny, Butcomb
Directions From Merryr
take B3219 north
Free House
Open 12-2.30 6-11.30
Bar food 12-1.45 7-8.45 Av main course £5
Restaurant 1 7-8.45 Av 3 course à la carte £12.50
Accommodation s£18 d£36

THURLESTONE Devon

The Village Inn
THURLESTONE Map 03 SX64
TQ7 3NN ☎ 01548 560382
A 100-year-old village pub with beams from a 16th-century ship which sailed in the Spanish Armada. It has recently been refurbished to include a fire as the focal point to the stylish surroundings. Innovative bistro-style food is served alongside traditional fare, all using fresh local produce. Principal beers: Palmers, Bass, 6X, Marstons Pedigree.
Directions A381 from Kingsbridge, R thru South Milton
Free House
Open 11.30-3 6-11
Bar food 12-2 6.30-9.30 Av main course £4.95

TRUSHAM Devon

Cridford Inn
TRUSHAM Map 03 SX88
TQ13 0NR ☎ 01626 853694
Originally a Saxon house, rebuilt as a hall in 1081, the inn is Britain's oldest domestic dwelling, retaining many of its medieval features. Local and regional foods are used in the bistro and restaurant menus, in dishes such as battered Brixham cod and roast duckling with port and orange sauce. Principal beers: Trusham, Broadside, Bass.
Free House
Open 12-2.30 6.30-11
Bar food 12.15-2 6.45-8.30 Av main course £7.50
Restaurant 7-8.45 Av 3 course à la carte £18.75 Av 4 course fixed price £18.75
Accommodation s£40 d£60

in full view, using fresh produce, local where possible. Principal beers: Palmers: IPA, Bridport Bitter, Zoo, Tally Ho! Guinness.
Directions Town centre
Free House
Open 10-11 10-10.30 (Sun 10-3,7-10.30)
Bar food 12-2.30 Av main course £5
Accommodation s£20 d£40

Shave Cross Inn
BRIDPORT Map 03 SY49
Marshwood Vale DT6 6HW
☎ 01308 868358
Set in the beautiful Marshwood Vale, this 14th-century thatched inn was the last stop for pilgrims on their way to the shrine of St Wita, and where travelling monks had their tonsures shaved. Food ranges from ploughman's through pasta and pies to a selection from the char-grill. Principal beers: Royal Oak, Badger Best, Draught Bass, Guinness.
Directions From Bridport take B3162 2m turn L signed 'Broadoak/Shave Cross' then Marshwood
Free House
Open 12-2.30 7-11
Bar food 12-2.30 7-9.30 Av main course £4

BUCKLAND NEWTON Dorset

Gaggle of Geese
BUCKLAND NEWTON Map 03 ST60
DT2 7BS ☎ 01300 345249
Built in 1834, originally as a village shop, this pub was known as the Royal Oak until about 18 years ago when the previous landlord began breeding geese. Popular pub dishes are supplemented by home-made blackboard specials such as lamb hot pot and haddock and prawn Mornay. Principal beers: Dorset Best, Bass, 6X, Oakhill.
Directions On B3143 N of Dorchester
Free House
Open 12-2.30 6.30-11
Bar food 12-2.30 7-11 Av main course £4
Restaurant 12-2.30 7-11 Av 3 course à la carte £10.50

CERNE ABBAS Dorset

The Royal Oak
CERNE ABBAS Map 03 ST60
23 Long St DT2 7JG ☎ 01300 341797
In its time this thatched 16th-century inn has been a blacksmith's shop and a coaching stop. There are three interconnecting rooms and a long bar with a flagstone floor and a huge collection of cups. Rough Dorset pâté, fresh fish, steaks and treacle tart are among the favourite dishes. Principal beers: Flowers IPA, Speckled Hen, 6X, Bass.

Directions On A352 N of Dorchester
Free House
Open 11-3 5.30-11 (Sun 12-3,5.30-10.30)
Bar food 12-2 6.30-9.30 Av main course £5.25
Restaurant 12-2 6.30-9.30

CORSCOMBE Dorset

The Fox Inn
CORSCOMBE Map 03 ST50
DT2 0NS ☎ 01935 891330
A thatched, stone-built inn, dating from 1640, with an inglenook fireplace and slate-topped bar, plus an oak conservatory with fabulous flowers. There are tables outside, and a stream under the trees. Food is freshly prepared from local ingredients, including lamb, rabbit, partridge and Lyme Bay crab. Principal beers: Exmoor, Spitfire, London Pride.
Directions From A37 between Yeovil & Dorcester follow signs for Halstock/Corscombe on R
Free House
Open 12-2.30 7-11
Bar food 12-2.30 7-11 Av main course £6.95
Restaurant 12-2.30 7-11 Av 3 course à la carte £15
Accommodation s£35 d£65

CRANBORNE Dorset

The Fleur-de-Lys
CRANBORNE Map 04 SU01
5 Wimborne St BH21 5PP
☎ 01725 517282
An ivy-clad village inn dating from the 1600s with an oak-beamed bar and restaurant. Judge Jeffreys, Rupert Brooke and Thomas Hardy all stayed here. 'Small bites' and basket meals are offered alongside grills, fish and vegetarian dishes, and specials such as venison in red wine. Principal beers: Badger Best, Tanglefoot.
Directions M27 onto B3081 to Cranborne
Hall & Woodhouse
Open 10.30-2.30 6-11.20 (Sun 12-3, 7-10.50)
Bar food 12-2 7-9.30 Av main course £5.95
Restaurant 12-2 7-9.30 Av 4 course fixed price £12.95
Accommodation s£20 d£32

DORCHESTER Dorset

Kings Arms Hotel
DORCHESTER Map 03 SY69
30 High East St DT1 1HF
☎ 01305 265353
A 300-year-old town centre pub where Thomas Hardy wrote one of his books. The bar offers a variety of good-sized home-made dishes, and the restaurant menu encompasses Chinese dim sum, lamb rogan josh, seafood fusilli, and port and Stilton steak, along with a range of fresh fish and vegetarian pasta dishes. Principal beers: Greenalls Original, Directors, Bass, Flowers.
Directions Town centre
Greenalls
Open 11-3 6-11.20
Bar food 12-2.30 6.30-9.30 Av main course £5
Restaurant 12-2.30 5.30-10 Av 3 course à la carte £12 Av 4 course fixed price £10.95
Accommodation s£44.25 d£44.25

EAST CHALDON Dorset

The Sailors Return
EAST CHALDON Map 03 SY78
DT2 8DN ☎ 01305 853847
An 18th-century thatched inn set in rolling Dorset countryside. Traditional home cooking is served, including locally caught fish, venison, pheasant and rabbit. Typical daily specials are pig roast with apple and cider sauce, fisherman's pie, and a choice of vegetarian dishes. Principal beers: Flowers IPA,Wadworths 6X,Caffreys.
Directions im S of A352 between Dorchester & Wool
Free House
Open 11-2.30 6-11
Bar food 12-2 6.30-9.30 Av main course £4
Restaurant 12-2 6.30-9.30 Av 3 course à la carte £9.50 Av 2 course fixed price £9.50

EAST MORDEN Dorset

The Cock & Bottle
EAST MORDEN Map 03 SY99
BH20 7DL ☎ 01929 459238
An original cob walled Dorset long house dating back some 300 years, serving usual and unusual bar meals. The à la carte menu uses all fresh produce, including roast partridge wrapped in smoked bacon on a port wine jus, and collops of monkfish with a herb crust. Principal beers: Badger Dorset Best, Badger IPA, Tanglefoot, Hofbrau lagers.
Directions From A35 W of Poole take B3075. Pub 2m on R
Hall & Woodhouse
Open 11-3 6-11
Bar food 12-2 6-9 Av main course £5.50
Restaurant 12-2 6-9 Av 3 course à la carte £15.50

GILLINGHAM Dorset

The Kings Arms Inn
GILLINGHAM Map 03 ST82
The Common, East Stour SP8 5NB
☎ 01747 838325
A friendly country pub with lovely views from the garden. Favourites from the traditional-style menu are Jen's home-made steak and kidney pie and Keith's beef and ale stew. There's also a choice of vegetarian dishes, ploughman's and burgers. Comforting puddings include chocolate cake, apple pie and spotted dick. Principal beers: Bass, Worthington, Carling Black Label, Carlsberg Export.
Directions On A30 W of Shaftsbury
Free House
Open 11.30-2.30 5-11
Bar food 12-2 6-9.30 Av main course £5.50
Restaurant 12-2 6-9.30 Av 3 course à la carte £11

GUSSAGE ALL SAINTS Dorset

The Drovers Inn
GUSSAGE ALL SAINTS Map 04 SU01
BH21 5ET ☎ 01258 840084
'The genuine article' is how the proprietor describes this 16th-century free house. Salads, sandwiches and ploughman's are available alongside full meals. The menu encompasses scrumpy pork, steak and mushroom pie, spicy curry, and lasagne, with an additional choice of fresh fish, vegetarian dishes and grills. Principal beers: Marstons Pedigree, Directors, Theakstons.
Free House
Open 11-11
Bar food 12-2.30 7-9.30 Av main course £5.25
Restaurant 12-2.30 7-9.30 Av 3 course à la carte £10

NORTH WOOTTON Dorset

The Three Elms
NORTH WOOTTON Map 03 ST61
DT9 5JW ☎ 01935 812881
Originally built as a cider house to serve adjacent farms, with splendid views of Dorset's Blackmoor Vale. The landlord has a huge collection of model cars. Main dishes feature Porterhouse steak with garlic and mushroom sauce, and royal ocean seafood platter. An excellent vegetarian selection includes broccoli and Brazil nut bake. Principal beers: London Pride, Butcombe, Spitfire, Ash Vine Bitter.
Directions From Sherborne take A352 to Dorchester then A3030. Pub 1 m on R
Free House
Open 11-2.30 6.30-11
Bar food 12-2 6.30-10 Av main course £5.75
Restaurant 12-2 6.30-10 Av 3 course à la carte £12
Accommodation s£20 d£35

PIDDLEHINTON Dorset

The Thimble Inn
PIDDLEHINTON Map 03 SY79
DT2 7TD ☎ 01300 348270
The River Piddle runs through the garden of this 200-year-old thatched pub in the heart of Hardy country. There's a good choice of home cooked food, including fresh fish, and meat dishes ranging from burgers through lasagne to T-bone steak. Vegetarian options and snacks are also available. Principal beers: Dorset Best, Old Thumper, Hardtackle.
Directions A35 westbound, R onto B3143, Piddlehinton 4m
Free House
Open 12-2.30 7-11
Bar food 12-2 7-9 Av main course £5.50
Restaurant 12-2 7-9 Av 3 course à la carte £11 Av 4 course fixed price £12

PLUSH Dorset

Brace of Pheasants
PLUSH Map 03 ST70
DT2 7RQ ☎ 01300 348357
A pretty 16th-century thatched inn situated in the fold of the Piddle Valley. Bar snacks include ploughman's, jacket potatoes, pasta parcels and pies, while typical main meals might be steaks from the char-grill, game pie or steamed supreme of salmon with a lobster, tarragon and prawn sauce. Principal beers: London Pride, Smiles, Bass.
Directions A35 onto B3143, 1m to Piddletrenthise, then R to Mappowder & Plush
Free House
Open 12-2.30 7-11
Bar food 12-2.30 7-11 Av main course £6.50
Restaurant 12-2.30 7-11 Av 3 course à la carte £15

PORTLAND Dorset

The Pulpit Inn
PORTLAND Map 03 SY67
Portland Bill DT5 2JT
☎ 01305 821237
On the tip of Portland Bill overlooking

contd.

the English Channel, the Pulpit specialises in fresh local seafood. Typical menu includes Portland crab salad, smoked mackerel, and fresh plaice fillet. Non-fish dishes include honey-roasted duck, leek and Stilton bake, and mushroom and nut fettucine. Principal beers: Bishops Tipple,Salisbury Best,Bass,Kronenberg.
Free House
Open 11.30-3.30 7-11.30
Bar food 12-2.30 7-10.30 Av main course £6
Restaurant 7-11 Av 3 course à la carte £15
Accommodation s£15 d£15

POWERSTOCK Dorset

Three Horseshoes Inn
POWERSTOCK Map 03 SY59
POWERSTOCK DT6 3TT
☎ 01308 485328
A stone-built country inn with original pine-panelled walls, set in a peaceful garden with a terrace overlooking the whole village - one of West Dorset's finest. Traditional English cooking is offered along with a choice of home-made pasta dishes: roast rack of Dorset lamb and pasta Parmigiani are typical examples. Principal beers: Palmers Bridport Bitter, Palmers IPA.
Directions E of A3066 (Bridport/ Beaminster rd)
Palmers Brewery
Open 11-3 6-11
Bar food 12-2 7-10
Restaurant 12-2 7-10
Accommodation s£30 d£40

PUNCKNOWLE Dorset

The Crown Inn
PUNCKNOWLE Map 03 SY58
Church St DT2 9BN ☎ 01308 897711
A 16th-century inn, frequented by smugglers from Chesil beach in the 18th century. Home-cooked dishes include steak and kidney pie cooked in Palmer's Tally Ho! and salmon and broccoli casserole. Puncknowle Apple Cake and sticky ginger pudding are among the tempting sweets served with local cream, ice cream or custard. Principal beers: Palmers.
Directions From A35, into Bridevally, thru Litton Cheney. From B3147, inland at Swyre.
Free House
Open 11-3 7-11 (Sun 12-3.30,7-10.30)
Bar food 11.30-2 7-9.30 Av main course £5
Accommodation s£20 d£18

SHERBORNE Dorset

Skippers Inn
SHERBORNE Map 03 ST61
Horsecastles DT9 3HE ☎ 01935 812753
A just out of town pub, popular with locals and visitors alike for the quality of its foods and ales. The home-cooked dishes include chicken liver pâté, grilled bass, steaks, and rabbit and mushroom pie. Bar food ranges from sandwiches to home-cooked ham and eggs. Principal beers: Wadworth 6X, Henrys, Bass, Adnams.
Directions From Yeovil A30 to Sherborne
Wadworth
Open 11-2.30 5.30-11 (Sun 12-2.30, 7-10.30)
Bar food 11-2.30 6.30-11 Av main course £4.20
Restaurant 11-2.30 6.30-11 Av 3 course à la carte £12.50 Av 3 course fixed price £12.50

White Hart
SHERBORNE Map 03 ST61
Bishops Caundle DT9 5ND
☎ 01963 23301
On the site of a monks' brewhouse, infamous Judge Jefferys once held courts here. There's a long history, but the inn's modern touches include children's play gear in the garden and special low fat dishes on the wide ranging menu. Home-made specialities include Somerset cider bake and scrumpy chicken. Principal beers: Dorset Best, Tanglefoot, Hofbrau lagers.
Directions On A3030 between Sherborne & Sturminster Newton
Badger
Open 11-2.30 6.30-11
Bar food 12-2 6.30-9.30 Av main course £5.50
Accommodation s£15 d£28

STUDLAND Dorset

The Bankes Arms Hotel
STUDLAND Map 04 SZ08
Watery Ln BH19 3AV
☎ 01929 450225
Five hundred yards from the beach, this Dorset pub is frequented by well-

INKTON Dorset

Fishermans Haunt Hotel
WINKTON Map 04 SZ19
Salisbury Rd BH23 7AS
☎ 01202 477283
Traditional fare is on offer at this old world inn, which faces the River Avon. Dishes include pan-fried Avon trout with almonds and garlic butter, and chicken Isabella, filled with ham and asparagus and topped with a Mornay sauce. There's also a choice of vegetarian dishes, such as mixed bean goulash. Principal beers: Gales, Bass.
Directions On B3347(Christchurch/ Ringwood rd)
Gales
Open 10.30-3 5-11 (Sat 10.30-11,Sun 12-10.30)
Bar food 12-2 7-10 Av main course £5
Restaurant 12-2 7-10 Av 3 course à la carte £13 Av 3 course fixed price £13
Accommodation s£42 d£60

Gloucestershire

AMBERLEY Gloucestershire

Amberley Inn Hotel
AMBERLEY Map 03 SO80
Culver Hill GL5 5AF ☎ 01453 872565
An impressive stone-built country inn with attractive gardens and a colourful mass of hanging baskets in summer. Traditional home-cooked food is served, including an all-day breakfast and spotted dick, in the bar, and home-made soup and Barnsley lamb chop in the restaurant. Principal beers: John Smiths smooth, John Smiths cask, Ruddles County, Theakstons XB.
Directions M5 J13 take A419 (towards Stroud) then A46
Free House
Open 7.30-11.30
Bar food 12-3 7-9.30 Av main course £5
Restaurant 11-3 7-9.30 Av 3 course à la carte £12.95 Av 4 course fixed price £12.95
Accommodation s£40 d£60

AA members can call AA Hotel Booking Service on 0990 050505 to book at AA recognised hotels and B & Bs in the UK and Ireland, or through our Internet site: http://www.theaa.co.uk/hotels

AMPNEY CRUCIS Gloucestershire

Crown of Crucis
AMPNEY CRUCIS Map 04 SP00
GL7 5RS ☎ 01285 851806
17th-century Cotswold coaching inn, situated beside the Ampney Brook overlooking the village cricket green. House specials and grills feature seafood penne pasta, traditional oxtail casserole, seared escalope of salmon, herb crêpes, and mushroom stroganoff. The Chef's daily specials appear on the blackboard. Principal beers: Archers Village Bitter, Wadworths 6X, Marstons Padigree, Stella Artois.
Directions On A417 3m E of Cirencester
Free House
Open 10-11
Bar food 12-2.30 7-10 Av main course £5
Restaurant 12-2.30 7-10 Av 3 course à la carte £15
Accommodation s£38 d£52

ANDOVERSFORD Gloucestershire

The Kilkeney Inn
ANDOVERSFORD Map 04 SP01
GL54 4LN ☎ 01242 820341
Formerly a row of Cotswold terraced

cottages. Main course dishes include tartlet of spinach, rice, cheese and pine nuts with tomato and coriander sauce, roast duck with port wine and gooseberry sauce, and pork fried in garlic butter and served with saffron rice and a mild peach curry sauce. Principal beers: Ruddles Best, John Smiths Extra Smooth.
Directions On A436 1m W of Andoversford
Free House
Open 11.30-2.30 6.30-11
Bar food 12-3
Restaurant 12-3 7-10.30 Av 3 course à la carte £15

BARNSLEY Gloucestershire

The Village Pub
BARNSLEY Map 04 SP00
GL7 5EF ☎ 01285 740421
300-year-old Cotswold building with local farming implements adorning the walls. A wide range of bar snacks available. Main course dishes typically include grilled Bibury trout, home-made steak and kidney pie, and char-grilled lamb steak with port wine and rosemary sauce. Principal beers: Oakhill Bitter, Wadworths 6X, Boddingtons, John Smiths.
Directions On B4425 3m NE of Cirencester
Free House
Open 11.30-3 6-11
Bar food 11.30-2 6.30-9.30 Av main course £5
Restaurant 11.30-2 6.30-9.30 Av 3 course à la carte £12.50

BISLEY Gloucestershire

The Bear Inn
BISLEY Map 03 SO90
George St GL6 7BD ☎ 01452 770265
Parts of this building date back to 1333, originally used as a court house and meeting room. Contains secret passages and a priest hole in the chimney. Offers a good selection of baguettes and burgers. Also, many home-made pies and casseroles, including rabbit and vegetable, and Moroccan spiced lamb hotpot. Principal beers: Bass, Tetleys, Flowers Original.
Directions E of Stroud off B4070
Free House
Open 11-2.30 6-11
Bar food 12-2 7-10 Av main course £5.70
Accommodation s£18 d£36

BLEDINGTON Gloucestershire

Kings Head Inn & Restaurant
BLEDINGTON Map 04 SP22
The Green OX7 6XQ
☎ 01608 658365
A 15th-century stone-built inn on the village green, by a brook with ducks. The interior retains its original character with old beams, pew seating, trestles and a large inglenook fireplace. The menu changes regularly, and has an adventurous slant to traditional pub food. Principal beers: Hook Norton, 6X.

Directions On B4450
Free House
Open 12-11
Bar food 12-2 7-10 Av main course £4.95
Restaurant 7-10 Av 3 course à la carte £14 Av 3 course fixed price £9.95
Accommodation s£40 d£60

BLOCKLEY Gloucestershire

The Crown Inn & Hotel
BLOCKLEY Map 04 SP13
High St GL56 9EX ☎ 01386 700245
Built of mellow local stone, this inn is situated in the heart of a secret village in the Cotswolds. Food is served in the bar (from toasted sandwiches to casserole of local pheasant); in the brasserie (specialising in fish), and from an international menu in the Coach House Restaurant. Principal beers: Goffs Jouster, Spitfire, Hook Norton.
Free House
Open 11-2.30 5.30-12
Bar food 12-2 7-10 Av main course £6.95
Restaurant 12-2 7-10 Av 3 course à la carte £25
Accommodation s£64 d£89

BROCKWEIR Gloucestershire

Brockweir Country Inn
BROCKWEIR Map 03 SO50
NP6 7NG ☎ 01291 689548
A village pub, dating back some 400 years, situated on Offa's Dyke Path by the River Wye and Brockweir Bridge. Popular items including ploughman's and haddock and chips are supplemented by home-made specials such as tuna fish bake or pork in cider, with traditional puddings to finish. Principal beers: Guinness.
Free House
Open 12-2.30 6-11 (Open all day Saturday)
Bar food 12-2 7-8.30 Av main course £5
Restaurant 12-2 7-8.30 Av 3 course à la carte £5
Accommodation s£28 d£40

CALCOT Gloucestershire

Gumstool Inn
CALCOT Map 04 SP01
GL8 8YJ ☎ 01666 890391
Part of handsome Calcot Manor, this pub's name derives from the local term for a ducking stool. Dine al fresco on the terrace in summer or by the cosy fire in winter on innovatively prepared dishes such as Gloucestershire Old Spot beer sausages or slow-roasted duck salad. Principal beers: 6X, Duckers Brew, Bass.
Directions Calcot lies on Jct of A4135 & A46, 3m W of Tetbury
Free House
Open 11.30-2 6-11 (open allday wknds May-Sept)
Restaurant 12-2 7-11 Av 3 course à la carte £15
Accommodation s£95 d£97

CHARLTON KINGS Gloucestershire

The Little Owl
CHARLTON KINGS Map 03 SO92
237 Cirencester Rd GL53 8EB
☎ 01242 529404
Double-fronted pub named after the local horse which won the 1981 Cheltenham Gold Cup. Among the main course dishes are pork fillet Annecy, truffled chicken, and slow-cooked duck legs with candied red cabbage. There is a vegetarian dish of the day which sometimes features spinach and mushroom cannelloni. Principal beers: Boddingtons, 6X, Hook Norton, Stella.
Directions M5 J11a take A417 E,A436 then L onto A435. Approx 2m to pub
Whitbread
Open 11.30-2.30 5.30-11
Bar food 12-2 6-10 Av main course £5
Restaurant 12-2 6-10 Av 3 course à la carte £18

CHEDWORTH Gloucestershire

Hare & Hounds
CHEDWORTH Map 04 SP01
Foss Cross GL54 4NN ☎ 01285 720288
Surrounded by beautiful Cotswold countryside on a remote stretch of the Fosse Way, this ancient pub has a low-slung 'cat-slide' slate roof and was once a haunt of Jack Matthews, the highwayman. Typical menu includes butternut squash curry, devilled chicken, pan-fried trout, and steak and kidney casserole with dumplings. Principal beers: Spitfire,Hook Norton,Wadworth 6X,Oakhill Bitter.
Directions On A429(Fosse Way)
Free House
Open 11-3 6-11 (Sun 12-3,7-10.30)
Bar food 12-2.30 7-9.45 Av main course £5.95
Restaurant 12-2.30 7-9.45

Seven Tuns
CHEDWORTH Map 04 SP01
Queen St GL54 4AA ☎ 01285 720242
Once a billet for Cromwell's troops, one of the oldest pubs in the region retains its original features. The seven 'tuns' are not barrels, but chimney pots, and peacocks stroll the charming walled garden, with a waterwheel as centrepiece. Aberdeen Angus prime steaks feature on a tempting menu. Principal beers: John Smith, Ruddles County, Georges Traditional.
Directions A40 then A429 towards Cirencester, after 5m R for Chedworth, 3m then 3rd turning on R
Free House
Open 11.30-3 6.30-11
Bar food 12-2 6.30-9 Av main course £8
Restaurant 12-2 6.30-9 Av 3 course à la carte £17

AA members can call AA Hotel Booking Service on 0990 050505 to book at AA recognised hotels and B & Bs in the UK and Ireland, or through our Internet site: http://www.theaa.co.uk/hotels

CHIPPING CAMPDEN Gloucestershire

Eight Bells Inn
CHIPPING CAMPDEN Map 04 SP13
Church St GL55 6JG ☎ 01386 840371
A 14th-century inn of Cotswold stone with open fires and old beams, providing warm, comfortable surroundings. An à la carte menu is served in a bar setting, with dishes such as hot seafood mousse with prawn and sherry sauce, haggis with mashed potato, and treacle tart. Principal beers: Donnington SBA, Abbott, Greene King, Tetley, Marstons Pedigree.
Free House
Open 11-3 6-11
Bar food 12-2.30 7-9.30 Av main course £7
Restaurant 12-2.30 7-9.30 Av 3 course à la carte £15
Accommodation s£38 d£48

CLEARWELL Gloucestershire

Wyndham Arms
CLEARWELL Map 03 SO50
GL16 8JT ☎ 01594 833666
Built in 1340 and situated in a valley at the edge of the Royal Forest of Dean. The bar snack menu ranges from Stilton puffed pears with orange mayonnaise to deep fried squid rings with Szechuan sauce. Lemon sole Cecilia and rainbow trout Cleopatra are among the restaurant's seafood dishes. Principal beers: Draught Bass, Guinness, Boddingtons Draught Flow.
Directions on B4231 1m S of Coleford
Free House
Open 11-11 (Sun 12-11)
Bar food 12-2 12-9.30 Av main course £4
Restaurant 12-2 12-9.30 Av 3 course à la carte £13.75 Av 3 course fixed price £18.25
Accommodation s£52.50 d£61

COLESBOURNE Gloucestershire

The Colesbourne Inn
COLESBOURNE Map 04 SP01
GL53 9NP ☎ 01242 870376
The emphasis is on a friendly, informal atmosphere at this 18th century former coaching inn, part of the Lord Lieutenant of Gloucestershire's estate and situated in a lovely area with historic interest. Dishes are prepared to order, so patiently await local Cockleford trout or duck, bacon and brandy pie. Principal beers: Wadworth 6x & IPA,Hall & Woodhouse Tanglefoot.
Directions On A435 N of Cirencester
Wadworth
Open 12-11 (Sun 12-10.30)
Bar food 12-2.30 7-10 Av main course £5
Restaurant 12-2.30 7-10 Av 3 course à la carte £15
Accommodation s£35 d£50

COLN ST ALDWYNS Gloucestershire

The New Inn
COLN ST ALDWYNS Map 04 SP10
GL7 5AN ☎ 01285 750651
Elizabethan coaching inn near the River Coln. Imaginative starters include cappuccino of butter with truffle oil, and pan fried grey mullet with an avocado salsa and garlic oil. Main courses range from Scottish beef with garlic, shallots and peppercorn cream sauce, to cannelloni of mushrooms with tarragon cream sauce, for vegetarians. Principal beers: Hook Norton, Wadworth 6X, Morland Original.
Directions Between Bibury(B4425) & Fairford(A417) 8m E of Cirencester
Free House
Open 11.30-11 (Winter closed 2.30-5.30)
Bar food 12-2 7-9.30 Av main course £10
Restaurant 12-2 7.30-9.30 Av 3 course fixed price £22.50
Accommodation s£59 d£87

EWEN Gloucestershire

The Wild Duck
EWEN Map 04 SU09
Drakes Island GL7 6BY ☎ 01285 770310
15-century Cotswold stone, Elizabethan inn situated in a quiet corner at the edge of the village. The blackboard menu includes grilled goats cheese with toasted French stick, smoked trout, Indonesian chicken stir fry, and Italian baked knuckle of ham. Game dishes are also served in the winter.

contd.

Directions Off A429 S of Cirencester.Centre of village
Free House
Open 11-11 (Sun 12-10.30)
Bar food 12-2 7-10 Av main course £5.95
Restaurant 12-2 7-10 Av 3 course à la carte £15
Accommodation s£49.50 d£69.50

FOSSEBRIDGE Gloucestershire

Fossebridge Inn
FOSSEBRIDGE Map 04 SP01
GL54 3JS ☎ 01285 720721
Lying at the side of the River Coln, the site of this Tudor inn has been a stopping place for travellers since Roman times. Rump of lamb in redcurrant and mint sauce, vegetable Wellington, baked cod in a cheese sauce glaze, or tagliatelle carbonara may be on today's menu. Principal beers: Hook Norton, Bass, 6X.
Directions On A429 (Fosse Way) 5m NE of Cirencester
Free House
Open 11-3 6-11
Bar food 11-2.30 6-11 Av main course £7.95
Accommodation s£49.50 d£59.50

GREET Gloucestershire

The Harvest Home
GREET Map 04 SP03
Evesham Rd GL54 5BH
☎ 01242 602430
Built at the turn of the century, this country inn is situated close to Sudeley Castle and the renowned Winchcombe Pottery. Menu includes baguettes, harvest pies and bakes, a seafood selection and various main course grills, such as chicken Cordon Bleu and zigeuner schnitzel. Vegetarian meals are listed on the blackboard. Principal beers: Hook Norton, Wadworths 6X, Fullers London Pride, Boddingtons BB.
Directions M5 J9 take A435 towards Evesham, then B4077 & B4078 towards Winchcombe
Whitbread
Open 11-3 6-11
Bar food 12-2 6.30-9.30 Av main course £5.80
Restaurant 12-2 6.30-9.30 Av 3 course à la carte £12.50

GUITING POWER Gloucestershire

The Hollow Bottom
GUITING POWER Map 04 SP02
Winchcombe Rd GL54 5UX
☎ 01451 850392
The pub formerly known as 'Ye Olde Inne' has been re-named. Locals have always called it the Hollow Bottom reflecting its location in the village. It is frequented by owners and trainers, so there's plenty of horse racing talk, and food includes ploughman's, steak and kidney pie and fresh trout. Principal beers: Goffs Jouster (Winchcombe), Hook Norton, Bass.
Directions From Cheltenham on A40 take A436 towards Stow-on-the-Wold. Village on L
Free House
Open 11-3 6-11
Bar food 12-2.30 7-9.30 Av main course £5.50
Restaurant 12-2.30 7-9.30 Av 3 course à la carte £10
Accommodation s£25 d£40

HINTON Gloucestershire

The Bull Inn
HINTON Map 03 ST77
SN14 8HG ☎ 0117 9372332
Beams, flag-stone floors and a vast peaceful garden at this sturdy, stone-built 450-year-old country pub, popular with the local riding fraternity. Expect jacket potatoes, omelettes, sandwiches and ploughmans in the bar, or steaks every which way, grilled darne of salmon, and Dover sole in the restaurant. Principal beers: Wadworth 6X, Henrys IPA, Draught Bass.
Directions From M4, A46 to Bath for 1m then R, 1m down hill, Bull on L
Wadworth
Open 11-3 7-11

Bar food 12-2 7-10.30 Av main course £4
Restaurant 12-2 7-9.30 Av 3 course à la carte £18

KINGSCOTE Gloucestershire

Hunters Hall
KINGSCOTE Map 03 ST89
GL8 8X2 ☎ 01453 860393
16th-century Cotswold stone coaching inn with low beamed ceilings. Among the main course dishes are fillet of beef Worcestershire with sweet onion *aumonière*, pheasant with rich cranberry and wild mushroom sauce, and stuffed cannelloni with Red Leicester sauce, continental salad and Provençale dressing. Principal beers: Uley, Bass, Courage.
Directions M5 J14 B4509/B4058 to Wooton-under-Edge then A4135 towards Tetbury. Village 2m on L
Free House
Open 7am-11pm
Bar food 12-2 6.30-9.30 Av main course £6.50
Restaurant 7-9.30 Av 3 course à la carte £15 Av 3 course fixed price £13.95
Accommodation s£45 d£60

LECHLADE Gloucestershire

The Trout Inn
LECHLADE Map 04 SU29
St Johns Bridge GL7 3HA
☎ 01367 252313
Boats are welcome at this 350-year-old pub, which is idyllically situated by the first lock on the River Thames. Dishes, including vegetarian and healthy eating options, are cooked to order and might include locally made sausages, vegetable lasagne, steak and mushroom pie and grilled salmon. Principal beers: Courage Best, Directors 6X.
Directions From A40 take A361 then A417. From M4 to Lechlade then A417 to Trout
Free House
Open 11-11
Bar food 12-2 7-10

AA members can call AA Hotel Booking Service on 0990 050505 to book at AA recognised hotels and B & Bs in the UK and Ireland, or through our Internet site: http://www.theaa.co.uk/hotels

LOWER APPERLEY Gloucestershire

The Farmers Arms
LOWER APPERLEY Map 03 SO82
Ledbury Rd GL19 4DR ☎ 01452 780172
Traditional country pub in the heart of Gloucestershire, between the Cotswolds and the Malverns. The Farmers Arms serves two real ales brewed on the grounds - Odda's Light and Sundowner Heavy. The menu may include duck stir fry, Cajun chicken, beef and ale pie, or paprika pork. Principal beers: Mayhems Oddas Light, Sundowner, Henrys IPA, Wadworth 6X.
Directions On B4213 SE of Tewkesbury (off A38)
Wadworth
Open 11-3 6-11
Bar food 11-2 6-10 Av main course £5.95
Restaurant 12-2 7-10 Av 3 course à la carte £16

NEWENT Gloucestershire

Three Choirs Vineyards Restaurant
NEWENT Map 03 SO72
Gl18 1LS ☎ 01531 890223
The only vineyard of this type in the country (similar to those in California or Australia), producing 250,000 bottles a year. The restaurant has a Californian atmosphere and modern English food, such as oak smoked wild salmon, and pork loin steak with braised red cabbage.
Directions M50 J3 to Newent then B4215 towards Dymock. Follow brown/cream signs
Open 12-2.30 7-9.30
Restaurant 12-2.30 7-9.30 Av 3 course à la carte £13

NYMPSFIELD Gloucestershire

Rose & Crown Inn
NYMPSFIELD Map 03 SO80
The Cross GL10 3TU ☎ 01453 860240
A warm friendly atmosphere, with a true Cotswold flavour, is promised at this 17th-century coaching inn. Plentiful quality food at affordable prices is served in both the bar and restaurant, including a good choice of vegetarian dishes, fish and steaks. Traditional hot puddings complete the picture. Principal beers: Uley Old Spot, Uley Bitter, Wickwar Bob, Old Peculiar.

contd.

Directions (M5 J13) off B4066 SW of Stroud
Free House
Open 11.45-11
Accommodation s£35.50 d£30

OAKRIDGE Gloucestershire

The Butcher's Arms
OAKRIDGE Map 03 SO90
GL6 7NZ ☎ 01285 760371
Converted butcher's shop located at the top of 'the Golden Valley', which has been designated an area of outstanding beauty. A full and varied restaurant menu is offered, while the bar menu specialises in 'Butcher's burgers' and potato wedge dishes, which all include chunky deep-fried jacket potato wedges. Principal beers: Archers Best, Goffs Jouster, Old Hooky, Tetley Bitter.
Free House
Open 11-3.30 6-11.30 (Sun, 7-10.30)
Bar food 12-3 6.30-11 Av main course £5
Restaurant 12-3 7.30-11 Av 3 course à la carte £16.50 Av 3 course fixed price £16.50

ODDINGTON (LOWER) Gloucestershire

The Fox
ODDINGTON (LOWER) Map 04 SP22
GL56 0UR ☎ 01451 870555
16th-century village pub situated in the heart of Gloucestershire's countryside. A constantly changing menu may feature Gloucestershire pie - chicken, ham and eggs in parsley sauce, local trout baked in newspaper, smoked haddock pie, Cotswold sausages, or rare roast sirloin of beef and Yorkshire pudding. Principal beers: Hook Norton BB, Marstons Pedigree, Smiles, Tanglefoot.
Directions A436 from Stow-on-the-Wold then R to Oddington
Free House
Open 12-3 6.30-11
Bar food 12-3 7-11 Av main course £7.95

OLDBURY-ON-SEVERN Gloucestershire

The Anchor Inn
OLDBURY-ON-SEVERN Map 03 ST69
Church Rd BS12 1QA
☎ 01454 413331
Opposite the River Severn, this traditional old stone inn features the south west's largest boules piste at the end of the large garden. The same menu in dining room and bars offers a good reasonably priced variety of international recipes. Try 'pimientos Rellenos' or classic poachers pie. Principal beers: Butcombe, Worthington, Theakstons, Black Sheep.
Directions From N A38 toward Bristol, 1 1/2m then R, village signed. From S A38 thru Thornbury
Free House
Open 11.30-2.30 6.30-11 (Sun 12-3.30, 7-10.30)
Bar food 11.30-2 6.30-9 Av main course £5
Restaurant 11.30-2 6.30-9.30 Av 3 course à la carte £10

SIDDINGTON Gloucestershire

The Greyhound
SIDDINGTON Map 04 SU09
Ashton Rd GL7 6HR ☎ 01285 653573
Cotswolds stone village pub, formerly a coach house. Main course dishes range from butterfly lamb chops, and escalope of pork in sherry and cream, to grilled salmon fillet, and breast of chicken in tarragon, cream and white wine. A mushroom Stroganoff is available for vegetarians. Principal beers: Wadworth 6X, IPA, Tanglefoot.
Directions A419 from Swindon, L at main roundabout, follow Siddington signs, pub at far end of village on R
Wadworth
Open 11.30-3 6.30-11
Bar food 12-2 7-10 Av main course £5.95

STOW-ON-THE-WOLD Gloucestershire

Coach and Horses
STOW-ON-THE-WOLD Map 04 SP12
Ganborough GL56 0QZ
☎ 01451 830208
250-year old inn built of Cotswold stone, with its own skittle alley and paddock for tying up horses. Blackboard menus may feature salmon, prawn and asparagus pancake, Cornish crab in Dijon mustard sauce, Stilton and broccoli lasagne, Cajun chicken, and monkfish in bacon with cream and garlic sauce. Principal beers: Donnington BB & SBA,Carlsberg, Guinness,Addlestones cider,Stowford Press.

Directions On A424 2.5m from Stow-on-the-Wold
Donnington Brewery
Open 11.30-3 6-11
Bar food 12-2 6.30-9.30 Av main course £5
Restaurant 12-2 6.30-9.30

STROUD Gloucestershire

The Ram Inn
STROUD Map 03 SO80
South Woodchester GL5 5EQ
☎ 01453 873329
An ancient building of Cotswold stone with open fires and beautiful views. The daily blackboard menus might offer pork chops with creamy apple and cider sauce, steaks, and halibut with Champagne sauce. The Farmers Lunch comprises soup and a roll, cheddar cheese, side salad, home-made pickles and an apple. Principal beers: Archers Best, Uley Old Spot, Woodfordes.
Directions A46 from Stroud to Nailsworth, R after 2m into S.Woodchester
Free House
Open 11-3 5.30-11 (Fri-Sat 11-11, Sun 12-10.30)
Bar food 12-2.30 6.30-9.30 Av main course £4.95
Restaurant 12-2.30 6.30-9.30 Av 1 course fixed price £4.95

TETBURY Gloucestershire

Trouble House Inn
TETBURY Map 03 ST89
Cirencester Rd GL8 8SG
☎ 01666 502206
The unusual name springs from the uprising outside the pub 135 years ago, and the two landlords who committed suicide. All the food is home-made from fresh ingredients, and might include chicken liver paté with toast, pork in a Stilton and apple sauce, and treacle tart. Principal beers: Wadworths 6X and IPA, Heineken Export, Boddingtons Smooth.
Directions On A433 between Tetbury & Cirencester
Wadworth
Open 11-2.45 6.15-11
Bar food 12-2 7-9.30 Av main course £5

TORMARTON Gloucestershire

Compass Inn
TORMARTON Map 03 ST77
GL9 1JB ☎ 01454 218242
Furnished at the turn of the century from original ship's fittings, at this traditional Cotswold stone, creeper covered inn in a prime countryside setting, thirsty riders park their horses in a provided field. Home-cooked fare is served with game, when in season, a speciality. Principal beers: Draught Bass, Smiles BB, Archers Village, Becks.
Directions From M4 A46 toward Stroud for 100yds then R
Free House
Open 7-11 (Sun 8-10.30)
Restaurant 7-9.30 Av 3 course à la carte £17 Av 2 course fixed price £15
Accommodation s£60 d£70

UPPER ODDINGTON Gloucestershire

Horse & Groom Inn
UPPER ODDINGTON Map 03 SP22
GL56 0XH ☎ 01451 830584
Small 16th-century Free House with a stream running through its landscaped garden. A range of char-grilled steak dishes are served with Stilton, red wine, mushroom and garlic sauces. Seafood meals include honey and almond trout, fillets of lemon sole with asparagus sauce, and broccoli and leek galette for vegetarians. Principal beers: Hook Norton, Ruddles, Stella, Fosters.
Directions Between A436 & B4450 E of Stow-on-the-Wold
Free House
Open 11.30-2.30 6-11
Bar food 12-2 6.30-9.30 Av main course £7.50
Restaurant 12-2 6.30-9.30 Av 3 course à la carte £13
Accommodation s£37.50 d£55

Somerset

APPLEY Somerset

The Globe Inn

APPLEY Map 03 ST02

TA21 0HT ☎ 01823 672327

Part cob, part slate, this building is over 500 years old and has two inglenook fireplaces. The small bar is set in a brick floored passageway. The same menu is offered throughout, with dishes such as fish soup, steak, and savoury vegetable crumble, plus a daily roast. Principal beers: Cotleigh Tawny.

Directions From M5 J6 take A38 towards Exeter. Village is signposted in 5m

Free House

Open 11-3 6.30-11 (Sun 12-3,7-10.30)

Bar food 12-2 7-10 Av main course £7

Restaurant 12-2 7-10

ASHCOTT Somerset

Ring o'Bells

ASHCOTT Map 03 ST43

High St TA7 9PZ ☎ 01458 210232

A large, friendly village pub catering for all with a great variety of dishes from Somerset Brie fritters to Mozzarella chicken to scrumptious Key Lime pie and cream, this hostelry dates from 1750 and features a large collection of bells and ephemera. Principal beers: Withy Cutter, Carling, Toby, Worthington.

Directions From M5 follow signs A39 & Glastonbury

Free House

Open 12-2.30 7-11

Bar food 12-2.30 7-10.30 Av main course £7

Restaurant 12-2.30 7-10.30 Av 3 course à la carte £10

ASHILL Somerset

Square & Compass

ASHILL Map 03 ST31

Windmill Hill TA19 9NX

☎ 01823 480467

A friendly one-bar pub with a dining room, overlooking the Blackdown Hills. There's a range of dishes served as starters or light meals, including prawns, paté and pasta, plus salads, sandwiches and jacket potatoes. Other options are steaks, fried fish and a choice of vegetarian fare. Principal beers: Exmoor Ale, Marstons Pedigree, Old Speckled Hen.

Directions From M5 J25 take A358. After 6m Windmill Hill is signposted on R

Free House

Open 12-2.30 6.30-11

Bar food 12-2 7-9.30/10. Av main course £5

Restaurant 12-2 7-9.30/10 Av 3 course à la carte £11.50

AXBRIDGE Somerset

The Oak House

AXBRIDGE Map 03 ST45

The Square BS26 2AP ☎ 01934 732444

Parts of this inn date from the 11th century, and much of its historic character is retained in the beams, stone walls, inglenook fireplaces and an ancient well linked to the Cheddar caverns. Dishes in the bistro include fresh Brixham salmon and a trio of Axbridge sausages. Principal beers: Smiles real ale, Keoghans.

Directions M5 J22. Take A38 to Bristol. Turn onto A371 to Cheddar/Wells. Turn L at Axbridge. Town centre

Free House

Open 12-3 7-11

Bar food 12-3 Av main course £3.85

Restaurant 12-3 7-11 Av 3 course à la carte £14

Accommodation s£42 d£57

BATCOMBE Somerset

The Batcombe Inn

BATCOMBE Map 03 ST63

BA2 6HE ☎ 01749 850359

A former toll house, cider house and smithy built in 1600 on the old toll road. The garden has a large pond, waterfall and children's adventure playground. Food ranges from 'lunchtime bites' to 'hearty helpings', all home-made, and a

range of fresh fish, meat and vegetarian dishes. Principal beers: Butcombe, Speckled Hen, Grolsch, Murphys.
Directions Take A359 from Frome to Bruton.Batcombe signed on R
Free House
Open 12-2.30 7-11
Bar food 12-2 7-9.30 Av main course £8
Restaurant 12-2 7-9.30

BATH Somerset

The Cross Keys
BATH Map 03 ST76
Midford Rd, Combe Down BA2 5RZ
☎ 01225 832002
On the upper outskirts of Bath, this old coaching inn's garden has a well-stocked aviary. On today's menu diners may find lamb chops with mint jelly, brie and mushroom pancake, or chicken curry. Home-made pies include pork and apple, beef and stilton, and fish and parsley. Principal beers: Founders, Seasonal Ale, Ushers Best, Courage Best.
Directions On B3110 S of Bath
Ushers
Open 11-2.30 6-11 (Sat-11-3,7-11 Sun 12-3,7-10.30)

The Olde Green Tree
BATH Map 03 ST76
12 Green St BA1 2JE ☎ 01225 448259
The pub can be traced back to 1752, but in 1923 it was extended and entirely panelled in oak, and parquet floors were laid in the three rooms. It is run on old fashioned lines with good beer, wine, food and company. Food ranges from bangers and mash to chicken curry. Principal beers: All from local micro breweries.
Directions Town centre
Free House
Open 11-11 (Sun 7-10.30)
Bar food 12-2.15 Av main course £4.50

BATHAMPTON Somerset

The George Inn
BATHAMPTON Map 03 ST76
Mill Lane BA2 6TR ☎ 01225 425079
A traditional country pub on the Kennet and Avon Canal in a quiet village location just a mile from Bath. Home-cooked food using fresh local produce includes Thai stir-fries (the house speciality), fresh fillet of salmon in a filo basket with Pernod sauce, and steaks from the grill. Principal beers: 6X, Courage Best, Fosters, Guinness.
Directions M4 J18 onto A46 L at traffic lights & follow signs for Bathampton
Free House
Open 11-3 6-11.30
Bar food 12-2 6.30-9.30 Av main course £7.50

BLAGDON Somerset

The New Inn
BLAGDON Map 03 ST55
Church St BS18 6SB
☎ 01761 462475
There are spectacular views of Blagdon Lake from this traditional inn at the heart of the Mendips. The extensive menu offers a range of sandwiches, salads and snacks, with heartier options such as steak and kidney pie; fish, chips and mushy peas, and couscous and cranberry lattice. Principal beers: Butcombe, IPA, Wadworths 6X.
Directions From Bristol take A38 S then A368 towards Bath
Wadworth
Open 11.30-2.30 7-11
Bar food 12-2 7-10 Av main course £5.50

BRADFORD-ON-TONE Somerset

White Horse Inn
BRADFORD-ON-TONE Map 03 ST12
TA4 1HF ☎ 01823 461239
A country pub in a picturesque village setting overlooking the church, just 200yds from the River Tone. Friendly service and value-for-money food is served, including home-made pasta bakes, curries and pies, grills and fish dishes. Sandwiches, jacket potatoes and basket meals are also available. Principal beers: Whitbread.
Directions N of A38 between Taunton & Wellington
Free House
Open 11.30-3 5.30-11
Bar food 12-2.15 6.30-10 Av main course £4.65
Restaurant 12-2.15 6.30-10 Av 3 course à la carte £10.50 Av 0 course fixed price £9.50

BRIDGWATER Somerset

Ashcott Inn
BRIDGWATER Map 03 ST33
50 Bath Rd TA7 9QQ
☎ 01458 210282
19th-century pub, originally part of farm buildings. Home-made specials include carbonara, chicken olives, and boeuf Bourguignonne. Among the seafood dishes are beer battered cod and salmon steak Hollandaise. Vegetarians can choose between a cauliflower and broccoli bake, vegetable lasagne or an Oriental stir-fry. Principal beers: Butcombe, Flowers original and IPA, Trophy, Murphys.
Directions M5 J23 follow signs for A39 to Bridgwater
Heavitree
Open 11-2.30 5.30-11(Sat-Sun all day opening)
Bar food 12-2.15 6.30-9.30 Av main course £3.75
Restaurant 12-2.15 6.30-9.30 Av 3 course à la carte £11

CASTLE CARY Somerset

The George Hotel
CASTLE CARY Map 03 ST63
Market Place BA7 7AH
☎ 01963 350761
Thatched, grade II listed 15th-century coaching inn. Dinner menu offers game terrine, and chorizo and egg salad, followed by local seafood dishes and duck in blackberries and cherry brandy sauce. A supper menu includes pheasant, duck and wild boar casseroled in a game sauce with herbs. Principal beers: Wilmots, Butcombe, Budvar, Kilkenny.

Directions From A303 take A371 at Wincanton, then N to Castle Cary
Free House
Open 10.30-3 6-11
Bar food 12-2 7-9 Av main course £8
Restaurant 12-2 7-9 Av 3 course à la carte £20
Accommodation s£40 d£75

CHARD Somerset

Hornsbury Mill
CHARD Map 03 ST30
Eleighwater TA20 3AQ
☎ 01460 63317
A 200-year-old working corn mill and museum, set in five acres of landscaped water gardens with a large resident duck population. There's fresh home-made bar food and a modern English restaurant menu with dishes such as saladette of seafood, and tipsy loin of pork with apple sauce.
Directions A358 to Chard, pub 2m before Chard
Free House
Open 10-4.30 6-11
Bar food 12-4.30 7-9 Av main course £6.95
Restaurant 12-2 7-9 Av 3 course à la carte £18 Av 4 course fixed price £17.50

CHURCHILL Somerset

Crown Inn
CHURCHILL Map 03 ST45
The Batch BS19 5PP ☎ 01934 852995
An amalgamation of two shops, a cottage and a coaching stop on the old Bristol to Exeter coach route, this inn specialises in home-made farmhouse-style lunches, using seasonal British produce, such as crab, lobster, rabbit and venison. Home-made soups are popular, plus rare roast beef sandwiches and locally produced faggots. Principal beers: Cotleigh, Palmers, PG, Otter.
Directions Take A38 S of Bristol.Turn R at Churchill traffic lights, then 1st L
Free House
Open 11.30-3.30 5.30-11
Bar food 12-2.15 Av main course £3.50

COMBE HAY Somerset

The Wheatsheaf
COMBE HAY Map 03 ST75
BA2 7EG ☎ 01225 833504
Beautiful gardens, recently terraced, are a feature at this 400-year-old country pub. The landlord shoots and fishes for the menu, and dishes

include breast of pheasant filled with a mushroom and spinach mousse, wrapped in bacon and served on a juniper, redcurrant and port sauce, along with traditional bar fare. Principal beers: Butcombes, Marstons Pedigree, Wadworths 6X, Courage Best.
Directions E of A367(S of Bath)
Free House
Open 12-2.30 6.30-10.30 (Sat 12-3,6.30-11,Sun 12-3,7-10.30)
Bar food 12-2 6.30-9.30 Av main course £5
Restaurant 12-2 6.30-9.30 Av 3 course à la carte £18

CROWCOMBE Somerset

Carew Arms
CROWCOMBE Map 03 ST13
TA4 4AD ☎ 01984 618631
Try wild boar and apple sausages or warm breast of pigeon salad from a menu with a difference at this unspoilt pub with views of the Brendon Hills from the garden. Locals can tell a few stories about the place, unusually furnished with pieces from old stations and dating from 1780. Principal beers: Exmoor Ale, Willmots.
Directions A358 direction of Minehead
Free House
Open 11-3 6-11
Bar food 12-2.30 Av main course £3.95
Restaurant 12-2.30 7-9.30 Av 3 course à la carte £13
Accommodation s£16

DINNINGTON Somerset

Rose & Crown Inn
DINNINGTON Map 03 ST41
TA17 8SX ☎ 01460 52397
Licensed for over 250 years, this genuine village pub serves good value home-cooked food. The daily menu is supplemented by blackboard specials, with a 'cheapie' like bangers and mash or a 'little treat' such as coquilles St Jacques Parisiennes. Traditional puddings include pear and ginger upside-down-cake. Principal beers: Butcombe, Spitfire, Brakspears, Wadworths 6X.
Directions N of A30 between Crewkerne & Chard
Free House
Open 11-4 6-11
Bar food 12-2.30 7-10 Av main course £3.25
Restaurant 12-2.30 7-10 Av 3 course à la carte £6

DUNSTER Somerset

The Exmoor House Hotel
DUNSTER Map 03 SS94
West St TA24 6SN ☎ 01643 821268
In the charming village of Dunster, close to Dunster Castle, this 16th-century Grade II listed Georgian building offers open fires and old beams, along with an inventive menu with English, American and French influences. Enjoy dishes like New England seafood chowder, a trio of local sausages, wild mushroom risotto and tarte tatin with cinnamon ice cream.
Directions A39 from Minehead, R onto A396
Free House
Open 9.30-10.30
Bar food 11.30-2.30 7.15-10.30 Av main course £4.95
Restaurant 7.30-10.30 Av 5 course fixed price £24.50
Accommodation s£45 d£65

EXEBRIDGE Somerset

Anchor Inn
EXEBRIDGE Map 03 SS92
TA22 9AZ ☎ 01398 323433
Situated on the banks of the River Exe, this 17th-century coaching inn, mentioned in RD Blackmore's novel *Lorna Doone*, is ideal for those exploring Exmoor. Trout fishing can be arranged. Bar menu may include Anchor gammon steak, local trout, or broccoli and cream cheese bake. Principal beers: 6X, Speckled Hen, Courage Best, Ushers Best.

contd.

Free House
Bar food 12-2 6-10 Av main course £4.50
Restaurant 12-2 6.30-10 Av 3 course à la carte £20 Av 3 course fixed price £20
Accommodation s£37 d£64

EXFORD Somerset

The Crown Inn
EXFORD Map 03 SS83
TA24 7QP ☎ 01643 831554
The first coaching inn on Exmoor, this hotel has a cosy village bar with a proper pub atmosphere and lovely food. Dishes include braised oxtail with creamed potatoes and red wine sauce, fillet of cod with bubble and squeak, and breast of chicken wrapped in Parma ham. Principal beers: Crown Bitter, Brakspear, Wadworths 6X.
Directions On B3224 (in Exmoor National Park)
Free House
Open 11-3 6-11
Bar food 12-2 6.30-9.30 Av main course £8
Restaurant 12-2 7-9.30 Av 3 course à la carte £24 Av 3 course fixed price £24
Accommodation s£40 d£80

FRESHFORD Somerset

The Inn at Freshford
FRESHFORD Map 03 ST76
BA3 6EG ☎ 01225 722250
A village inn with extensive gardens and riverside walks, serving traditional home-cooked meals. Bar food ranges from sandwiches to steaks, while the à la carte restaurant offers roast shoulder of lamb with Dijon mustard and honey; daily fresh fish, steaks and vegetarian dishes such as nut roast. Principal beers: Courage Cask Ales.
Directions 1m from A36 between Beckington & Limpley Stoke
Free House
Open 11-3 6-11
Bar food 12-3 6-11 Av main course £5.95
Restaurant 12-3 6-11 Av 3 course à la carte £15

FROME Somerset

The Horse & Groom
FROME Map 03 ST74
East Woodlands BA11 5LY
☎ 01373 462802
Just a minute away from Longleat House, this small country inn provides freshly cooked quality food. Fresh bread is made daily, and dishes might include Cornish crab dumplings with dill sauce, Tuscany pork escalope with tomatoes, basil, mozzarella and roasted pine kernels, and a brazil nut and chocolate tart. Principal beers: Batemans XB, Wadworths 6X, Greene King IPA, Butcombe Bitter.
Directions Just off Frome By-pass(A361 Shepton Mallet/Devizes rd)
Free House
Open 11.30-2 6.30-9
Bar food 12-2 6.30-9 Av main course £6
Restaurant 12-2 6.30-9 Av 3 course à la carte £17

GLASTONBURY Somerset

The Who'd a Thought It Inn
GLASTONBURY Map 03 ST53
17 Northload St BA6 9JJ
☎ 01458 834460
An 18th-century inn with a large collection of local artefacts and interesting memorabilia. The gents toilet has won the South West Loo of the Year Award three years running. Traditional pub grub includes home-made pies, roasts, vegetarian and fish dishes. Principal beers: Palmers of Bridport.
Directions A39
Free House
Open 11-11 (Sun 12-3, 7-10.30)
Bar food 12-2.15 5.45-9.15 Av main course £5
Accommodation s£29.50 d£49

ILCHESTER Somerset

Ilchester Arms
ILCHESTER Map 03 ST52
The Square BA22 8LN ☎ 01935 840220
An ivy-clad 18th-century building with a lunchtime menu, full evening à la carte, and summer barbecues with a Cajun influence. Bar food includes traditional bangers and mash, fresh fish and steak and kidney pie, and the restaurant menu has French leanings.
Directions Just off A30, 4 1/2m N of Yeovil
Free House

Open 12-4 6-11
Bar food 12-3 7-11 Av main course £14
Restaurant 12-3 7-11 Av 3 course à la carte £22.50

ILMINSTER Somerset

New Inn
ILMINSTER Map 03 ST31
Dowlish Wake TA19 0NZ
☎ 01460 52413

A 350-year-old pub built of Moolham stone, which is full of fossils, and the beams inside are liberally bedecked with hops. Food ranges from sandwiches to steaks, and the Swiss landlady's continental style shows through - fondue, carbonnade and raclette are all popular. Principal beers: Butcombe, Theakston Old Peculiar, Wadworths 6X.
Directions From Ilchester follow signs for Kingstone then Dawlish Wake
Free House
Open 11-3 6-11
Bar food 12-2.30 6.30-9.30 Av main course £4.50
Restaurant 12-2.30 6.30-9.30 Av 3 course à la carte £14

KILVE Somerset

The Hood Arms
KILVE Map 03 ST14
TA5 1EA ☎ 01278 741210

At the foot of the Quantock Hills, this 17th-century coaching inn is especially suitable for families. A meal may include venison casserole with apricot brandy, crispy duck in black cherry sauce, or stilton and spinach lasagne. Principal beers: Exmoor, Cotleigh, Flowers Original.
Free House
Open 11-2.30 6-11
Bar food 12-2.30 6-11 Av main course £5.50
Restaurant 12-2.30 6-11 Av 3 course à la carte £13
Accommodation s£25 d£40

KINGSDON Somerset

Kingsdon Inn
KINGSDON Map 03 ST52
TA11 7LG ☎ 01935 840543

There is a good atmosphere at this local pub, a listed thatched and beamed building with log fires, overlooking the village green. Food is purchased from local suppliers and cooked to order. Dishes include ploughman's, fish soup, half a roast duck with scrumpy sauce, and treacle tart and cream. Principal beers: Smiles Best, Oakhill, London Pride, Pedigree.
Directions From A303 take A372 towards Bridgwater then B3151
Free House
Open 11-3 6-11
Bar food 12-2 7-10 Av main course £5

KNAPP Somerset

The Rising Sun Inn
KNAPP Map 03 ST32
TA3 6BG ☎ 01823 490436

A listed 15th-century Somerset long house, this inn retains many original features. Dishes include a good choice of seafood from Brixham and St Mawes, such as John Dory with sun-dried tomatoes, anchovies and capers. Other options might be steaks, mushroom stroganoff or roast mallard. Principal beers: Exmoor, Bass, Boddingtons.
Directions M5 J25 A358 then A378 follow signs for North Curry/Knapp
Free House
Open 11.30-2.30 6.30-11
Bar food 12-2 Av main course £5
Restaurant 12-2 7-10 Av 3 course à la carte £17
Accommodation s£25 d£36

LANGFORD BUDVILLE Somerset

The Martlet Inn
LANGFORD BUDVILLE Map 03 ST12
TA21 0QZ ☎ 01823 400262

Parts of this building date back to 1607, and lots of original features remain, including old doors and beams. There's a children's play area and the garden overlooks farmland to the rear. Dishes include ploughman's with local cheeses, whole plaice, steaks and a creamy vegetable pasta bake. Principal beers: Exmoor, Cotleigh.
Directions Take B3187 from Wellington for 2 1/2m, then L at Lang. Bud. sign
Free House
Open 12-3 7-11
Bar food 12-2.30 7-9.30 Av main course £5

LANGLEY MARSH Somerset

The Three Horseshoes

LANGLEY MARSH Map 03 ST02

TA4 2UL ☎ 01984 623763

This ancient stone and tiled building is a country pub with genuine locals and no nonsense. All the food is home cooked and a full vegetarian menu is offered. Options include home-made deep-pan pizzas, jacket potatoes, and dishes such as beef curry, fish pie and runner bean crumble. Principal beers: Palmers IPA, Otter Ale, Ringwood Best, Butcombe.

Directions M5 J25 take B3227 to Wiveliscombe. From square follow signs for Langley Marsh.1m

Free House

Open 12-2.30 7-11

Bar food 12-2.30 7-11 Av main course £4.95

LUXBOROUGH Somerset

Royal Oak Inn

LUXBOROUGH Map 03 SS93

TA23 0SH ☎ 01984 640319

A rural inn of great character with a thatched roof, flagstone or cobbled floors, low beams and open fires, situated beside a stream in the valley of the Brendon hills. Snack and evening menus are supplemented by specials such as fresh fish, game pie, and speciality chicken or steak dishes. Principal beers: Cotleigh Tawny, Exmoor Gold, Flowers IPA, Beamish.

Directions From A38 (Taunton/ Minehead) at Washford take minor rd S thru Roadwater

Free House

Open 11-3.30 6-11 (Sun 12-3,7-10.30)

Bar food 12-2 7-10 Av main course £4.95

Restaurant 12-2 7-10

Accommodation s£22.50 d£35

MELLS Somerset

The Talbot Inn

MELLS Map 03 ST74

High St BA11 3PN ☎ 01373 812254

An authentic coaching inn, set in a beautifully preserved village, where the passage of the last 500 years has gone virtually unnoticed. Wholesome fresh ingredients are used in the traditional bar fare, and in the restaurant top quality English produce is treated with French imagination and flair. Principal beers: Bass, Butcombe, 6X.

Directions From A36(T), R onto A361 to Frome, then A362 towards Radstock, 1/2m then L to Mells 2 1/2m

Free House

Open 12-2.30 6-11

Bar food 12-2.30 7-12 Av main course £5

Restaurant 12-2.30 7-12 Av 3 course à la carte £14

Accommodation s£20 d£35

MONTACUTE Somerset

The Phelips Arms

MONTACUTE Map 03 ST41

The Borough TA15 6XB

☎ 01935 822557

Built of local hamstone, this 18th-century inn is one of a square of similar buildings in the centre of the village, and was used in the filming of *Sense and Sensibility.* The menu ranges from sausages and mash to jambalaya, with treacle tart or lemon brûlée to finish. Principal beers: Palmers IPA, Palmers Tally Ho, Palmers 200.

Directions From Cartgate r'about on A303 follow signs for Montacute

Free House

Open 11-2.30 6-11 (Sun 12-3,7-10.30)

Bar food 12-2 6-10 Av main course £5.50

Accommodation s£25 d£40

NETHER STOWEY Somerset

The Cottage Inn

NETHER STOWEY Map 03 ST13

Keenthorne TA5 1HZ ☎ 01278 732355

Dating from the 16th/17th-century, the Cottage has always been a coaching inn, and until about 15 years ago cider was made on site. There is a bar menu of club sandwiches, fish dishes, char-grill

specialities and other popular fare, plus half a dozen daily specials such as stir-fried lemon chicken. Principal beers: Butcombe, Exmoor, Farmhouse Cider, Bass.
Directions M5 J23 follow A39 signs for Cannington/Minehead. Inn on A39
Free House
Open 11-11 (Sun closed 3-7)
Bar food 12-2.15 6.15-9.30 Av main course £5

NORTH PERROTT Somerset

The Manor Arms
NORTH PERROTT Map 03 ST40
TA18 7SG ☎ 01460 72901
A listed 16th-century building, lovingly restored, with an inglenook fireplace, flagstone floor, oak beams and local Ham stone walls. The bar food is all home-made, from the paté served as a starter to the tartare sauce accompanying the fried fish. Exciting international dishes are offered in the restaurant, again all home-made. Principal beers: Butcombe, Worthington, Bass, Caffreys.
Directions From A30 (yeovil/Honiton rd) take A3066 towards Bridport
Free House
Open 11.30-2.30 6.45-11
Bar food 12-2.30 7-11 Av main course £4.50
Restaurant 12-2.30 7-11 Av 3 course à la carte £12
Accommodation s£17.50 d£32

NUNNEY Somerset

The George at Nunney
NUNNEY Map 03 ST74
Church St BA11 4LW
☎ 01373 836458
17th-century coaching inn close to Nunney's 13th-century moated castle. A la carte main course dishes feature breast of duckling with toasted almonds, sautéed diced monkfish in a gentle pepper sauce, and fillet of Angus steak with port wine sauce, topped with truffles and mozzarella cheese. Principal beers: Bass, 6X, Stones, Worthington.
Directions 0.25m N of A361
Free House
Open 12-3 7-11
Bar food 12-3 7-11 Av main course £6
Restaurant 12-3 7-11 Av 3 course à la carte £10 Av 3 course fixed price £8

OVER STRATTON Somerset

The Royal Oak
OVER STRATTON Map 03 ST41
TA13 5LQ ☎ 01460 240906
400-year old inn with flagstone floors, rag-rolled walls, and a granite and oak bar. Garden features a 'junior assault course'. Typical menu includes gateau of roasted vegetables, cod in beer batter, salmon and spinach parcel with prawn and mushroom sauce, whole dressed crab, and seafood linguini. Principal beers: Badgers Best, Tanglefoot, Stratton Ale.
Directions A3088 from Yeovil, L onto A303, Over Stratton on R after South Petherton
Badger
Open 11-3 6-11
Bar food 12-2.30 7-10 Av main course £6
Restaurant 12-2.30 7-10 Av 3 course à la carte £18

PORLOCK Somerset

The Ship Inn
PORLOCK Map 03 SS84
High St TA24 8QD ☎ 01643 862507
13th-century thatched coaching inn situated in Exmoor National Park, within walking distance of the sea. Specials typically include roast beef, local sea bass, and Exmoor lamb with redcurrant sauce and apricots. Among the other dishes on offer are local trout with almonds, and vegetarian tagliatelle. Principal beers: Cotleigh, Bass, Courage.
Directions A358 to Williton, then A39 to Porlock
Free House
Open 10.30-11
Bar food 12-2 6.30-9.30 Av main course £5.50
Accommodation s£27.50 d£45

PRIDDY Somerset

New Inn
PRIDDY Map 03 ST55
Priddy Green BA5 3BB ☎ 01749 676465
Originally a farmhouse, dating from the 15th century, the New Inn became a pub in the 18th-century to serve the local lead miners. Specialities are fresh fish straight from the harbour at Looe and traditional English fare such as steak and ale pie and spotted dick with custard. Principal beers: Bass, Fullers, Wadworth, Carling.

contd.

Directions From M4 J18: take A39 R to Priddy 3m before Wells. From J19:through Bristol onto A39. From M5 J21: A371 to Cheddar, then B3371
Free House
Open 11.30-3 7-11.45
Bar food 12-2 7-10 Av main course £5.50
Restaurant 12-2 7-10
Accommodation s£21 d£32.50

RUDGE Somerset

The Full Moon at Rudge
RUDGE Map 03 ST85
BA11 2QF ☎ 01373 830936
There's been a coaching inn or hostelry on this site since the early 1700s, which was once at the crossroads of the main drovers' routes. The inn retains its small rooms, stone floors and scrubbed tables of old. Robust British fare is served, including entrecôte of beef with Stilton sauce. Principal beers: Butcombe, Bass 6X.
Directions From A36(Bath/Warminster rd) follow signs for Rudge
Free House
Open 12-3 6-11
Bar food 12-3 Av main course £5.50
Restaurant 6.30-9.30 Av 3 course à la carte £20
Accommodation s£35 d£45

SALTFORD Somerset

Riverside Inn
SALTFORD Map 03 ST66
The Shallows BS18 3EZ
☎ 01225 873862
Welcoming pub that celebrates its delightful location by the River Avon with a nautical theme. Wholesome cooking of traditional pub staples includes bangers and mash, lasagne and salad, and beef and ale pie. Beef Stroganoff and duck in kirsch and black cherry sauce star in the evening. Principal beers: Wadworth 6X, Henrys IPA, Bass, Old Timer.
Directions Midway between Bristol & Bath on A4
Wadworth
Open 11-11
Bar food 12-2.30 7-10 Av main course £4.95
Restaurant 12-2.30 7-10 Av 3 course à la carte £17

SPARKFORD Somerset

The Sparkford Inn
SPARKFORD Map 03 ST62
High St BA22 7JN ☎ 01963 440218
Flagstone floors, open fires and antique furnishings are features of this old coaching inn. Bar food includes soup and sandwiches, local cheese and hot pies, and there is a daily lunchtime carvery. In the evening the à la carte menu offers steak specialities, local duck and fresh fish. Principal beers: Bass, 6X, London Pride, Worthingtons Best Bitter.
Directions just off A303 N of Yeovil
Free House
Open 11-2.30 6.30-11 (Sun 12-3,7-10.30)
Bar food 12-2.20 7-10 Av main course £4.95
Restaurant 12-2 7-9.30 Av 3 course à la carte £15
Accommodation s£28 d£28

STANTON WICK Somerset

The Carpenters Arms
STANTON WICK Map 03 ST66
BS18 4BX ☎ 01761 490202
Converted from a row of miners cottages, this country inn promises a warm welcome, with a log fire in winter. A choice from filled baguettes to Thai green curry is offered in Coopers Parlour, and dishes such as char-grilled king scallops and roast Barbary duck in the restaurant. Principal beers: Bass, Butcombe, 6X, Worthingtons.
Directions From A37(Bristol/Wells rd) take A368 towards Weston-S-Mare take 1st R
Free House
Open 11-11
Bar food 12-2 7-10 Av main course £6.75
Restaurant 12-2 7-10 Av 3 course à la carte £20
Accommodation s£52.50 d£69.50

STAPLE FITZPAINE Somerset

The Greyhound Inn
STAPLE FITZPAINE Map 03 ST21
TA3 5SP ☎ 01823 480227
Built as a hunting lodge, c17th century, the pub is set in an area of outstanding natural beauty. There are three bars and a separate oak panelled restaurant. Food, all home-made, is

offered from a bar menu and a daily blackboard, including local seafood, game and vegetarian dishes. Principal beers: Exmoor Ale, Flowers Original, Flowers IPA, Boddingtons Gold.

Directions From M5, A316 to the A303, after 3m R to village
Free House
Open 12-3 5-11
Bar food 12-2 7-10 Av main course £3.95
Restaurant 12-2 7-10 Av 3 course à la carte £15

STOKE ST GREGORY Somerset

Rose & Crown
STOKE ST GREGORY Map 03 ST32
Woodhill TA36 6EW ☎ 01823 490296
200-year-old cottage style pub situated near a nature reserve. Bar menu offers a wide selection of grilled steaks and seafood. The main menu includes dishes such as local skate meunière, Scotch salmon Hollandaise, and scrumpy chicken. Vegetarian options feature nut roast chasseur, and seafood risotto. Principal beers: Thomas Hardy Bitter, Royal Oak, Withy Cutter, Yeoman Bitter.
Directions M5 J25 A358 then A37 thru N Cerney to Stoke St Gregory church on R. Pub 0.5m on L
Free House
Open 11-3 7-11
Bar food 12.30-3 7-10 Av main course £5.50
Restaurant 12.30-3 7-10 Av 3 course à la carte £12 Av 3 course fixed price £12
Accommodation s£25 d£38

WATERROW Somerset

The Rock Inn
WATERROW Map 03 ST02
TA4 2AX ☎ 01984 623293
The most miserable landlord in Somerset presides over this old coaching inn - according to the local young farmers! The Rock is literally built into the rock face, in a lovely green valley beside the River Tone. A traditional range of food is offered alongside a good vegetarian selection. Principal beers: Cotleigh Tawny, Exmoor Gold, John Smiths Extra Smooth.
Directions From Taunton take B3227.Waterrow approx 14m.
Free House
Open 7-12 (7am till 12 midnight)
Bar food 11-2 6-10 Av main course £3.20
Restaurant 11-2 6-10 Av 3 course à la carte £12
Accommodation s£20 d£40

WELLS Somerset

The Fountain Inn/Boxers Restaurant
WELLS Map 03 ST54
1 St Thomas St BA5 2UU
☎ 01749 672317
The labourers who assisted the stonemasons building Wells Cathedral, 50 yards away, stayed at this 15th-century hostelry. Dishes range from ploughman's with Wells' own Cathedral City Cheddar, in the bar, to pan-fried breast of chicken with wild mushroom and spinach stuffing and Marsala sauce, served in Boxers Restaurant. Principal beers: Milligans, Ushers Best, Ushers Seasonal, Founders Ale.
Directions City centre,at junc of A371 & B3139

contd.

Ushers
Open 10.30-2.30 6-11 (Sun 12-3,7-10.30)
Bar food 12-3 6-12 Av main course £6
Restaurant 12-2 6-10 Av 3 course à la carte £15

WEST CAMEL Somerset

The Walnut Tree

WEST CAMEL Map 03 ST52
Fore St BA22 7QW ☎ 01935 851292
This inn enjoys a peaceful village setting. The same menu is offered throughout, with starters such as Greek salad and home-made salmon and cod terrine, followed by a range of steaks, chicken breast wrapped in bacon and vegetarian cheese filos. Sweets include Pavlova and sticky toffee pudding. Principal beers: Bass, Butcombe, Kilkenny.
Directions Off A303 between Sparkford & Yeovilton Air Base
Free House
Open 11-3 5.30-11
Bar food 12-2 7.15-9.30 Av main course £10
Restaurant 12-2 7.15-9.30 Av 3 course à la carte £15
Accommodation s£39.50 d£49.50

WEST HUNTSPILL Somerset

Crossways Inn

WEST HUNTSPILL Map 03 ST34
TA9 3RA ☎ 01278 783756
17th-century inn of Dutch architecture, situated on the edge of Sedgemoor and within easy reach of the sea. Bar snacks, home-made pies and char-grilled steaks on offer. Specialities include broccoli, chicken and ham Mornay, mushroom Stroganoff, and a curried nut roast for vegetarians. Principal beers: Royal Oak, Flowers Original and IPA, Trophy, Guinness.
Directions On A38 3.5m from M5 J22/23
Free House
Open 10.30-3.30 5.30-11
Bar food 12-2.30 6.30-9.30 Av main course £4.80
Restaurant 6.30-10 Av 3 course à la carte £9.50 Av 2 course fixed price £8
Accommodation s£24 d£34

WEST PENNARD Somerset

Apple Tree Inn

WEST PENNARD Map 03 ST53
BA6 8ND ☎ 01749 890355
Old stone building surrounded by open fields with views of the Mendip Hills. Regular dishes include char-grilled steaks and chops, home-made chicken Kiev and lasagne, and escargots Bourguignonne. Cashew and nut paella, and moussaka with red wine sauce are on offer to vegetarians. Principal beers: Bass and Butcombe bitter.
Directions On A361(Glastonbury/Shepton Mallet) between West Pennard & Pilton
Free House
Open 11-2.30 6-11
Bar food 12-2.30 6.30-11 Av main course £5
Restaurant 12-2.30 2.30-11 Av 3 course à la carte £14

WHEDDON CROSS Somerset

The Rest and Be Thankful Inn

WHEDDON CROSS Map 03 SS93
TA24 7DR ☎ 01643 841222
In the highest village on Exmoor, The Rest & Be Thankful, once a coaching inn, obtained its name because the stage coaches climbing the steep hill to Wheddon Cross needed to rest and be thankful. The menu includes fish, steaks, sandwiches and salads. There is a skittle alley. Principal beers: Ruddles County, Old Speckled Hen, Theakstons, XB.
Directions 20m W of Taunton
Free House
Open 9.30-3 6.30-11
Bar food 12-2 7-10 Av main course £5
Restaurant 12-2 7-10 Av 3 course à la carte £12
Accommodation s£23 d£46

WITHYPOOL Somerset

Royal Oak Inn

WITHYPOOL Map 03 ST56
TA24 7QP ☎ 01643 831506
Situated on the edge of Exmoor National Park, this pub has boasted some famous guests, including President Eisenhower and the author of *Lorna Doone*, R.D. Blackmore. Roasted tenderloin of Somerset pork, escalope of venison, roasted quail, or lamb's kidneys in French mustard and garlic sauce may be on the menu. Principal beers: Flowers IPA, Pedigree.

Directions From M5 thru Taunton on B3224, then B3223 to Withypool
Free House
Open 11-2.30 6-11 (Sun 12-3, 7-10.30)
Bar food 12-2 6.30-9.30 Av main course £6
Restaurant 12-1.30 7-9 Av 3 course à la carte £22 Av 3 course fixed price £22
Accommodation s£33 d£33

WOOLVERTON Somerset

Red Lion
WOOLVERTON Map 03 ST75
Bath Rd BA3 6QS ☎ 01373 831050
Once a court room, this 400-year-old building has a lovely stone floor and an open fire. It is decorated in Elizabethan style and is, of course, haunted. Good home cooking is served, ranging from baskets of chips to steaks. Options include chicken, fish, curry, chilli and steak pie. Principal beers: 6X, IPA.
Directions On the A36 between Bath & Warminster
Wadworth
Bar food 12-2.15 7-9.30 Av main course £4.95

Wiltshire

ALDERBURY Wiltshire

The Green Dragon
ALDERBURY Map 04 SU12
Old Rd SP5 3AR ☎ 01722 710263
14th-century pub situated on a hill with fine views of Salisbury. The specials board changes daily and typically features pumpkin and sweet potato soup, venison casseroled in red wine and juniper, and pork, potato and cardamom curry. Main menu offers creamy mushroom Stroganoff, and cheese, spinach and pepper stuffed mushrooms. Principal beers: Dorset Best, Tanglefoot, Hard Tackle, Munchener.

Directions 1m off A36 (Southampton/Salisbury rd)
Hall & Woodhouse
Open 11-2.30 (Sat-Sun 11-3) 6-11
Bar food 12-2 7-9 Av main course £5.50

AXFORD Wiltshire

Red Lion Inn
AXFORD Map 04 SU27
Kennet Rise SN8 2HA
☎ 01672 520271
18th-century inn on the banks of the Kennet Valley. A la carte starters include deep fried camembert with a pineapple sauce, and baked brie with redcurrant jelly. Seafood dishes range from halibut steak poached in white wine and dill, to salmon steak lightly grilled in butter and fennel. Principal beers: Hook Norton, 6X, Whitbread.
Directions M4 J15, A246 to Marlborough town centre. Follow signs for Ramsbury. Inn 3m
Free House
Open 11-3 6.30-11
Bar food 11-3 6.30-11 Av main course £5
Restaurant 11-3 6.30-11 Av 3 course à la carte £20
Accommodation s£35 d£45

BARFORD ST MARTIN Wiltshire

Barford Inn
BARFORD ST MARTIN Map 04 SU03
SP3 4AB ☎ 01722 742242
Legend has it that Charles Dickens sat in the Barford snug to write one of his novels. The inn has a large salad bar and a typical menu includes mushroom Stroganoff, pork Valentine in Spanish tomato sauce, toad-in-the-hole, and 'the National Dish of Israel' - falafel with humus and salad. Principal beers: Dorset

contd.

Best, Tanglefoot, Dempseys.
Directions W on A30 5m from Salisbury toward Shaftesbury
Hall & Woodhouse
Open 11-11
Bar food 12-2.30 7-9.30 Av main course £6
Restaurant 12-2.30 7-9.30 Av 3 course à la carte £10 Av 3 course fixed price £10
Accommodation s£28 d£40

BECKHAMPTON Wiltshire

Waggon & Horses
BECKHAMPTON Map 04 SU06
SN8 1QJ ☎ 01672 539418
A beautiful thatched coaching inn dating back 400 years and close to the Avebury Stone circles, a friendly, informal atmosphere awaits at this hostelry mentioned in Dickens' Pickwick Papers'. Sample home-cooked food, perhaps Cajun shrimps followed by beef and Stilton pie. Principal beers: Wadworths, IPA, 6X, Old Timer.
Wadworth
Open 11-11 (Sun 12-10.30)
Bar food 11.45-6 6-10 Av main course £5.50
Restaurant 11.45-6 6-10

BOX Wiltshire

The Quarrymans Arms
BOX Map 03 ST86
Box Hill SN13 8HN
☎ 01225 743569/742954
A 300-year-old miners' pub with splendid views of the Colerene Valley. The main menu offers Stilton and asparagus pancake, poached mushrooms with white wine, bacon and mustard sauce, rack of lamb with port, thyme and redcurrant sauce, and sea bass supreme. Principal beers: Butcombe, 6X, Bob, Gem.
Directions Phone the pub for accurate directions
Free House
Open 11-3 6-11 (Thu-Sat open all day) (Sun 6-10.30)
Bar food 12-3 7-10 Av main course £4.50
Restaurant 12-3 7-10 Av 3 course à la carte £12.50
Accommodation s£25 d£30

BRADFORD ON AVON Wiltshire

The Canal Tavern
BRADFORD ON AVON Map 03 ST86
49 Frome Rd BA15 1LE
☎ 01225 867426 865232
Kennet and Avon canalside pub displaying all manner of waterways memorabilia. A selection of steak grills is available, including prime fillet with pâté and Stilton in a rich wine sauce. Other main course dishes are roast duckling with apricot and brandy sauce, vegetarian moussaka, and couscous and cranberry lattice. Principal beers: Wadworths 6X, IPA, Old Timer, Bass.
Directions From Bath A4 to Bathford roundabout then A363
Wadworth
Open 11-3 6-11
Bar food 12-2.30 7-10 Av main course £4.50
Restaurant 12-2.30 7-10 Av 3 course à la carte £14

BRINKWORTH Wiltshire

The Three Crowns
BRINKWORTH Map 04 SU08
SN15 5AF ☎ 01666 510366
On the village green overlooking the Vale of White Horse, this pub has a stone-flagged conservatory furnished with individual antique pine tables. Exotic meats are a feature of the restaurant menu, including ostrich, kangaroo and crocodile. Aberdeen Angus steaks, fish, and vegetarian dishes also appear. Principal beers: Wadworth 6X, Bass, Boddingtons, Archers.
Directions A3102 to Wootton Bassett, then B4042, 5m to Brinkworth
Whitbread
Open 10-3 6-11
Bar food 12-2 Av main course £5
Restaurant 12-2 6.15-9.30 Av 3 course à la carte £15

BROMHAM Wiltshire

The Greyhound Inn
BROMHAM Map 03 ST96
SN15 2HA ☎ 01380 850241
This friendly, family run pub offers a scrumptious mixture of fare. 'Ravishing' lunches are freshly baked rolls with an array of fillings. At any time, savour the choice of 'beginnings' and 'middlings' - devilled whitebait and chicken Verluccio perhaps - with a home-made apricot Pavlova - just one 'ecstatic ending'. Principal beers: Wadworth 6X, Flowers, Caffreys, Wadworth IPA.

Directions Chippenham rd A342 from Devizes for 4m. L into Bromham
Free House
Open 11-2.30 6.30-11 (Sun 12-3, 7-10.30)
Bar food 11-2 6.30-10.30 Av main course £6.50
Restaurant 11-2 6.30-10.30 Av 3 course à la carte £12

BURBAGE Wiltshire

Three Horseshoes Inn
BURBAGE Map 04 SU26
Stibb Green SJ8 3AE ☎ 01672 810324
Good old-fashioned English country cooking is the order of the day at this quaint 300 year old thatched pub decorated with railway artefacts. Try fisherman's hotpot or Wiltshire Fidgetty pie, but go international for a luxury Swiss or German ice cream or 'Louisiana Lovebite' pudding. Principal beers: Wadworth IPA & 6X.
Wadworth
Open 12-2.30 6-11
Bar food 12-2 7-9 Av main course £5.50

BURTON Wiltshire

The Old House at Home
BURTON Map 03 ST87
SN14 7LT ☎ 01454 218227
The extensive menu at this ivy-clad country pub offers a great choice of freshly cooked dishes from around the world. Chef's specials include tropical chicken on a creamed curry sauce with pineapple rice, Milano mushrooms flamed in brandy, and braised monkfish with a puff pastry crouton. Principal beers: Bass Old Timer, Smiles Best, Wadworths 6X.
Directions On B4039 NW of Chippenham
Free House
Open 11.30-2.30 7-11
Bar food 11.30-2.30 7-11 Av main course £9

CHIPPENHAM Wiltshire

The Crown at Tolldown
CHIPPENHAM Map 03 ST97
Tolldown Dyrham SN14 8HZ
☎ 01225 891231
Classic village local, yet minutes from the M4/J18. Home-made pies, quiches and curries feature daily, with specials ranging from double chicken breast in port and Stilton cream sauce, and pork coriander casserole, to poached salmon in a prawn and cream sauce. Traditional roasts for Sunday lunch. Principal beers: Wadworth 6X, IPA Tanglefoot, John Smiths, Old Timer Summersault.
Directions From M4 S toward Bath on A46, pub 3/4m on L
Wadworth
Open 12-2.30 7-11
Bar food 12-2.15 7-9.30 Av main course £6

COLLINGBOURNE DUCIS Wiltshire

The Shears Inn & Country Hotel
COLLINGBOURNE DUCIS Map 04 SU25
The Cadley Rd SN8 3ED
☎ 01264 850304
A 17th-century drovers' and shearers' inn set in a peaceful hollow of Wiltshire countryside. Baguettes and baked potatoes are offered in the bar, and there's an extensive restaurant menu, with roast half shoulder of lamb among the house specialities, and seafood including moules marinière. Principal beers: Morlands, Whitbread, Boddingtons, Stella.
Directions On A338 NW of Andover & Ludgershall
Free House
Open 11-3 5.30-11
Bar food 12-2 6.30-9 Av main course £4.50
Restaurant 12-2 6.30-9 Av 3 course à la carte £13.50

CORSHAM Wiltshire

Methuen Arms Hotel
CORSHAM Map 03 ST87
2 High St SN13 0HB ☎ 01249 714867
The oldest part of this hotel was a nunnery in the early 14th century, and the ancient stone walls with mullioned windows and oak beams still stand today. Both traditional and cosmopolitan food is served, with daily specials such as steak and kidney pie and tropical chicken with wild rice.
Directions Town centre,on A4 between Bath & Chippenham
Free House
Open 11-2.30 6-11
Bar food 12-2 6-9.30 Av main course £4.50
Restaurant 12-2 6-9.30
Accommodation s£33 d£39

contd.

CORSLEY HEATH Wiltshire

The Royal Oak Inn

CORSLEY HEATH Map 03 ST84

BA12 7PR ☎ 01373 832238

Originally a home for monks, this 16th-century inn incorporates 15th-century stables, and is situated on the edge of the Longleat Estate. The menu reflects an imaginative approach to country cooking; dishes including hand-made sausages, traditional fish and chips, and Guinness beef casserole. Principal beers: Wadworth 6X,Bass,Boddingtons bitter.

Directions On A362 between Warminster & Frome

Wadworth

Open 11.30-3 6-11

Bar food 12-2.30 6-9 Av main course £5.50

DEVIZES Wiltshire

The Elm Tree

DEVIZES Map 04 SO06

Long St SN10 1NJ ☎ 01380 723834

16th-century coaching inn with a function room for hire and a courtyard garden. Italian cooking is a speciality and a typical menu includes a wide range of pizzas, risotto Bolognese, Arrabbiata, lasagne al forno, and tiramisu for dessert. Principal beers: Wadworths 6X, Henrys IPA, Stella, Heineken.

Wadworth

Open 12-3 6-11

Bar food 12-2 6-11 Av main course £3.50

Accommodation s£17.50 d£32

Fox & Hounds

DEVIZES Map 04 SO06

Nursteed Rd SN10 3HJ ☎ 01380 723789

One of the earliest victims of 'ram-raiding', this thatched former farmhouse was hit by a steamroller in the 1900's. It remains unspoilt, though, and offers fresh home-cooking, simple or with a twist. 'Hot fish combo' includes a pineapple and prawn kebab, calamari and greenlip mussels. Principal beers: Wadworths 6X, IPA, Summersault.

Directions Located on A342 direction of Andover, 1m from Devizes town boundary

Wadworth

Open 11-3 5-11

Bar food 12-2.30 6.30-10 Av main course £5.75

Restaurant 12-3 6.30-10 Av 3 course à la carte £14.50

EAST KNOYLE Wiltshire

The Fox and Hounds

EAST KNOYLE Map 03 ST83

The Green SP3 6BN ☎ 01747 830573

Enjoy fine ale and good value food at this true countryman's pub, occupying a wonderful position overlooking the village green and beyond across the Blackmore Vale. Large menu incorporates tasty sandwiches to homemade puddings while specials could include a local bison burger!

Directions Off A303 onto A350 for 200yds, then R. Pub 1 1/2m on L

Free House

Open 11-2.30 6-11

Bar food 12-2.30 7-10.30 Av main course £5.50

FONTHILL GIFFORD Wiltshire

Beckford Arms

FONTHILL GIFFORD Map 03 ST93

SP3 6PX ☎ 01747 870385

18th-century inn adjacent to the William Beckford Estate. Typical blackboard specials are game casserole, fresh Poole plaice with a prawn and almond beurre noisette, and venison sausages with a shallot and red wine reduction. Main course dishes include lamb cutlets with wild mushroom and

Spanish brandy sauce. Principal beers: Courage Best, Wadworth 6X, John Smiths, Thatchers.
Directions 2m from A303 (Fonthill Bishop turning) halfway between Hindon & Tisbury at crossroads next to Beckford estate
Free House
Open 12-3 6-11
Bar food 12-3 6-1 Av main course £4.95
Restaurant 12-3 6-11 Av 3 course à la carte £15 Av 3 course fixed price £11.95
Accommodation s£34.50 d£54.50

FORD Wiltshire

The White Hart
FORD Map 03 ST87
SN14 8RP ☎ 01249 782213
An attractive stone-built coaching inn dating from 1553, with a terrace overlooking the Bybrook River. Food ranges from ploughman's and cold roast beef to oak smoked eel on potato salad, suprème of chicken filled with mushroom duxelles on red wine sauce, and hot toffee pudding. Principal beers: Spitfire, Tanglefoot, Hook Norton, Smiles Best.

Directions Off A420 between Chippenham & Bristol
Free House
Open 11-3 5-11
Bar food 12-2 7-10 Av main course £5
Restaurant 12-2 7-10 Av 3 course à la carte £19
Accommodation s£45 d£65

GREAT HINTON Wiltshire

The Linnet
GREAT HINTON Map 03 ST95
BA14 6BU ☎ 01380 870354
This mid-18th century cosy pub used to be part of an old woollen mill in this tiny Wiltshire village. Both bar and restaurant offer the same menu which includes vegetarian dishes. Specials often include home made pies, seafood platters and fresh local trout. Principal beers: Wadworth 6X & IPA.
Directions Just off the A361 Devizes to Trowbridge rd
Wadworth
Open 11-2.30 6.30-11
Bar food 12-2 6.30-10 Av main course £6.10
Restaurant 12-2 6.30-10 Av 3 course à la carte £11.50

HEYTESBURY Wiltshire

The Angel Inn
HEYTESBURY Map 03 ST94
High St BA12 0ED ☎ 01985 840330
Close to the River Wylye, this 17th-century coaching inn was frequented by pilgrims on their way to Plymouth and the New World. Today's menu may feature wild boar and apple sausages, mushrooms stuffed with leek and Stilton in filo pastry, or rack of lamb with vegetables and new potatoes. Principal beers: Ringwood Best, Marstons Pedigree, Timothy Taylor Landlord.
Directions From A303 take A36 toward Bath, 8m, Heytesbury on L
Free House
Open 11.30-3 6.30-11
Bar food 12-2.15 7-9.30 Av main course £6.25
Restaurant 12-2.15 7-9.30 Av 3 course à la carte £13.75
Accommodation s£37.50 d£49

HINDON Wiltshire

The Lamb at Hindon
HINDON Map 03 ST93
SP3 6DP ☎ 01747 820573
The oldest part of this posting inn

contd.

dates from the 17th century, and Silas White, leader of the notorious Moonrakers, based his activities here. There is an Anglo-French menu in the restaurant, and traditional dishes such as game casserole and grilled plaice are offered in the bar. Principal beers: Archibald Beckett, Ashvine Lionheart, Wadworth 6X.
Directions From A303 take B3089 towards Salisbury
Free House
Open 8-11
Bar food 12-2 7-10 Av main course £5.95
Restaurant 12-2 7-9.30 Av 3 course à la carte £19 Av 3 course fixed price £19
Accommodation s£30

HORNINGSHAM Wiltshire

The Bath Arms
HORNINGSHAM Map 03 ST84
BA12 7LY ☎ 01985 844308
Built in the early 18th century as a priory house, becoming a pub in 1763, the Bath Arms is situated in the picturesque village by the exit of Longleat House. The menu offers a full range of dishes, including fresh fish, vegetarian fare and plenty of home-made desserts. Principal beers: Smiles:Best, Golden Brew, Heritage, Smiles seasonal beers.
Directions Off B3092 S of Frome
Smiles
Open 11-11 (Winter closed 3-5.30)
Bar food 12-2.30 6-9.30 Av main course £5.95
Restaurant 12-2.30 6-9.30 Av 3 course à la carte £10
Accommodation s£29 d£42

HORTON Wiltshire

The Bridge Inn
HORTON Map 04 SU06
SN10 2JW ☎ 01380 860273
Only 2 miles from Devizes, this recently renovated inn is situated next to the Kennet and Avon canal, and has a large garden with its own barbecue. Chicken breast with black pudding stuffing wrapped in Parma ham, ratatouille crumble with basil dressing, or seafood pie may be on today's menu. Principal beers: IPA, 6X, Murphys, Heineken.
Directions A361 from Devizes, R at 3rd roundabout
Wadworth
Open 11.30-3 (Sun 3.30) 6.30-11
Bar food 12-2.30 7-9.30 Av main course £4.75
Restaurant 7-9.30 Av 3 course à la carte £13.95 Av 3 course fixed price £13.95
Accommodation s£17.50 d£35

KILMINGTON Wiltshire

The Red Lion Inn
KILMINGTON Map 03 ST73
KILMINGTON BA12 6RP
☎ 01985 844263
Relatively unchanged 15th-century coaching inn covered with creepers and decorated with flower boxes. Overlooked by White Sheet Hill. Menu may feature creamy fish pie, Cornish pasties, vegetable lasagne, or lamb and apricot pie. Home-cooked ham a speciality. Principal beers: Butcombe Bitter, Wadworth 6X, Guinness Bitter, Toby.
Directions B3092 off A303 then L at Kilmington Street
Free House
Open 11.30-2.30 6.30-11
Bar food 12-1.50 Av main course £3.95
Accommodation s£25 d£30

LACOCK Wiltshire

The George Inn
LACOCK Map 03 ST96
4 West St SN15 2LH ☎ 01249 730263
Dating from 1361, this inn is steeped in history, and a major feature is the grand open fireplace where a crackling log fire burns in winter. Dishes include grilled steaks - kangaroo and ostrich among them - duck, sausage and orange pie, battered cod and a three cheese and pasta bake. Principal beers: Wadworth 6X, IPA Old Timer.
Directions M4 J17 take A350 S
Wadworth
Open 10-11 (Sun 10-10.30)
Bar food 12-1.45 6-9.45
Restaurant 12-1.45 6-9.45 Av 3 course à la carte £15
Accommodation s£25 d£35

Red Lion Inn
LACOCK Map 03 ST96
1 High St SN15 2LQ ☎ 01249 730456
Dating from the early 1700s, this pub is prominently positioned in the village recently immortalised in TV series of *Pride & Prejudice, Moll Flanders* and *Emma*. The bar offers sandwiches, basket meals and home-made specials. A la carte dishes include Stilton mushrooms, honey-glazed lamb and sticky toffee pudding. Principal beers: Farmers Glory, IPA, Wadworths 6X, Draught Guinness.
Directions Just off A350 between Chippenham & Melksham
Wadworth
Open 11.30-3 5.30-11 (Summer 11.30-11)
Bar food 12-2.30 6-9 Av main course £5.95
Restaurant 6-9 Av 3 course à la carte £14.95
Accommodation s£45 d£60

LIMPLEY STOKE Wiltshire

The Hop Pole Inn
LIMPLEY STOKE Map 03 ST76
Woods Hill, Lower Limpley Stoke BA3 6HS ☎ 01225 723134
The Hop Pole dates from 1580, the name coming from the hop plant, which still grows outside the pub. Home-made pies, including steak and ale, are a speciality of the house, and there's a choice of fish, steaks and vegetarian dishes. Bar snacks encompass chip butties and samosas with salad. Principal beers: Courage Best, Butcombe, Bass.
Directions Off A36
Free House
Open 11-3 6-11
Bar food 12-2.15 6.30-10 Av main course £4.50
Restaurant 12-2.15 6.30-10 Av 3 course à la carte £15

LOWER WOODFORD Wiltshire

The Wheatsheaf
LOWER WOODFORD Map 04 SU13
SP4 6NQ ☎ 01722 782203
18th-century inn situated in the Woodford Valley near the River Avon. The large menu offers an interesting range of starters, such as Cajun chicken wings, fish dishes, curries and home-made pies. Good vegetarian selection including potato, leek and Stilton bake, mushroom and nut fettucine, and spinach and mushroom lasagne. Principal beers: Badger Dorset Best, Tanglefoot.
Directions Take A360 N of Salisbury. Village signposted 1st R turn
Hall & Woodhouse
Open 11-2.30 (3pm on Sat/Sun) 6.30-11
Bar food 12-2.30 7-10 Av main course £5.50

MALMESBURY Wiltshire

The Smoking Dog
MALMESBURY Map 03 ST98
62 The High St SN16 9AT
☎ 01666 825823
Built in the 1700s from Cotswold stone, and situated near the River Avon. Look out for the picture of a dog puffing on a pipe. The lunch menu includes bagels topped with smoked salmon and scrambled egg, beef and Guinness pie, and poached egg on ham and avocado with Hollandaise sauce. Principal beers: Wadworth 6X, Marstons Pedigree, Archers Best, Guinness, Scrumpy Jack.

Free House
Open 11.30-11 (Sun-12-10.30)
Bar food 12-2 7-9.30 Av main course £8
Restaurant 12-2 7-9.30 Av 3 course à la carte £16

MARTEN Wiltshire

Tipsy Miller
MARTEN Map 04 SU26
SA8 3SH ☎ 01264 731372
Built on the site of a 17th-century inn, the Tipsy Miller has a large garden surrounded by fine countryside views and overlooked by Wilton windmill, Wiltshire's only working windmill. Menu

contd.

ranges from Dover sole and smoked chicken, to kangaroo in a red wine sauce, and ostrich served 'Hunter's style.' Principal beers: 6x, Bass, Carling, Caffreys. Guinness.

Directions 6m SW of Hungerford on A338
Free House
Open 11-3 6-11
Bar food 11-3 6-11 Av main course £4.50
Restaurant 11-3 6-11 Av 3 course à la carte £17.50

MELKSHAM Wiltshire

Kings Arms Hotel
MELKSHAM Map 03 ST96
Market Place SN12 6EX
☎ 01225 707272

Once an important coaching house on the London to Bath route, warmth and hospitality are offered by this traditional market place inn. Choose from the set menu or à la carte, perhaps pan-fried sardines followed by chicken coriander, in the comfort of the Wedgwood decorated dining room. Principal beers: 6X, IPA, John Smiths.
Wadworth
Open 11-2.30 5-11
Bar food 12-2 6-9 Av main course £6
Restaurant 12-2 7-9 Av 3 course à la carte £15.50 Av 3 course fixed price £13.50
Accommodation s£32 d£58

MERE Wiltshire

Old Ship Inn
MERE Map 03 ST83
Castle St BA12 6JE ☎ 01747 860258

You are assured of a warm welcome at this 16th-century coaching inn. Architectural features include stone walls, flagstone floors and an original elm stairway. Home-cooked dishes are served in the bar, and there is a full à la carte menu in the oak-beamed restaurant. Principal beers: Tanglefoot and Badger Best.
Directions W of Stonehenge just off A303
Badger
Open 11-11 (Sun 12-10.30)
Bar food 12-2.30 6.30-9 Av main course £5
Restaurant 12-2.30 7.30-9 Av 3 course à la carte £15
Accommodation s£32 d£53

NORTH NEWNTON Wiltshire

The Woodbridge Inn
NORTH NEWNTON Map 04 SU15
A345 SN9 6JZ ☎ 01980 630266

A 16th-century country inn, situated in an area of outstanding natural beauty between Stonehenge and Avebury Circle. It is well known for its unique menu of international and traditional British cooking. Options include fish Creole, sizzling hoi sin beef, Mexican fajitas, and Barnsley chops. Principal beers: Wadworths, 6X, Farmers Glory, IPA.
Directions From M4 J15 take A345 through Marlborough & Pewsey
Wadworth
Open 11-11 (Sun 12-3, 7-10.30)
Bar food 11-10.30 11-10.30 Av main course £4.50
Restaurant 12-2.30 6-10 Av 3 course à la carte £12.50
Accommodation s£27 d£32.50

NUNTON Wiltshire

The Radnor Arms
NUNTON Map 04 SU12
SP5 4HS ☎ 01722 329722

Built as a cottage in the mid-18th century, becoming a pub in about 1853, the Radnor Arms is set in a small village overlooking water meadows. The name comes from Lord Radnor, landowner of the Longford Estate. Freshly prepared dishes are served including an extensive choice of fish. Principal beers: Tangle Foot, Dorset Best, IPA, Guinness.
Directions From Salisbury ring road take A338 to Ringwood. Nunton signposted on R
Hall & Woodhouse
Open 11-3 6-11
Bar food 12-2 7-9.30 Av main course £7.50

PEWSEY Wiltshire

The French Horn
PEWSEY Map 04 SU16
Marlborough Rd ☎ 01672 562443
The pub is situated on Pewsey Wharf. Prisoners from the Napoleonic War, released to build the canal, were summoned to the pub for food by the sound of a French horn. Fresh fish specials supplement both the bar and restaurant menus, and everything is made on the premises. Principal beers: Wadworth 6X, IPA, Stella, Carlsberg.
Directions A338 thru Hungerford, at Burbage take B3087 to Pewsey
Wadworth
Open 12-2.30 6-11
Bar food 12-2.30 6.30-9.30 Av main course £5.50
Restaurant 12-2.30 6.30-9.30 Av 3 course à la carte £15

PITTON Wiltshire

The Silver Plough
PITTON Map 04 SU23
White Hill SP5 1DZ ☎ 01722 712266
A traditional village pub with beamed bars full of interesting old artefacts. Bar food ranges from sandwiches to steaks, using fresh local ingredients. Typical restaurant dishes are smoked seafood salad, medallions of pork with caramelised apples and Calvados sauce, and banoffee pie. Principal beers: Tanglefoot, Badger Best.
Directions From Salisbury take A30 towards Andover, Pitton signposted approx 3m from Salisbury
Badger
Open 11-3 (Sun 12-3) 6-11 (Sun 7-10.30)
Bar food 12-2.30 6.30-9.30 Av main course £6
Restaurant 12-2 7-9 Av 3 course à la carte £17 Av 3 course fixed price £12.95

ROWDE Wiltshire

The George and Dragon
ROWDE Map 03 ST96
High St ☎ 01380 723053
Traditional Wiltshire pub that specialises in dishes using fresh fish from Cornwall. The blackboard menu may offer skate, Dover sole, cod, seabass, turbot, hake, monkfish, or squid. A non-fish meal may include spicy chick pea stew, pan-fried calves liver, or wild rabbit risotto.
Principal beers: Bunces Pigswill, Hopback or Ashvine, Butcombe, Wadworths 6X.
Free House
Open 12-3 7-11
Bar food 12-2 7-10
Restaurant 12-2 7-10 Av 3 course à la carte £20 Av 3 course fixed price £10

SALISBURY Wiltshire

Kings Arms Hotel
SALISBURY Map 04 SU12
7a-11 St Johns St SP1 2SB
☎ 01722 327629
The King's Arms was built nearly a century before Salisbury Cathedral and is a perfect base for those visiting the ancient city. 'Pippins' - the restaurant - may feature fresh grilled rainbow trout, tagliatelle Bolognese, or Cajun spiced prawns on its menu. Food is also available in one of the two bars. Principal beers: Flowers, 6X, Boddingtons, Whitbread.
Free House
Open 11-11
Bar food 11-3 6-10 Av main course £4.50
Restaurant 11-3 6-10 Av 3 course à la carte £15 Av 3 course fixed price £12.95
Accommodation s£40 d£58

SEEND Wiltshire

Bell Inn
SEEND Map 03 ST96
Bell Hill SN12 6SA ☎ 01380 828338
Cromwell's troops once stayed here when advancing on Devizes Castle and in 1685, a troop downed a whole cask of liquor before routing the Duke of Monmouth's rebellion. Enjoy tipsy mushrooms to Tuscan trout while admiring stunning views in a setting carefully refurbished to retain old world charm. Principal beers: Wadworth 6X, IPA, Heineken, Kronenberg.
Wadworth
Open 11-3 5.30-11
Bar food 12-2.30 6.30-10 Av main course £5.50
Restaurant 12-2.30 6.30-10

SHERSTON Wiltshire

The Rattlebone Inn
SHERSTON Map 03 ST96
Church St SN16 0LR ☎ 01666 840871
John Rattlebone fought in 1016 to defeat King Canute. He was fatally wounded in

contd.

the stomach, and used a tile to cover it until the battle ended, when he was brought to the site of the Rattlebone Inn to die. It is said he still resides in ghostly form. In this quintessential English setting, sample the varied menu including lamb with raspberry and mint, smoked haddock au gratin, and raspberry Whim Wham. Principal beers: Abbot Ale, Smiles Best, Sherston Pale Ale, Bass.

Directions M4 J18 take A46 towards Stroud,then B4040 thru Acton Turville,then to Sherston

Smiles

Open 11.30-3 (Sat 11.30-11,Sun 12-10.30)

Bar food 12-2 7-10 Av main course £4.50

Restaurant 12-2 7-10

STAPLEFORD Wiltshire

The Pelican Inn

STAPLEFORD Map 04 SU03

Warminster Rd SP3 4LT

☎ 01722 790241

A 250-year-old coaching inn with stone walls, an inglenook fireplace, stables converted into a restaurant, and a large rear garden popular with families. Meals are cooked to order, and dishes range from bar snacks to plaice Dieppe, vegetarian lasagne and char-grilled steaks. Principal beers: Ringwood Best, Ringwood 49'er, Otter Bitter.

Directions On A36 7m W of Salisbury

Free House

Open 11-2.30 6-11 (Sun 12-3, 7-10.30)

Bar food 12-2 6.30-9.30 Av main course £6

Restaurant 12-2 6.30-9.30 Av 3 course à la carte £15

STOURHEAD Wiltshire

Spread Eagle Inn

STOURHEAD Map 03 ST73

BA12 6QE ☎ 01747 840587

Built in 1720 as an inn for visitors to Stourhead Estate, the Spread Eagle is set in the middle of the beautiful National Trust property. Wholesome home-cooked fare is served in the bar, including various home-made pies. More exotic dishes are offered from the extensive à la carte menu. Principal beers: Courage Cask Ales.

Directions N of A303 off B3092

Free House

Open 10-11

Bar food 10-3 6-10 Av main course £4.95

Restaurant 12-3 6-10

TOLLARD ROYAL Wiltshire

King John Inn

TOLLARD ROYAL Map 03 ST91

SP5 5PS ☎ 01725 516207

A Victorian pub, opened to supply the necessary refreshment to workers at the Tollard Royal Iron Foundry. The village is situated on the edge of Cranborne Chase, an area of outstanding natural beauty. Traditional home-cooked dishes are offered from a frequently changing blackboard menu. Principal beers: Smiles, Tisbury, Eldridge Pope.

Directions From Shaftsbury take A30 towards Salisbury then B3081

Free House

Open 12-2.30 6.30-11

Bar food 12-2.30 7-9.30 Av main course £6

Restaurant 12-2.30 7-9.30

Accommodation s£33.50 d£40

UPTON LOVELL Wiltshire

Prince Leopold

UPTON LOVELL Map 03 ST94

BA12 0JP ☎ 01985 850460

Built as a local shop and post office in 1887, and named after Queen Victoria's youngest son, this pub enjoys splendid views of the Wylye Valley. The menu may include a variety of Balti dishes, poached salmon, Wylye Valley lamb, 'Old Granddad Southern Steak', or pancakes with stir-fry vegetable stuffing. Principal beers: Ringwood, Bass 6X, Beamish, Websters.

Directions South of A36 between Warminster & Salisbury

Free House

Open 12-3 7-11

Bar food 12-3 7-11 Av main course £6.50

Restaurant 12-3 7-11 Av 3 course fixed price £13.50

WANBOROUGH Wiltshire

Shepherds Restaurant
WANBOROUGH Map 04 SU28
Foxhill SN4 0DR ☎ 01793 790266
Dating from the 15th century, and very much a resting place for shepherds, this pub is now believed to be the only one actually on the Ridgeway. All the food is freshly prepared and includes home-made burgers, pastas and home-cooked ham. Vegetarians are also catered for. Principal beers: Flowers IPA, Boddingtons, Wadworth 6X, Fullers London Pride.
Directions M4 J15 towards Swindon.1st r'about take 3rd exit.Thru' Upper Wanborough.At x-rd turn R
Whitbread
Open 11-3 6-11
Bar food 11.30-2.30 6-10.30 Av main course £5
Restaurant 11.30-2.30 6-10.30 Av 3 course à la carte £15

WOODFALLS Wiltshire

The Woodfalls Inn
WOODFALLS Map 04 SU12
The Ridge SP5 2LN ☎ 01725 513222
Built in 1868 as an ale house and coaching inn on the northern edge of the New Forest, the inn closed in the early 80s, re-opening in 1992 restored to its former glory. English fare, including fresh local fish, is served in the bar, and there is a full restaurant menu. Principal beers: Ringwood, Gales, HSB, Courage.

Directions B3079 to Brook, B3078 to Telegraph Corner, B3080 to Woodfalls
Free House
Open 7.30-11
Bar food 12-2.30 6.30-10 Av main course £5.95
Restaurant 12-2.30 7-9.45 Av 3 course à la carte £16.95 Av 4 course fixed price £16.95
Accommodation s£39.95 d£50

WOOTTON RIVERS Wiltshire

Royal Oak
WOOTTON RIVERS Map 04 SU16
SN8 4NQ ☎ 01672 810322
Situated in the middle of a picturesque village, close to the Kennet and Avon canal, the Royal Oak is a 16th-century thatched free house with a wealth of oak beams. The menu offers an extensive choice including snacks, basket meals, salads, fish, steaks and vegetarian dishes. Principal beers: Wadsworth 6X, IPA , Ushers.
Directions 4m S of Marlborough off A346
Free House
Open 10.30-3.30 6-11
Bar food 12-2 7-9.30 Av main course £6
Restaurant 12-2 7-9.30 Av 3 course à la carte £15
Accommodation s£20 d£30

South & South-East England

Historic London plus a plethora of traditional heritage towns, stately homes and English gardens are the hallmarks of this region set amidst ranges of rolling chalk downland.

• Bedfordshire • Berkshire •
• Buckinghamshire • Greater London •
• Hampshire • Hertfordshire • Kent •
• London • Surrey • Sussex, East •
• Sussex, West • Wight, Isle of •

Bedfordshire

ASTWICK Bedfordshire

Tudor Oaks Lodge
ASTWICK Map 04 TL23
Taylor's Rd SG5 4AZ ☎ 01462 834133
Specialising in micro-brewery guest beers, this beamed lodge has 5 fireplaces made of handmade brick and a Jacobean staircase. Speciality dishes include tournedos Rossini, chicken Valdostana, and steak pizzaiola, while the specials board may offer grilled rainbow trout, 'truckers breakfast', or home-made steak pie. Principal beers: Boddingtons.

Directions 4m S of A1(M) J9
Free House
Open 7am-11
Bar food 12-2.30 6-10.30 Av main course £5.50
Restaurant 7-10 Av 3 course à la carte £15
Accommodation s£30 d£35

BOLNHURST Bedfordshire

Ye Olde Plough
BOLNHURST Map 04 TL05
Kimbolton Rd MK44 2EX
☎ 01234 376274
Built in 1480, burnt down in 1989 and re-opened in 1991 following an archaeological re-build, this pub has regained its Grade II listing. There is a resident ghost called Cedric who is fascinated by the food, so different from his day, with dishes such as smoked fish lasagne and Thai prawn curry. Principal beers: Hook Norton, Ruddles Best, Directors.
Directions Off B660 N of Bedford
Free House
Open 12-2.30 7-11 (Sun 7-10.30)
Bar food 12-2.30 7-9.30

BROOM Bedfordshire

The Cock
BROOM Map 04 TL14
23 High St SG18 9NA ☎ 01767 314411
Unusually, this pub has no bar. Drinks are served from a servery in the floor. Luckily there are tables so diners can sit down to a meal which may include breast of Cajun chicken, dover sole, mushroom stroganoff, or a range of ploughmans' and 'mega' sandwiches. Principal beers: IPA, Rayments, Abbot.
Directions Off B658 SW of Biggleswade
Greene King
Open 12-3 6-11
Bar food 12-2.30 7-9.30
Restaurant 12-2.30 7-9.30 Av 3 course à la carte £14

EATON BRAY Bedfordshire

The White Horse
EATON BRAY Map 04 SP92
Market Square LU6 2DG
☎ 01525 220231
250-year-old village green pub with an unusual central bar servery. Good choice of bar food including steaks, seafood and a *Nora Batty* stocking filler which contains meat and Yorkshire pudding. A main course could start with quail eggs and asparagus, followed by peppercorn duck or beef Provençale. Principal beers: Friary Meux Bitters, Flowers IPA, Carlsberg lager, Labbatts lager.
Directions Take A5 N of Dunstable then A5050 1m turn L & follow signs
Free House
Open 11.30-2.30 6.30-11
Bar food 12-2.30 7-9.15 Av main course £5
Restaurant 12-2.30 7-9.15 Av 3 course à la carte £12

KEYSOE Bedfordshire

The Chequers
KEYSOE Map 04 TL06
Brook End MK44 2HR ☎ 01234 708678
Home-made dishes prepared from fresh ingredients are served at this free house. Starters or snacks include home-made soup or pâté, followed perhaps by trout with Noilly Prat, almonds and cream or a robust steak and ale pie. The blackboard menu offers daily specials including vegetarian dishes. Principal beers: Stowford Pross cider, Hook Norton, Lodon Pride, McEwans.

Directions On B660 N of Bedford
Free House
Open 11.30-2.30 6.30-11
Bar food 12-2 7-9.45 Av main course £5.50

LINSLADE Bedfordshire

The Globe Inn
LINSLADE Map 04 SP92
Globe Ln, Old Linslade LU7 7TA
☎ 01525 373338
The Globe stands by the Grand Union Canal and is also close to the River Ouzel, Linslade Wood and the Greensand Ridge. Food on offer may include scrumpy chicken-stuffed chicken breast cooked in scrumpy cider, duck with Cointreau and orange sauce, or beef and ale pie. Principal beers: London Pride, Theakston, Pedigree.
Directions A5 S to Dunstable, follow signs to Leighton Buzzard (A4146)
Free House
Open 11-3 6-11 (Sun 12-4,7-10.30)
Bar food 12-2.30 7-10 Av main course £5.95
Restaurant 12-2.30 7-10 Av 3 course à la carte £22

ODELL Bedfordshire

The Bell
ODELL Map 04 SP95
Horsefair Ln MK43 7AG
☎ 01234 720254
A 16th-century thatched pub with a wealth of oak beams and an inglenook fireplace. There is a large garden, close to the River Ouse, with an aviary of birds, rabbits and a pet goose. Traditional home-made fare is served - hot and cold dishes - using best quality produce. Principal beers: Greene King, IPA, Abbot Ale, Rayments.
Greene King
Open 11-2.30 6-11 (Sun 7-10.30)
Bar food 12-2 7-9.30 Av main course £5.25

AA members can call AA Hotel Booking Service on 0990 050505 to book at AA recognised hotels and B & Bs in the UK and Ireland, or through our Internet site: http://www.theaa.co.uk/hotels

RADWELL Bedfordshire

The Swan Inn
RADWELL Map 04 TL05
Felmersham Rd MR43 7HS
☎ 01234 781351
A Grade II listed stone-built pub with a thatched roof, the Swan is situated near the river and has a very large garden. The blackboard menus offer snacks such chicken burrito, pasta, ploughman's and quiche. Main courses include monkfish and prawns in cream sauce, and sirloin steak. Principal beers: IPA Bitter, Bombardier, Guinness, Murphys.
Directions Off A6 N of Bedford
Charles Wells
Open 12-2.30 6-11
Bar food 12-2 7-9
Restaurant 12-2 7-9 Av 3 course à la carte £13

WOBURN Bedfordshire

The Black Horse
WOBURN Map 04 SP93
1 Bedford St MK17 9QB
☎ 01525 290210
Traditional country inn dating from 1824, situated near Woburn Abbey. The pub is famous in the area for being home to the Woburn Oyster Festival. Naturally fresh oysters are part of the menu, along with other seafood dishes, such as mussels with white wine, and Scottish steaks. Principal beers: Ruddles Best, Marstons Pedigree, London Pride.
Directions On main road through Woburn
Free House
Open 11-3 6-11 (Sat-Sun 11-11)
Bar food 12-2.30 6.30-10 Av main course £4.25
Restaurant 12.-2.30 6.30-10 Av 3 course à la carte £15

Berkshire

ALDERMASTON Berkshire

The Hinds Head
ALDERMASTON Map 04 SU56
Wasing Ln RG7 4LX ☎ 01189 712194
Dating back to the 15th-century, this inn, with clock and bell tower, must be one of the few remaining with village lock-up still attached. Latter, last used in 1865. Typical dishes include lamb in honey and red wine, home-made curries, and contd.

gammon in honey and cider sauce. Principal beers: Courage Best, Fullers London Pride.
Directions M4 J12, then A4 towards Newbury, then L on A340 towards Basingstoke, 2m to the village
Free House
Open 11-3 5-11.30
Bar food 12-2 6.30-9.30 Av main course £6.25
Accommodation s£40 d£57.50

ASCOT Berkshire

Royal Foresters Hotel

ASCOT Map 04 SU96
London Rd SL5 8DR ☎ 01344 884747
An 18th-century building situated near Ascot race course. Bar food includes ploughman's, bacon and cheese burger, lasagne and fish and chips. There is also a 120-seater Beefeater chain restaurant. Principal beers: Morlands.
Directions On A329 midway between Ascot & Bracknell
Free House
Open 11-11
Bar food 12-10 12-10 Av main course £5
Restaurant 12-2.30 5-10.30 Av 3 course à la carte £15
Accommodation s£41 d£41

ASHMORE GREEN Berkshire

The Sun in the Wood

ASHMORE GREEN Map 04 SU56
Stoney Ln RG18 9WF ☎ 01635 42377
At this friendly country pub tucked in the Berkshire countryside and surrounded by mature woodland, fresh food tempts with an interesting flair such as suprême of shark with a tomato and garlic sauce or steamed salmon and crab sausage with a saffron and parsley sauce. Principal beers: Wadworth 6X, Henrys IPA.
Directions A34 Robin Hood roundabout, L to Shaw, at mini roundabout R then 7th L into Stoney Lane, 1 1/2m pub on L
Free House
Open 12-2.30 6-11
Bar food 12-2.15 6.30-9.45 Av main course £6.50
Restaurant 12-2.15 6.30-9.45

CHIEVELEY Berkshire

The Blue Boar Inn

CHIEVELEY Map 04 SU47
North Heath, Wantage Rd RG20 8UE
☎ 01635 248236
The 'blue boar' was left at this pub by Cromwell's men prior to the Battle of Naseby in 1644, and to this day sits outside on a plinth. Traditional pub grub is served in the bar, while the restaurant offers steaks, char-grills and roasts, plus some vegetarian options. Principal beers: Wadworths 6X, Fullers London Pride, Boddingtons.
Directions Off B4494 S of Wantage
Free House
Open 11-3 6-11
Bar food 12-3 7-11 Av main course £6.95
Restaurant 12-3 7-11 Av 3 course à la carte £23.50
Accommodation s£49 d£59

COOKHAM Berkshire

Bel and The Dragon

COOKHAM Map 04 SU88
High St SL6 9SQ ☎ 01628 521263
One of the oldest licensed houses in England, the inn was built of wattle and daub as a house of refreshment for people attending church. The name comes from the Apocrypha (Bel was an idol of the Babylonians). There is an extensive French menu and a choice of bar meals. Principal beers: Brakspear, Henley Real Ale.
Free House
Open 11.30-2.30 5.30-11 (Sun 12-3, 7-11)
Bar food 12.15-2.30 7-9 Av main course £6
Restaurant 12.15-2.30 7-9.30 Av 3 course à la carte £18.50

COOKHAM DEAN Berkshire

Chequers Inn Brasserie
COOKHAM DEAN Map 04 SU88

Dean Ln SL6 9BQ ☎ 01628 481232

17th-century village inn with oak beams and open fire. Among the seafood dishes on offer are poached salmon with prawns and chervil, and sautéed collops of monkfish with garlic and ginger. Other main course meals include Chinese style pork chilli, and roasted breast of duck with orange and Cointreau. Principal beers: London Pride, Marstons, Pedigree.

Directions From A4094 in Crookham High St take R fork after r'way bridge into Dean Lane. Pub in 1m.

Free House

Open 12-3 6-11

Bar food 12-2.30 6 9.30 Av main course £8

Uncle Tom's Cabin
COOKHAM DEAN Map 04 SU88

Hills Ln SL6 9NT ☎ 01628 483339

This 300 year old pub takes pride in the use of fresh ingredients and individual preparation of every item on the menu, which ranges from stuffed jacket potatoes, baguettes and home-made burgers to authentic Indian Balti dishes. Principal beers: Benskins, Lowenbrau, Carlsberg, Guinness.

Directions A4 towards Maidenhead, over bridge, R & on to Cookham High st, thru town over railway line, past Whyteladies Ln, pub on L

Carlsberg Tetley

Open 11-3 5.30-11 (Sun 12-3, 7-10.30)

Bar food 12-2 7.30-10 Av main course £6

CRAZIES HILL Berkshire

The Horns
CRAZIES HILL Map 04 SU78

RG10 8LY ☎ 0118 9401416

Originally a hunting lodge with a recently renovated barn now resembling a medieval hall. Among the starters are Gruyère cheese and spinach tartlets with warm gazpacho sauce, and crabcakes with home-made tartare sauce. Main dishes include lamb steak with redcurrant and mint, and duck with plum sauce. Principal beers: Brakspear Ordinary, Special, Old, OBJ.

Directions Off A321 NE of Wargrave

Brakspear

Open 11.30-2.30 6-11

Bar food 12-2 7-9.15 Av main course £6

Restaurant 12-2 7-9.15 Av 3 course à la carte £16

CURRIDGE Berkshire

The Bunk Traditional Inn
CURRIDGE Map 04 SU47

RG18 9DS ☎ 01635 200400

A traditional inn dating back about 150 years, with beams, brasses and a log fire in the attractive bar. The approach to food is very flexible, the à la carte menu can be taken in the restaurant, bar, conservatory or patio, and vice versa with the bar menu. The food is largely traditional British. Principal beers: Arkells 3B, 6X, London Pride, Carlsberg Export.

Directions M4 J13/A34 S 0.75m take 1st exit. 1m turn L,pub 400yds

Free House

Open 11-11

Bar food 12-4 6.30-12 Av main course £7.50

Restaurant 12-5 6.30-12 Av 3 course à la carte £18

DORNEY Berkshire

The Palmer Arms
DORNEY Map 04 SU97

Village Rd SL4 6QW ☎ 01628 666612

18th-century pub close to Dorney Court and the River Thames. Offers a range of bar snacks, and light pasta dishes. Main course options range from chicken fillet in wild mushroom sauce, and boeuf Bourguignonne, to seafood Mornay, and breast of duck with cranberry sauce. Principal beers: Rebellion IPA, Courage Best, Theakstons Old Peculiar, Fosters.

Directions Onto A4 then B3026 across M4 to Dorney

Free House

Open 11-3 6-11

Bar food 12-3 6.30-11 Av main course £4.95

Restaurant 12-3 6.30-11 Av 3 course à la carte £15

EAST ILSLEY Berkshire

The Swan
EAST ILSLEY Map 04 SU48

RG20 7LF ☎ 01635 281238

The Swan, set in a peaceful downland village, is largely 17th century, though it may incorporate some earlier building. Bar snacks, such as ploughman's and burgers, are served as well as full meals

contd.

with dishes such as spicy chicken joints, mussels Provençale and toffee, apple and pecan pie. Principal beers: Morlands Original, Old Speckled Hen, Bombardier.
Directions 5m N of J13 on A34. 18m S of Oxford M4.
Morland
Open 10.30-2.30 6-11
Bar food 12-2 6-10 Av main course £6
Restaurant 12-2.30 6-11 Av 3 course à la carte £11
Accommodation s£33 d£48

FRILSHAM Berkshire

The Pot Kiln
FRILSHAM Map 04 SU57
RG18 0XX ☎ 01635 201366
Formerly a centre for many old crafts, including farming, pottery, hurdle, besom and brickmaking, the pub has stood here for at least 400 years, and there is now a micro-brewery in the converted calf building. Simple wholesome food is served, including hot filled rolls, casseroles, pies and fresh vegetables. Principal beers: West Berkshire, Morlands, Arkells.
Directions A34 towards Oxford, 1st L to Chieveley, then 1st R to Hermitage. 2nd L onto B4009, 2nd R to Yattendon, R on sharp L bend, on for 1m
Free House
Open 12-3 6.30-11 (closed Tues morning)
Bar food 12-2 7-9.30 Av main course £5.90

GREAT SHEFFORD Berkshire

The Swan Inn
GREAT SHEFFORD Map 04 SU37
Newbury Rd RG17 7DS
☎ 01488 648271
Overlooking the River Lambourn in the heart of an area best known for sheep-farming and racehorses, the Swan was built in 1881 and has a large riverside patio. Chicken tikka, honey-roasted stincotta, grilled whole plaice, or broccoli and cream cheese bake may be on today's menu. Principal beers: Wadworth 6X, Courage Best, John Smiths, and Butts Ales.
Directions 1.5m north of M4 J14 on A338
Eldridge Pope
Open 11-3 (Sun 12-3) 6-11 (Sun 7-10.30)
Bar food 12-2.30 6.30-9.30 Av main course £5.95
Restaurant 12-2.30 6.30-9.30 Av 3 course à la carte £13

HARE HATCH Berkshire

The Queen Victoria
HARE HATCH Map 04 SU37
The Holt RG10 9TA ☎ 01189 402477
A country cottage-style building dating back 300 years, this inn welcomes a wide range of customers and offers quality food at sensible prices. Favourite dishes are port and Stilton pâté with garlic bread, lamb with rosemary, Mexican beef taco shells, and lentil, basil and sun-dried tomato sausages. Principal beers: Brakspears PA, SPA, Old, Premium Smooth.
Directions On A4 between Reading & Maidenhead
Brakspear
Open 11-11
Bar food 11.30-3 6.30-11 Av main course £5

HURLEY Berkshire

The Rising Sun
HURLEY Map 04 SU88
High St SL6 5LT ☎ 01628 824274
In traditional surroundings, this pub has an open log fire in winter, and old, beamed ceilings. The evening menu offers garlic mushrooms with cheese, calves' liver with bacon and onions, and honey glazed chicken with cashew nuts. Principal beers: Brakspears, Heineken, Stella.
Directions Off the A4130 from Maidenhead
Whitbread
Open 11.30-3 5.30-11
Bar food 12-2 7-9.30 Av main course £5
Restaurant 12-2 7-9.30

HURST Berkshire

Wheelwrights Arms
HURST Map 04 SU77

Davis Way RG10 0TR ☎ 01189 344100

A traditional old pub, a former wheelwrights workshop, majoring in beams, open fires and a warm welcome. Food has an international flavour with chicken satay, deep-fried calamari, and stir-fried beef and black bean sauce in amongst the familiar steaks, fish and chips, and chicken, ham and leek pie. Principal beers: 6X, Farmers Glory, Henrys IPA, Tanglefoot.

Directions A329 (M) exit at Winnersh, follow signs to Wokingham, 1 1/2m after leaving A329 L at Winnersh station, then 1m, pub on R

Wadworth

Bar food 12-2.30 6.30-9 Av main course £3.50

Restaurant 12-2.30 6.30-9 Av 3 course à la carte £11 Av 3 course fixed price £7.75

INKPEN Berkshire

The Swan Inn
INKPEN Map 04 SU36

Craven Rd RG17 9DX ☎ 01488 668326

A friendly village pub, mainly 17th-century, with three open fires and many oak beams. The owners have their own organic farm shop, so the menu features organic beef and produce from their nearby farm. Dishes include beef curry, cottage pie, fruit crumble and rice pudding. Principal beers: Adnams Bitter & Mild, Butts Bitter, Barbus.

Directions S down Hungerford High St, L to common, R to Inkpen, pub 3m

Free House

Open 12-2.30 7-11 (Sun 12-3, 7-10.30)

Bar food 12-2 7-9.30 Av main course £6

KINTBURY Berkshire

The Dundas Arms
KINTBURY Map 04 SU36

53 Station Rd RG17 9UT
☎ 01488 658263

Kennet and Avon canalside pub with a jetty for food and drinks. Typical main course dishes are roast breast of duck with lemon grass sauce, fried skate with capers and butter, and braised veal with ginger, coriander and lime leaf sauce. There is also an impressive champagne and wine list. Principal beers: Shepherd Neame Spitfire, Morlands Original Bitter, Bass, Bombardus.

Directions M4 J13 take A34 to Newbury,then A4 to Hungerford, turn L to Kintbury. Pub 1m after r'way & canal bridges

Free House

Open 11-2.30 6-11

Bar food 12-2 7-9 Av main course £8

Restaurant 7.30-9 Av 3 course à la carte £25

Accommodation s£55 d£65

KNOWL HILL Berkshire

Bird In Hand Country Inn
KNOWL HILL Map 04 SU87

Bath Rd RG10 9UP ☎ 01628 826622

This friendly country inn, parts of which date from the 14th century, has been in the same family for the last three generations. There is an emphasis on traditional fare, including fish and chips, Lancashire hot pot and steak and kidney pudding. Snacks are also served in the bar. Principal beers: Brakspears, London Pride.

Directions Follow A404(M) for 2m, onto A4 for 3m, pub on R

Free House

Open 11-3 5.45-11

contd.

Open 11-3 5.45-11
Bar food 12-2.30 6-10 Av main course £7
Restaurant 12-2 7-10 Av 3 course à la carte £15 Av 3 course fixed price £15
Accommodation s£55 d£70

NEWBURY Berkshire

The White Hart Inn

NEWBURY Map 04 SU46

Kintbury Rd, Hamstead Marshall RG20 0HW ☎ 01488 658201

An English country inn with Italian food, reflecting the partnership of an Italian chef and his English wife. There is a range of omelettes, pasta dishes, steak and fish options supported by daily specials, such as pork with apricots and mushrooms, grilled on a skewer and served with risotto and salad. Principal beers: Wadworths 6X, Ringwood Best.
Directions A4, 2m past Speen, L at crossroads, cross railway & canal, L at jct, R at next jct, inn 300yrds on R
Free House
Open 12-2.30 6-11
Bar food 12-2.30 6-11 Av main course £8.50
Restaurant 12.30-2.30 7-11 Av 3 course à la carte £18.50
Accommodation s£45 d£65

READING Berkshire

Fishermans Cottage

READING Map 04 SU77

224 Kennet Side RG1 3DW
☎ 0118 9571553

Situated on the tow path of the Kennet and Avon canal, the main bar of this pub is shaped like a canal barge. There is also a conservatory, with a warm relaxed atmosphere. Dishes include omelettes, fish and chips, home-made pies and specials such as aubergine, tomato and mozzarella gratin. Principal beers: Fullers London Pride, ESB, Fullers Chiswick Bitter.
Directions L from Kings Rd into Orts Rd then Canal Way turning
Fullers
Open 11.30-3 5.30-11 (Fri-Sun & summer 11.30-11)
Bar food 12-2.30 6.30-9.30 Av main course £4.50

STANFORD DINGLEY Berkshire

The Bull Inn

STANFORD DINGLEY Map 04 SU57

RG7 6LS ☎ 01734 744409

A 15th-century timber framed building extended in the 18th century, the Bull is frequented by locals and has a good pub atmosphere. The menu of traditional bar fare - ploughman's, baked potatoes and drunken fish pie - is supplemented by 'specials' such as chicken curry or coquille St Jacques. Principal beers: West Berks brewery, Brakspears, Bass, Tennants lager.
Directions M4 J12 A4/A340 towards Pangbourne.1st L to Bradfield. Thru' Bradfield, 0.3m take L into Back Lane. At end turn L, pub 0.25m on L
Free House
Open 12-3 7-11
Bar food 12-3 7.30-10.30

The Old Boot Inn

STANFORD DINGLEY Map 04 SU57

RG7 6LT ☎ 01734 744292

An 18th-century free house, this family-run business is set in idyllic surroundings close to the river which runs through the village. Two chefs prepare the meals from fresh produce, with dishes such as game sausages with creamed potatoes, and monkfish and salmon Royale. Principal beers: Archers, Spitfire, Brakspears Special, London Pride.
Directions M4 J12,A4/A340 to Pangbourne.1st L to Bradfield.Thru' Bradfield follow signs for Stanford Dingley
Free House
Open 11-3 6-11
Bar food 12-2.30 6-10 Av main course £6.95
Restaurant 12-2.30 6-10 Av 3 course à la carte £18

WALTHAM ST LAWRENCE Berkshire

The Bell

WALTHAM ST LAWRENCE Map 04 SU87

The Street RG10 0JJ ☎ 0118 9341788

Since 1608, when it was left to the village in trust, the rent from this pub has been donated to the needy of Waltham St Lawrence. A selection from this charitable menu may include local rabbit stew, chicken lasagne, venison in red wine, or harvest leek and vegetable crumble. Principal beers: Brakspears, Wadworths 6X, Bass.

Directions On B3024 E of Twyford (from A4 turn at Hare Hatch)
Free House
Open 11-3 6-11
Bar food 12-2 7-9.30 Av main course £5.50
Restaurant 12-2 7-9.30

WINKFIELD Berkshire

Rose & Crown
WINKFIELD Map 04 SU97
Woodside, Windsor Forest SL4 2DP
☎ 01344 882051
A traditional country pub and restaurant situated on the Windsor side of Ascot Racecourse. Baguettes, baked potatoes and a range of popular dishes are offered at lunchtime, and the evening menu may have crab pâté, and lamb Wellington with mushroom and Madeira sauce. Principal beers: Broadside, Bombardier, Moorlands Original, Fosters.
Directions M3 J3 from Ascot race course on A332 take 2nd exit from Heatherwood Hosp r'about,then 2nd turn L
Morland
Open 11-11 (Sun 12-7)
Bar food 12-2.30 7-9.30 Av main course £5
Restaurant 12-2.30 7-9.30 Av 3 course à la carte £15
Accommodation d£37.50

WINTERBOURNE Berkshire

The Winterbourne Arms
WINTERBOURNE Map 04 SU47
RG16 8BB ☎ 01635 248200
A classic country pub serving high quality restaurant food. All meals are made with fresh produce, and even the ice cream and pasta is made on the premises. Dishes include seafood chowder, roast new season's lamb with tarragon sauce, and a trio of liqueur ice creams. Principal beers: Flowers, Bass, Brakspears, Fullers.
Directions From M4 S on A34, 1st slip road
Free House
Open 11.30-3 6-11
Bar food 12-2.30 6-11 Av main course £8.95
Restaurant 12-2.30 6-11 Av 3 course à la carte £15 Av 3 course fixed price £7.95

YATTENDON Berkshire

The Royal Oak Hotel
YATTENDON Map 04 SU57
The Square RG18 0UF ☎ 01635 201325
Located in the unspoilt village of Yattendon, this 16th- century coaching inn, now with 3 AA rosettes, once served Oliver Cromwell. If he could eat there today he might enjoy honey-glazed hock of braised ham with lentil casserole, tournedos Rossini or saddle of venison Grand Veneur. Principal beers: Banks, Fullers.
Directions From M4 J12, A4 to Newbury 1m. 3rd exit on 2nd roundabout then 1st left, to Bradfield, then follow signs to Yattendon
Free House
Open 12-3 6-11
Bar food 12-2 7-9.30 Av main course £9.50
Restaurant 12.30-2 7.30-9.30 Av 3 course à la carte £38 Av 2 course fixed price £16.50
Accommodation s£75 d£90

Buckinghamshire

AMERSHAM Buckinghamshire

The Hit or Miss
AMERSHAM Map 04 SU99
Penn St HP7 0PX ☎ 01494 713109
Country pub with its own cricket pitch, pavilion and team -hence the name. Off the pitch, chef Robin Davies offers an international menu. Diners may sample Chinese marinated duck with rice, pan-fried tilapia with crab and ginger sauce, or Peruvian breast of chicken with chilli and peanut sauce. Principal beers: Fullers London Pride, Brakspear PA.

Free House
Open 11-11 (Sun 12-10.30)
Bar food 12-3 6-11 Av main course £6.95
Restaurant 12-2.30 7-10 Av 3 course à la carte £25

AYLESBURY Buckinghamshire

Bottle & Glass
AYLESBURY Map 04 SU29
Gibraltar HP17 8TY ☎ 01296 748488
Bursting with character, this is a very pretty mid-16th-century, thatched pub with a friendly welcome in a charming hamlet. Seafood is their speciality: try Scottish salmon with wild mushrooms and ginger and coriander sauce, sole fillets with beurre blanc, or Cornish lobster Thermidor. Principal beers: Morrells Varsity, Oxford Bitter & Mild, Kronenbourg.
Directions On A418 between Thame & Aylesbury
Morrells
Open 11-3 6-12
Bar food 12-2.15 6.30-10.15 Av main course £7
Restaurant 12-2.15 6.30-10.15 Av 3 course à la carte £22

BEACONSFIELD Buckinghamshire

The Greyhound
BEACONSFIELD Map 04 SU99
Windsor End HP9 2JN ☎ 01494 673823
16th-century drover's tavern in a secluded village location opposite a parish church. Home-made pies, such as chicken and leek, or pork, apple, bacon and cider are a speciality, as are an interesting variety of bubble and squeak dishes. Principal beers: Courage Best, Fullers London Pride, 6X.
Directions Follow signs to Beaconsfield Old Town, left at central roundabout
Free House
Open 11-3 5.30-11
Bar food 12-2.15 7-10
Restaurant 12-2.15 7-10 Av 3 course à la carte £14

The Royal Standard of England
BEACONSFIELD Map 04 SU99
Brindle Ln, Forty Green HP9 1XT
☎ 01494 673382
Charles II renamed this pub in 1660 in gratitude for providing him with shelter during the Civil War. Stained glass windows and authentic decor provide the setting for an extensive buffet bar, traditional pub meals and a taste of the Royal Standard's chutney, an exclusive recipe for over 300 years. Principal beers: Marstons Pedigree, Owd Roger, Brakspears.

Directions A40 to Beaconsfield. R at Church roundabout onto B474 towards Penn. Left onto Forty Green Road 1mile
Free House
Open 11-3 5.30-11 (Sun 12-3,7-10.30)
Bar food 12-3 6.30-11 Av main course £6
Restaurant 12-3 6.30-11 Av 0 course fixed price £3.15

BLEDLOW Buckinghamshire

The Lions of Bledlow
BLEDLOW Map 04 SP70
Church End HP27 9PE ☎ 01844 343345
Asked to describe the special character of this 16th-century inn, the landlord mentioned the old rambling open bar and the old rambling open customers! Originally three cottages, it is situated at the foot of the Chilterns overlooking the village green, and offers a varied menu using fresh local ingredients. Principal beers: Wadworth 6X, Courage Best, Theakston XB, John Smiths.
Directions M40 J6 take B4009 to Princes Risborough thru Chinnor into Bledlow.
Free House
Open 11.30-3 6-11
Bar food 12-2 7-9.30 Av main course £5
Restaurant 12-2 7-9.30 Av 3 course à la carte £11

BOLTER END Buckinghamshire

The Peacock
BOLTER END Map 04 SU79
HP14 3LU ☎ 01494 881417
The oldest part of this pub dates from 1620, featuring original beams and a fireplace dating from the early 1800s. It is

situated on top of the Chiltern Hills overlooking the common. Traditional English food is served with Mediterranean and Asian specials, and tempting home-made puddings. Principal beers: Tetleys, Brakspears, Bass.
Directions A40 thru Stokenchurch, then B482
Free House
Open 11.45-2.30 6-11
Bar food 12-2 7-9.45 Av main course £6

BUCKINGHAM Buckinghamshire

The Wheatsheaf

BUCKINGHAM Map 04 SU63

Main St, Maids Moreton MK18 1QR ☎ 01208 815433

All the charm of an English pub is evident at this thatched 17th-century establishment, with the addition of an attractive conservatory restaurant. The bar offers a good choice of snacks, while restaurant fare includes grills, Desperate Dan pie, breaded plaice and fresh vegetable bake. Principal beers: Hook Norton.
Directions From M1 J13 take A421 to Buckingham, then take A413.
Free House
Open 12-3 6-11
Bar food 12-3 7-11
Restaurant 12-3 7-11

CHALFONT ST GILES Buckinghamshire

Ivy House

CHALFONT ST GILES Map 04 SU99

London Rd HP8 4RS ☎ 01494 872184

Former coach house, this 200 year-old inn has distinctive arched windows and veranda. The ghost of a friendly stable lad has a habit of turning things on and off. Main course dishes include pan-fried pork escalopes with Welsh rarebit sauce, and lamb with port and red berry sauce. Principal beers: London Pride, Brakspears, 6X, Flowers.
Directions On the A413 2m S of Amersham & 1 1/2m N of Chalfont St Giles
Free House
Open 12-3 6-11
Bar food 12-3 6.30-10.30
Restaurant 12-3 6.30-10.30 Av 3 course à la carte £16 Av 3 course fixed price £16

The White Hart

CHALFONT ST GILES Map 04 SU99

Three Households HP8 4LP
☎ 01494 872441

Genuine hospitality, good food and service are promised at this 100-year-old pub, which was renovated five years ago, and is located in a quiet semi-rural setting. Food ranges from ploughman's and burgers to home-made steak and kidney pie and fresh haddock in beer batter. Principal beers: Morland Original Cask Bitter, Morland Old Speckled Hen, Guinness, Stella.
Directions Off A413 (Denham/Amersham)
Morland
Open 11.30-2.30 (Sun 12-3) 6-11 (Sun 7-10.30)
Bar food 12-2 6.30-9.30
Restaurant 12-2 6.30-9.30 Av 3 course à la carte £14

CHENIES Buckinghamshire

The Red Lion

CHENIES Map 04 TQ09

Chenies Village, Chorleywood WD3 6ED
☎ 01923 282722

A small country free house, owner run, offering friendly service, good beer, food and wine. Specialities include the "internationally famous" Chenies lamb pie; pasta with smoked salmon and courgettes in a pesto sauce, and escalope of pork stuffed with peanut and mushroom with rum sauce. Principal beers: Benskins Best Bitter,Notley Ale, Wadworth 6X,Lion Pride.

Directions Between Rickmansworth & Amersham on A404
Free House
Open 11-2.30 5.30-11
Bar food 12-2 7-10 Av main course £6.50

CHESHAM Buckinghamshire

The Black Horse Inn
CHESHAM Map 04 SP90
Chesham Vale HP5 3NS
☎ 01494 784656
A listed building, just under 500 years old, with a wealth of beams, an interesting book collection and a vast number of foreign bank notes. There is a huge pond in the garden with ducks and terrapins. Old English food is offered, including a range of pies, pheasant casserole and fish dishes. Principal beers: Adnams, Black Horse Stallion, Benskins, Burton.
Directions A41 from Berkhamstead, A416 thru Ashley Green, 3/4m before Chesham R to Vale Rd, btm of Mashleigh Hill follow rd for 1m, inn on L
Benskins
Open 11.45-2.30 6-11
Bar food 12-2 6-9.30
Restaurant 12-2 6-9.30 Av 3 course à la carte £10

The Swan
CHESHAM Map 04 SP90
Ley Hill HP5 1UT ☎ 01494 783075
A beamed 16th-century pub with its own large garden, backing on to fields and woodlands and facing the golf course, common and cricket ground. The same traditional pub menu is offered throughout, including steaks, home-made pies and international favourites such as chilli, curry and lasagne. Principal beers: Benskins, Burton, Tetley.
Directions E of Chesham by golf course
Allied Domecq
Open 11-2.30 5.30-11
Bar food 12-2 7-9
Restaurant 12-2 7-9

CHICHELEY Buckinghamshire

The Chester Arms
CHICHELEY Map 04 SP94
MK16 9JE ☎ 01234 391214
An unspoilt country pub situated within a few hundred metres of the National Trust's Chicheley Hall. Traditional English home cooking is offered, including honey-glazed ham, deep fried plaice, nut roast and apple pie. Ploughman's and cold buffet dishes are also available. Principal beers: Greene King, IPA, Abbot.
Directions Faces A422, 2m from Newport Pagnell, 4m from M1 J14
Greene King
Open 11-3 6-11
Bar food 12-2 7-9 Av main course £5
Restaurant 12-2 7-9 Av 3 course à la carte £9

CHOLESBURY Buckinghamshire

The Full Moon
CHOLESBURY Map 04 SP90
Hawridge Common HP5 2UH
☎ 01494 758959
An ale house since 1693, this inn retains much of its original character. The atmosphere is warm and friendly, and children and animals are made most welcome. Dishes include char-grilled lamb chops, peppered pork steaks, chicken curry, and vegetarian options such as black bean chilli. Principal beers: Bass, London Pride, Boddingtons.
Directions At Tring on A41 take turn for Wiggington & Cholesbury
Free House

Open 12-3 (Mon-Fri closed 3-5.30.Sat open all day) 5.30-11 (Sat 12-11,Sun 12-4,7-10.30)
Bar food 12-2 6-9
Restaurant 12-2 6-9 Av 3 course à la carte £10

CUDDINGTON Buckinghamshire

Annie Bailey's
CUDDINGTON Map 04 SP71
Upper Church St HG18 0AP
☎ 01844 291215
Named after the establishment's landlady of 1847. There's a wide selection of sandwiches (including Annie Baileys triple decker club sandwich), salads and snacks. Main courses range from breast of Lunesdale duck on honey and black bean sauce, to saddle of lamb with a spicy Swiss chard farci. Principal beers: Brakspears, Murphys, Heineken.
Free House
Open 12-2.30 (Sun, 12-4) 6.30-11
Bar food 12-2.30 6.30-11 Av main course £8
Restaurant 12-2.30 6.30-11 Av 3 course à la carte £20 Av 3 course fixed price £18

FAWLEY Buckinghamshire

The Walnut Tree
FAWLEY Map 04 SU78
RG9 6JE ☎ 01491 638360
A 50's pub, with warm decor and comfortable seating, the Walnut Tree is located in the Chiltern Hills with wonderful views some 400ft above Henley-on-Thames. Renowned for its food, bar meals encompass ploughman's, chicken oriental, and stuffed aubergine, while the carte centres on prime cuts cooked to order. Principal beers: Brakspears Bitter and Special, Guinness, Stella Artois.
Directions From Henley on A4155(towards Marlow)turn L at 2nd sign for Fawley.Turn R at village green
Brakspear
Open 12-3 6-11
Bar food 12-3 6-11
Restaurant 12-3 6-11 Av 3 course à la carte £15
Accommodation s£35 d£45

FORD Buckinghamshire

The Dinton Hermit
FORD Map 04 SP70
Water Ln HP17 8XH ☎ 01296 748379
'The Dinton Hermit' was John Bigg, born 1629 in Dinton. Local legend claims he was the Masked Executioner of Charles I, and so ashamed of this deed that he became a hermit, residing in a cave. It is a small, village pub with home-made food – try turkey breast in celery sauce with prawn and rice pyramids, Stilton and asparagus pancake, or raspberry meringue Chantilly. Principal beers: ABC, 6X, Carlsberg, Guinness.
Directions Off the A418 between Aylesbury & Thame
Free House
Open 11-2.30 6-11
Bar food 12-2 7-9.30

GREAT BRICKHILL Buckinghamshire

The Old Red Lion
GREAT BRICKHILL Map 04 SP93
Ivy Ln MK17 9AG ☎ 01525 261715
250-year-old pub with fine views over the Vale of Aylesbury. The menu offers a wide range of bar meals including sandwiches, ploughman's lunches and home-made steak and mushroom pie. Vegetarian options include vegetable lasagne and broccoli and cream cheese bake. Principal beers: Adnams, Greene King IPA, Flowers Original, Boddingtons.
Whitbread
Open 12-2.30 5.30-11
Bar food 12-2 7-9 Av main course £5

GREAT MISSENDEN Buckinghamshire

The George Inn
GREAT MISSENDEN Map 04 SP80
94 High St HP16 0BG ☎ 01494 862084
Ancient fireplaces and oak beams characterise this 15th-century coaching inn, which enjoys a village setting in the Chiltern Hills. Interesting menus in the bar and restaurant range from the traditional to the bizarre, with dishes as diverse as cod and chips and scallop and pancetta shashlik. Principal beers: Adnams, Wadworths 6X, Greene King, Bass.
Directions Off A413 between Aylesbury & Amersham
Greenalls
Open 7-11 (Sat 9-11) (Sun 9-3.30, 7-10.30)

contd.

Bar food 12-2 6.30-9.15 Av main course £4.75
Restaurant 12-2 6.30-9.30 Av 3 course à la carte £12 Av 3 course fixed price £15
Accommodation s£58.75 d£58.75

The Hampden Arms

GREAT MISSENDEN Map 04 SP80

Great Hampden HP16 9RQ
☎ 01494 488255

A mock Tudor building, 400 years old in parts, in the heart of woodland bordering the Chequers estate. The extensive menu is traditional in style, ranging from prawn cocktail and snails with garlic butter, through steaks, baked trout and chicken curry. There are separate brunch and vegetarian menus. Principal beers: Abbot Ale, Thomas Hardy, Tetley Cask.
Directions From M40 take A4010, R before Princes Risborough, Great Hampden signposted
Free House
Open 12-2.30 7-11
Bar food 12-2 7-9.30 Av main course £4.95
Restaurant 12-2 7-9.30 Av 3 course à la carte £15

The Rising Sun

GREAT MISSENDEN Map 04 SP80

Little Hampden HP16 9PS
☎ 01494 488393 488360

Set among charming beech woods, the Rising Sun has been a pub since 1750 and, as it is only a short walk from Chequers, has often been visited by past Prime Ministers. The menu may feature roast pheasant, dressed Norfolk crab, braised loin of pork, or deep-fried fillet of plaice. Principal beers: Dortmunder Union, Adnams, Brakspear, Marstons Pedigree.
Directions From A413 N of Gt Missenden. Take Rignall Rd on L (signed Princes Risborough) 2.5m turn R signed 'Little Hampden only'
Free House
Open 11.30-2.30 (Sun 12-3) 6.30-11
Bar food 12-2 7-9 Av main course £7.95
Restaurant 12-2 7-9 Av 3 course à la carte £18.50 Av 3 course fixed price £16.95
Accommodation s£25 d£40

HADDENHAM Buckinghamshire

The Green Dragon

HADDENHAM Map 04 SP70

8 Churchway HP17 8AA
☎ 01844 291403

An old coaching inn situated near the 12th-century church, the village green and pond. At lunchtime dishes include starters, fresh fish, pies and casseroles, and there's a light menu of omelettes and salads. In the evening, choose from a range of original dishes with a French influence. Principal beers: Heineken, Stella Artois, Marston Pedigree, Murphys.
Directions From the M40 A329 to Thame, then A418, 1st R after entering Bucks
Whitbread
Open 11.30-3 6.30-11.30
Bar food 12-2.30 7-9.30
Restaurant 12-2.30 7-9.30

KINGSWOOD Buckinghamshire

Crooked Billet

KINGSWOOD Map 04 SP61

Bicester Rd HP18 0QJ ☎ 01296 770239

Located in peaceful Buckinghamshire countryside, The Crooked Billet has been a pub for about 200 years and is believed to be haunted by Fair Rosamund, a girlfriend of Charles I. Specials may include prawn and salmon lasagne, Jamaican chicken curry, cauliflower and nut Mornay, or steak, ale and mushroom pie. Principal beers: Friary Meux, Calders, Tetley Cask, Carlsberg.
Directions On A41 between Aylesbury & Bicester
Free House
Open 11-3 6-11
Bar food 12-2.30 6.30-9.30 Av main course £4
Restaurant 12-2.30 6.30-12 Av 3 course à la carte £15

LACEY GREEN Buckinghamshire

Pink & Lily
LACEY GREEN Map 04 SP80
Pink Rd HP27 0RJ ☎ 01494 488308
Unusual name derived from head butler, Mr Pink, of nearby Hampden House, who lived in sin with Miss Lilley when the building was a coaching inn. Poet, Rupert Brooke, was a regular visitor. Specials include halibut in green pea sauce, trout fillets in Pernod and cream, and leek and Stilton bake. Principal beers: Brakspear, Hobgoblin, Caffreys.
Directions Off A4010 S of Princes Risborough
Free House
Open 11.45-3 6-11
Bar food 12-2 6.30-9.30 Av main course £4.95

LONG CRENDON Buckinghamshire

The Angel Inn
LONG CRENDON Map 04 SP60
47 Bicester Rd HP18 9EE
☎ 01844 208268
A Grade I listed wattle and daub building with exposed beams and open fires. Modern English and European cuisine is served, with an emphasis on seafood and local products. Dishes might include lobster bisque, roast fillet of monkfish wrapped in Parma ham, and pear tarte tatin. Principal beers: Ruddles Rumpus, Boddingtons, Stella Artois.
Directions A418 to Thame, B4011 to L Crendon, Angel on B4011
Free House
Open 12-2.30 7-10.30
Restaurant 12-2.30 7-10.30 Av 3 course à la carte £20 Av 3 course fixed price £16.75
Accommodation s£45 d£55

Mole & Chicken
LONG CRENDON Map 04 SP60
Easington Ter HP18 9EY
☎ 01844 208387
17th-century end of terrace which used to be a village shop. For starters there are Madeira marinated herring fillets and home-made duck liver pâté. House specialities include Peri Peri chicken roasted with lemons and chillies, and shoulder of lamb with honey, garlic and rosemary sauce. Principal beers: Abbot Ale, Tetley, Boddingtons.
Directions Off B4011 N of Thame
Free House
Open 12-3 6-12 (Sun open all day)
Bar food 12-2 7-10 Av main course £8.95
Restaurant 12-2 7-10

MARLOW Buckinghamshire

The Kings Head
MARLOW Map 04 SU88
Church Rd, Little Marlow SL7 3RZ ☎ 01628 484407
Built in the 1650s, this village pub is situated within easy walking distance of the River Thames. Famous for its crooked chimney. Offers a wide selection of starters, toasties, sandwiches and jacket potatoes. Home-made specials are listed on the blackboard and typically include chicken Wellington and Mexican tacos.
Directions M40 J4 take A4040 S 1st A4155
Free House
Open 11-3 5.30-11
Bar food 12-2 7-10 Av main course £5.95
Restaurant 12-2 7-10

MARSWORTH Buckinghamshire

The White Lion
MARSWORTH Map 04 SP91
Startops End HP23 5LJ
☎ 01442 822325
15th-century inn situated on the banks of the Grand Union Canal, close to a bird sanctuary. Bar menu typically features steak, red wine and mushroom pie, supreme of chicken with crab and lobster sauce, vegetable pie with creamy cheese sauce, and whole local trout with tomato and basil stuffing. Principal beers: Adnams Broadside, London Pride, Ruddles Best, Ruddles County.
Directions Off B485 north of Tring
Free House
Open 12-12
Bar food 12-2.30 6-10 Av main course £5.50
Restaurant 12-2.30 6-10 Av 3 course à la carte £18

MOULSOE Buckinghamshire

The Carrington Arms
MOULSOE Map 04 SP94
Cranfield Rd MK16 0HB
☎ 01908 218050
Named after the Carrington family whose unusual and unexplained crest features an elephant with a pink ear. Bar snacks include venison casserole, mushroom and spinach pasta, Pacific oysters and caviar. Steak meals are Aberdeen Angus, and the seafood selection, which changes daily, includes red snapper, lobster, tilapia, sea bass and marlin. Principal beers: Charles Wells Bombardier, Fargo Velvet, Boddingtons, Theakstons Old Peculier.

Directions M1 J14 take rd signed 'Cranfield & Moulsoe'. Pub 1m on R
Free House
Open 11-2.30 6-11
Bar food 12-2 6.30-10 Av main course £6
Restaurant 12-2 6.30-10
Accommodation s£38.50 d£38.50

PRINCES RISBOROUGH Buckinghamshire

Red Lion
PRINCES RISBOROUGH Map 04 SP80
Upper Icknield Way, Whiteleaf HP27 0LL
☎ 01844 344476
A 17th-century inn surrounded by National Trust land with old thatched cottages. The pub has a nautical theme and a large collection of antiques. There are attractive beer gardens with barbecues in summer. Traditional English food is served, including a range of fish dishes. Principal beers: Brakspears PA, Hook Norton Best, Old Speckled Hen.
Directions A4010 thru Princes Risbro', then R into 'Holloway', go to end of road, R, pub on L
Free House
Open 11.30-3 5.30-11 (wknd 11.30-3, 6/7-10.30)
Bar food 12-2 7-9.30 Av main course £4.50
Restaurant 12-2 7-9.30 Av 3 course à la carte £9 Av 3 course fixed price £9.95
Accommodation s£29.50 d£39.50

TURVILLE Buckinghamshire

The Bull & Butcher
TURVILLE Map 04 SU79
RG9 6QU ☎ 01491 638283
Small country pub built in 1550. Overlooked by the windmill featured in the film *Chitty Chitty Bang Bang*. Main course dishes include venison pie, chicken breast in brandy, Stilton and cream sauce, and salmon and spinach tagliatelle. Vegetable hotch potch pudding for vegetarians. Principal beers: Brakspears, Heineken, Stella, Murphys.
Directions M40 J5 follow signs for Ibstone.Turn R T-junc.Pub 0.25m on L
Brakspear
Open 11-11 (Mon-Sat, closed 3-6) 12-10.30 (Sun, closed 3-7)
Bar food 12-2 7-9.45 Av main course £8

WADDESDON Buckinghamshire

The Five Arrows Hotel
WADDESDON Map 04 SP71
High St HP18 0JE ☎ 01296 651727
Grade II listed hotel built as part of the Waddesdon Estate by Baron Ferdinand de Rothschild in 1887. Among the starters are aubergine stuffed with feta and sun dried tomato, and a salad of Parma ham, salami, melon and figs. Main dishes include pistachio stuffed guinea fowl with rich wine sauce. Principal beers: Chiltern Brewery Beechwood, Fullers ESB, Fullers London Pride.
Directions On A41 6m NW of Aylesbury
Free House
Open 11-3 (Mon-Sat) 6-11 (Sun 7-10.30)
Bar food 12-3 7-11
Restaurant 12-3 7-11 Av 3 course à la carte £18.50
Accommodation s£55 d£70

WEST WYCOMBE Buckinghamshire

The George and Dragon Hotel
WEST WYCOMBE Map 04 SU89
High St HP14 3AB ☎ 01494 464414
This village coaching inn may have some grisly history -the pub has two ghosts

and the nearby caves were host in the 18th century to the infamous Hellfire Club - but things are different now. Copenhagen chicken, pheasant breasts on a bed of red cabbage or beef Wellington may be on today's menu. Principal beers: Courage Best.
Directions M40 North, J5, L onto A40, 4m into village. M40 South, J4, A4010 to T jct, L onto A40, village 1/2 m
Free House
Open 11-2.30 5.30-11 (Sun 11-11)
Bar food 12-2 6-9.30 Av main course £6.50
Accommodation s£52 d£62

WOOBURN COMMON Buckinghamshire

Chequers Inn
WOOBURN COMMON Map 04 SU98
HP10 0HF ☎ 01628 529575
A 17th-century coaching inn set in the Chiltern countryside with its own large garden. Interesting bar food, served in generous portions, includes home-made spicy pork, apple and leek sausages, and beef burgers with bacon and cheese. The Dining Room offers an extensive choice for more formal meals. Principal beers: Marstons Best Bitter, Marstons Pedigree, Timothy Taylor Landlord, London Pride.

Directions M40 J2 thru' Beaconsfield towards H Wycombe.1m turn L into Broad Lane. Inn 2.5m
Free House
Open 10-11
Bar food 12-2.30 6.30-9.30 Av main course £7.50
Restaurant 12-2.30 6.30-9.30 Av 3 course à la carte £20
Accommodation s£67.50 d£72.50

Greater London

KESTON Greater London

The Crown
KESTON Map 05 TQ46
Leaves Green BR2 6OG
☎ 01959 572920
Not far from Biggin Hill, this pub has old beams and a garden with a barbeque. Jazz nights are held occasionally. The bar menu offers traditional pub fare, while the restaurant specialises in English and European cuisine. Principal beers: Master Brew, Spitfire, Hurlimann, Steinbock.
Directions A21 onto A232, then L onto A233, pub 4m
Shepherd Neame
Open 11-3 5-11
Bar food 12-2 7-9.30 Av main course £5.95
Restaurant 12-2 7-9.30 Av 3 course à la carte £15

UXBRIDGE Greater London

The Turning Point
UXBRIDGE Map 04 TQ08
Canal Cottages, Packet Boat Ln, Cowley Peachey UB8 2JF
☎ 01895 440550
This is the point on the Grand Union Canal where horsedrawn barges were able to be turned around, and the building housed employees who repaired the barges. The waterside bar and restaurant offer pleasant surroundings for a comprehensive selection of snacks and freshly cooked meals.
Directions From M4 J4 2m N on A408
Free House

contd.

Open 11-11
Bar food 12-9.30 12-9.30 Av main course £4.95
Restaurant 12-2.30 7-9.30 Av 3 course à la carte £16.95 Av 3 course fixed price £16.95

Hampshire

BASINGSTOKE Hampshire

The Dean Gate Inn
BASINGSTOKE Map 04 SU65
Deane RG25 3AX ☎ 01256 780226
Formerly a tollgate on the Andover to London road, the building dates back 300 years. It is said that Jane Austen stabled her horses here when her father was vicar of Steventon. Good home-cooked food is served, including burgers, grills, vegetarian dishes and specialities such lasagne and steak pie. Principal beers: Ushers BB, Founders, Four Seasons Ale.
Directions B3400 between Oakley & Overton
Free House
Bar food 12-2.30 7-9.45 Av main course £5.95
Restaurant 12-2.30 7-9.45 Av 3 course à la carte £13 Av 2 course fixed price £5.95
Accommodation d£35

BEAUWORTH Hampshire

The Milburys
BEAUWORTH Map 04 SU52
SO24 0PB ☎ 01962 771248
The Milbury's is in an area of outstanding natural beauty and its 300 year old well reputedly hides the valuables secreted by besieged King Stephen's Castle. Choose from a menu featuring light baked avocado with Stilton and smoked salmon to lobster Thermidor or a simpler Chef's lasagne. Principal beers: Directors, King Alfred, Pendragon, Ballards.
Directions A272 toward Petersfield, after 6m R for Beauworth
Free House
Open 10.30-2.30 6-11
Bar food 12-2 6-10 Av main course £6.50
Accommodation s£27.50 d£38.50

BENTLEY Hampshire

The Bull Inn
BENTLEY Map 04 SU74
☎ 01420 22156
From this 15th century inn offering a traditional welcome and perhaps a meeting with the resident ghost, observe the view over the River Wey while contemplating a wide ranging menu from interesting baguettes to oriental specialities. Principal beers: Fullers London Pride, Gales HSB, Wadworths 6X, Courage Best.
Directions 2m out of Farnham on the A31 towards Winchester
Free House
Open 11-11
Bar food 11.45-3.30 6.30-12 Av main course £7.50
Restaurant 11.45-3.30 6.30-12 Av 3 course à la carte £20 Av 3 course fixed price £20

BENTWORTH Hampshire

The Sun Inn
BENTWORTH Map 04 SU64
Sun Hill GU34 5JT ☎ 01420 562338
Originally two 17th-century cottages in a quiet lane on the edge of the village. Bar snacks include sandwiches, filled jacket potatoes and desserts. Daily blackboard specials might feature spinach roulade with bacon and cream cheese, giant Yorkshire pudding and beef, plus a variety of pasta dishes for vegetarians. Principal beers: Hampshire Special, Gales HSB, Ringwood Best, Diggers Gold.
Free House
Open 12-3 6-11
Bar food 12-2 7-9.30 Av main course £6

BOLDRE Hampshire

The Red Lion Inn
BOLDRE Map 04 SZ39
Rope Hill SO41 8NE ☎ 01590 673177
Head for this peaceful inn bordering the New Forest and find a heritage dating back to 1650 - enhanced by tapestries made by the present landlady's mother. Bar menu available. Restaurant menu may include traditional jugged hare to innovative vegetarian choices. Principal beers: Websters Green Label, Hardy Country Ale, Royal Oak, Tetley Smooth.

Directions 1/4m E off A337, 1m N of Lymington
Eldridge Pope
Open 11-3 6-11
Bar food 11-3 6-11 Av main course £7.50
Restaurant 11.30-3 6-11 Av 3 course à la carte £15

BURITON Hampshire

The Five Bells
BURITON Map 04 SU71
High St GU31 5RX ☎ 01730 263584
Named after the five bells of Buriton church, this 17th-century inn is situated on the South Downs. Fresh fish such as swordfish, crab, red snapper and sea bass make up an important part of the menu. Game dishes using pheasant and partridge are also a house speciality. Principal beers: Friary Meux, Burton Ale, Ballards Best, Ringwood Best.
Free House
Open 11-2.30 (3.00 at w/e) 5.30-11
Bar food 12-2 6.30-10 Av main course £7

CADNAM Hampshire

The White Hart
CADNAM Map 04 SU31
Old Romsey Rd SO40 2NP
☎ 01703 812277
Situated on the edge of the New Forest with its own paddock. Blackboard menu changes daily. Typical meals include roast pheasant on a bed of spinach with beetroot jus, aubergine fritters with grilled vegetables and pesto, and wild boar steak in honey mead pie. Principal beers: 6X, Flowers, Speckled Hen, Courage Best.
Directions M27 J1 Just off r'about to Lyndhurst
Whitbread
Open 11-3 6-11
Bar food 11.30-2 6-9.30 Av main course £7.50
Restaurant 11.30-2 6-9.30 Av 3 course à la carte £17.50

CHALTON Hampshire

The Red Lion
CHALTON Map 04 SU71
PO8 0BG ☎ 01705 592246
Hampshire's oldest pub, dating from 1147, with a thatched roof, inglenook fireplace, beams, open fires and antique furniture. It is surrounded by rolling hills and there are lovely views from the garden. A snack menu is offered, with main courses chalked up on the blackboard. Principal beers: Gales Best,Butser IPA,HSB Winter Brew.
Directions just off A3 between Horndean & Petersfield
Gales
Open 11-3 6-11 (Sun 12-3,7-10.30)
Bar food 12-2 6.45-9.30 Av main course £6.60
Restaurant 12-2 6.45-9.30 Av 3 course à la carte £12

CHARTER ALLEY Hampshire

The White Hart
CHARTER ALLEY Map 04 SU55
White Hart Ln RG26 5QA
☎ 01256 850048
Dating from 1815, but considerably extended, this village pub has quite a reputation for its range of over 300 real ales. Good value home-cooked food is served, including bar snacks, steaks, seafood and dishes such as beef Madras, Lamb Waterloo and sticky toffee

contd.

pudding. Principal beers: Harveys Best Bitter, Morrells Mild, Greene King Abbot Ale.
Directions From M3 J6 take A339 towards Newbury. Take turning to Ramsdell. Turn right at church, then 1st left into White Hart Lane.
Free House
Open 12-2.30 7-11
Bar food 12-2 7-9 Av main course £5.25
Restaurant 12-2 7-9 Av 3 course à la carte £13

CLANVILLE Hampshire

The Red Lion Country Inn
CLANVILLE Map 04 SU34
SP11 9HN ☎ 01264 771007
A traditional country inn, built of brick and flint, whose facilities include a lounge bar, restaurant, function suites, a patio courtyard, large car park and a helicopter landing pad. The food ranges from burgers and baguettes to stir-fried king prawns, steaks, and pine-nut and vegetable Wellington. Principal beers: Hampshire Brewery, King Alfreds, Ruddles Best, Flowers.
Free House
Open 11-3 6-11 (Sun 12-3, 7-10.30)
Bar food 12-2.30 6.30-9.30 Av main course £4.95
Restaurant 12-2.30 6.30-9.30 Av 3 course à la carte £11.95

CRAWLEY Hampshire

Fox & Hounds
CRAWLEY Map 04 SU43
SO21 2PR ☎ 01962 776285
Savour home-cooking and a variety of fish at this lovely pub beside the duckpond in a beautiful, peaceful village. Choose daily changing specials from the blackboard such hot Stilton, celery and apple bake or Test Valley trout with prawns and mushrooms in brandy . Principal beers: Gales, Wadworths 6X, Stella, Carlsberg.
Directions A34 onto A272 then 1st R into Crawley
Free House
Open 11.30-2.30 6.30-11
Bar food 12-2 7-9.30 Av main course £6.95
Restaurant 12-2 7-9.30
Accommodation s£45 d£65

DUMMER Hampshire

The Queen Inn
DUMMER Map 04 SU54
Down St RG25 2AD ☎ 01256 397367
You can dine by candlelight at this 16th-century village pub, with its low beams and huge open log fire. Everything is home made, from the soup and light bites to the famous fish and chips with beer batter. The steak and kidney pudding is only for the heartier appetite! Principal beers: Courage Best, Directors, Marstons Pedigree.
Directions M3 J7 Turn into Dummer Village
Free House
Open 11-3 (Sun 12-3) 5.30-11 (Sat 6-11, Sun 7-10.30)
Bar food 12-2.30 7-10 Av main course £6.95
Restaurant 12-2.30 7-10 Av 3 course à la carte £23 Av 4 course fixed price £10.95

EAST MEON Hampshire

Ye Olde George Inn
EAST MEON Map 04 SU62
Church St GU32 1NH
☎ 01730 823481
Originally a pair of 15th-century cottages, this country inn is situated near the River Meon. Meat and fowl dishes include pheasant with cranberry confit, duck with citrus and juniper sauce, and venison with prune and red wine sauce. Vegetarian options include red onion tarte tatin, and wild mushroom risotto. Principal beers: Old Dray, Cheriton Pots, Greene King IPA, London Pride.
Directions S of A272 (Winchester/ Petersfield) turning 1.5m from Petersfield on L opp church
Free House
Open 11-11 (Sun-12-10.30)
Bar food 12-2.30 7-10 Av main course £5.50
Restaurant 12-2.30 7-10 Av 3 course à la carte £18 Av 3 course fixed price £10.95
Accommodation s£25 d£50

EASTON Hampshire

The Chestnut Horse
EASTON Map 04 SU53
SO21 1EG ☎ 01962 779257
Set in a small, quaint village with thatched cottages and beautiful countryside, this traditional pub has a wishing well in the garden. There is a long menu with good choices such as savoury pancakes, grilled tuna steak with capers, chicken Provençale, and ratatouille and cheese suet pudding. Principal beers: Bass,Courage Best,Chestnut Horse Special.
Directions From M3 J9 take A33 towards Basingstoke,then B3047.Take 2nd R
Free House
Open 11-3 6-11
Bar food 12-2 7-9.45 Av main course £4.50
Restaurant 12-2 7-9.45 Av 3 course à la carte £15

Cricketers Inn
EASTON Map 04 SU53
SO21 1EJ ☎ 01962 779353
200 yards from the River Itchen, this traditional village pub is a noted venue for real ale fans, while the local cricket team is one of Hampshire's top sides. One menu for restaurant and bar offers a range including open toasties, doorstop sandwiches, roast cod, and gammon steak. Principal beers: Ringwood, Cheriton, Otter, Hopback.
Directions M3 J9,A33 towards Basingstoke. Turn R at Kingsworthy onto B3047. 0.75m turn R for Easton
Free House
Open 11.30-3 6-11
Bar food 12-2.30 6.30-9.30 Av main course £4.95
Restaurant 12-2.30 6.30-9.30 Av 3 course à la carte £9.95 Av 2 course fixed price £4.95
Accommodation s£17 d£35

EAST TYTHERLEY Hampshire

Star Inn
EAST TYTHERLEY Map 04 SU22
SO51 0LW ☎ 01794 340225
17th-century coaching inn overlooking farmland. Both pub and adjacent cricket green were featured in the TV series *Gentlemen and Players*. Bar menu offers a good selection of home-made dishes, grills, and vegetarian options. Typical restaurant meals include hot salmon steak, and sole filled with crabmeat and scallops. Principal beers: HSB Ringwood, Theakstons.
Directions N of Romsey off B3084
Free House
Bar food 10.30-2 6-9 Av main course £5.95
Restaurant 12-2 7-9 Av 3 course à la carte £20
Accommodation s£35 d£60

EMSWORTH Hampshire

The Sussex Brewery
EMSWORTH Map 04 SU70
36 Main St, Hermitage PO10 8AU
☎ 01243 371533
Known locally as 'Dirty Dick's' after the owner who turned his front room into a bar in 1920, this sometime brewery dates from the 17th century, though the facade is later. The menu features 49 traditionally made sausages, some vegetarian, served with mashed, chipped or baked potatoes. Principal beers: Hall & Woodhouse Badger, Tanglefoot & IPA, Ballards, Bass.
Directions On the A259 coast road, between Havant and Chichester
Free House
Open 11-11 (Sun 12-10.30)
Bar food 12-2 7-9.30 Av main course £5.50
Restaurant 12-2 7-9.30 Av 3 course à la carte £12

FORDINGBRIDGE Hampshire

The Augustus John
FORDINGBRIDGE Map 04 SU11
116 Station Rd SP6 1DG
☎ 01425 652098
Named after the famous British painter who spent the last 30 years of his life in Fordingbridge and used this pub. Lunchtime specials feature steak and Guinness casserole, and haddock topped with Welsh rarebit. Main courses include pork fillet with brandy and apricot, and sea bass with Pernod and fennel. Principal beers: Popes, Hardys, Bass, Tetleys.
Eldridge Pope
Open 11.30-11

The Compasses Inn
FORDINGBRIDGE Map 04 SU11
Damerham SP6 3HQ ☎ 01725 518235
Dating back over 400 years, the Compasses once had its own brewery and the old brew tower is still standing. Imaginative freshly prepared dishes, using fresh local produce, include battered aubergine with Stilton sauce; bratwurst, curry dip and chips, and fricassée of seafood and tagliolini nero. Principal beers: Compasses Ale, Ringwood Best, Summer Lightning.
Directions NW of A338 at Fordingbridge
Free House
Open 11-3 6-11
Bar food 12-2 7-9.30 Av main course £5
Restaurant 12-2 7-9.30 Av 3 course à la carte £15
Accommodation s£29.50 d£25

HOOK Hampshire

Crooked Billet
HOOK Map 04 SU75
London Rd RG27 9EH
☎ 01256 762118
Keep the children occupied in the play area while watching wildlife on the River Whitewater at this easy-to-find roadside pub. Dishes include tried and tested favourites from toasties to steaks with a wide range of home-made specials such as Italian lamb stew or fresh poached salmon. Principal beers: Courage, Best, Directors, Fosters.
Directions From M3 J5 follow signs for A30/Hook.Pub 1m outside Hook
Free House
Open 11.30-3 6-11
Bar food 11.30-3 6-11 Av main course £6

IBSLEY Hampshire

Olde Beams Inn
IBSLEY Map 04 SU10
Salisbury Rd BH24 3PP ☎ 01425 473387
The cruck beam is still clearly visible from the outside this thatched 14th-century building, and English, Italian and French influences are apparent in the menus. Dishes include Scotch beef steaks, roasted guinea fowl with a redcurrant and port sauce, and a choice of fresh fish and vegetarian options. Principal beers: Ringwood bitter, Eldridge Pope, Wadworths 6X, Bass.

Directions On A338 between Ringwood & Salisbury
Free House
Open 11-3 6-11
Bar food 12-2 6.30-10 Av main course £6.70
Restaurant 12-2 6.30-10 Av 3 course à la carte £13 Av 3 course fixed price £10

LINWOOD Hampshire

Red Shoot Inn
LINWOOD Map 04 SU10
Toms Ln BH24 3QT ☎ 01425 475792
The owners of this establishment pride themselves on maintaining 'real ale and real food in a real country pub.' Set in the heart of the New Forest, there is live rock music every Sunday evening and occasional jazz. The menu offers speciality sausages and steaks, crusty bread snacks and sandwiches. Principal beers: 6X, Wadworth IPA, Farmers Glory.
Wadworth
Open 11-3 6-11 (Sun 12-10.30, summer 11-11)
Bar food 12-2 6.30-9.30 Av main course £5

LONGPARISH Hampshire

The Plough Inn
LONGPARISH Map 04 SU44
SP11 6PB ☎ 01264 720358
As it is only 100 yards away from the river this 400-year old pub is regularly visited by the local duck population. Typical menu includes scallops Mornay, lobster Thermidor, shoulder of lamb kleftico, wild boar sausage, and salmon Hollandaise. Principal beers: Heineken, Stella, King Alfreds, Flowers.
Directions Off A303 4m S of Andover
Whitbread
Open 11-4 6-11
Bar food 12-3 6.30-11 Av main course £5.95

Restaurant 12-2.30 6.30-11 Av 3 course à la carte £20 Av 3 course fixed price £20
Accommodation s£25 d£40

LOWER WIELD Hampshire

The Yew Tree Inn

LOWER WIELD Map 04 SU64

SO24 9RX ☎ 01256 389224

Situated under a 350-year-old yew tree overlooking the village cricket green. Light meals include smoked Scottish salmon with fresh lime, while main courses on offer range from toasted brioche with lightly scrambled eggs and seasoned with fresh truffle, to pigeon breast with toasted pine kernels and walnut oil. Principal beers: Cheriton Brewhouse, Pots and Diggers Gold.
Directions Off A339 between Basingstoke & Alton
Free House
Open 12-3 6-11 (except Mon)
Bar food 12-2 7-9.30 Av main course £4.25
Restaurant 12-2 7-9.30 Av 3 course à la carte £15

LYMINGTON Hampshire

Bosun's Chair

LYMINGTON Map 04 SZ39

Station St SO41 3BA
☎ 01590 675140

Close to the marina, this nautically themed pub caters well to the sailing community and visitors to the New Forest. Its name refers to the lookout chair on board a yacht. On offer are speciality sausages and pies, lots of fish dishes (naturally), and steaks. The local favourite is cheese, cream and garlic potatoes. Principal beers: Wadworth 6X,IPA,Becks.
Directions M27,then A337 thru Lyndhurst/Brockenhurst.Follow signs for station.
Wadworth
Open 10.30-11 (Sun 12-10.30,Summer 10.30-11)
Bar food 12-3 6.30-11 Av main course £4.95
Restaurant 12-3 6.30-11 Av 3 course à la carte £12
Accommodation s£30 d£40

The Chequers Inn

LYMINGTON Map 04 SZ39

Lower Woodside SO41 8AH
☎ 01590 673415

A listed building, dating from 1670, next to the West Solent salt marshes. It is a proudly 'unimproved' pub with old beams and low ceilings and no carpet or upholstery. The food is fresh and wholesome; fish is a speciality, with crabs and lobsters in summer and local game in season. Principal beers: Wadworths 6X, Bass, London Pride, Heineken.
Directions From Lymington take A337 towards New Milton.Turn L at White Hart PH then L into Ridgeway Lane.Pub 1m
Free House
Open 11-3 6-11 (Sat-Sun 11-11)
Bar food 12-2 7-10 Av main course £4.75
Restaurant 12-2 7-10 Av 3 course à la carte £15

Waggon & Horses

LYMINGTON Map 04 SZ39

Undershore Rd SO41 5SB
☎ 01590 672517

Only a few hundred metres from the Isle of Wight Ferry, this 17th-century inn was the scene of a bizarre shooting accident in the 19th century. Today's menu may feature venison in red wine, beef and Stilton cobbler, seafood Provençale, or chicken pasta in white wine sauce. Principal beers: Bass, Flowers, John Smiths, 6X.
Wadworth
Open 11-3 6-11
Bar food 12-2.30 6-10 Av main course £6
Restaurant 12-2.30 6-10 Av 3 course à la carte £15 Av 2 course fixed price £4.98

MATTINGLEY Hampshire

The Leather Bottle

MATTINGLEY Map 04 SU75

Reading Rd RG7 8JU ☎ 0118 9326371

A typical country inn, dating from 1714, with beams and inglenook fireplaces, surrounded by open countryside. There's one menu for the whole pub, offering a choice of snacks and full meals, supplemented by blackboard specials. Dishes include grills, fish, curries and vegetarian options. Principal beers: Courage Best, Directors, John Smiths, Fosters.

Directions From M3 J5 follow signs for Hook.Pub is 3m from Hook on B3349 (Reading rd)

Free House

Open 11-2.30 6-11 (Sun 12-3, 6.30-10.30)

Bar food 12-2 7-10 Av main course £6.50

Restaurant 12-2 7-10

MICHELDEVER Hampshire

The Dever Arms

MICHELDEVER Map 04 SU53

Winchester Rd SO21 3DG

☎ 01962 774339

A friendly village pub with an original wattle and daub building, old beams and an open fire. Bar food includes ploughman's and hot dishes such as cottage pie, lasagne and breaded scampi. The restaurant offers moules marinière, braised wild rabbit, steaks, and specialities such as chicken Boursin. Principal beers: Marstons Best, Pedigree, & Mild, Guinness.

Directions Take A30 from Winchester towards Basingstoke.After Kingsworthy turn L after petrol station.Pub 0.5m on L

Marstons

Open 12-3 6-11

Bar food 12-2.30 6-10.30 Av main course £4.50

Restaurant 12-2.30 6-10.30 Av 3 course à la carte £15

NORTH WALTHAM Hampshire

The Fox

NORTH WALTHAM Map 04 SU54

RG25 2BE ☎ 01256 397288

Formerly village cottages which were built in 1624. Splendid views across fields and farmland. Home-made dishes include beef in ale, chicken chasseur, and lamb and leek casserole. Roast venison, rabbit pie, and wild boar sausages are typical game dishes. The fish menu offers halibut, monkfish and shark. Principal beers: Milligans Mist, Ushers Spring Fever, Ushers Best bitter, Ushers Founders.

Directions From M3 J7 take A30 towards Winchester. Village signposted on R

Ushers

Open 11-3 5.30-11.30 (Sat-Sun all day opening)

Bar food 12-2 7-10 Av main course £3

Restaurant 12-2 7-10 Av 3 course à la carte £7

ODIHAM Hampshire

The Grapevine Bistro Restaurant

ODIHAM Map 04 SU75

121 High St RG29 1LA

☎ 01256 701122

The restaurant is on the ground floor of an elegant bay-windowed Georgian building. Frequently changing blackboard menus might offer fresh mussels poached in a light curry sauce, baked turbot with a polenta and dill crust, and dark chocolate and pecan nut tartlets served with clotted cream.

Directions Off the A287 between North Warnborough and Farnham

Restaurant 12-2 6-10.30 Av 3 course à la carte £19

OVERTON Hampshire

Red Lion

OVERTON Map 04 SU54

High St RG25 3HQ ☎ 01256 773225

There is a warm, friendly atmosphere, well kept cellar and over 200 dishes to choose from in two separate restaurants, smoking or non-smoking. Try a game in the skittle alley before Thai honey and ginger chicken, steak and ale pie or a vegetarian choice. Principal beers: John Smiths, Fosters, Guinness.

Free House

Open 11.30-3 5.30-11

Bar food 12-2.30 6.30-9.30 Av main course £3.50

Restaurant 12-2.30 6.30-9.30 Av 3 course à la carte £11

OWSLEBURY Hampshire

The Ship Inn

OWSLEBURY Map 04 SU52

Whites Hill SO21 1LT ☎ 01962 777358

Despite its name this village pub is nowhere near the sea. It's a friendly place, 300 years old and cosy with original beams. The garden is large, with a fish pond and summer marquee. Dishes are cooked to order and include salmon en croûte, lamb jalfrezi, and steak and mushroom pie. Principal beers: Batemans Mild, Marstons Best, Pedigree, Stella.

Directions M3 J11 take B3335 follow signs for Owslebury

Marstons

Open 11-3 (Sat 11-11,Sun 12-10.30) 6-11

Bar food 12-2 6.30-9.30

Accommodation d£38

PILLEY Hampshire

The Fleur de Lys

PILLEY Map 04 SZ39

Pilley St SO41 5QG ☎ 01590 672158

The oldest pub in the New Forest; established as an inn in 1096. Two lively ghosts and a 14th-century wishing well. Lunchtime snacks include pizza, seafood and steaks. An *Old Times* special menu offers rabbit broth with dumplings, vegetarian broth with noodles, plus pheasant and venison dishes.

Free House

Open 11.30-3 (Fri-Sat, 11-11.30) 6-11 (Sun, 11.30-10.30)

Bar food 12-2.30 6-9.30 Av main course £7.25

Restaurant 12-2.30 6-9.30 Av 3 course à la carte £15 Av 3 course fixed price £14.99

PORTSMOUTH & SOUTHSEA Hampshire

The Wine Vaults

PORTSMOUTH & SOUTHSEA Map 04 SZ69

43-47 Albert Rd PO5 2SF

☎ 01705 864712

An amalgamation of four Victorian shopfronts with split-level floors and church pew seating. Vacuum cleaners, bikes and pipe clips are among the curios on display, and the downstairs brewery is in full view. Bar food, Mexican meals, and a daily choice of five meat and five veggie specials are offered. Principal beers: Offyatrolli, Whippersnapper, Impaled Ale, Stinger.

Free House

Open 11-11 (Mon-Sat) 12-10.30 (Sun)

ROCKBOURNE Hampshire

The Rose & Thistle

ROCKBOURNE Map 04 SU11

SP6 3NL ☎ 01725 518236

A 16th-century pub set in lovely countryside serving some interesting bar food, such as herring roes on toast and scrambled eggs with smoked salmon and prawns. In the restaurant look out for duck breast with a creamy mustard sauce, and monk fish in an oriental sauce. Principal beers: Marstons Pedigree, Wadworths 6X, Courage Best.

Free House

Open 11-3 6-11

Bar food 12-3 6-11 Av main course £6

Restaurant 12-3 6-11 Av 3 course à la carte £15

ROMSEY Hampshire

Old Horse & Jockey

ROMSEY Map 04 SU32

23 Maidstone SO51 8HG

☎ 01794 519515

Originally a coaching inn - Romsey's oldest - the pub was a veterinary practice for 25 years until it was re-converted in 1996. There is traditional pub food and a bistro-brasserie style menu with dishes such as lobster sausage, seared fillet of lamb Niçoise, and brioche butter pudding. Principal beers: Directors, John Smiths, Theakstons Old Peculiar, Becks Draught.

Directions A36 onto A3090 (A31) to Romsey, pub 1st building on L

Free House

contd.

Open 11-2.30 6-11 (Sun 12-2.30, 7-10.30)
Bar food 11-2 6-9.30 Av main course £9
Restaurant 11-2 6-9.30 Av 3 course à la carte £20

ROWLANDS CASTLE Hampshire

Castle Inn

ROWLANDS CASTLE Map 04 SU71
1 Finchdean Rd PO9 6DA
☎ 01705 412494
Built in the mid-19th century, this listed building is only 200 yards from the 500 acre Stansted Park. A typical restaurant menu may include pan-fried duck breast or darne of salmon with tarragon sauce, while the bar will be serving curries, sandwiches, and children's meals. Principal beers: Gales Butser, HSB, Best Smooth, Keg Best.
Directions N from Havant on B2149 to R's Castle, Pass green, under railway bridge, pub 1st on left opp Stansted Pk
Gales
Open 11.30-3 6-11 (Sun 12-10.30, Fri 11.30-3, 5.30-11, Sat 11.30
Bar food 12-2 7-9 Av main course £4
Restaurant 12-2 7-9 Av 3 course à la carte £12
Accommodation s£18 d£28

ST MARY BOURNE Hampshire

The George Inn

ST MARY BOURNE Map 04 SU45
SP11 6BG ☎ 01264 738340
A Grade II listed village inn overlooking the Bourne Rivulet. The Oyster and Seafood Bar, probably unique outside London, specialises in the delights of fresh seafood. Other specialities include braised oxtail in red wine and lamb roasted in English mustard, rosemary and honey. There's an impressive wine list, too. Principal beers: Ringwood 49, Wadworths 6X, Courage Best, Old Speckled Hen.
Free House
Open 11-3 6-11
Bar food 12-2 7-9.30 Av main course £5.95
Restaurant 12-2 7-9.30 Av 3 course à la carte £17
Accommodation s£45 d£50

SHEDFIELD Hampshire

Terracotta Room at the Vineyard

SHEDFIELD Map 04 SU51
Wickham Vineyard, Botley Rd
SO32 2HL ☎ 01329 835454
Part of Wickham Vineyard, this restaurant is open all day from morning coffee to evening meals, including snacks, lunches and cream teas. The Australian influenced menus offer smoked fillet of emu, satay of kangaroo fillet and char-grilled crocodile tail with pineapple and coconut sauce.
Directions off A334 between Wickham & Botley
Open 10.30-5 7-11
Restaurant 12-5 7-9.30 Av 3 course à la carte £10

SHERFIELD ENGLISH Hampshire

The Hatchet Inn

SHERFIELD ENGLISH Map 04 SU22
SO31 6FP ☎ 01794 322487
This 17th-century country inn, lying in the Test Valley on the borders of the New Forest offers a tasty range of bar snacks, or an à la carte menu offering fresh ideas such as medallions of fillet steak sate with a peanut cream chilli sauce. Principal beers: Bass, London Pride, John Smiths, Caffreys.
Directions From Salisbury A36, A27
Free House
Bar food 12-2 7-9.15 Av main course £4.50
Restaurant 12-2 7-9.15 Av 3 course à la carte £15.50

SPARSHOLT Hampshire

The Plough Inn

SPARSHOLT Map 04 SU43
Main Rd SO21 2NW ☎ 01962 776353
Traditional, rustic country pub on the edge of Sparsholt village with a donkey paddock and extensive gardens. Today's specials may include roast breast of duck with nectarines and peach schnapps, wild mushroom tagliatelle, salad of quail with cherry stuffing, or rack of lamb with redcurrant and rosemary. Principal beers: Henry's IPA, Wadworths 6X, Murphys, Dry Blackthorn.
Directions From Winchester take B3049(A272) W
Wadworth

Open 11-3 6-11 (Sun-12-3,6-10.30)
Bar food 12-2 6-9 Av main course £6
Restaurant 12-2 6-9 Av 3 course à la carte £14

STEEP Hampshire

Harrow Inn
STEEP Map 04 SU72
GU32 2DA ☎ 01730 262685
Unspoiled country inn built in the 17th century, and serving beer from barrels behind the bar. Sweetcorn mushroom quiche, home-made Scotch eggs, or cottage pie may be on the menu. There are also home-made smoked hams which are used in a variety of dishes. Principal beers: Flowers Original, Marston Pedigree, Wadsworth 6X.
Directions From A3 onto A272 thru Sheet, back across A3 into Steep
Free House
Open 12-2.30 6-11 (Sat 11-3, 6-11, Sun 12-3, 7-10.30)

STOCKBRIDGE Hampshire

Mayfly
STOCKBRIDGE Map 04 SU33
Testcombe SO20 6AZ
☎ 01264 860283
Stunning riverside setting for this sturdily built country pub with extensive outdoor seating, conservatory, and numerous bar areas. All day food is a plus, especially the popular hot and cold buffet featuring chicken tandoori, quiches, cold cuts, oak-smoked River Test trout, and an extensive selection of cheeses. Principal beers: Boddingtons, Flowers Original.
Directions Between A303 & A30, 3m from Andover & Stockbridge
Whitbread
Open 10-11

Vine Inn
STOCKBRIDGE Map 04 SU33
High St SO20 6HF ☎ 01264 810652
A 316-year-old listed coaching inn, by the River Itchen, with old beams, antique furniture and open fires. Home-made food using fresh local produce is offered from blackboard menus. Shellfish is a speciality, and there is a popular hot seafood platter. Bar food ranges from ploughman's to beef and Boddington pie. Principal beers: Whitbread Gold and Best Bitter.
Directions Town centre
Free House
Open 11-11
Bar food 12-3 7-10 Av main course £5.50
Accommodation s£30 d£40

STRATFIELD TURGIS Hampshire

The Wellington Arms
STRATFIELD TURGIS Map 04 SU65
RG27 0AS ☎ 01256 882214
Originally a farmhouse, built in the 17th century, this Grade II listed building is situated on the Duke of Wellington's estate in rural North Hampshire. Bar food ranges from sandwiches to marinated chicken supreme, while the restaurant might offer home cured gravadlax and beef Wellington. Principal beers: Dorset Best, Tanglefoot, Hofbrau, Dempseys.
Directions A33
Free House
Open 11-11
Bar food 12-2.30 6-10 Av main course £6.95
Restaurant 12-2 6.30-9.30 Av 3 course à la carte £25 Av 3 course fixed price £17.95
Accommodation s£70 d£80

TICHBORNE Hampshire

The Tichborne Arms
TICHBORNE Map 04 SU53
SO24 0NA ☎ 01962 733760
There has been a pub on this site since the 1400s, but the present building of brick and thatch dates from 1939 when its predecessor burnt down. Ploughman's, toasties and jacket potatoes are offered from the menu and there are home-made specials such as steak, ale and Stilton pie. Principal beers: Flowers IPA, Wadworth 6X, Fuggles IPA, Boddingtons.
Directions off A31 towards Alresford, after 200yds R at sign for Tichborne
Free House
Open 11.30-2.30 6-11
Bar food 12-1.45 6.30-9.45 Av main course £5.25 *contd.*

UPPER FROYLE Hampshire

The Hen & Chicken Inn
UPPER FROYLE Map 04 SU74
GU34 4JH ☎ 01420 22115
Royalty and highwaymen alike have patronised this 16th-century coaching inn, which retains its traditional atmosphere with large open fires, panelling and beams. The same menu is offered in the bar, restaurant or garden, with items ranging from baguettes and burgers to baked cod or beef stir-fry. Principal beers: Old Pray, Hook Norton, Courage Best, London Pride.

Directions 6m from Farnham on A31 on R
Free House
Bar food 11.30-3 6.30-12 Av main course £12
Restaurant 11.30-3 6.30-12 Av 3 course à la carte £22 Av 3 course fixed price £22

WELL Hampshire

The Chequers Inn
WELL Map 04 SU74
RG29 1TL ☎ 01256 862605
Snugly atmospheric rooms with low beams and wooden pews are enhanced by a large open fire, 18th-century prints and sepia photographs at this 16th-century inn. Modern Australian cooking with Asian and Eastern influences is offered, with dishes ranging from burgers with bacon and Brie to seared Kangaroo fillet. Principal beers: Badgers IPA, Dorset Best, Tanglefoot, Hoffbrau Premium & Export.
Directions From Odiham: halfway down High St turn R into Long Lane, follow for 3m, L at T jct, pub 1/4m top of hill
Hall & Woodhouse
Open 11-3 6-11 (all day at weekends)
Bar food 12-2.30 7-10 Av main course £8
Restaurant 7-10 Av 3 course à la carte £19 Av 3 course fixed price £19

WHERWELL Hampshire 4

The White Lion
WHERWELL Map 04 SU34
SP11 7JF ☎ 01264 860317
Set in one of the Test Valley's prettiest thatched villages, easily found from main routes, this former coaching inn has many a tale to tell. The same menu, staple favourites with chalkboard specials such as prawns in filo pastry and breast of duck, serves bar, restaurant and courtyard garden. Principal beers: Flowers, Boddingtons, Castle Eden.
Directions Off A303 onto B3048, pub in village on B3420
Greenalls
Open 10-2.30 6-11
Bar food 12-2 7-9.30 Av main course £5.25
Restaurant 12-2 7-9.30 Av 3 course fixed price £12
Accommodation s£22 d£36

WHITCHURCH Hampshire

The Red House Inn
WHITCHURCH Map 04 SU44
21 London St RG28 7LH
☎ 01256 895558
16th-century coaching inn near the River Test. Dishes include char-grilled swordfish with pesto and black olive tapenade, roast pheasant with pearl barley and rich Madeira sauce, plus a vegetarian option of semolina gnocchi with gorgonzola and mushrooms. Theme menus have included a *Pasta Night* and a *Cajun Night*. Principal beers: Old Wardour, Diggers Gold, Cheriton Pots, XB.
Free House
Open 11-11
Bar food 12-2 6.30-9.30 Av main course £5.50
Restaurant 12-2 6.30-9.30 Av 3 course à la carte £13.95 Av 3 course fixed price £16.50

Watership Down Inn
WHITCHURCH Map 04 SU44
Freefolk Priors RG8 7NJ ☎ 01256 892254
Built in 1840, previously called The Freefolk Arms. Name changed in the mid-1970s to celebrate the success of local author Richard Adams' novel *Watership Down,* which was based on nearby landmarks. Basket meals, ploughmans and sandwich snacks are available. Also fish platters, lasagnes and a wide selection of curries. Principal beers: Bunny Hop Mild, Archers Best, Brakspears PA.
Directions On B3400 between Basingstoke & Andover
Free House
Open 11.30-3.30 6-11
Bar food 12-2.30 6-9.30 Av main course £5

WHITSBURY Hampshire

The Cartwheel Inn
WHITSBURY Map 04 SU11
Whitsbury Rd SP6 3PQ
☎ 01725 518362
Built at the turn of the century as a wheelwright's and shop, this listed tile and slate-roofed building has been a pub since the 1920s. Food ranges from ploughman's, salads and jacket potatoes to steaks, chicken curry and local rainbow trout. The vegetarian choice includes cashew paella. Principal beers: Adnams Broadside, Ringwood, Guinness.
Directions Off the A338 between Salisbury & Fordingbridge
Free House
Open 11-2.30 6-11
Bar food 12-2.30 7-9.30 Av main course £6
Restaurant 12-2.30 7-9.30

WINCHESTER Hampshire

Wykeham Arms
WINCHESTER Map 04 SU52
75 Kingsgate St SO23 9PE
☎ 01962 853834
A traditional town hostelry named after the founder of Winchester College. Old school desks feature in the bar. Once named 'Fleur de Luce' until French names were banned during the Napoleonic wars, France now gently influences the menu. Try French onion soup and whole black bream with gazpacho dressing. Principal beers: Bass, Hardys, Royal Oak, Popes Traditional.
Directions Near Winchester College & Winchester Cathedral
Eldridge Pope
Open 11-11
Restaurant 12-2.30 6.30-9 Av 3 course à la carte £15
Accommodation s£69.50 d£79.50

WOODLANDS Hampshire

The Game Keeper
WOODLANDS Map 04 SU31
268 Woodlands Rd SO40 7GH
☎ 01703 293093
Situated in the heart of the New Forest, this cosy country pub offers a friendly and relaxed atmosphere, with log fires in winter. Ploughman's, basket meals and baguettes are served in the bar, and home-made pies and desserts are specialities of the restaurant, along with steak, ribs and fish. Principal beers: Wadworth 6X, IPA.
Directions A35 from Lyndhurst then L
Wadworth
Open 11-11 (winter 11-2.30, 5-11)
Bar food 12-2 6.30-9.30 Av main course £3.50
Restaurant 12-2 6.30-9.30 Av 3 course à la carte £6.95

Hertfordshire

ARDELEY Hertfordshire

The Jolly Waggoner
ARDELEY Map 05 TL32
SE2 7AH ☎ 01438 861350
Antique furniture and ancient beams typify this 500- year-old village pub. Log fires warm in the winter months whilst the well-kept garden is popular in the summer. Diners could sample calves liver with Roquefort cheese and horseradish, locally made sausages, home-made beefburgers, or sirloin of Scotch beef Provençale. Principal beers: IPA and Abbot.
Greene King
Open 12-2 6.30-11
Bar food 12-2 6.45-9.30 Av main course £7.50
Restaurant 12-1.45 7-9.30 Av 3 course à la carte £20

BARLEY Hertfordshire

The Fox & Hounds
BARLEY Map 05 TL43
High St SG8 8HU ☎ 01763 848459
15th-century inn once used as a hunting lodge by James I. Inglenook fireplaces, low ceilings and stone floors provide the setting for a menu which may feature seared spiced salmon with tomato salsa, honey roasted chicken, spaghetti Bolognese, cashew nut paella, or venison in red wine pie. Principal beers: Adnams Southwold, Broadside.
Directions A505 onto B1368 at Flint Cross, pub 4m
Free House
Bar food 12-1.45 Av main course £6.50
Restaurant 12-1.45 6.30-9.30 Av 3 course à la carte £10

BUNTINGFORD Hertfordshire

The Sword in Hand
BUNTINGFORD Map 05 TL32
Westmill SG9 9LQ ☎ 01763 271356
Early 15th-century inn, once the home of the Scottish noble family, Gregs. Pub's name taken from a motif within their family crest. Daily specials feature salmon en croûte with tangy lemon sauce, lamb in rosemary and apple sauce, prawns in creamy Creole sauce, and duck in Morello cherry sauce. Principal beers: Rayments Bitter, Greene King IPA, Abbot Ale, Marstons Pedigree.
Directions Off A10 1.5m S of Buntingford
Free House
Open 12-2 6-11
Bar food 12-2.30 6.30-9.30 Av main course £3.50
Restaurant 12-2.30 6.30-9.30 Av 3 course à la carte £12

CHIPPERFIELD Hertfordshire

The Royal Oak
CHIPPERFIELD Map 04 TL00
11 The Street WD4 9BH
☎ 01923 266537
Conversation is an important part of the character of this pub, dating from 1787 and easily located at the main crossroads of the village. A simple menu offers home-cooked favourites from potted shrimps to steak or a selection of freshly roasted cold meats. Principal beers: Draught Youngs Special, Youngs Bitter, Draught Bass.
Directions Off M25 at Kings Langley, 1st turning L in High St
Free House
Open 12-3 6-11
Bar food 12.30-2.30 7.30-9 Av main course £7

FLAUNDEN Hertfordshire

The Bricklayers Arms
FLAUNDEN Map 04 TL00
Hogpits Bottom HP3 0PH
☎ 01442 833322
At this traditional country pub in beautiful countryside, settle into the snug oak beamed atmosphere to sample freshly prepared dishes with an international influence. Cajun red snapper is one of the fish dishes and vegetarians could try broccoli and walnut bake from a good selection. Principal beers: Fullers London Pride, Marstons Pedigree, Brakspear Special, Ringwood Old Thumper.
Free House
Open 11.30-2.30 6-11
Bar food 12-2 7-9 Av main course £6
Restaurant 12-2 7-9 Av 3 course à la carte £20

The Green Dragon
FLAUNDEN Map 04 TL00
HP3 0PP ☎ 01442 832269
A freehouse with traditional features including open fires, old beams and antique furniture. The bar menu includes snacks, light bites and 'dragon fillers' such as steak and kidney pie. A typical restaurant dish is roast pork chimera, with a curried sauce and sautéed banana. Principal beers: Marstons Pedigree, Greene King Abbot, IPA.
Directions B4505 from Hemel to Bovington then S to Flaunden
Free House
Open 11-3 5.30-11 (Sat 11-11, Sun 12-3,7-10.30)
Bar food 12-2 7-9 Av main course £8
Restaurant 12-2 7-9.30 Av 3 course à la carte £18

HINXWORTH Hertfordshire

Three Horseshoes
HINXWORTH Map 04 TL24
High St SG7 5HQ ☎ 01462 742280
A small thatched, beamed and timbered pub with a dining extension into the garden. One menu is offered throughout, a daily changing blackboard using local

produce, game and a varied selection of fresh fish. Dishes include 'Harry Pig' sausages made from free-range pork, roast Whitby cod, and red lentil cannelloni. Principal beers: Greene King IPA, Abbot Ale, Guinness, Strongbow.
Directions E of A1 between Biggleswade and Baldock
Greene King
Open 11.30-2.30 5.30-11 (Sun 12-2.30, 7-10.30)
Bar food 12-2 7-9.30
Restaurant 12-2 7-9.30 Av 3 course à la carte £15

KNEBWORTH Hertfordshire

The Lytton Arms
KNEBWORTH Map 04 TL22
Park Ln SG3 6QB ☎ 01438 812312
Built in 1887 the Lytton Arms is popular with ramblers, horse riders and cyclists, and has served over 1700 different real ales in under a decade. Grilled butterfly chicken breast, vegetable tikka masala Kiev, home-made lasagne, or O'Keefe speciality sausages may be on today's menu. Principal beers: London Pride, Bass, Theakstons.

Directions From A1(M)take A602.At Knebworth turn R at rail station.Follow signs 'Codicote'.Pub 1.5m on R
Free House
Open 11-11
Bar food 12-2 6.30-9.30 Av main course £5.50

LITTLE HADHAM Hertfordshire

The Nags Head
LITTLE HADHAM Map 05 TL42
The Ford SG11 2AX ☎ 01279 771555
Dates from 1595 and one of the oldest buildings in the village. Situated near the River Avon. Blackboard specials typically feature grilled sea bass, poached skate wing, and breast of duck in brandy and orange sauce. Evening menu includes a range of steak dishes and fresh rainbow trout Grenobloise. Principal beers: Greene King, Abbot, IPA, Wexford.
Directions M11 J8 take A120 towards Puckeridge & A10. At traffic lights in L.Hadnam turn L. Pub 0.75m on R
Greene King
Open 11-11 (Mon-Sat closed 2.30-6) 12-10.30 (Sun closed 3-7)
Bar food 12-2 6-9 Av main course £4.25
Restaurant 12-2 6-9 Av 3 course à la carte £11.50

MUCH HADHAM Hertfordshire

Jolly Waggoners
MUCH HADHAM Map 05 TL41
Widford Rd SG10 6EZ ☎ 01279 842102
The pub was built in 1840 and two older cottages were incorporated into it in 1975, to provide the pleasant restaurant area with its open fire and views of the Ash Valley. Good home-cooked food is served including pies, steaks, lasagne, vegetarian dishes and snacks. Principal beers: McMullens AK, Bass, Directors, Fosters.
Directions On the B1004 between Bishops Stortford & Ware
Free House
Open 12-3 6.30-11 (Sun 12-3, 7-10.30)
Bar food 12-3 6.30-11 Av main course £6
Restaurant 12-3 6.30-11 Av 3 course à la carte £12

SARRATT Hertfordshire

The Cock Inn
SARRATT Map 04 TQ09
Church End, Church Ln WD3 6HH
☎ 01923 282908
The pub, opposite the village church, used to be the resting place of the cock horse who pulled carts up the hill from the mill. Bar food ranges from a

contd.

sandwich to a pie, pasta or fish dish, and the restaurant offers international fare, such as lamb Dijonnaise and roast forest duckling. Principal beers: Fullers, Brakspears, Shepherd Neame.
Directions Between M25 J18 and the A404 opposite St Clement Danes school
Free House
Open 11-3 5.30-11 (Sat 11-11, Sun 12-10.30)
Bar food 11-2.30 6-10 Av main course £5
Restaurant 12-2.30 7-10 Av 3 course à la carte £20

TEWIN Hertfordshire

The Plume of Feathers
TEWIN Map 04 TL21
Upper Green Rd AL6 0LX
☎ 01438 717265
Built in 1596, this historic inn, a former hunting lodge of Elizabeth I and later the haunt of highwaymen, now boasts several ghosts including a 'lady in grey'. Enjoy fresh country-style dishes; monkfish tails in the bar or a nest of pigeon breasts in the à la carte restaurant. Principal beers: Courage Best, Wadsworths 6X, Speckled Hen.
Directions E from A1 J6 toward WGC, follow B1000 toward Hertford, Tewin signed on L
Free House
Open 11-2.30 6-11
Bar food 12-2 7-9 Av main course £5.95
Restaurant 12-2.30 7-9 Av 3 course à la carte £16.95

WALKERN Hertfordshire

The White Lion
WALKERN Map 04 TL22
31 The High St SG2 7PA
☎ 01438 861251
A heavily timbered 16th-century coaching inn with original inglenooks, stone floors and low ceilings. There are roaring log fires in the winter and a patio and beer garden for summer use. The menu ranges from snacks through hot red jungle chicken curry to the hearty Lion's Share mixed grill. Principal beers: Greene King IPA, Abbot Ale, Wexford Irish Cream ale.
Directions B1037 from Stevenage
Greene King
Open 11-3 5-11 (Sat 11-11, Sun 12-5)
Bar food 12-3 5-11 Av main course £6
Restaurant 12-3 5-11 Av 3 course à la carte £15

WARE Hertfordshire

The Sow & Pigs
WARE Map 05 TL31
Cambridge Rd, Thundridge SG12 0ST
☎ 01920 463281
There is a predominantly porcine theme to this village pub, with piggy pictures and lots of little pigs in display cabinets (also pig roasts on Bank Holiday Mondays). Good food is served in generous portions, from USA-style salad sandwiches to Yorkshire fish with home-made chips and mushy peas. Principal beers: Adnams, Shipstones, Wadworth 6X, Stella Artois.
Directions On A10 just N of Ware turn off. Adj to entrance of Hanbury Manor
Greenalls
Open 11-11
Bar food 11.30-2.30 6-9.30 Av main course £5.50
Restaurant 11.30-2.30 6-9.30 Av 3 course à la carte £15

WATTON-AT-STONE Hertfordshire

George & Dragon
WATTON-AT-STONE Map 04 TL31
SG14 3TA ☎ 01920 830285
There's a clubby, convivial atmosphere at this village centre pub, which dates from about 1550 (look out for the old drunks' lock-up opposite). The menu, the same for the bar and restaurant, includes steak, burgers and chicken Kiev, while blackboard specials offer fresh fish and game dishes, all home made. Principal beers: Greene King IPA, Abbot Ale, Guinness, Murphys.

Directions Off A602 between Stevenage & Ware

Greene King
Open 11-2.30 6-11 (Sun 11-2.30,3-7)
Bar food 12-2 7-10 Av main course £5.75
Restaurant 12-2 7-10 Av 3 course à la carte £12.50

WESTON Hertfordshire

The Rising Sun
WESTON Map 04 TL23
21 Halls Green SG4 7DR
☎ 01462 790487
Set in picturesque Hertfordshire countryside, The Rising Sun is especially welcoming to those with children. Play equipment, a children's menu, and tuck shop in summer are provided. Adults should enjoy the choice from a menu which may offer spicy sausage grill, shellfish platter, or steak and kidney pie. Principal beers: McMullens A.K, Country, Gladstone, Bass.
Directions A1(M)J9 take A6141(dual c'way)towards Baldock(take outside lane)& turn R towards Graveley.100yds take 1st L
Free House
Open 11.30-2.30 6-11
Bar food 12-2 6.15-10 Av main course £5

Kent

ASHFORD Kent

Royal Oak Inn
ASHFORD Map 05 TR04
Charing Village TN27 0HU
☎ 01233 712612
Situated near Leeds Castle and well placed for visits to Canterbury and Rochester Cathedrals. Seafood dishes range from fillets of rainbow trout, to salmon steak with cream and tarragon sauce. Other main courses include wild rabbit pie, game pie, spicy beef burritos, and cheese, broccoli and mushroom pie for vegetarians. Principal beers: Bass, London Pride, Shepherd Neame.
Directions From Ashford A20 to 1st major roundabout, signs to Charing Village
Free House
Open 11-2.30 6-11
Bar food 12-2.30 7-9.30 Av main course £8.50
Restaurant 12-2.30 7-9.30 Av 3 course à la carte £15
Accommodation s£35 d£45

BIDDENDEN Kent

The Three Chimneys
BIDDENDEN Map 05 TQ83
TN30 7HN ☎ 01580 291472
15th-century country pub, a mile and a half from Biddenden village, set in the Kentish Weald, an area famous for its hops and cherries. Seasonal blackboard menus may offer fricassee of veal, Kentish lamb pie, venison steak in Rob Roy sauce, or celery and ham Mornay. Principal beers: Harveys Best, Harveys Old Ale, Brakspears, Adnams Best.
Free House
Open 11-2.30 6-11
Bar food 12-2 6.30-10 Av main course £6
Restaurant 12-2 6.30-10 Av 3 course à la carte £14

BOROUGH GREEN Kent

The Brickmakers Arms
BOROUGH GREEN Map 05 TQ65
Maidstone Rd, St Mary's Platt TN15 8JJ
☎ 01732 883594
Main road pub that welcomes families and can cater for weddings. Bar menu offers home-cooked food, while the restaurant has an a la carte menu. Daily specials are available, and fresh fish is a speciality. Principal beers: Master Brew, Spitfire, Hurlimann

Directions on A25 in St Mary's Platt
Shepherd Neame
Open Winter 11-3 5.30-11 (Sun 12-3, 7-10.30, Sun & Summer 11-11)
Bar food 12-2.30 6.30-9.30 Av main course £5.50
Restaurant 12-2.30 6.30-9.30 Av 3 course à la carte £12

South & South East (& Isle of Wight)

BOYDEN GATE Kent

The Gate Inn
BOYDEN GATE Map 05 TR26
CT3 4EB ☎ 01227 860498
A 'talkers' pub', with no music or fruit machines, in a very rural location. Politically correct 'ploughperson's', light meals (veg flan and cold ham), spicy hot-pots and burgers feature, and 'torpedoes' (filled chunks of French bread) are a speciality - look out for the chilli dog with Tabasco, Dragonfire and onions. Principal beers: Shepherd Neame, Master Brew Bitter, Spitfire Ale, Bishops Finger.
Directions From Canterbury on A28 turn L at Upstreet
Shepherd Neame
Open 11-2.30 6-11 (Sat 11-3,6-11/Sun 12-3,7-10.30)
Bar food 11-2.30 6-11 Av main course £3

BRABOURNE Kent

The Five Bells
BRABOURNE Map 05 TR14
Canterbury Rd TN25 5LP
☎ 01303 813334
Fresh fish is always available at this 16th century pub, beautifully situated at the foot of the North Downs Way. Pheasant and venison pie, or kidneys in red wine may also be available. Principal beers: Courage, Shepherd Neame, Ruddles County.
Directions 5m E of Ashford
Free House
Bar food 12-3 6.30-10
Restaurant 12-3 6.30-10

BURHAM Kent

The Golden Eagle
BURHAM Map 05 TQ76
80 Church St ME1 3SD ☎ 01634 668975
Oriental food, with all the delectable flavours of China, Thailand, Malaysia and Singapore, is offered in a traditional pub setting at the Golden Eagle. Red hot chilli chicken and pork Babibangang can be enjoyed along with panoramic views of the Medway Valley and the North Downs. Principal beers: Wadworth 6X, Marstons Pedigree, Whitbread Best, Stella.
Directions From M2 J3 or M20 J6 take A229 Burpham is 2m on Pilgrims Way
Free House
Open 11-2.30 6.15-11
Bar food 12-2 7-10 Av main course £7
Restaurant 12-2 7-10 Av 3 course à la carte £12 Av 3 course fixed price £16.50

CHIDDINGSTONE Kent

Castle Inn
CHIDDINGSTONE Map 05 TQ54
TN8 7AH ☎ 01892 870247
Owned and conserved by the National Trust since 1939, Chiddingstone village is charming and unspoilt. Quenching thirsts since 1730, The Castle has an open kitchen where diners may see staff prepare dishes such as skate wings with black butter, pigeon and mushroom pie, or boiled beef and carrots. Principal beers: Larkins, Harveys, Guinness, Becks.

Directions S of B2027 between Tonbridge & Edenbridge
Free House
Bar food 11-6.30 6.30-10.45 Av main course £5.20
Restaurant 12-2 7.30-9.30 Av 3 course à la carte £19.50 Av 3 course fixed price £19.50

CHILHAM Kent

The White Horse
CHILHAM Map 05 TR05
The Square CT4 8BY ☎ 01227 730355
Set in the picturesque Tudor square of Chilham, the White Horse was built in 1460 and has been a pub for over 250 years. Home-made specials are offered from the blackboard menu, including pies, curries, pasta dishes and vegetarian options, as well as sandwiches, ploughman's and salads. Principal beers: Fremlins, Flowers O/B, Boddingtons, Heineken.
Directions Take A28 from Canterbury then A252,turn L 1m
Whitbread

Open 11-11 (Sun 12-10.30)
Bar food 12-2.30 7-9 Av main course £4.95
Restaurant 7-9 Av 3 course à la carte £11

CHILLENDEN Kent

The Griffins Head
CHILLENDEN Map 05 TR25
CT3 1PS ☎ 01304 840325
A friendly and warm welcome awaits you at this typical, old English pub, built in 1286 as a farm and given to monks to farm in the 16th century. Inside are open fires and old beams, with barbecues at weekends in summer. Home-cooked food includes steak and Guinness pie, grilled sardines and game. Principal beers: Shepherd Neame.
Directions A2 from Canterbury towards Dover,then B2046.Village on R
Shepherd Neame
Bar food 12-2 7-9.30 Av main course £5
Restaurant 12-2 7-9.30 Av 3 course à la carte £15

CLIFFE Kent

The Black Bull
CLIFFE Map 05 TQ77
186 Church St ME3 7AD
☎ 01634 220893
Tapestries, the restaurant at The Black Bull specialises in Malaysian, Indonesian and Chinese cuisine, so nasi goreng or pajri nanas may be on the menu. Vegetarians may like to try Lohan Chai, or 'Buddhist vegetables ensemble for the Gods'! The area is also ideal for walking and bird watching. Principal beers: Black Bull Special, Old Peculiar, Speckled Hen, Wadworths 6X.
Directions On B2000 N of Rochester
Free House
Open 12-2.30 7-11 (Sun, 7-10.30)
Restaurant 12.30-3 7-10 Av 3 course à la carte £18.50 Av 4 course fixed price £20.50

EASTLING Kent

Carpenters Arms
EASTLING Map 05 TQ95
The Street ME13 0AZ ☎ 01795 890234
A 14th-century country pub with oak beams, two inglenook fireplaces and a candlelit restaurant with a brick tile floor. Traditional bar food is served along with grills and daily specials. Restaurant dishes include snails in garlic and corn-fed quail with Stilton cheese sauce. Principal beers: Masterbrew, Bishop's Finger, Spitfire, Guinness.
Directions A251 towards Faversham, then A2, 1st L Brogdale Rd, 4m to Eastling
Shepherd Neame
Open 11-4 6-11 (Sun 12-4, 7-10.30)
Bar food 12-2.30 6.30-10.30 Av main course £6
Restaurant 12-2.30 6.30-10.30 Av 3 course à la carte £15 Av 3 course fixed price £10
Accommodation s£35 d£45

EYNSFORD Kent

Swallows' Malt Shovel Inn
EYNSFORD Map 05 TQ56
Station Rd DA4 0ER ☎ 01322 862164
Situated near the River Darenth, this pub offers a good selection of snacks and light lunches such as moules marinière and Mediterranean prawns. Main course dishes range from lobster Thermidor, grilled sea bass, and monkfish in garlic butter, to home-made venison pie, and a vegetable curry for vegans. Principal beers: London Pride, Flowers Original, Pedigree, Brakspears.
Directions A20 to Brands Hatch, then on A225, 1m to pub
Free House
Open 11-3.30 7-11
Bar food 12-3.30 7-11.30 Av main course £5
Restaurant 12-3.30 7-11.30 Av 3 course à la carte £12

FAVERSHAM Kent

The Albion Tavern
FAVERSHAM Map 05 TR05
Front Bents, Faversham Creeks
ME13 7DH ☎ 01795 591411
Situated close to Swale Creek. Main course specials range from fillet of sole with a prawn, white wine, mushroom and cream sauce, and lamb rump with a blackcurrant and red wine sauce, to pot roast partridge with apple and blackberry sauce. Principal beers: Shepherd Neame.
Directions From Faversham take A2 W.In Ospringe turn R just before Ship Inn at Shepherd Neame Brewery 1m turn L over creek bridge

contd.

Shepherd Neame
Open 11-3 6.30-11
Bar food 12-2 7-10 Av main course £6
Restaurant 12-2 7-10 Av 3 course à la carte £15 Av 4 course fixed price £15.50

Shipwrights Arms
FAVERSHAM Map 05 TR05
Hollowshore ME13 7TU
☎ 01795 590088
Step back in time at this fascinating 17th century pub in a peaceful backwater which draws water from its own artesian well and generates its own electricity. Local shipwrights' and river traffic enjoy home cooking; pork satay, chicken casserole or salmon. The ghost of a Dutch sea captain also visits. Principal beers: Shepherd Neame, Master Brew, Spitfire, Hurlimann.
Directions M2 towards Canterbury
Free House
Open 11-11 (Sun 12-10.30)
Bar food 12-3/4 7-9/10 Av main course £3
Restaurant 12-3/4 7-9/10

FORDCOMBE Kent

Chafford Arms
FORDCOMBE Map 05 TQ54
TN3 0SA ☎ 01892 740267
Run by a dinosaur (according to the landlord), this is an old fashioned pub, tile-hung and creeper-clad, opposite the village green and cricket club. Home-cooked food is served with fish as a speciality, including local trout, hot crab Newburg and fresh Dover sole from Hastings. Principal beers: King and Barnes, Larkins, London Pride.
Directions On B2188(off A264) between Tunbridge Wells & E Grinstead
Whitbread
Open 11-3 6-11
Bar food 12.30-2 7.30-9.30 Av main course £5.95
Restaurant 12.30-2 7.30-9.30 Av 3 course à la carte £15 Av 3 course fixed price £15

AA members can call AA Hotel Booking Service on 0990 050505 to book at AA recognised hotels and B & Bs in the UK and Ireland, or through our Internet site: http://www.theaa.co.uk/hotels

FORDWICH Kent

Fordwich Arms
FORDWICH Map 05 TR15
King St CT2 0DB ☎ 01227 710444
Fordwich is the smallest town in England, with its own town hall and mayor, and the inn, with its lovely garden, is beside the River Stour. There's a bar snack menu, and a weekender and party menu for the oak-panelled dining room, plus occasional gourmet evenings. Principal beers: Flowers, Fremlins, Boddingtons.
Directions Follow A28 from A2, on approaching Sturry R at 'Welsh Harp' pub into Fordwich Rd
Whitbread
Open 11-11 (Sun 12-3, 7-10.30)
Bar food 12-2.30 6.30-10 Av main course £6
Restaurant 12-2.30 6.30-10 Av 3 course à la carte £10

GOUDHURST Kent

The Star & Eagle
GOUDHURST Map 05 TQ73
High St TN17 1AL ☎ 01580 211512
A constantly changing menu is presented at this 14th-century inn which was once the headquarters of the 18th-century 'Hawkhurst Gang' of robbers and smugglers. Murphy's pie, butterfly trout fillets, breast of Barbary duck, home cooked ham, or 'sizzling fajitas' may be among the courses that diners can sample. Principal beers: Fremlins, Flowers Original, Boddingtons.
Directions On A262 E of Tunbridge Wells
Whitbread
Open 11-11
Bar food 12-2.30 7-9.30 Av main course £6
Restaurant 12-2.30 7-9.30 Av 3 course à la carte £15
Accommodation s£35 d£53

HADLOW Kent

The Artichoke Inn
HADLOW Map 05 TQ65
Park Rd, Hamptons TN11 9SR
☎ 01732 810763
Located in a conservation hamlet of mostly listed houses, this ragstone timber framed inn dates from 1483. Home-made pies are a speciality - chicken and

mushroom, steak and kidney or vegetable - and home-made pasta dishes. There is also a choice from the char-grill, including steaks and chops. Principal beers: Youngs Ordinary, Greene King Abbot, Fullers London Pride.

Directions From Tonbridge take A26.In Hadlow turn L into Carpenters Lane.L at junc,2nd on R.

Free House

Open 12-3 6.30-11

Bar food 12-2 7-9.30 Av main course £6.25

Restaurant 12-2 7-9.30 Av 3 course à la carte £12

HERNHILL Kent

Red Lion

HERNHILL Map 05 TR06

The Green NE13 9JR ☎ 01227 751207

Beams and flagstone floors are all part of the charm at this 14th-century hostelry. Dishes include the pie of the day, fresh fish, steaks and roast duck. Mushroom and spinach strudel might be among the vegetarian options, and there are home-made sweets to finish. Principal beers: Shepherd Neame, Master Brew, Hancocks, Fosters.

Directions S of A299 between Faversham & Whitstable

Free House

Open 11-11

Bar food 11-3 6-11 Av main course £6

Restaurant 11-3 6-11 Av 3 course à la carte £12 Av 3 course fixed price £9.95

IDEN GREEN Kent

The Peacock

IDEN GREEN Map 05 TQ73

Goudhurst Rd TN17 2PB

☎ 01580 211233

Grade II listed building dating from the 12th-century with low beams and inglenook fireplace. A wide range of snacks and light meals is available. Main meals include various curries, chicken and oyster pie, lamb and apricot pie, and home-made lasagne and moussaka. Principal beers: Masterbrew, Spitfire, Hurlimann.

Directions A21 from Tun Wells to Hastings, onto A262, pub 1 1/2m past Goudhurst

Shepherd Neame

Open 12-11 (Sun 12-4, 7-10.30)

Bar food 12-2.15 7-9 Av main course £5

IGHTHAM Kent

George & Dragon

IGHTHAM Map 05 TQ55

The Street TN15 9HH ☎ 01732 882440

The Duke of Northumberland was imprisoned in this 16th-century building after the discovery of the Gunpowder Plot. It is a fine example of Tudor architecture in a historic village setting. There is a lunch menu of home-made bar food, and a full à la carte in the evening. Principal beers: Master Brew, Spitfire, Hurlimann.

Directions From M20, A20 then A227 towards Tonbridge

Shepherd Neame

contd.

Open 11-3 6-11 (Sun 12-3, 7-10.30, Summer open all day)
Bar food 12-2.30 6.30-9.30 Av main course £5.50
Restaurant 12-2.30 6.30-9.30 Av 3 course à la carte £12

IVY HATCH Kent

The Plough

IVY HATCH Map 05 TQ55

High Cross Rd TN15 0NL
☎ 01732 810268

Fish and shellfish are favoured ingredients at this 300-year old pub which employs a number of French staff from a catering school in Grenoble. Some seafood dishes which may be on the menu are marinated herring in madeira, steamed skate Grenobloise, fresh dressed lobster, and Cajun style pan-fried tuna. Principal beers: Lakins, Adnams.
Directions M25 J5 take A25 towards Borough Green follow signs for Ivy Hatch
Free House
Open 11.30-3 6-11
Restaurant 12-2 7-10 Av 3 course à la carte £22 Av 3 course fixed price £15.95

LENHAM Kent

The Harrow Inn

LENHAM Map 05 TQ85

Hubbards Hill, Warren St ME17 2ED
☎ 01622 858727

Maybe meet a ghostly regular at this historic hostelry, once the forge and rest house for pilgrims en route to Canterbury, in a peaceful hamlet atop the North Downs. Fresh, seasonal market produce carefully prepared may include poached suprême of guinea fowl or even sautéed kangaroo steak. Principal beers: Shepherd Neame, Master Brew, Becks, Caffreys.
Directions A20 thru Lenham, take sign for Warren St on L, pub on R
Free House
Open 11.30-2.30 7-10.30
Bar food 11.30-2.30 7-10.30
Restaurant 11.30-2.30 7-10.30
Accommodation s£39.50 d£49.50

LINTON Kent

The Bull Inn

LINTON Map 05 TQ75

Linton Hill ME17 4AW ☎ 01622 743612

A 17th-century black beamed, white walled pub with a beautiful garden overlooking the Weald of Kent. Barbecues are held on summer Sundays from 5-8pm. Light bites and fresh home-cooked produce are served, along with specials such as Teriyaki tuna steak and chicken Brindisi. Principal beers: Shepherd Neame, Master Brew, Spitfire.

Directions A229 thru Maidstone to Linton
Shepherd Neame
Open 11-3 5-11 (Sat-Sun in Summer, open all day)
Bar food 12-2.30 6.30-9.30 Av main course £6
Restaurant 12-2.30 6.30-9.30 Av 3 course à la carte £15

NEWNHAM Kent

The George Inn

NEWNHAM Map 05 TQ95

44 The Street ME9 0LL
☎ 01795 890237 890587

Situated in the heart of the Kent hop fields and orchards, with a panelled bar which runs the length of the building. Among the main course dishes are lamb Solfredo cooked in white wine and herbs, and Scotch salmon fillet poached in orange and ginger sauce. Vegetarian options are also available. Principal beers: Shepherd Neame Master Brew, Bishops Finger, Spitfire.
Directions 5m SW of Faversham
Shepherd Neame
Open 11.10-3 6.30-11
Bar food 12-2.15 7-9.30 Av main course £5.50
Restaurant 12-2.15 7-9.30 Av 3 course à la carte £15

PAINTERS FORSTAL Kent

The Alma
PAINTERS FORSTAL Map 05 TQ95
ME13 0DU ☎ 01795 533835
Typical weather-boarded Kent inn situated in the heart of apple orchard country. Among the home-made dishes are sizzling chicken, rib-eye of beef, steak and kidney pudding, and beef and beer casserole. Home-made desserts include fresh strawberry cheese cake, and steamed fruit pudding with butterscotch sauce and cream. Principal beers: Shepherd Neame, Masterbrew, Spitfire, Hurlimann.
Directions A251 S then R thru Whitehill
Shepherd Neame
Open 10.30-3 6.30-11
Bar food 12-2 7-9.30 Av main course £6

PLUCKLEY Kent

The Dering Arms
PLUCKLEY Map 05 TQ94
Station Rd TN27 0RR ☎ 01233 840371
A former hunting lodge, the Dering Arms is built in the same style as the manor house of the Dering Estate, with beautiful Dutch gables. Pies, ploughman's, soup, and sausage and chips are typical of the bar food, while the restaurant specialises in fresh fish and game in season. Principal beers: Goachers Dering Ale, Maidstone Dark, Porter.
Directions M20 J8 take A20 to Ashford.Then R onto B2077 to Pluckley
Free House
Open 11-3 6-11
Bar food 11.30-3 7-11 Av main course £5
Restaurant 11.30-3 7-11 Av 3 course à la carte £16
Accommodation s£28 d£36

RINGLESTONE Kent

The Ringlestone Inn
RINGLESTONE Map 05 TQ85
Ringlestone Rd, Twixt Harrietsham & Wormhill ME17 1NX ☎ 01622 859900
Many original features remain at this listed 16th-century former monks' hospice, including brick and flint walls and floor, medieval furniture and candlelight. Pies made with country wines are the house speciality, such as duck and damson wine, vegetable and nut, and beef with black beer and raisin wine. Principal beers: Bishops Finger, Spitfire, Harveys, Abbot.

Directions M20 J8 take A20 then B2163.After Hollingbourne turn R at x-rd by water tower
Free House
Open 12-3 6.30-11 (Sat-Sun 12-11)
Bar food 12-2 7-9.30 Av main course £5.85
Restaurant 12-2 7-9.30 Av 3 course à la carte £17.50 Av 3 course fixed price £9.95
Accommodation s£40 d£50

SELLING Kent

The Rose and Crown
SELLING Map 05 TR05
Perry Wood ME13 9RY
☎ 01227 752214
16th-century pub situated on top of Crown Hill with views across acres of woodland. The standard menu comprises home-made pies, curries, seafood snacks, filled jacket potatoes and a selection of desserts. House specials include prawn Creole and Mexican chicken. Also offers a good choice of real ales. Principal beers: Goachers Maidstone Ale, Harveys Best, Adnams Southwold, Murphys.
Free House
Open 11-3 7-11
Bar food 12-2 7-9.30
Restaurant 12-2 7-9.30

SHIPBOURNE Kent

The Chaser Inn
SHIPBOURNE Map 05 TQ55
Stumble Hill TN11 9PE ☎ 01732 810360
A Colonial-style building, dating from the 1880s, with an impressive porticoed front. It stands next to the church overlooking the village green. Fresh fish is the speciality of the restaurant, and traditional English fare including home-made pies and puddings is served in the

contd.

bar. Principal beers: Harveys Sussex Best,Shepherd Neame Best.
Directions On A227 N of Tonbridge
Free House
Open 11-3 5-11.30
Bar food 12-2 6.30-9.30 Av main course £7.50
Restaurant 12.30-2 7.30-9.30 Av 4 course fixed price £22.50

SMARDEN Kent

The Chequers Inn
SMARDEN Map 05 TQ84
TN27 8QA ☎ 01233 770217
The deeds of this inn, which dates back to 1387, decree the landlord to allow villagers to draw water from the pond. Most come nowadays for a friendly welcome, bar snack or blackboard specials such as fillet of red snapper Meunière, crispy roast duckling or pork Hawaiian. Principal beers: Draught Bass, London Pride, Old Speckled Hen, Youngs Special.
Free House
Open 10.30-3 6-11
Bar food 12-2.30 6.30-10 Av main course £6
Restaurant 12-2.30 6.30-10 Av 3 course à la carte £13.50
Accommodation s£20 d£40

SMARTS HILL Kent

The Bottle House Inn
SMARTS HILL Map 05 TQ54
Coldharbour Rd TN11 8ET
☎ 01892 870306
Built in 1492, the inn is full of oak beams, with a low ceiling, open fire and copper bar top. The adventurous daily menu might offer sizzling chicken fajitas, rack of hickory smoked ribs, and king prawns and mussels with tagliatelle and orange and green ginger sauce. Principal beers: Larkins, Harveys, Burton Ale.
Directions From Tunbridge Wells take A264 W then B2188 N
Free House
Open 11-2.30 6-11
Bar food 12-2 7-10 Av main course £7.95
Restaurant 12-2 7-10 Av 3 course à la carte £18

SPELDHURST Kent

The George and Dragon
SPELDHURST Map 05 TQ54
Speldhurst Hill TN3 0NN
☎ 01892 863125
Dating from 1213, this is one of the oldest three pubs in England. It was used as a stopping off point by knights off to the Crusades, and there are grooves in the fireplace where they sharpened their swords. The food has a continental influence, and there's plenty of fresh seafood. Principal beers: Harveys Best and Pale, Bass, Guinness.
Free House
Open 11-11
Bar food 12-2.30 6-9.30 Av main course £7.95
Restaurant 12-2.30 6-10 Av 3 course à la carte £17.50 Av 3 course fixed price £15

TUNBRIDGE WELLS (ROYAL) Kent

The Crown Inn
TUNBRIDGE WELLS (ROYAL) Map 05 TQ53
The Walks, Groombridge TN3 9QH
☎ 01892 864742
Sir Arthur Conan Doyle was a regular visitor to this 16th-century coaching inn and used it as a location in the Sherlock Holmes story 'Valley of Fear.' Other visiting sleuths can choose from a menu that may include Speldhurst sausages, breast of chicken 'Rebecca', or grilled trout in dill and white wine sauce. Principal beers: Harveys IPA, Directors, Ruddles County.
Directions Take A264 W of Tunbridge Wells, then B2110 S
Free House
Open 11-3 6-11
Bar food 12-2 7-9.30 Av main course £5
Restaurant 7-9.30 Av 3 course à la carte £11
Accommodation s£23 d£38

The Hare on Langton Green
TUNBRIDGE WELLS (ROYAL) Map 05TQ53
Langton Rd, Langton Green TN3 0JA
☎ 01892 862419
A large, bay-fronted Edwardian building on the edge of the village green. The food is prepared on the premises, and there's an emphasis on hearty portions and value for money. Dishes include fresh fish, steaks, crispy duck with oriental vegetables, and spinach and wild

mushroom pancakes. Principal beers: Rayments, Greene King IPA, Abbot Ale.
Directions On A264 W of Tunbridge Wells
Free House
Open 11.30-11 (Sun 12-10.30)

Sankey's Cellar Wine Bar
TUNBRIDGE WELLS (ROYAL) Map 05 TQ53
39 Mount Ephraim TN4 8AA
☎ 01892 511422
Set in a Victorian villa, in a 'city' ambience, seafood is the speciality. Fresh, direct from the source, classic Whitstable oysters , stuffed Brittany clams or Portuguese Cataplana may be the choices on a daily changing menu. Principal beers: Harveys Best, Shepherd Neame, Larkins, Adnams.
Directions on the A26
Open 11-11 (Sat 11-3. 6-12)
Restaurant 12-4 7-12.30 Av 3 course à la carte £25 Av 3 course fixed price £23.50

WROTHAM Kent

The Green Man
WROTHAM Map 05 TQ65
Hodsoll St, Ash-cum-Ridley TN15 7LE
☎ 01732 823575
An 18th-century brick and timber building with impressive floral displays in summer. The interior is warmly decorated with hops, horse brasses and local pictures. There's a large garden with a pets' corner and children's play area. Traditional, continental and Far Eastern dishes are served. Principal beers: Pedigree, 6X, Fremlins, Boddingtons.
Directions Off A227 between Wrotham & Meopham
Whitbread
Open 11-2.30 6.30-11
Bar food 12-2 7.30-9.45 Av main course £5

LONDON

EC1

The Eagle
EC1 Map E4
159 Farringdon Rd EC1R 3AL
☎ 0171 8371353
A popular pub serving Mediterranean-style food chalked up on a blackboard menu, with lots of grills - Italian sausages and black bream with Romesco sauce for example. Other options might be caldeirada, a Portuguese fish stew, and to finish the Portuguese custard tart is recommended. Principal beers: Marstons Pedigree,Boddingtons,Wadworth 6X,Heineken.
Free House
Open 12-11
Bar food 12.30-2.30 6.30-10.30 Av main course £7.50

The Peasant
EC1 Map 05 TQ38
240 St John St EC1V 4PH
☎ 0171 336 7726
Converted Victorian pub with original mosaic floor and ceramic mural. In contrast, the upstairs restaurant is of a modern minimalist design. Typical dishes include Thai chicken and coconut broth, poached pear and watercress salad with salted almonds and Pecorino, and lamb juniper sausages with roast potatoes, shallots and wild mushrooms. Principal beers: Budvar, Rolling Rock, Weiss Beer, Kriek.
Free House
Open 12-12
Bar food 12.30-3.30 6.30-11
Restaurant 12.30-3.30 6.30-11 Av 3 course à la carte £18.50 Av 2 course fixed price £12.50

NW1

The Chapel
NW1 Map B4
48 Chapel St NW1 5DP
☎ 0171 4029220
Anglo-Mediterranean food is served at this relaxed establishment, which has stripped floors, old pine tables and chairs, free newspapers and a display of local artists' paintings. Typical dishes are stuffed chicken wings, cod and salmon with pesto hollandaise, and rich chocolate mousse.

contd.

Directions By A40 Marylebone Rd & Old Marylebone Rd junc. Off Edgware Rd by tube station
Free House
Open 12-11 12-10.30 (Sun-closed 4-7)
Bar food 12-2.30 7-10.00 Av main course £7

The Engineer
NW1 Map 05 TQ38
65 Gloucester Av, Primrose Hill NW1 8JH
☎ 0171 7220950
Stylish Primrose Hill pub designed in 1841 by Isambard Kingdom Brunel. Minimalist decor acts as backdrop to modern British cooking based on free-range/organic produce. Salmon fishcakes with caper aïoli, char-grilled squid with chilli, ginger and garlic, and lamb, sweet potato and roast garlic stew, show the style. Principal beers: Guinness, Caffreys, Grolsch, Greene King IPA.
Directions Off Regents Pk Rd, on corner of Princess Rd
Bass
Bar food 12-3 7-11 Av main course £7
Restaurant 12-3 7-11 Av 3 course à la carte £20 Av 2 course fixed price £7.50

The Globe
NW1 Map B4
43/47 Marylebone Rd, Marylebone NW1 5JY ☎ 0171 9356368
Opposite Baker Street tube station and built in 1735, this three storey pub has been frequented by such luminaries as Charles Dickens and Alfred Lord Tennyson and is a favourite with tourists. Specials include cannelloni, Caribbean chicken, chilli, and a variety of fish dishes.
Directions nr Baker St tube
Scottish & Newcastle
Open 11-11 (Sun 12-10.30)
Bar food 11-3.30 Av main course £5

The Lansdowne
NW1 Map 05 TQ38
90 Gloucester Av, Primrose Hill NW1 8HX
☎ 0171 483 0409
Famous rock stars can often be spotted at this relaxed, traditionally-styled dining pub in secluded Primrose Hill. What was once a seedy strip joint now boasts a constantly changing menu that may offer Jerusalem artichoke soup, goat's cheese and roast onion tart or guinea fowl cooked in milk with mash and cabbage. Principal beers: Greene King IPA, London Pride.
Bass
Open 12-11
Bar food 12.30-2.30 7-10 Av main course £7

The Queens
NW1 Map 05 TQ38
49 Regents Park Rd, Primrose Hill NW1
☎ 0171 5860408
Victorian pub situated in central London. A wide range of snacks, savouries and blackboard specials is available. Main courses range from warm bacon and oyster mushroom salad with garlic croutons and goats cheese sauce, to pan-fried calves liver on swede purée with caramelised onions and sweet pepper sauce. Principal beers: Youngs.
Directions Nearest tube station - Chalk Farm
Youngs
Open 11-11.30
Bar food 12-2.30 7-10
Restaurant 12-2.30 12-2.30 Av 3 course à la carte £15

NW8

Crocker's Folly
NW8 Map A4
24 Aberdeen Place NW8 8JR
☎ 0171 2866608
Named after Frank Crocker who opened this pub in 1898. Nowadays, closely associated with cricket because of its proximity to Lord's. The public bar houses much cricketing memorabilia. Daily specials typically include duck liver and orange pâté, roast pheasant with port and almonds, and various home-made pies. Principal beers: Gales, Brakspears, Greene King, Theakstons.
Directions Nearest tube station - Warwick Avenue
Free House

Open 11-11 (Sun 12-10.30)
Restaurant 12-2.30 6-9.30 Av 3 course à la carte £10

SE16

Mayflower Inn
SE16 Map 05 TQ37
117 Rotherhithe St, Rotherhithe SE16 4NF ☎ 0171 2374088
The ship The Mayflower is believed to have begun her historic voyage to the New World from the Mayflower steps by the present day inn, which was then known as the Spread Eagle. Dishes include steak and ale pie, mushroom balti, fillet of plaice, and Cajun chicken. Principal beers: Abbot Ale, IPA, Stella, Kronenberg.
Directions From A2 off at Surrey Keys roundabout onto Brunel Rd, 3rd L onto Swan Rd, at T jct L, 200m to pub on R
Greene King
Open 11-11 (Winter 12-11)
Restaurant 12-2 7.30-10 Av 3 course à la carte £14

SW1

The Albert
SW1 Map D2
52 Victoria St SW1H 0NP
☎ 0171 2225577 2227606
The Albert has a division bell and a collection of prime minister pictures – no wonder, as it is 500 yards from Buckingham Palace and Whitehall. This is the place to celebrity spot, from cabinet ministers to theatre stars. A traditional menu offers roasts, specials and a dessert trolley. Principal beers: Theakstons Best & Old Peculiar,Directors,Courage Best,John Smiths Smooth.
Scottish & Newcastle
Open 11-11 (Sun 12-10.30)
Bar food 11-10.30 Av main course £4.25
Restaurant 12-11 Av 3 course à la carte £13.95 Av 3 course fixed price £13.95

The Clarence
SW1 Map D3
53 Whitehall SW1A 24P
☎ 0171 930 4808
In the grounds of the Palace of Whitehall, next to the original Scotland Yard building, and opposite the War Rooms, The Clarence is one of a very few public houses that has to obtain its license from Buckingham Palace. Swordfish steak, chicken chasseur, or beefsteak and ale pie may be on the menu here. Principal beers: Theakstons Best, Theakstons Old Peculiar, Greene King, Abbot Ale.
Scottish & Newcastle
Open 11-11 (Sun 12-1.30)
Restaurant 12-3 6-11 Av 3 course fixed price £15

The Orange Brewery
SW1 Map C1
37-39 Pimlico Rd SW1W 8NE
☎ 0171 730 5984
Four-storey Victorian pub with original working gas lamps. Beers and lagers are brewed on site from a full mash brew. Bar snacks include a selection of pies such as lamb and rosemary, and beef and beer. Among the types of sausages are pork and leek, Cajun, and orange and herb. Principal beers: All ales brewed on premises.
Directions Nr Sloane Sq or Victoria tube stations
Scottish & Newcastle
Open 11-11
Bar food 12-3 6-10 Av main course £4.25

SW3

The Cross Keys
SW3 Map 05 TQ38
1 Lawrence St, Chelsea SW3 5NB
☎ 0171 349 9111
This historic Chelsea haunt, these days more by celebrities than the landlord murdered in 1911, dates back to 1765. Recently refurbished by the talented Weller Brothers, a choice of bar, leafy conservatory or gallery settings offers a relaxed, stylish ambience to sample delicious food with a Mediterranean accent . Principal beers: Kronenberg, Fosters, Guinness, John Smiths.
Free House
Open 12-11 (Sun 12-10.30)
Bar food 12-3 6-9 Av main course £5
Restaurant 12-3 7-12 Av 3 course à la carte £15 Av 3 course fixed price £10.50

The Front Page
SW3 Map B1
35 Old Church St SW3 5BS
☎ 0171 3522908
A pub has stood on this site since the early 17th century. The Front Page is a traditional, smart version with wooden panelling, wooden floors and large tables. The menu features a wide variety of dishes such as spicy coconut and mushroom soup, Cumberland sausages and fettucine with asparagus. Principal beers: Brakspears, Theakstons, Fosters, Kronenberg.
Free House
Open 11-11 (Sun 12-10.30)
Bar food 12-2.30 7-10.30 Av main course £6

SW5

O'Neills
SW5 Map 05 TQ38
326 Earl's Court Rd SW5 9BQ
☎ 0171 3739172
A Victorian brewery-turned-bar established by the eponymous Irishman who worked his way up through the ranks to first manage then buy out the business. The Irish theme is taken up in the food which ranges from boxty pancakes, through Finnegan's fry, to Kiss the Blarney Cake. Principal beers: Caffreys, Guinness, Carling, Grolsch.
Bass
Open 12-11

SW6

Jim Thompson's Oriental Bar Restaurant Bazaar
SW6 Map B1
617 Kings Rd SW6 2ES
☎ 0171 731 0999
Situated in London's fashionable King's Road, this once ordinary lads' pub has been transformed into an Oriental bar and restaurant, specialising in south-east Asian cuisine from countries such as Thailand, Malaysia, Vietnam, Cambodia and Indonesia. The lavish interior decor conjures up the decidedly exotic atmosphere of an Oriental bazaar. Principal beers: Tiger, Elephant, Carlsberg, Becks.
Directions Nearest tube station - Fulham Broadway
Free House
Open 12-12
Bar food 12-7.30 Av main course £5
Restaurant 12-11 Av 3 course à la carte £16 Av 3 course fixed price £9.95

SW10

The Chelsea Ram
SW10 Map 05 TQ38
32 Burnaby St SW10 0PL
☎ 0171 351 4008
Busy pub situated in central London. House specials are listed on the blackboard menu. Main course dishes include home cured salmon with pesto linguini with a tomato and tarragon coulis, braised lamb shanks with bubble and squeak served with a mint jus, and Chelsea Ram salad Niçoise with chicken. Principal beers: Youngs.
Directions Nearest tube station- Earls Court
Youngs
Open 11-3 5.30-11.30
Bar food 12-2.30 7-10 Av main course £8
Restaurant 12-2.30 7-10 Av 3 course à la carte £15

W1

The Argyll Arms
W1 Map C4
18 Argyll St, Oxford Circus W1V 1AA
☎ 0171 734 6117
A tavern has stood on this site since 1740, but the present building is mid-Victorian and is notable for its stunning floral displays. The most famous of the distinguished sandwiches in the bar is the hot salt beef, while the restaurant offers traditional roast beef and pies. Principal beers: Tetley, Pedigree, IPA.
Directions Nearest tube station -Oxford Circus
Allied Domecq
Open 11-11
Bar food 11-3 5-7.30 Av main course £5.50
Restaurant 11-3 6-7.30

The Glassblower
W1 Map D3
42 Glasshouse St W1R 6JY
☎ 0171 7348547
A traditional English pub in the heart of the West End, and ideally placed for visiting shops and theatres, The Glassblower has an international menu with the emphasis on traditional English dishes. The speciality of the house is fish and chips and an eclectic sausage

collection, from Cumberland to Cajun. Principal beers: Theakston Best, XB, Old Peculiar, Courage Directors.
Scottish & Newcastle
Open 11-11 (Sun 12-10.30)

W2

The Prince Bonaparte
W2 Map 05 TQ38
80 Chepstow Rd W2 5BE
☎ 0171 2295912
A large Victorian pub, airy and open plan, offering modern British cooking with Eastern, African and Mediterranean influences. Typical dishes are Middle Eastern vegetarian plate, with aubergine, houmous, tabouleh and feta; Cumberland sausages with roast red onions, mash and gravy, and Moroccan lamb tagine with almond cous-cous and harissa. Principal beers: Staropramen, Boddingtons, London Pride, Grolsch.
Bass
Open 12-11
Bar food 12-3 6.30-10.30 Av main course £7.50
Restaurant 3 6.30-10.30 Av 3 course à la carte £14.50

WC1

Cittie of Yorke
WC1 Map E4
22-23 High Holborn WC1V 6BS
☎ 0171 2427670
A pub has been on this site since 1430 and the current building dates from the 17th century. Bar features paintings of illustrious patrons of the past, such as Dickens, Sir Thomas More, and William Morris. A menu of traditional pub food may include lasagne, black pudding, or sausage and mash. Principal beers: Old Brewery Bitter.
Samuel Smith
Open 11-11
Bar food 12-2.30 5.30-10 Av main course £4.25

WC2

Prince of Wales
WC2 Map D4
150-151 Drury Ln, Convent Garden WC2B 5TB
☎ 0171 8365183 0171 2409935
Opened in 1852, this pub is a useful venue for those visiting the many theatres in London's West End. Covent Garden is closeby for shopping and an abundance of street entertainment. Traditional bar food is served such as steak and mushroom pies or roast pork with apple sauce. Principal beers: Old Peculiar, Theakstons Best, Becks, Fosters.
Scottish & Newcastle
Open 11-11 (Mon-Sat) 12-10.30 (Sun)

Surrey

ABINGER Surrey

The Volunteer
ABINGER Map 04 TQ14
Water Ln, Sutton RH5 6PR
☎ 01306 730798
Dating from the 15th-century, this inn has a pond, waterfall and terraced lawns. A wide selection of hot and cold bar snacks are available, plus main courses such as roast duck with black cherry sauce, local game, and rump steak, ale and mushroom pie. Principal beers: Ansells, Sussex, Greene King, Pedigree.
Directions Off B2126 S of A25(Dorking/Guildford)
Free House
Open 11-3 6-11
Bar food 12-2.15 7-9.30 Av main course £6
Restaurant 12-2.15 7-9.30 Av 3 course à la carte £15
Accommodation s£20 d£35

BLACKBROOK Surrey

The Plough at Blackbrook
BLACKBROOK Map 04 TQ14
RH5 4DS ☎ 01306 886603
A part 17th-century, part Victorian pub built over the Blackbrook, on the edge of Holmwood Common, with a large cottage garden at the back. Bar snacks

contd.

and basket meals are served in addition to the international menu, including peppered mackerel, moussaka, steaks and chicken curry. Principal beers: Sussex, Festive, Broadwood, Porter.
Directions Follow A24, L after Dorking Golf Club, Blackbrook signed
King & Barnes
Open 11-2.30 6-11 (Sun 12-3, 7-11)
Bar food 12-2 7-9 Av main course £5.25

BRAMLEY Surrey

Jolly Farmer Inn
BRAMLEY Map 04 TQ04
High St GU5 0HB ☎ 01483 893355
Family run for 25 years, this 350-year-old village pub specialises in good ale and award-winning food. There is also a bistro in the 400-year-old barn. An extensive choice of dishes is produced from market fresh produce including fish, Scotch beef and game in season. Principal beers: Dorset Best, Tongham Tea, Theakston Best, Old Peculiar.
Directions Onto A281, Bramley 3m S of Guildford
Free House
Open 10-3 6-11
Bar food 12-2 6.45-10 Av main course £7.50
Restaurant 12-2 7-9.30 Av 3 course à la carte £17
Accommodation s£30 d£40

CHIDDINGFOLD Surrey

The Crown Inn
CHIDDINGFOLD Map 04 SU93
The Green GU8 4TX ☎ 01428 682255
Once a resting place for Cistercian monks and pilgrims, this Grade II listed building, said to be the oldest established inn in England, has accommodated Elizabeth I and Edward VI. Bar food ranges from simple snacks to steaks, and the panelled restaurant offers a range of seafood, grills and roasts. Principal beers: Charles
Wells Eagle, Badger Best, Tanglefoot, Wadworth 6X.
Directions On A283 between Milford and Petworth
Badger
Open 8-11
Bar food 12-2.30 7-9.30 Av main course £5.50
Restaurant 12-2.30 7-9.30 Av 3 course à la carte £19
Accommodation s£47 d£57

COBHAM Surrey

The Cricketers
COBHAM Map 04 TQ16
Downside KT11 3NX ☎ 01932 862105
A careful blend of old and new architectural features characterises this pub which overlooks the old cricket green. Home-made duck and orange pâté, and deep fried brie with redcurrant jelly are among the starters. Main courses include grilled wing of skate with capers, and nut and mushroom fettucine. Principal beers: Yorkshire, Ruddles County, Websters, Theakstons Best.
Directions From A3 take A245 towards Cobham, 2nd r'about turn R, then 1st R opp Waitrose. Pub 1.5m
Free House
Open 11-2.30 3-12
Bar food 12-2 6.30-10 Av main course £6
Restaurant 12.15-2.30 7.15-11 Av 3 course fixed price £19.95

COLDHARBOUR Surrey

The Plough Inn
COLDHARBOUR Map 04 TQ14
RH5 6HD ☎ 01306 711793
17th-century coaching inn near Leith Hill, the highest point in South East England. Home-made meals figure prominently on the menu, ranging from venison and wild rabbit and smoky bacon pies, to roast pheasant and orange stuffing, and broccoli and Stilton flan for vegetarians. Principal beers: Hall & Woodhouse Dorset Best, Tanglefoot, Wadworths 6X, Adnams Broadside.
Directions M25 J9 - A24 to Dorking. Take A25 towards Guildford. Coldharbour signposted from the one-way system
Free House
Open 11.30-3 6-11 (Sat-Sun 11.30-11)
Bar food 12-2.30 7.30-9.30 Av main course £6.50
Restaurant 12-2.30 7.30-9.30 Av 3 course à la carte £12
Accommodation d£35

COMPTON Surrey

The Harrow Inn
COMPTON Map 04 SU94
The Street GU3 1EG ☎ 01483 810379
Situated in an attractive Surrey village, part of this beamed building dates from the 15th century. Freshly prepared food

includes innovative fish, seafood and game. Try the lemon sole and salmon Doria with wine, cream and cucumber or pork tenderloin with bacon, prunes and a mushroom sauce. Principal beers: Harveys Sussex, Tetleys, Greene King IPA, Burton ale.
Directions 3m S of Guildford on A3 then B3000
Allied Domecq
Open 11-3 5.30-11 (Closed Sun evenings)
Bar food 12-3 6-11 Av main course £6
Restaurant 12-3 6-11 Av 3 course à la carte £20
Accommodation s£30 d£37.50

EGHAM Surrey

The Fox and Hounds

EGHAM Map 04 TQ07

Bishopgate Rd, Englefield Green TW20 0XU ☎ 01784 433098

A good English pub, located on the Royal Park, convenient for walkers and riders. Dishes include home-made steak and kidney pudding, Cumberland sausage with mash and onion gravy, slow roasted half shoulder of lamb with garlic and rosemary, and a selection of fresh fish and game from the blackboard. Principal beers: Greene King,Courage.
Directions From village green turn L into Castle Hill Rd, then R into Bishops Gate Rd
Free House
Open 12-3 6-9.45
Bar food 12.15-2.15 7.15-9.45 Av main course £2.50
Restaurant 12.15-2.15 7.15-9.45 Av 3 course à la carte £25 Av 3 course fixed price £25

ELSTEAD Surrey

The Woolpack

ELSTEAD Map 04 SU94

The Green GU8 6HD ☎ 01252 703106

Built as a wool-bale store in the 18th century, this village inn has plenty of wool industry memorabilia on display, and there are log fires, settles, window seats and spindle backed chairs. The food, on blackboard menus, might include chicken satay, African lamb stew, and salmon with Pernod and fennel. Principal beers: Abbot Ale, Harveys PA, Tetley, Youngs PA.
Directions Milford exit off A3
Ind Coope
Open 11-2.30 6-11
Bar food 12-2.30 7-11
Restaurant 12-2.30 7-11 Av 3 course à la carte £13.50

EWHURST Surrey

The Windmill Inn

EWHURST Map 04 TQ04

Pitch Hill GU6 7NN ☎ 01483 277566

Rebuilt after a fire in 1906. The original inn was the haunt of 18th-century smugglers who used its false roof to store contraband. Nowadays, bar meals include duck and chicken legs in orange sauce and rabbit stew; while restaurant regulars are lobster thermidor and wild mushroom risotto with chopped truffle. Principal beers: Hogs Back Tea, Charles Wells Bombardier, Harveys Pale Ale, Courage
Free House
Open 12-11 (Mon-Sat) 12-10.30 (Sun)
Bar food 12-2.30 7-9.30 Av main course £6
Restaurant 12-2.30 7-9.30 Av 3 course à la carte £25

HASCOMBE Surrey

The White Horse

HASCOMBE Map 04 TQ03

GU8 4JA ☎ 01483 208258

16th-century pub with views of the surrounding hills. The impressive blackboard menu is changed regularly and might include swordfish steak, venison casserole and roast pheasant. Imaginative vegetarian options such as aubergine and spinach bake, and hazelnut roast en croûte with apple and mint sauce, are also available. Principal beers: King and Barnes Sussex, Badger Best, Wadworths 6X.
Ind Coope
Open 11-3 (w/e 11-11) 5.30-11
Bar food 12-2.30 7-10 Av main course £6.50
Restaurant 12-3 7-12 Av 3 course à la carte £22 Av 3 course fixed price £22

MICKLEHAM Surrey

King William IV

MICKLEHAM Map 04 TQ15

Byttom Hill RH5 6EL ☎ 01372 372590

Late 18th-century pub located on a hillside overlooking Norbury Park and the Mole Valley. Lunchtime and evening specials are changed every day. Fresh fish

contd.

is usually available and vegetarian meals, such as mushroom and aubergine bake or red cabbage hot pot with sour cream and chives, are among the blackboard specialities. Principal beers: Tea (Hogs Back brewery), Hop Garden Gold, Badgers Best Bitter, Adnams Best Bitter.
Free House
Open 11-3 6-11
Bar food 12-2 7-9.30 Av main course £6.50

The Running Horses
MICKLEHAM Map 04 TQ15
Old London Rd RH5 6DU
☎ 01372 372279
One of the oldest buildings in the village, this 16th-century coaching inn was built for the London to Dorking run. Bar food includes mussels, large sandwiches and hot crusty baguettes, while the restaurant offers new English cuisine using all fresh ingredients. Principal beers: London Pride, Youngs, King & Barnes, 6X.
Directions Off A24 between Leatherhead & Dorking
Allied Domecq
Open 11-3 5.30-11
Bar food 12-2.30 7-9.30 Av main course £3.75
Restaurant 12-2.30 7-9.30 Av 3 course à la carte £14

NEWDIGATE Surrey

The Six Bells
NEWDIGATE Map 04 TQ14
Village St RH5 5DH ☎ 01306 631276
Opposite the church in the quiet village of Newdigate, this pub was originally a row of cottages built in the 15th century. An extensive bar menu offers everything from baked potatoes and ploughmans to full Sunday lunches, vegetarian specials, and Susan's special pies. Principal beers: Ansells, Youngs, Sussex, Pedigree.

Directions A24 S of Dorking L at Beare Green r'about
Free House
Open 11-3 6-11
Bar food 12-2.15 7-9.30 Av main course £6
Restaurant 12-2.15 7-9.30

OCKLEY Surrey

Bryce's at The Old School House
OCKLEY Map 04 TQ14
RH5 5TH ☎ 01306 627430
Converted 18th-century boys' school and tea room with a strong emphasis on fish in the restaurant. The menu may include pan-fried skate with caper butter, red snapper Cantonese, swordfish steak, or baked Selsey crab. The bar also has a full menu with similar dishes. Principal beers: King & Barnes Sussex, Broadwood & Festive.
Directions 8m S of Dorking on A29
King & Barnes
Open 11-3 6-11
Bar food 12-3 7-10 Av main course £7
Restaurant 12-3 7-10 Av 3 course à la carte £21.50 Av 3 course fixed price £21.50

PIRBRIGHT Surrey

The Royal Oak
PIRBRIGHT Map 04 SU95
Aldershot Rd GU24 0DQ
☎ 01483 232466
The front extension of this pub has an ancient door and a stained glass window originally from a church, and there are large award-winning gardens to relax in. The standard menu is supplemented by daily specials such as mustard and mango gammon, rattle snake junction steak and coconut cream chicken. Principal

beers: Fuggles, Youngs Special, Flowers O.B, Flowers IPA.
Directions M3 J3 take A322 towards Guildford, then A324 towards Aldershot
Whitbread
Open 11-11 (Sun 12-10.30)
Bar food 12-2 6.30-9.30 Av main course £5.95

SHERE Surrey

The White Horse Inn
SHERE Map 04 TQ04
Middle St GU5 9HS ☎ 01483 202518
In a beautiful village (touristy in summer), this is a 15th-century traditional pub with huge beams and two large, open fires. It is said to have been popular with smugglers in the 18th century. There is an interesting (short) menu including Cajun sausages and vegetable Korma. Principal beers: Theakstons,6X,Fosters,Holstein.
Directions South of A25 between Guildford & Dorking
Scottish & Newcastle
Open 11-11 (Sun 12-10.30)
Bar food 12-2.30 7-9.30 Av main course £6.95

THURSLEY Surrey

Three Horseshoes
THURSLEY Map 04 SU93
Dye House Rd GU8 6QD
☎ 01252 703268
The accent is on conversation and relaxation at this traditional establishment offering panoramic views of tranquil countryside. The constantly varying menu features fresh, home-cooked fare with a cosmopolitan influence. Don't ask for chips but sample crab filled mushrooms, lamb Bourguignonne and Victorian sherry trifle. Principal beers: Gales HSB, Butser, Fullers London Pride.
Directions Thursley exit from A3, between Milford & Hindhead
Free House
Open 12-3 6-11
Bar food 12-2 7-9 Av main course £6
Restaurant 12-2 7-9 Av 3 course à la carte £15
Accommodation s£30 d£40

WEST CLANDON Surrey

Onslow Arms
WEST CLANDON Map 04 TQ05
The Street GU4 7TE ☎ 01483 222447
17th-century hostelry that takes pride in its extensive menu and carvery. Moules marinière, home-made noodles with seafood, roast duckling in orange sauce, and calves' liver in Dijon mustard sauce, are supplemented by daily specials. Handy for both Gatwick and Heathrow. Principal beers: Courage, Whitbread, Youngs, King & Barnes.
Directions FromA3 take A247
Free House
Bar food 12-2 7-9.30 Av main course £4.25
Restaurant 12-2 7-11 Av 3 course à la carte £17 Av 3 course fixed price £14.95

WINDLESHAM Surrey

Brickmakers Arms
WINDLESHAM Map 04 SU96
Chertsey Rd GU20 6HT
☎ 01276 472267
First class food and quality wines draw a clientele from all over southern England to this pub/restaurant which, backing on to Sunningdale Golf Club, is something of a 'nineteenth hole'. Inclusive or à la carte, menus feature mouth-watering, innovative dishes. Try roast monkfish with chorizo and tomato sauce. Principal beers: Courage Best, Fullers London Pride.

Directions On B386 between Bagshot & Longcross
Free House
Open 11.30-3 5-11
Bar food 12-2.30 6-10 Av main course £10
Restaurant 12-2.30 6-10 Av 3 course à la carte £25 Av 3 course fixed price £17.50

WITLEY Surrey

The White Hart
WITLEY Map 04 SU93
Petworth Rd GU8 5PH ☎ 01428 683695
16th-century coaching inn with illustrious connections. George Elliot based characters in her novel 'Middlemarch' on the clientele, the original sign is in the Victoria and Albert, and Richard II used the pub as a hunting lodge. Menu may include tuna and cheese bake, steak and kidney in ale pie, or salmon and broccoli lasagne. Principal beers: Masterbrew, Spitfire, Hurliman.

Directions On main A283 between Milford & Chiddingfold
Shepherd Neame
Open 11-2.30 5.30-11 (Wknd 11-11)
Bar food 12-2 6-10 Av main course £4.50
Restaurant 12-2 6-10 Av 3 course à la carte £10

Sussex, East

ALCISTON Sussex, East Map 05 TQ50

Rose Cottage Inn
ALCISTON Map 05 TQ50
BN26 6UW ☎ 01323 870377
Small 17th-century cottage style pub close to the South Downs Way. Blackboard specials are regularly changed, but typically include rabbit and bacon pie, beef and ale pie, char-grilled lamb steak with cream of tarragon sauce, and venison braised in port and Guinness. Principal beers: Harveys.
Directions Off A27 between Eastbourne & Lewes
Free House
Open 11.30-3 6.30-11
Bar food 12-2 7-10 Av main course £5.50
Restaurant 7-9 Av 3 course à la carte £13.50

ARLINGTON Sussex, East

Old Oak Inn
ARLINGTON Map 05 TQ05
BN26 6SJ ☎ 01323 482072
Originally built as a poorhouse for the village in 1733, situated at the edge of Abbots Wood near Michelham Priory. Bar snacks and main course dishes are served. The latter include fried goujons of sole, grilled Cajun chicken breast, and roast duck with blackcurrant and cranberry sauce. Principal beers: Dorset Best Bitter, Harveys.
Directions N of A27 between Polegate & Lewes
Free House
Open 11-3 6-11
Bar food 12-2 7-9 Av main course £5
Restaurant 7-9 Av 3 course à la carte £12.95

BARCOMBE Sussex, East

The Anchor Inn
BARCOMBE Map 05 TQ41
Anchor Ln BN8 5BS ☎ 01273 400414
Built in 1790 on the banks of the River Ouse with fine views of the South Downs. A wide selection of house specials include roast pork with apple and cider sauce, grilled halibut with fresh herb sauce, sirloin steak with shallot sauce, and lamb cutlets with thyme and Madeira sauce. Principal beers: Badger, Tanglefoot, Harveys.
Directions L from A26 (Lewes/ Uckfield rd)
Free House
Open 11-11.30 (Sun 12-11)
Bar food 12-3 6-9 Av main course £5.50
Restaurant 12-3 7-9 Av 3 course à la carte £20
Accommodation s£30 d£52

BERWICK Sussex, East

The Cricketers Arms
BERWICK Map 05 TQ50
BN26 6SP ☎ 01323 870469
Converted from 17th-century flint cottages at the foot of the South Downs, the Cricketer's remains a traditional pub. Favourites such as steak and kidney pudding and local cod in batter are supported by daily specials including a vegetarian dish and maybe wild boar

sausages or pork in cider. Principal beers: Harveys traditional best bitter.
Directions Off A27 between Polegate & Lewes(follow signs for Berwick Church)
Free House
Open 11-3 6-11
Bar food 12-2.15 6.30-9.30 Av main course £5

BLACKBOYS Sussex, East

The Blackboys Inn
BLACKBOYS Map 05 TQ52
Lewes Rd TN22 5LG ☎ 01825 890283
Half-timbered coaching inn, mostly dating from the early 17th-century, set in woodland grounds with a pond. Main course menu features braised pheasant with red wine and sweet chestnuts, venison marinated with port, redcurrants and juniper berries, lobster Thermidor, and baked crab Mornay. Desserts include Blackboys Boat and crème brulée. Principal beers: Harveys Best Pale, Armarda(summer), Old(winter).
Directions On B2102 between Uckfield & Heathfield
Harveys of Lewes
Open 11-3 6-11
Bar food 12-3 6.30-11 Av main course £6.50
Restaurant 12-3 7-11 Av 3 course à la carte £14

BRIGHTON Sussex, East

The Greys
BRIGHTON Map 04 TQ30
105 Southover St BN2 2UA
☎ 01273 680734
Venture off the beaten track to find this small bar where the Belgian Chef prepares specialities from his home country and around the world. Sample magret of duck with Belgian beer and black cherries or cassoulet of king prawns with fennel and Pastis in a informal atmosphere. Principal beers: Flowers Original, Chiswick, Spinaker Classic, Guinness.
Free House
Open 11-3 5.30-11 (wknd 11-11)
Bar food 12-2 7-9 Av main course £6.95

AA members can call AA Hotel Booking Service on 0990 050505 to book at AA recognised hotels and B & Bs in the UK and Ireland, or through our Internet site: http://www.theaa.co.uk/hotels

CHIDDINGLY Sussex, East

The Six Bells
CHIDDINGLY Map 05 TQ51
BN8 6HE ☎ 01825 872227
A large country freehouse, with a beer garden and fish pond, serving a good selection of pub food, including ploughman's, pigman's (ham, salad and French bread) and shepherd's pie. There's a choice of vegetarian fare, such as Stilton and walnut pie, plus popular pasta, curry and chilli dishes. Principal beers: Directors, John Smiths, Harveys.
Directions E of A22 between Hailsham & Uckfield(turn opp Golden Cross PH)
Free House
Open 11-3 6-11
Bar food 11-2.30 6-10.30 Av main course £3

COWBEECH Sussex, East

Merrie Harriers
COWBEECH Map 05 TQ61
BU27 4JQ ☎ 01323 833108
200-year-old country pub with low beamed ceiling and open fireplaces. Lunchtime specials feature pork and mushroom Stroganoff, and home-made turkey and ham pie. The main menu includes breast of duck with home-made Morello cherry sauce, and gammon steak with home-made apricot and brandy sauce. Principal beers: Harveys and Whitbread.
Free House
Open 11-2.30 6-11
Bar food 12-2 6-9

EWHURST GREEN Sussex, East

The White Dog Inn
EWHURST GREEN Map 05 TQ72
Village St TN31 5TD ☎ 01580 830264
A 16th-century country inn, with brick and stone floors and a large inglenook fireplace. It overlooks Bodiam Castle to the rear, and has lovely gardens with facilities for caravans. Speciality dishes include crevettes with garlic butter, steaks, and chicken Dijonnaise. Bar snacks are also available. Principal beers: Harveys, London Pride, Stella, Fosters.
Directions Between Staplecross & Bodiam off B2165 & B2244
Free House
Open 12-3.30 6.30-Closing (Except for Mon Nights)

contd.

Bar food 12-3.30 7-Closing Av main course £5
Restaurant 12-3.30 7-Closing Av 3 course à la carte £16

EXCEAT Sussex, East

The Golden Galleon
EXCEAT Map 05 TV59
Exceat Bridge BN25 4AB
☎ 01323 892247
Popular eighteenth-century inn that is believed to have inspired Rudyard Kipling's 'Song of the Smugglers'. Italian owner brings the taste of the Med to pub staples such as roast chicken (in olive oil and rosemary), and the menu is dotted with Italian specialities. Real ale comes from the pub's own micro-brewery. Principal beers: Cuckmere Haven, Harveys Armada, Greene King Abbot.
Directions On the A259 1 1/2m E of Seaford
Free House
Bar food 12-2 6-9

FLETCHING Sussex, East

The Griffin Inn
FLETCHING Map 05 TQ42
TN22 3SS ☎ 01825 722890
16th-century inn with open fireplaces, sloping floors and priest hole. Bar meals include rabbit pie with lentils, spicy Thai-style crab claws, and Italian sausages with beans and polenta. Thursdays Fish Fest features pan-fried skate wing with capers and black butter, and salmon with roasted almonds and lemon Hollandaise. Principal beers: Harveys Best, Tanglefoot, T.E.A, Courage Directors.
Directions From East Grinstead take A22 then A275.Village signed on L
Free House
Open 12-3 6-11 (Sun 7-11)
Bar food 12-2.30 7-9.30 Av main course £6
Restaurant 12.30-2.30 7.30-9.30
Accommodation s£40 d£50

FOREST ROW Sussex, East

Black Peter's Bar at Brambletye Hotel
FOREST ROW Map 05 TQ43
The Square RH18 5EZ ☎ 01342 824144
Built in 1866, later converted into a hotel. Sir Arthur Conan Doyle was a regular visitor, and the hotel is mentioned in the Sherlock Holmes story *The Adventure of Black Peter.* Main courses include duck marinated in ginger and redcurrant, mushroom Stroganoff, and beef Wellington on a rich port sauce. Principal beers: Harveys, Theakstons, Directors.
Directions On A22 S of East Grinstead
Free House
Open 10-11
Bar food 12-2.30 6.15-10 Av main course £5
Restaurant 12-2.30 6.15-10 Av 3 course à la carte £15 Av 4 course fixed price £15
Accommodation s£35 d£50

GUN HILL Sussex, East

The Gun Inn
GUN HILL Map 05 TQ51
TN21 0JU ☎ 01825 872361
This cottage-style inn gets its name from the area's iron industry. Some of the first canons were cast here. It's a favourite with walkers as the Wealden Way runs through the garden. Fillet steak Wellington or Alison's pasta are among the freshly prepared recipes served informally in the bar. Principal beers: Harveys, Adnams, Larkins.
Directions Take A22 from Eastbourne, then A267.At Little Chef follow signs for Gun Hill, pub is 2m on right.
Free House
Open 11-3 6-11 (Summer & Wkends 11-11) (Sun 12-11)
Bar food 12-3 6-11 Av main course £6
Accommodation d£36

HARTFIELD Sussex, East

Anchor Inn
HARTFIELD Map 05 TQ43
Church St TN7 4AG ☎ 01892 770424
Situated in the heart of Winnie the Pooh country, on the edge of Ashdown Forest, is this 14th-century pub with stone floors and a very large inglenook fireplace. Food includes bar snacks and dishes such as spaghetti with seafood, smoked haddock Monte Carlo, lamb kebab and sirloin steak. Principal beers: Fremlins, Harveys, Flowers, Marstons Pedigree.
Directions B2110 E of Forest Row
Free House
Open 11-11
Bar food 12-2 6-10 Av main course £4
Restaurant 12-2 7-9.30 Av 3 course à la carte £17.50
Accommodation s£30 d£40

KINGSTON (NEAR LEWES) Sussex, East

The Juggs
KINGSTON (NEAR LEWES) Map 05 TQ30
The Street BN7 3NT ☎ 01273 472523
Rambling fifteenth-century inn with delightful garden and interesting selection of freshly cooked food. Busy, busy, busy, but electronic pagers inform visitors when the food is ready. Expect steak and kidney pie, locally made sausages, and outstanding home-made desserts - the summer pudding is highly recommended. Principal beers: Harveys Best Bitter, King & Barnes, Stella Artois, Merrydown Premium.

Directions Off A27 E of Brighton
Free House
Open 11-3 6-11
Bar food 12-2 6-9.30 Av main course £6
Restaurant 12-2 6-9.30 Av 3 course à la carte £12

LITLINGTON Sussex, East

Plough & Harrow
LITLINGTON Map 05 TQ50
BN26 5RE ☎ 01323 870632
Full of character, this listed 15th-century village pub, with oak beams and an inglenook fireplace, has an abundance of railway memorabilia. Food in the bar and the Dining Car restaurant includes home-made soups and pies, local crab, char-grilled steaks and a range of snacks. Principal beers: Hall & Woodhouse, IPA, Badger, Tanglefoot.
Directions S of A27 between Lewes & Polegate
Free House
Open 11-3 6.30-11
Bar food 11.30-2.30 7-10 Av main course £6
Restaurant 11.30-2.30 7-10

MAYFIELD Sussex, East

The Middle House
MAYFIELD Map 05 TQ52
High St TN20 6AB ☎ 01435 872146
Originally built for Sir Thomas Gresham, founder of the London Stock Exchange, this Elizabethan building is Grade I listed and has a Grinling Gibbons carved fireplace. A varied menu may include calves liver Jerez, roast leg of lamb, wild forest mushroom rosti, or Dover sole grilled with lobster and prawns. Principal beers: Everards original, Harveys best, Greene King, Abbot.
Directions E of A267 S of Tunbridge Wells
Free House
Open 11-11
Bar food 12-2 7-9.30
Restaurant 12-2 7-9.30 Av 3 course à la carte £20 Av 3 course fixed price £15
Accommodation s£45 d£55

OLD HEATHFIELD Sussex, East

Star Inn
OLD HEATHFIELD Map 05 TQ52
TN21 9AH ☎ 01435 863570
Originally built to house the stonemasons who worked on the village church in the 14th century, the Star has an award-winning garden, the view from which was painted by Turner. Typical menu ranges from jacket potatoes and ploughmans', to poached salmon and baked aubergine topped with brie. Principal beers: Harveys, Youngs, Greene King.
Free House
Open 11.30-3 5.30-11
Bar food 12-2.15 7-9.30 Av main course £5.95
Restaurant 12-2.15 7-9.30 Av 3 course à la carte £15

UPPER DICKER Sussex, East

The Plough
UPPER DICKER Map 05 TQ50
Coldharbour Rd BN27 3QJ
☎ 01323 844859
Built in the 17th century as a farmhouse The Plough has been a pub since the late 18th century. Its situation in the heart of the East Sussex countryside makes it ideal for walkers. A menu of home-cooked food is on offer with a choice of daily specials. Principal beers: Master Brew, Spitfire, Hurlimann.

contd.

Directions Off A22 W of Hailsham
Shepherd Neame
Open 11-3 6-11 (Sun 12-3, 7-10.30, Summer wknd 11-11)
Bar food 12-2.30 6-9.30 Av main course £3.95
Restaurant 12-2.30 6-9.30

WARBLETON Sussex, East

The Warbill in Tun Inn
WARBLETON Map 05 TQ61
Church Hill TN21 9BD ☎ 01435 830636
12th-century alehouse whose peculiar name is thought to be a play on the name of the village Warbleton. Its colourful history involves smugglers, priest holes and The Beatles, who drank here with manager Brian Epstein. House specialities include Barnsley chops, vegetable lasagne, lemon sole fillets and Mediterranean beef casserole. Principal beers: Harveys Best, Directors, John Smiths, Guinness.
Free House
Open 11-3 7-11 (10.30 Sun)
Bar food 12-2.30 7-11
Restaurant 12-3 7-11.30 Av 3 course à la carte £13.50 Av 3 course fixed price £9.25

WEST FIRLE Sussex, East

The Ram Inn
WEST FIRLE Map 05 TQ40
BN8 6NS ☎ 01273 858222
17th-century coaching inn situated at the foot of the South Downs. Handy for Glyndebourne Opera House. Typical dishes from the bar menu range from steak and mushroom pie cooked in Irish stout, and roast chicken coated in Indian spices, to mushroom and leek lasagne with white wine cream. Principal beers: Otter Bitter, Harveys Best Bitter.

Directions Off A27 3m E of Lewes
Free House
Open 11.30-3 7-11 (Sun 12-3, 7-10.30)
Bar food 12-2 7-9 Av main course £8
Accommodation d£50

WITHYHAM Sussex, East

The Dorset Arms
WITHYHAM Map 05 TQ01
TN7 4BD ☎ 01892 770278
Hops, flowers and hanging baskets adorn this tile-hung pub on the village green. There's a traditional bar serving pub grub, and a pretty cottage-style restaurant offering a blackboard menu with dishes such as liver and bacon, spinach and pasta bake and sticky toffee pudding. Special menus are available at weekends. Principal beers: Harvey's Best,Pale Ale.

Directions on B2110 2 miles E of Hartfield
Harveys of Lewes
Open 11.30-3 5.30-11
Bar food 12-2 7.30-9.30 Av main course £5
Restaurant 12-2 7.30-9.30 Av 3 course à la carte £10.50 Av 3 course fixed price £12.50

Sussex, West

AMBERLEY Sussex, West

The Bridge Inn
AMBERLEY Map 04 TQ01
Houghton Bridge BN18 9LR
☎ 01798 831619
Inhabiting a 250-year-old, Grade II listed building, the Bridge has a homely atmosphere, with original oil and watercolour paintings and open fires. Blackboard specials feature tasty dishes such as grilled sardines, rainbow trout and liver and bacon, and there are special menus for occasions such as Valentine's Day and Hallowe'en. Principal beers: Gales Best Bitter,Boddingtons,Marstons Pedigree, Flowers Original, Morlands Speckled Hen.
Directions 5m N of Arundel on B2139
Free House
Open 11-3 5.45-11.30
Bar food 11-2.30 7-11 Av main course £6.25
Restaurant 11-2.30 7-11 Av 3 course à la carte £14 Av 3 course fixed price £15

ARDINGLY Sussex, West

The Avins Bridge Restaurant & Bar
ARDINGLY Map 05 TQ32
College Rd RH17 6SH
☎ 01444 892390
At this turn of the century railway/ coaching hotel in quiet village location, the food's main theme is English with some European influences. Try freshly prepared dishes like seafood ravioli with lobster sauce or peppered fillet of lamb, then indulge in orange syllabub with tuiles biscuits. Principal beers: King & Barnes Festival, Carlsberg.
Open 12-3 7-11
Restaurant 12-3 7-11 Av 3 course à la carte £18

ASHURST Sussex, West

The Fountain Inn
ASHURST Map 04 TQ11
BN44 3AP ☎ 01403 710219
Originally a farm cottage, dating back 400 years, this friendly pub has low beams, a slabstone floor and a large inglenook fireplace. The imaginative menu offers a good range of dishes including home-made soup, lamb and apricot casserole, rainbow trout, vegetable koulibiak, treacle tart and hot chocolate fudge cake. Principal beers: Chadiwcks, John Smiths, Courage Best, Fullers London Pride.
Directions On B2135 N of Steyning
Free House
Open 11-2.30 6-11
Bar food 12-2 7-9.30 Av main course £5.95
Restaurant 12-2 7-9.30

BILLINGSHURST Sussex, West

Burdocks
BILLINGSHURST Map 04 TQ02
59 High St RH14 9QP
☎ 01403 782750
Named after a previous owner's dog, this village restaurant and tea-room dates from the 16th-century. Breakfast, morning coffee, afternoon tea, lunch and evening meals. Sun-dried tomato and mushroom pasta, venison casserole, treacle tart and sticky toffee pudding are blackboard regulars. Sunday brunch is a speciality, as are the interesting sandwiches.
Directions Town centre
Restaurant 11.30-finish 7-finish Av 3 course à la carte £11

Ye Olde Six Bells
BILLINGSHURST Map 04 TQ02
76 High St RH14 9QS ☎ 01403 782124
Dating back to 1436 this Sussex pub boasts flagstone floors, an Inglenook fireplace, and the legend of a cursed tunnel to the nearby church. One of Sotheby's auction-rooms is also in the village. Cauliflower cheese, cottage pie, or lasagne may be on today's menu. Principal beers: King & Barnes Sussex Ale, Broadwood Ale & Festive, Guinness.

contd.

Directions Village centre
King & Barnes
Open 11-2.30 5.30-11 (Sun 12-3, 7-10.30)
Bar food 12-2 7-9 Av main course £3.65

BURPHAM Sussex, West

George & Dragon
BURPHAM Map 04 TQ00
BN18 9RR ☎ 01903 883131
17th-century pub, situated near the River Avon and a Saxon burial ground. Splendid views of Arundel Castle from nearby cricket green. Dinner menu ranges from sautéed lambs kidneys in sherry cream sauce, red mullet and scallop duet, to open cannelloni, and chicken breast served in whisky and oyster sauce. Principal beers: Harveys Best, Arundel ASB, Courage Directors, Woodfords.
Directions Off A27 1m E of Arundel, signed Burpham
Belchers
Open 11-2.30 6-11
Bar food 12-2 7-9.45 Av main course £5.60
Restaurant 12.15-2 7.15-9.45 Av 3 course fixed price £19.50

CHILGROVE Sussex, West

The White Horse at Chilgrove
CHILGROVE Map 04 SU81
PO18 9HX ☎ 01243 535219
A pub with restaurants, dating from 1765, situated in a peaceful South Downs village opposite the large village green. The menus are on the wall, offering traditional English fare with home-made ices in the bar, and English and French cuisine in the restaurants, supported by an extensive wine list. Principal beers: Ballard Best Bitter.
Directions On B2141 between Chichester and Petersfield
Free House
Open 11-2.30 6-11
Bar food 12-3 6-11 Av main course £7.50
Restaurant 12-3 7-12 Av 3 course à la carte £19.50 Av 3 course fixed price £19.50
Accommodation s£35 d£35

COMPTON Sussex, West

Coach & Horses
COMPTON Map 04 SU71
The Square PO18 9HA ☎ 01705 631228
The atmosphere is lively in the half panelled Village Bar of this 15th-century coaching inn. There's bar billiards and the old stables are used as a skittle alley. Local game and fresh fish figure prominently, and while the menus are similar, the restaurant offers more choice than the bar. Principal beers: Fullers ESB.
Directions On B2146 S of Petersfield
Free House
Open 11-2.30 6-11
Bar food 12-2 6-9.30 Av main course £5
Restaurant 12-2 6-9.30 Av 3 course à la carte £15

COPTHORNE Sussex, West

Hunters Moon Inn
COPTHORNE Map 04 TQ33
Copthorne Bank RH10 3JF
☎ 01342 713309
This pub, surrounded by quiet green fields, is part of a village which was once a haven for smugglers and poachers. A typical menu - using legally obtained ingredients - includes oven-baked duck breast, red snapper fillet, Highland smoked salmon platter, and chestnut and parsnip crumble in spinach cream sauce. Principal beers: Badger, Spitfire.
Directions Copthorne Way to r'about, 1st exit L, on to T Jct, R into Copthorne Bank
Free House
Open 11-3 5-11
Bar food 12-2
Restaurant 7-9.30 Av 3 course à la carte £16.50
Accommodation s£25 d£50

EARTHAM Sussex, West

The George Inn
EARTHAM Map 04 SU90
PO18 0LT ☎ 01243 814340
Within a mile of the South Downs Way, this 18th-century traditional pub is a good spot for a well-earned rest on a good walk. There is a barbecue and herb garden. The menu has specials such as breast of Magret duck with mead and caramelised pineapple, Olde English pies, speciality steaks, and farmer's brunches. Principal beers: ASB,Gales Best,BBB.

Directions From A27 at Tangmere r'about follow signs for Crockerhill/Eartham
Gales
Open 11-3 6.30-11
Bar food 12-2.30 6-9.30 Av main course £5.95
Restaurant 12-2 7-9 Av 3 course à la carte £15

FERNHURST Sussex, West

The Red Lion
FERNHURST Map 04 SU82
The Green GU27 3HY ☎ 01428 653304
Revive at this cosy 15th century village pub close to popular walking routes from a wide choice of home-cooked dishes. Spicy Armenian lamb or homemade fishcakes with tomato salsa could be followed by a delicious raspberry linzer torte. Principal beers: King & Barnes, Wadworth 6X, Adnams, Guinness.
Directions From A3 at Hindhead take A287 to Haslemere, then A286 to Fernhurst
Free House
Open 11-3 5-11
Bar food 11-3 5-11 Av main course £6
Restaurant 11-3 7-11 Av 3 course à la carte £15

HALNAKER Sussex, West

Anglesey Arms
HALNAKER Map 04 SU90
PO18 0NQ ☎ 01243 773474
At this traditional English country pub set in a picturesque village close to 'Glorious Goodwood' the constantly changing daily specials may include Selsey lobster salad or , in the bar, a tasty array of snacks from calamares to quiche. Principal beers: Friary, Burton, Greene King, Carlsberg.
Directions 4m from centre of Chichester on A285
Free House
Open 11-3 6-11 (Sun 12-3, 7-10.30)
Bar food 12-2 7.30-10 Av main course £9
Restaurant 12-2 7.30-10 Av 3 course à la carte £15 Av 3 course fixed price £8.50

KIRDFORD Sussex, West

The Half Moon Inn
KIRDFORD Map 04 TQ02
RH14 0LT ☎ 01403 820223
A beamed 17th-century coaching inn, with an interesting inglenook fireplace, in a village setting opposite the 14th-century church. Sandwiches, fresh fish, skins and ribs are offered in the bar, while the restaurant menu is slanted towards seafood, with some meat and vegetarian dishes. Principal beers: Arundel, Flowers, Boddingtons, 6X.
Directions Off A272 between Billingshurst & Petworth. At Wisborough Green follow signs 'Kirdford'
Whitbread
Open 11-11
Bar food 12-2.30 7-9.30 Av main course £4
Restaurant 12-2.30 7-9.30 Av 3 course à la carte £20
Accommodation s£25 d£40

LOWER BEEDING Sussex, West

Jeremy's at the Crabtree
LOWER BEEDING Map 04 TQ22
Brighton Rd RH13 6PT ☎ 01403 891257
Writer Hilaire Belloc was a visitor to this inn which has a Georgian dining room and an original 16th-century beamed bar. Marinated pigeon and caramelised pear salad, seared tuna on egg noodles, or cod fillet with watercress and basil butter may be on today's menu. Principal beers: Sussex.
Directions 4m SE of Horsham on A281
Free House
Open 11-3.30 6-11.20
Bar food 12.30-2 7.30-10 Av main course £9.50
Restaurant 12.30-2.30 7.30-9.30

LURGASHALL Sussex, West

The Noah's Ark
LURGASHALL Map 04 SU92
The Green GU28 9ET ☎ 01428 707346
Built in 1537, this pub overlooks the village green where cricket is the summer highlight. Starters feature mussels in garlic butter and watercress soup. The main course menu includes home-made curries, steaks and various omelettes, plus moussaka, calves liver and bacon, and vegetable Cumberland pie. Principal beers: Rayments Special Bitter, Greene

contd.

King, seasonal ales.
Directions Off A283 N of Petworth
Greene King
Open 11.30-3, 6-11 (Sat-Sun open all day)
Bar food 12-2 7.30-10 Av main course £5.75
Restaurant 12-2 7.30-10 Av 3 course à la carte £15.75

MIDHURST Sussex, West

The Elsted Inn
MIDHURST Map 04 SQ82
Elsted Marsh GU29 0JT
☎ 01730 813662
A Victorian local, built to serve the long gone railway station (hence the old railway photos). The simple surroundings belie the quality of the food - look out for hand-made sausages and raised pies, Sussex bacon pudding, fishcakes with crab or salmon, and the pub's favourite pud, treacle tart. Principal beers: Ballards: Trotton, Best, Wild, Wassail.
Directions From Midhurst take A272 W.After 4m take L signed 'Elsted & Harting'(NB Elsted Marsh also known as Lower Elsted)
Free House
Open 11-3 5.30-11
Bar food 12-2.30 7-9 Av main course £4.95
Restaurant 12-2.30 7-9 Av 3 course à la carte £15
Accommodation s£25 d£45

OFFHAM Sussex, West

Black Rabbit
OFFHAM Map 04 TQ00
Mill Ln BN18 9PB ☎ 01903 882828
This popular inn, thought uniquely named, is located on a sheltered stretch of the River Arun enjoying unspoiled views of Arundel Castle. All tastes and appetites are catered for in the Boathouse restaurant at lunchtime or for a cosier dinner, follow creamy garlic mushrooms with salmon Royale. Principal beers: Dorset Best, Tanglefoot, Hard Tackle, Badger IPA.
Directions Go from Arundel Bridge on the Mill Road past the Wildfowl Trust and keep straight on for 300yrds
Hall & Woodhouse
Open 11-11
Bar food 12-3 6.30-10.30 Av main course £4.50
Restaurant 12-3.30 6.30-10.30 Av 3 course à la carte £11.95 Av 3 course fixed price £11.95

OVING Sussex, West

The Gribble Inn
OVING Map 04 SU90
PO20 6BP ☎ 01243 786893
Atmospheric thatched country inn with an abundance of beams, bric-a-brac and an old-fashioned cottage garden, the former home of poet/writer Rose Gribble. Their own on-site brewery supplies the ale, the food is simple pub fare - home-made soups, scrumpy chicken, country ham, braised steak, fish and chips. Principal beers: Gribble Inn, Pigs Ear, Ewe Brew, Reg's Tipple.
Directions From A27 take A259, at roundabout after 1m turn L, 1st R, 1st L to Oving
Badger
Open 11-3 6-11
Bar food 12-2.30 6.30-9.30 Av main course £5.95

PETWORTH Sussex, West

The Halfway Bridge Inn
PETWORTH Map 04 SU92
Halfway Bridge GU2 9BP
☎ 01798 861281
Built in 1710 as a coaching inn, overlooking the River Lod. Main dishes range from smoked haddock with bubble & squeak and poached egg, and grilled bream with roasted vegetables and an orange butter sauce, to wild boar steak with an apple and scrumpy sauce. Principal beers: Gales HSB, Cheriton Brewhouse Pots Ale, Fullers London Pride.
Directions On A272
Free House
Open 11-3 6-11
Bar food 12-2 7-10 Av main course £7.95
Restaurant 12-2 7-10 Av 3 course à la carte £15

ROWHOOK Sussex, West

The Chequers Inn
ROWHOOK Map 04 TQ13
RH12 3PY ☎ 01403 790480
16th-century inn named after the chequer tree in its garden. Interesting soups on offer include cream of celery and Stilton, and cream of leek and almond. Among the other dishes are game casserole, and breaded aubergine with wild mushrooms and four cheeses in spicy tomato sauce. Principal beers: Brakspears, London Pride, Flowers Original.
Directions Off A29 NW of Horsham
Free House
Open 11-3 6-11
Bar food 12-2.30 7-10 Av main course £5.95
Restaurant 12-2.30 7-10 Av 3 course à la carte £12.50

RUSPER Sussex, West

Star Inn
RUSPER Map 04 TQ23
High St RH12 4RA ☎ 01293 871264
15th-century coaching inn, said to be the oldest pub in Sussex. The menu is styled as a newspaper, 'The Daily Star', and may feature feta cheese goujons wrapped in spinach leaves, shellfish platter, or 'Hog's Breath' chilli, as well as a selection of baguettes, sandwiches, jacket potatoes, and salads. Principal beers: London Pride, Pedigree, Brakespear, Strongs Country.
Directions A24 S, at Capel roundabout take Rusper turning
Whitbread
Open 11-11 (Sun 12-10.30)
Accommodation s£30 d£45

SOUTH HARTING Sussex, West

The Ship Inn
SOUTH HARTING Map 04 SU71
GU31 5PZ ☎ 01730 825302
17th-century inn constructed from a ship's timbers, hence its name. Speciality pastry dishes include salmon en croûte and game pie. Among the main courses are veal scallopine, honey-roast shank of pork, and chicken tikka masala. A range of bar snacks is also available. Principal beers: Palmers.
Directions From Petersfield take B2146 towards Chichester
Free House
Open 11-11 (Winter,Tue-Thu closed 3-5)
Bar food 12-2.30 7-9.30 Av main course £6
Restaurant 12-2.30 7-9.30

The White Hart
SOUTH HARTING Map 04 SU71
High St GU31 5QB ☎ 01730 825355
16th-century inn with oak beams and inglenook fireplaces, overlooking the South Downs. Among the interesting starters are moules bonne femme, mushrooms d' amour, and smoked salmon mousse. The main course dishes include chicken Penang, Malaysian-style lamb kopa and, for vegetarians, avocado and corn bake. Principal beers: Burton, Friary, Pedigree.
Directions From Petersfield take B2146 towards Chichester
Free House
Open 11-3 6-11
Bar food 11-3 7-11 Av main course £5.25
Restaurant 11-3 7-11 Av 3 course à la carte £15 Av 3 course fixed price £15

STEDHAM Sussex, West

Hamilton Arms/Nava Thai Restaurant
STEDHAM Map 04 SU82
Hamilton Arms School Ln GU29 0NZ
☎ 01730 812555
Named after Emma Hamilton, Lord Nelson's mistress, the pub is located in a picture postcard village opposite the common. This is the first English pub cum-Thai restaurant, and while the bar offers the usual pub grub, the restaurant serves traditional Thai cuisine, inspired by the Thai landlady. Principal beers: Ballards Best, Fullers London Pride, Courage Directors.
Directions Off A272 between Midhurst & Petersfield
Free House
Open 11-3 6-11
Bar food 12-2.30 6-10.30 Av main course £5.25
Restaurant 12-2.30 6-10.30 Av 3 course à la carte £16 Av 4 course fixed price £17

STOPHAM Sussex, West

White Hart at Stopham Bridge
STOPHAM Map 04 TQ01
RH20 1DS ☎ 01798 873321
A traditional country pub, situated on the banks of the River Arun beside the Stopham Bridge (c1306), which is

contd.

closed to traffic. It has a seafood restaurant with an extensive range, plus separate meat and vegetarian menus. Dishes include smoked eel fillets and red snapper Cantonese. Principal beers: Flowers, Ruddles, King & Barnes Sussex.
Directions Off the A283 between Petworth & Pulborough, 1st turning on L, past Pulborough railway bridge, opposite 'Country Gardens'
Whitbread
Open 11-3 6.30-11
Bar food 12-2.30 6.30-9.30 Av main course £4.75
Restaurant 12-2.30 6.30-9.30
Av 3 course à la carte £17.50

SUTTON Sussex, West

White Horse Inn
SUTTON Map 04 SU91
The Street RH20 1PS ☎ 01798 869221
A Georgian inn, constructed of stone under a tiled roof, in a village setting at the north foot of the South Downs. Blackboard menus apply to both the bar and restaurant, favouring fresh fish with dishes such as English cod and chips, and char-grilled tuna steak with fresh mango salsa. Principal beers: Courage Best, Arundel Best, Youngs PA, Youngs Special.
Directions 4m S of Pulborough turn R at foot of Bury Hill, follow Roman Villa signs, on for 1m to Sutton
Free House
Open 11-3 6-11
Bar food 12-2 7-10 Av main course £5.90
Restaurant 12-2 7-10 Av 3 course à la carte £16
Accommodation s£48 d£58

TILLINGTON Sussex, West

The Horse Guards Inn
TILLINGTON Map 04 SU92
GU28 9AF ☎ 01798 342332
Made up of three cottages, this 300-year-old inn is in a lovely setting overlooking the South Downs. Its name changed in the 1850s when the Horse Guard regiment came to Petworth Park to guard French prisoners of war. Dishes include poached scallops and pan-fried venison steak. Principal beers: King and Barnes-Sussex Bitter, Hall and Woodhouse-Badger Best.
Directions On A272 1m W of Petworth.Inn next to church
Free House
Open 11-3 6-11
Bar food 12-2 7-10 Av main course £5.50
Restaurant 12-2 7-10
Accommodation d£55

WARNHAM Sussex, West

The Greets Inn
WARNHAM Map 04 TQ13
47 Friday St RH12 3QY
☎ 01403 265047
14th-century village inn with oak beams, inglenook fireplace and prize winning garden. The main course menu ranges from beef and Guinness pie, and chicken and Stilton roulade, to chicken and avocado Stroganoff, and spinach and ricotta parcels with basil and tomato sauce. Principal beers: Flowers Original, Brakspears, Fullers London Pride, Heineken.
Directions Off A24 N of Horsham
Whitbread
Open 11-2.30 6-11
Bar food 12-2.30 7-10.30 Av main course £8.50
Restaurant 12-2.30 7-10.30 Av 3 course à la carte £14

Wight, Isle of

BEMBRIDGE Wight, Isle of

The Crab & Lobster Inn
BEMBRIDGE Map 04 SZ68
32 Foreland Fields Rd PO35 5TR
☎ 01983 872244
Clifftop inn with splendid views across the Solent and English Channel. As the name suggests, local seafood is the house speciality in both

bar snacks and main courses. The latter include lobster thermidor, grilled whole lemon sole, poached salmon with watercress sauce, and grilled avocado with crabmeat. Principal beers: Real ales and lagers.
Free House
Open 11-3 6-11
Bar food 12-2.30 6.30-9 Av main course £5.50
Restaurant 7-9 Av 3 course à la carte £16.50

BONCHURCH Wight, Isle of

The Bonchurch Inn
BONCHURCH Map 04 SZ57
Bonchurch Shute PO38 1NU
☎ 01938 852611
Coaching inn with a cobbled courtyard built in 1838, and within easy reach of the beach. Bar food is available, as well as a selection of Italian specials such as seafood or Milanese risotto, cannelloni with spinach and tagliatelle vegetarian. Fish meals include king prawns Genovese, and scampi laced with brandy. Principal beers: Directors Best, Speckled Hen.
Free House
Open 11-3.30 6.30-11
Bar food 11-3 6.30-9.30 Av main course £5
Restaurant 6.30-9 Av 3 course à la carte £12
Accommodation s£17.50 d£35

CHALE Wight, Isle of

Clarendon Hotel & Wight Mouse Inn
CHALE Map 04 SZ47
PO38 2HA ☎ 01983 730431
17th-century inn with live music every night of the year, 'Mouse World' indoor play area, a selection of 365 whiskies, a Shetland pony, and a fine view of Chale Bay and the Needles. Typical menu includes fisherman's pie, steak and mushroom pudding, lamb kebabs, and grilled Dover sole. Principal beers: Strongs Country Bitter, Boddingtons, Wadworths 6X, Gales HSB.

Directions S on the A3055
Free House
Open 11-12 (Sun 12-10.30)
Restaurant 12-3 7-9.30 Av 3 course à la carte £9 Av 3 course fixed price £13.50
Accommodation s£25 d£50

FRESHWATER Wight, Isle of

The Red Lion
FRESHWATER Map 04 SZ38
Church Place PO40 9BP
☎ 01983 754925
Built in the 12th-century and situated next to the church. The River Yar and causeway are nearby. Starters include crab and Stilton stuffed mushrooms. Main menu features duck breast with cranberry and orange sauce, and marinated trout wrapped in bacon. Also a choice of home-made ice creams. Principal beers: Flowers Original, London Pride, 6X, Goddards.
Directions In Freshwater follow signs for parish church
Whitbread
Open 11.30-3 5.30-11 (Sun 12-3, 7-10.30)
Bar food 12-2 6.30-9 Av main course £7

NITON Wight, Isle of

Buddle Inn
NITON Map 04 SZ57
St Catherines Rd PO38 2NE
☎ 01983 730243
16th-century building, formerly a farmhouse, that has been used as pub since the 1700s. Within easy reach of a small beach and harbour. Lunchtime menu offers a wide selection of snacks and light meals, while the Chef's specials include curried chicken, fresh local plaice, and Dorset apple cake. Principal beers: Flowers Original, Bass, Abbot Ale, 6X.
Directions Take A3055 from Ventnor.In Niton take 1st L signed 'to the lighthouse'.
Whitbread
Open 11-11 (Sun 12-10.30)
Bar food 11.30-2.45 6-9.30 Av main course £4.75

contd.

SEAVIEW Wight, Isle of

Seaview Hotel & Restaurant
SEAVIEW Map 04 SZ69
High St PO34 5EX ☎ 01983 612711
Built by William Caws in 1826. An Edwardian facade was added in 1906. First course menu ranges from chive and dill blinis with prawns in Pernod and fennel dressing, to hot crab ramekin. main course dishes include roasted salmon with anchovy and pink peppercorns, and duck breast with caramelised marmalade and crispy onions. There is also an impressive wine list.
Directions Town centre
Free House
Open 10.30-3 6-11
Bar food 12-2 7-9.30 Av main course £8.95
Restaurant 12-2 7.30-9.30 Av 3 course à la carte £20
Accommodation s£40 d£70

VENTNOR Wight, Isle of

The Spyglass Inn
VENTNOR Map 04 SZ57
The Esplanade PO38 1JX
☎ 01983 855338
Built around 1830, and situated at the western end of Ventnor Esplanade with fine views over the English Channel. Contains a large collection of seafaring memorabilia. Specials include beef braised in red wine, and crab and lobster bisque. Vegetarian dishes include vegetable Kiev, and tortellini with spinach and ricotta cheese. Principal beers: Dorset Best, Tanglefoot, Wadworth 6X.
Directions Town centre
Free House
Open 10.30-11
Bar food 12-2.15 7-9.30 Av main course £5
Restaurant 12-2.15 7-9.30
Accommodation d£40

Central England & East Anglia

Birthplace of the University, the Industrial Revolution, and William Shakespeare, the landscape varies from the unspoilt fenlands to the industrial heartlands with the rich heritage of middle England in between.

• Cambridgeshire • Derbyshire •
• Essex • Leicestershire •
• Lincolnshire • Norfolk •
• Northamptonshire •
• Nottinghamshire • Oxfordshire •
• Rutland • Staffordshire • Suffolk •
• Warwickshire • West Midlands •

Cambridgeshire

BYTHORN Cambridgeshire

The White Hart
BYTHORN Map 04 TL07
PE18 0QN ☎ 01832 710226
A meal at Bennett's, the restaurant at this Cambridgeshire pub, could feature spicy fish gumbo or celeriac salad with rémoulade sauce for starters, an entrée of calves liver, saddle of hare, or veal sweetbreads, followed by burnt Cambridgeshire cream or praline parfait for dessert. Principal beers: Wexford Irish Cream Ale, Greene King IPA, Harp, Stella.
Directions 0.5m off A14 (Kettering/ Huntingdon rd)
Free House
Open 11-3 6-11
Bar food 12-2 7-10 Av main course £7
Restaurant 12-2 7-10 Av 4 course fixed price £23.50

CAMBRIDGE Cambridgeshire

The Cambridge Blue
CAMBRIDGE Map 05 TL45
85/87 Gwydir St CB1 2LG
☎ 01223 361382
A terraced pub dating from the late 19th century, with two simply furnished bars and a conservatory. The large garden features chickens and a model railway. Vegetarians are well catered for, typical dishes including vegetable lasagne, samosas, nut roast, ploughman's pie and chicken curry. Principal beers: Nethergate IPA, Bitter, Golden Gate, Old Growler.
Directions Town centre
Nethergate Brewery
Open 12-2.30 6-11
Bar food 12-2 7-9.30 Av main course £3.95

Free Press
CAMBRIDGE Map 05 TL45
Prospect Row CB1 1DU
☎ 01223 368337
Located in a back street not far from the centre of Cambridge this traditional town pub is named after a local 19th-century pro-temperance journal! Menu may include pork and cider casserole, Persian lamb, homity pie, rumbledethumps, or Zorba pie (lamb with black olives). Principal beers: IPA, Abbot.
Greene King
Open 12-2.30 (wknd 12-3) 6-11
Bar food 12-2 6-9 Av main course £4.25

DRY DRAYTON Cambridgeshire

The Black Horse
DRY DRAYTON Map 05 TL36
Park St CB3 8DA ☎ 01954 781055
A 350-year-old village pub with exposed wooden beams and open fires, the Black Horse has a charming ambience. A comprehensive menu offers ploughmans, jacket potatoes, burgers, vegetarian dishes, fish and main courses such as gammon steak with peach slices, as well as daily specials and sandwiches.
Directions Just outside Cambridge between the A14 & A428
Free House
Open 11-2.30 6.30-11 (Sun 12-3, 7-10.30)
Bar food 12-2 7-9 Av main course £5

DUXFORD Cambridgeshire

The John Barleycorn
DUXFORD Map 05 TL44
3 Moorfield Rd CB2 4PP
☎ 01223 832699
Traditional thatched and beamed English country pub situated close to Cambridge. The same menu is served in both bar and restaurant, and may include venison and vegetable pie, Turkish lamb, smoked haddock with poached eggs, or Irish stew with parsley dumplings. Principal beers: IPA, Abbot, Dark Mild, Kronenberg.
Directions Off A505 S of Cambridge
Greene King
Open 12-2.30 6.30-11
Bar food 12-2.30 6.30-11 Av main course £8
Restaurant 12-2.30 6.30-11 Av 3 course à la carte £14

ELSWORTH Cambridgeshire

The George & Dragon
ELSWORTH Map 05 TL36
41 Boxworth Rd CB3 8JQ
☎ 01954 267236
Set in a pretty village just outside Cambridge, this pub has one menu and three separate dining areas, each with its own appeal. Dishes include breast of chicken and ribs in a barbecue sauce, mushroom and spinach lasagne, grilled steaks and a selection of salads. Principal beers: Greene King, Ruddles, Tetleys.
Directions SE of A14 between Cambridge & Huntingdon
Free House
Open 11-3 6-11
Bar food 12-2 6.15-9 Av main course £7
Restaurant 12-2 6.15-9 Av 3 course à la carte £15

ELTISLEY Cambridgeshire

The Leeds Arms
ELTISLEY Map 04 TL25
The Green PE19 4TG
☎ 01480 880283
Named after local landowners, the Leeds Arms is located opposite the village green where the local cricket team play in season. Escalopes of pork Holstein, cashew nut and vegetable stir-fry, scampi Thermidor, or steak Rossini may be on the menu. Principal beers: Greene King, Hook Norton, Websters Yorkshire Bitter.
Directions On the A428 between Cambridge & St Neots
Free House
Open 11.30-2.30 6.30-11
Bar food 12-2 7-9.45 Av main course £7.50
Restaurant 12-2 7-9.45 Av 3 course à la carte £12.50

ELY Cambridgeshire

The Red Lion
ELY Map 05 TL58
47 High St, Stretham CB6 3JQ ☎ 01353 648132
A 17th-century coaching inn, painstakingly renovated, with a lovely conservatory restaurant. It is situated in the centre of the village, in a conservation area. Snacks and meals are served in the bar and there is a full restaurant menu with dishes such as steak pie and salmon and broccoli Mornay. Principal beers: Tetley, Greene King, Old Speckled Hen, Bass Mild.
Directions From Ely take A10 towards Cambridge
Free House
Open 11-3 6.30-11
Bar food 12-2 7-9 Av main course £4.95
Restaurant 12-2 7-9 Av 3 course à la carte £11 Av 3 course fixed price £7.95
Accommodation s£31 d£35

FEN DITTON Cambridgeshire

Ancient Shepherds
FEN DITTON Map 05 TL46
High St CB5 8ST ☎ 01223 293280
Dates back to 1540. The name derives from the ancient order of Shepherders who used to meet here. A wide selection of sandwiches and baguettes are available. Main courses on offer include duck with Cointreau and marmalade sauce, lamb and apricot pie, rib eye steak, and nut Wellington for vegetarians. Principal beers: Benskins,Tetleys, Flowers, Carlsberg.
Directions From A14 take B1047 signed Cambridge/Airport
Free House
Open 11-3 6-11
Bar food 12-2.15 7-9.15 Av main course £7.50

contd.

Restaurant 12-2.15 7-9.15 Av 3 course à la carte £15

FENSTANTON Cambridgeshire

King William IV
FENSTANTON Map 05 TL36
High St PE18 9JF ☎ 01480 462467
There is a warm atmosphere in this charming, thatched pub, built in the 17th century, and retaining inglenooks and old beams. Most appetites are catered for, with a sandwich menu and main menu (try mussels with cheddar croutons or tuna steak with lemon spinach). On Wednesday there's live jazz and R&B. Principal beers: Abbot, IPA, Rayments.
Directions Off the A14 between Cambridge & Huntingdon
Greene King
Open 11-3.30 6-11 (Sun 11-11)
Bar food 11.30-2.15 6.45-10 Av main course £4
Restaurant 11.30-2.15 6.45-10 Av 3 course à la carte £12

FOWLMERE Cambridgeshire

The Chequers
FOWLMERE Map 05 TL44
High St SG8 7SR ☎ 01763 208369
Civilised sixteenth-century inn made famous by Samuel Pepys, who slept here in 1600. Modern British cooking is the order of the day, with the likes of sautéed pigeon breasts on raw spinach and truffoil salad, or roast duck with stir-fried vegetables and oriental ginger, anise and chilli sauce, served in the bar or restaurant. Principal beers: Adnams Broadside.
Directions From M11 A505, 2nd R to Fowlmere
Free House
Open 12-2.30 6-11
Bar food 12-2 7-10 Av main course £7
Restaurant 12-2 7-10 Av 3 course à la carte £7

GODMANCHESTER Cambridgeshire

Black Bull
GODMANCHESTER Map 04 TL24
32 Post St PE18 8AQ ☎ 01480 453310
17th-century coaching inn with large inglenook fireplace. The blackboard menu typically offers pan fried chicken, peppered pork, poached salmon, and steak and ale pie. Wednesday is fish night, featuring fresh cod from Grimsby. Vegetarian options include vegetable Stroganoff, and leek and pasta bake. Principal beers: Flowers, Boddingtons, Castle Eden, Banks & Taylor.
Directions Off A1198 S of Huntington
Whitbread
Open 11-2.30 6-11 (Sun 12-10.30)
Bar food 12-2 6-10 Av main course £6
Accommodation s£19 d£35

GOREFIELD Cambridgeshire

Woodmans Cottage
GOREFIELD Map 09 TF41
90 High Rd PE12 4NB ☎ 01945 870669
A friendly pub and restaurant with lively licensees and locals. Adventurous bar food includes specials such as rogan josh, Chinese chilli beef, nut roast and pork in a blanket. There's a comprehensive carte, with fish, steaks and vegetarian options, and a very tempting sweet trolley. Principal beers: Tennants,Caffreys, Worthington Bass, Toby IPA.
Free House
Open 11-2 (Sun 12-3) 7-11
Bar food 11-2 7-11 Av main course £5
Restaurant 12-2.30 7-11 Av 3 course à la carte £11.30 Av 0 course fixed price £10

GREAT CHISHILL Cambridgeshire

The Pheasant
GREAT CHISHILL Map 05 TL43
24 Heydon Rd SG8 8SR
☎ 01763 838535
A small 18th-century pub with beams and a flagstone floor, the Pheasant has a large garden with panoramic views of the countryside. Dishes range from smoked haddock and salmon fishcakes in the bar to honey glazed duck breast on ginger flavoured Thai vegetables in the à la carte restaurant. Principal beers: Nethergates, Adnams Best Bitter, Ruddles Best Bitter.
Directions Off B1039 between Royston & Saffron Walden
Free House
Open 12-2.30 6-11
Bar food 12-2 7-9.30 Av main course £5.50
Restaurant 12-2 7-9.30 Av 3 course à la carte £16

HILDERSHAM Cambridgeshire

The Pear Tree
HILDERSHAM Map 05 TL34
CB1 6BU ☎ 01223 891680
A small one-bar village pub where the walls are adorned with photographs and press cuttings of the 1933 Hildersham football team, famous for never winning. Daily specials include crispy crab pancakes, diced beef cooked in Guinness, steak dishes, vegetable and nut strudel, and a selection of home-made puddings. Principal beers: Greene King IPA, Abbot Ale, Guinness, Strongbow.
Greene King
Open 12-2.30 6.30-11.20
Bar food 12-2 6.30-9.30 Av main course £5

HINXTON Cambridgeshire

The Red Lion
HINXTON Map 05 TL44
High St CB10 1QY ☎ 01799 530601
Interesting knick-knacks, pictures and stuffed animals catch the eye at this recently extended 16th-century inn. The menu offers plenty of fresh fish, steaks and dishes such as chicken Kiev and roast duck with orange and Grand Marnier sauce. To finish there could be profiteroles or treacle sponge pudding. Principal beers: Boddingtons, Adnams, IPA-Greene King.
Directions 1m from M11 J9, 2m from M11 J10
Free House
Open 11-2.30 6-11 (Sun 12-3,7-10.30)
Bar food 12-2 7-10

HOLYWELL Cambridgeshire

The Old Ferryboat Inn
HOLYWELL Map 05 TL37
PE17 3TG ☎ 01480 463227
A strong contender for the oldest inn in Britain, this atmospheric, thatched building on the River Ouse is steeped in both charm and history. Daily specials such as sautéed chicken breast with mushrooms, onions and red wine, and lemon sole stuffed with crabmeat in a seafood sauce, back up the standard menu. Principal beers: Bass, Nethergates, Courage.
Directions A14 A1096, from Cambridge then A1123 R to Holywell
Free House

Open 11.30-3 6-11
Restaurant 12-2 6-10 Av 3 course à la carte £12.50
Accommodation s£44.50 d£55

HORNINGSEA Cambridgeshire

The Plough & Fleece
HORNINGSEA Map 05 TL46
High St CB5 9JG ☎ 01223 860795
The style of architecture reflects the influence of the Dutch who came to drain the fens in the 17th-18th century. The unusual fireplace in the public bar was built by a local blacksmith about 100 years ago. Traditional dishes include Romany rabbit, ham hot pot and figgy sly pie. Principal beers: Greene King, Guinness, Harp, Kronenbourg.
Directions From A14 eastbound take B1047. Top of slip rd turn L. Pub opp garden centre.
Greene King
Open 11.30-2.30 7-11
Bar food 12-2 7-9.30 Av main course £5
Restaurant 12-2 7-9.30 Av 3 course à la carte £10

HUNTINGDON Cambridgeshire

The Old Bridge House
HUNTINGDON Map 04 TL27
1 High St PE18 6TQ ☎ 01480 52681
One menu is offered, whether you eat in the relaxed Terrace or in the more formal restaurant. Modern international dishes include red mullet in tempura batter, and pheasant and chicken sausage. Besides its range of real ales, the inn has a notable selection of fine wines. Principal beers: Adnams Best, Guinness, Carlsberg, Stella.

contd.

Directions Huntingdon signposted from A1 & A14 from Cambridge
Free House
Open 11-11 (Sun 12-11)
Accommodation s£79.50 d£89.50

KEYSTON Cambridgeshire

The Pheasant Inn
KEYSTON Map 04 TL07
Village Loop Rd PE18 0RE
☎ 01832 710241
One extensive menu is offered throughout this lovely thatched inn. So you can eat what you like, a snack or a full blown meal, where you like, in the traditional bar with its oak beams, open fires and simple wooden furniture or in the more luxurious surroundings of the small restaurant. Principal beers: Adnams.
Directions Signposted from A14 W of Huntingdon
Free House
Open 12-2 6-10
Bar food 12-2 6-10
Restaurant 12-2 6-10 Av 3 course à la carte £15.25

KIMBOLTON Cambridgeshire

The New Sun Inn
KIMBOLTON Map 04 TL16
20-22 High St PE18 0HA
☎ 01480 860052
16th-century inn situated in the Georgian high street opposite Kimbolton Castle. Specials include home-made steak and kidney pudding, mushroom Stroganoff, and lamb sweetbreads in wine, shallots and cream sauce. Other main course dishes include guinea fowl wrapped in bacon with a black cherry and Calvados sauce. Principal beers: Wells.
Directions From A1 N, B645 for 7m, From A1 S B661 for 7m, From A14 B660 for 5m
Charles Wells
Open 11-2.30 6-11 (Sun 12-10.30)
Bar food 12-2.15 7-9.30 Av main course £4.50
Restaurant 12-2 7-9.30 Av 3 course à la carte £17

MADINGLEY Cambridgeshire

The Three Horseshoes
MADINGLEY Map 05 TL36
High St CB3 8AB ☎ 01954 210221
Thatched pub close to Cambridge with an impressive wine list featuring around 100 wines. An interesting menu strong on vegetable accompaniment, offers dishes such as crostini of pigeon, marinated buffalo mozzarella and baked Chavignol crottin. Principal beers: Adnams, Stella, Guinness.
Directions From M11 J14 take A428 W. Village on R
Free House
Open 11.30-3 6-11
Bar food 12-2 6.30-10
Restaurant 12-2 6.30-10 Av 3 course à la carte £20

NEWTON Cambridgeshire

The Queen's Head
NEWTON Map 05 TL44
CB2 5PG ☎ 01223 870436
Friendly conversation is the order of the day at this traditional country pub. There's one old beamed bar and a very different Victorian bar, reflecting the pub's development over the centuries. Simple home-made food is served: Aga-baked potatoes, soup, toast and beef dripping, or freshly cut sandwiches. Principal beers: Adnams Bitter, Adnams Broadside.
Directions 6m S of Cambridge on B1368, 1 1/2m off A10 at Harston
Free House
Open 11.30-2.30 6-11 (Sun 12-2.30,7-10.30)
Bar food 12-2.15 6.30-9.30 Av main course £3.50

PETERBOROUGH Cambridgeshire

Charters Café Bar
PETERBOROUGH Map 04 TL19
Town Bridge PE1 1DG
☎ 01733 315700
On the River Nene, Charters is a floating barge right in the centre of Peterborough, believed to be the largest converted barge in Great Britain. The interior has open fires and old beams and the varied menu includes Greek salad, chicken Szechuan, salmon en croûte, Cajun chicken, and steaks. Principal beers: Bass, London Pride, Tiger, JNB.
Free House
Open 12-11
Bar food 12-2.30 Av main course £2
Restaurant 12-2.15 7-10 Av 3 course à la carte £15

REACH Cambridgeshire

The Kings
REACH Map 05 TL56
8 Fair Green CB5 0JD ☎ 01638 741745
Formerly a farmhouse, overlooking the village green where an annual fair has been held since 1201. Basic pub food is available such as home-made soups, *King's Skins* (potatoes with bacon, melted cheese and sweet chilli sauce), and pan-fried baby poussin with garlic and herbs. Principal beers: Greene King, Elgoods, Old Chimneys, Fenland Brewery.
Directions Off the B1102 between Cambridge & Burwell
Free House
Open 12-3 7-11

STILTON Cambridgeshire

The Bell Inn
STILTON Map 04 TL18
Great North Rd PE7 3RA
☎ 01733 241066
The Bell, built in 1642, was home to 18th-century landlord Cooper Thornhill, who is known as the man who made Stilton cheese famous. The cheese can be found in some of the dishes on a menu which may also feature coriander lamb, Normandy pork terrine, ginger glazed duck, or grilled trout Marsala. Principal beers: Tetley Bitter, Marstons Pedigree, Greene King.
Free House
Open 12-2.30 6-11

Bar food 12-2 6.30-9.30 Av main course £7
Restaurant 12-2 7-9.30 Av 3 course à la carte £22.50 Av 3 course fixed price £16.95
Accommodation s£40 d£55

SUTTON Cambridgeshire

The Anchor Inn
SUTTON Map 05 TL47
Bury Ln, Sutton Gault CB6 2BD
☎ 01353 778537
Originally built to house Scottish prisoners of war who were digging the New Bedford river in the 16th-century, this family-run inn offers a varied menu which may include parsnip and mushroom galette with almondine potatoes, chicken, leek and bacon crumble, and an interesting selection of cheeses. Principal beers: Nethergate IPA, Adnams.
Directions From A14, B1050 to Earith, take B1381 to Sutton. Sutton Gault on left.
Free House
Open 12-3 7-11
Bar food 12-2 7-9 Av main course £9
Restaurant 12-2 7-9 Av 3 course à la carte £20 Av 3 course fixed price £13.50
Accommodation s£45 d£57.50

Derbyshire

ALFRETON Derbyshire

White Horse Inn
ALFRETON Map 08 SK45
Badger Ln, Woolley Moor DE55 6FG
☎ 01246 590319
A 300-year-old village local with a relatively unchanged tap room, set in two acres of gardens with panoramic views of the Amber Valley. There's a good

contd.

choice of food, including tipsy beef, quiche, creamy chicken pie and breaded plaice. Puds include jam roly poly and sticky toffee meringue. Principal beers: Draught Bass.
Directions From A632(Matlock/Chesterfield rd) take B6036.Pub 1m beyond Ashover
Free House
Open 11.30-2.30 6-11 (Sun, 12-3,5-10.30)
Bar food 11.30-2 6.30-9 Av main course £3.95
Restaurant 11.30-2 6.30-9 Av 3 course à la carte £10

ASHBOURNE Derbyshire

The Green Man
ASHBOURNE Map 07 SK14
St Johns St DE6 1GH ☎ 01335 345783
Located in the heart of Ashbourne this 17th-century coaching inn has two bars, the Johnson and the Boswell. Typical specials board includes pork Valentine, trio of lamb chops, beef goulash, chicken Korma, and Derbyshire oatcakes. Principal beers: Fosters, Mansfield, Old Speckled Hen.
Directions In town centre off A52
Free House
Open 11-11 (Sun 12-10.30)
Bar food 12-2.30 6-8.30 Av main course £4.95
Accommodation s£30 d£40

BAKEWELL Derbyshire

Aitch's Wine Bar & Bistro
BAKEWELL Map 08 SK26
4 Buxton Rd DE45 1DA
☎ 01629 813895
Once the stables/garage of a nearby hotel, this wine bar has created a colourful Mediterranean atmosphere in the 200-year-old building. Light meals are served in the bar, while typical bistro dishes are spicy Thai fish cakes, char-grilled chicken with plum and chilli sauce, and chocolate truffle cake. Principal beers: Gillespies stout, Theakstons bitter, Draught Becks lager.
Open 12-3 7-11
Bar food 12-3 Av main course £6.50
Restaurant 12-3 7-11 Av 3 course à la carte £20 Av 3 course fixed price £18

The Lathkil Hotel
BAKEWELL Map 08 SK26
Over Haddon DE45 1JE
☎ 01629 812501
Built in the early 19th century, the Lathkil Hotel offers panoramic views of the hills and dales of the Peak District as well as a meeting place for many local riders. A meal may include roast guinea fowl, lobster bisque, New Zealand green lip mussels, or baked rainbow trout. Principal beers: Wards and Vaux.
Free House
Open 11.30-3 6.30-11
Bar food 12-2 7-9 Av main course £5.25
Restaurant 7-9 Av 3 course à la carte £16.50
Accommodation s£35 d£55

The Mowsal Head Hotel
BAKEWELL Map 08 SK26
Mowsal Head DE45 1NL
☎ 01629 640250
Overlooking beautiful Monsal Dale and the viaduct, this hotel was rebuilt in 1883 to serve the railway station. A diverse range of food is available in the bar, tea-room or restaurant. Specialities include home-made pies, colonial goose with apricot and honey stuffing, and Bakewell tart. Principal beers: Mowsal Best, Hartington Bitter, Theakstons Best, Pedigree.
Free House
Open 10.30-11.30
Bar food 12-2.30 6-9.30 Av main course £5.50
Accommodation d£40

BIRCHOVER Derbyshire

The Druid Inn
BIRCHOVER Map 08 SK26
Main St DE4 2BL ☎ 01629 650302
200-year-old pub covered in creepers in summer and autumn, situated near the Rowtar Rocks. Main course dishes range

from marinated rack of lamb with redcurrant and gooseberry sauce, and Derbyshire pheasant with venison casserole, to South African bobotie. Vegetarian options include Mexican mole, and lentil, carrot and nut rissoles. Principal beers: Mansfield Cask Bitter, Speckled Hen.
Directions From A6 between Matlock & Bakewell take B5056, signed Ashbourne.Take 2nd L to Birchover
Free House
Open 12-3 7-11
Bar food 12-2 7-9 Av main course £8.80
Restaurant 12-2 7-9 Av 3 course à la carte £14.50

BIRCH VALE Derbyshire

The Waltzing Weasel Inn
BIRCH VALE Map 07 SK08
New Mills Rd SK22 1BT
☎ 01663 743402
Enjoying stunning views of Kinder Scout - the highest peak in Derbyshire - the restaurant at this charming inn is locally renowned and ideally placed for walkers. Diners may sample beef in whisky, braised grouse, or duck and cherry pie. Principal beers: Marstons Bitter,Marstons Pedigree.
Free House
Open 12-3 6-11
Bar food 12-2 7-9.30 Av main course £9
Restaurant 12-2 7-9 Av 3 course à la carte £24.50 Av 3 course fixed price £24.50
Accommodation s£45 d£65

BRASSINGTON Derbyshire

Ye Olde Gate Inne
BRASSINGTON Map 08 SK25
Well St DE4 4HJ ☎ 01629 540448
Constructed in 1616 from local stone and salvaged Armada timbers, this coaching post was a makeshift hospital in the Civil War, and is only 3 miles from Carsington Water. Typical menu includes Cajun chicken, a variety of omelettes, and beef in ale. Principal beers: Marstons Pedigree, Head Brewers Choice.
Directions 3m NW of Carsington Water
Marstons
Open 12-2.30 6-11
Bar food 12-1.45/2 7-9 Av main course £6

CASTLETON Derbyshire

Ye Olde Cheshire Cheese Inn
CASTLETON Map 07 SU18
How Ln S33 8WJ ☎ 01433 620330
Muddy boots are welcome at this family-run, 17th-century free house in the heart of the Peak District National Park. A typical menu includes roast wild boar, game pie, pheasant, smoked chicken, and home-made pies. Principal beers: Mansfield, Old Baily, Old Speckled Hen, White Rabbit.
Directions A625 from Sheffield
Free House
Open 8-1
Accommodation s£25 d£45

DARLEY ABBEY Derbyshire

The Abbey
DARLEY ABBEY Map 08 SK33
Darley St DE22 1DX
☎ 01332 558297
The simple medieval hall house, formerly a monastic guest house, makes a striking pub. It offers good home-cooking, from a thick slice of ham with eggs, or a hot sandwich stuffed with Lincolnshire sausage and fried onions, to blackboard specials such as chicken Kiev, and plaice and salmon goujons. Principal beers: Old Brewery Bitter, Ayingzrbrau Lager, Pil Prinz.
Directions A38 onto A6 to Duffield Rd
Samuel Smith
Open 11.30-2.30 6-11 (Sun-Sat open all day)
Bar food 12-2 Av main course £4.25

DERBY Derbyshire

Brunswick Inn
DERBY Map 08 SK33
1 Railway Ter DE1 2RU
☎ 01332 290677
Traditional old railway pub where seventeen hand pumps dispense excellent real ales, some brewed at their own Brunswick Brewery next door. Food is down-to-earth, and takes in home-made soups, hot cobs filled with beef and Stilton, or sausage and onion, and chicken, celery, leek and mushroom pie.
Directions A25 to Derby, pub just before railway station
Free House
Open 11-11 (Sun 12-10.30)
Bar food 11.30-2.30 Av main course £3

DOE LEA Derbyshire

Hardwick Inn
DOE LEA Map 08 SK46
Hardwick Park S44 5QS
☎ 01246 850245
Built in 1607 from locally quarried sandstone, the inn stands on the south gate of Hardwick Park leading from Hardwick Hall. Traditional home-cooked meals are served in the bar and carvery restaurant: steaks and salads, fresh fish and 'specials' such as pork and sage casserole, rabbit pie or venison in red wine. Principal beers: Scotch Bitter, Old Peculiar, XB, Theakstons.
Directions M1 J29 take A6175.0.5m L(signed Stainsby/Hardwick Hall)After Stainsby/2.5m turn L at staggered junc
Free House
Restaurant 12-2 7-9 Av 3 course à la carte £10.75 Av 3 course fixed price £10.75

EYAM Derbyshire

Miners Arms
EYAM Map 08 SK27
Water Ln S30 1RG ☎ 01433 630853
Best known for the suffering it endured during the plague, the village of Eyam is also home to this 17th-century inn and restaurant. Guinea fowl forestière, escalope of pork with cream and apricots, or sautéed monkfish may be on the menu. Principal beers: Tetleys, Stones.
Directions Off B6521, 5m S of Bakewell
Free House
Open 12-3 7-11
Bar food 12-2 Av main course £5.50
Restaurant 12-2 7-9 Av 3 course à la carte £17
Accommodation s£25 d£50

GRINDLEFORD Derbyshire

The Maynard Arms
GRINDLEFORD Map 08 SK27
Main Rd S30 1HP ☎ 01433 630321
Overlooking the Derbyshire Hills and the Hope Valley, the Maynard Arms was built in 1898. Diners here can choose from a menu which may offer peppered monkfish, ballotine of duck, prawn linguini, or Cajun-style vegetable lasagne. Breakfast is available any time. Principal beers: Boddingtons, Old Speckled Hen, Wadworth.
Directions M1 J29 onto A619 to Baslow, onto A623 to Calver, R into Grindleford
Free House
Open 12-3 6-11
Bar food 12-2 6-9.30 Av main course £5.50
Restaurant 12-2 7-9.30 Av 3 course à la carte £15.95 Av 4 course fixed price £15.95
Accommodation s£59 d£69

HASSOP Derbyshire

Eyre Arms
HASSOP Map 08 SK27
DE45 1NS ☎ 01629 640390
Built around the time of the Civil War, this unspoilt, ivy-clad inn comes complete with oak beams, open fires and a resident Cavalier ghost. The extensive menu ranges from steak and kidney pie, battered cod and chips and gammon steak with pineapple, to the more exotic chicken korma and lamb balti. Principal beers: Marston Pedigree, John Smiths, Black Sheep.

Directions A6 then A619 toward Sheffield, 1/2m take B6001 to Hathersake & Hassop
Free House
Open 11.30-3 6.30-11
Bar food 12-2.30 6.30-9 Av main course £6

HAYFIELD Derbyshire

The Royal Hotel
HAYFIELD Map 07 SK08
Market St SK22 2EP ☎ 01663 742721
Set on one of the highest points in the Peak District, and originally built in the 18th century as a parsonage, the Royal Hotel now offers jazz every Sunday and a full menu every day. It may include Cajun cod fillet, Texas rib-eye steak, or steak, kidney and Beamish pie. Principal beers: John Smiths, Marstons, Theakstons.
Directions Off the A624
Free House
Open 12-3 6-11 (Weekend 12-11)
Bar food 12-3 6.30-10 Av main course £6
Restaurant 12-3 7-10 Av 3 course à la carte £12 Av 2 course fixed price £7.95
Accommodation s£29.50 d£49

HOGNASTON Derbyshire

The Red Lion Inn
HOGNASTON Map 08 SU25
Main St DE6 1PR ☎ 01335 370396
Located in the sleepy village of Hognaston, this 17th-century pub overlooks Carsington Water and has a special menu of home-made desserts. A meal here may include roast quail in port and cranberry sauce, haggis with 'neeps and tatties', or chicken rogan josh on the bone. Principal beers: Marstons Pedigree.
Free House
Open 12-3 6-11
Bar food 12-2 6.30-9 Av main course £7.95
Restaurant 12-2 6.30-9 Av 3 course à la carte £14.50
Accommodation s£40 d£65

HOPE Derbyshire

Cheshire Cheese Inn
HOPE Map 07 SK18
Edale Rd S30 2RF ☎ 01433 620381
On the old cheese route (hence the name), this 400-year-old inn is characterised by beams, open fires and antique brass and copperware. All the food is freshly cooked and includes rabbit, bacon and vegetable pie, fresh Grimsby fish, Derbyshire pork sausages and sticky toffee pudding. Principal beers: Wards.
Directions On A625 between Sheffield & Chapel-en-le-Frith
Free House
Open 12-3 (Sat open all day) 6.30-11
Bar food 12-2.30 6.30-9 Av main course £6.75
Restaurant 12-2.30 6.30-9 Av 3 course fixed price £14
Accommodation d£45

LITTLE LONGSTONE Derbyshire

Packhorse Inn
LITTLE LONGSTONE Map 07 SK17
Main St DE45 1NN ☎ 01629 640471
Originally built in 1520 and established as a pub over 200 years ago, the Packhorse has a long history in Little Longstone and hosts a folk club every Wednesday night. Roast chicken, liver, bacon and onions, or steak and kidney pie may be part of a typical menu. Principal beers: Marstons, Pedigree
Directions From A6, A6020, turn L
Marstons
Open 11.30-3.30 5-11
Bar food 12-2.30 6.30-9.30 Av main course £5
Restaurant 12-2.30 6.30-9.30 Av 3 course à la carte £10 Av 3 course fixed price £10

LITTON Derbyshire

Red Lion Inn
LITTON Map 07 SU17
SK17 8QU ☎ 01298 871458
A 400-year-old stone-built inn with church pew seating and open fires. Food is freshly prepared, and dishes from a spring menu include half a pheasant casseroled in wine and herbs, minted roast lamb, and salmon grilled with dill sauce. Rhubarb crumble and treacle sponge are among the traditional puddings. Principal beers: Boddingtons.
Free House
Open 7-11
Bar food 12-2 7-9

ROWSLEY Derbyshire

The Grouse & Claret
ROWSLEY Map 08 SK26
DE4 2EL ☎ 01629 733233
The name of this friendly pub refers not to food and wine, but to angling – the Grouse and Claret is a fishing fly. It is said to be the start of the journey for JB Priestley's *Good Companions.* Traditional pub fare includes steaks and sandwiches, as well as specials such as minted lamb casserole and Sheltie haddock. Principal beers: Riding Bitter, Mansfield Bitter, Old Baily Deakins Ale.
Directions On A6 between Matlock & Bakewell
Mansfield Brewery
Open 11-11 (Sun 12-10.30)
Bar food 12-2.30 6-9.30 Av main course £4.75
Accommodation s£20 d£35

SHARDLOW Derbyshire

The Clock Warehouse
SHARDLOW Map 08 SK43
London Rd DE72 2GL
☎ 01332 792840
Built in 1781, originally a grain storehouse. Situated along the Trent & Mersey Canal near Shardlow Lock. Daily specials are displayed on the blackboard menu. Other dishes range from Cajun chicken, tuna steak with lemon and pepper butter, and New Orleans smokey, to steak and ale pie, and vegetable tikka masala. Principal beers: Mansfield Bitter, Riding, Old Baily.
Directions On A6 3m from M1 J24
Mansfield Brewery
Open 11.30-11 (Sun 12-11)

The Old Crown
SHARDLOW Map 08 SK43
Cavendish Bridge DE72 2HL
☎ 01332 792392
In the heart of the Derbyshire countryside this riverside pub offers a wide selection of food. Today's menu may include meatballs in onion gravy, smoked haddock Charentaise, Japanese prawns, or mushroom balti. There is also a full bar menu featuring jacket potatoes, sandwiches, baguettes, salad and a children's menu. Principal beers: Pedigree, Bass, Landlord, Batemans XXXB.
Directions M1 J24 take A6 towards Derby turn L before river bridge into Shardlow
Free House
Open 11-3 5-11
Bar food 12-2 Av main course £6

STANTON BY DALE Derbyshire

The Chequers Inn
STANTON BY DALE Map 08 SK21
Dale Rd DE7 4QF ☎ 0115 9320946
In 1846 this pub was established as a grocer's shop and beer house. A brief history of the next 150 years is currently on sale - with proceeds to the cricket club! It is a typical country pub offering a good pint of beer and ploughman's, toasties and daily specials in the bar. Principal beers: Bass Draught, Carling, M&B Mild,Caffreys.
Directions From M1 J25 take A52 towards Derby.Follow signs for Sandiacre then Stanton by Dale
Bass
Open 11-2.30 6-11 (Sat-Sun 11-11)
Bar food 12-2 Av main course £3.50

TIDESWELL Derbyshire

The George Hotel
TIDESWELL Map 07 SK17
Commericial Rd SK17 8NU
☎ 01298 871382
Situated nearly 1200 feet above sea level amid the Peak District's most attractive locations, this 18th-century coaching inn offers a full bar menu which may feature lamb and apricot pie, peppered pork, 'The George Giant Yorky Pudding', or leek and mushroom crumble. Principal beers: Kimberley Classic.
Directions A619 to Baslow, A623 towards Chapel en le Frith, 1/4m off A623
Free House
Open 11-3 7-11
Bar food 12-2 7-9 Av main course £5.35
Accommodation s£25 d£46

TISSINGTON Derbyshire

Bluebell Inn
TISSINGTON Map 07 SK15
DE6 1NH ☎ 01335 350317
Converted 17th-century farmhouse which can cater for banquets, functions and wedding parties of up to 150. Diners

here can choose from a menu that may offer seafood Boursin, turkey steak tandoori, wheat and walnut casserole, or fusilli Provençale with ground beef. Jazz club last Wednesday in the month. Principal beers: Bass, Guinness, Caffreys
Directions 3m N of Ashbourne on A515
Free House
Open 12-3 6.30-11.45
Bar food 12-2.30 6.30-9.30 Av main course £5.50
Restaurant 12-2.30 6.30-9.30 Av 3 course à la carte £12

Essex

ARKESDEN Essex

Axe & Compasses
ARKESDEN Map 05 TL43
CB11 4EX ☎ 01799 550272
'Relax at the Axe' is the motto of this old thatched pub, which lies opposite the stream that passes through the pretty village. Steaks, pasta, fresh fish and vegetarian dishes are served in the bar, while the restaurant offers monkfish with roasted red pepper sauce and rack of lamb with rosemary. Principal beers: IPA, Abbot, Harp, Kronenbourg.
Directions From Buntingford take B1038 towards Newport.Take a left turn for Arkesden.
Greene King
Open 11.30-2.30 6-11
Bar food 12-2 6.45-9.30 Av main course £6.50
Restaurant 12-2 6.45-9.30 Av 3 course à la carte £15

BLACKMORE END Essex

The Bull Inn
BLACKMORE END Map 05 TL73
CM7 4DD ☎ 01371 851037
In a quiet village location, this grade II listed building provides a warm and welcoming atmosphere. Typical dishes are lamb cutlets with a herb crust, and guinea fowl with cabbage, bacon and thyme dumplings. Restaurant food is also available in the bar with the addition of sandwiches and snacks. Principal beers: Greene King IPA, Adnams, Boddingtons, Murphys.
Free House
Open 12-3 6.30-11
Bar food 12-1.45 7-9.45
Restaurant 12-1.45 7-9.45 Av 3 course à la carte £18

BURNHAM-ON-CROUCH Essex

Ye Olde White Harte Hotel
BURNHAM-ON-CROUCH Map 05 TQ99
The Quay CM0 8AS ☎ 01621 782106
Built in the 1600s with many of its original beams and fireplaces now exposed. Overlooks the River Crouch with its own jetty on the quay. Main course specials include fresh trout au Breton, rabbit with red wine, tomato and rosemary sauce, and roast goose breast in hot Cumberland sauce. Principal beers: Tolly, Adnams, Crouch Vale.
Free House
Open 11-11
Bar food 12-2 7.30-9.30 Av main course £4.20
Restaurant 12-2 7.30-9.30 Av 3 course à la carte £15 Av 3 course fixed price £12.50
Accommodation s£19.80 d£36.30

CASTLE HEDINGHAM Essex

The Bell Inn
CASTLE HEDINGHAM Map 05 TL73
St James St CO9 3EJ ☎ 01787 460350
15th-century coaching inn with a large function room where Disraeli once made a speech. A nearby Norman keep was used for the BBC's production of *Ivanhoe*. Seafood includes New Zealand green lipped mussels and rainbow trout. Thai chicken curry, cannelloni, and home-made toffee and banana pie are also served. Principal beers: Shepherd Neame Masterbrew, Greene King IPA, Greene King Abbot Ale.
Directions On A1124(A604) N of Halstead, turn R to Castle Hedingham
Grays
Open 11.30-3 (Sun, 12-3) 6-11 (Sun, 7-10.30)
Bar food 12-2 7-10 Av main course £5.50

CLAVERING Essex

The Cricketers
CLAVERING Map 05 TL43
CB11 4QT ☎ 01799 550442
16th-century village Free House with imaginative main course dishes which include fillet of monkfish tail lightly coated in pink peppercorns and sliced on to a honey oyster sauce, and breast of pheasant stuffed with a chestnut farci of thigh meat and sliced on to a juniper berry sauce. Principal beers: Flowers, Adnams.
Directions From M11 J10 take A505 east. Then A1301, B1383. At Newport take B1038
Free House
Open 10.30-3 6-11
Bar food 12.00-3.00 7.00-12.00 Av main course £8
Restaurant 12-3 7-12 Av 3 course à la carte £22 Av 3 course fixed price £22
Accommodation s£50 d£60

COLCHESTER Essex

Rose & Crown Hotel
COLCHESTER Map 05 TL92
East St CO1 2TZ ☎ 01206 866677
Reputed to be the 'oldest inn in England's oldest town', the Rose & Crown retains much of its character, particularly in the Tudor bar. The food is Italian influenced with plenty of pasta, alongside steaks, roast lamb, and chicken breast aromatica, with forest mushrooms, fresh tarragon and white wine sauce. Principal beers: Broadside, Adnams, Tetleys.
Free House
Open 10-2.30 7-11
Bar food 12-2 7-10 Av main course £6
Restaurant 12-2 7-10 Av 3 course à la carte £20
Accommodation s£59.50 d£59.50

DEDHAM Essex

Marlborough Head Hotel
DEDHAM Map 05 TM03
Mill Ln CO7 6DH ☎ 01206 323250
Following a fascinating history associated with the wool trade, this 550-year-old building with its wonderful beams and fireplaces has been an inn since 1704. Wholesome home-made dishes are served, including Aga-roasted back bacon steak, fried trout with almond butter, and brazil nut and fine bean bake. Principal beers: Greene King
Directions E of A12, N of Colchester
Allied Domecq
Open 10-11 (Sun 11-10.30)
Bar food 12-2.30 7-9.30 Av main course £6.50
Accommodation s£32.50 d£50

The Sun Hotel
DEDHAM Map 05 TM03
High St CO7 6DF ☎ 01206 323351
500-year old pub located opposite the church in the quiet village of Dedham, which was once the home of painter John Constable. A typical menu includes rainbow trout almondine, Suffolk sausage selection, gammon and peaches, Spanish lamb, and 'Chicken George'. Principal beers: Adnams, Greene King, Courage.
Directions Off A12
Free House
Open 11-11 (Sun 12-10.30)
Bar food 12-2.30 6.30-9.30 Av main course £5.95
Restaurant 6.30-9.30 Av 3 course à la carte £15
Accommodation s£38 d£55

ELSENHAM Essex

The Crown
ELSENHAM Map 05 TL52
High St CM22 6DG ☎ 01279 812827
The Crown has been a pub for nearly three hundred years, and has retained many oak beams and a large open

fireplace. Fish dishes and savoury stuffed pancakes are a speciality, as are the home-made ice creams: try marmalade and gin, Drambuie and hazelnut, or brown bread! Principal beers: Crouchvale, Spitfire, Marstons Pedigree, Tetleys.
Directions M11 J8 towards Takeley L at traffic lights
Free House
Open 11-3 6-11 (Sun 12-3,7-11)
Bar food 12-3 7.30-10.30
Restaurant 12-3 7.30-10.30 Av 3 course à la carte £12

FEERING Essex

The Sun Inn
FEERING Map 05 TL82
Feering Hill CO5 9NH ☎ 01376 570442
The owners of this 14th-century pub promise that "here you're only a stranger once." There is a varied and imaginative menu, ostrich and kangaroo are among the more exotic ingredients, with plenty of dishes from the landlord's homeland of Malta. Real ale is enthusiastically served and beer festivals are held twice a year.
Free House
Open 11-3 6-11
Bar food 12-2 6-10 Av main course £4

GOSFIELD Essex

The Green Man
GOSFIELD Map 05 TL72
The Street CO9 1TP ☎ 01787 472746
A traditional pub in an attractive village setting, The Green Man offers a range of dishes from ploughman's, sandwiches and jacket potatoes to steak and kidney pudding, curry and lasagne. Other options include a buffet of cold meats with salads and pickles, and a selection of fresh fish. Principal beers: Greene King, IPA & Abbot, Wexford, Guinness.
Directions Braintree A131 then A1017
Free House
Open 11-3 6-11 (Sun 12-3, 7-10.30)
Bar food 12-2 6.30-9 Av main course £10
Restaurant 12-2 6.30-9 Av 3 course à la carte £13

GREAT BRAXTED Essex

Du Cane Arms
GREAT BRAXTED Map 05 TL81
The Village CM8 3EJ ☎ 01621 891697
The Du Cane family's original property was demolished and rebuilt in 1936, about half a mile away, with a six foot wall all around the estate to ensure privacy. The menus offer international dishes such as smoked eel Smetana, fettucine capricciosa, and steak Midani with hot chilli sauce. Principal beers: Adnams, Courage, Green King, Carlsberg.
Directions Great Braxted signed between Witham and Kelvedon on A12
Free House
Open 11.30-3 6.30-11
Bar food 11.30-2.30 6.30-9.30 Av main course £5
Restaurant 11.30-2.30 6.30-9.30 Av 3 course à la carte £16.50

GREAT YELDHAM Essex

The White Hart
GREAT YELDHAM Map 05 TL73
Poole St CO9 4HJ ☎ 01787 237250
Dating back 500 years, this half-timbered building is set in four and a half acres of well kept gardens by a tributary of the River Colne. Home-made dishes range from a sandwich of mozzarella, plum tomato and salami to char-grilled breast of chicken with gorgonzola, polenta and Mediterranean vegetables. Principal beers: Adnams Best, Ridleys IPA, Fullers London Pride, Marstons Pedigree.
Directions On A604 between Haverhill & Halstead
Free House
Open 11-3 6-11
Bar food 12-2 6.30-10 Av main course £7.50
Restaurant 12-2 6.30-10 Av 3 course à la carte £14 Av 2 course fixed price £7.50

HARLOW Essex

Rainbow & Dove
HARLOW Map 05 TL41
Hastingwood Rd CM17 9JX
☎ 01279 415419
A 16th-century mail coach stop between London and Norwich, this pub has plenty of atmosphere. Eating is informal with quality bar food and a range of daily specials such as fresh hake cutlet with lemon sauce, chicken kebabs with rice, and spinach cannelloni. Principal beers: Flowers Original, Bass, Carlsberg, Tetley.
Directions M11 J7 take A414 towards Chipping Ongar.Take L into Hastingwood Rd

contd.

Free House
Open 11.30-3 6-11
Bar food 11.30-2.30 7-9.30 Av main course £4.50

HIGH EASTER Essex

The Cock & Bell Inn
HIGH EASTER Map 05 TL61
The Street CM1 4QW ☎ 01245 231296
14th-century, Grade II listed, timber framed building at the centre of the village, opposite the 12th-century church. Entrées include Barbary duck breast with a sauce of peaches in brandy. Main course menu features salmon steak poached in Grenadine, white wine and prawn sauce, and vegetarian Kiev. Principal beers: Mauldons, London Pride, Nethergate, Crouch Vale.
Free House
Open 12-3 7-11
Bar food 12-2.30 7-10 Av main course £4.95
Restaurant 12-3 7-10 Av 3 course à la carte £16.95 Av 4 course fixed price £12.95
Accommodation s£29.50 d£39.50

HORNDON ON THE HILL Essex

Bell Inn & Hill House
HORNDON ON THE HILL Map 05 TQ68
High Rd SS17 8LD ☎ 01375 673154
Five hundred years old, this inn is heavily beamed with flagstone floors, high back settles and log fires. Its pretty courtyard is appreciated in summer. Robust fare includes meat pasties and puddings, roast cod on a tomato tart with basil pesto, and pigeon breasts with haggis, potato rösti and thyme. Principal beers: Highgate IPA, Fullers London Pride, Draught Bass.
Free House
Open 11-2.30 6-11
Bar food 12-2 6.30-10 Av main course £8
Restaurant 12-2 6.30-10 Av 3 course à la carte £20.50
Accommodation d£45

LANGHAM Essex

The Shepherd and Dog
LANGHAM Map 05 TM03
Moor Rd CO4 5NR ☎ 01206 272711
Customers from a 50-mile radius are attracted to this friendly village pub in the Dedham Vale. Traditional country cooking includes fresh salmon with lobster sauce and duck breast with redcurrants and walnuts, alongside fried cod, chops, and steak and kidney pudding. Principal beers: Greene King Draught, Nethergate.
Directions A12 toward Ipswich, 1st turning on L out of Colchester, marked Langham
Free House
Open 11-3.3 5.30-11.20
Bar food 12-3.30 6-12.30 Av main course £5.95
Restaurant 12-3.30 6-12.30 Av 3 course à la carte £15

LEIGH-ON-SEA Essex

Crooked Billet
LEIGH-ON-SEA Map 05 TQ88
51 High St SS9 2EP
☎ 01702 714854
Set in the picturesque fishing village of Old Leigh, this 16th-century inn is full of character with open fires, beams and local pictures. Garden seating overlooks the cockle boats and the estuary. Bar snacks and daily specials are served including local seafood. Principal beers: Tetleys, Burton Ale, Adnams, Benskins.
Directions A13 towards Southend, follow signs for Old Leigh
Allied Domecq
Open 11-11 (Sun 12-10.30)
Bar food 12-2.30 Av main course £3.95

LITTLE CANFIELD Essex

The Lion & Lamb
LITTLE CANFIELD Map 05 TL52
CM6 1SR ☎ 01279 870257
A large roadside pub with a reputation for good food and a warm welcome. Snacks, steaks and popular dishes, including home-made steak and kidney pie, are served in the bar. The restaurant offers dishes such as roast rack of lamb plus a fish and vegetarian selection. Principal beers: Ridleys (local brews), Stella, Fosters, Heineken.
Directions M11 J8 A120 towards Braintree
Ridley & Sons
Open 11-2.30 6-11
Bar food 12-2 6.30-10 Av main course £6
Restaurant 12-2 6.30-10 Av 3 course à la carte £15

LITTLE DUNMOW Essex

Flitch of Bacon
LITTLE DUNMOW Map 05 TL62
The Street CM6 3HT
☎ 01371 820323
Ham is a speciality of this 15th-century pub, served in a home-baked pie, or with eggs and sauté potatoes. It is the home of the 'Dunmow Flitch', which was taken to couples who had not repented of marriage after a year and a day. Local game and fresh fish also feature. Principal beers: Greene King IPA.
Directions A120 to Braintree for 10m, turn off at Little Dunmow, 1/2m pub on R
Free House
Open 12-3 6-11
Bar food 12-2.30 6-9 Av main course £6.50
Restaurant 12-2.30 6-9 Av 3 course à la carte £12
Accommodation s£29.60 d£49.60

LITTLE WALTHAM Essex

The Dog and Gun
LITTLE WALTHAM Map 05 TL71
Boreham Rd CM3 3NF
☎ 01245 360211
Home cooked food, served in generous portions at competitive prices, is offered at the Dog & Gun. Dishes include steaks, pork fillet with whisky, fajitas, sizzling lamb with a hot chilli sauce and daily seafood specials. Steamed puddings or maybe a Louisiana Lovebite (an ice cream gateau) complete the meal. Principal beers: Greene King.
Free House
Open 11-3 6-11
Bar food 12-3 6.30-9.30
Restaurant 12-3 6.30-9.30 Av 3 course à la carte £15

NORTH FAMBRIDGE Essex

The Ferry Boat Inn
NORTH FAMBRIDGE Map 05 TQ89
Ferry Ln CM3 6LR ☎ 01621 740208
The first Queen Elizabeth DID NOT sleep at this 500-year-old Essex pub. There are loads of beams, stone floors, open fires, a duck pond, river walks and marshes all around. Home cooked fare is served in large portions, with dishes such as French onion soup, steak and kidney pie and jam roly poly. Principal beers: IPA, Old Speckled Hen.
Directions From Chelmsford take A130 S then A132 to South Woodham Ferrers, then B1012. R to village
Free House
Open 11-3 6.30-11
Bar food 12-2 7-10 Av main course £4
Restaurant 12-2 7-9.30 Av 3 course à la carte £6.50

RICKLING GREEN Essex

The Cricketers' Arms
RICKLING GREEN Map 05 TL52
CB11 3YE ☎ 01799 543210
Originally an Elizabethan cottage, this building became an ale house at some point in the 18th century and was extended in 1874 when it acquired a full license. There is an extensive menu including fresh fish, grills, kebabs, vegetarian dishes, balti curries, and mussels, which have to be the house speciality. Principal beers: Flowers IPA, Best Bitter, Carlsberg, Stella.
Directions M11 J8 take A120 W(signed Hertford).At 3rd r'about turn R onto B1383
Free House
Open 12-3 6-11
Bar food 12-3 7-10 Av main course £7.50

STOCK Essex

The Hoop
STOCK Map 05 TQ69
21 High St CM4 9BD ☎ 01277 841139
Fish dishes and traditional country fare are the specialities of The Hoop, a 15th-century building with its own large garden, accommodating weekend barbecues and an annual beer festival. Look out for daily fish specials, braised steak and dumplings, apple pie, and

contd.

spotted dick with custard. Principal beers: Mighty Oak, Nethergate, Crouchvale, Adnams.
Free House
Open 10-11 (Sun 12-10.30)

TILLINGHAM Essex

Cap & Feathers Inn
TILLINGHAM Map 05 TL90
South St CM0 7TH ☎ 01621 779212
A typical Essex wood-clad pub, built in the middle of the 15th century, retaining lots of character in its beams, wooden floors, open fires, warped walls and sloping ceilings. Food ranges from soups and sandwiches to home-smoked beef fillet, steaks, vegetarian dishes and daily fresh fish. Principal beers: Crouch Vale, IPA, Willie Warmer.
Directions From Chelmsford take A414 & follow signs for Burnham-on-Crouch/then signs for Tillingham
Free House
Open 11-11 (Winter 11-3,6-11)
Bar food 12-2 7-9.30 Av main course £5.25
Restaurant 12-2 7-9.30 Av 3 course à la carte £7 Av 2 course fixed price £6.50
Accommodation s£20 d£30

WENDENS AMBO Essex

The Bell
WENDENS AMBO Map 05 TL53
Royston Rd CB11 4JY ☎ 01799 540382
Dating from 1576, this listed building has lots of beams and two inglenook fireplaces. It's a real village pub, cosy and friendly, with a stream and ducks at the bottom of the garden. Traditional pub food is served, including steak and kidney pudding and fish and chips. Principal beers: Adnams.
Directions Near Audley End train station
Free House
Open 11.20-2.30 6-11
Bar food 12-2 7-9 Av main course £5.50
Restaurant 12-2 7-9

WICKHAM BISHOPS Essex

The Mitre
WICKHAM BISHOPS Map 05 TL81
2 The Street CM8 3NN
☎ 01621 891378
Called 'The Mitre' because the Bishops of London used to stay in the village, this early 19th-century pub is just how pubs used to be. Food is freshly cooked to order and includes a range of bar snacks, chunky steak pie, chicken thermidor, whole tail breaded scampi and vegetable curry. Principal beers: Ridleys, Stella Artois, Guinness.
Directions Off B1018 between Witham and Maldon
Ridley & Sons
Open 11.30-11
Bar food 12-2.30 7-9.30 Av main course £5
Restaurant 12-2.30 7-9.30 Av 3 course à la carte £10

WIVENHOE Essex

The Black Buoy Inn
WIVENHOE Map 05 TM02
Black Buoy Hill CO7 9BS
☎ 01206 822425
Principal beers: Greene King, IPA & Abbot, Flowers IPA, Tolly Old Strong.
Directions From Colchester take A133 towards Clacton,then B1027, B1028.In Wivenhoe turn left after church into East St.
Free House
Open 11.30-2.30, 6.30-11 (Sun 12-3, 7-10.30)
Bar food 12-2 Av main course £4.75
Restaurant 12-2 7-9.30 Av 3 course à la carte £11.50 Av 3 course fixed price £13.95

YOUNG'S END Essex

The Green Dragon
YOUNG'S END Map 05 TL71
CM7 8QN ☎ 01245 361030
Originally a house and stables, these days the stables have been integrated into the pub and are now the restaurant area. All the old beams have been retained, along

with the hay rack and feeding trough. Traditional English fare is served, along with some curries and a large selection of seafood. Principal beers: Greene King IPA, Abbot Ale, Kronenbourg, Harp Scrumpy Jack.

Directions M11 J8 take A120 towards Colchester. At Braintree b'pass take A131 S
Greene King
Open 11.30-2.15 6-11
Bar food 12-3 6.30-11 Av main course £6
Restaurant 12-3 6.30-11 Av 3 course à la carte £15 Av 3 course fixed price £12.55

Leicestershire

CASTLE DONINGTON Leicestershire

The Nag's Head
CASTLE DONINGTON Map 08 SK42
Hilltop DE74 2PR ☎ 01332 850652
Low beamed ceilings, open fires, scrubbed pine tables and colour washed walls set the scene at this small country pub. The food, offered from a chalk board menu, is modern European in style. Imaginative dishes include sliced fillet of beef in Cajun spices with tzatziki, and pan-fried blackened swordfish steak with crème fraiche. Principal beers: Banks, Marstons Pedigree.

Marstons
Open 11.30-2.30 5.30-11
Bar food 12-2 5.30-7 Av main course £4
Restaurant 12-2 6-9 Av 3 course à la carte £19

CROXTON KERRIAL Leicestershire

Peacock Inn
CROXTON KERRIAL Map 08 SK82
1 School Ln NG3 1QR ☎ 01476 870324
Seventeenth-century coaching inn in the glorious Vale of Belvoir. Fresh local trout and seasonal game from nearby estates feature on a menu that can also offer pan-fried monkfish with a green peppercorn sauce in the restaurant, and homely steak and kidney pie or proper fish and chips in the bar.
Free House
Accommodation s£30 d£35

GLOOSTON Leicestershire

The Old Barn Inn & Restaurant
GLOOSTON Map 04 SP79
St Andrew's Ln LE16 7ST
☎ 01858 545215
The same menu is served throughout the Old Barn, which is a 16th-century inn complete with oak beams and log fires. The food is described as 'adventurous European with vegetarian options', such as roast breast of duck in a honey, olive and cumin sauce, or celeriac and apple bake. Principal beers: Speckled Hen, Theakstons best bitter, Guinness, Coors.
Free House
Open 12-3 (Sunday only) 7-11 (Mon-Sat)
Bar food 12-3 7-11
Restaurant 12-3 7-11 Av 3 course à la carte £15 Av 3 course fixed price £13.25

HALLATON Leicestershire

The Bewicke Arms
HALLATON Map 04 SP79
1 Eastgate LE16 8UB
☎ 01858 555217
Picturesque thatched inn located in the village of Hallaton, which is famous for Easter Monday Hare Pie Scrambling and the ancient ceremony of Bottle Kicking! After these strenuous activities diners may sit down to chicken puttanesca, aubergine and chick pea moussaka,

contd.

beery beef casserole, or the Bewicke banger. Principal beers: Ruddles Best, Ruddles County, Marstons Pedigree, Caffreys.
Directions S of A47 between Leicester & A47/A6003 junc
Free House
Open 12-3 7-11
Bar food 12-2 7-9.45 Av main course £6.80
Restaurant 12-2 7-9.45

HOSE Leicestershire

Rose & Crown
HOSE Map 08 SK72
43 Bolton Ln LE14 4SE
☎ 01949 860424
Converted from 19th-century cottages, this pub has been sympathetically modernised and has a patio, large car park and a paddock beyond. Hearty, good-value meals are served, including a range of steaks, home-made pies and battered fish. Other options might be mushroom stroganoff or a seafood platter. Principal beers: Guinness.
Directions Off A606 N of Melton Mowbray
Free House
Open 12-3 7-11 (Sun 7-10.30)
Bar food 12-2 7-10 Av main course £7.50

KEGWORTH Leicestershire

Cap & Stocking
KEGWORTH Map 08 SK42
20 Borough St DE74 2FF
☎ 01509 674814
A proper local, simply furnished, with coal fires, displays of stuffed fish and birds and a cast iron range. The back room has French windows onto a sheltered garden. The menu includes filled rolls and burgers, pizzas and ploughman's, and dishes such as beef stroganoff and chicken curry. Principal beers: Hancocks HB, M+B Mild, Draught Bass, Guinness Caffreys.
Directions Village centre
Bass
Open 11.30-3 6.30-11
Bar food 11.30-2.30 6.30-9 Av main course £5.25

LEICESTER Leicestershire

Welford Place
LEICESTER Map 04 SK50
9 Welford Place LE1 6ZH
☎ 0116 2470758
A building of high ceilings, huge windows and some elegance, this Victorian former gentleman's club is an oasis of calm in the heart of the city. Appropriate home-made fare is served from breakfast till dinner, with strong Italian and French influences around a core of traditional English dishes. Principal beers: Ruddles Best and County.
Directions Town centre
Free House
Open 8-12

LOUGHBOROUGH Leicestershire

The Swan in The Rushes
LOUGHBOROUGH Map 08 SK51
21 The Rushes LE11 5BE
☎ 01509 217014
A 30s tile-fronted real ale pub with two drinking rooms, a cosmopolitan atmosphere and no frills. Healthy home-cooked food is served (no chips), including ploughman's lunches, beef and mushrooms in Guinness, pork and potato balti, and Stilton and broccoli quiche. Principal beers: Archers Golden, Hoegaarden, Batemans XXXB, Greene King.
Directions Town centre
Free House
Open 11-11
Bar food 12-2.30 6-8.30 Av main course £5
Restaurant 12-2.30 6-8.30 Av 3 course à la carte £12 Av 3 course fixed price £12
Accommodation s£20 d£30

MARKET BOSWORTH Leicestershire

The Black Horse
MARKET BOSWORTH Map 04 SK40
17 Market Place CV13 0LF
☎ 01455 290278
A traditional inn in the market place of an old country town, offering a relaxed and informal atmosphere. Diners are welcome to have a one dish meal or a full three courses. Choose from local trout, chicken breast in truffle sauce, or the chef's pie of the day, among other dishes. Principal beers: John Smiths, Tetley, Pedigree.

Free House
Open 11-3 (Sat-Sun, no closing) 6-11
Bar food 12-2.30 6-10 Av main course £7.95

Softleys Restaurant
MARKET BOSWORTH Map 04 SK04
Market Place CV13 0JS
☎ 01455 290464
A small family-run hotel and restaurant in the centre of the picturesque market town. Food is cooked to order using fresh ingredients and recipes from around the world, such as marinated tiger prawns and pork, grilled and served with satay sauce, and breast of chicken with lime and coriander butter. Principal beers: Adnams, Hook Norton, Wadworths.
Open 11-3 7-11
Bar food 11-3 7-11 Av main course £6
Restaurant 11-3 7-11 Av 3 course à la carte £18
Accommodation s£40 d£55

MARKET HARBOROUGH Leicestershire

The Queens Head Inn
MARKET HARBOROUGH Map 04 SP75
Main St, Sutton Bassett LE16 8HP
☎ 01858 463530
Unspoilt village pub set in the picturesque Welland Valley. Daily blackboard dishes might include starters such as Rutland mushroom and chicken, ham or asparagus terrine with pistachio nuts. Typical main course dishes are partridge pudding, and fresh mussels and king prawns cooked in a spicy tomato and red pepper sauce. Principal beers: Adnams Southwold, Ruddles County, Bass.
Free House
Open 11.45-3 6.30-11
Bar food 11.45-2 7-9.30 Av main course £6.25
Restaurant 7-10 Av 3 course à la carte £15

The Sun Inn
MARKET HARBOROUGH Map 04 SP78
Main St, Marston Trussel LE16 9TY
☎ 01858 465531
A 17th-century village inn in the heart of hunting, shooting and fishing country. Quality bar lunches are served, and typical restaurant dishes are roasted quail with a game farce, on a marbled balsamic dressing and roasted beetroot, and whole roast lobster laid onto spinach spaghetti with a citrus beurre blanc. Principal beers: Everards, Ruddles, Bass
Directions S of A4304 between Market Harborough & Lutterworth
Free House
Open 12-3 6.30-11
Bar food 12-2 6.30-9.30 Av main course £7
Restaurant 12-2 6.30-9.30 Av 3 course à la carte £18 Av 5 course fixed price £18.95
Accommodation s£38 d£50

MEDBOURNE Leicestershire

The Nevill Arms
MEDBOURNE Map 04 SP89
12 Waterfall Way LE6 8EE
☎ 01858 565288
A country pub with a beamed bar and large open fire, set by a stream with a thriving duck population. Home-made soups, casseroles and traditional puddings are the staple fare, such as curried parsnip soup, braised beef with mushrooms and red wine, and walnut pudding with hot fudge sauce. Principal beers: Ruddles, Adnams
Free House
Open 12-3 (Sunday) 12-2.30 (Mon-Sat)
Bar food 12-2 7-10 Av main course £5
Accommodation s£32.50 d£39.95

MOUNTSORREL Leicestershire

The Swan Inn
MOUNTSORREL Map 08 SU51
10 Loughborough Rd LE12 7AT
☎ 0116 2302340
Many original features, including exposed beams and open fireplaces, have been retained at this listed building, which dates from 1688. The varied menu offers home cooked dishes from around the world, including lasagne, enchiladas, Yangtse chicken and beef casseroled in Old Peculiar. Principal beers: Batemans XB, Old Peculier, Theakstons XB, Wadworths 6X.

contd.

Free House
Open 12-2.30 5.30-11
Bar food 12-2.30 6.30-11 Av main course £6
Restaurant 12-2.30 6.30-11 Av 3 course à la carte £11
Accommodation s£20 d£32

OLD DALBY Leicestershire

The Crown Inn
OLD DALBY Map 08 SK62
Debdale Hill LE14 3LF
☎ 01164 823134
Log fires, fresh flowers and antique furniture feature at this 16th-century pub. The emphasis is on fresh food, with home-made bread, pickles, and herbs from the garden. Expect wild rabbit Bourguignonne with fresh pasta, or monkfish marinated in five spices with sweet garlic purée and beurre citronelle. Principal beers: Mansfield bitter, Black Sheep, Smooth Brew, Batemans XB.
Free House
Open 12-3 6-11
Bar food 12-2 6-10 Av main course £10.95
Restaurant 7-10 Av 3 course à la carte £22

REDMILE Leicestershire

Peacock Inn
REDMILE Map 08 SK73
Church Corner NG13 0GA
☎ 01949 842554
On the banks of the old Grantham canal, this stone-built 18th-century inn offers a wide menu. Fresh lobster on a bed of tagliatelle, grilled seabass with king prawns, or ostrich steak with walnut and port under onion and potato rosti may be on the menu today. Principal beers: Timothy Taylors, Pedigree, Tetleys, Bass.
Directions From A1 take A52 towards Nottingham
Free House
Open 11-11
Bar food 12-2.30 6.30-11 Av main course £7.95
Restaurant 12-2 7-11 Av 3 course fixed price £14.95
Accommodation s£65 d£75

SIBSON Leicestershire

The Cock Inn
SIBSON Map 04 SK30
Main St CV13 6LB ☎ 01827 880357
One of England's oldest inns, dating from about 1250, and a refuge of the notorious highwayman Dick Turpin in the 1730s. Traditional home-cooked meals are served incorporating continental-style dishes, ranging from sandwiches to entrecôte Stilton. Other options include curry, lasagne and roast Barbary duckling. Principal beers: Draught Brew XI, Draught Bass.
Directions On A444 between Nuneaton & M42 J11
Free House
Open 11.30-2.30 6.30-11
Bar food 11.30-2 6.30-9.45 Av main course £6.25
Restaurant 11.30-2 6.30-9.45 Av 3 course à la carte £17.55

SILEBY Leicestershire

The White Swan
SILEBY Map 08 SK61
Swan St LE12 7NW ☎ 01509 814832
The White Swan is proud of its reputation for good value home-cooked food. Dishes include pork and garlic paté served with hot croissants; pot roasted pheasant with cider and shallots, and whole baked seabass with prawns, lemon and butterpat. Vegetarian dishes are also featured. Principal beers: Shipstoes, Ansells bitter, Marstons Pedigree, Tetleys.
Free House
Open 11.45-3 7-11
Bar food 12-2 7-10 Av main course £5.95
Restaurant 12-2 7-10 Av 3 course à la carte £16.50

SOMERBY Leicestershire

The Old Brewery
SOMERBY Map 08 SK71
High St LE14 2PZ ☎ 01664 454866
Home of the Parish Brewery, which produces the award-winning Parish Special Bitter and Baz's Bonce Blower, this inn has been a labour of love for Barrie Parish and Jim Cantrell. But food is important too as a typical menu featuring spicy Cajun chicken, Somerby sausages, and Somerby hot pot demonstrates. Principal beers: Parish Special Bitter.

Directions Between Melton Mowbray & Oakham off the A606 at Leesthorpe
Free House
Open 11-2.30 6-11 (Sun 12-11)
Bar food 11.45-2 6.45-10
Accommodation d£25

THORPE LANGTON Leicestershire

The Bakers Arms
THORPE LANGTON Map 04 SP79
Main St LE16 7TS ☎ 01858 545201
A thatched property with exposed beams and big open fires in the winter. There's a welcoming atmosphere and the cosy rooms are pine furnished on quarry-tiled floors. The food is all home-made and typical dishes are prawns in garlic mayonnaise, and steak, kidney and Guinness pie. Principal beers: Burton, Tetley.
Directions S of Leicester on the A6 take L turn marked 'The Langtons'
Free House
Open 11-6.30 (Sat-Sun 12-2.30)
Bar food 12-2 6.30-9.30 Av main course £10
Restaurant 12-2 6.30-9.30 Av 3 course à la carte £16.95

WALCOTE Leicestershire

The Black Horse Inn
WALCOTE Map 04 SP58
Littleworth Rd LE17 4JU
☎ 01455 552684
Authentic Thai cooking is served at the Black Horse. The simple menu lists types of dishes cooked with the meat of your choice - perhaps beef, pork, chicken or prawn. These include Phat Khing, stir-fried meat with ginger and onion, and Kaeng Phed, meat with spices and herbs in coconut cream. Principal beers: HOB Bitter, Timothy Taylor Landlord, Hook Norton.
Free House
Open 12-2.3 (Mon-Tue closed) 6.30-11
Bar food 12-2 7-9.30 Av main course £6

WOODHOUSE EAVES Leicestershire

The Pear Tree Inn
WOODHOUSE EAVES Map 08 SK51
Church Hill LE12 8RT ☎ 01509 890243
Set in the heart of Charnwood Forest, the Pear Tree has been managed by the same family for three generations. A typical menu may feature seafood goujons, char-grilled nut cutlets, or home-made

beefburgers, as well as ploughmans', sandwiches and baps, and chalk-board daily specials. Principal beers: Burton Ale, Tetley Trad, Marstons Pedigree, Kilkeny.
Directions Village centre
Free House
Open 11.30-3 6-11.30
Bar food 12-2 7-10 Av main course £6.50
Restaurant 12-2 7-10 Av 3 course à la carte £12

Lincolnshire

ALLINGTON Lincolnshire

The Welby Arms
ALLINGTON Map 08 SK84
The Green NG23 2EA ☎ 01400 281361
Built as a farmhouse in the 17th century, this pub has been licensed for the last 100 years and stands on the village green. Tasty home-cooked food is served, including lunchtime snacks. Typical dishes are mariner's pie, beef Szechuan and ratatouille and pasta bake. Principal beers: John Smiths, Draught Bass, TT Landlord.
Directions From Grantham take either A1 north or A52 west, Allington is 1.5m.
Free House
Open 12-2.30 5.30-11
Restaurant 12-2.30 6.30-10 Av 3 course à la carte £11.50

ASWARBY Lincolnshire

The Tally Ho Inn
ASWARBY Map 08 TF03
NG34 8SA ☎ 01529 455205
Originally a farmhouse, this 17th-century inn is surrounded by parkland on which sheep graze contentedly. Exposed beams, stone walls and log fires create a warm ambience. Dishes include hot smoked salmon tartlets, beef and horseradish casserole, and date and walnut pudding. Principal beers: Batemans, Bass.

contd.

Directions From A1 take Grantham exit onto A52 towards Boston. Take A15 towards Sleaford.
Free House
Open 12-3 6-11
Bar food 12-2.30 6.30-10
Restaurant 12-2.30 7-10 Av 3 course à la carte £15
Accommodation s£30 d£45

BARNOLDBY LE BECK Lincolnshire

The Ship Inn
BARNOLDBY LE BECK Map 08 TA20
Main Rd DN37 0BG ☎ 01472 822308
The inside of this 200-year-old inn is like a Pandora's box of interesting bric-a-brac, fresh flowers and vines. Home cooking with bistro flair is offered, with specials such as rustic pan-fried lamb steak, parfait of duckling with smoked bacon in a cherry brandy sauce, and croustade of seafood Mornay. Principal beers: Directors, Youngers, Flowers Original, Boddingtons Gold, Theakstons Best.
Directions Off A46/A18 SW of Grimsby
Free House
Open 11-3 6.30-11
Bar food 12-2 7-9.30 Av main course £7
Restaurant 12-2 7-9.30

BICKER Lincolnshire

Ye Olde Red Lion
BICKER Map 08 TF23
PE20 3EF ☎ 01775 821950
An old world pub, established in 1663, and originally called the Sailors' Rest. There is a range of steaks, beefburger and fish dishes, and home-made specialities such as beef and mushroom pie, crispy chicken and a daily vegetarian dish. Desserts include fruit tart, profiteroles and spotted dick. Principal beers: Batemans and Bass.
Directions 8m W of Boston on A52
Free House
Open 11-3 (Sat-Sun Open All Day) 6-11
Bar food 11-2.30 6-9.30 Av main course £6
Restaurant 11-2.30 6-9.30 Av 3 course à la carte £10

AA members can call AA Hotel Booking Service on 0990 050505 to book at AA recognised hotels and B & Bs in the UK and Ireland, or through our Internet site: http://www.theaa.co.uk/hotels

BOURNE Lincolnshire

The Wishing Well Inn & A La Carte Restaurant
BOURNE Map 08 TF02
Main St, Dyke PE10 0AF
☎ 01778 422970
Situated in the centre of the village, with inglenook fireplaces and original beams. A wide choice of bar snacks is available, plus home-made vegetarian options such as Wellington vegetables flavoured with saffron and ginger. Duck à l'orange, salmon en croûte, and breaded lemon sole are among the main course dishes.
Directions 1m N of Bourne off A15 between Peterborough & Lincoln
Free House
Open 11-12
Bar food 11.45-2 6-10 Av main course £5.50
Restaurant 11.45-1.30 7-10 Av 3 course à la carte £18 Av 2 course fixed price £8

COLEBY Lincolnshire

The Bell Inn
COLEBY Map 08 SK96
Far Ln LN5 0AH ☎ 01522 810240
An 18th-century inn full of character and charm with low beamed ceilings, open log fires and a barrel shaped bar with lots of international number plates. Doorstep sandwiches are a house speciality, and in the panelled restaurant freshly made dishes are served in generous portions. Principal beers: Bass, Flowers Original, Tetley.
Directions 8m S of Lincoln on A607.In village turn right at church.
Free House
Open 11.30-11 (Apr-Dec, Closed 3.30-5.30)
Bar food 11.30-2 5.30-10 Av main course £3.50

Restaurant 11.30-2 5.30-10 Av 3 course fixed price £13
Accommodation d£34.50

CONINGSBY Lincolnshire

The Old Lea Gate Inn
CONINGSBY Map 08 TF25
Leagate Rd LN4 4RS ☎ 01526 342370
'Satisfying the hungry traveller since 1542', this inn continues a noble tradition with a wide choice of home-cooked dishes, including grills, fish and specialities such as rack of lamb with mint sauce, chicken balti with rice and naan bread, and steak and kidney pie. Principal beers: Taylors Landlord, Batemans XB, Marstons Pedigree.
Directions Off B1192 just outside Coningsby
Free House
Open 11.30-3 12.30-9
Bar food 12-2 7-10 Av main course £5
Restaurant 12-2 7-9.30 Av 3 course à la carte £13

CORBY GLEN Lincolnshire

The Woodhouse Inn
CORBY GLEN Map 08 TF02
NG33 4NS ☎ 01476 550316
Built in 1839 as an inn and horse transport business, the stables have now been converted to provide accommodation. The only Sardinian oven in Britain is located in the garden. The wood-burning brick-built construction brings an authentic Mediterranean flavour to many dishes on the menu. Principal beers: Theakstons, Ruddles, Youngers.
Directions 4m E of A1 Colsterworth roundabout on the A151
Free House
Open 11-11.30
Bar food 12-3 7-12 Av main course £4.75
Restaurant 12-3 7-12 Av 3 course à la carte £13.50
Accommodation s£32.50 d£39.50

EWERBY Lincolnshire

Finch Hatton Arms
EWERBY Map 08 TF14
43 Main St NG34 9PJ ☎ 01529 460363
Built as an inn during the 1870s, this small hotel retains a 'local' atmosphere in the bar. The same extensive menu is offered in both the bar and the comfortable restaurant, including moussaka, lasagne and chicken tikka masala, plus steaks, fish and vegetarian dishes. Principal beers: Draught Bass, Worthington Cask Bitter, Caffreys, Carling.
Directions 2m N of Kirkby-la-Thorne Jct of A17. Also 2m E of A153 between Sleaford & Anwick
Free House
Open 11.30-3 6.30-11
Restaurant 12-2 7-10 Av 3 course à la carte £15 Av 4 course fixed price £9.50
Accommodation s£36 d£54

FREISTON Lincolnshire

Kings Head
FREISTON Map 08 TF34
Church Rd PE22 0NT ☎ 01205 760368
Originally two 14th-century cottages. Lunchtime menu offers a wide selection of snacks and light meals such as home-made steak and kidney pie, and home-made chicken and mushroom pie. In the evenings, the choice includes Dambuster grill, duck with orange sauce, and lasagne verde. Principal beers: Batemans, Bass, Stella.
Batemans
Open 11-11
Bar food 12-2 7.30-9.30 Av main course £4.95

FROGNALL Lincolnshire

The Goat
FROGNALL Map 08 TF11
155 Spalding Rd PE6 8SA
☎ 01778 347629
The same comprehensive menu is offered throughout this welcoming country pub. The garden looks out onto open fields. Extensions to the original 1640 ale house include a large family dining room with amusements for children. Hearty specials may include game pie, jumbo Yorkshires or chicken Balti. Principal beers: Adnams, Bass

contd.

Directions A1 to Peterborough, A15 to Market Deeping, A16 to Spalding, pub about 1 1/2m from jct of A15 & A16
Free House
Open 11-2.30 6-11 (Sun 12-3, 7-10.30)
Bar food 12-2 6.30-9.30 Av main course £5.50
Restaurant 12-2 6.30-9.30 Av 3 course fixed price £8.50

GEDNEY DYKE Lincolnshire

The Chequers
GEDNEY DYKE Map 09 TF42
PE12 0AJ ☎ 01406 362666
Local artists display their pictures at this traditional East Anglian pub offering great value light meals, or locally sourced specialities such as Lincoln red fillet of beef with smoked salmon and wild mushroom sauce, or the day's choice of fresh seafood. Principal beers: Adnams, Abbot, Elgoods, Old Speckled Hen.
Directions From King's Lynn take A17, 1st roundabout after Long Sutton take B1359
Free House
Open 12-2.30 7-11
Bar food 12-2 7-9/9.30 Av main course £7.50
Restaurant 12-2 7-9/9.30 Av 3 course à la carte £14.50

GRANTHAM Lincolnshire

The Beehive Inn
GRANTHAM Map 08 SK93
10/11 Castlegate NG31 6SE
☎ 01476 567794
Grantham's oldest pub, the Beehive is also the only English pub with a 'living sign'. Located high in a lime tree in front of the pub is a working beehive. A traditional, old English welcome is matched by traditional home-cooked fare such as chilli con carne, gammon, pan-fried steak and ploughman's – which originated here. Principal beers: Batemans XB.
Directions A52 to town centre, L at Finkin St, pub at end
Free House
Open 11.30-11
Bar food 11.30-3 Av main course £2.95

HAGWORTHINGHAM Lincolnshire

George & Dragon
HAGWORTHINGHAM Map 08 TF36
Main Rd PE23 4NA ☎ 01507 588255
The hosts at this traditional country inn take pride adapting to their customers' every need. A truly international choice of dishes is offered including Chinese, Mexican , English, French, Italian. On summer weekends the ice cream garden serves an array of flavours from peanut to cheesecake. Principal beers: John Smiths, Batemans.
Directions Take A158 to coast
Free House
Bar food 12-2 5-9.30 Av main course £5

HECKINGTON Lincolnshire

The Nags Head
HECKINGTON Map 08 TF14
34 High St NG34 9QZ ☎ 01529 460218
Overlooking the green of a village boasting the only 8 sailed windmill in the country, this white painted 17th-century coaching inn reputedly once played host to Dick Turpin. A typical menu might offer pears and Stilton grilled on toast and turkey chestnut lasagne. Principal beers: Wards Best, Double Maxim.
Directions 5m E of Sleaford on A17
Wards
Open 11-3 5-11
Bar food 12-2 7-9 Av main course £6
Accommodation s£22 d£32

LINCOLN Lincolnshire

Wig & Mitre
LINCOLN Map 08 SK97
30 Steep Hill LN2 1TL ☎ 01522 535190
A 14th-century property renovated in the 1970s, with original beams and open fires. Modern British food is served in the bar and restaurant, ranging from sandwiches and toasted Lincolnshire plum bread to daily fresh fish and pan-fried fillet steak with a bacon and potato rosti. Principal beers: Samuel Smiths.
Directions Adjacent to Lincoln Cathedral
Free House
Open 8-11

LONG BENNINGTON Lincolnshire

The Reindeer
LONG BENNINGTON Map 08 SK84
Main Rd NG23 5EH ☎ 01400 281382
A small, welcoming pub with exposed beams and cosy fireplaces set in a pretty, bustling village within easy reach of the main A1. The imaginative menu offers giant Yorkshire pud filled with beef and mushroom cooked in Guinness to vegetable Tikka Masala. Leave room for locally made farmhouse ice cream. Principal beers: John Smiths, Ruddles County, Old Speckled Hen, Theakstons XB.
Directions 7m North of Grantham on the A1
Free House
Open 11-3 7-11
Bar food 11.30-2 7-10
Restaurant 11.30-2 7-10 Av 3 course à la carte £16

MARSTON Lincolnshire

Thorold Arms
MARSTON Map 08 SK84
Main St NG32 2HH ☎ 01400 250899
Built in 1842 as an estate house which farmed and brewed ale, Thorold being the name of the landowners. There's an extensive choice of food, including a range of pizzas, bar steaks, curries and jacket potatoes. The fixed-price menu might include beef stroganoff, chicken chasseur and red trout in almonds. Principal beers: Hardy Hanson, Wards, Worthington, Bass.
Directions Off A1 N of Grantham
Free House
Open 12-4 7-11
Bar food 12-2.45 7-9.45 Av main course £3.50
Restaurant 12.15-2.30 7-9.30 Av 3 course à la carte £10.25 Av 3 course fixed price £6.25
Accommodation s£22.50 d£45

NAVENBY Lincolnshire

Kings Head
NAVENBY Map 08 SK95
High St LN5 0EE ☎ 01522 810367
A warm, friendly welcome awaits at this quaint 17th-century stone village inn, frequented by the Red Arrows flying team. Settle by the inglenook under beamed ceilings in the non-smoking restaurant or in the bar to study a varied menu: steaks with sauces, fish and puddings from the blackboard. Principal beers: Bass, Tetleys, Friary Meux.
Directions From Lincoln, A607 to Navenby
Free House
Open 12-11
Bar food 12-2 7-10
Restaurant 12-2 7-10

NEWTON Lincolnshire

The Red Lion
NEWTON Map 08 TF03
NG34 0EE ☎ 01529 497256
The village of Newton has only sixteen houses, and is 10 miles from anywhere, so this pub will be ideal for those looking for some peace and quiet. There are three menus: the Cold Carvery, the Hot Carvery (available at weekends only) and a blackboard bar menu. Principal beers: Bateman's XXXB, Draught Bass.
Directions 10m E of Grantham on A52
Free House
Open 11.30-3 6-11.30
Bar food 12-2 7-10 Av main course £7
Restaurant 12-2 7-10 Av 3 course à la carte £13.75

OLD SOMERBY Lincolnshire

Fox & Hounds
OLD SOMERBY Map 08 SK93
NG33 4AB ☎ 01476 564121
This traditional free house in a small, picturesque village is noted in the area for its home-cooked fare: roasts, steaks and Grimsby fish which includes poached halibut in a fennel, cream and parsley sauce or a 'whale' sized seafood platter. Principal beers: Ruddles, Marstons, Courage.
Directions From A1 take A52 E, after 3m take B1176, then 1m to Old Somerby
Free House
Open 11-2.30 7-11.30

contd.

Bar food 12-2.30 7-10 Av main course £5
Restaurant 12-2.30 Av 3 course à la carte £10.15

PARTNEY Lincolnshire

Red Lion Inn
PARTNEY Map 09 TF46
PE23 4PG ☎ 01790 752271
Parts of this Lincolnshire inn may date back up to 400 years, but reports of a ghost seem to be unsubstantiated. Typical menu includes Lincolnshire sausages, chicken and cranberry cobbler, cod and courgette bake, pork in cream and wine, or leek and mushroom lasagne. Principal beers: Bass, Batemans.
Directions On the A16 from Boston, or A158 from Horncastle
Free House
Open 11-2.30 7-11 (Sun 12-2.30, 7-10.30)
Bar food 12-2 7-9.30 Av main course £6
Accommodation s£25 d£35

RAITHBY Lincolnshire

Red Lion Inn & Le Baron Restaurant
RAITHBY Map 08 TF36
PE23 4DS ☎ 01790 753727
Set in the attractive village of Raithby, this Tudor-style listed inn specialises in Indian food and pizzas. Menu may include lamb pasanda, duck breast in redcurrant sauce, Sicilian pizza, spinach and ricotta cannelloni, or fennel pie. Principal beers: Raithby Bitter.
Directions Take A158 from Horncastle, R at Sausthorpe, keep L into Raithby
Free House
Open 12-3.30 (wknds, BHs only) 7-11
Bar food 12-3 7.30-10.30 Av main course £5
Restaurant 12-3 7.30-10.30 Av 3 course à la carte £12.50
Accommodation s£20 d£32

ROTHWELL Lincolnshire

The Nickerson Arms
ROTHWELL Map 08 TF19
Hill Rise LN7 6AZ ☎ 01472 371300
Originally the village forge, and said to be haunted by an old cellarman, this village inn dates back to the 16th century. Dishes on offer might include roast goose with ginger, mango and spring onion glaze, or homemade steak and Guinness pie with smoked mussels. Principal beers: Batemans, Fuller London Pride, Courage Directors, Marstons Pedigree.
Directions A46 towards Lincoln, L to Swallow, Rothwell 3m
Free House
Open 12-3 7-11
Bar food 12-2 7-9.30 Av main course £5.50
Restaurant 12-2 7-9.30 Av 3 course à la carte £18

SAXILBY Lincolnshire

The Bridge Inn
SAXILBY Map 08 SK87
Gainsborough Rd LN1 2LX
☎ 01522 702266
Canalside pub near Lincoln. Bar snacks and blackboard specials are available. Main course menu offers a selection of steak and seafood dishes, including sirloin à la creme with brandy, cream and mushroom sauce, poached plaice with prawn cream sauce, grilled fresh trout, and deep fried calamari. Principal beers: John Smiths, Theakstons, Best, Directors.
Directions Just off A57 W of Lincoln
Free House
Open 11.30-2.30 7-11
Bar food 11.30-2 7-various Av main course £5.75
Restaurant 11.30-2 7-Various

SPALDING Lincolnshire

The Ship Inn
SPALDING Map 08 TF22
Reservoir Rd, Surfleet-Seas-End
PE11 4DH ☎ 01775 680384
Dating back to 1640, this pub is situated at the confluence of the rivers Glen, Welland and Vernatts Drain. Home-made pies include steak and kidney, veal and ham, and chicken

and vegetable. Other main dishes range from roast pheasant and confit of duck, to grilled trout and halibut steak. Principal beers: Marstons, Pedigree.
Directions Off A16 (Spalding to Boston)
Free House
Open 12-3 7-11 (flexible openings, min hours shown)
Bar food 12-3 Av main course £3
Restaurant 7-11 Av 3 course à la carte £10
Accommodation d£35

SPRINGTHORPE Lincolnshire

The New Inn
SPRINGTHORPE Map 08 SK88
14-16 Hill Rd DN21 5PY
☎ 01427 838254
A terraced pub, circa 1880, in an idyllic setting on the village green. The landlord, who sometimes delights his customers with an impromptu song, is also a qualified masseur, and has been known to treat customers as they wait for their food. Home-style cooking is provided by the landlady. Principal beers: Batemans XXXB, Marstons Pedigree.
Directions Off A631 SE of Gainsborough
Free House
Open 12-2 7-11
Bar food 12-2 7-11 Av main course £5
Restaurant 12-2 7-11 Av 3 course à la carte £10 Av 4 course fixed price £8.50

STAMFORD Lincolnshire

The George at Stamford
STAMFORD Map 04 TF00
71 St Martins PE9 2LB ☎ 01780 755171
The George is a beautiful 16th-century coaching inn with log fires, an oak panelled restaurant for formal dining and a walled monastery garden. The Garden Lounge menu offers a range of pasta dishes, a cold buffet, and other options ranging from stir-fried chilli squid to Nelsons Lincolnshire sausages and mash. Principal beers: Adnams, Ruddles.
Directions Town centre
Free House
Open 7am-11pm
Restaurant 12.30-2.30 7.30-10.30 Av 3 course à la carte £30 Av 2 course fixed price £13.50
Accommodation s£72 d£95

St Peter's Inn and The Bistro
STAMFORD Map 04 TF00
11 St Peter's St PE9 2DQ
☎ 01780 763298
Thai style wok dishes are a speciality at this 18th-century pub and bistro in the conservation area of Stamford. As well as Thai style chicken or vegetable curry, the menu here may offer feta cheese omelette, pasta carbonara, fillet steak royale, or St Peter's mussel surprise. Principal beers: Marstons
Directions From A1 take A6121 to Stamford.Pub 1m on R
Free House
Open 12-2.30 (Tue-Thurs) 12-9 (Fri-Sun)
Bar food 12-2 Av main course £6.95
Restaurant 12-2 6.30-9 Av 3 course à la carte £12

TETFORD Lincolnshire

The White Hart Inn
TETFORD Map 09 TF37
East Rd LN9 6UU ☎ 01507 533255
Built around 1520, this three-bar country pub was frequented by Dr Johnson and Tennyson - though not at the same time! There's a frequently changing menu of home-cooked food. Items from the specials board include steak and beer pie, rabbit fricassée, seafood gratin, and vegetarian bake. Principal beers: Batemans XXXB, Adnams Best Bitter, Fullers London Pride.
Directions From Louth take A16 S Tetford signed on R
Free House
Open 12-3 7-11
Bar food 12-2 7-9 Av main course £5.50
Restaurant 12-2 7-9 Av 3 course à la carte £11

WADDINGHAM Lincolnshire

Brandy Wharf Cider Centre
WADDINGHAM Map 08 SK99
Brandy Wharf DN21 4RJ
☎ 01652 678364
Set in an orchard of some 170 apple and pear trees, this traditional tavern has a 200-yard frontage against the River Ancholme and serves no beer - only cider. Typical menu includes Herefordshire scrumpy cider sausage, steak and vegetable pie, rainbow trout,

contd.

and vegetarian lasagne. Principal beers: Cider Only.
Directions On the B1205 between S Kelsey & Waddingham
Open 12-3 7-11
Bar food 12-2 7-9.45 Av main course £4.50

WOODHALL SPA Lincolnshire

Abbey Lodge Inn
WOODHALL SPA Map 08 TF16
Tattershall Rd, Kirkstead LN10 6UQ
☎ 01526 352538
Named after Kirkstead Abbey, of which little remains, this traditional pub is in a 200-year-old Grade II listed building. They offer good home-cooked dishes, with vegetarian options, chicken and fish dishes, followed by desserts like spotted dick and custard, or peach meringue basket. Principal beers: Bass.
Free House
Open 10.30-2.30 6.30-11
Bar food 12-2 7-10 Av main course £5.50
Restaurant 12-2 7-10 Av 3 course à la carte £10

WOOLSTHORPE Lincolnshire

Rutland Arms
WOOLSTHORPE Map 08 SK83
NG32 1NY ☎ 01476 870360
Better known to locals as the 'Dirty Duck', this family pub sits at the side of the Grantham canal, in the shadow of Belvoir Castle. Specialities include Bobby T's freshly-caught cod and haddock, grilled pork cutlet, roast beef and Yorkshire pudding, and rainbow trout with almond butter. Principal beers: Castle Eden, Flowers Original, Trophy.
Free House
Open 11-3 6-11
Bar food 11-3 6-9.30 Av main course £5
Restaurant 11-3 6-9.30 Av 3 course à la carte £11

Norfolk

BAWBURGH Norfolk

Kings Head
BAWBURGH Map 05 TG10
Harts Ln NR9 3LS
☎ 01603 744977
A cosy 17th-century pub with low beamed ceilings and large open fires, plus a courtyard and garden outside. Food is cooked to order, and there's plenty to choose from: snacks, grills and fish, home-made pies, vegetarian dishes and favourites such as burgers, curry and chilli. Principal beers: Adnams, Boddingtons, Flowers Original, Marstons Pedigree.
Directions From A47 W of Norwich take B1108 W
Free House
Open 11-11 (Sun 12-10.30)
Bar food 12-2 7-10 Av main course £6.75
Restaurant 12-2 7-10 Av 3 course à la carte £18

BINHAM Norfolk

Chequers Inn
BINHAM Map 09 TF93
Front St NR21 0AL ☎ 01328 830297
Set in the picturesque flint village of Binham not far from the Norfolk coast, the Chequers Inn was built in the 17th century and is in charitable trust to the village. Chicken Penang, wild boar and pheasant pie, stuffed quail, or Stilton and leek bake may be on today's menu. Principal beers: Greene King IPA and Abbot, Adnams Best, Adnams Broadside, Draught Bass.
Directions On B1388 between Wells-next-the-Sea & Walsingham
Free House

Open 11.30-3 5.30-11.30 (Sun 12-3,7-10.30)
Bar food 12-2 6-9 Av main course £5
Restaurant 6-9
Accommodation d£36

BLICKLING Norfolk

The Buckinghamshire Arms

BLICKLING Map 09 TG12
Blickling Rd NR11 6NF ☎ 01263 732133
Late 17th-century coaching inn, originally built for guests and servants of nearby Blickling Hall. Lunch menu offers a wide selection of snacks, salads, and home-made pies and lasagnes. Dinner menu includes grilled steak dishes, and pasta meals such as pasta linguini with smoked salmon, prawns and cream. Principal beers: Reepham Brewery, Adnams.
Directions From Cromer (A140) take exit at Aylsham onto B1354
Free House
Open 11-3 6-11
Bar food 12-2.30 7-9 Av main course £5.95
Restaurant 12-2.30 7-9 Av 3 course à la carte £16
Accommodation s£40 d£60

BRANDON CREEK Norfolk

The Ship

BRANDON CREEK Map 05 TL69
PE38 0PP ☎ 01353 676228
The Ship was built in 1640 on the site of an old blacksmith's forge. There are various grisly stories of murder and ghosts, so make sure you ask the right questions! An extensive menu covers soup of the day to a monster mixed grill, accompanied by live music in winter. Principal beers: Tetley Keg, Adnams, Abbot Ale, Butcombe.
Directions S of Downham Market on A10
Free House
Open 11-3 6-11
Bar food 12-2.30 6.30-9.30 Av main course £5.50
Restaurant 12-2.30 6.30-9.30 Av 3 course à la carte £10 Av 2 course fixed price £5

BRESSINGHAM Norfolk

The Old Garden House

BRESSINGHAM Map 05 TM08
IP22 2AG ☎ 01379 687405
16th-century thatched pub where families are welcome, and events such as Burns Night and Chinese New Year are celebrated in style. The menu may include fillet of wild boar in a red wine sauce, pasta Florentine or, for the younger diner, Dizzy Dinosaurs and Cheesy Chicken Feet! Principal beers: Old Roosters, Adnams, Directors.
Free House
Open 12-3 6 11
Bar food 12-2.30 7-9.30 Av main course £6
Restaurant 12-2.30 7-9.30 Av 3 course à la carte £15

BURNHAM MARKET Norfolk

The Hoste Arms

BURNHAM MARKET Map 09 TF84
The Green PE31 8HD
☎ 01328 738257
17th-century inn overlooking the village green. Typical lunch menu starters are marinated anchovies with dill and shallot dressing, or terrine de campagne with red onion chutney and croûtons. Main courses include collops of monkfish with spring onion risotto, and aubergine, tomato and goats cheese with pimento vinaigrette. Principal beers: Woodfordes Wherry, Greene King.
Directions From Fakenham take B1355 N to Burnham Market
Free House
Bar food 12-2 7-9 Av main course £8.95
Restaurant 12-2 7-9 Av 3 course à la carte £17
Accommodation s£60 d£96

BURNHAM THORPE Norfolk

The Lord Nelson

BURNHAM THORPE Map 09 TF84
Walsingham Rd PE31 8HN
☎ 01328 738241
There is no bar at this pub, the ale is served straight from the barrel. It was Nelson's local in the 1780s and little has changed since, even the wooden settles and stone-flagged floors remain. Home-cooked food includes a vegetarian menu and fish and game specials. Principal beers: Abbot,Greene King IPA & Mild, Nelsons Revenge(Woodfordes).

contd.

Free House
Open 11-3 6-11 (Sun 12-3,7-10.30)
Bar food 12-2 7-9 Av main course £6.95

CLEY NEXT THE SEA Norfolk

George & Dragon Hotel
CLEY NEXT THE SEA Map 09 TG04
High St NR25 7NR ☎ 01263 740652
Rebuilt at the turn of the century in classic Edwardian style, this village hotel overlooks a shallow lake popular with kingfishers, herons and visiting bird watchers. A good selection of sandwiches and light meals are available such as Cley cider pickled herrings and calamari. Main courses include Norfolk steak dishes and curries. Principal beers: Greene King, IPA, Abbot.
Directions On coast road (A149). Centre of village
Free House
Open 11-3 (Winter, 11.30-2.30) 6-11 (Winter, 6.30-11)
Bar food 12-2 7-8.45 Av main course £5
Restaurant 12-2 7-8.45 Av 3 course à la carte £12
Accommodation s£35 d£45

DOCKING Norfolk

Pilgrims Reach
DOCKING Map 09 TF73
High St PE31 8NH ☎ 01485 518383
16th-century inn once popular with pilgrims. A good selection of appetisers such as lobster bisque with brandy and cream, baked goats' cheese wrapped in pastry with warm pear sauce, and turtle soup with dry sherry. Main dishes include grilled Dover sole and roast duckling with orange and lime glaze. Principal beers: Adnams, Greene King, Carlsberg.
Directions From Hunstanton take A1495 then B1454 or A149 E then B1153
Free House
Open 12-3 7-11.30
Bar food 12-2 7-9.30 Av main course £7
Restaurant 7-10.30 Av 3 course à la carte £20

AA members can call AA Hotel Booking Service on 0990 050505 to book at AA recognised hotels and B & Bs in the UK and Ireland, or through our Internet site: http://www.theaa.co.uk/hotels

EASTGATE Norfolk

Ratcatchers Inn
EASTGATE Map 09 TG12
Easton Way NR10 4HA
☎ 01603 871430
A 200-year-old pub with a great atmosphere, where rat catchers used to meet to collect 'a penny a tail'. Everything is home made - bread, herb oils and chutneys - and there's an extensive choice including vegetarian dishes, seafood, grills, pies, eastern and continental food. Principal beers: Bass, Adnams.
Directions Off A140, past Norwich Airport take B1149 to Holt, thru Horsford, 6m then pub signed
Free House
Open 12-2.30 6-11 (Sun 12-3, 7-10.30)
Bar food 12-2.30 6-11 Av main course £7
Restaurant 12-2.30 6-11 Av 3 course à la carte £13

ERPINGHAM Norfolk

Saracen's Head
ERPINGHAM Map 09 TG13
Wolterton NR11 7LX ☎ 01263 768909
Set amongst rolling Norfolk hills and built in 1806, the Saracen's Head claims to be individualistic and to have an addictive atmosphere. Visitors can decide for themselves by sampling from a menu that may include crab and whitefish fishcakes, grilled fillet of Scottish salmon, or escalope of veal Milanese. Principal beers: Adnams Bitter.
Directions W of A140 N of Aylsham.Take L turn follow signs 'Calthorpe'.Thru' Calthorpe 1m on R
Free House
Open 11-3 6-11
Bar food 12.30-2 7.30-9 Av main course £7.25
Restaurant 12.30-2 7.30-9 Av 3 course à la carte £13.50
Accommodation s£35 d£45

GREAT BIRCHAM Norfolk

King's Head Hotel
GREAT BIRCHAM Map 09 TF73
PE31 6RJ ☎ 01485 578265
Italian food is the speciality of this house - a friendly village hotel. Starters include fish salad, house paté and a range of pasta dishes. To follow, chicken, veal and pork are offered in creamy sauces, along

with grilled steaks and some fish options such as salmon with anchovy butter. Principal beers: Ancocks, Worthington BB, Bass.
Free House
Open 11-2 7-9.30
Bar food 12-2 7-9.30 Av main course £7
Restaurant 12-2.30 7-9.30 Av 3 course à la carte £18
Accommodation s£37 d£57

GREAT RYBURGH Norfolk

The Boar Inn
GREAT RYBURGH Map 09 TF92
NR21 0DX ☎ 01328 829212
300-year-old village inn opposite the church. A good selection of sandwich snacks and starters, such as smoked mackerel and tandoori chicken tikka, and home-made pizzas. Main courses include rahmschnitzel, roast duck with black cherry sauce, and courgette and pasta bake for vegetarians. Principal beers: Adnams, Carlsberg, Kilkenny, Guinness.
Directions Off A1067 4m S of Fakenham
Free House
Open 11-2.30 6.30-11
Bar food 12-2 7-9.30 Av main course £5.50
Restaurant 12-2 7-9.30 Av 3 course à la carte £11
Accommodation s£18 d£35

HAPPISBURGH Norfolk

The Hill House
HAPPISBURGH Map 09 TG33
NR12 0PW ☎ 01692 650004
A 16th-century coaching inn with original beams, large fireplaces and a cobbled rear yard. (The stables have been converted into a children's bar.) Food includes snacks and popular dishes such as plaice princess, with prawns, peppercorns and cream, and steaks with a choice of sauces. Principal beers: Shepherd Neame, Scotts, Wolf, John Bull.
Directions From A149 N of Gt Yarmouth take B1151 then L onto B1159 take 3rd R
Free House
Open 12-3 7-11 (Sat-Sun & summer 12-11)
Bar food 12-2 7-9.30 Av main course £4.50
Restaurant 12-2 7-9.30 Av 3 course à la carte £9
Accommodation s£10 d£20

HEMPSTEAD Norfolk

Hare and Hounds
HEMPSTEAD Map 09 TG13
Baconsthorpe Rd NR25 6LD
☎ 01263 713285
Flint building dating from 1620 complete with original beams. Blackboard specials typically include game pie in herby crust, jugged hare, toad in the hole, and soused herring. Vegetarians options include mushroom Stroganoff, and aubergine and kidney bean casserole. Enjoys regular visits from local folk musicians. Principal beers: Hare of the Hound (own ale) Abbot, WoodfordesWherry, Adnams.
Directions From Holt follow signs for Baconsthorpe. Pub 1.5m from Holt(pub not actually in Hempstead)
Free House
Open 11.30-3 (Sun 12-3) 5.30-11 (Sun 7-10.30)
Bar food 12-2 6-9.30 Av main course £4.95

HETHERSETT Norfolk

Kings Head Public House
HETHERSETT Map 05 TG10
36 Norwich Rd NR9 3DD
☎ 01603 810206
An attractive 17th-century roadside inn with a beamed snug bar, a comfortable lounge bar with an inglenook fireplace, and a separate dining room. A good choice of sandwiches and toasties is offered at lunchtime, while the specials board offers spinach and mushroom lasagne, poached salmon, chilli, steaks and omelettes. Principal beers: Courage Directors, Marstons Pedigree, Morlands Old Speckled Hen, John Smiths.

contd.

Directions Old Norwich Road just off B1172 Cringleford to Wymondham road. 5m SW of Norwich
Free House
Open 11-2.30 5.30-11
Bar food 12-2.30 6.30-9.30 Av main course £5.75

HORSEY Norfolk

Nelson Head
HORSEY Map 09 TG42
The Street NR29 4AO
☎ 01493 393378 01692 581016
16th-century country pub specialising in Austrian cuisine, situated in an area ideal for bird-watching, sailing and fishing. Today's menu may include Austrian dishes such as weiner schnitzel with salad, or znaimer gulash with noodles. Other dishes may be Golden Pond trout, roast duckling, and double lamb chop with tomato and courgettes. Principal beers: Woodfordes Wherry, Nelsons Revenge.
Directions On coast rd (B1159) between West Somerton & Sea Palling
Free House
Open 11-2.30 7-11
Bar food 11-2 7-9.30 Av main course £5
Restaurant 11-2 7-9.30 Av 3 course à la carte £10

KING'S LYNN Norfolk

The Tudor Rose Hotel
KING'S LYNN Map 09 TG62
St Nicholas St PE30 1LR
☎ 01553 762824
Dating from about 1500, the building retains many original features, such as the fireplace, beams, and splendid crown post roof. Snacks and light meals are served in the panelled front bar, while the restaurant menu might offer steak or salmon fillet with herb crust. Principal beers: Batemans XB,Woodfordes Wherry,Bass.
Directions Town centre
Free House
Open 11-11 (Sun 7-10.30)
Bar food 12-2 7-9 Av main course £3.95
Restaurant 7-9
Accommodation s£30

AA members can call AA Hotel Booking Service on 0990 050505 to book at AA recognised hotels and B & Bs in the UK and Ireland, or through our Internet site: http://www.theaa.co.uk/hotels

MUNDFORD Norfolk

Crown Hotel
MUNDFORD Map 05 TG89
Crown Rd IP26 5HQ ☎ 01842 878233
Principal beers: Woodfordes Wherry, Sam Smiths, Marstons Pedigree.
Directions Take A11 to Barton Mills intersection, then A1065 to Brandon & thru to Mundford
Free House
Open 11-11
Bar food 12-3 7-10 Av main course £5.75
Restaurant 12-3 7-10 Av 3 course à la carte £18
Accommodation s£32.50 d£49.50

NORWICH Norfolk

Adam & Eve
NORWICH Map 05 TG20
Bishopsgate NR2 2RZ ☎ 01603 667423
The oldest pub in Norwich, dating from 1249. Originally a brewhouse for the workmen building Norwich Cathedral. Several ghosts from the nearby monks' cemetery are said to haunt the pub. Daily specials are listed on the blackboard. Other dishes include game pie, and Elizabethan pork cooked in cider and rosemary. Principal beers: Adnams, BB, Wadworths 6X, John Smiths.
Free House
Open 11-11 (Sun 12-10.30)
Bar food 12-7 Av main course £4.50

Ribs of Beef
NORWICH Map 05 TG20
24 Wensum St NR3 1HY
☎ 01603 619517
One-bar riverside pub named after one of Henry VIII's favourite dishes. The original building was destroyed by the Great Fire of Norwich in 1507. Bar food offers a wide range of sandwiches, salads and omelettes, Norfolk ham being a favoured ingredient. Noted for its choice of real ales. Principal beers: Woodfordes, Wolf, Reepham, Adnams.
Open 10.30-11 (Mon-Sat) 12-10.30 (Sun)
Bar food 12-2.30 Av main course £4.35

SNETTISHAM Norfolk

The Rose & Crown
SNETTISHAM Map 09 TF63
Old Church Rd PE31 7LX
☎ 01485 541382
Built to accommodate the workmen who constructed Snettisham Church in 1397, and situated near some of West Norfolk's splendid beaches. House specialities range from Armenian lamb, and home-made beef and spinach lasagne, to Thai style stir fry. Vegetarian dishes typically include mushroom Stroganoff and home-made vegetable chilli. Principal beers: Woodfordes, Adnams, Bass.
Directions Off A149 N of King's Lynn
Free House
Open 11-11
Bar food 12-2.30 6-10 Av main course £7.50
Restaurant 12-2.30 6-10

STIFFKEY Norfolk

Stiffkey Red Lion
STIFFKEY Map 09 TF94
44 Wells Rd NR23 1AJ ☎ 01328 830552
Overlooking the River Stiffkey and close to the National Seal Sanctuary, this traditional village pub specialises in beer from local micro-breweries. A typical menu includes fresh local dressed crab, game and ale casserole, organic pork and leek sausages, and a variety of grilled locally-caught fish. Principal beers: Woodfordes Wherry, Greene King, Adnams Southwood.
Directions Take A149 from Wells toward Cromer, 5m then L
Free House
Open 11-3 6-11
Bar food 12-2 6-9 Av main course £6
Restaurant 12-2 6-9 Av 3 course à la carte £16

STOW BARDOLPH Norfolk

The Hare Arms
STOW BARDOLPH Map 05 TF60
PE34 3HT ☎ 01366 382229
Located in the quiet Norfolk village of Stow Bardolph, The Hare Arms proudly offers 'a sophisticated international cuisine'. Pork steak in cider sauce, jambon à la creme, Madeira chicken, snails in garlic butter, or 'Carpet Bagger' steak may be on today's menu. Principal beers: Rayments, Wexford, Greene King.
Directions From King's Lynn take A10 to Downham Market.After 9m village signed on L
Greene King
Open 11-2.30 6-11 (Sun 12-3,7-10.30)
Bar food 12-2 7-10 Av main course £6
Restaurant 12-2 7-9.30 Av 3 course à la carte £20 Av 3 course fixed price £16.75

SWANTON MORLEY Norfolk

Darbys Freehouse
SWANTON MORLEY Map 09 TG01
Elsing Rd NR20 4JT ☎ 01362 637647
Converted by the current owner from two tied cottages, this freehouse specialises in guest beers from a range of micro-breweries. Beef and Guinness pie, smoked duck tagliatelle, or Torbay sole with smoked salmon, prawns and vermouth sauce may turn up on the menu. Principal beers: Woodfordes, Tanlgefoot, Adnams.
Directions From A47 (Norwich/King's Lynn) take B1147 to Dereham
Free House
Open 11-2.30 6-11 (Sat 11-11,Sun 11-2.30,6-10.30)
Bar food 12-2 7-9.45 Av main course £6
Restaurant 12-2 7-9.45 Av 3 course à la carte £12.50
Accommodation s£25 d£43

THOMPSON Norfolk

The Chequers Inn
THOMPSON Map 05 TL99
Griston Rd IP24 1PX ☎ 01953 483360
Taller visitors will have to stoop in this pub which is one of the longest thatched buildings in Norfolk, as the ceiling in less than 6 feet. Sitting down to eat should be no problem though. The menu may include home-made steak and kidney pie, trout almondine, or mushroom nut fettucine. Principal beers: Adnams, Tetley, Fullers, Carlsberg.
Directions 1m off A1075 (Thetford/Watton rd)
Free House
Open 11-3 6-11
Bar food 11.30-2 6.30-10

AA members can call AA Hotel Booking Service on 0990 050505 to book at AA recognised hotels and B & Bs in the UK and Ireland, or through our Internet site: http://www.theaa.co.uk/hotels

THORPE MARKET Norfolk

Green Farm Restaurant & Hotel
THORPE MARKET Map 09 TG23
North Walsham Rd NR11 8TH
☎ 01263 833602
A 16th-century flint-built farmhouse with Dutch gables, situated on the village green, once thought to have been a small monastery. Typical dishes are Cromer crab cakes, breast of roast Norfolk duckling with a rhubarb and gin compôte, and a choice of charcoal grilled steaks. Principal beers: Greene King IPA, Woolfe Bitter, Tetleys, Carlsberg.
Directions Situated on A149
Free House
Open 11-2.30 6.30-11
Bar food 12-2 7-10 Av main course £7
Restaurant 7-10 Av 3 course à la carte £17.95 Av 4 course fixed price £17.95
Accommodation s£45 d£55

TITCHWELL Norfolk

Titchwell Manor Hotel
TITCHWELL Map 09 TF74
PE31 8BB ☎ 01485 210221
Traditional small hotel close to the shore in an area of outstanding natural beauty. Also close by are golf courses, the RSPB Titchwell Reserve and Sandringham House. Food on offer may include pigeon breast in puff pastry, sauté of razor fish, queen scallops, calamari and mussels, or tagine of halibut. Principal beers: Wexford Irish, Greene King.
Directions A149(coast rd) between Brancaster & Thornhall
Free House
Open 12-2.30 6-11
Bar food 12-2.30 6.30-10 Av main course £12
Restaurant 12-2 6.30-9.30 Av 3 course à la carte £22 Av 3 course fixed price £22
Accommodation s£35 d£70

TOFT MONKS Norfolk

Toft Lion
TOFT MONKS Map 05 TM49
NR34 0EP ☎ 01502 677702
A proper local, as it has been since 1650, this thatched village pub serves simple home-made food, including vegetarian specials. Meals range through ploughman's, hot dogs and burgers, salads, fish and chips and shepherd's pie. Treacle tart and apple crumble are favourite puddings. Principal beers: Adnams Best Bitter,Adnams Broadside, Woodfordes Wherry.
Directions Take A146 from Beccles, then A143
Free House
Open 11.30-2.30 (Sun 12-3.30) 5-11 (Sun 7-10.30)
Bar food 12-2 7-9 Av main course £3.50

UPPER SHERINGHAM Norfolk

The Red Lion Inn
UPPER SHERINGHAM Map 09 TG14
The Street NR26 8AD ☎ 01263 825408
Within easy reach of Sheringham Park and breath-taking coastal walks this 17th-century flint and brick village pub has plenty of authentic charm. It also offers a menu which may include 'Drunken Thumper' - casseroled rabbit, Stilton stuffed flat mushrooms, or devilled lambs kidneys and rice. Principal beers: Woodfordes Wherry, Greene King IPA, Caffreys.
Directions A140(Norwich to Cromer) then A148 to Sheringham/Upper Sheringham
Free House
Open 11.30-3.20 6.30-11.20
Restaurant 12-3 7-11
Accommodation s£18 d£36

WARHAM ALL SAINTS Norfolk

Three Horseshoes
WARHAM ALL SAINTS Map 09 TF94
NR23 1NL ☎ 01328 710547
Became an alehouse in 1725. With gas lighting, stone floors and a good range of bar snacks and vegetable, fish and game home-made pies. Other dishes include plaice in watercress sauce, roast shoulder of lamb, mackerel smokie hot-pot, and Warham cheesy mushroom bake. Principal beers: Greene King, Woodfordes.
Directions From Wells A149 to Cromer,

then R onto B1105 to Warham
Free House
Open 11.30-3 6-11
Bar food 12-2 6.30-9 Av main course £5.50
Restaurant 12-2 6.30-9 Av 3 course à la carte £9.50
Accommodation s£20 d£40

WINTERTON-ON-SEA Norfolk

Fishermans Return
WINTERTON-ON-SEA Map 09 TG41
The Lane NR29 4BN ☎ 01493 393305
This 300 year old brick and flint pub has had George Bernard Shaw and Wilkie Collins among its patrons. If you should follow in their footsteps you may find spicy aubergine soup, mushrooms in Stilton sauce with tagliatelle, or baked lamb in ginger and rhubarb sauce on the menu. Principal beers: Blues and Bloater, Adnams, Theakstons.
Directions N of Gt Yarmouth on B1159
Free House
Open 12-2.30 6-11 (Sat-Sun 12-11, winter 6.30-11)
Bar food 12-2 6.30-9.30
Accommodation s£30 d£45

WOODBASTWICK Norfolk

The Fur & Feather
WOODBASTWICK Map 09 TG31
Slad Ln NR13 6HQ ☎ 01603 720003
The inn is Woodforde's Brewery flagship, just five years old, converted from two cottages that had been used as brewery offices. There's a good choice of dishes, including several for vegetarians. Options include Woodforde's pie, with diced beef and mushrooms cooked in 'Norfolk Nog'. Principal beers: Mild Broadsman, Wherry, Gt Eastern, Nog.
Woodforde's
Open 11-3 6-11
Bar food 12-2 6.30-9.30 Av main course £6.25
Restaurant 12-2 7-9 Av 3 course à la carte £13 Av 3 course fixed price £13

Northamptonshire

ASHBY ST LEDGERS Northamptonshire

The Olde Coach House Inn
ASHBY ST LEDGERS Map 04 SP56
CV3 8UN ☎ 01788 890349
There's plenty to do at this 19th-century inn. 1998 should see events such as Bank Holiday pig roasts, a beer festival, and an Easter egg hunt. The menu may offer spinach pasta carbonara, three bone rack of lamb, or tuna steak baked with banana and brandy butter. Principal beers: St Ledger Ale, Jennings Cumberland, Everards Old Original.
Directions M1 J11 follow signs A361/Daventry.Village on L
Free House
Open 12-2.30 6-11
Bar food 12-2 6-9.30 Av main course £8
Restaurant 12-2 6-9.30 Av 3 course à la carte £14
Accommodation s£46 d£56

BADBY Northamptonshire

The Windmill Inn
BADBY Map 04 SP55
Main St NN11 6AN ☎ 01327 702363
A traditional 16th-century village inn with flagstones, real fires, inglenook seating and a thatched roof. Tables at the front face one of the village greens. Meals range from the 'steakwich' and ploughman's to a variety of home-cooked fare including a choice of English, French and Cajun dishes. Principal beers: Highgate Dark, Wadworth 6X, Flowers OB, Bass Special.
Directions M1 J16 take A45 to Daventry then A361 S. Village 2m
Free House
Open 11.30-2.30 5.30-11
Bar food 12-2.30 7-9.30 Av main course £5.25
Restaurant 12-2.30 7-9.30 Av 3 course à la carte £12.75
Accommodation s£42 d£49.50

CASTLE ASHBY Northamptonshire

Falcon Hotel
CASTLE ASHBY Map 04 SP85
NN7 1LF ☎ 01604 696200
Claimed to be the prettiest hotel in the county, the 400-year-old Falcon stands in the centre of a privately owned village. Restaurant fare includes poached lobster with whisky sauce, and medallions of venison and pigeon breast with mushrooms and red wine. Bar food is similar, offered alongside traditional bar snacks. Principal beers: Adnams, John Smiths, Marstons, Guinness.
Directions S of A45 between Northampton & Wellingborough
Free House
Open 12-3 6.30-11
Bar food 12-2 7-9.30

contd.

Restaurant 12.30-2 7-10 Av 3 course à la carte £23 Av 3 course fixed price £19.50
Accommodation s£65 d£75

CLIPSTON Northamptonshire

The Bulls Head
CLIPSTON Map 04 SP78
Harborough Rd LE16 9RT ☎ 01858 525268
There are coins in the beams of this 17th-century village pub, apparently left by US airmen for a pint on their return. Snacks include a 'steakwich bap' or ploughman's with pate or cheese. More substantial dishes are 'drunken Bull pie', steaks, chilli, chicken Kiev, fresh fish and vegetarian lasagne. Principal beers: Batemans, Ruddles, Greene King.
Directions On B4036 S of Market Harborough
Free House
Open 11.30-2.30 6.30-11
Bar food 11.30-2 6.30-9.30 Av main course £5.95

COSGROVE Northamptonshire

The Navigation Inn
COSGROVE Map 04 SP74
Thrupp Wharf, Castlethorpe Rd MK19 7BE ☎ 01908 543156
A traditional canal-side pub with many narrow boat associations. The menu offers home-cooked grills, deep-fried cod and ever popular lasagne and chilli, alongside sandwiches and ploughman's. There's a vegetarian choice, such as mushroom stroganoff, and daily blackboard specials including game and fresh fish. Principal beers: Frog Island, Hook Norton, Speckled Hen, Wadworths 6X.
Directions From A5 W of Milton Keynes take A508 N.Take 2nd R, 1st L.Inn 0.5m
Free House
Open 11-3.30 6-11
Bar food 12-2.30 7-9.30

CRICK Northamptonshire

The Red Lion Inn
CRICK Map 04 SP57
52 Main St NN6 7TX ☎ 01788 822342
A thatched, stone-built coaching inn dating from the 1600s. Dishes include rainbow trout, moussaka and roast duckling. At lunchtime there is a choice of savoury bakes, such as leek and smoky bacon, the daily roast, steak, and fried fish, along with sandwiches, ploughman's, and hot and cold sweets. Principal beers: Websters, Pedigree, Theakstons XB.
Directions M1 J18 0.75m E on A428
Free House
Open 11.30-2.30 6.30-11 (Sun 12-3,7-10.30)
Bar food 12-1.45 7-9

FOTHERINGHAY Northamptonshire

The Falcon Inn
FOTHERINGHAY Map 04 TL09
PE8 5HZ ☎ 01832 226254
Crusty bread sandwiches and all home-made dishes are served at this early 19th-century pub. Wholesome soups, smoked fish and home-made patés might be followed by braised rabbit, roast duckling or vegetarian lasagne. Blackberry and apple crumble and banoffee cream pie are among the tempting puddings. Principal beers: Elgoods Cambridge, Adnams, Ruddles County, Bass.
Directions N of A605 between Peterborough & Oundle
Free House
Open 10.30-3 6-11 (Sun 12-3,7-11)
Bar food 12.15-2 6.45-9.45 Av main course £5
Restaurant 12.15-2 6.45-9.45

GRAFTON REGIS Northamptonshire

The White Hart
GRAFTON REGIS Map 04 SP74
Northampton Rd NN12 7SR ☎ 01908 542123
A warm welcome is promised at this family-run pub, which has open fires

in winter and a large beer garden. The owner-chef uses the best fresh produce, adding an interesting twist to some everyday items. Dishes include fried fish, and pork, chicken and steak with a choice of sauces. Principal beers: Greene King Abbot, IPA.
Directions M1 J15 on A508 between Northampton & Milton Keynes
Free House
Open 11.30-3 6-11
Bar food 12-2.30 6-9.30 Av main course £4
Restaurant 12-2.30 6-9.30 Av 3 course à la carte £10

HARRINGTON Northamptonshire

The Tollemache Arms

HARRINGTON Map 04 SP78

High St NN6 9NU ☎ 01604 710469

A thatched 16th-century country inn with bar food comprising grills and seafood, specials such as venison pie, and a choice of Tollemache Fayre, including pasta, sweet and sour chicken and Cumberland sausage. Blanquette of spring lamb, slowly cooked with leeks, shallots and thyme, is a speciality of the restaurant. Principal beers: Eagle IPA, Bombardier.
Directions E of A508 S towards Market Harborough(take turning at Kelmarsh)
Charles Wells
Open 12-2.30 6-11
Bar food 12-2.15 6.45-9 Av main course £5.25
Restaurant 12-2.15 6.45-9

HARRINGWORTH Northamptonshire

The White Swan

HARRINGWORTH Map 04 SP99

Seaton Rd NN17 3AF
☎ 01572 747543

Memorabilia from the nearby USAF wartime airfield, local pictures and old trades' tools are displayed at this stone-built 15th-century coaching inn. Food is freshly prepared from local produce and includes home-made soup and paté, steak, stuffed chicken breast grilled with Stilton, lasagne, fresh salmon, and Chicago-style pork spare ribs. Principal beers: Greene King, Marstons Pedigree.
Directions Off B672 NE of Corby
Free House
Open 11.30-2.30 6.30-11
Bar food 12-2 7-10 Av main course £7.50
Restaurant 12-2 7-10 Av 3 course à la carte £13.50
Accommodation s£34 d£45

KETTERING Northamptonshire

The Overstone Arms

KETTERING Map 04 SP87

Stringers Hill, Pytchley NN14 1EU
☎ 01536 790215

An 18th-century coaching inn, with its own orchard and country garden, in the village of Pytchley. There is a varied menu with favourites such as Guinness pie (with steak and mushrooms), fish dishes, grills, pasta and vegetarian options. This is supported by a list of daily specials. Principal beers: Ruddles, Websters, Kronenbourg, Carling.
Free House
Open 12-3 7-11
Bar food 12-3 7-11 Av main course £12
Restaurant 12-3 7-11 Av 3 course à la carte £12

LITTLE HARROWDEN Northamptonshire

The Lamb

LITTLE HARROWDEN Map 04 SP87

Orlingbury Rd NN9 5BH
☎ 01933 673300

Traditional English fare is offered at this friendly pub, which has evolved over the years from its 17th-century origins. Bar snacks include a generous banger butty, scampi, and steak sandwiches, while steak and kidney pie and wild boar are specialities of the cellar restaurant. Principal beers: Charles Wells Eagle, Bombardier, Adnams Broadside, Speckled Hen.
Charles Wells
Open 11-2.30 7-11
Bar food 12-4 7-9.30 Av main course £5.95
Restaurant 12-2 7-9.30

OUNDLE Northamptonshire

The Mill at Oundle
OUNDLE Map 04 TL08
Barnwell Hill PE8 5PB
☎ 01832 272621
Visitors to this converted watermill can see the River Neve flow under the bar, or dine next to the water and watch the boats go by. A meal here may consist of chicken Valdostana, mushroom Parmigiana, ranch combo platter, or a selection of burgers, pizzas, or Mexican dishes. Principal beers: Courage, Caffreys, Beamish, Fosters.
Directions A14 Thrapston exit, A605 toward Peterborough, 8m Oundle turning, 1m to pub
Free House
Open 11-3 6.30-11
Bar food 12-3 6.30-11 Av main course £7.50
Restaurant 12-3.30 7-11 Av 3 course à la carte £12.50 Av 4 course fixed price £11.75

SIBBERTOFT Northamptonshire

The Red Lion
SIBBERTOFT Map 04 SP68
43 Welland Rise LE16 9UD
☎ 01858 880011
Unspoilt village pub operating the same menu in bar and restaurant. Typical menu includes fish pie, beef lasagne, steak and kidney pudding, and mushroom and nut fettucini. Specials include steak and stilton pie, monkfish and stuffed lambs hearts. Principal beers: Bass, Everards Beacon, Batemans XB, Caffreys.
Directions From Market Harborough take A4304,then A50.After 1m turn L
Free House
Open 11-11 (Mon-Tue evening only)
Bar food 12-2 7-10 Av main course £7.95

STAVERTON Northamptonshire

The Countryman
STAVERTON Map 04 SP56
Daventry Rd NN11 6JH
☎ 01327 311815
There is a warm, homely atmosphere at this 16th-century stone-built pub. Sandwiches and ploughman's are served in the bar, while the restaurant offers traditional pub dishes, plus healthy meats recommended by the Heart Foundation: bison, ostrich, venison and kangaroo, as well as fish and vegetarian dishes. Principal beers: Everards Tiger, Marstons Pedigree, Theakstons XB.
Free House
Open 12-3 6-11
Bar food 12-2 6-9 Av main course £6.25
Restaurant 12-2 6-9 Av 3 course à la carte £18

STOKE BRUERNE Northamptonshire

The Boat Inn
STOKE BRUERNE Map 04 SP74
NN12 7SB ☎ 01604 862428
The Boat is a traditional thatched canal-side inn, opposite the canal museum by the lock. The bar menu offers a good selection from burgers and ploughman's to full home-cooked meals. Restaurant dishes include simple steaks, lobster and more exotic fare such as ostrich and kangaroo meat. Principal beers: Robinsons Best, Marstons Pedigree, Wadworths 6X, Old Speckled Hen.
Free House
Open 9am-11pm (3-6 closed Mon-Fri in winter)
Restaurant 12-2 7-9.30 Av 3 course à la carte £15 Av 3 course fixed price £13.95

SULGRAVE Northamptonshire

The Star Inn
SULGRAVE Map 04 SP54
Manor Rd OX17 2SA ☎ 01295 760389
Grade II listed farmhouse with flagstone floors and open fireplaces, only 200 yards from Sulgrave Manor, ancestral home of George Washington. Today's menu may feature grilled chicken breast with apple,

thyme and bacon sauce, steak and mushroom pie, seafood risotto, or spinach and ricotta flan. Principal beers: Hook Norton, Best Bitter, Old Hooky, Best Mild.
Directions M40 J11 follow brown signs for golf course, then for Sulgrave Manor
Free House
Open 11-2.30 6-11
Bar food 12-2 6.30-9.30 Av main course £8
Restaurant 12-2 6.30-9.30
Accommodation s£30 d£50

UPPER BENEFIELD Northamptonshire

Benefield Wheatsheaf Hotel
UPPER BENEFIELD Map 04 SP98
PE8 5AN ☎ 01832 205245
Stone-built, with a Colly Weston roof, this inn dates from 1645. Bar food offers both cosmopolitan and traditional English dishes with fresh fish from the board. The restaurant's seasonal carte includes Delhi chicken, Jamaican-style steak, and ostrich with a rosemary sauce. Principal beers: Dortmunder, John Smiths, Carlsberg, Stella.
Free House
Open All day opening
Bar food 12-2 6-9.45 Av main course £6.95
Restaurant 12-2 6-9.45 Av 3 course à la carte £17
Accommodation s£42 d£52

WADENHOE Northamptonshire

The King's Head
WADENHOE Map 04 TL08
Church St PE8 5ST ☎ 01832 720024
A thatched 17th-century pub, owned, like most of the houses in the village, by the Wadenhoe Trust. Simple home-made fare is served in the bar - soup, sandwiches, baguettes and toasties - while the restaurant offers dishes such as smoked salmon mousse, and steak and kidney casserole with herb dumplings. Principal beers: Adnams, Pedigree, Guiness, Stella.
Free House
Open 12-3 (not Monday) 6-11
Bar food 12-2 Av main course £3
Restaurant 7-9 Av 3 course à la carte £12.50
Accommodation s£30 d£50

WELFORD Northamptonshire

Shoulder of Mutton Inn
WELFORD Map 04 SP68
12 High St NN6 6HT
☎ 01858 575375
A 17th-century low beamed village pub, with an open-plan interior supported by arches. It is a friendly place, well patronised by locals. Garlic battered chicken goujons, vegetarian tagliatelle, seafood platter and chicken tikka masala appear on the cosmopolitan menu. Principal beers: Worthington Draught, Draught Bass, Carling.
Directions 2m N of A14 J1
Free House
Open 12-2.30 7-11 (Thurs pm only)
Bar food 12-2.30 7-11 Av main course £5.95

Nottinghamshire

BEESTON Nottinghamshire

Victoria Hotel
BEESTON Map 08 SK53
Dovecote Ln NG9 1JG ☎ 0115 925 4049
Converted Victorian railway hotel, specialising in traditional ales and fine whiskies, and known for its stained glass and acid-etched windows. Menu may include Lincolnshire sausages and champ, pork afelia, goats cheese salad with ruby grapefruit and mange tout, or home-made game pie with sloe gin. Principal beers: Bramcote Hemlock, Everards Tiger, Batemans XB, Marstons Pedigree.
Directions M1 J25 take A52 E. R at Nurseryman PH & R opp Rockaway Hotel into Barton St 1st L
Free House
Open 11-11

COLSTON BASSETT Nottinghamshire

The Martins Arms Inn
COLSTON BASSETT Map 08 SK73
School Ln NG12 3FN ☎ 01949 81361
A listed building, this traditional pub dates from around 1690 and is situated in a conservation village in the heart of the Vale of Belvoir. Interesting food, in both the bar and restaurant, ranges from speciality sandwiches on warm ciabatta to wild

contd.

rabbit Bourguignonne with fresh pasta. Principal beers: Marstons Pedigree, Bass, Batemans.
Directions M1 J22, take A50 then A46 North towards Newark. Colston Bassett is situated East of Cotgrave.
Free House
Open 12-3 6-11
Bar food 12-3 6-10
Restaurant 12-3 7 Av 3 course à la carte £25
Accommodation s£35 d£60

ELKESLEY Nottinghamshire

Robin Hood Inn
ELKESLEY Map 08 SK68
High St DN22 8AJ ☎ 01777 838259
An old village pub close to the 12th-century church, the Robin Hood offers the same menu throughout the house. Typical dishes are pan-fried chicken liver with grapes and balsamic vinegar; char-grilled salmon fillet with tomato salsa, and hot cinnamon flavoured apple pie with whipped cream and ice cream. Principal beers: Boddingtons, Murphys, Marstons Pedigree.
Whitbread
Open 11.30-3 6.30-11 (Sat 11-11)
Bar food 12-2 7-9.30 Av main course £6
Restaurant 12-2 7-9.30 Av 3 course à la carte £16

NORMANTON ON TRENT Nottinghamshire

The Square & Compass
NORMANTON ON TRENT Map 08 SK75
Eastgate NG23 6RN ☎ 01636 821439
Those with children are very welcome at this 400 year old village pub close to Robin Hood country. The Gun Room restaurant is decorated with old shotguns, stuffed birds and shooting memorabilia, and has a menu specialising in locally shot game. Principal beers: Stones, Mansfield, Adnams.
Directions Off A1 & B1164 N of Newark-on-Trent
Free House
Open 12-3 6-11
Bar food 12-2.30 7-9.45 Av main course £4.25
Restaurant 12-2.30 7.30-10.30 Av 3 course à la carte £11
Accommodation d£20

NOTTINGHAM Nottinghamshire

Fellows Morton & Clayton
NOTTINGHAM Map 08 SK54
54 Canal St NG1 7EH
☎ 01159 506795
City centre location near the canal. Bar snacks, light meals and salads are available with main course dishes such as rump steak, tandoori chicken, chilli con carne, home-made lasagne and home-made steak kidney pie. Principal beers: Boddingtons, Fellows, Claytons, TT Landlord.
Free House
Open 11-11
Bar food 11.30-2.30 Av main course £4
Restaurant 11.30-2.30 Av 3 course à la carte £5

Lincolnshire Poacher
NOTTINGHAM Map 08 SK54
161-163 Mansfield Rd TG1 3FR
☎ 0115 9411584
Unspoilt country pub where "conversation is the name of the game." A typical menu may feature Lincolnshire sausages, leek and sweet potato soup, spinach and ricotta brioche, or chicken piri piri. The Poacher also hosts occasional blues and folk nights. Principal beers: Batemans XB, XXXB, Mild, Victory.
Directions M1 J26 Town centre
Batemans
Open 11-11 (Sun 12-10.30)

Ye Olde Trip to Jerusalem
NOTTINGHAM Map 08 SK54
1 Brewhouse Yard, Castle Rd NG1 6AD
☎ 0115 9473171
Claiming to be the oldest pub in England, this welcoming establishment dates to 1070 AD and is associated with the soldiers who went to the crusades with Richard the Lionheart. It is reputedly haunted. Snacks and sandwiches are augmented by specials like chicken Jerusalem (with Stilton and celery). They have story-telling on the second Tuesday of every month. Principal beers: Kimberley Classic, Marstons Pedigree.
Free House
Open 11-11 (Sun 12-10.30)

SCAFTWORTH Nottinghamshire

King William
SCAFTWORTH Map 08 SK69
DN10 6BL ☎ 01302 710292
Situated in a small hamlet on a private estate, the King William is on the banks of the River Idle and is especially welcoming to those with children. Today's specials may include lamb and apricot curry, *Pork King Billy*, or steak and ale pie. Principal beers: Flowers Original, Boddingtons.
Directions 1m SW of Bawtry just off A631
Free House
Open 11-5 12-11 (Sat & Sun 12-3.30,7-11)
Bar food 12-3 5.30-9.30 Av main course £4

THURGARTON Nottinghamshire

The Red Lion
THURGARTON Map 08 SK64
Southwell Rd NG14 7GP
☎ 01636 830351
Scene of a gruesome murder in 1936, this 14th-century inn began life as the alehouse of nearby Thurgaton Priory. Those not put off by the framed newspaper account of the murder in the bar, may be tempted by a selection of dishes such as grilled liver and bacon, Cumberland sausage or Barnsley chop. Principal beers: John Smiths, Ruddles County, Courage Directors.
Directions On A612 between Nottingham & Southwell
Free House
Open 11.30-2.50 6.30-11.30
Bar food 12-2 7-10 Av main course £5.25
Restaurant 12-2 7-10 Av 3 course à la carte £12

WEST LEAKE Nottinghamshire

Star Inn
WEST LEAKE Map 08 SK52
Melton Ln LE12 5RQ ☎ 01509 852233
Civilised eighteenth-century country inn known locally as Leake Pit House due to a supposed cockpit in the garden. The printed menu lists standard items such as steaks, mixed grill and scampi. Daily changing specials run to spicy parsnip soup, lamb paprika, Russian fish pie and vegetable cannelloni. Principal beers: Bass, Theakston XB, Gibbs, Salisbury BB.
Directions A6 toward Loughborough, 1/3m L to Kingston, over canal, R to Sutton Bonnington, over crossroad
Free House
Open 11-2.30 6-11 (Sun 12-3, 6-10.30)
Bar food 12.30-2 6.30-8.30 Av main course £5

Oxfordshire

ARDINGTON Oxfordshire

The Boars Head
ARDINGTON Map 04 SU48
Church St OX12 8QA ☎ 01235 833254
200-year-old pub situated on a privately owned estate in the Vale of the White Horse. Starters include smoked chicken with mango and jalapenos. Typical main dishes are roast venison with red wine and juniper pancakes, honeyed duck on a parsnip purée, and pork in orange and mustard sauce. Principal beers: Morlands, Fullers London Pride, Marstons Pedigree.
Directions Off A417 W of Wantage
Free House
Open 11.30-3 6-11
Bar food 12-2 7-9 Av main course £10.50
Restaurant 12-2 7-9

BANBURY Oxfordshire

The Marston Inn
BANBURY Map 04 SP44
Marston-St-Lawrence ox17 2DB
☎ 01295 711906
Built in the 15th century, originally as three cottages, the property was seized by Cromwell prior to the Battle of Edgehill and sold to raise money for his army. It is a traditional pub (with no eating or children in the bar). Restaurant dishes include moules marinière and Elizabethan casserole. Principal beers: Hook Norton.
Hook Norton
Open 12-3 7-11
Restaurant 12.15-2 7.15-9.30 Av 3 course à la carte £15 Av 3 course fixed price £5

Roebuck Inn
BANBURY Map 04 SP44
Stratford St, Drayton OX15 6EN
☎ 01295 730542
A 16th-century stone-built inn with old beams and open fires. Traditional bar food, vegetarian dishes and Mexican specialities are all available in the bar. In

contd.

the restaurant, the chef's pâté might be followed by swordfish steak with grapefruit salsa, or roast local duck. Principal beers: Hook Norton, London Pride, Spitfire, Boddingtons.
Directions On A422 W of Banbury
Free House
Open 11-2.30 (Sun 12-3) 6-11 (Sun 7-10.30)
Bar food 11.30-2.30 6.30-10.30 Av main course £5.50
Restaurant 12-2.30 7.15-11.30 Av 3 course à la carte £16
Accommodation s£26 d£36

BARNARD GATE Oxfordshire

The Boot Inn
BARNARD GATE Map 04 SP41
OX8 6XE ☎ 01865 881231
Named after the owner's interest in collecting boots. Footwear formerly belonging to celebrities such as George Best, Ian Botham, and The Bee Gees is on display. House *Old Favourites* include chicken breast marinated in honey, soy and lemon, seafood Thermidor, and char-grilled Aberdeen Angus rib-eye steak. Principal beers: Hook Norton, London Pride.
Directions off the A40 between Witney & Eynsham
Free House
Open 11-3 6-11.30
Restaurant 12-2.15 6.30-10 Av 3 course à la carte £19

BINFIELD HEATH Oxfordshire

Bottle & Glass
BINFIELD HEATH Map 04 SU77
RG9 4JT ☎ 01491 575755
Thatched 15th-century inn situated on an old drovers' route at the edge of the Chilterns. Blackboard menu changes regularly. Typical dishes are grilled oysters and mussels in garlic butter, rump steak cooked with red wine and apricots, smoked salmon, and loin of pork with apple sauce and stuffing. Principal beers: Brakspears.
Directions N of B4155 between Reading & Henley
Brakspear
Open 11-3 6-11
Bar food 12-1.45 7-9.30 Av main course £7

BRIGHTWELL BALDWIN Oxfordshire

The Lord Nelson Inn
BRIGHTWELL BALDWIN Map 04 SU69
OX9 5NP ☎ 01491 612330
Find this attractive pub in a scenic setting, perhaps via one of the many footpaths in the area. Relax by the open log fire or in the garden in summer to sample perhaps pork chops with apricot sauce or seafood crêpes from the regularly changing menu. Principal beers: Ruddles Best, Courage Best.
Directions Off the B4009 between Watlington & Benson
Free House
Open 11.30-3 6.30-11
Bar food 12-2 7-9.30 Av main course £6
Restaurant 12-2 7-9.30 Av 3 course à la carte £15

BURCOT Oxfordshire

The Chequers
BURCOT Map 04 SU59
OX14 3DP ☎ 01865 407771
Partly dating back to the 16th century and originally a staging post for barges on the Thames, this inn has been managed by the same team for the last twenty years. Various imaginatively themed food events have included a French evening, an Italian evening, and a Valentine's chocolate fondue evening! Principal beers: Ushers, Brakspears, Ruddles.
Directions On A415 (Dorchester/Abingdon rd)
Free House
Open 11-2.30 6-11
Bar food 12-2 6.30-9-9.30 Av main course £5.50
Restaurant 12-2 6.30-9-9.30 Av 3 course à la carte £10

BURFORD Oxfordshire

The Angel at Burford
BURFORD Map 04 SP21
14 Witney St OX18 4SN
☎ 01993 822438
16th-century Cotswold inn with open fires, flagstone floors and secluded walled garden. Formerly frequented by the notorious smugglers of Burford. Dinner menu includes beef with a shallot and garlic confit on peppery brandy sauce, and ostrich steak en croûte flavoured with fleur de thym on a juniper berry sauce. Principal beers: Goffs brewery

Jouster, Morlands Original, Marstons Pedigree, Bass.
Directions Town centre
Free House
Open 12-3 6-11
Bar food 12-2.30 7-9 Av main course £5.50
Restaurant 12-2.30 7-9 Av 3 course fixed price £20
Accommodation s£38 d£47

Golden Pheasant
BURFORD Map 04 SP21
91 High St OX18 4QA
☎ 01993 823223
Country inn with large open fireplaces and flagstone floors. Starters feature lobster and crab fritters with a mango and red pepper chutney, while main course meals range from char-grilled sea bass with sea salt and marsh samphire, to blackened monkfish with a lime and coriander butter. Principal beers: Theakstons, Directors.
Directions A134 from Colchester then B1087
Free House
Open 9-11
Bar food 12-3.30 7-11 Av main course £7.95
Restaurant 7-11 Av 3 course à la carte £25.30
Accommodation s£50 d£70

The Inn for All Seasons
BURFORD Map 04 SP21
The Barringtons OX18 4TN
☎ 01451 844324
Dating from the 17th century, this coaching inn has been a quarry cottage, petrol station and off license. A tunnel still runs from the quarry and local potholers hope soon to knock on the bar floor for a pint. Traditional pies, ploughman's and seasonal dishes are served. Principal beers: Wadworth 6X, Bass, Whichwood Ales, Grand Slam Badger.

Directions M5 J9/10, take A40 E towards Oxford
Free House
Open 11-2.30 6-10.30
Bar food 11-2.30 6-9.30 Av main course £7
Restaurant 11-2.30 6-9.30 Av 3 course à la carte £16.50 Av 3 course fixed price £16.50
Accommodation s£30 d£60

The Lamb Inn
BURFORD Map 04 SP21
Sheep St OX18 4LR ☎ 01993 823155
15th-century, Cotswold stone inn with flagged floors and oak beams. Cream of parsnip and coriander soup, roasted pepper and avocado tartlet with chilli salsa, and pan fried escalope of venison with an apple, redcurrant and black pepper sauce, are regular features on the dinner menu. Principal beers: Wadworths, Hook Norton.

Free House
Open 11-11
Bar food 12-2 Av main course £6.50
Restaurant 12.30-2 7-9 Av 3 course à la carte £24
Accommodation s£57.50 d£90

CHADLINGTON Oxfordshire

The Tite Inn
CHADLINGTON Map 04 SP32
Mill End OX7 3NY ☎ 01608 676475
The name means spring source leading to mill pond and the spring feeding the trough of this, one of the oldest buildings in the area, has never run dry. Dishes freshly prepared and home-cooked at this family run pub range from fresh garlic mushrooms to boeuf Bourguignonne. Principal beers: Archers Village.
Directions 3m S of Chipping Norton
Free House
Open 12-2.30 6.30-11

contd.

Bar food 12-2.30 7-11 Av main course £5.50
Restaurant 12-3 7-11 Av 3 course à la carte £14

CHARLBURY Oxfordshire

The Bell House
CHARLBURY Map 04 SP31
Church St OX7 3PP ☎ 01608 810278
On the banks of the River Evenlode, this 17th-century inn offers an ideal base for cycling, walking, or touring holidays. Honey glazed duck with blackberry and apple sauce, oven-baked salmon and king prawns, or braised game casserole with parsnips may be on today's menu.
Free House
Open 11-11
Bar food 12-2.30 6.30-9.15 Av main course £3
Restaurant 12.30-2.15 7-9.15 Av 3 course à la carte £15
Accommodation s£55 d£75

CHINNOR Oxfordshire

Sir Charles Napier
CHINNOR Map 04 SP70
Spriggs Alley OX9 4BX
☎ 01494 483011
An assortment of furniture and wonderful sculptures are features of this interesting establishment, which is situated on the top of the Chiltern Hills overlooking fields and beech-woods. Dishes include crostini of pigeon and mushrooms with truffle oil, and char-grilled tuna with confit of fennel and sauce vierge. Principal beers: Wadworth,6X.
Directions M40 J6 take B4009 towards Princes Risborough.In Chinnor R at r'about.Spriggs Alley 2m
Free House
Bar food 12.00-2.00 7.00-10.00
Restaurant 12.00-2.00 7.00-10.00 Av 2 course fixed price £14.50

CHIPPING NORTON Oxfordshire

Chequers
CHIPPING NORTON Map 04 SP32
Goddards Ln OX7 5NP
☎ 01608 644717
Town centre pub with low beamed ceilings and inglenook fireplace, next door to the theatre. Bar meals include home-made honey and cider roast ham,

duck breast and cashew nut stir fry, and roasted vegetables with an Oriental sauce. Principal beers: Chiswick, London Pride, ESB.
Directions Town centre, next to theatre
Fullers
Open 11-2.30 5.30-11
Bar food 12-2 6-9 Av main course £5.50
Restaurant 6.30-10 Av 3 course à la carte £12.50

CHURCH ENSTONE Oxfordshire

Crown Inn
CHURCH ENSTONE Map 04 SP32
Mill Ln OX7 4NN ☎ 01608 677262
This 17th-century pub lying off the main road to the 'gateway to the Cotswolds' has recently been refurbished and offers imaginative ideas such as marinated anchovies with lentil salad and warm salad of duck, duck livers and celeriac.
Free House
Accommodation s£32 d£45

CLIFTON Oxfordshire

Duke of Cumberland's Head
CLIFTON Map 04 SP43
OX15 0PE ☎ 01869 338534
Close to Edge Hill, this 16th century listed building had associations with Royalist troops during the Civil War. In quiet open countryside this

establishment likes to preserve a peaceful atmosphere in which to enjoy English and French dishes from Oxfordshire sausages to fillet of beef Richelieu. Principal beers: Warden, Hook Norton, Adnams.
Directions A4260 from Banbury, then B4031 from Deddington
Free House
Open 12-2.30 7-11
Bar food 12-2.30 7-9.30 Av main course £8
Restaurant 12-2.20 7-11 Av 3 course à la carte £20
Accommodation s£25 d£45

CUDDESDON Oxfordshire

Bat & Ball Inn
CUDDESDON Map 04 SP50
28 High St OX44 9HJ ☎ 01865 874379
In a picturesque village with views over the Chilterns and Berkshire Downs, this old coaching inn is renowned for its collection of cricketing memorabilia. Baguettes feature on the bar menu or try warm bacon and avocado salad followed by baked trout Balmoral and a frozen chocolate parfait. Principal beers: Wadworth 6X, Brakspear Bitter.
Directions Pass thru Wheatley towards Garsington, take only L turn, signed Cuddesdon
Free House
Open 12-2.30 5-11
Bar food 12-2.30 6.30-9.30 Av main course £5.75
Restaurant 12-2.30 6.30-9.30 Av 3 course à la carte £16.50
Accommodation s£35 d£45

CUMNOR Oxfordshire

Bear & Ragged Staff
CUMNOR Map 04 SP40
Appleton Rd OX2 9QH
☎ 01865 862329
When Richard Cromwell stayed here in 1650 the Bear and Ragged Staff was already over three centuries old. A typical menu includes rare breast of goose, rosti and port, feuilleté of Angus beef with mushroom compote, cassoulet of Cornish scallops, and tranchon of monkfish, glazed shallots and Pinot Noir. Principal beers: Morrells Oxford Bitter, Varsity & Graduate, Bass.
Directions A420 from Oxford, R to Cumnor on B4017
Morrells
Open 12-3 5.30-11
Bar food 12-2.15 7-10 Av main course £10
Restaurant 12-2.15 7-10 Av 3 course à la carte £22 Av 3 course fixed price £14.95

The Vine Inn
CUMNOR Map 04 SP40
11 Abingdon Rd OX2 9QN
☎ 01865 862567
A friendly welcome awaits at this village pub where the menu offers adventurous options such as fillet of ostrich with port and cranberry sauce or kangaroo with sweet chilli sauce in addition to more traditional dishes. Principal beers: Wadworth 6X, Adnams, Speckled Hen, Marston Pedigree.
Directions A420 from Oxford, R onto B4017
Free House
Open 11-2.30 6-11
Bar food 12.30-2.15 6.30-9.15 Av main course £4.95
Restaurant 12.30-2.15 6.30-9.15 Av 3 course à la carte £15
Accommodation s£35 d£50

DORCHESTER-ON-THAMES Oxfordshire

The George
DORCHESTER-ON-THAMES Map 04 SU59
High St OX10 7HH ☎ 01865 340404
The bare-brick, oak-beamed restaurant at this 15th-century coaching inn may have seafood terrine, bacon and Brie chicken, or vegetable Wellington on its menu. There is also an extensive wine list and a special executive rate which makes The George ideal for conferences. Principal beers: Brakspears.
Directions Just off A4170 (Oxford/Henley rd)
Free House
Open 11-11
Bar food 12-2 7-9.30 Av main course £7.50
Restaurant 12-2 7-9.30 Av 3 course à la carte £25
Accommodation s£57.50 d£75

DUNS TEW Oxfordshire

The White Horse Inn
DUNS TEW Map 04 SP42
OX6 4JS ☎ 01869 340272
A Cotswold village pub, circa 16th century, with log fires, flagstone floors

contd.

and low wooden beams. The bar offers snacks along with traditional pies and puds, while a restaurant meal might comprise spiked spiced kidneys, pavé of cod fillet in filo pastry, and a choice of old fashioned puddings. Principal beers: Hook Norton, Courage Best, Theakstons Best.
Directions M40 J11, A4260, follow signs to Deddington and then onto Duns Tew
Free House
Open 12-11 (Sun 12-10.30)
Bar food 12-2 7-9 Av main course £5.50
Restaurant 12-2 7-9 Av 3 course à la carte £17
Accommodation s£35 d£55

FARINGDON Oxfordshire

The Lamb at Buckland
FARINGDON Map 04 SU29
SN7 8QH ☎ 01367 870484
An 18th-century stone-built village pub offering high quality food in a friendly and informal atmosphere. There's an imaginative choice of dishes, ranging from lobster and shellfish fricassée to roast grouse with all the trimmings, and you can eat where you like, in the bar, restaurant or even the garden. Principal beers: Askells, Broadside.
Directions Just off A420 3m E of Faringdon
Free House
Open 8.30am-3pm 5.30pm-11pm
Bar food 12-2 6.30-9.30 Av main course £6.50
Restaurant 12-2 6.30-9.30 Av 3 course fixed price £16.95
Accommodation s£35 d£35

The Leather Bottle Restaurant & Lounge
FARINGDON Map 04 SU29
Challow Station SN7 8NT
☎ 01367 710155
18th-century thatched building in the tiny village of Challow Station, not far from Lambourn in the 'Valley of the Racehorse.' Turkey steak, salmon, prawns, crab, lamb or lemon sole may feature on today's menu.
Directions On A417 between Faringdon & Wantage, 1m S of Stanford in the vale
Free House
Open 11.45-3 6.30-11
Bar food 11.45-3 6.30-11 Av main course £6
Restaurant 11.45-3 6.30-11 Av 3 course à la carte £18 Av 2 course fixed price £9.95

FYFIELD Oxfordshire

The White Hart
FYFIELD Map 04 SU49
Main Rd OX13 5LN ☎ 01865 390585
A 15th-century chantry house with well preserved original features. The atmosphere is relaxed and friendly and there is a large garden with a play area and lots of seating. The same menu is served throughout offering freshly prepared traditional and international dishes. Principal beers: Hook Norton,Wadworth 6X, Old Peculier, Boddingtons.
Directions Just off A420, 8m SW of Oxford
Free House
Open 11-3 6-11
Bar food 12-2 7-10 Av main course £7
Restaurant 12-2 7-10 Av 3 course à la carte £12

GORING Oxfordshire

Miller of Mansfield
GORING Map 04 SU68
High St RG8 9AW ☎ 01491 872829
An ivy-covered 18th-century, beamed inn, close to the Thames in the Goring Gap, an area of outstanding natural beauty. It offers a varied menu of dishes such as steak, mushroom and Guinness pie; nut wellington; chicken breast stuffed with Stilton and wrapped in bacon, and goujons of chicken with barbecue sauce. Principal beers: Courage, Theakstons, Ruddles, Kronenbourg.
Directions From Pangbourne A329 to Streatley, then R on B4009, 1/2m to Goring.
Free House
Open 11-11 (Sun 12-10.30)
Bar food 12-2 6.30-10 Av main course £4.50
Restaurant 12-2 6.30-10 Av 3 course à la carte £14
Accommodation s£29.50 d£45

GREAT TEW Oxfordshire

The Falkland Arms
GREAT TEW Map 04 SP42
OX7 4DB ☎ 01608 683653
500-year-old thatched inn with flagstone floors and inglenook fireplace. Named after Lord Falkland who lived in the nearby manor house. Bar meals feature pork in cider and whole grain mustard sauce. A la carte dishes include grilled

lemon sole, and chicken in orange and ginger sauce. Principal beers: Adnams, Hook Norton, Wadworth.
Directions From Banbury take A361, then B4022
Wadworth
Open 11-2.30 6-11.30 (Summer 11-11.30)
Bar food 12-2 Av main course £11.50
Restaurant 7-9
Accommodation s£40 d£50

HENLEY-ON-THAMES Oxfordshire

The Five Horseshoes
HENLEY-ON-THAMES Map 04 SU78
Maidensgrove RG9 6EX
☎ 01491 641282
Superb views can be enjoyed from the restaurant of one of the highest pubs in the Chilterns dating from the early 1700s. A selection of grills, game and light warm salads such as goats cheese with pine kernels is supplemented in the summer months by the Sunday barbecue. Principal beers: Brakspears.
Directions A4130 from Henley, onto B480
Brakspear
Open 11.30-2.30 6-11
Bar food 12-2 7-10 Av main course £7
Restaurant 12-2 7-10 Av 3 course à la carte £16.95 Av 3 course fixed price £10

The Fox Inn
HENLEY-ON-THAMES Map 04 SU78
RG9 6DB ☎ 01491 574134
Close to beech woods and sloping fields, the Fox is a red-brick, creeper-clad pub that was built in 1936. Goujons of plaice, moussaka, or prime beefburger may be on the menu alongside a selection of sandwiches, ploughmans', and salads. Principal beers: Brakspears, Heineken, Stella Artois, Guinness.
Directions On A4130 between Henley & Nettlebed
Brakspear
Open 11-3 7-11 (Sun 12-3,7-10.30)
Bar food 11.30-2.30 7-10 Av main course £5

The Golden Ball
HENLEY-ON-THAMES Map 04 SU78
Lower Assendon RG9 6AH
☎ 01491 574157
A friendly atmosphere in a beamed 16th century setting can be enjoyed by cosy open fires or, in the warm months, from the garden. A good choice includes handmade individual pies like steak, stout and oyster, filled jacket potatoes and tempting homemade puddings. Principal beers: Brakspear.
Directions A4130, R onto B480, pub 300yrds on L
Free House
Open 11-3 6-11
Bar food 11.45-2.15 6.45-9.45 Av main course £5.95

HOOK NORTON Oxfordshire

The Gate Hangs High
HOOK NORTON Map 04 SP33
Banbury Rd OX15 5DF
☎ 01608 737387
'The gate hangs high and hinders none/Refresh and pay and travel on.' This rhyme reflects the pub's former role as a tollgate en route to Banbury Market. All the soups, patés, main courses and sweets are home-made, and there is a wide choice of steaks, fish, pasta and chicken. Principal beers: Hook Norton, Old Hookey.
Directions Off A361 SW of Banbury
Hook Norton
Open 11.30-3 6.30-11
Bar food 12-2 7-9.30 Av main course £6
Restaurant 12-2 7-9.30 Av 3 course à la carte £14.50

LOWER WOLVERCOTE Oxfordshire

The Trout Inn
LOWER WOLVERCOTE Map 04 SP41
195 Godstow Rd OX2 8PN
☎ 01865 554485
Built in 1138, destroyed by Henry VIII and rebuilt with stones from Godstow Nunnery, this Thames-side inn is on a weir that feeds a pond teeming with fish. The menu of popular dishes, such as beef and ale pie and cod and chips, is supplemented by blackboard specials - including trout. Principal beers: Bass.
Directions From A40 at Wolvercote r'about(N of Oxford) follow signs for Wolvercote
Bass
Open 11-11 (Sun 12-10.30)

MIDDLE BARTON Oxfordshire

The Fox Inn
MIDDLE BARTON Map 04 SP42
Endostone Rd OX7 7BN
☎ 01864 340338
At this characterful 14th century inn with open fires set in lovely countryside, the Italian owner offers a wide range of pasta dishes and Mediterranean influenced salads alongside traditional English fare. Principal beers: Hook Norton.
Free House
Open 12-3 5-11
Bar food 12-2.30 7-10 Av main course £4.95
Restaurant 7-10 Av 3 course à la carte £15

MINSTER LOVELL Oxfordshire

The Mill & Old Swan
MINSTER LOVELL Map 04 SP31
OX8 5RN ☎ 01993 774441
600-year-old inn situated in the valley of the River Windrush near Oxford. Richard III was a regular visitor. Dinner menu offers cream of parsnip and cider soup, monkfish and mussels with saffron and chive velouté, and sautéed calves liver on celeriac purée with a rich Madeira and veal gravy. Principal beers: Guinness, Caffreys.
Directions On A4095 W of Whitney
Free House
Open 12-2.30 7-9.30
Bar food 12-2.30 7-9.30 Av main course £6
Restaurant 12-2.30 7-9.30 Av 3 course à la carte £17.95
Accommodation s£60 d£80

MOULSFORD Oxfordshire

The Beetle & Wedge Hotel
MOULSFORD Map 04 SU58
Ferry Ln ☎ 01491 651381
This famous Thames-side hotel has two restaurants, the more informal being the Brasserie-style Boathouse. The Dining Room offers more formal elegance in ambience and service.
Principal beers: Wadworth 6X, Adnams, Tanglefoot.
Directions Off A329 between Reading & Oxford
Free House
Bar food 12.30-2 7.30-10
Restaurant 12.30-2 7.30-10

MURCOTT Oxfordshire

The Nut Tree
MURCOTT Map 04 SP51
OX5 2RE ☎ 01865 331253
A thatch over white stone inn set in five acres of grounds fronted by a duck pond. All freshly cooked meals are served, including fish, steaks, pies, curries, and maybe calves' liver and bacon or duck breast with Madeira sauce. Principal beers: Morrells Smooth, Morrells Bitter, Whichwood Grand Slam, Hampshire Br.
Directions M40 J9 take A34 towards Kidlington.Then B4027 S.Murcot on L
Free House
Open 11-4 6.30-11
Bar food 11-4 6.30-11
Restaurant 11-4 6.30-11

NORTH MORETON Oxfordshire

The Bear
NORTH MORETON Map 04 SU58
High St OX11 9AT ☎ 01235 813236
A 16th-century beamed village pub with large open fireplaces. Similar food is served in both the bar and restaurant, from seasonal menus with dishes such as sizzling snails in garlic butter, Thai marinated chicken, and pork Marsala, supplemented by blackboard specials. Principal beers: Hook Norton, Becks.
Directions Off A4130 between Didcot & Wallingford
Free House
Open 12-3 6.30-11
Bar food 12-3 6.30-11 Av main course £8
Restaurant 12-3 6.30-11 Av 3 course à la carte £15

NORTH NEWINGTON Oxfordshire

The Roebuck Inn
NORTH NEWINGTON Map 04 SP44
Banbury Rd OX15 6AB
☎ 01295 730444
A 16th-century stone-built pub with a warm atmosphere, large inglenook fireplace and beautiful location. There's an informal bistro style throughout the pub, with blackboard menus and dishes with English, Mediterranean and Far Eastern flavours, such as fillet steak, lamb stifado and Thai chicken curry. Principal beers: Morland Original, London Pride, Old Speckled Hen.
Directions Off B4035 W of Banbury
Free House
Open 12-3 7-11
Bar food 12-3 7-11

NUFFIELD Oxfordshire

The Crown
NUFFIELD Map 04 SU68
RG9 5SJ ☎ 01491 641335
A heavily beamed, traditional pub set in a village on the edge of the Chilterns on the Ridgeway Path, the Crown offers a selection of tasty dishes from deep fried Brie with hot cranberry sauce to roast pork hobbler with apple gravy, vegetarian Kiev or daily fresh fish. Principal beers: Brakspears.
Directions Follow Henley signs, then Wallingford rd on L past turning for village
Brakspear
Open 11-2.30 6-11 (Sat 11-3,6-11 Sun 12-3,7-10.30)
Bar food 12-2 6.30-9 Av main course £6.95

OXFORD Oxfordshire

Anchor
OXFORD Map 04 SP50
2 Hayfield Rd, Walton Manor OX2 6TT
☎ 01865 510282
A 30s-style art deco pub with a warm and friendly atmosphere. The name comes from the pub's proximity to the canal and river. Dishes from around the world include penne and pesto bake, Thai red chicken curry and pork Dijonnaise, and bar food such as samosas, burgers and chilli. Principal beers: Wadworth 6X, Henrys IPA, Tanglefoot.
Directions A34 Oxford Ring Road(N), exit Peartree Roundabout, 1 1/2m then R at Polstead Rd, follow rd to bottom, pub on R
Wadworth
Open 12-11
Bar food 12-2.30 6-8.30 Av main course £4.50
Restaurant 12-2.30 6-8.30 Av 3 course à la carte £9.50

The Nosebag Restaurant
OXFORD Map 04 SP50

6-8 St Michael's St OX1 2DV
☎ 01865 721033
The Nosebag Restaurant is a 15th-century building, in the centre of Oxford, with oak beams, Laura Ashley decor and classical music to set the ambience. There is an imaginative blackboard menu of freshly prepared dishes. Specialities include home-made soups, casseroles, pasta bakes and imaginative vegetarian dishes.

contd.

Open Mon 9.30-5.30, Fri-Sat 9.30-10.30 Sun 9.30-9)

The White House
OXFORD Map 04 SP50
2 Botley Rd OX2 0AB ☎ 01865 242823
Set back from a busy road, the White House is an oasis of calm; newly renovated in modern style, but retaining a traditional, friendly pub feel. It offers an eclectic range of high-quality food at pub prices, such as salmon fishcakes, wild mushroom ravioli and Kilkenney ale sausage. Principal beers: Wadworths 6X,Abbot,Tetley,Old Speckled Hen.
Directions 2 minutes walk from rail station
Allied Domecq
Open 11-11 (Sun 12-10.30)
Bar food 12-3 6-9.30 Av main course £4.50
Restaurant 12-3 6-9.30 Av 3 course à la carte £15 Av 3 course fixed price £15

PISHILL Oxfordshire

The Crown Inn
PISHILL Map 04 SU78
RG9 6HH ☎ 01491 638364
15th-century coaching inn at the foot of the Chilterns. The 400-year old thatched barn is ideal for functions. Menu may include rack of lamb with redcurrant and mint sauce, mushrooms stuffed with fennel, garlic and peppers, or tuna steak in prawn and white wine sauce. Principal beers: Brakspear Bitter, Fullers London Pride, Marstons Pedigree.
Directions On B480 off A4130 NW of Henley-on-Thames
Free House
Open 11.30-2.30 6-11
Bar food 12-2 7-10 Av main course £6.95
Restaurant 12-2 7-10 Av 3 course à la carte £16.50
Accommodation d£75

SHENINGTON Oxfordshire

The Bell
SHENINGTON Map 04 SP34
OX15 6NQ ☎ 01295 670274
A pretty 18th-century pub, situated on the village green, with open fires and flagstone floors. The blackboard menus offer freshly prepared and home-cooked dishes including lamb and lime casserole, salmon in cucumber sauce, double chocolate mousse and sticky toffee pudding. Principal beers: Hook Norton Flowers, Bass.
Directions M40 J11 take A422 to Stratford. Village is signposted 3m N of Wroxton
Free House
Bar food 12-2.30 6.30-10 Av main course £7.50
Restaurant 12-2.30 6.30-10 Av 3 course à la carte £10

SHIPTON-UNDER-WYCHWOOD Oxfordshire

The Shaven Crown Hotel
SHIPTON-UNDER-WYCHWOOD Map 04 SP21
High St OX7 6BA ☎ 01993 830330
At the heart of the Cotswolds yet off the tourist trail, this village inn has a monastic history. One of the oldest licensed premises in England, the medieval courtyard leads to the Monk's Bar for venison sausages braised in red wine or the restaurant for gravlax followed by sirloin Bordelaise. Principal beers: Hook Norton,Tetleys,Guinness.
Directions From M40 J11 take A361 through Chipping Norton to Shipton-under-Wychwood.
Free House
Open 11-11 (Sun 11-10.30)
Bar food 12-2 6-9 Av main course £5.25
Restaurant 12-2 7.30-9 Av 3 course fixed price £18.50
Accommodation s£35 d£72

SOUTH MORETON Oxfordshire

The Crown Inn
SOUTH MORETON Map 04 SU58
High St OX11 9AG ☎ 01235 812262
A village pub dating from the 1850s decorated and furnished to a high standard in a country style. It promises good food, good ale and good ambience. The blackboard menu offers traditional British and some European dishes,

including a vegetarian selection. Principal beers: Tanglefoot, Adnams, Wadworth 6X.
Directions From Didcot take A4130 towards Wallingford.Village on R
Wadworth
Open 11-3 5.30-11
Bar food 12-2 7-9.30 Av main course £6.50
Restaurant 12-2 7-9.30

SOUTH STOKE Oxfordshire

The Perch and Pike
SOUTH STOKE Map 04 SU58
RG8 0JS ☎ 01491 872415
At this quiet,17th-century pub/restaurant, furnished principally with antiques, all food is cooked to order. Have a drink in the garden or by the fire while awaiting char-grilled fillet of honeyed chicken with sweet peppers or roasted fillet of red mullet with tapénade and tomato salad. Principal beers: Brakspear's PA & Special.
Directions Between Goring and Wallingford just off B4009
Brakspear
Open 12-2 11-6 (Sun 7-10.30)
Bar food 12-2 7-9 Av main course £9.95

SPARSHOLT Oxfordshire

The Star Inn
SPARSHOLT Map 04 SU38
Watery Ln OX12 9PL
☎ 01235 751539 751001
Frequented by many leading jockeys and trainers, this 400-year-old inn is in the heart of racing and hunting country. The racing theme is taken up in the menu, which might offer prawn platter, peppered pork, a vegetarian Tuscan bean garlic crostini, and steamed treacle sponge with custard. Principal beers: Morlands, Worthington, Fosters, Guinness.
Directions Off B4507 4m W of Wantage
Free House
Open 12-3 6-11 (Sat 12-11,Sun 12-10.30)
Bar food 12-2 7-9.30
Restaurant 12-2 7-9.30 Av 3 course à la carte £13
Accommodation d£50

STADHAMPTON Oxfordshire

The Crazy Bear & Ragged Staff
STADHAMPTON Map 04 SU69
Bear Ln OX44 7UR ☎ 01865 890714
It may be 400 years old, but this is by no means a traditional pub. Here there are fish tanks for toilet cisterns, and a large bear (relating to local legend) dressed according to the season. Bar, restaurant and brasserie food is served, using fresh produce delivered daily. Principal beers: Brakspears,London Pride,Old Speckled Hen.
Directions M40 J7 take A329 towards Wallingford
Free House
Open 12-11
Bar food 12-3(Sun 5) 7-10.30 Av main course £8.95
Restaurant 12-3(Sun 5) 7-10.30 Av 3 course à la carte £25 Av 3 course fixed price £16.95
Accommodation s£50 d£60

STEEPLE ASTON Oxfordshire

Red Lion
STEEPLE ASTON Map 04 SP42
South Side OX6 3RY ☎ 01869 340225
A traditional pub for the congregation of kindred souls to enjoy beers, wines and spirits without distractive technology. Food is prepared to order, in the bar at lunchtime and the dining room in the evening. There is game from autumn to winter and crab and lobster in spring and summer. Principal beers: Tanglefoot, Hook Norton, Wadworths 6X.
Directions Off A4260 between Oxford & Banbury
Free House
Open 11-3 6-11 (Sun 7-10.30)
Bar food 12-2 7.30-9 Av main course £4.80
Restaurant 7-9.30 Av 3 course à la carte £19

STEVENTON Oxfordshire

The Cherry Tree
STEVENTON Map 04 SU49
33 High St OX13 6RZ ☎ 01235 831222
An inventive range of fare is offered in an atmosphere of old world charm at this inviting roadside tavern. Begin with nachos or Thai style fish cakes or try ale soused sausages billed as 'drunken toads in the hole' with sticky toffee pudding to finish. Principal beers: Wadworth, Henry's IPA, 6X, Farmers Glory.
Directions Leave A34 at Milton Interchange, follow signs for Steventon, go into village, over railway bridge, pub on R
Wadworth
Open 11.30-11 (Sun 12-10.30)'

contd.

Bar food 12-2 7-9 Av main course £6.50
Restaurant 12-2 7-9 Av 3 course à la carte £14.95

STOKE ROW Oxfordshire

Crooked Billet
STOKE ROW Map 04 SU68
RG9 5PU ☎ 01491 681048
Built in 1642, this off-the-beaten-track pub was once the hideout of notorious highwayman, Dick Turpin, who was romantically attached to the landlord's daughter, Bess. Typical main dishes include skate wing baked Thai style, and venison casserole cooked in herbs and claret. A good vegetarian selection is also available. Principal beers: Brakspears.
Directions From Henley to Oxford A4130.Turn L at Nettlebed for Stoke Row
Brakspear
Open 12-3 7-11
Bar food 12-2.30 7-10 Av main course £11.95
Restaurant 12-2.30 7-10 Av 3 course à la carte £20 Av 3 course fixed price £13.95

SUTTON COURTENAY Oxfordshire

The Fish
SUTTON COURTENAY Map 04 SU59
4 Appleford Rd OX14 4NQ
☎ 01235 848242
The present Fish is Victorian, built on the site of a previous village inn, and it has recently been stylishly refurbished. There is a strong emphasis on wine with 12-15 house wines available by the glass. The menu offers fish, fresh from the Channel coast, Angus beef and classic desserts. Principal beers: Morland .
Directions From A415 in Abingdon take B4017 then L onto B4016 to village
Morland
Open 12-3.30 6-11.30 (Sun 7-11)
Bar food 12-3.30 Av main course £5
Restaurant 12-3.30 7-11 Av 3 course à la carte £15.95

THAME Oxfordshire

Abingdon Arms
THAME Map 04 SP70
21 Cornmarket OX9 2BL
☎ 01844 260116
'The Abo' is the oldest pub in Thame and has been completely refurbished after a recent fire. Live music is presented at weekends in a separate barn. The bar menu may include Miller's tortillas, liver, bacon and onions, or a selection of jacket potatoes, burgers, and 'Abo doorsteps.' Principal beers: Vale Ale, Hook Norton, Tetley Bitter, Wadworths 6X.
Free House
Open 11-11 (Sun 12-10.30)
Bar food 12-2.30 6-9 Av main course £4

WESTON-ON-THE-GREEN Oxfordshire

The Chequers
WESTON-ON-THE-GREEN Map 04 SP51
OX6 8QH ☎ 01869 350319
17th-century coaching inn built of Cotswold stone. Bar offers a traditional English pub menu while the restaurant is devoted to Thai food. Menu includes soups, Kwaitiew noodle dishes, Pad (stir fry), Kaeng (Thai curry), Khoa (rice dishes), salads, and Pla (fish and seafood). Principal beers: Fullers, London Pride, ESB.
Directions M40 J9 A34 S take 1st exit
Fullers
Open 11.30-3 6-11
Bar food 12-2.30 6.30-10.30 Av main course £2.45
Restaurant 12-2.30 6.30-10.30

WOODSTOCK Oxfordshire

The Feathers Hotel
WOODSTOCK Map 04 SP41
Market St OX20 1SX ☎ 01993 812291
Just a few miles from Oxford this 17th-century country town hotel was originally four separate houses and is

decorated with antiques throughout. Menu may offer honey-baked ham salad with herb vinaigrette, seabass fillet with creamed leaks and rosemary, or pot roasted guinea fowl with broccoli and tapenade. Principal beers: Wadworths 6X.
Directions From M40 J9 take 1st L in Woodstock. Hotel on L
Free House
Open 11-3 6-10.30
Bar food 12.30-2.15 7.30-9.15 Av main course £7.50
Restaurant 12.30-2.15 7.30-9.15 Av 3 course à la carte £30 Av 2 course fixed price £16.50
Accommodation s£88 d£105

WOOTTON Oxfordshire

The Killingworth Castle Inn

WOOTTON Map 04 SP41
Glympton Rd OX20 1EJ
☎ 01993 811401
A coaching inn built in 1637, the Killingworth Castle has retained its original beams and fireplaces. Folk singers bring a cheer on Friday nights and there is always the West Oxford way footpath. The specials and snacks include Cajun butterfly chicken, sandwiches and lemon brûlée. Principal beers: Morland.
Directions Exit A34 onto B4027, cross over A4260, pub on N edge of Wootton
Morland
Open 12-2.30 6.30-11 (open all day summer wknds)
Bar food 12-2 7-9 Av main course £6.50
Accommodation s£25 d£35

WYTHAM Oxfordshire

White Hart

WYTHAM Map 04 SP40
OX2 8QA ☎ 01865 244372
In the pretty, thatched village of Wytham (owned by Oxford University), this attractive, creeper-covered pub has flagstone floors and open fires. It has frequently been used in the television series *Inspector Morse*. There is a salad, cold meat, and quiche buffet, as well as hot dishes, and in summer excellent barbecues. Principal beers: ABC, Tetley, Burton.
Directions Just off A34 NW of Oxford
Allied Domecq
Open 11.30-2.30 6-11 (Summer-Sat 11.30-11,Sun 12-10.30)
Bar food 12-2 7-9 Av main course £6

Rutland

EMPINGHAM Rutland

White Horse Inn

EMPINGHAM Map 04 SK90
Main St LE15 8PS
☎ 01780 460221 460521
Situated close to Rutland Water, the largest man-made lake in Europe, the White Horse dates from the 17th century and was originally a court house. A typical menu may feature Rutland fillet steak, red mullet, Glastonbury lamb, or Irish mussels. Conference facilities for up to 60 are available. Principal beers: Oakham Ales, Ruddles, John Smiths, Directors.
Directions From A1 take A606 signed Oakham & Rutland Water
Scottish & Newcastle
Open 7am-11pm
Bar food 12-2.15 7.15-10 Av main course £5.95
Restaurant 12-2.15 7.15-10 Av 3 course à la carte £19 Av 3 course fixed price £16.95
Accommodation s£37 d£45

GLASTON Rutland

The Monckton Arms Hotel

GLASTON Map 04 SK80
LE15 9BP ☎ 01572 822326
This 16th-century farmhouse in the heart of Rutland countryside is famed for food. A comprehensive choice includes hearty home made favourites like cottage pie or, for the more daring palate, kangaroo or ostrich are among the house specials. Principal beers: John Smiths, Bass, Ruddles Best & County.
Directions From M1, Glaston is on A47 towards Peterborough, 20m outside Leicester.
Free House
Open 11-11 (Sun 12-3, 7-11)
Bar food 12-2.30 7-10 Av main course £5.95
Restaurant 12-2.30 7-10 Av 3 course à la carte £18
Accommodation s£35 d£48

AA members can call AA Hotel Booking Service on 0990 050505 to book at AA recognised hotels and B & Bs in the UK and Ireland, or through our Internet site: http://www.theaa.co.uk/hotels

OAKHAM Rutland

The Blue Ball
OAKHAM Map 04 SK80
6 Cedar St, Braunston-in-Rutland LE15 8QS ☎ 01572 722135
14th-century village pub which hopes to offer high class cuisine at reasonable rates. Table d'hôte menu may include panfried seabass on a bed of sautéed fennel with tomato and shallot sauce, char-grilled steak Rossini with red wine sauce, or Parma ham and Parmesan salad tossed in a raspberry dressing.
Directions From A1 take A606 to Oakham.Village SW of Oakham
Free House
Open 12-3 6-11
Bar food 12-2 7-10 Av main course £8
Restaurant 7-9.30 Av 3 course à la carte £18.95 Av 2 course fixed price £14.95

WING Rutland

The Cuckoo Inn
WING Map 04 SK80
3 Top St LE15 8SE ☎ 01572 737340
A truly traditional village pub dating from the 17th century, the Cuckoo was so named after the villagers tried to fence in a cuckoo in order to hear its call throughout the year. A traditional menu includes breaded plaice, lamb casserole, steaks and snacks. Principal beers: Pedigree, Carlsberg, Guinness, Murphys.
Directions A6003 from Oakham, R then L
Free House
Open 11.30-2.30 6.30-11 (Sun 11.30-4, 7-10.30)

Staffordshire

ABBOTS BROMLEY Staffordshire

The Crown Inn
ABBOTS BROMLEY Map 07 SK02
Market Place WS15 3BS
☎ 01283 840227
Originally a coaching inn, this traditional country pub is situated in the middle of a conservation village and is associated with the Horn Dance, a ritual dating from 1246 that takes place every September. Dishes include steaks, chicken balti, salmon with hollandaise sauce and cauliflower cheese. Principal beers: Cidermaster, Banks Mild, Bass, Carling.
Directions From Uttoxeter take A518, then B5013 & B5234 to Abbots Bromley

Free House
Open 12-3.20 6-11.20 (Sat 12-11.20)
Bar food 12-2.30 6-9.30 Av main course £5.25
Restaurant 12-2.30 6-9.30 Av 3 course à la carte £8.95
Accommodation s£20 d£40

The Royal Oak
ABBOTS BROMLEY Map 07 SK02
Bagot St WS15 3DB
☎ 01283 840117
There is a friendly village atmosphere at this black and white pub, with its open fires, beamed ceilings and oak panelled restaurant. Dishes range from steak to nut roast, and breaded scampi to a trio of pan-fried Mediterranean style fish. A choice of bar snacks is also available. Principal beers: Marstons.
Free House
Open 12-3 6.30-11
Bar food 12-2 7-10
Restaurant 12-2 7-10

BUTTERTON Staffordshire

The Black Lion Inn
BUTTERTON Map 07 SK05
ST13 7SP ☎ 01538 304232
Dating from 1782, this inn has changed little in character, with its numerous rambling rooms and interesting brassware, china and whisky jugs. There's traditional pub food in the bar, along with daily specials, and a French-influenced menu in the restaurant, which offers steaks, chicken and fish dishes. Principal beers: Gillespies, Youngers, Theakstons Best, Pedigree.
Directions From A52 (between Leek & Ashbourne) take B5053
Free House
Open 12-3 7-11
Bar food 12-2 7-9 Av main course £5

Restaurant 12-2.30 7-10.30 Av 3 course à la carte £10 Av 3 course fixed price £10

CRESSWELL Staffordshire

Izaak Walton Inn

CRESSWELL Map 07 SJ93

Cresswell Ln ST11 9RE ☎ 01782 392265

Civilised surroundings are offered at this pleasant country pub and restaurant. The extensive menu includes steak specialities; the chef's own curries, pies and bakes; fresh fish and a choice of vegetarian dishes. Additional daily specials might be pork and pineapple curry or grilled red snapper. Principal beers: Marstons.

Directions Just off A50 SE of Stoke-on-Trent

Free House

Open 12-3 6-11

Bar food 12-2 6-10 Av main course £5

Restaurant 12-2 6-10 Av 3 course à la carte £12 Av 3 course fixed price £7.95

NORBURY JUNCTION Staffordshire

Junction Country Inn & Restaurant

NORBURY JUNCTION Map 07 SJ72

ST20 0PN ☎ 01785 284288

Situated near the Shropshire Union Canal, this pub offers a range of bar snacks and light lunches. Typical meals on the blackboard menu include moules marinière, pan-fried lemon sole, steak and ale pie, and Barbary duck. Vegetarian options include macaroni cheese, and broccoli and mushroom Mornay. Principal beers: Banks, Marstons.

Free House

Bar food 11.30-2.30 6-9.30 Av main course £5.50

Restaurant 12-2.30 7-10 Av 3 course à la carte £15 Av 3 course fixed price £15

TATENHILL Staffordshire

Horseshoe Inn

TATENHILL Map 08 SK22

Main St DE13 9SD ☎ 01283 564913

A busy, welcoming environment where locals and visitors mix happily is a feature of this characterful old pub, at the centre of a peaceful village nestled in a lovely valley. Home-made fare includes oven-baked smoked mackerel with gooseberry sauce and leek and sesame roasted salmon fillet. Principal beers: Marstons Pedigree, Smooth Brewed.

Directions A38 S of Burton-on-Trent

Marstons

Open 11-3 5.30-11 (Sat-Sun all day)

Bar food 12-2 6-10 Av main course £5

Restaurant 12-2 6-10

TUTBURY Staffordshire

Ye Olde Dog & Partridge Inn

TUTBURY Map 08 SK22

High St DE13 9LS ☎ 01283 813030

Built in the 15th-century. Later came to prominence in connection with bull running, devised by John of Gaunt, which centred around nearby Tutbury Castle. Main course dishes include roast Staffordshire leg of pork with chunky apple and raisin sauce and crackling, and roast Aylesbury duck with black cherry sauce. Principal beers: Marstons Smooth, Pedigree.

Directions Off A50 NW of Burton upon Trent

Free House

Open 12-2 6-9.45

Bar food 12-2 Av main course £3.25

Restaurant 12-2 6-9.45 Av 3 course à la carte £15 Av 2 course fixed price £7.20

Accommodation s£36 d£44

YOXALL Staffordshire

The Crown

YOXALL Map 07 SK11

Main St DE13 8NQ ☎ 01543 472551

A cosy, friendly village pub with old beams and open fires. Simple but tasty food is served, including sandwiches, snack dishes and salads. Main courses range through pizzas, grills and dishes such as fillet of duckling, breaded plaice, and Barnsley chops with mint and redcurrant gravy. Principal beers: Marstons Pedigree.

Directions On A515 N of Lichfield

Marstons

Bar food 12-2 6-9 Av main course £4.25

Restaurant 12-2 6-9

AA members can call AA Hotel Booking Service on 0990 050505 to book at AA recognised hotels and B & Bs in the UK and Ireland, or through our Internet site: http://www.theaa.co.uk/hotels

Suffolk

ALDEBURGH Suffolk

The Mill Inn
ALDEBURGH Map 05 TM45
Market Cross Place IP15 5BJ
☎ 01728 452563
A genuine traditional fisherman's inn frequented by the local lifeboat crew - the licensee is a longstanding member - The Mill stands opposite the 17th century Moot Hall, a half timbered landmark on this stretch of Heritage coast. Home cooked 'pub grub' satisfies appetites sharpened by the sea air and naturally features the day's catch. Principal beers: Adnams Bitter, Broadside, seasonal ales.
Directions Follow Aldeburgh signs from A12 on A1094. Pub last building on L before sea
Adnams
Open 11-11 (Sun 12-10.30)
Bar food 12-2 7-9 Av main course £5.50
Restaurant 12-2 7-9 Av 3 course fixed price £10
Accommodation s£19 d£38

BARDWELL Suffolk

Six Bells Inn
BARDWELL Map 05 TL97
The Green IP31 1AW
☎ 01359 250820
It's well worth exploring the lovely Suffolk countryside to locate the cosy atmosphere of this 16th century inn which appeared in several episodes of the television series *'Dads Army'*. Imaginative, varied dishes might include pan-fried fillet of halibut with artichoke hearts, bacon and olive oil. Principal beers: Adnams Best, Theakstons Best.
Directions From Bury St Edmunds take A143 towards Diss. 8m, L at turning for Bardwell Windmill, pub on L
Free House
Open 12-2 (Wknd 12-2.30) 6.30-11
Bar food 12-2/2.30 6.30-10.30/11 Av main course £6.50
Restaurant 12-2/2.30 6.30-10.30/11 Av 3 course à la carte £16 Av 3 course fixed price £12.50
Accommodation s£30 d£45

BECCLES Suffolk

Swan House Restaurant
BECCLES Map 05 TM48
Newmarket NR34 9HE
☎ 01502 713474
16th-century former tavern, close to St. Michael's church where Lord Nelson's parents were married. Within easy reach of the River Waveney. Among the lunchtime specials are sautéed chicken livers, and spinach, mozzarella and potato bake. The a la carte menu includes baked Nile perch with asparagus and dill cream sauce. Principal beers: Adnams.
Directions Town centre
Free House
Open 11-11
Bar food 12-2 Av main course £3.25
Restaurant 12-2 7-9.30 Av 3 course à la carte £15.50 Av 3 course fixed price £10.95

BLYFORD Suffolk

Queens Head Inn
BLYFORD Map 05 TM47
Southwold Rd IP19 9JV
☎ 01502 478404
This 15th-century thatched inn features open fires, beams and antique settles. Two smugglers who met their end whilst transferring booty via a secret passage to the local church reputedly still haunt. Interesting food offered to more peaceful clients includes an impressive Greek-style baked lamb special. Principal beers: Adnams Best Bitter, Broadside, Tally Ho.
Directions From A12 at Blythburgh take B1123 for 1 m
Adnams
Open 11-3 6.30-11.30
Bar food 12-2.15 7-9 Av main course £5.25
Restaurant 12-2.15 7-9 Av 3 course à la carte £12
Accommodation d£50

BRANDESTON Suffolk

The Queens Head
BRANDESTON Map 05 TM26
The Street IP13 7AD ☎ 01728 685307
Approximately 400 years old, this village pub has wooden panelling, quarry tile floors and open fires. There is an extensive bar and evening menu, the former ranging from sandwiches to local

sausages with fries, the latter including smoky bacon chicken, steak, and spicy fish kebabs. Principal beers: Adnams.
Directions Stowmarket, A14 then A1120. Follow signs to Earl Soham, R at village green to Brandeston.
Adnams
Open 11.30-2.30 6-11 (Sun 12-3, 7-10.30)
Bar food 12-1.50 7-9.30 Av main course £4.50
Accommodation s£17 d£34

BURY ST EDMUNDS Suffolk

The Nutshell
BURY ST EDMUNDS Map 05 TL86
17 The Traverse IP33 1VJ
☎ 01284 764867
The Nutshell is a thatched pub which claims to be the smallest pub in Great Britain, with an area of 15 ft x 7 ft 6 in – hence the name. It is very popular, despite the fact that they do not serve food (presumably not enough elbow room!). Principal beers: Greene King IPA, Abbot Ale.
Greene King
Open 11-11 (all day open)

CHELSWORTH Suffolk

The Peacock Inn
CHELSWORTH Map 05 TL94
The Street IP7 7HV ☎ 01449 740758
Riverside 14th-century pub, believed to be the oldest building in the village. Bar menu features snacks and light lunches such as honey roast ham with mango chutney. Other dishes include Stilton creamed mushrooms, salmon and dill fishcakes, and Chelsworth beef patties. Principal beers: Adnams, Greene King IPA.
Free House
Open 12-3 6.30-11
Bar food 12-2 7-9.45
Restaurant 12-2 7-9.45 Av 3 course à la carte £18
Accommodation s£35 d£45

COCKFIELD Suffolk

Three Horseshoes
COCKFIELD Map 05 TL95
Stow's Hill IP30 0JB ☎ 01284 828177
Originally a thatched Long Hall dating back to 1350, the old beams are supported by one of the oldest king posts in Suffolk. Set in open country close to historic Lavenham, the garden features a gazebo. Hearty fare could include a half roast chicken in creamy Cajun sauce special.
Directions A134 towards Sudbury, then L, 4m then onto A1141 towards Lavenham
Greene King
Open 12-3 6-11 (Sun 12-3, 7-10.30)
Bar food 12-2 6-9.30 Av main course £3.95
Restaurant 12-2 6-9.30 Av 3 course à la carte £12

COTTON Suffolk

The Trowel & Hammer Inn
COTTON Map 05 TM06
Mill Rd IP14 4QL ☎ 01449 781234
A sprawling thatched and tiled 15th-century pub with a pretty restaurant and a large garden full of hollyhocks and roses. Bar and restaurant menus reflect seasonal availability of fresh produce with dishes ranging from lasagne and chips to roast tail of monkfish with saffron sauce. Principal beers: Adnams, Greene King, Nethergate.
Directions From A14 follow signs to Haughley,then Bacton,then turn left for Cotton.
Free House
Open 11.30-3 (Sat 11.30-11,Sun 12-10.30) 6-11
Bar food 11.30-2 6.30-10.30 Av main course £6
Restaurant 11.30-2 6.30-10.30 Av 3 course à la carte £16 Av 3 course fixed price £13

DUNWICH Suffolk

The Ship Inn
DUNWICH Map 05 TM47
St James St IP17 3DT
☎ 01728 648219
Much of this once thriving port has disappeared into to the sea, leaving a village of period buildings, among which is this old smugglers inn. The menus are based on fresh local produce with fish as a speciality, including fish cakes with salsa dip and excellent fish and chips. Principal beers: Adnams, Greene King.
Directions N on A12 from Ipswich thru Yoxford, R signed Dunwich
Free House
Open 11-3 6-11

contd.

Bar food 12-2 7-9.30 Av main course £4.75
Restaurant 12-2 7-9.30
Accommodation s£35 d£50

EASTBRIDGE Suffolk

The Eels Foot Inn

EASTBRIDGE Map 05 TM46

IP16 4SN ☎ 01728 830154

Edge of village pub surrounded by fields and marshland, close to Minsmere Bird Reserve. Formerly three cottages, one of which was the cobbler's. Pub named after one of his tools. Most of the food is home-made, including steak, pork and venison casseroles, fish pies, and vegetable lasagne for vegetarians. Principal beers: Adnams Bitter, Mild, Broadside, Extra.

Directions At Yoxford on A12 take B1122(signed Leiston/Sizewell). Turn L at Theberton
Adnams
Open 11-3 7-11
Bar food 12-2 7-9 Av main course £4.95
Accommodation s£15 d£16.50

ERWARTON Suffolk

The Queens Head

ERWARTON Map 05 TM23

The Street IP9 1LN ☎ 01473 787550

A country pub with 16th-century black oak beams and open fires, offering views over the fields to ships on the Stour. The home-cooked dishes might include deep-fried whitebait with lemon, salad and bread; beef and ale casserole topped with dumplings, and deep dish apple pie. Principal beers: Greene King, Adnams.

Directions From Ipswich take B1456 to Shotley
Free House
Open 11-3 6.30-11
Bar food 12-2 7-10 Av main course £6.50
Restaurant 12-2 7-10 Av 3 course à la carte £12.50

FRAMSDEN Suffolk

The Dobermann Inn

FRAMSDEN Map 05 TM15

The Street IP14 6HG
☎ 01473 890461

All the original wood and brickwork is intact at this small country pub, which dates from 1590. The menu ranges from sandwiches to full three-course meals. Favourites include the Trencher Special Grill, of gammon with sausage, egg, tomato peas and chips. There's also a good choice of fish and veggie dishes. Principal beers: Adnams.

Directions S of A1120 (Stowmarket/Yoxford)
Free House
Open 12-3 7-11
Bar food 12-2 7-9
Restaurant 12-2 7-9 Av 3 course à la carte £13.50
Accommodation s£25 d£35

HADLEIGH Suffolk

The Marquis of Cornwallis

HADLEIGH Map 05 TM04

Upper Layham IP75 5JZ
☎ 01473 822051

A beamed, 16th-century country inn with two acres of garden leading down to the River Brett. The menu ranges from snacks to full meals, with daily specials such as liver and bacon casserole, grilled skate wing and Malay chicken curry. Vegetarian options are always available. Principal beers: Adnams Southwold.

Directions From Colchester take A12 then B1070 towards Hadleigh. Layham signed on L
Free House
Open 11-3 6-11
Bar food 12-2 7-9.30 Av main course £5.25
Restaurant 12-2 7-9.30 Av 3 course à la carte £13
Accommodation s£29 d£41

HARTEST Suffolk

The Crown

HARTEST Map 05 TL85

The Green IP29 4DH ☎ 01284 830250

Set on the village green, next to the church, this 15th-century building was once known as Hartest Hall and still has the original manorial court. The inn is heavily beamed and there's a large inglenook fireplace in the bar. One menu is offered throughout with an emphasis on fresh Lowestoft fish. Principal beers: Greene King, Abbot, IPA, Wexford.

Directions On B1066 S of Bury St Edmunds
Greene King
Open 11-2.30 6-11
Bar food 12-2 6.30-9.30 Av main course £6.50
Restaurant 12-2 6.30-9.30 Av 3 course à la carte £12.50

HOLBROOK Suffolk

The Compasses

HOLBROOK Map 05 TM13
Ipswich Rd IP9 2QR
☎ 01473 328332

Situated on the Shotley peninsula, The Compasses is in an area of outstanding natural beauty and also has a fine collection of over 1000 keyrings! Chilli bean bake, chicken Alexander, or cod and prawn Mornay could be on the menu, while the beef lasagne is locally renowned. Principal beers: Tetleys, Benskins, Carlsberg, Guinness.

Directions From A137 S of Ipswich, take B1456/B1080
Free House
Open 11-2.30 6-11
Bar food 11.30-2.15 6-9.30 Av main course £6
Restaurant 11.30-2.15 6-9.30 Av 3 course fixed price £11.50

HONEY TYE Suffolk

The Lion

HONEY TYE Map 05 TL93
CO6 4NX ☎ 01206 263434

A busy dining pub with low beamed ceilings and an open log fire, offering a wide range of drinks including real ales and an interesting wine list. There's one menu throughout, with dishes such as poached salmon steak with lime sauce, and braised leg of lamb with orange and rosemary. Principal beers: Greene King IPA, Adnams Bitter, Fosters, Carlsberg.

Directions On A314 between Colchester & Sudbury
Free House
Open 11-3 6-11 (Sun 12-10.30)
Bar food 12-2 6.30-9.30 Av main course £6.90
Restaurant 12-2 6.30-9.30

HORRINGER Suffolk

Beehive

HORRINGER Map 05 TL86
The Street IP29 5SN ☎ 01284 735260

Thatched cottage-style flintstone pub built in the mid-19th century. Ickworth House and Ickworth Park are close by. Typical bar menu includes Suffolk ham with pickles, pancake cannelloni with rich meat sauce, wild mushroom risotto, smoked salmon with ribbon noodles, and mild Thai chicken curry. Principal beers: Greene King.

Directions From A14, 1st turning for Bury St Edmunds, sign for Westley & Ickworth Park
Greene King
Open 11.30-2.30 7-11
Bar food 12-2 7-9.30 Av main course £7.95

ICKLINGHAM Suffolk

The Red Lion

ICKLINGHAM Map 05 TL77
The Street IP28 6PS
☎ 01638 717802

16-century inn situated at the edge of the King's Forest, close to the River Lark. Furnished with antiques and rugs. A la carte menu includes starters such as goats cheese in filo pastry with spiced damson and raisin chutney, plus main courses like roast Barbary duck with cherry brandy sauce. Principal beers: Wexfords, Greene King.

contd.

Directions On A1101 between Mildenhall & Bury St Edmunds
Greene King
Open 11-10.30
Bar food 12-2.30 6-10 Av main course £7.95
Restaurant 12-2.30 6-10 Av 3 course à la carte £20

KERSEY Suffolk

The Bell Inn
KERSEY Map 05 TM04
IP7 6DY ☎ 01473 823229
At this fascinating inn dating from 1320, sited in a pretty village location, notice the worn cobbled corridor. It used to be stables route but now leads to home-cooked English fare. Feast on lobster Thermidor, or an English pie followed by an old fashioned spotted dick pudding. Principal beers: Adnams, Nethergate, Courage, Theakston.
Directions R off A1141 from Ipswich, 1 1/2m Kersey on L, follow signs for Kersey Street
Free House
Open 11-3 6.30-11.20
Bar food 12-3 7-9.30 Av main course £5.95
Restaurant 12-3 7-9.30 Av 3 course à la carte £14

LAVENHAM Suffolk

Angel Hotel
LAVENHAM Map 05 TL94
Market Place CO10 9QZ
☎ 01787 247388
At the heart of one of England's best preserved medieval towns, good food and friendly service are offered at this historic inn first licensed in 1420. Home-cured or smoked meat and fish feature, or savour carrot and coriander soup and venison fillet with blackberry and apple. Principal beers: Adnams, Mauldons White Adder, Nethergate Bitter, Greene King.
Directions From Bury St Edmunds, A134 to Sudbury, after 3m L onto A1141 to Lavenham.
Free House
Open 11-11 (Sun 12-10.30)
Bar food 12-2.15 6.45-9.15 Av main course £15
Restaurant 12-2.15 6.45-9.15 Av 3 course à la carte £15
Accommodation s£39.50 d£65

LAXFIELD Suffolk

The Kings Head
LAXFIELD Map 05 TM27
Gorams Mill Ln IP13 8DW
☎ 01986 798395
There is no bar at this old fashioned village pub, the beer is served from the tap room. The building dates from the 14th century and retains its original high backed settles, tiled floors and open fires. All the food is home cooked from traditional, well loved recipes. Principal beers: Adnams Best, Broadside, Greene King IPA.
Free House
Open 11-3 6-11 (Sun 12-3, 7-10.30)
Bar food 12-2 7-9

LEVINGTON Suffolk

The Ship Inn
LEVINGTON Map 05 TM23
Church Ln IP10 0LQ ☎ 01473 659573
14th-century, Grade II listed thatched building near the River Orwell. Among the seafood meals are king prawns in garlic butter, and salmon and broccoli bake. Other dishes include braised steak in leek and Stilton sauce, chicken in asparagus sauce and, for vegetarians, vegetable paella with cashew nuts. Principal beers: Greene King IPA, Abbot, Burton Ale, Flowers IPA.
Directions off the A14 towards Felixstowe
Free House
Open 11.30-3 6-11
Bar food 12-2 7-9 Av main course £5.95
Restaurant 12-2 7-9 Av 3 course à la carte £11

LIDGATE Suffolk

Star Inn
LIDGATE Map 05 TL75
CB8 9PP ☎ 01638 500275
500-year-old pub where the blackboard menu changes regularly and there's an interest in Catalan food. Typical dishes include Mediterranean fish soup, paella, Catalan salad, lamb in garlic and wine, venison in port, kidneys in sherry, pork with apricots, steak in Stilton sauce, monkfish marinière, and chicken aux herbes. Principal beers: Greene King.
Directions From Newmarket, clocktower in High st, follow signs toward Clare on B1063. Lidgate 7m from Newmarket
Greene King
Open 11-3 5-11
Bar food 12.30-2 7.30-10 Av main course £8.50
Restaurant 12.30-2 7.30-10 Av 3 course à la carte £15.50 Av 3 course fixed price £12.50

LINDSEY Suffolk

White Rose Inn
LINDSEY Map 05 TL94
Rose Green IP7 6LG ☎ 01787 210664
In idyllic rural surroundings, this 15th-century thatched and beamed inn specialises in quality cuisine at affordable prices, complemented by fine wines. Leek and Stilton tartlet, chicken breast with wild mushroom fricassée and Summer pudding with a bramble coulis are temptations from a regularly varying selection. Principal beers: Greene King & Adnams Bitters, Guinness, Carlsberg, Kronenbourg.
Directions From A1071 take A1141, take 2nd turning to Kersey & follow signs to St James Chapel, pub approx 1/2m beyond chapel
Free House
Open 12-3.30 6-11.30
Restaurant 12.30-3 7-11 Av 3 course à la carte £20

MELTON Suffolk

Wilford Bridge
MELTON Map 05 TM25
Wilfrord Bridge Rd IP12 2PA
☎ 01394 386141
Busy pub close to the world famous Saxon Sutton Hoo burial ship. Offers a wide selection of snacks and light meals. Char-grilled chicken dishes include chicken Dijonnaise and chicken piri piri. Vegetarian options feature vegetable and Stilton pie, and vegetable and bean casserole. Principal beers: Adnams, John Smith, Guinness, Kilkenny.
Directions Head to the coast from the A12, follow signs to Bawdsey & Orford, cross railway lines, next pub on L
Free House
Open 11-3 6.30-11
Bar food 11.30-2 6.30-9.30 Av main course £6
Restaurant 11.30-2 6.30-9.30 Av 3 course à la carte £12.50

NAYLAND Suffolk

White Hart at Nayland
NAYLAND Map 05 TL93
High St CO6 4NF ☎ 01206 263382
At this medieval coaching house, in a quaint riverside village, Chef Patron Mark Prescott and partner Michel Roux have created an interesting culinary venue. From a typical dinner menu, one of six starters may feature superb native oysters, with main dishes such as breast of woodpigeon. Principal beers: Adnams, Greene King, IPA, Stella.
Free House
Open 12-3 6.30-11

contd.

Bar food 12-2.30 6.30-9.30 Av main course £8.50
Restaurant 12-2.30 6.30-9.30 Av 3 course fixed price £16

ORFORD Suffolk

Jolly Sailor Inn
ORFORD Map 05 TM45
Quay St IP12 2NU ☎ 01394 450243
Situated right by the quay at Orford, this lovely old smuggler's inn is made up of several cosy rooms served via counters and hatches from the central cubicle. Naturally, fresh local fish is a feature, alongside local game in season and home-cooked dishes prepared from personal recipes. Principal beers: Adnams.
Directions On B1084 E of Woodbridge
Adnams
Open 11.30-2.30 7-11 (Sun 12-2.30, 7-10.30)
Bar food 12-2 7.15-8.45 Av main course £5
Accommodation d£35

RATTLESDEN Suffolk

Brewers Arms
RATTLESDEN Map 05 TL95
Lower Rd IP30 0RJ ☎ 01449 736377
Definitely a 'destination pub', the Brewers Arms is in a very rural location. It has a wealth of beams, dating from the 17th century, and the original village bread oven. Food is all home-made, with dishes such as monkfish Thermidor and pan-fried pork with carrot and coriander sauce. Principal beers: Greene King.
Directions From A14 take A1088 toward Woolpit, Rattlesden 2.8m from Woolpit
Greene King
Open 12-11 (Sun 12-10.30)
Bar food 12.30-2 7-9.30 Av main course £4.50
Restaurant 12.30-2 7-9.30 Av 3 course à la carte £14

REDE Suffolk

The Plough
REDE Map 05 TL85
IP29 4BE ☎ 01284 789208
Choose from a bistro-style selection at this half-thatched, half-tiled hostelry on the village green, easily found from the main A413. Examples include pheasant braised with apples and cider or Moroccan chicken fillet or a speciality steak. Principal beers: Greene King IPA, Abbot Ale.
Directions on the A143 between Bury St Edmonds and Haverhill
Greene King
Open 11-3 7-11
Bar food 11-3 7-9.30 Av main course £5.95
Restaurant 11-3 7-9.30 Av 3 course à la carte £16

RICKINGHALL Suffolk

Hamblyn House Hotel
RICKINGHALL Map 05 TM07
The Street IP22 1BN ☎ 01379 898292
350-year-old beamed hotel with open fires. Said to be haunted by the mysterious 'Lavender Lady'. The restaurant menu features pot roasted guinea fowl with redcurrants and port, fillet of pork stuffed with prunes and walnuts, and pan-fried goose breast with orange Calvados sauce. Principal beers: St Peters.
Directions Signed on A143 between Diss & Bury St Edmunds
St Peters Brewery
Open 12-3 6-11
Bar food 12-2.30 7-9.30 Av main course £5.95
Restaurant 12-2.30 7-9.30 Av 3 course à la carte £20
Accommodation s£39.50 d£59.50

RISBY Suffolk

The White Horse Inn
RISBY Map 05 TL86
Newmarket Rd IP28 6RD
☎ 01284 810686
17th-century coaching inn with open fires, exposed beams and period furniture including a large mirror in the bar used by judges preparing for sessions in 17th and 18th centuries. Menu offers up to 25 main courses and a variety of daily

specials. Principal beers: Adnams, Bass, Whitbread, Greene King.
Directions A14 from Bury St Edmunds
Free House
Open 11-3.30 6-11
Bar food 11-2.30 6-10 Av main course £4.75
Restaurant 11-2.30 6-10 Av 3 course à la carte £12 Av 4 course fixed price £12.50

ST PETER SOUTH ELMHAM Suffolk

St Peter's Hall
ST PETER SOUTH ELMHAM Map 05 TM38
NR35 1NQ ☎ 01986 782322
Medieval and Tudor hall which has its own brewery. Built in 1996, it not only produces 'traditional' beers, but also more unusual beers such as honey porter, blackcurrant, and gooseberry. Items on the 'Bill of Fare' may include tortellini with artichoke, steamed Scottish salmon escalope, or pan-fried duck magret. Principal beers: St Peters
Directions From A40 S of Diss take B1077
Open 11-11
Bar food 11.30-2.30 6-9.30 Av main course £6.95

SAXTEAD GREEN Suffolk

Old Mill House
SAXTEAD GREEN Map 05 TM26
IP13 9QE ☎ 01728 685064
17th-century coaching inn with pond, overlooking the village green. Interesting starters include peaches and Stilton, and sautéed kidneys in brandy sauce. Among the main course dishes are veal escalopes Viscayenne, grilled halibut steak, lamb cutlets garnished with artichoke hearts, and braised venison in red wine, onion and mushroom sauce. Principal beers: Fosters, Kronenbourg, Beamish, Adnams.
Directions Nr junction of A1120 & B1119 opp Saxstead windmill
Free House
Open 11-3 6.30-11
Bar food 12-2.30 7-9.30 Av main course £5.95
Restaurant 12-2.30 7-9.30 Av 3 course à la carte £15

SNAPE Suffolk

The Crown Inn
SNAPE Map 05 TM35
Bridge Rd IP17 1SL ☎ 01728 688324
This 15th century inn lies just a stone's throw from The Maltings, home of the famed Aldeburgh music festival. In an unspoilt landscape, this traditional pub serves fare with flair: pigeon breast and bacon salad or crayfish tails with mango starters simply whet the appetite. Principal beers: Adnams, Broadside, Carlsberg, Bulmers.
Directions A12 N to Lowestoft, R to Aldeburgh, then R again in Snape at crossroads by church, pub at bottom hill
Adnams
Open 12-3 6-11 (Sun 12-3, 7-10.30)
Bar food 12-2 7-9.30 Av main course £6.95
Restaurant 12-2 7-9.30
Accommodation s£35 d£50

SOUTHWOLD Suffolk

Crown Hotel
SOUTHWOLD Map 05 TM57
The High St IP18 6DP
☎ 01502 722275
There is a busy bar and restaurant trade at this 16th-century coaching inn, which is a flagship for Adnams Wine Merchants and offers a list of up to 300 wines. The menus are rustic in style with dishes such as roast rack of lamb with flash-fried liver and cassoulet of mixed beans. Principal beers: Adnams, Broadside, Mild (summer), Old (winter), Best Bitter.
Directions S of Lowestoft off A12
Adnams
Open 10.30-3 6-11
Bar food 12.15-2 7-10 Av main course £8

contd.

Restaurant 12.30-1.30 7.30-9.30 Av 3 course fixed price £21.25
Accommodation s£43 d£65

STOKE-BY-NAYLAND Suffolk

The Angel Inn
STOKE-BY-NAYLAND Map 05 TL93
CO6 4SA ☎ 01206 263245
Renovated 16th-century inn situated in one of British painter John Constable's favourite villages. Main course dishes range from steamed fillets of salmon and halibut with dill sauce, and honey glazed rack of lamb, to roast duckling with cassis sauce, and griddled wing of skate. Home-made puddings include raspberry Bavarois. Principal beers: Greene King, IPA, Abbot Ale, Adnams Best.
Directions From A12 take Colchester R turn, then A134, 5m to Nayland. From A12 S take B1068
Free House
Open 11-2.30 6-11
Bar food 12-2 6.30-9 Av main course £8.50
Restaurant 12-2 6.30-9 Av 3 course à la carte £16
Accommodation s£45 d£59

THORNHAM MAGNA Suffolk

The Four Horseshoes
THORNHAM MAGNA Map 05 TM17
Wickham Rd IP23 8DH
☎ 01397 678777
Discover this ancient 12th-century thatched inn with its own well, wealth of beams and mischievous ghost in a picturesque village. The frequently changing menu combines old favourites and modern classics such as home-made steak and kidney pudding or pan-fried skate wing with black butter. Principal beers: Courage Best & Directors,Adnams Southwold & Broadside.
Directions From Diss on A140 turn rt and follow signs for Finningham, 1/2 mile turn right for Thornham Magna
Free House
Open 12-2.30 7-11
Bar food 12-2 7-10 Av main course £6.50
Restaurant 12-2 7-10 Av 3 course à la carte £20
Accommodation s£30 d£40

WALBERSWICK Suffolk

Bell Inn
WALBERSWICK Map 05 TM47
Ferry Rd IP18 6TN ☎ 01502 723109
600-year-old inn overlooking the village green and a short distance from the beach. A wide range of bar snacks is available. House specials range from chicken balti, and Cajun chicken with noodles, to salmon and fennel tart. Desserts include toffee and banana crumble , and honey, apple and clove tart. Principal beers: Adnams Bitter, Broadside, Extra Mild.
Directions On the A12 signed just before Blythburgh
Adnams
Open 11-3 6-11
Bar food 12-2 6-9 Av main course £5.50
Restaurant 12-2 6-9 Av 3 course à la carte £10
Accommodation s£40 d£60

Warwickshire

ALCESTER Warwickshire

The Moat House Inn
ALCESTER Map 04 SP05
Birmingham Rd, Kings Coughton B49 5QF ☎ 01789 762984
One of the oldest buildings in Warwickshire, rebuilt in 1478, and retaining its period character with low ceilings, beams and open fires. Food crosses the international range with dishes such as rabbit pie, sweet and sour pork, chicken curry and lasagne, plus fish and vegetarian options. Principal beers: Courage Brands, John Smiths, Guinness, Fosters.
Directions On A435 between Studley & Alcester
Free House
Open 11.30-3 6-11.30

ALDERMINSTER Warwickshire

The Bell
ALDERMINSTER Map 04 SP24
01789 ☎ 01789 450414
Special events are a regular staple of The Bell's calendar, so much so that a newsletter is produced to keep customers informed. 1997 included Gilbert & Sullivan, A Taste of India, and an evening with Stefan Buczacki. The menu is also an attraction, and may include tomato and basil sausages, venison and steak pie, or Somerset rarebit. Principal beers: Hook Norton, IPA, Guinness, Marstons Pedigree.
Directions just off A3400 S of Stratford-upon-Avon
Free House
Open 12-3 7-11
Restaurant 12-2 7-9.30 Av 3 course à la carte £15 Av 2 course fixed price £6.50

BAGINTON Warwickshire

The Old Mill Hotel
BAGINTON Map 04 SP37
Mill Hill CV8 3AH ☎ 01203 302241
A working mill until the 1920s, the original mill wheel is still visible in the restaurant at this hotel. Popular dishes include grills, burgers, battered haddock, lasagne, Cajun chicken, chilli con carne and steak and kidney pudding. Vegetarian dishes such as mushroom pilau are flagged. Principal beers: J Smith, Courage, Fosters, Kronenberg.
Directions Just off A45 & A46
Scottish & Newcastle
Open 11-3 5-11
Bar food 12-2 6-9.30 Av main course £4.50
Restaurant 12-2 6-9.30 Av 3 course à la carte £10.50
Accommodation s£37 d£37

BROOM Warwickshire

Broom Tavern
BROOM Map 04 SP05
High St B50 4HL ☎ 01789 773656
William Shakespeare had connections with this 16th-century inn, and the pub sign depicts the Bard under a crab tree which once stood nearby. Duck Montmorency, 'Surf and Turf': sirloin steak and Japanese prawns, chicken chasseur, Cumberland cottage pie, or Broom Tavern salad may be available from a varied menu. Principal beers: Whitbread, Boddingtons IPA, Caffreys, Guinness.
Directions N of B439 W of Stratford-upon-Avon
Free House
Open 11-3 6.30-11
Bar food 12-2 6.45-9.30 Av main course £6.50
Restaurant 12-2 6.45-9.30 Av 3 course à la carte £12

EATHORPE Warwickshire

The Plough Inn
EATHORPE Map 04 SP36
Fosse Way CV33 9DQ ☎ 01926 632557
A friendly, old fashioned country pub, with beams and open fires, in a small village setting. The menu comprises local favourites such as the famously huge Brontosaurus Grill, deep-fried scampi and 'Green Cuisine' vegetarian dishes. Daily specials reflect the Italian owner's roots. Principal beers: Stella Artois, Guinness, Tetleys, Bass.
Directions A46 then A423 into Fosse Way
Free House
Open 12-2.30 7-11
Bar food 12-2.30 7-11 Av main course £4
Restaurant 12-2.30 7-11 Av 3 course à la carte £12 Av 3 course fixed price £4.95

EDGEHILL Warwickshire

The Castle Inn
EDGEHILL Map 04 SP34
OX15 6DJ ☎ 01295 670255
An octagonal tower on the summit of Edgehill, some 700ft above sea level, opened in 1750 to commemorate the 100th anniversary of the Battle of

contd.

Edgehill. It became an inn in 1822, providing its patrons with views of several counties from the garden. Popular bar food and grills are served. Principal beers: Hook Norton.
Directions M40 then A422, travel 6m until Upton House, then turn R go 1 1/2m
Hook Norton
Open 11.15-2.30 6.15-11
Bar food 12-2 6.30-9 Av main course £4.50
Accommodation s£25 d£49.50

ETTINGTON Warwickshire

The Houndshill
ETTINGTON Map 04 SP24
Banbury Rd CV37 7NS
☎ 01789 740267
Just 4 miles from Stratford-upon-Avon, this family-run inn is perfectly suited for visitors to the Heart of England. Cotswold pork sausages, Warwickshire ham, steak and kidney pie, or Thai chicken and lamb curry may be on the menu. Principal beers: Theakstons Best and Theakstons XB.
Directions On A422 SE of Stratford-upon-Avon
Free House
Open 12-3 6-11
Bar food 12-2 6.30-9.30 Av main course £5.50
Restaurant 12-2 6.30-9.30 Av 3 course à la carte £12.50

GREAT WOLFORD Warwickshire

Fox & Hounds Inn
GREAT WOLFORD Map 04 SP23
CV36 5NQ ☎ 01608 674220
Dating from 1540, old settles, dog grates, open fires, flagged floors and baking ovens are all features of this old world pub. Typical bar dishes include prime beef in Guinness and Cotswold casserole, while the restaurant offers salmon en croute with crab mouse or stuffed quails with paté. Principal beers: Spitfire, Hook Norton, 6X, CHB.
Directions Off A44 NE of Moreton-in-Marsh
Free House
Open 12-3 7-11
Bar food 12-2 7-9.30 Av main course £4.50
Restaurant 12-2 7-9.30 Av 3 course à la carte £15

LONG COMPTON Warwickshire

The Red Lion
LONG COMPTON Map 04 SP23
Main St CV36 5JS ☎ 01608 684221
Dating from 1743, this Grade II listed coaching inn, built of Cotswold stone, retains many original features and is situated in an area of outstanding natural beauty. The traditional bar/bistro menu is supplemented by two blackboard menus of more unusual dishes and fresh fish. Principal beers: Webster, Ruddles, John Smiths, Directors.
Directions On A3400 between Shipton on Stour & Chipping Norton
Free House
Open 11-2.30 6-11
Bar food 12-2 7-9 Av main course £5.50
Restaurant 7-9 Av 3 course à la carte £15

LONG ITCHINGTON Warwickshire

The Harvester
LONG ITCHINGTON Map 04 SP46
Church Rd CV23 8PE
☎ 01926 812698
Very much a village pub, the Harvester is centrally located by the church and pond, with old photos of Long Itchington on display. Home-made lasagne, chilli, curry and chicken Florentine are offered in the bar, while in the restaurant quality steaks are served with home sauces and fresh vegetables. Principal beers: Hook Norton Bitter, Old Hooky.
Directions Off A423 E of Leamington Spa
Free House
Open 11-3 6-11
Bar food 12-3 6-10.30 Av main course £3.50
Restaurant 12-3 6-10.30 Av 3 course à la carte £12.50

LOWER BRAILES Warwickshire

The George Hotel
LOWER BRAILES Map 04 SP33
High St OX15 5HN ☎ 01608 685223
Dating from the 16th century with 17th and 18th-century additions, this hotel, recently completely refurbished, retains many historic features. There is a garden with old fruit and walnut trees, a stone-laid patio and a barbecue. Dishes range from seafood platter to prime fillet steak. Principal beers: Hook Norton.

Directions B4035 toward Shipston on Stour
Hook Norton
Open 12-3 6-11
Bar food 12-2 7-9.30 Av main course £5
Restaurant 12-2 7-9.30 Av 3 course à la carte £15

LOWSONFORD Warwickshire

Fleur De Lys
LOWSONFORD Map 04 SP16
Lapworth St B95 5HJ
☎ 01564 782431
Converted from three cottages and a mortuary, this pub is where the original Fleur de Lys pies were made. It's alongside the Stratford-upon-Avon to Birmingham canal, and has a large garden. The style is casual dining with traditional pies, bangers and mash, vegetable korma and lemon chicken. Principal beers: Flowers Original, Wadworth 6X.
Directions Off A3400 (Birmingham to Stratford)
Whitbread
Open 11-11 (Sun 10.30-12)
Bar food 12-2.30 6-9.30 Av main course £6

MONKS KIRBY Warwickshire

The Bell Inn
MONKS KIRBY Map 04 SP48
Bell Ln CV23 0QY
☎ 01788 832352
Centuries ago the Bell was the gate house for the priory, then eventually became a brew house and inn. The menu offers an extensive choice of both English and Spanish food, embracing Paco's tapas, fish and grills, and Spanish specialities such as paella served in its iron cooking dish. Principal beers: Flowers, Boddingtons, Murphys.
Directions Off B4027 & B455 W of Lutterworth
Free House
Open 12-2.30 7-11
Bar food 12-2.30 7-11 Av main course £3.75
Restaurant 12-2.30 7-11 Av 4 course fixed price £12.75

PRINCETHORPE Warwickshire

The Three Horseshoes
PRINCETHORPE Map 04 SP47
Southam Rd CV23 9PR ☎ 01926 632345
19th-century inn that overlooks the Warwickshire countryside. Typical menu includes chicken Cordon Bleu, spinach and walnut lasagne, and rainbow trout. The blackboard menu is changed daily and may include braised steak, cottage pie, monkfish Thermidor, or duck in pepper sauce. Principal beers: Adnams, Theakstons, Ruddles County, John Smiths.
Directions On A423 at crossroads of B4455 & B4453
Free House
Open 11-2.30 6-11
Bar food 11.30-2 6-10 Av main course £4.50
Accommodation s£20 d£30

RATLEY Warwickshire

The Rose and Crown
RATLEY Map 04 SP34
OX15 6DS ☎ 01295 678148
900 years old this year, this Hornton stone-built village pub is reputedly haunted by a fugitive Roundhead who was discovered in the chimney and beheaded in the hearth! The inn is also famous for its views of surrounding countryside, and offers a varying menu of old-fashioned 'pub grub'. Principal beers: Bombadier, Eagle IPA, Tanglefoot, Old Speckled Hen.
Directions Follow Edgehill signs
Free House
Open 12-2.30 6-11
Bar food 12-2.30 6-11 Av main course £5.95

STRATFORD-UPON-AVON Warwickshire

The Dirty Duck
STRATFORD-UPON-AVON Map 04 SP25
Waterside CV37 6BA ☎ 01789 297312
Frequently visited by members of the Royal Shakespeare Company, this traditional inn is partly Elizabethan, and overlooks the River Avon. A typical menu (shaped like a stage with curtains) features pork Dijonnaise, Henry VIII's traditional roast beef, spinach and mushroom lasagne, and horseshoe gammon. Principal beers: Whitbread Original, Flowers IPA, Boddingtons.

contd.

Whitbread
Open 11-11
Restaurant 12-2 6-10 Av 3 course à la carte £15

TEMPLE GRAFTON Warwickshire

The Blue Boar
TEMPLE GRAFTON Map 04 SP15
B49 5NR ☎ 01789 750010
The Blue Boar, an ale house since the early 1600s, has a 35ft glass covered well in the restaurant bar, the pure water from which has been used for brewing for many years. Bar food ranges from ploughman's to chicken curry, while the restaurant might offer Halibut Belle Mennaire. Principal beers: Hook Norton, Theakstons XB, Old Speckled Hen, Directors.
Free House
Open 11.30-3 6-11.30 (Sun 12-4, 7-10.30)
Bar food 12-2.15 6.30-10 Av main course £5.95
Restaurant 12-2.15 6.30-10 Av 4 course fixed price £10.95
Accommodation s£45 d£65

WARWICK Warwickshire

The Tilted Wig
WARWICK Map 04 SP26
11 Market Place CV34 4SA
☎ 01926 410466
A restaurant, bar and brasserie all rolled into one, set in historic Warwick, two minutes walk from the castle. The name comes from its proximity to the Crown Court. A wide variety of food includes snacks, burgers, a Tex Mex selection, char-grill dishes and vegetarian options. Principal beers: Tetley, Marstons, Pedigree, Castlemaine 4X.
Directions From M40 J15 follow A429 into Warwick, after 1 1/2m L into Brook St and on into Market Place

Free House
Open 11-11
Bar food 11-10 Av main course £5

WELFORD-ON-AVON Warwickshire

The Four Alls
WELFORD-ON-AVON Map 04 SP15
Binton Rd CV37 8PW
☎ 01789 750228
17th-century inn situated on the banks of the River Avon, two miles from Stratford. The menu includes a selection of snacks, salad platters, and traditional pies. Main course dishes range from salmon béarnaise, and lemon chicken, to vegetarian options such as vegetable korma, and cannelloni Provençale. Principal beers: Stella Artois, Heineken.
Directions B439 from Stratford then L
Whitbread
Open 11-11
Bar food 12-2.30 6.30-10 Av main course £4
Restaurant 12-2.30 6.30-10 Av 3 course à la carte £8

WHATCOTE Warwickshire

Royal Oak
WHATCOTE Map 04 SP24
CV36 5EF ☎ 01295 680319
The Royal Oak has been an ale house since 1168, originally for the workers building churches in the area. All home-cooked food and fresh vegetables are offered, with dishes such as chef's paté and toast, fresh trout, chicken in garlic, steaks, and mushroom en croute. Principal beers: Hook Norton Traditional Beer, Theakstons Bitter, Guinness.
Hook Norton
Open 12-3 6-11
Bar food 12-3 6.30-10.30 Av main course £6
Restaurant 12-3 6.30-10.30 Av 3 course à la carte £12

WILMCOTE Warwickshire

The Mary Arden Inn
WILMCOTE Map 04 SP15
The Green CV37 9XJ ☎ 01789 267030
Named after William Shakespeare's mother, whose house is opposite, this recently refurbished inn is family-run and only 3 miles from Stratford-upon-

Avon. Menu may include salmon en croûte, venison casserole, lamb rump steak, avocado aux champignons, or sausage and mash. Principal beers: Theakstons, Fosters, Becks, John Smiths.
Directions A46 to A3400 toward Birmingham, L into Featherbed Ln and on to T Jct, pub opposite
Free House
Open 11-11 (Nov-March closed 3-5.30)
Bar food 12-2.30 6.30-9.30 Av main course £5.95
Restaurant 12-2.30 6.30-9.30 Av 3 course à la carte £18
Accommodation s£40 d£55

WITHYBROOK Warwickshire

The Pheasant
WITHYBROOK Map 04 SP48
Main St CV7 9LT ☎ 01455 220480
17th-century coaching inn with flagstones and inglenook fireplace, situated near a brook. The menu offers a selection of home-made pies and curries. Main dishes range from Cajun-style chicken breast, smoked trout and poached salmon, to venison pie, braised pheasant and roast duck in orange sauce. Principal beers: Directors, Fosters, Kronenbourg, John Smiths.
Directions Off B4112 NE of Coventry
Free House
Open 11-3 6.30-11
Bar food 12-2 6.30-10 Av main course £7.50

WOOTTON WAWEN Warwickshire

The Bulls Head
WOOTTON WAWEN Map 04 SP16
Stratford Rd B95 6BD ☎ 01564 792511
A 16th-century black and white timbered inn, with rugs on flagstone floors, old beams and open fires. The same menu is served throughout, with fresh fish and seafood, the house speciality, offered from a daily blackboard. Other options include steaks and kebabs from the char-grill. Principal beers: Marstons, Pedigree, London Pride, Adnams.
Directions On A3400
Free House
Open 12-3 6-11
Bar food 12-2.30 7-10 Av main course £10
Restaurant 12-2.30 7-10 Av 3 course à la carte £18

West Midlands

BARSTON West Midlands

Bulls Head
BARSTON Map 04 SP27
Barston Ln B29 0JU ☎ 01675 442830
A traditional pub in a small village setting. The building dates back to 1490, and there's a priest hole in the private lounge that dates back to Cromwell's time. Bar food includes sandwiches, steaks and sausage and chips. The evening menu offers steaks, fresh fish and chicken dishes. Principal beers: Bass, Brew, Tetley, Carling.
Directions M42 J5 take A4141 towards Warwick.Turn L 0.25m.Straight on at staggered junc.Pub 1m
Free House
Open 11-2.30 5.30-11 (Sun 12-10.30)
Bar food 12-2 7-8.30 Av main course £3.75
Restaurant 12-2 7-8.30 Av 3 course à la carte £8.25 Av 3 course fixed price £9.50

COVENTRY West Midlands

The Rose and Castle
COVENTRY Map 04 SP37
Ansty CV7 9HZ ☎ 01203 612822
Small, canalside pub with moorings available. A wide range of bar snacks and light meals is available. Seafood dishes include goujons of plaice, cod Mornay, and grilled halibut with prawns. Vegetarian options feature vegetable lasagne, and mushrooms baked with tomato, chilli sauce and cheese. Principal beers: Tetley, Bass.
Directions From junc of M6/M69 at Walsgrave follow signs for Ansty. 0.75m to pub
Free House

contd.

Open 12-3 (Sat-Sun, all day opening) 6-11
Bar food 12-3 6-11 Av main course £5.50

NETHERTON West Midlands

Little Dry Dock
NETHERTON Map 07 SO98
Windmill End DY2 9HU
☎ 01384 235369
The bar is made from a canal boat at this characterful canal-side pub. Sample 'the famous Mad O'Rourke speciality pies'; the 'Desperate Dan', steak and kidney cooked in Guinness, is served complete with horns. Fridays offer live and lively Irish folk music. Principal beers: Lumphammer, Burton Ale, Old Speckled Hen.
Free House
Open 11-3 6-11 (Sun 12-3, 7-10.30)
Bar food 12-2.30 6-10 Av main course £5

STOURBRIDGE West Midlands

The Retreat Bar & Bistro
STOURBRIDGE Map 07 SO88
157 Hagley Rd, Old Swinford DY8 2JJ
☎ 01384 396290
A stylish bar and bistro in a village setting offering a range of food from snacks to full meals. Dishes include giant New Zealand mussels, and roast baby chicken with tomato and fresh tarragon sauce; or hot avocado with port and grilled Stilton from the separate vegetarian menu. Principal beers: Boddingtons, Flowers original.
Directions On A491
Open 12-3 7-11
Bar food 12-2.15 7-10 Av main course £6.50
Restaurant 12-3 7-1 Av 3 course à la carte £17.50

WEST BROMWICH West Midlands

The Vine
WEST BROMWICH Map 07 SP09
Roebuck St B70 6RD ☎ 0121 5532866
Real ale and curry is the winning combination at this popular pub. Home-made tandoori dishes, curries and balti meals are prepared to traditional recipes by the landlord and his wife, and there is an authentic Indian barbecue serving sizzling chicken and lamb tikka kebabs. Prices are equally attractive. Principal beers: M&B Mild, Brew IV, Guinness, Caffreys.
Free House
Open 11.30-2.30 5-11 (Fri-Sun all day)
Bar food 12-2 5-10.30
Restaurant 12-2 6-9.30 Av 3 course à la carte £7

WOLVERHAMPTON West Midlands

Barley Mow
WOLVERHAMPTON Map 07 SO99
Penn Common WV4 5JN
☎ 01902 333510
Dated 1630, this tiny pub was a site for anti-aircraft guns in WWII, and may have been a rest stop for Lady Godiva on her ride into Coventry. Specialities include 'Mighty Mow Yorkies': Yorkshire pudding with various fillings, 'Barley Mow Mega Grill', home-made spicy meatloaf, and 'Simon's Special Breakfast'. Principal beers: Burton, ABC, Holdens.
Directions Town centre near Penn Golf Club
Free House
Open 12-3 6.30-11
Bar food 12-2 6.30-9.30 Av main course £5

RADITIONAL
COUNTRY ALES
POTTERIES
ANIC
OUT
BREWERY
T ALES

Wales & The Marches

Fierce historical independence and individuality marks the principality. Spectacular mountain ranges and a Gulf Stream coastline are guarded by the battlements of the unspoilt Marches countryside.

• Bridgend • Caerphilly • Cardiff •
• Carmarthenshire • Ceredigion •
• Conwy • Denbighshire •
• Flintshire • Gwynedd •
• Herefordshire • Isle of Anglesey •
• Monmouthshire • Pembrokeshire •
• Powys • Shropshire • Swansea •
• Vale of Glamorgan •
• Worcestershire • Wrexham •

Bridgend

KENFIG Bridgend

Prince of Wales Inn
KENFIG Map 03 SS88
CF33 4PR ☎ 01656 740356
Dating from 1440, this stone-built inn has been many things in its time - school, hotel and courtroom - and it's the only pub that still holds a weekly Sunday school. The landlord's own home-grown veg and salad appears wherever possible on the menu, and fresh fish is a speciality. Principal beers: Bass Triangle, Worthingtons, Marstons Pedigree.
Directions M4 J37 into North Cornelly & follow signs for nature reserve, Kenfig
Free House
Open 11-4 6-11
Bar food 12-2.30 7-10 Av main course £5
Restaurant 12-2.30 7-10

Caerphilly

CAERPHILLY Caerphilly

The Courthouse
CAERPHILLY Map 03 ST18
Cardiff Rd CF83 1FN
☎ 01222 888120
14th-century Welsh longhouse overlooking Caerphilly Castle. Specials change weekly and typically feature Mediterranean lamb stew and pasta, and ratatouille pie. The all-day menu includes home-made curries and pies, salmon cutlet with parsley sauce, beef Wellington, and Chinese-style chicken. Principal beers: Courage Best.
Free House
Open 11-11
Bar food 12-5.30 5.30-9.30 Av main course £4
Restaurant 12-5.30 5.30-9.30 Av 3 course à la carte £8.50

Cardiff

CREIGIAU Cardiff

Caesars Arms
CREIGIAU Map 03 ST08
Cardiff Rd CF4 8NN ☎ 01222 890486
Large country pub and restaurant where fresh fish is bought daily. Specialities include whole sea bass baked in rock salt, spicy bajan fishcakes, plus local dishes like cockles laverbread. Also available are honeyed roast Barbary duck, grilled leg of Welsh lamb and venison with port and redcurrant sauce. Principal beers: Hancocks Bitter, Flowers IPA, Murphys.
Directions 1m from M4 J34
Free House
Open 12-2.30 (Sun, 12-7) 6-12.30
Restaurant 12-2.30 7-12.30 Av 3 course à la carte £15

Carmarthenshire

ABERGORLECH Carmarthenshire

The Black Lion
ABERGORLECH Map 02 SN53
SA32 7SN ☎ 01558 685271
Small, 16th-century village inn on the banks of the River Cothi. Seafood dishes include pink trout with prawns and asparagus. A range of steak meals are also available such as steak au poivre. Vegetarian options feature three bean casserole, and leek and mushroom crumble. Principal beers: Worthington Real Ale, Addlestones Cider, Welsh, Worthington Dark.
Directions From Carmarthan take A40 eastwards,then B4310 signposted Brechfa & Llansawel.
Free House
Open 12-11 (Sun 12-10.30)
Bar food 12-2 7-9 Av main course £4.50
Restaurant 12-2 7-11 Av 3 course à la carte £12

LLANARTHNE Carmarthenshire

Golden Grove Arms
LLANARTHNE Map 02 SN52
SA32 8JJ ☎ 01558 668551
200-year-old coaching inn, formerly a farm. Within easy reach of Dryslwyn, Dinefwr and Carreg Cennen castles, with fine views of the Black Mountains. Main course dishes range from fillet of salmon with chive butter sauce, to venison marinated in port and rosemary, served with port and redcurrant sauce. Principal beers: Buckleys BB, Kronenbourg, Reverend James, Special Vat.
Directions B4300 from Carmarthen
Free House
Open 12-12
Bar food 12-2 6-9.30 Av main course £5.95

Restaurant 12-2 6-9.30 Av 3 course à la carte £15.20 Av 2 course fixed price £5.50
Accommodation s£25 d£35

LLANDEILO Carmarthenshire

The Castle Brewery
LLANDEILO Map 02 SN62
113 Rhosmaen St SA19 6EN
☎ 01558 823446
All the ales at this inn are brewed on the premises to an award-winning standard. It is a late Georgian ale house comprising two bars three snugs and a large open courtyard. Home cooked dishes range from hot baguettes and dragon sausages to trout with almonds and rump steak. Principal beers: Watkins BB, Watkins OSB.
Tomos Watkin & Sons
Open 12-11
Bar food 12-2.15 5.30-9 Av main course £5.50
Restaurant 12-2.15 5.30-9 Av 3 course à la carte £10.50
Accommodation s£25 d£40

PONT-AR-GOTHI Carmarthenshire

The Salutation Inn
PONT-AR-GOTHI Map 02 SN52
SP32 7NG ☎ 01267 290336
Situated in the gentle countryside of the Towy Valley, this 18th-century roadside inn offers a warm welcome to locals and travellers alike. Duck breast in plum and wine sauce, salmon with citrus and ginger sauce, pork stroganoff, or Texas steak in Mexican chilli may be on today's menu.
Directions On A40 between Carmarthen & Llandeilo
Felinfoel

Ceredigion

LLWYNDAFYDD Ceredigion

Crown Inn & Restaurant
LLWYNDAFYDD Map 02 SN35
SA44 6BU ☎ 01545 560396
Built in 1799, the Crown is situated in a wooded valley with extensive award-winning gardens just 1.5 miles from the beautiful cove of Cwmtudu. The inn specialises in home-cooked local meat and fish, and most of the dishes are daily specials marked on the board. Principal beers: Flowers Original, IPA, Wadworths 6X, Guinness.
Directions Off A487 NE of Cardigan
Free House
Open 12-3 6-11
Bar food 12-2.30 6-9.30 Av main course £6
Restaurant 12-2 6-9.30 Av 3 course à la carte £16

Conwy

CAPEL CURIG Conwy

Cobdens Hotel
CAPEL CURIG Map 06 SH75
LL24 0EE ☎ 01690 720243
Situated at the foot of Moel Siabod in the centre of Snowdonia, the back bar of this 230-year-old pub is built onto the mountain rock face. Food is freshly prepared from local produce and dishes include Welsh lamb chops, and fishcakes of fresh and smoked salmon. Principal beers: Tetley's, Cambrian, ABC.
Directions A55 to Bangor, A5 to Capel Curig
Free House
Open 11-11 (Sun 12-11)
Bar food 12-2.30 6.30-9 Av main course £7
Restaurant 12-2.30 6.30-9 Av 3 course à la carte £12.50 Av 4 course fixed price £13
Accommodation s£29.50 d£59

CONWY Conwy

The Groes Inn
CONWY Map 06 SH77
LL32 8TN ☎ 01492 650545
Built around 500 years ago in the River Conwy Valley, the Groes Inn gained its licence in 1573, reputedly making it the first Licenced House in Wales. A speciality is the home-made ice cream. Flavours include Cream of Summer Roses, coconut and Malibu, and After Eight Mint. Principal beers: Banks, Marstons Pedigree, Grolsch, Wrexham lager.
Directions Off A55 to Conwy, L at mini r'about by Conwy castle onto B5106, 2 1/2m inn on R
Free House
Open 12-3 6.30-11
Bar food 12-2 6.30-9 Av main course £6.50
Restaurant 12-2 6.30-9 Av 3 course à la carte £17.50 Av 4 course fixed price £17.50
Accommodation s£55 d£70

GWYTHERIN Conwy

Lion Inn Hotel & Restaurant

GWYTHERIN Map 06 SH86

LL22 8UU ☎ 01745 860244

The original inn is thought to be over 300 years old, but various extensions have been added over the years. There is a fairly comprehensive bar menu using mainly fresh local produce, and a more adventurous restaurant menu with themed weekend specials - Indian, Greek, seafood and so on. Principal beers: Ansells Mild, Wexford Irish bitter, Marstons Pedigree, Carlsberg lager.

Directions 4m off A548 (Llanrwst/ Abergale rd)

Free House

Open 12-11 (weekdays, closed 2.30-6) 12-10.30 (Sundays, closed 4-7)

Bar food 12-2.30 6.30-10.30 Av main course £5

Restaurant 12-2.30 6.30-10.30 Av 3 course à la carte £14

Accommodation s£24.50 d£39.50

LLANDUDNO JUNCTION Conwy

The Queens Head

LLANDUDNO JUNCTION Map 06 SH87

Glanwydden LL31 9JP ☎ 01492 546570

Located in the tiny village of Glanwydden, this country pub was once a wheelwright's cottage and retains much of its original style. Typical dishes, served in generous portions, include deep fried Pencarreg cheese with cranberry preserve, and a house speciality seafood platter with Marie Rose dip and new potatoes. Principal beers: Benskins, Ind Coope Burton, Tetleys.

Carlsberg Tetley

Open 3-11

Bar food 12-2 6-9

LLANNEFYDD Conwy

The Hawk & Buckle Inn

LLANNEFYDD Map 06 SH97

LL16 5ED ☎ 01745 540249

Situated in a hamlet of 140 souls, this 17th-century coaching inn has views over rolling fields to the sea beyond. Both the bar and restaurant menus offer a good choice of food based on local produce. Meat, fish and vegetarian dishes are listed in European and ethnic styles. Principal beers: Caffreys, Guinness, Worthington Bitter, Carling.

Free House

Open 12-2 7-11

Bar food 12-2 7-9.30 Av main course £6

Restaurant 7-10.30 Av 3 course à la carte £18

Accommodation s£38 d£50

Denbighshire

BODFARI Denbighshire

The Dinorben Arms

BODFARI Map 06 SJ07

LL16 4DA ☎ 01745 710309

Warm hospitality awaits locals and visitors alike at this historic hostelry in the heart of the Clwyd Vale. Its well could be the legendary Deifar's Well, believed to possess magical properties. Home-cooked daily specials, smorgasbord at lunchtime or on certain evenings, try the farmhouse buffet or carvery. Principal beers: Tetley Bitter, Ind Coope Burton Ale, Guinness, Beamish.

Directions Come off A55 onto B5122 through Caerwys, R onto A541, R after 2 1/2m in Bodfari. Pub 100yrds of B541 next to church

Free House

Open 12-3 6-11

Bar food 12-3 6-10.15 Av main course £4.75

Restaurant 12-3 6-10.15 Av 3 course à la carte £14 Av 3 course fixed price £8.95

LLANFERRES Denbighshire

The Druid Inn

LLANFERRES Map 07 SJ16

Ruthin Rd CH7 5SN ☎ 01244 810225

At this 17th century coaching inn, overlooking the Alyn Valley and the Craig Harris mountains, a daily blackboard menu features imaginative home-cooked food such as a halibut steak with cheese and herb crust or ham wrapped asparagus in cheese sauce.

Principal beers: Burtonwood Bitter, Forshans, Buccaneer, Top Hat.
Directions A494 from Mold, Druid Inn 4 1/2m on R
Burtonwood
Open 11.30-3 5.30-11 (Sun open all day)
Bar food 11.30-3 5.30-10 Av main course £5.95
Restaurant 11.30-3 5.30-10 Av 3 course à la carte £12
Accommodation s£22.50 d£36.50

LLANGOLLEN Denbighshire

The Famous Britannia Inn
LLANGOLLEN Map 07 SJ27
Horseshoe Pass LL20 8DW
☎ 01978 860144
The original building dates back to the 13th-century when it accommodated monks from the nearby Valle Crucis Abbey. Main course dishes include pork Orleans, salmon St. Emilion, chicken Provençale, and roast duck flamed in cognac served with an orange and brandy sauce. Principal beers: Old Peculier,Theakstons Best, IPA, Youngers.
Directions From Llangollen take A542 N 2m
Free House
Open 12-3.30 5-11
Bar food 12-3.30 5.30-11 Av main course £4.95
Restaurant 7.30-10.30 Av 3 course à la carte £14.95 Av 3 course fixed price £14.95
Accommodation s£25 d£40

LLANYNYS Denbighshire

Cerrigllwydion Arms
LLANYNYS Map 06 SJ16
LL16 4PA ☎ 01745 890247
Dates from around 1400 when it was built by Edward Edwards, attorney of Cerrigllwydion Hall, for the benefit of his churchgoers. A wide selection of snacks and light lunches is available. Main dishes include lamb cutlets in honey and mustard, and salmon with prawn and cream sauce. Principal beers: Bass, Tetley.
Directions A525 towards Denbigh, R after 1 1/2m, then L and 1m to pub
Free House
Bar food 12-3 7-11 Av main course £5
Restaurant 12-3 7-11 Av 3 course à la carte £13.50

Flintshire

BABELL Flintshire

Black Lion Inn
BABELL Map 03 SN83
CH8 8PZ ☎ 01352 720239
Locally produced food and wines are served at this 13th-century inn. Bar meals and snacks are not available, but there is a dinner and a supper menu. Dishes might include roast duckling with black cherry sauce, rabbit casserole, and poached cod fillet thermidor. Principal beers: Trophy Bitter, Boddingtons Bitter, Heineken.
Directions S of A55 between Holywell & St Asaph
Free House
Bar food 7.30-10
Restaurant 7.15-9.45 Av 3 course à la carte £16 Av 4 course fixed price £16

CILCAIN Flintshire

White Horse Inn
CILCAIN Map 07 SJ16
CH7 5NN ☎ 01352 740142
Dating from the 14th century, this cosy inn enjoys a lovely village setting. All the dishes are home-made, prepared and cooked by the owner using local produce where possible. Specialities include mixed game pie, Thai chicken, lamb cobbler and mushroom stroganoff, with traditional hot puddings to finish. Principal beers: Thwaites, Ansells mild, Pedigree, Speckled Hen.
Directions From Mold take A541 towards Denbigh. After approx 6m turn L
Free House
Open 12-3 5.30-11 (Sun, 7-10.30)
Bar food 12-2 7.30-9.30 Av main course £6

HALKYN Flintshire

Britannia Inn
HALKYN Map 07 SJ27
Pentre Rd CH8 8BS
☎ 01352 780272
500-year-old inn with splendid views of the Dee Estuary and Wirral. Typical main course dishes range from minted lamb and barley casserole, honey lamb steak, and pork Espana, to home-made steak and kidney pie, and lasagne *Verdi* for vegetarians. Principal beers: J W Lees, G B Cask Mild, Moonraker Strong Ale, Golden Original Lager.

contd.

Directions Off A55 on B5123
J W Lees
Open 11-11 (Sun 12-10.30)
Bar food 12-2.30 6.30-9.30 Av main course £5
Restaurant 12-2.30 6.30-9.30 Av 3 course à la carte £9

Gwynedd

ABERDYFI Gwynedd

Penhelig Arms Hotel & Restaurant
ABERDYFI Map 06 SN69
LL35 0LT ☎ 01654 767215
A traditional inn dating from 1750, gutted and refurbished in 1982 and continually upgraded to be a recent AA Hotel of the Year for Wales. Dishes might include a game terrine with Cumberland sauce, haddock baked with ginger and chilli with green garlic sauce, and dark chocolate truffle cake. Principal beers: Mansfield, Tetley, Pedigree, Draught Bass.
Directions On A493(coastal rd) W of Machynlleth
Free House
Open 11.30-3.30 6-11
Bar food 12-2.30 7-9.30 Av main course £7
Restaurant 12-2.30 7-9.30 Av 0 course fixed price £19
Accommodation s£39 d£68

BONTDDU Gwynedd

The Halfway House
BONTDDU Map 06 SH61
LL40 2UE ☎ 01341 430635
Halfway between Dogellau and Barmouth, the proximity of this striking half-timbered building to the lovely Mawddach Estuary ensures fresh fish is always available, including red sea bream, local salmon or trout. Also available is homemade Welsh steak and mushroom pie. Principal beers: Marstons Pedigree,Guinness,Carlsberg.
Directions On A436 between Dolgellau & Barmouth
Free House
Open 12-3 6-11
Bar food 12-2 7-9 Av main course £5.50
Restaurant 12-2 7-9 Av 3 course à la carte £7.95

LLANBERIS Gwynedd

Pen-Y-Gwryd
LLANBERIS Map 06 SH56
Nantgwynant LL55 4NT
☎ 01286 870211
The home of British mountaineering, and base for the successful 1953 Everest team, this cosy inn is in Snowdonia National Park. The food is British with some Danish influences. Typical dishes are prawns baked with spinach and cream, roast leg of lamb with mint sauce, and rhubarb and ginger crumble. Principal beers: Bass Real Ale, Theakstons/Welsh Bitter.
Directions From Caernarfon take A4086 at Pen-y-Gwryd take A498 S
Free House
Open 11-11
Bar food 12-2 Av main course £3.50
Restaurant 7.30-8 Av 3 course à la carte £15
Accommodation s£20 d£40

LLANENGAN Gwynedd

The Sun Inn
LLANENGAN Map 06 SH22
LL53 7LG ☎ 01758 712660
A friendly, country pub, the Sun has an interesting garden with three baths, two toilets and a sink full of plants! There's a map in the bar showing where and when several ships sank at nearby Hell's Mouth beach. Traditional pub food includes steaks, lasagne and banana splits. Principal beers: Tetley,Burton.
Directions From Pwllheli take A499 S to Abersoch.Then 1.5m towards Hells Mouth Beach
Carlsberg Tetley
Open 12-2 6-11 (Summer 12-11)
Bar food 12-2 5.30-9 Av main course £6

MAENTWROG Gwynedd

Grapes Hotel
MAENTWROG Map 06 SH64
LL41 4HN ☎ 01766 590208 590365
In the heart of Snowdonia, this family-run, 17th-century coaching inn has a unique atmosphere. It has been frequented by Lloyd George and Lilly Langtry, and has and piano-playing ghost. The home-cooked food ranges from a cheese sandwich to sea bass with spring onions, ginger and ham. Principal beers: Bass Draught, Pedwar Bawd, Cambrian, Carling.
Directions A5 thru Corwen to Bala, A487 to Maentwrog, onto A496, pub 100yrds
Free House
Open 11-11 (Sun 12-10.30)
Bar food 12-2.15 6-9.30 Av main course £7
Accommodation s£25 d£50

PENMAENPOOL Gwynedd

George III Hotel
PENMAENPOOL Map 06 SH61
LL40 1YD ☎ 01341 422525
Beautifully situated at the head of the Mawddach Estuary, the main part of this hotel dates from 1650, while the lodge was a Victorian waiting room, ticket office and station master's house. Seafood is a speciality, along with Welsh lamb, pheasant and a variety of home-made dishes. Principal beers: Cambrian Original Real Ale, Ruddles Real Ale, John Smiths.
Directions From Dolgellau take A493 W
Free House
Open 11-11
Bar food 12-2.30 6.30-9.30 Av main course £5.45
Restaurant 12-2 7-9 Av 3 course à la carte £19
Accommodation s£37.50 d£70

PORTHMADOG Gwynedd

The Ship
PORTHMADOG Map 06 SH53
Lombard St LL49 9AP ☎ 01766 512990
Dating from 1824, this is the oldest pub in Porthmadog. A daily changing specials board typically features lamb in Dijon mustard, beef in ale pie, avocado and corn bake, and vegetable salsa. Seafood dishes include grilled halibut with lemon sauce, and salmon with lobster and brandy sauce. Principal beers: Abbot Ale, Old Speckled Hen, Draught Burton Ale, Tetley Bitter.
Directions From the A55 take the A470 S toward the coast
Allied Domecq
Open 11-11
Bar food 12-2.15 6.30-9.30 Av main course £6
Restaurant 5.30-11 Av 3 course à la carte £15

TUDWEILIOG Gwynedd

Lion Hotel
TUDWEILIOG Map 06 SH23
LL53 8ND ☎ 01758 770244
Village inn with courtyard, situated near the coast. A selection of bar snacks is available. Among the main course options are lamb or chicken balti, rainbow trout, steak and kidney pie, and chicken tikka masala. Vegetarian dishes include tagliatelle Niçoise, wheat casserole, and spinach cannelloni. Principal beers: Marston Pedigree, Boddingtons, Theakston BB, Theakston Mild.
Directions A499 from Carmarthen, B4417 Tudweiliog
Free House
Bar food 12-2 6-9.30 Av main course £5
Accommodation s£24 d£38

Herefordshire

AYMESTREY Herefordshire

Riverside Inn & Restaurant
AYMESTREY Map 03 SO46
HR6 9ST ☎ 01568 709440
16th-century inn, built on the site of a monastery on the banks of the River Lugg. Typical main course dishes

contd.

include mushroom Stroganoff, roast Welsh lamb with juniper sauce, and local pheasant braised in red wine and herbs. Nut roast with chestnut stuffing and red wine sauce, for vegetarians. Principal beers: Woodhampton Ales, Otter Ales, Boddingtons.
Directions On A4110 15m N of Hereford
Free House
Open 12-3 6.30-11
Bar food 12-3 7-11 Av main course £5
Restaurant 12-3 7-11 Av 3 course à la carte £17.50
Accommodation s£25 d£40

CAREY Herefordshire

Cottage of Content
CAREY Map 03 SO53
HR2 6NG ☎ 01432 840242
Relax and enjoy excellent food, wine and beer at this small medieval country inn in a quiet location. Ale has been served here since 1485. Fish and game in season is the speciality. Taste the oak smoked salmon, perhaps a Hereford steak, then the orange and brandy pudding. Principal beers: Hook Norton,Old Hooky.
Directions From A40 W of Ross-on-Wye take A49 towards Hereford.Follow signs for Hoarworthy,then Carey
Free House
Open 12-2 7-11 (Sun 7-10.30)
Bar food 12-2 7-11
Restaurant 12-2 7-11 Av 3 course à la carte £13.50

DORSTONE Herefordshire

The Pandy Inn
DORSTONE Map 03 SO34
WR3 6AN ☎ 01981 550273
Built by Richard De Brita in 1185 to house his workers while constructing Dorstone Church, this is the oldest inn in Herefordshire. The menu typically includes game soup laced with port, pheasant with peverada sauce, casserole of wild boar with rosemary and orange, and braised venison with juniper berries. Principal beers: Draught Bass, Hereford Beer, Worthington, Tetley.
Directions Off B4348 W of Hereford
Free House
Open 12-3.30 7-11
Bar food 12-3 7-10 Av main course £5.50
Restaurant 12-3 7-10 Av 3 course à la carte £12

FOWNHOPE Herefordshire

The Green Man Inn
FOWNHOPE Map 03 SO53
HR1 4PE ☎ 01432 860243
Set in peaceful village surroundings this country inn dates from 1485, the first year of Henry VII's reign. It has low oak beams, an attractive garden, and is close to the meandering River Wye. Dishes include grilled trout, roast chicken, beef stroganoff, and a variety of steaks. Principal beers: Courage Directors, Marstons Pedigree, Sam Smith, Hook Norton.
Directions From M50 take A449 then B4224 to Fownhope
Free House
Bar food 12-2 6-10 Av main course £4.95
Restaurant 12-2 7-9 Av 3 course à la carte £14.50
Accommodation s£31 d£51

HAMPTON BISHOP Herefordshire

The Bunch of Carrots
HAMPTON BISHOP Map 03 SO53
HR1 4JR ☎ 01432 870237
Recently restored, this 250-year-old pub is situated 20 yards from the River Wye, and one story explaining its unusual name relates to a fisherman catching a large salmon from a lure carved from a carrot. There's a good choice of food and the carvery is a new feature. Principal beers: Bass, Boddingtons, Hook Norton, Smiles.
Directions From Hereford take A4103, A438, then B4224
Free House
Open 11-3 6-11
Bar food 12-2.30 6-10 Av main course £5.50

HEREFORD Herefordshire

The Crown & Anchor
HEREFORD Map 03 SO54
Cotts Ln, Lugwardine HR1 4AB
☎ 01432 851303
A small 16th-century black and white building with a pretty front garden and patio. Inside there are exposed beams and a huge fireplace with log fires in

winter. There's a good range of fish, meat and vegetarian dishes, ranging from sausage and chips to lemon chicken with sweet pepper sauce. Principal beers: Worthingtons BB, Bass, Hobsons BB.
Directions 2 miles from Hereford city centre on A438, turn left into Lugwardine
Free House
Open 11-11.30
Bar food 12-2 7-10

HOWLE HILL Herefordshire

The Crown
HOWLE HILL Map 03 SO62
HR9 5SP ☎ 01989 764316
Roses round the door greet visitors to this simple 19th-century country pub nestling in a sheltered spot of this scattered hamlet. The barber visits on the first Tuesday of each month. Get a haircut or simply enjoy a homemade pie or pudding in the bar. Principal beers: Whitbread, Marstons Pedigree.
Directions End M50 thru Ross to B4234, 1st L after entering Walford, then 1st R signed Howle Hill
Free House
Open 12-2.30 (except Tues) 7-11
Bar food 12-2 7-9.30 Av main course £5

LEDBURY Herefordshire

The Feathers Hotel
LEDBURY Map 03 SO73
High St HR8 1PS ☎ 01531 635266
A striking black and white Elizabethan coaching inn, with exposed beams and log fires. Quills Restaurant offers modern Anglo-French cooking, while dishes in Fuggles Brasserie include home-made salmon fishcakes, spiced coconut lamb cutlets and a strudel of roasted Mediterranean vegetables and Ricotta cheese. Principal beers: Worthington Best Bitter, Draught Bass.
Directions Town centre
Free House
Open 11-11 (Sun 12-10.30)
Bar food 12-2 7-9.30 Av main course £7.50
Restaurant 12-2.30 7-9.30 Av 3 course à la carte £25 Av 3 course fixed price £14.95
Accommodation s£49 d£65

The Talbot
LEDBURY Map 03 SO73
14 New St HR8 2DX ☎ 01531 632963
This Grade II listed pub is over 400 years old and was once the scene of fighting between cavaliers and roundheads. The oak-panelled restaurant's menu may feature baked mozzarella with Parma ham, loin of pork with sage, onion and cider cream, or venison fillet with redcurrant and port. Principal beers: Hancocks HB, Marstons, Saddlers Celebrated, Caffreys.
Directions follow Ledbury signs, turn into Bye St, 2nd L into Woodley Rd, over bridge to jct, L into New St. Talbot on R
Free House
Open 11.30-3 5-11
Bar food 12-2.30 6.30-9.30 Av main course £5.50
Restaurant 12-2.30 6.30-9.30 Av 3 course à la carte £15
Accommodation s£31.50 d£31.50

LEOMINSTER Herefordshire

The Royal Oak Hotel
LEOMINSTER Map 03 SO45
South St HR6 8JA ☎ 01568 612610
A town centre coaching inn dating back to before 1723 and retaining many original features. Home-cooked food is served in the bar, and a more adventurous menu is offered in the restaurant. Daily specials include a range of home-made pies, a roast, and deep fried cod in batter. Principal beers: Brains S.A Wood Bitter, Tennants Extra.
Directions Town centre
Free House
Open 10-2.30 6-10.30
Bar food 12-2 6.30-9 Av main course £4.50
Restaurant 12-2 6.30-9 Av 3 course à la carte £14 Av 3 course fixed price £10.25
Accommodation s£31.50 d£45

LITTLE COWARNE Herefordshire

The Three Horseshoes Inn
LITTLE COWARNE Map 03 SO65
HR7 4RQ ☎ 01885 400276
Previously used a Court House, this pub's typical fare ranges from Stilton, walnut, apple and celery strudel, and wild rabbit casserole with blackberries, to breast of chicken in apricot and brandy sauce, and salmon fillet in champagne sauce. Loganberry, damson, and melon and ginger home-made ice creams are also

contd.

available. Principal beers: Ruddles County, Websters Yorkshire Bitter, John Smiths, Theakston XB.
Directions Off A456 (Hereford/Bromyard).At Stokes Cross, take turning signed Little Cowarne/Pencombe
Free House
Open 11-3 6.30-11 (Sun 11-3, 7-10.30)
Bar food 12-3 6.30-11 Av main course £4.95
Restaurant 12-3 6.30-11 Av 3 course à la carte £14 Av 2 course fixed price £7.25
Accommodation s£18 d£36

MUCH MARCLE Herefordshire

The Slip Tavern
MUCH MARCLE Map 03 SO63
HR8 2NG ☎ 01531 660246
Taking its name from a landslip which occurred in 1575, this family run pub is peacefully surrounded by cider orchards and countryside. An extensive menu of home-cooked fare includes the increasingly popular beef cooked in brown ale with mushrooms and onions, the Marcle fish bake and a tempting array of special puddings. Principal beers: Hook Norton, Wadworths 6X, Flowers IPA, Flowers.
Directions On the A438 between Hereford & Tewkesbury
Free House
Open 11-2.30 6.30-11
Bar food 12-2.30 7-11 Av main course £5.50
Restaurant 7-11 Av 3 course à la carte £14

PEMBRIDGE Herefordshire

The Cider House Restaurant
PEMBRIDGE Map 03 SO35
Dunkerton's Cider Mill HR6 9ED
☎ 01544 388161
The mill makes organic ciders from traditional cider apples. The restaurant has been established, in two 450-year-old barns, to allow visitors to enjoy a glass of cider with food. Organic produce is used where possible, with home-made bread, pickles, local cheeses and meat from the farm. Principal beers: Dunkertons Ciders, Caledonian.
Directions W on A44 from Leominster, L in Pembridge centre by New Inn, 1m on L
Open Mon-Sat 10-5 & Thurs-Sat 7-10
Bar food 12-2.30 Av main course £4
Restaurant 12-2.30 7-10 Av 3 course à la carte £15

New Inn
PEMBRIDGE Map 03 SO35
Market Square HR6 9DZ
☎ 01544 388427
The treaty ending the Wars of the Roses is believed to have been signed in the Court Room of this 14th century coaching inn, which looks out over the market square. The menu may include salmon with prawns, aubergine and pepper pie, or lamb and redcurrant hotpot. Principal beers: Ruddles County, Ruddles Best, Theakstons Best, John Smiths Smooth.
Free House
Open 9-3 6-11
Restaurant 12-2 7-9 Av 3 course fixed price £14
Accommodation s£18.50 d£37

RUCKHALL Herefordshire

The Ancient Camp Inn
RUCKHALL Map 03 SO43
HR2 9QX ☎ 01981 250449
Built on the site of an Iron Age fortress, the Ancient Camp has spectacular views of the River Wise, and allows patrons free fishing on its own stretch of river. Today's menu may include monkfish in bacon with saffron cream, crab and spinach ravioli, or venison with garlic potatoes. Principal beers: Woods Parish Bitter, Hook Norton Bitter.
Directions Take A465 from Hereford, then B4349.Follow signs 'Belmont Abbey/Ruckhall'
Free House
Bar food 12-3 Av main course £7.50
Restaurant 7-11 Av 3 course à la carte £20
Accommodation s£40 d£50

ST OWEN'S CROSS Herefordshire

The New Inn
ST OWEN'S CROSS Map 03 SO52
HR2 8LQ ☎ 01989 730274
There's a friendly welcome at this 16th-century coaching inn, which has a

wealth of oak beams and a large inglenook fireplace. All the food is cooked to order, including deep-fried whitebait, honey roast lamb, a choice of pasta dishes and a vegetarian pancake with mushrooms and asparagus. Principal beers: Smiles, London Pride, Wadworth 6X, Tetleys.
Directions Off A4137 W of Ross-on-Wye
Free House
Open 12-2.30 6-11
Bar food 12-2.30 6-11 Av main course £8
Restaurant 12-2.30 6-11
Accommodation s£35 d£60

SELLACK Herefordshire

The Lough Pool Inn
SELLACK Map 03 SO52
HR9 6LX ☎ 01989 730236
A 17th-century inn with a lovely setting in the Wye Valley. There are flowers in season and warming fires in winter. Food ranges from bar snacks to more exotic fare such as wild boar, goat and ostrich. Specialities are moules marinière, Herefordshire beef steak and vegetarian dishes. Principal beers: Wye Valley, Bass, John Smiths, Caffreys.
Directions Off A49 N of Ross-on-Wye
Free House
Open 11.30-2.30 6.30-11.20
Bar food 12-2.30 7-10.30 Av main course £5
Restaurant 12-2.30 7-10.30 Av 3 course à la carte £13

SHOBDON Herefordshire

The Bateman Arms
SHOBDON Map 03 SO46
HR6 9LX ☎ 01568 708374
400-year-old, black and white coaching inn. Usual starters include grilled goats cheese with damson relish, and baked Dorset crab pot. Main courses range from supreme of chicken with honey and orange, and poached fillet of sea bass with fresh herbs, to pan fried duck breast with bramble sauce. Principal beers: Woods Parish Bitter, Bass,.
Directions On B4362 off A4110 NW of Leominster
Free House
Open 12-2.30 7-11
Bar food 12-2 7-10 Av main course £6.50
Restaurant 12-2 7-10 Av 3 course à la carte £12

WALTERSTONE Herefordshire

Carpenters Arms
WALTERSTONE Map 03 SO32
HR2 0DX ☎ 01873 890353
Dating back over 300 years, this popular Black Mountains pub retains lots of character, with beams, antique furniture and a leaded fireplace, where open fires burn all winter. The food ranges from bar snacks to home-cooked dishes such as chilli, chicken curry, plaice and steak. Principal beers: Wadworth 6X, Worthington Best, Albright bitter.
Directions Off the A465 between Hereford & Abergavenny at Pandy
Free House
Open 11-11
Bar food 12-3 7-9.30 Av main course £5
Restaurant 12-3 7-9.30

WEOBLEY Herefordshire

Ye Olde Salutation Inn
WEOBLEY Map 003 SO45
Market Pitch HR8 8SJ ☎ 01544 318443
The Oak Room Restaurant is at the heart of this friendly village inn. All dishes are cooked to order, and might include seared king scallops on a crisp pasta biscuit with red pepper and basil; braised guinea fowl with port and sage, and fresh lemon tart with raspberry coulis. Principal beers: Hook Norton Best Bitter, Flowers Original Bitter, Boddingtons Bitter.
Directions On A4112 12m NW of Hereford
Free House
Open 11-3 7-11 (Fri-Sat open all day)
Bar food 12-3 7-11 Av main course £6
Restaurant 12-3 7-11 Av 3 course à la carte £22
Accommodation s£36 d£60

WHITNEY-ON-WYE Herefordshire

Rhydspence Inn
WHITNEY-ON-WYE Map 03 SO24
HR3 6EU ☎ 01497 831262
Originally a 14th-century manor house, this inn has splendid views of the Wye Valley. A stream marking the border between England and Wales runs through the garden. Typical dishes include tarragon chicken, caramelised onion and Feta cheese gateau served with orange and endive

contd.

salad, and stuffed sweet capsicum peppers. Principal beers: Robinson Best, Dunkerton Draught cider, Brains, Bass.
Directions 17m W of Hereford on A438
Free House
Open 11-2.30 7-11
Bar food 11-2 7-9.30 Av main course £6.50
Restaurant 11-2 7-9.30 Av 3 course à la carte £20
Accommodation s£27.50 d£55

WINFORTON Herefordshire

The Sun Inn
WINFORTON Map 03 SO24
HR3 6EA ☎ 01544 327677
Conventiently located for visiting Hay-on-Wye, Brecon, Hereford, and the Black Mountains, the Sun is also able to provide facilities for canoeing, pony-trekking, and hang-gliding. Typical menu includes guinea fowl breast in mushroom sauce, steak and Guinness pie, and grilled sewin fillet. Ploughmans' are a speciality. Principal beers: Woods Parish, Jennings, Flowers, Brains.
Free House
Open 11-3 6.30-11
Bar food 12-2 7-9.30 Av main course £7
Accommodation s£30 d£45

WOOLHOPE Herefordshire

The Butchers Arms
WOOLHOPE Map 03 SO63
HR1 4RF ☎ 01432 860281
A black and white half-timbered building dating from the 14th century, in idyllic rural surroundings. The small restaurant opens for Sunday lunch and Saturday dinner, and bar meals are available all week. Dishes range from sandwiches and deep-fried meals with chips to Woolhope rabbit pie. Principal beers: Hook Norton Best Bitter, Hook Norton Old Hooky.
Directions Off B4224 between Hereford & Ross-on-Wye
Free House
Open 11.30-3 6.30-11
Bar food 12-2.15 7-10
Restaurant 12-2.15 7-10

The Crown Inn
WOOLHOPE Map 03 SO63
HR1 4QP ☎ 01432 860468
Built in 1750 next to the 13th-century church, the pub is a focal point of village life. A large selection of home-made dishes and grills is served in the bar and restaurant. These include fish cakes, lamb stew with dumplings, tandoori chicken masala, and spotted dick with custard. Principal beers: Smiles BB, Hook Norton BB, Tetley BB, Worthington BB.
Free House
Open 12-11 12-10.30 (Sun 12-10.30)
Bar food 12-2.30 opening-11 Av main course £6
Restaurant 12-2.30 opening-11 Av 3 course à la carte £12

Isle of Angelsey

BEAUMARIS Isle of Anglesey

Ye Olde Bulls Head Inn
BEAUMARIS Map 06 SH67
Castle St LL58 8AP ☎ 01248 810329
A town centre coaching inn commandeered by Cromwell's General Myton in 1645 while his forces lay siege to the nearby castle. Other celebrated guests include Charles Dickens and Dr Johnson. Modern British fare is served in the restaurant and the bar offers home-made terrines, sausages and pies. Principal beers: Draught Bass & Worthington, Keg Stones, Caffreys,Bass Mild.
Directions From Menai Bridge take A545 to Beaumaris
Free House
Open 11-11 (Sun 12-10.30)
Bar food 12-2.30 Av main course £6
Restaurant 12-1.30 7.30-9.30 Av 3 course à la carte £25 Av 3 course fixed price £20.95
Accommodation s£47 d£77

Monmouthshire

ABERGAVENNY Monmouthshire

Clytha Arms
ABERGAVENNY Map 03 SO21
Clytha NP7 9BW ☎ 01873 840206
A former dower house, this building became a pub in 1952. The old pub on the Usk River having been washed away in 1942. Imaginative bar food includes smoked sewin with scrambled egg, and

black pudding with fried apple. The restaurant menu ranges from roast lamb to Caribbean fruit curry. Principal beers: Banks, Brains bitter, Bass, Guinness.
Directions From junc A449/A40 (E of Abergavenny) follow signs for 'Old Road Abergavenny/Clytha'
Free House
Open 11.30-3 6-11
Bar food 12.30-2.15 7.30-9.30 Av main course £6
Restaurant 12.30-2.15 7.30-9.30 Av 3 course à la carte £18 Av 3 course fixed price £11.95
Accommodation s£45 d£50

Llanwenarth Arms Hotel
ABERGAVENNY Map 03 SO21
Brecon Rd NP8 1EP ☎ 01873 810550
Situated on the bank of the River Usk, this hotel dates back to the 16th-century. Splendid views of the Blorenge Mountain and Usk Valley. Starters include mushrooms sautéed with bacon, cream and Malmsey Madeira with a cheddar cheese topping. Main dishes include double breast of pheasant in port wine sauce. Principal beers: Bass, Ruddles County, John Smiths.
Directions On A40 between Abergavenny & Crickhowell
Free House
Open 11-3 6-11
Bar food 12-2 7-10 Av main course £10
Restaurant 12-2 7-10 Av 3 course à la carte £19
Accommodation s£45 d£55

Walnut Tree Inn
ABERGAVENNY Map 03 SO21
Llandewi Skirrid NP7 8AW
☎ 01873 852797
Italian dishes are the speciality here. Typical examples are pappardelle with rabbit sauce, carpaccio of monkfish with deep fried capers and balsamic vinegar, tagliolini with crab, pasta n'casciata, and puntarelle salad with wild rocket and anchovy dressing. Other dishes include fillet of sea bass, and Llanover salt duck with preserves.
Directions 3m NE of Abergavenny on B4521
Free House
Open 12-4 7-12
Restaurant 12-3 7-10.30

BETTWS-NEWYDD Monmouthshire

Black Bear Inn
BETTWS-NEWYDD Map 03 SO30
NP5 1JN ☎ 01873 880701
A 17th-century inn, in the beautiful Usk Valley, with stone walls and floor in the bar area and a racehorse theme in the restaurant. Quiches, fresh fish and ploughman's figure on the bar menu, while restaurant dishes include lobster, suprême of chicken with Stilton cheese, and glazed lemon tart. Principal beers: Slaters Premium, Original and Bitter, Bath SPA, Stella.
Directions Off B4598 N of Usk
Free House
Open 12-2.30 6-12.30
Bar food 12-2 6-12 Av main course £5.30
Restaurant 12-2 6-12.30 Av 3 course à la carte £20 Av 3 course fixed price £11.95

CHEPSTOW Monmouthshire

Castle View Hotel
CHEPSTOW Map 03 ST59
16 Bridge St NP6 5EZ
☎ 01291 620349
Situated opposite Britain's oldest stone-built castle is this 300-year-old, ivy-clad hotel. There is an emphasis on regional produce in dishes such as deep-fried Pencarreg cheese, pan-fried Welsh lamb with rosemary and redcurrant jelly, and a vegetarian lasagne Llanboidy made with laver bread cheese. Principal beers: Tetley cask conditioned, Castlemaine 4X, Carlsberg Export.
Directions Opposite Chepstow Castle
Free House
Open 12-2.30 6-11

contd.

Bar food 12-2.30 6.30-9.30 Av main course £3.95
Restaurant 12-2 6.30-9.30 Av 3 course à la carte £14.95 Av 3 course fixed price £14.95
Accommodation s£39.95 d£49.95

LLANTRISANT Monmouthshire

Greyhound Inn
LLANTRISANT Map 03 ST39
NP5 1LE ☎ 01291 672505 673447
Country charm and modern comforts combine at this rurally situated, friendly inn located in the heart of the Usk Vale. Old favourites and specials from the blackboard such as fresh Usk salmon or a vegetarian cashew nut roulade offer value for money. Principal beers: Flowers Original, Marstons Pedigree, Wadworths 6X, Green King Abbot Ale.
Directions Take A449 from J24 toward Monmouth, 1st jct go to Usk, L into Usk sq. then 2nd L posted Llantrisant, 2 1/2m to inn
Free House
Open 11-3 6-11
Bar food 11.45-2.15 6.15-10.30 Av main course £6
Accommodation s£40 d£50

LLANVAPLEY Monmouthshire

Red Hart Inn
LLANVAPLEY Map 03 SO31
NP7 8SN ☎ 01600 780227
An old fashioned country pub, where families are welcome, opposite the 12th-century parish church. Home cooked food with an international flavour is served, including Italian, Indian, and Thai-style dishes. A particular favourite is the high quality char-grilled rump steak. Principal beers: Hancocks HB, Allbright, Bass, Carling Black Label and Premier.
Directions On B4233 E of Abergavenny
Free House
Open 12-3 6-11
Bar food 12-2.30 6-12 Av main course £8
Restaurant 12-2.30 6-12 Av 3 course à la carte £15

AA members can call AA Hotel Booking Service on 0900 050505 to book at AA recognised hotels and B & Bs in the UK and Ireland, or through our Internet site: http://www.theaa.co.uk/hotels

PENALLT Monmouthshire

The Boat Inn
PENALLT Map 03 SO51
Lone Ln NP5 4AJ
☎ 01600 712615
350-year-old riverside pub situated in the Wye Valley. A range of light meals and cold meals is available. Main dishes include spicy beef Florentine, pork in cider hot pot, and Yale chilli. Vegetarian options feature vegetable Turkari curry, and leek, roast parsnip and Stilton bake. Principal beers: Old Peculier, Adnams Broadside, Spitfire, Archers Golden.
Directions From Monmouth take A466.In Redbrook the pub car park is signposted. Park & walk across rail bridge over R Wye
Free House
Open 11.30-3 6-11 (Sun 12-4, 6.30-10.30) (Sat 11-11)
Bar food 12-2.30 6-9.30 Av main course £4.40

SHIRENEWTON Monmouthshire

The Carpenters Arms
SHIRENEWTON Map 03 ST49
Usk Rd NP6 6BU
☎ 01291 641231
A 400-year-old building with flagstone floors and open fires, furnished with antiques of all descriptions. Country-style cooking is served in the bar from a chalk board menu that might offer home-made soup, chicken and smoky bacon pie, paella, pork steak in blue cheese, and bread and butter pudding. Principal beers: Old Roger, Timothy Taylor Landlord, London Pride, 6X.
Directions M48 J2 take A48 to Chepstow then A4661,B4235.Village 3m on L
Free House

Open 11-2.30 6-11
Bar food 11.30-2 7-9.30 Av main course £4.50

Tredegar Arms
SHIRENEWTON Map 03 ST49
The Square NP6 6RQ ☎ 01291 641274
Curios, farm implements and a sugar tong collection decorate the interior of this beautiful, old fashioned, village square local. Snack on a granary sandwich or choose a home-cooked blackboard special such as lamb 'Bill-a-Bong' or 'Bullyhole Pepper Pot Pie'. Principal beers: Hancocks HB, Hook Norton, Brains Dark, Bass.
Directions From Chepstow B4235, L towrd Caldicot
Free House
Open 12-3 6-11.30 (open all day Sat)
Bar food 12-2 7-9 Av main course £3.50
Restaurant 12-2 6.45-9.30 Av 3 course à la carte £12.50
Accommodation s£25 d£40

TAL-Y-COED Monmouthshire

The Halfway House Inn
TAL-Y-COED Map 03 SO41
NP7 8TL ☎ 01600 780269
Originally a drovers' inn, dating from the 17th-century, then a coaching inn on the London to Fishguard route (halfway between Monmouth and Abergavenny). Traditional home produced bar meals are offered, and there's an à la carte restaurant serving local meat, fish and poultry, plus vegetarian dishes. Principal beers: Felinfoel traditional bitter and Double Dragon, Bass, Whitbread, Carling.
Directions On B4233 (between Abergavenny & Ross-on-Wye)
Free House
Open 12-3.30 6-11
Bar food 12-2 7-9.30 Av main course £3.50
Restaurant 12-2 7-9.30 Av 3 course à la carte £11

TRELLECK Monmouthshire

The Lion Inn
TRELLECK Map 03 SO50
NP5 4PA ☎ 01600 860322
Situated opposite the church, this village pub was built in 1580 as a brew house. Traditional British pub food is served, supplemented by an ever changing specials board. There's a vegetarian choice including pasta bake and bean chilli, home-made pies, fish and chips and peppered rump steak. Principal beers: Tetleys, Carlsberg,Guinness,Bass.
Directions From A40 just south of Monmouth take B4293 and follow signs for Trelleck
Free House
Open 12-3 6-11 (Mon 7-11,Sat 6.30-11,Sun closed even.)
Bar food 12-2 6-9.30 Av main course £4.50
Accommodation d£30

TRELLECK GRANGE Monmouthshire

The Fountain Inn
TRELLECK GRANGE Map 03 SO40
NP6 6QW ☎ 01291 689303
A 17th-century drovers' inn with a beamed bar and restaurant. Pies, pasta and curries are staples in the bar, while in the restaurant there's local trout, Wye salmon, jugged hare, and Tudor roast venison (marinated in red wine and herbs), along with steaks, lamb, pork and tempting home-made puddings. Principal beers: Brains Smooth, Butcombe Bitter, Wadworths 6X.
Directions Off A466
Free House
Open 12-3 6-11
Bar food 12-2.30 7-10.30 Av main course £6
Restaurant 12-2.30 7-10.30 Av 3 course à la carte £15 Av 3 course fixed price £10
Accommodation s£18 d£30

USK Monmouthshire

The Nags Head Inn
USK Map 03 SO30
Twyn Square NP5 1BH ☎ 01291 672820
A beamed 500-year-old inn, filled with antiques and bric-a-brac, in one of the prettiest little towns in Wales. Situated just a quarter of a mile from the River Usk, it is not surprising that fresh salmon appears on the menu, alongside local game in season. There's also a good vegetarian selection. Principal beers: Brains, Buckleys, Carlsberg, Murphys.
Directions On A472
Free House
Open 10.30-3 5.30-11
Bar food 11.30-3 5.30-11
Restaurant 11.30-3 5.30-11

Pembrokeshire

AMROTH Pembrokeshire

The New Inn
AMROTH Map 02 SN10
SA67 8NW ☎ 01834 812368
A beautiful Flemish chimney and inglenook fireplace are features of this 400-year-old smugglers inn. The dining room overlooks the sunken forest on the beach, which is only a stone's throw away. Specialities are seafood, including fresh lobster and crab, home-made dishes and prime steaks. Principal beers: Burton Ale, Tetley Draught.
Directions A48 to Carmarthen, A40 to St Clears, A477 to Llanteg then L
Free House
Open 11.30-3 5.30-11
Bar food 12-2 5.30-9 Av main course £5
Restaurant 5.30-9

BROAD HAVEN Pembrokeshire

The Galleon Inn
BROAD HAVEN Map 02 SM81
SA62 3JW ☎ 01437 781467
The Galleon, just across the road from the beach, is run by an ex-sea captain who has lived in Hong Kong, hence the nautical theme in the pub and the Eastern influence in the food. Sizzling prawns and spicy duck are offered alongside fresh local trout and pork à la Normande. Principal beers: Flowers IPA, Boddingtons, Wadworth 6X, Stella Artois.
Directions A40 to Carmarthen, A40 to Haverfordwest, B4341 to Broad Haven
Free House
Open 12-11
Bar food 12-2.30 6-8.30 Av main course £4.75
Restaurant 12-2.30 7-10 Av 3 course à la carte £15

CAREW Pembrokeshire

Carew Inn
CAREW Map 02 SN00
SA70 8SL ☎ 01646 651267
A traditional stone-built country inn situated opposite the Celtic cross and Norman castle, just a stone's throw from Carew mill pond. Good value food is served in generous portions, including snacks, steaks and spaghetti Bolognese and daily specials such as Thai green curry and salmon fishcakes. Principal beers: Reverend James(Crown Buckley), Worthington Draught Bass.
Directions From A477(N of Tenby) take A4075.Inn 400yds opp castle & Celtic cross
Free House
Open 12-2.30 4.30-11 (Sat & Summer 11-11,Sun 12-3,7-10.30)
Bar food 12-2 7-9 Av main course £4.50
Restaurant 12-2 7-9 Av 3 course à la carte £9.95
Accommodation s£15 d£25

CILGERRAN Pembrokeshire

Pendre Inn
CILGERRAN Map 02 SN14
Pendre SA43 ☎ 01239 614223
Free-range hens roam the garden of this 14th-century inn located at the foot of the Preseli hills. The menu concentrates on local produce and may include stuffed trout, game pie, Welsh lamb cooled in honey, apricot stuffed breast of chicken in pastry, or Yorkshire puddings with various fillings. Principal beers: Buckleys Smooth, Worthington BB, Bass.
Directions Off A478 south of Cardigan
Free House
Open 11.30-11.30
Bar food 12-2.30 6.30-10 Av main course £4.50

HAVERFORDWEST Pembrokeshire

The Georges Restaurant & Cafe Bar
HAVERFORDWEST Map 02 SM91
24 Market St SA61 1NH
☎ 01437 766683
Named after the George family, who ran a brewery here, the Georges has retained many original features, including a friendly ghost in the cellar. The menu features world-wide dishes such as Hungarian goulash and Normandy crab bake as well as tempting Belgian ice cream sundaes and traditional English fare! There is occasional live folk music. Principal beers: Marstons Pedigree, Worthington Cask, Wadworth 6X.

Directions on the A40
Open 10.30-10.30
Bar food 11.45-2.30 6-9.30 Av main course £5
Restaurant 11.45-2.30 6-9.30 Av 3 course à la carte £16 Av 3 course fixed price £10.95

LAMPHEY Pembrokeshire

The Dial Inn
LAMPHEY Map 02 SN00
SA71 5NU ☎ 01646 672426
Locals believe the Dial Inn is named after the sun dial once positioned over the entrance (now gone). It is a traditional thatched village pub with old beams and fresh flowers. The specials board offers variety including Welsh fillet steak, cashew nut roast and Glamorgan cheese sausages. Principal beers: Worthington BB,HB,Bass,Guinness.
Directions Just off A4139(Tenby to Pembroke rd)
Free House
Open 11-3 6-11
Bar food 12-2 7-9 Av main course £6
Restaurant 7-9 Av 3 course à la carte £15

LANDSHIPPING Pembrokeshire

The Stanley Arms
LANDSHIPPING Map 02 SN01
SA67 8BE ☎ 01834 891227
A 200-year-old pub with an original slate floor in the public bar. There is a large beer garden with views of Cleddau Estuary and Picton Castle, and abundant hanging baskets in summer. The emphasis is on home-cooked food with specialities such as lamb and apricot pie. Principal beers: Worthington, Bass.
Directions Off A40 at Canaston Bridge onto A4075, R at Cross Hands
Free House
Open 12-3 6-11
Bar food 12-2 7-9.30 Av main course £5.25

LETTERSTON Pembrokeshire

The Harp Inn
LETTERSTON Map 02 SM92
31 Haverfordwest Rd SA62 5UA ☎ 01348 840061
Extensive bar meal choice from home-baked ham salad to curry offers value for money. Steaks, with a choice of mouthwatering sauces from au poivre to chilli pepper and tomato, are a speciality in the restaurant where the feature is a lovely inglenook fireplace.
Directions Located on main A40
Free House
Open 11-11
Bar food 12-2.30 6.30-9.30 Av main course £4.50
Restaurant 12-2.30 7-9.30 Av 3 course à la carte £13 Av 3 course fixed price £6.50

NEVERN Pembrokeshire

Trewern Arms
NEVERN Map 02 SN04
SA42 0NB ☎ 01239 820395
In a tranquil village setting, this picturesque, ivy clad, 16th-century inn on the banks of the river Nevern offers a warm welcome to ramblers, travellers and locals. The congenial 'Brew House' bar offers range of simple, satisfying fare: battered cod, vegetarian lasagne, or study the salad bar. Principal beers: Flowers Original, Flowers IPA, Castle Eden.
Directions On the A487 between Cardigan and Fishguard
Free House
Open 11-3 6-11

contd.

Bar food 12-2 6-9 Av main course £6
Restaurant 7-9 Av 3 course à la carte £15
Accommodation s£30 d£45

PEMBROKE DOCK Pembrokeshire

Ferry Inn

PEMBROKE DOCK Map 02 SM90

Pembroke Ferry SA72 6UD
☎ 01646 682947

Originally the home of the Pembroke ferry, this traditional inn is ideal for those interested in life on the river. There's plenty of fish on the menu including sea bass, brill, turbot, cod, plaice, and shellfish. Beef en croûte, pork tenderloin, or Stilton, celery and apple Wellington may also be available. Principal beers: Hancocks HB, Draught Bass.
Directions A477, off A48, R at garage, signs for Cheddar Bridge, L at roundabout
Free House
Open 11.30-2.45 6.30-11
Bar food 12-2 7-10 Av main course £5
Restaurant 7-9 Av 3 course à la carte £14

PORTHGAIN Pembrokeshire

The Sloop Inn

PORTHGAIN Map 02 SM83

SA62 5BN ☎ 01348 831449

A well known, traditionally built harbour-side pub in a village setting, offering popular bar food: sandwiches, filled baguettes and Cajun spiced chicken and chips in a basket for example. Dishes from the bistro menu include mussels marinière, grilled crab thermidor, straightforward steaks and tropical vegetable curry. Principal beers: Felinfdel Double Dragon, Worthington BB, Stella, Carling.
Free House
Open 11-3 6-11
Bar food 12-2.30 6-9.30 Av main course £4.50
Restaurant 12-2.30 6-9.30 Av 3 course à la carte £15

ROSEBUSH Pembrokeshire

Tates at Tafarn Newydd

ROSEBUSH Map 02 SN02

SA66 7RA ☎ 01437 532542

There's a convivial atmosphere at this 17th-century coaching inn, which was associated with the drovers taking cattle from London to Ireland. The cosmopolitan menus include chicken suprême baked with 40 cloves of garlic, and salmon with grilled couscous and salsa verde. Lemon fudge tart features among the tempting desserts. Principal beers: Buckleys Best Bitter, Reverend James, Guinness, Harp.
Directions From A40 between Haverfordwest & Camarthan take B4313 N
Free House
Open 11-11 (Sun 12-10.30)
Bar food 12-2.30 7-9.30 Av main course £7
Restaurant 12-2.30 7-9.30

STACKPOLE Pembrokeshire

Armstrong Arms

STACKPOLE Map 02 SR99

SA71 5DF ☎ 01646 672324

Although it's only been a pub for five years, this listed building is over 500 years old and has an ancient elm ceiling. Food ranges from Welsh rarebit and filled croissant, to beef, Guinness and mushroom pie, or noisettes of Welsh lamb with redcurrant, cranberry and orange sauce. Principal beers: Charles Wells Bombardier.
Directions From Pembroke take B4319 & follow signs for Stackpole
Free House
Open 11.30-3 6.30-11
Restaurant 12-2 6.30-9 Av 3 course à la carte £15

WOLF'S CASTLE Pembrokeshire

The Wolfe Inn

WOLF'S CASTLE Map 02 SM92

SA62 5LS ☎ 01437 741662

A traditional Welsh village pub and restaurant, by a freshwater salmon and trout river, with three dining rooms warmed by open fires. Food is freshly prepared and cooked to order, ranging from sandwiches to steaks and vegetable lasagne to escalope of lamb filled with chopped leek and

Caerphilly cheese. Principal beers: Flowers IPA, Heineken, Stella, Labbatts.
Directions On A40 between Haverfordwest and Fishguard
Free House
Open 11-11
Bar food 12-3 6.30-10.30 Av main course £9
Restaurant 12-3 6.30-10.30 Av 3 course à la carte £13
Accommodation s£20 d£28

Powys

BERRIEW Powys

Lion Hotel & Restaurant
BERRIEW Map 07 SJ10
SY21 8PQ ☎ 01686 640452 640844
Discover this 17th century inn next to the church in a pretty village. Blackboard specials or à la carte feature Welsh and English specialities with a hint of the Far East: Welsh venison with red wine, mushrooms and juniper berries or Thai chicken with fresh ginger and spring onion. Principal beers: Bass, Worthington, Guinness.
Directions 5m from Welshpool on A483, 9m from Newtown, R to Berriew
Free House
Open 11-3 5.30-11
Bar food 12-2 7-9 Av main course £7
Restaurant 12-2 7-9 Av 3 course fixed price £8.95
Accommodation s£50 d£80

CARNO Powys

Aleppo Merchant Inn
CARNO Map 06 SN99
SY17 5LL ☎ 01686 420210
Named after his ship by a retired sea captain, a landlord around the turn of the century, this village pub, located in beautiful countryside between the Snowdonia and Brecon national parks, dates from the 17th century. Try lobster bisque and Welsh lamb from the traditional menu. Principal beers: Boddingtons, Brains.
Directions From Newtown, A489 and A470
Free House
Open 11.30-2.30 6-11
Bar food 12-2 6.30-9 Av main course £5
Restaurant 12-2 6.30-9 Av 3 course à la carte £12

COEDWAY Powys

Ye Old Hand and Diamond
COEDWAY Map 07 SJ31
SY5 9AR] ☎ 01743 884379
Close to the Shropshire border and the River Severn, this 19th-century inn still retains much of its original character and has had the same chef for around twenty years. Typical menu includes Welsh lamb chops, pork Normandy, venison, pheasant, and grilled trout and almonds. Principal beers: Bass, Worthington, Caffreys, Guinness.
Free House

CRICKHOWELL Powys

The Bear
CRICKHOWELL Map 03 SO21
Brecon Rd NP8 1BW ☎ 01837 810408
An historic 14th century coaching inn situated in a small market town in the Brecon national park, this charming establishment is very much the hub of the local community. Welsh lamb and locally caught salmon are always favourites on a menu featuring fresh produce and home grown herbs. Principal beers: Bass, Ruddles Best, John Smith, Yorkshire Bitter.
Directions M4, A449, A40, thru Abergavenny
Free House
Open 10-3 6-11
Bar food 12-2 6-10 Av main course £8
Restaurant 12-2 7-9.30 Av 3 course à la carte £22
Accommodation s£45 d£56

Gliffaes Country House Hotel
CRICKHOWELL Map 03 SO21
NP8 1RH ☎ 01874 730371
A fine country house with grounds including six acres of formal garden offering good value light lunches such

contd.

as chicken with raspberry and walnut oil dressing, the fare combines the best national and Mediterranean specialities. Three course dinner could feature Welsh lamb with cous cous, roast garlic and rosemary. Principal beers: John Smith, Carlsberg.
Directions 1m off the A40, 2 1/2m W of Crickhowell
Free House
Open 12-3 6-11
Bar food 12-2.30 7.30-9.15 Av main course £5.50
Restaurant 12.30-2.30 7.30-9.15 Av 3 course à la carte £20.95 Av 0 course fixed price £20.95
Accommodation s£36.50 d£73

Nantyffin Cider Mill
CRICKHOWELL Map 03 SO21
Brecon Rd NP8 1SG ☎ 01873 810775
Converted from a 16th-century cider mill, Nantyffin retains many original features, including the crush and press. The same menu of freshly prepared dishes is offered throughout, with dishes such as oak smoked salmon, and venison with smoked pear and game sauce. Principal beers: Felin Foel, Double Dragon, Speckled Hen, William Spensers.
Directions At junction of A40 & A479, 1.5m west of Crickhowell
Free House
Open 12-3 6-11
Bar food 12-3 6-11 Av main course £7.50
Restaurant 12-3 6-11 Av 3 course à la carte £18 Av 0 course fixed price £11.95

ELAN VILLAGE Powys

Elan Valley Hotel
ELAN VILLAGE Map 03 SN96
LD6 5HN ☎ 01597 810448
At the gateway to Wales's magnificent lakeland, this former Victorian fishing lodge caters for locals and tourists in a welcoming atmosphere. Wales meets the Mediterranean in a interesting menu offering Greek lamb moussaka to 'Crempog bwyd a mor', Welsh seafood pancakes. Principal beers: Hancocks HB.
Directions A44 to Rhayader then B4518 for 2m
Free House
Open 11-11.30
Bar food 12 9.30 Av main course £4.25
Restaurant 7-9 Av 3 course fixed price £10
Accommodation s£25 d£45

HAY-ON-WYE Powys

The Famous Old Black Lion
HAY-ON-WYE Map 03 SO24
Lion St HR35 5AD ☎ 01497 820841
Dating from around 1380, this listed building has plenty of character with old beams, open fires, prints, pots and a candlelit area at night. Extensive menus are offered in the King Richard Bar and the Cromwell Restaurant, dishes ranging from stir-fry chicken with noodles to spicy peppered venison. Principal beers: Old Black Lion, Flowers, Boddingtons.
Directions Town centre
Free House
Open 11-11
Bar food 12-3 7-10.30 Av main course £6.95
Restaurant 12-3 7-11 Av 3 course à la carte £18
Accommodation s£22 d£48

Kilverts Inn
HAY-ON-WYE Map 03 SO24
The Bullring HR3 5AG ☎ 01497 821042
A town centre hotel where food is served in the beamed bar, with its growing collection of hats, or Colin's Restaurant. The former offers quality pub fare, while the restaurant may have beef Bourguignonne, or grilled trout fillets glazed with lime zest, ginger and Demerara sugar. Principal beers: Castle Eden, Bass, Boddingtons, Murphys.
Directions Take A49 from M50, then L onto B4348 into Hay-on-Wye

Free House
Open 10.30-11
Bar food 12-2 7-9.30 Av main course £6
Restaurant 12-2 7-9.30 Av 3 course à la carte £17 Av 3 course fixed price £15
Accommodation s£25 d£50

LLANDRINDOD WELLS Powys

The Llanerch 16th-Century Inn
LLANDRINDOD WELLS Map 03 SO06
Llanerch Ln LD1 6BG ☎ 01597 822086
Traditional standards of hospitality are maintained at this 16th-century staging post. Original features include a Jacobean staircase and an inglenook fireplace. There is an extensive menu of snacks and meals, and additional specials might be curry of the week or salmon in herb butter. Principal beers: Hancocks HB, Worthington Creamflow, Albright.
Directions behind the railway station
Free House
Open 11.30-3 6-11
Bar food 12-2.15 6-9.30 Av main course £4.95
Restaurant 12-2.15 6-9.30 Av 3 course à la carte £12.50 Av 3 course fixed price £6.95
Accommodation s£27.50 d£45

LLANFIHANGEL-NANT-MELAN Powys

Red Lion Inn
LLANFIHANGEL-NANT-MELAN Map 03 SO15
LD8 2TN ☎ 01544 350220
Old-fashioned former drovers inn on the edge of Radnor Forest where food is taken seriously. The daily blackboard advertises such things as braised Welsh lamb, monkfish with cockles and bacon, and Welsh cheese ploughmans. Steak is properly matured Welsh Black or Hereford. Principal beers: Carlsberg, Tetley, Hook Norton.
Directions A483 to Crossgates then R onto A44
Free House
Open 11.30-2.30 6.30-11
Restaurant 12-2 7-9 Av 3 course à la carte £15

LLANFYLLIN Powys

Cain Valley Hotel
LLANFYLLIN Map 06 SJ11
High St SY22 5AQ ☎ 01691 648366
400-year-old Grade II listed coaching inn with Jacobean staircase. A short drive from the Berwyn Mountains and Lakes Vyrnwy and Bala. A la carte menu features sirloin steak with Stilton and walnut butter, and pork stuffed with apricots, herbs, walnuts and served with a red wine sauce. Principal beers: Draft Worthington, Bass, Ansells, Tetleys.
Directions A5 Shrewsbury bypass, A458 to Welshpool, A490 to Llanfyllin
Free House
Open 11-11.45 (Sun 12-11.15)
Bar food 12-2 7-9 Av main course £5
Restaurant 12-2 7-9 Av 3 course à la carte £15
Accommodation s£32 d£54

LLANGATTOCK Powys

The Vine Tree Inn
LLANGATTOCK Map 03 SO21
The Legar NP8 1HG ☎ 01873 810514
Situated in the beautiful Usk Valley overlooking the medieval bridge, the Vine Tree is predominantly a dining pub, giving good value for money in a cheerful atmosphere. Traditional, freshly prepared food includes home-baked bread, fresh fish and local vegetables and meat. Principal beers: Flower IPA, Welsh Bitter, Heineken, Stella.
Directions Take A40 W from Abergavenny then A4077 from Crickhowell
Free House
Open 12-3 6-11
Bar food 12-2.30 6-10 Av main course £8
Restaurant 12-2.30 6-10 Av 3 course à la carte £8

LLYSWEN Powys

The Griffin Inn
LLYSWEN Map 03 SO13
LD3 0UR ☎ 01874 754241
A traditional stone and timbered inn, dating from the 15th century, with a large inglenook and open fires and displays of fishing memorabilia. The country-style cooking features fresh water fish, game in season and Welsh cheeses, with dishes such as piscatorial pie and roast partridge. Principal beers: Brains, Thomas Watkins, Flowers IPA.
Directions On A470 (Brecon to Builth Wells rd)
Free House
Open 12-3 7-11

contd.

Bar food 12-3 7-11 Av main course £5
Restaurant 7-9 Av 3 course à la carte £18.65 Av 3 course fixed price £15
Accommodation s£34.50 d£60

MACHYNLLETH Powys

Dolbrodmaeth Inn
MACHYNLLETH Map 06 SH70
Dinas Mawddwy SY20 9LP
☎ 01650 531333

In a tranquil, riverside setting amid mountain scenery, popular with anglers, the inn was restored in 1980 after a fire. Bistro-style lunches are offered or for dinner in the candlelit restaurant , sample locally caught trout, steak Diane or a conscientiously prepared vegetarian special. Principal beers: Ind Coope, Burton Ale, Tetley Draught.
Directions A54 to A458, W to jct with A470, R for 1/2m, edge of Dinas Mawddwy on L between road and river
Free House
Open 11-11
Bar food 12-2 7-9
Restaurant 12-2 7-9 Av 3 course à la carte £13 Av 3 course fixed price £13
Accommodation s£38 d£50

MONTGOMERY Powys

Dragon Hotel
MONTGOMERY Map 07 SO29
SY15 6PA ☎ 01686 668359

17th-century former coaching inn situated near Montgomery Castle. Bar menu offers a good selection of snacks and main courses, such as lamb cutlets grilled with mint and red wine gravy, plaice fillet with orange and almond butter, and mushroom Stroganoff and deep fried Brie with cranberry dip, for vegetarians. Principal beers: Flowers IPA, Stella Artois, Carling, Worthington.
Directions A483 toward Welshpool, R onto B4386 then B4385
Free House
Open 8-11
Bar food 12-2 7-9 Av main course £6.95
Restaurant 12-2 7-9 Av 3 course fixed price £17.25
Accommodation s£42 d£72

PENYBONT Powys

Severn Arms Hotel
PENYBONT Map 03 SO16
LD1 5UA ☎ 01597 851224

Meat dishes at this village hotel range from pork tenderloin pan-fried with onions and mushrooms and served with a rich creamy sauce flavoured with Martini, to sirloin steak served with a rich brandy and red wine sauce. Among the fish and vegetarian meals are grilled trout with almonds, and broccoli and cream cheese bake. Principal beers: Bass, Worthington, Brains, John Smiths.
Directions On A44 at Jct with A488
Free House
Open 11-2.30 6-11
Bar food 11-2.30 6.30-10 Av main course £4.50
Restaurant 6.30-8.45 Av 4 course fixed price £13.90
Accommodation s£28 d£50

TALYBONT-ON-USK Powys

Star Inn
TALYBONT-ON-USK Map 03 SO12
LD3 7YX ☎ 01874 676635

A traditional 200-year-old village pub with a beer garden and a mooring on the canal. There is a good range of food, from beefburgers, faggots and chips to home-made specialities such as carbonnade of beef (casseroled in

Irish stout), and a spinach and leek pasta bake. Principal beers: Double Dragon, Freeminers, Wye Valley, Old Peculiar.
Free House
Open 11-3 6-11 (Sat-Sun 11-11)
Bar food 12-2.15 6.30-9.30 Av main course £4.50
Accommodation s£25 d£40

TRECASTLE Powys

Castle Coaching Inn
TRECASTLE Map 03 SN83
LD3 8UH ☎ 01874 636354
A listed 17th-century coaching inn set amid the splendour of the Brecon Beacons National Park. Home-cooked bar food is served, and a fixed-price four-course dinner menu is available in the restaurant by prior booking. Dishes range from liver and bacon suet pudding to country lentil crumble. Principal beers: Worthington Creamflow, Grolsch, Carling Black Label, Scrumpy Jack.
Directions On A40 W of Brecon
Free House
Open 11.30-11
Bar food 12-2.30 6.30-9.45 Av main course £6.95
Restaurant 7-9.30 Av 3 course à la carte £15.95 Av 4 course fixed price £15.95
Accommodation s£41 d£43.50

Shropshire

BRIDGNORTH Shropshire

The Lion O'Morfe
BRIDGNORTH Map 07 SO79
Upper Farmcote WV15 5PS
☎ 01746 710678
Became a country pub in the early 1850s. 'Morfe' is derived from the Welsh name meaning 'marsh'. A wide selection of bar meals are available, including home-made dishes like seafood lasagne, tuna pasta bake, and leek, cheese and onion hot pot. The blackboard menu changes daily. Principal beers: Banks Bitter, Banks Mild, Draught Bass, Caffreys.
Directions Off A458 (Bridgnorth/ Stourbridge) 2.5m from Bridgnorth follow signs for Claverley on L,0.5m up hill on L
Free House
Open 11.30-2.30 7-11
Bar food 12-2 7-9

COALPORT Shropshire

The Woodbridge Inn & Restaurant
COALPORT Map 07 SJ60
TF8 7JE ☎ 01952 882054
A 16th-century coaching inn overlooking the Severn Gorge by Coalport Bridge. The garden offers riverside seating and a weekend barbecue, weather permitting. Food ranges from bar snacks to coq au vin, steaks and vegetable balti in the restaurant. Principal beers: Courage Directors,John Smiths, Shropshire Lad, Bombadier.
Directions Off A442 S of Telford
Scottish Courage
Open 12-12 (winter 12-3,5.30-11)
Bar food 12-2.30 5.30-9.30 Av main course £3.95
Restaurant 7-10 Av 3 course à la carte £12

HEATHTON Shropshire

The Old Gate Inn
HEATHTON Map 07 SO89
WV5 7EB ☎ 01746 710431
A warm welcome is assured at this 16th-century country inn, which has a lovely south-facing garden with good hardwood furniture for summer dining. Popular steaks, lasagne and scampi are supplemented by specials such as pan-fried fillet of seabass with lobster and cod cake and lobster cream sauce. Principal beers: Enville Ale, Timothy Taylor Landlord, Old Speckled Hen, Tetley.
Directions From Bridgnorth take A454 towards Wolverhampton. Village on minor rd on R
Free House
Open 12-2.30 6.30-11
Bar food 12-2 6.30-9 Av main course £7.95

HODNET Shropshire

The Bear Hotel
HODNET Map 07 SJ62
TF9 3NH ☎ 01630 685214
A warm ambience and fascinating tales await at this former coaching inn with a wealth of beams, nooks and crannies and unusual glass floor panel looking down onto the cellar garden. Chefs' prepare a range from snacks to full à la carte and specials such as luxury fishcakes or fidget pie. Principal beers:

contd.

Theakstons, Marston Pedigree, John Smiths, Kronenbourg.
Directions A442 to Jct with A53, or M6 J15, take A53
Free House
Open 11-7
Bar food 12-2 6.30-10.30 Av main course £5
Restaurant 12-2 6.30-10.30 Av 3 course à la carte £15
Accommodation s£30 d£50

HOPTON WAFERS Shropshire

The Crown at Hopton
HOPTON WAFERS Map 07 SO67
DY14 0NB ☎ 01299 270372
A 16th-century coaching inn of great character, offering a choice of minor and major courses, the former serving as a starter or snack. Among the lighter options are pasta, salads and savouries such as king prawns in garlic butter. Major dishes include spiced lamb meatballs, chicken satay, and seafood pancake. Principal beers: Abbot Ale, Boddingtons Bitter, Marstons Pedigree, Stella Artois.
Directions On A4117
Free House
Open 12-3 6-11
Bar food 12-3 6-9.30 Av main course £8
Restaurant 12-2.30 7.30-9.30 Av 3 course à la carte £24 Av 3 course fixed price £24
Accommodation s£45 d£70

LLANFAIR WATERDINE Shropshire

Red Lion Inn & Restaurant
LLANFAIR WATERDINE Map 07 SO27
LD7 1TV ☎ 01547 528214
16th-century drover's inn, situated in a remote riverside setting. Blackboard specials include gammon steak glazed in a mustard and ginger sauce and topped with sautéed fresh nectarines, steak chasseur, and lamb en croûte with a stuffing of onion, mushroom, apricot and thyme and served with a Périgourdine sauce. Principal beers: Tetleys, Pedigree, Wye Valley, Dorothy Goodbody.
Free House
Open 12-2.30 (except Tue) 7-12
Bar food 12-2 7-9 Av main course £5.60
Restaurant 7-9 Av 3 course à la carte £14

LUDLOW Shropshire

The Church Inn
LUDLOW Map 07 SO57
Buttercross SY8 1AW ☎ 01584 872174
A Georgian building at the centre of the medieval town, this inn has a lounge bar smartness plus its own busy restaurant. Lunchtime fare ranges from freshly-cut sandwiches to steak and kidney pie. The longer evening menu offers chicken chasseur, grilled trout, rump steak and curry. Principal beers: Gillespies Stout, Ruddles County, Websters Yorkshire, Pedigree.
Directions Town centre
Free House
Open 11-11
Bar food 12-2 6-9 Av main course £4.75
Restaurant 12-2 6-9 Av 3 course à la carte £10
Accommodation s£28 d£45

Unicorn Inn
LUDLOW Map 07 SO57
Corve St SY18 1DU ☎ 01584 873555
Built in 1635 on the banks of the River Corve, The Unicorn is a good place for walkers and mountain bikers, and hosts a jazz festival in summer. Blackboard menus may include roast duck, wild boar steak, haddock Mornay, Cumberland sausages, or bacon, mushroom and cauliflower bake. Principal beers: Worthington Best, Draught Bass.
Directions A49 to Ludlow
Free House
Open 12-3 6-11
Bar food 12-2.15 6-9.15 Av main course £5
Restaurant 12-2.15 6-9.15
Accommodation s£20 d£20

MADELEY Shropshire

The New Inn
MADELEY Map 07 SJ60
Blists Hill Open Air Museum, Legges Way TF7 5DU ☎ 01952 586309
This Victorian pub set in the Blist's Hill Open Air Museum, is part of the complex of Ironbridge Gorge Museums which celebrate Britain's 19th century industrial heritage. Staff dress in Victorian costumes, the pub is gaslit, and there is sawdust on the floors. Bar meals and snacks are available. Principal beers: Banks Mild & Bitter, Draught Bulmers.

Directions Between Telford & Broseley
Free House
Open 11-5 (July-Sept 11-6)
Bar food 12-2.30 Av main course £4.90
Restaurant 12-2.30 Av 3 course à la carte £4.90

MINSTERLEY Shropshire

The Stables Inn
MINSTERLEY Map 07 SJ30
Drury Ln, Hopesgate SY5 0EP
☎ 01743 891344
17th-century drovers inn. The original stables and outbuildings are still standing across the yard. Fine countryside views, with a visible gathering of curlews in spring and summer. Bar menu ranges from home-made beef and Guinness pie, and rainbow trout, to chicken Kiev, and tomato and vegetable tagliatelle for vegetarians. Principal beers: Tetley Bitter, Bomberdier Bitter, Ansells Mild, Carlsberg.
Directions From Shrewsbury A488 turn L at r'about in Misterely. At Plox Green x-roads turn R. Pub approx 3m.
Free House
Open 12-3 7-11 (Sun 7-10.30)
Bar food 12-2 7-9.15 Av main course £5
Restaurant 12-2 7-9.15 Av 3 course à la carte £10

MORVILLE Shropshire

Acton Arms
MORVILLE Map 07 SO69
WV16 4RJ ☎ 01746 714209
Believed to have been built from the remains of a priory demolished in the 16th century, the Acton Arms is described as England's most frequently haunted inn. Freshly cooked traditional meals include the Catch of the Day and prime steaks from the griddle. Principal beers: Banks Mild & Bitter & Smoothpour.
Directions On the A458, 3m W of Bridgnorth
Free House
Open 12-3 6.30-11.20
Bar food 12-2.30 7-11 Av main course £5.50
Restaurant 12-2.30 7-11 Av 3 course à la carte £12

AA members can call AA Hotel Booking Service on 0990 050505 to book at AA recognised hotels and B & Bs in the UK and Ireland, or through our Internet site: http://www.theaa.co.uk/hotels

MUCH WENLOCK Shropshire

The George & Dragon
MUCH WENLOCK Map 07 SO69
2 High St TF13 6AA
☎ 01952 727312
A bustling, friendly town local, housing a fascinating collection of old brewery and pub artefacts, this 16th century free house offers good hearty home cooking. Tasty bar food for lunch or evening; restaurant meals could feature home baked ham or steak and stout pie. Principal beers: Hook Norton, Everards.
Directions on A458 halfway between Shrewsbury & Bridgnorth
Free House
Open 11-2.30 6-11
Bar food 12-2 6.30-9 Av main course £5.75
Restaurant 12-2 6.30-9 Av 3 course à la carte £14

Longville Arms
MUCH WENLOCK Map 07 SO69
Longville in the Dale TF13 6DT
☎ 01694 771206
Simple, hearty country cooking such as casseroles of pheasant, venison or rabbit are popular along with fresh trout or salmon at this pub situated in most beautiful part of Shropshire. It is a convenient base for exploring Long Mynd, the Stretton Hills and more local landmarks. Principal beers: Draught Bass, Murphy Stout, Carling Lager, Caffreys.
Directions From Shrewsbury take A49 to Church Stretton, then B4371 to Longville
Free House
Open 12-3 7-11
Bar food 12-2 7-9 Av main course £4.50
Restaurant 12-2 7-9 Av 3 course à la carte £8
Accommodation s£17.50 d£35

The Talbot Inn
MUCH WENLOCK Map 07 SO69
High St TF13 6AA ☎ 01952 727077
Ministering to the needs of the weary traveller for six centuries, this inn fronts onto the historic High Street, but has a quiet courtyard garden. Freshly made sandwiches and home-cooked English dishes are offered, including game in season, market fresh fish and fillet steak, followed by traditional home-made puddings. Principal beers: Directors, John Smiths, Theakstons.
Free House

contd.

Open 9-2.30 6.15-11 (Sun 10-2.30, 7-10.30)
Bar food 12-2 7-9.30 Av main course £5.50
Restaurant 7-9.30 Av 3 course à la carte £13
Accommodation s£40 d£80

Wenlock Edge Inn
MUCH WENLOCK Map 07 SO69
Hill Top, Wenlock Edge, TF13 6DJ
☎ 01746 785678
On top of Wenlock Edge, a 400-million-year-old coral reef, this family-run country inn features an inglenook fireplace and original beams. An interesting menu offers popular flans such as smoked chicken and asparagus, as well as pan-fried fish, organically reared beef, and chicken with Gruyère and smoked ham. Principal beers: Hobsons Best & Town Crier, Ruddles Best, Murphys, Merrydown.
Directions 4 1/2m from Much Wenlock on B4371
Free House
Open 11.30-2.30 2.30-11 (Sun 12-2.30, 6.30-10.30)
Bar food 12-2 7-9 Av main course £6.50
Restaurant 12-2 7-9 Av 3 course à la carte £12
Accommodation s£45 d£65

MUNSLOW Shropshire

The Crown
MUNSLOW Map 07 SO58
SY7 9ET ☎ 01584 841205
Originally a coaching inn with a panelled Tudor interior behind a Georgian facade, this pub has its own micro-brewery visible from the bar. Meals are cooked to order, including traditional bar food with fresh fish, vegetarian and Thai dishes, and an evening menu of mostly French-influenced dishes. Principal beers: Banks Mild, Marstons Pedigree, Boys Pale Ale, Munslow Ale.
Directions On B4368 between Craven Arms & Much Wenlock
Free House
Open 12-2.30 7-11
Bar food 12-2 7-9.30 Av main course £5.50
Restaurant 7-9.30 Av 3 course à la carte £15

NESSCLIFFE Shropshire

The Old Three Pigeons Inn
NESSCLIFFE Map 07 SJ31
SY4 1DB ☎ 01743 741279
Unusual 15th-century pub built of sandstone, ship's timbers and wattle and daub, with a 16th-century highwayman's carved wooden seat by the fireplace, and a Russian tank and fire engine in the back garden! Menu may include peppered sirloin steak and honey roast chicken, as well as up to twenty different fish dishes. Principal beers: Whitbreads, John Smiths.
Directions On A5
Free House
Open 11.30-3 7-11
Bar food 12-3.30 7-10.30 Av main course £4.95
Restaurant 12-3.30 7-10.30 Av 3 course à la carte £15

NORTON Shropshire

Hundred House Hotel & Country Inn
NORTON Map 07 SJ70
Bridgnorth Rd (A442) TF11 9EE
☎ 01952 730353
Everyone is welcome at this friendly inn, where local farmers mix with international businessmen from Telford. There's a restaurant and a brasserie with similar food, all freshly cooked using local produce. Look out for Severn salmon, Norton free-range chicken and Bridgnorth pork sausages. Principal beers: Heritage Bitter, Aurics Old Ale, Everards Tiger, Everards Mild.
Directions On A442
Free House
Open 10.30-3.30 6-11
Bar food 12-2.30 6-10 Av main course £7.95
Restaurant 12-2.30 6-10 Av 3 course à la carte £25
Accommodation s£65 d£79

OSWESTRY Shropshire

The Bradford Arms
OSWESTRY Map 07 SJ22
Llanymynech SY22 6EJ ☎ 01691 830582
Dating from 1760, this old coaching inn was Victorianised in 1901. Both bar and restaurant menus offer modern English cooking including fresh fish, steaks and vegetarian dishes. There is a good choice of sweets too, including chocolate fudge cheesecake, treacle tart and lemon

pudding. Principal beers: Riegele (Augsburg), Kronenbourg, Marstons, Guinness.
Directions On A483
Free House
Open 12-2.30 7-12
Bar food 12-2.30 7-11 Av main course £6.95
Restaurant 7-12 Av 3 course à la carte £18.95

PICKLESCOTT Shropshire

Bottle & Glass Inn

PICKLESCOTT Map 07 SO49

SY6 6NR ☎ 01694 751345

The Bottle & Glass is a 17th-century tavern with a wealth of oak beams, low ceilings and log fires. Traditional home-made pies, such as steak and kidney or game, are a staple in the bar, along with basket meals, while the restaurant offers a choice of grills, lasagne and curry. Principal beers: Bass, Worthington.
Directions Turn off A49 at Dorrington between Shrewsbury & Church Stretton
Free House
Bar food 12-3 7-9 Av main course £4.95
Restaurant 12-3 7-9 Av 3 course à la carte £11 Av 2 course fixed price £7.95
Accommodation s£20 d£35

SHREWSBURY Shropshire

Boathouse Inn

SHREWSBURY Map 07 SJ41

New St SY3 8JQ ☎ 01743 362965

Situated on the bank of the River Severn, this 15th century inn overlooks the site of the annual Shrewsbury Flower Festival. Enjoy a summer weekend barbecue in the large beer garden. Choice on the menu includes a range of steaks, home-cooked specials and flavoured sausages. Principal beers: Heineken, Stella, Boddingtons, Fuggles.
Free House
Open 11-11
Bar food 12-2.30 5-8
Restaurant 12-2.30 5-8

Henry's Restaurant

SHREWSBURY Map 07 SJ41

Butcher Row SY1 1UW
☎ 01743 353117

A former butcher's shop, this 14th-century timber-framed building is located in the heart of the town, perched above a fashion shop. Home-made pasta and battered cod appear on the bar menu, while the restaurant offers citrus shark steak, escalope of pork with Stilton and sage, and an extravagant paella Valenciana. Principal beers: Tetley Bitter, Carlsberg lager.
Directions Town centre
Open 11.30-2.15 6.30-10
Bar food 11.30-3 Av main course £3.95
Restaurant 11.30-3 6.30-12 Av 3 course à la carte £12 Av 3 course fixed price £8.75

WEM Shropshire

The Raven Inn

WEM Map 07 SJ52

Tilley SY4 5HE ☎ 01939 234419

17th-century village inn where the menu offers a selection of snacks and light lunches. Main course dishes include poached salmon in prawn and dill sauce, sirloin steak in red wine and mushroom sauce, spinach and cheese pie, and char-grilled lamb steak in a coriander, orange and coconut cream sauce. Principal beers: Marsdens Pedigree, Carlsberg, Guinness.
Directions A49 to Whitchurch onto B5063, R at T jct, sharp L signed Tilley
Free House
Open 11.30-3 6-11.30
Bar food 12-2.30 6-11.30 Av main course £6
Restaurant 12-2.30 6-11.30 Av 3 course à la carte £10

WHITCHURCH Shropshire

Willey Moor Lock Tavern

WHITCHURCH Map 07 SJ54

Tarporley Rd SY13 4HF
☎ 01948 663274

Built as a lock-keepers cottage in the 1790s and converted into a pub in the 1970s, the Willeymoor features original beams, canal paintings and a teapot collection. A meal here may feature home-made steak pie, Willeymoor grill, lasagne, or freshly battered cod. Principal beers: Scotch bitter, Theakstons Best, Theakstons Mild, Guinness.

contd.

Directions 2m N of Whitchurch on A49 (Warrington/Tarporley)
Free House
Open 12-2.30 6-11 (Sun 7-10.30)
Bar food 12-2 6-9 Av main course £5

Swansea

REYNOLDSTON Swansea

King Arthur Hotel
REYNOLDSTON Map 02 SS48
Higher Green SA3 1AD
☎ 01792 391099
There is a relaxed and informal atmosphere at this 250-year-old former coaching inn. The menu is the same for the bar and restaurant, offering traditional meals, cooked on the premises, with an emphasis on seasonal produce including fresh fish, game and local specialities, such as bacon, laverbread and cockles. Principal beers: Double Dragon, Worthington, Bass, Carling Black Label.
Directions Just N of A4118 SW of Swansea
Free House
Open 11-11
Bar food 12-2.30 6-9.30 Av main course £6
Restaurant 12-2.30 6-9.30 Av 3 course à la carte £10.50 Av 2 course fixed price £7.50
Accommodation s£30 d£45

Vale of Glamorgan

EAST ABERTHAW Vale of Glamorgan

Blue Anchor Inn
EAST ABERTHAW Map 03 ST06
CF62 3DD ☎ 01446 750329
This historic Welsh inn was established in 1380, and its open fires,

antique furniture, beams and thatch ensure an old world atmosphere. Diners here can choose from a menu that may feature braised escalopes of venison, red sea-bream fillet on a bed of spinach, or roast leg of Welsh lamb. Principal beers: Buckleys Best, Theakstons Old Peculier, Wadworths 6X, Boddingtons.
Free House
Bar food 12-2 6-8 Av main course £5
Restaurant 12.-2.30 7-9.30 Av 3 course à la carte £20

PENMARK Vale of Glamorgan

Six Bells Inn
PENMARK Map 03 ST06
CF62 3BP ☎ 01446 710229
A pub with a history, the Six Bells appeared on the first Ordnance Survey map of 1623, and it has a Norman archway at the front door. Typical dishes include moules marinière, pan-fried sirloin of Welsh beef with game chips and garlic butter, and passion fruit crème brûlée. Principal beers: Hancocks HB, Worthington Creamflow, Carling Black Label, Grolsch.
Directions M4 J33 take A4045,follow signs for 'Cardiff Wales airport' then 'Penmark'
Free House
Open 12-11 (Sun 12-10.30)
Bar food 12-3 Av main course £5.50
Restaurant 12-3 7-10 Av 3 course à la carte £20
Accommodation s£15 d£20

ST HILARY Vale of Glamorgan

The Bush Inn
ST HILARY Map 03 ST07
CF71 7PD ☎ 01446 772745
Situated opposite the Norman church, this thatched, 15th-century pub enjoys a very pretty village setting. Inside there is a large inglenook fireplace complementing the warmth of the atmosphere. Wholesome, traditional food is cooked on the premises, ranging from Welsh rarebit to steak and ale pie. Principal beers: Hancocks Home Brew, Bass, Whitbread, Premier and Black Label.
Directions S of A48, E of Cowbridge
Welsh Brewers
Open 11.30-11 (Mon-Tue 11.30-3,5-11)

Bar food 12-3 7-10 Av main course £4.50
Restaurant 12-3 7-10 Av 3 course à la carte £15 Av 3 course fixed price £9.95

Worcestershire

BEWDLEY Worcestershire

Little Pack Horse
BEWDLEY Map 07 SO77
31 High St DY12 2DH ☎ 01299 403762
400-year-old pub with elm timber bar and mosaic wall. A selection of Mad O' Rourke's distinctive pies are available, such as Famous Desperate Dan pie, Poultry Pig & Fungi pie, and for vegetarians, Allotment pie and Back Garden pie. Other dishes include venison stew, and braised oxtail soaked in ale. Principal beers: Lump Hammer Burton, Speckled Hen.
Free House
Open 11-3, 6-11 (Sat-Sun all day opening)
Bar food 12-2 6.30-9.30 Av main course £4

BREDON Worcestershire

Fox & Hounds Inn & Restaurant
BREDON Map 03 SO93
Church St GL20 7LA
☎ 01684 772377
Thatched, 16th-century inn near to Bredon's 11th-century tithe barn and the River Avon. House specialities include fillet au poivre, lamb loin char-grilled with a redcurrant sauce, and Thai style chicken. Vegetarian options feature mushroom Stroganoff and vegetable tikka masala. Principal beers: Boddingtons, Banks Bitter, Marstons Pedigree, Old Speckled Hen.
Directions M5 J9 into Tewkesbury take B4080 towards Pershore. Bredon 3m.
Whitbread
Bar food 12-2.30 6.30-10 Av main course £4.50
Restaurant 12-2.30 6.30-10 Av 3 course à la carte £14.50

BRETFORTON Worcestershire

The Fleece Inn
BRETFORTON Map 04 SP04
The Cross WR11 5JE ☎ 01386 831173
Originally a medieval farmhouse, the Fleece, which is described by staff as 'a living museum', has been a pub since 1848 and is now owned by the National Trust. Typical menu includes steak and kidney pie, Gloucester sausages, and ratatouille lasagne. Principal beers: Uley Beer, Everards.
Directions B4035 from Evesham
Free House
Open 11-2.30 6-11
Bar food 12-2 7-9 Av main course £4.50

CASTLEMORTON Worcestershire

The Robin Hood
CASTLEMORTON Map 03 SO73
WR13 6BS ☎ 01684 833212
Situated at the base of the Malvern hills, this 15th-century timbered pub is ideal for unwinding after a walk on Castlemorton Common. Diners may enjoy 'Friar's gammon', minced gammon with cheese and leek, trout with almonds, Cumberland sausage in onion gravy, or a selection of home-made desserts. Principal beers: Flowers, Theakstons.
Directions On B4208 (Worcester/Gloucester rd)
Free House
Open 11.30-3 7-11 (Sun 11.30-11)
Bar food 12-2 7-9.30 Av main course £4.50
Restaurant 12-2 7-9.30 Av 3 course à la carte £10

KEMPSEY Worcestershire

Walter de Cantelupe Inn
KEMPSEY Map 03 SO84
Main Rd WR5 3NA ☎ 01905 820572
Named after a 13th century Bishop of Leicester who resided in the village, this

contd.

individual establishment combines traditional features ornamented with a touch of the Orient. International flavours are added to robust British dishes using seasonal ingredients such as pork casserole with fresh lime, coconut and spices. Principal beers: Marstons Bitter, Timothy Talyors Landlord.
Directions 4m S of Worcester City centre, on A38
Free House
Open 11.30-2.30 5.30-11 (Sun 11.30-2.30, 7-10.30)
Bar food 12-2 6-9.30 Av main course £4.75
Restaurant 12-2 6-9/9.30 Av 3 course à la carte £12.75

KNIGHTWICK Worcestershire

The Talbot at Knightwick
KNIGHTWICK Map 03 SO75
WR6 5PH ☎ 01886 821235
500-year-old coaching inn overlooking the River Teme. Typical starters feature four cheese tagliatelle, and pork, orange and cognac pâté. Main course dishes range from Middle Eastern lamb casserole, and turbot fillet with sorrel mousse and saffron sauce, to St. David's rabbit, and wild mushroom tart for vegetarians. Principal beers: Hobsons, Bass, Worthington.
Directions A44 through Worcester, 8m W turn onto B4197
Free House
Bar food 12-2 6.30-9.30 Av main course £8.95
Restaurant 12-2 6.30-9.30 Av 3 course à la carte £16.20
Accommodation s£24.50 d£42

MALVERN Worcestershire

Farmers Arms
MALVERN Map 03 SO74
Birts St, Birtsmorton WR13 6AP
☎ 01684 833308
A 15th-century black and white building in a quiet parish just off the Malvern Hills. Food ranges from bar snacks, through dishes such as Hereford pie, chilli, lasagne and macaroni cheese, to rump steak or trout with almonds. Puddings include apple pie, treacle tart and gateaux. Principal beers: Hook Norton, Old Hookey.
Directions On B4208 S of Great Malvern
Free House
Open 11-2.30 6-11
Bar food 11-2 6-10 Av main course £3.50

OMBERSLEY Worcestershire

Kings Arms
OMBERSLEY Map 03 SO86
Main Rd WR9 0EW ☎ 01905 620142
A crooked black and white pub, built in 1411, with cosy beamed bars and large inglenook fireplaces filled with bric-a-brac. It is in a village setting opposite the church. The food is old English - oxtail braised in stout, and poacher's pot - with some continental dishes. Principal beers: Bass, Worthington, Carling Premier, Heineken.
Directions Just off A449
Free House
Open 11-3 5.30-11
Bar food 12.15-2.15 6-10.30 Av main course £7.50

PENSAX Worcestershire

The Bell Inn
PENSAX Map 03 SO76
WR6 6AE ☎ 01299 896677
Built around 1840 as a hunting lodge, the Bell is a black and white inn, beautifully

situated with idyllic valley views from the lounge. The traditional bar serves a constantly changing range of ales (over 400 a year), and there is a choice of popular home-cooked bar food. Principal beers: Hook Norton.
Directions From Kidderminster A456 to Clows Top, B4202 towards Abberley, pub 2m on L
Free House
Open 12-2.30 5-11 (Sun 12-10.30)
Bar food 12-2 6-9.30 Av main course £4.95

POWICK Worcestershire

The Halfway House
POWICK Map 03 SO85
Bastonford WR2 4SL ☎ 01905 831098
Situated at the foot of the Malvern Hills, halfway between between Worcester and Malvern. A good selection of bar snacks is available. Among the home-made meals are vegetarian chilli, vegetable lasagne and vegetable curry. Other typical main courses include chicken Marengo, trout Italienne, and mushroom Stroganoff. Principal beers: Marstons, Timothy Taylors, Heineken, Stella Artois.
Directions From A15 J7 take A4440 then A449
Free House
Open 12-2.30 6-11
Bar food 12-2 6.30-9 Av main course £8.50
Restaurant 12-2 6.30-9 Av 3 course à la carte £15

WYRE PIDDLE Worcestershire

The Anchor Inn
WYRE PIDDLE Map 03 SO94
Main St WR10 2JB ☎ 01386 552799
The gardens of this 17th-century inn gently slope to the River Avon, offering a perfect view of the surrounding countryside. The bar menu includes pies, fresh fish, cold meats and home-made puddings, while the restaurant menu may offer escargots Bourguignonne, fillet mignon, mushroom ravioli, or Drambuie haggis. Principal beers: Hook Norton Best Bitter, Flowers IPA, Marstons Pedigree, Flowers Original.
Directions From M5 J6 take A4538 S towards Evesham
Free House
Open 11-2.30 6-11
Bar food 12-2 7-9.15 Av main course £6.50
Restaurant 12-2 7-9.15 Av 3 course à la carte £12.50

Wrexham

HANMER Wrexham

Hanmer Arms Village Hotel
HANMER Map 07 SJ43
SY13 3DE ☎ 01948 830532
Village hotel close to a 19th-century church and within easy reach of Hanmer Mere. House specialities feature fillet of beef Rossini, seafood Provençale, Scotch salmon, and roast duck served with orange and Cointreau sauce. Vegetarian options include aubergine lasagne, vegetable moussaka, and mushroom Stroganoff. Principal beers: Tetley Traditional Bitter, Calders Cream Ale,Carlsberg Lager.
Directions Between Wrexham & Whitchurch on A539, off A525
Free House
Open 12-3 6-11
Bar food 12-3 6-10.30 Av main course £8.50
Restaurant 12-3 6-10.30 Av 3 course à la carte £12.50 Av 3 course fixed price £11.50
Accommodation s£19 d£25

MARFORD Wrexham

Trevor Arms Hotel
MARFORD Map 07 SJ35
LL12 8TA ☎ 01244 570436
Built in the early 1800s as a coaching inn, and situated on a hill with fine views of the Cheshire Plain. The Chef's recommendations include lamb with creamed leeks served with pink peppercorn sauce, fillet steak stuffed with prawns and served with dill sauce, and king prawns flamed in Pernod. Principal beers: Greenalls, Tetleys, Caffreys, Labatts.
Directions off A483 onto B5102 then R onto B5445 into Marford
Free House
Open 11-11
Bar food 12-2.30 6-11 Av main course £5
Restaurant 12-2.30 6-11 Av 3 course à la carte £15 Av 3 course fixed price £6.75
Accommodation s£29.50 d£35.50

Northern England

Prehistoric sites, Roman forts, sparsely populated peaceful villages, pretty landscapes and the stunning scenery of the Lake District sit alongside great industrial conurbations and Victorian seaside resorts.

• Cheshire • Cumbria • Co Durham •
• Greater Manchester • Lancashire •
• Merseyside • Northumberland •
• Tyne & Wear
• Yorkshire, East Riding of •
• Yorkshire, North • Yorkshire, South •
• Yorkshire, West •

Cheshire

BARTHOMLEY Cheshire

The White Lion Inn
BARTHOMLEY Map 07 SJ75
CW2 5PG ☎ 01270 882242
A thatched, traditional, rural pub, dating from 1614, the White Lion has connections with the Bartholomew Massacre during the English Civil War, as well as several reports of ghosts. Listen to the stories while enjoying a sandwich or ploughmans. Principal beers: Burtonwood Bitter, James Forshaws, Top Hat, Buccaneer.
Burtonwood
Open 11.30-11 (Thurs 5-11, Sun 12-10.30)
Bar food 12-2 Av main course £2

BOLLINGTON Cheshire

The Church House Inn
BOLLINGTON Map 07 SJ97
Church St SK10 5PY ☎ 01625 574014
Convenient for both the natural landscape of the Peak District National Park and the bright lights of Manchester, this village inn has a varied menu. Diners may enjoy diced lamb in cranberry and ginger sauce, swordfish steak in a white wine and tarragon sauce, or Bollington-made black pudding. Principal beers: Theakston, Tetley, Jennings, Kilkenny.
Directions Macclesfield turnoff on A34, thru Prestbury, follow Bollington signs.
Free House
Open 12-3 5.30-11
Bar food 12-2 6.30-9.30 Av main course £6
Accommodation s£27.50 d£37.50

BROOMEDGE Cheshire

The Jolly Thresher
BROOMEDGE Map 07 SJ75
Higher Ln WA13 0RN ☎ 01925 752265
Named after Lord De Trafford, who disguised himself as a farm labourer to escape the Roundheads, this pub has a function room, its own bowling green, and is locally famous for its cod and chips. Menu may also include Barnsley lamb chop or Virginia ham and pineapple. Specials board changes daily. Principal beers: Billy Westwoods Bitter, Hydes Anvil BB.
Directions A56
Hydes Anvil
Open 11.30-3 5.30-11
Bar food 12-2 Av main course £4.95
Restaurant 12-2 7-9 Av 3 course à la carte £9.85

BROXTON Cheshire

The Copper Mine
BROXTON Map 07 SJ45
Nantwich Rd CH3 9JH ☎ 01829 782293
The Copper Mine has log fires and a pretty conservatory overlooking glorious countryside. Its name commemorates the copper mining industry that once flourished in this area. There is live country music on Monday, which you can enjoy while sampling the vast menu, from chicken Yakatori to cod in crispy batter. Principal beers: Burtonwood, Bass, Caffreys, Carling.
Directions A41 from Chester, L at r'about onto A534, pub 1/4m on L
Free House
Bar food 12-2.30 7-9.30 Av main course £7
Restaurant 12-2.30 7-9.30

BURLEYDAM Cheshire

Combermere Arms
BURLEYDAM Map 07 SJ64
SY13 4AT ☎ 01948 871223
The 16th-century Combermere Arms is a black and white coaching inn with oak beams and open fires. It is reputedly haunted by a monk from the local abbey. Home-cooked traditional food using local produce is available daily, including drunken steak and kidney pie, fish dishes, burgers and salads. Principal beers: Bass, Worthington, Carling, Caffreys.
Directions On the A525 from Whitchurch
Free House
Open 11-11
Bar food 12-2.30 6-9.30 Av main course £6.50
Restaurant 12-2.30 6-9.30

BURWARDSLEY Cheshire

The Pheasant Inn
BURWARDSLEY Map 07 SJ55
CH3 9PF ☎ 01829 770434
It might take some finding but this 300 year old half timbered pub's setting is known as the gem of Cheshire at the top of the rolling Peckforton Hills. The

owners' Highland cattle graze in adjacent fields. Beef is a speciality and all dishes are carefully prepared using fresh seasonal ingredients. Principal beers: Draft Bass, Stones, Caffreys, Guinness.

Directions From Chester A41 to Whitchurch, after 4m L to Burwardsley
Free House
Open 11.30-3 6.30-11
Bar food 12-2.30 7-9.30 Av main course £6.50
Restaurant 12-2.30 7-9.30 Av 3 course à la carte £15
Accommodation s£45 d£60

EATON Cheshire

Plough Inn Hotel
EATON Map 07 SJ86
Macclesfield Rd CW12 2NH
☎ 01260 280207
The Plough is a 17th-century, Grade II listed, timber-framed inn complete with ghost – the Lady in Grey. It is 5 minutes from the Peak National Park and has a warm, friendly atmosphere. The menu has French and traditional dishes like moules marinière, saumon aux crevettes, steak and old ale pie and Coronation chicken. Principal beers: Banks, Marstons.
Directions just off A536(Congleton to Macclesfield rd)
Free House
Open 12-2 6.30-11
Bar food 12-2 6.30-9.30 Av main course £7
Restaurant 12-3 7-11 Av 3 course à la carte £39.50 Av 3 course fixed price £39.50
Accommodation s£45 d£60

AA members can call AA Hotel Booking Service on 0990 050505 to book at AA recognised hotels and B & Bs in the UK and Ireland, or through our Internet site: http://www.theaa.co.uk/hotels

HANDLEY Cheshire

The Calveley Arms
HANDLEY Map 07 SU45
Whitchurch Rd CH3 9DT
☎ 01829 770619
Old coaching inn located in a quiet Cheshire village. Old beams and open fires provide the setting for bar meals which may include duck St Clements with caramelized fruits, escargots Bourguignons, wild boar with damson and juniper juice, or panfried monkfish with shallots, rosemary and white wine. Principal beers: Boddingtons, Burtonwood, Castle Eden.
Directions 4m S of Chester, take signposted turning then 300yds to pub
Free House
Open 12-3 5.30-11 (Sun 12-3, 7-10.30)
Bar food 12-2.30 6-9.30 Av main course £5.50

LITTLE BUDWORTH Cheshire

Shrewsbury Arms
LITTLE BUDWORTH Map 07 SJ56
Chester Rd, Little Budworth CW6 5EY ☎ 01829 760240
Retaining much of its original farmhouse atmosphere, this inn dates back 250 years, though it was much altered in Victorian times. Dishes range from rolls, sandwiches and jacket potatoes in the bar to restaurant specials such as duck a l'orange, smoked fish casserole and lamb rogan josh. Principal beers: Frederic Robinsons Best Bitter, Harthways Mild, Tennants Extra, Carling Black Label.
Directions S of A54 between Chester & Winsford
Robinson's
Open 11.30-3 6-11
Bar food 12-2 6-9.30 Av main course £5.25
Restaurant 12-2 6-9.30 Av 3 course à la carte £10 Av 3 course fixed price £5.65

MALPAS Cheshire

The Cholmondeley Arms
MALPAS Map 07 SJ44
SY14 8BT ☎ 01829 720382
Children are welcome at this converted village schoolhouse adjacent to the parks and gardens of Cholmondeley Castle. Home-made puddings are a speciality and a constantly changing menu may

contd.

also offer goat's cheese soufflé, rabbit braised with wine and Cholmondeley salmon fish cakes. Principal beers: Marstons, Boddingtons, Greene King IPA.
Directions on A49, between Whitchurch & Tarporley
Free House
Open 11-3 6.30-11
Accommodation s£32 d£38

OVER PEOVER Cheshire

The Dog Inn
OVER PEOVER Map 07 SJ77
Well-Bank Ln WA16 8UP
☎ 01625 861421
An old world pub in a pretty village setting in the heart of the Cheshire countryside. The food, served in hearty portions, is popular with a clientele from a 40-mile radius. Dishes include black pudding, roast beef and Yorkshire pudding, poached salmon in cucumber sauce, and home-made fruit pies. Principal beers: Tetley bitter, Boddingtons, Flowers IPA, Addlestones Cider.
Directions From Knutsford take A50 south.Turn L at 'The Whipping Stocks'.Pub in 2m
Free House
Open 11-3 5.30-11 (Sun 12-3,7-10.30)
Bar food 12-2.30 6.30-9 Av main course £7.95
Accommodation d£57.50

Ye Olde Parkgate Inn
OVER PEOVER Map 07 SJ77
Stocks Ln WA16 8TU ☎ 01625 861455
Ivy covered village pub offering traditional home cooking. Menu may include prawns Waldorf, rainbow trout with almonds and dry sherry, black pudding with garlic butter and fried potato wedges, or chicken breast with orange sauce. Parkgate "pie of the day" and "roast of the day" are also available. Principal beers: Samuel Smiths.
Directions A50 from Knutsford. Inn 3m on L after Radbroke Hall
Samuel Smith
Open 11-11 (Sun 12-10.30)
Bar food 12-2 6.30-9.30 Av main course £5.50

AA members can call AA Hotel Booking Service on 0990 050505 to book at AA recognised hotels and B & Bs in the UK and Ireland, or through our Internet site: http://www.theaa.co.uk/hotels

PENKETH Cheshire

The Ferry Tavern
PENKETH Map 07 SJ58
Station Rd WA5 2UJ
☎ 01925 791117 791116
A 17th-century inn that lays claim to being the home of the original "ferry 'cross the Mersey". Children, walkers and horse riders are well catered for, while the restaurant menu may feature grilled black pudding topped with Stilton, Cumberland sausage "imported" from Cumbria, and Barbary duck breast tagliatelle. Principal beers: Directors, Ruddles, Pedigree, Websters.
Directions A57 - A562, Fiddler's Ferry signposted
Free House
Open 12-2 5.30-11
Bar food 12-2 6-7.30 Av main course £5
Restaurant 12-2 6-9 Av 3 course à la carte £10

POTT SHRIGLEY Cheshire

The Cheshire Hunt
POTT SHRIGLEY Map 07 SJ97
1 Hedgerow, Spuley Ln SK10 5DA
☎ 01625 573185
A regular meeting place for the North East Cheshire Hunt, this village inn is situated in the Peak District National Park. There is a daily varied specials board and a bar meal may include Cheshire Hunt pâté, mushroom and nut fettucini or Bollington's Own black pudding. Principal beers: Boddingtons, Marstons, Bass, Carlsberg.
Free House
Open 12-3 5.30-11
Bar food 12-2.30 7-10 Av main course £5.50
Restaurant 12-2.30 7-10 Av 3 course à la carte £16

PRESTBURY Cheshire

The Legh Arms & Black Boy Restaurant
PRESTBURY Map 07 SJ87
SK10 4DG ☎ 01625 829130
Centrally located in historic Prestbury village, this 15th-century pub and restaurant takes pride in catering for special occasions. An extensive menu may include thinly sliced panfried calves

liver, wild duckling braised in Clementine and Grand Marnier, or spinach and mushroom roulade in puff pastry. A wide choice of speciality coffees is also available. Principal beers: Frederic Robinsons.

Directions From M6 thru Knutsford to Macclesfield, turn to Prestbury at Broken Cross. Pub in village centre

Robinson's

Open 8-12

Bar food 12-2 7-10 Av main course £5.50

Restaurant 12-2 7-10 Av 3 course à la carte £10.95 Av 3 course fixed price £10.95

SMALLWOOD Cheshire

The Bulls Head

SMALLWOOD Map 07 SJ86

Newcastle Rd CW11 0TY

☎ 01477 500247

Traditional coaching inn with award winning garden. A good selection of snacks and light meals is available. Typical main course dishes include Japanese prawn platter, poached salmon with champagne or Hollandaise sauce, Alabama chilli, and Somerset pork with cream, cider and mustard. Principal beers: Tetleys Bitter, Marstons Pedigree, Guinness, Carlsberg.

Directions From M6 J17 follow signs for Congleton.At traffic lights turn R onto A5. Pub is 1.5m on L.

Ansells

Open 11.30-3 6.30-11

Bar food 12-2 6.30-10 Av main course £6.50

Restaurant 12-2 6.30-10 Av 3 course à la carte £11

SWETTENHAM Cheshire

The Swettenham Arms

SWETTENHAM Map 07 SJ86

CW12 2LF ☎ 01477 571284

A heavily timbered 17th-century pub, tucked behind the parish church, and surrounded by delightful gardens. The varied and creative menu specialises in old English cooking using the freshest local produce. Dishes include casserole of rabbit and pot-roast spring chicken. Principal beers: Thomas Greenall Original, Irish Kilkenny, Tetley bitter, Guinness.

Directions M6 J18 to Holmes Chapel, then A535 towards Jodrell Bank. 3m take rd on R (Forty Acre Lane) to Swettenham

Free House

Open 11-3 (Sun 12-3) 6-11 (Sun 7-10.30)

Restaurant 12-2.30 7-9.30 Av 3 course à la carte £15

TUSHINGHAM CUM GRINDLEY Cheshire

Blue Bell Inn

TUSHINGHAM CUM GRINDLEY Map 07 SJ54

SY13 4QS ☎ 01948 662172

Built as a coaching inn in 1667, this is a very friendly pub with a three-piece suite in the bar from where conversation flows. Once haunted by a duck (killed by its owner, the landlord), this particular bird does not appear on the menu! But steaks, scampi, rainbow trout, Cumberland sausage and smoked mussels do. Principal beers: Hanby Ales "Drawwell".

Directions On the A49 N of Whitchurch

Free House

Open 12-3 6-11

Restaurant 12-3 6-11 Av 3 course à la carte £8.50

WARMINGHAM Cheshire

The Bears Paw Hotel

WARMINGHAM Map 07 SJ76

School Ln CW11 9QN

☎ 01270 526317

Country hotel close to the River Wheelock. Luncheon menu ranges from lamb cutlets with redcurrant and rosemary sauce, and chicken breast wrapped in smoked bacon with Stilton and port sauce, to broccoli and cauliflower bake for vegetarians. Seafood dishes include grilled halibut fillets with lemon, prawns and almonds. Principal beers: Flowers IPA, London Pride, Old Speckled Hen, Pedigree.

Directions From M6 J18 take A54 then A533 towards Sandbach. Follow signs for village

Free House

Open 11-11 (Sun 12-10.30)

Bar food 12-2 6-9.30 Av main course £5.25

Restaurant 12-2 7-12 Av 3 course à la carte £15 Av 4 course fixed price £14

Accommodation s£50 d£66

WILDBOARCLOUGH Cheshire

Cat & Fiddle
WILDBOARCLOUGH Map 07 SJ96
Buxton Rd SK11 0AR ☎ 01298 23364
This 19th-century inn located on the Cheshire plain, is the second highest in England at 1,690 feet above sea level. Good views of Jodrell Bank and the Mersey estuary. Bar menu includes tagliatelle, jacket potatoes, sandwiches, salads, and seafood platter. Principal beers: Frederic Robinson.
Directions On the A537 between Macclesfield & Buxton
Robinson's
Open 11-3 6.30-11
Bar food 11.30-2.30 7-9.30 Av main course £5.50

WINCLE Cheshire

The Ship Inn
WINCLE Map 07 SJ96
SK11 0QE ☎ 01260 227217
The ship on the sign is the Nimrod, used by Shackleton on an Antarctic expedition, but the ice has already been broken in this redstone pub, which is reputedly the oldest licensed premises in Cheshire. This is a good area for walking, and the bar offers a regularly varied blackboard menu. Principal beers: Boddingtons.
Directions Leave A54 at Fourways Motel Crossroads, towards Danebridge, Ship 1/2m before bridge on L
Free House
Open 12-3 7-11
Bar food 12-2.30 7-9.30 Av main course £5

WYBUNBURY Cheshire

The Swan
WYBUNBURY Map 07 SJ64
Main Rd CW5 7NE
☎ 01270 841280
Registered as an alehouse in 1580, situated next to the church in the village centre. Main course includes a range of steak, poultry and seafood dishes, such as farmhouse grill, duckling with orange and Cointreau sauce, and rainbow trout with roasted almonds. Vegetarian options include mushroom and nut fettucine. Principal beers: Marstons, Boddingtons, Bass.
Directions M6 J16 towards Chester/Nantwich.Turn L at traffic lights in Wybunbury
Free House
Open 7-11
Bar food 12-3 6-9.30 Av main course £5.50
Restaurant 12-3 6-9.30 Av 3 course à la carte £15

Cumbria

AMBLESIDE Cumbria

Drunken Duck Inn
AMBLESIDE Map 07 NY30
Barngates LA22 0NG ☎ 015394 36347
Set in 60 private acres in the heart of Cumbria's scenic lakeland, this 16th-century inn has its own tarn and micro-brewery. A regularly changing menu may offer fennel, orange and butterbean bake, Moroccan lamb tagine, or chicken and tomato pie. Puddings are a speciality. Principal beers: Drunken Duck, Yates, Jennings.
Directions A592 from Kendal, follow signs for Hawkshead, 2 1/2m sign for inn on R, 1m up the hill
Free House
Open 11.30-3 6-11 (Sun 12-3, 6-10.30)
Bar food 12-2 6.30-9 Av main course £6.95
Restaurant 12-2 6.30-9 Av 3 course à la carte £16.50
Accommodation s£47.50 d£65

APPLEBY-IN-WESTMORLAND Cumbria

The Royal Oak Inn
APPLEBY-IN-WESTMORLAND Map 12 NY62
Bongate CA16 6UN ☎ 017683 51463
Situated in Bongate, the oldest part of historic Appleby-in-Westmorland, this welcoming and comfortable pub aims to make its guests feel relaxed. It is a

medieval coaching inn, and renowned for its food. Try Mrs Beaton's little brown shrimps, twice baked soufflé, Mrs Ewbank's Cumberland sausage or something from the blackboard. Principal beers: Yates Bitter, Black Sheep Bitter, Fraoch,Theakstons Best Bitter.
Directions M6 J38 take A66 east.Village on B6542 on R.
Free House
Open 11-3 6-11
Bar food 11-3 6-11
Restaurant 12-2 6.30-9
Accommodation s£30 d£60

ARMATHWAITE Cumbria

The Dukes Head Hotel
ARMATHWAITE Map 12 NY54
Front St CA4 9PB ☎ 016974 72226
Cumbrian village pub nestling in the Eden Valley, a location which offers a variety of diversions, including fishing, walking, bird watching and historical touring. A full menu includes "probably the best roast duckling in Cumbria", venison steak, grilled English sirloin steak, and poached plaice. Principal beers: Boddingtons, Tetleys, Whitbread.
Directions A6, take Armathwaite turning
Free House
Open 11-3 6-11
Bar food 12-2 6.30-9 Av main course £6
Restaurant 12 2 6.30-9 Av 3 course fixed price £7.75
Accommodation s£26 d£46

ASKHAM Cumbria

The Punchbowl Inn
ASKHAM Map 12 NY52
CA10 2PF ☎ 01931 712443
An easy-to-find haven, this 18th-century coaching inn on the village green offers the best in old world charm and hospitality. A light lunch could include salmon and prawn crust with main courses from a wide choice of interestingly named dishes such as Measand meatloaf. Principal beers: Castle Eden, Old Speckled Hen, Guinness, Murphys.
Directions From M6 N on A6 for 7m
Whitbread
Open 12-3 7-11
Bar food 12-2 6.30-9 Av main course £6
Accommodation s£19.50 d£39

BARBON Cumbria

The Barbon Inn
BARBON Map 07 SD68
LA6 2LJ ☎ 015242 76233
A 17th-century coaching inn, off the main road, nestling at the foot of the Yorkshire Dales. Bar food ranges from sandwiches to steak and kidney pie, and the set-price dinner menu might offer spiced pancakes with smoked haddock, and escalope of venison with wild mushrooms and cream. Principal beers: Theakstons.
Directions 3.5m N of Kirkby Lonsdale on A683
Free House
Open 12-3 6.30-11
Bar food 12-2 7-9 Av main course £5.50
Restaurant 12.30-1.30 7.30-9 Av 5 course fixed price £16.95
Accommodation s£32 d£55

BASSENTHWAITE Cumbria

The Pheasant
BASSENTHWAITE Map 11 NY23
CA13 9YE ☎ 017687 76234
A 16th-century inn near Bassenthwaite Lake with 60 acres of grounds running down to Thornthwaite Forest. Traditional English fare is offered in both the bar and restaurant, such as pork and ham pie; Cumberland sausage platter; trout with prawn and pesto sauce, or roast pork with sage and onion dressing. Principal beers: Scotch Bitter, Old Speckled Hen.
Directions A66 to Cockermouth, 8m N of Keswick on L
Free House
Open 11.30-2.30 5.30-10.30
Bar food 12-2 Av main course £6
Restaurant 12.30-2 7-8.30 Av 3 course à la carte £21 Av 4 course fixed price £21
Accommodation s£62 d£52

BEETHAM Cumbria

The Wheatsheaf Hotel
BEETHAM Map 07 SD47
LA7 7AZ ☎ 015395 62123
In the charming village of Beetham, the Wheatsheaf is close to the Lake District and Yorkshire Dales. The high-standard cuisine includes home-made hot pot with red cabbage, Cumberland sausage, crispy

contd.

roast duckling, and a sweet trolley. Principal beers: Boddingtons, Theakstons, Tetley.
Directions On A6 5m N of J35
Free House
Open 11-3 6-11 (Sun 12-3, 7-10.30)
Bar food 11.45-2 6-8.45 Av main course £4
Restaurant 12-1.15 7-8.45 Av 3 course à la carte £9.25
Accommodation s£30 d£40

BLENCOGO Cumbria

The New Inn
BLENCOGO Map 11 NY14
CA7 0BZ ☎ 016973 61091
A late Victorian sandstone pub, with an open fire and a friendly atmosphere, in a farming hamlet with fantastic views of the north Cumbrian fells. Dishes range from sandwiches to traditional roasts at lunchtime, with a more varied evening selection including tempting home-made sweets. Principal beers: Theakstons Bitter, Boddingtons Manchester Gold, Carlsberg Export, Castlemain 4X.
Directions Toward Wigton on B5305, then B5302 toward Silloth, after 4m Blencogo is signed on L
Free House
Open 12-3 7-11
Bar food 12-3 7-9 Av main course £9

BUTTERMERE Cumbria

Bridge Hotel
BUTTERMERE Map 11 NY11
CA13 9UZ ☎ 017687 70252
A perfect Lakeland retreat, standing next to an old packhorse bridge which in its day carried Wordsworth, Ruskin and Southey to marvel at the Buttermere fells and their twin lakes, this traditional 18th-century inn offers good food and a warm welcome, as well as accommodation. Principal beers: Carlsberg, Guinness, Tetley, Burtons.
Directions Take B5289 from Keswick
Free House
Open 10.30am-10.40pm
Bar food 12-2.30 6-9.30 Av main course £4.95
Restaurant 7-8.30 Av 5 course fixed price £19
Accommodation s£41 d£82

CANAL FOOT Cumbria

The Bay Horse Hotel and Restaurant
CANAL FOOT Map 07 SD37
LA12 9EL ☎ 01229 583972
Lying at the waters edge of the Leven Estuary, this 17th-century hotel and restaurant offers an impressive and imaginative menu which uses local produce wherever possible. There is also an informative and extensive wine list. Day cookery courses are available in the spring and autumn. Principal beers: Mitchell Best, Mitchell Lancaster.
Directions signed from Ulverston on A590
Free House
Open 7-11
Bar food 12-2 Av main course £8
Restaurant 12-1.30 7.30 Av 3 course à la carte £25 Av 3 course fixed price £15.75
Accommodation s£80 d£55

CARTMEL Cumbria

The Cavendish
CARTMEL Map 07 SD37
LA11 6QA ☎ 015395 36240
Cartmel's oldest hostelry, dating back 450 years, is situated within the village walls, and has its own micro-brewery. Pub lunches range from sandwiches through pasta to Cumbrian hot pot with local black pudding, and more formal meals are served in the restaurant, including fish, local venison and vegetarian dishes. Principal beers: Cartmel.
Directions M6 J36 take A590 follow signs for Cartmel.In village take 1st L
Free House
Open 11.30-11
Bar food 12-2.15 6-9.30 Av main course £5.40
Restaurant 12-2.15 6-9.30
Accommodation s£35 d£50

CASTERTON Cumbria

Pheasant Inn
CASTERTON Map 07 SD67

LA6 2RX ☎ 015242 71230

Situated between the Yorkshire Dales and the Lake District, this 18th-century coach house served briefly as the World War II headquarters of King Peter of Yugoslavia. A meal here may include oven-baked doctor fish, Loch Fyne mussels cooked in white wine, or Aberdeen Angus steak. Principal beers: Theakston, Bombardier, McEwans, Guinness.

Directions From M6, A65 7m, L onto A683 at Devils Bridge, 1m to Casterton

Free House

Open 11-3 6-11

Bar food 12-3 6.30-10

Restaurant 7-9 Av 3 course à la carte £17

Accommodation s£37.50 d£64

CROSTHWAITE Cumbria

The Punch Bowl
CROSTHWAITE Map 07 SD49

LA8 8HR ☎ 015395 68237

16th-century coaching inn offering superb views of the idyllic Lyth Valley. A varied menu may include aubergine and polenta with gorgonzola, fillet of salmon antiboise, roasted tuna steak, or roast leg of pork with fennel stuffing. Principal beers: Theakstons Best, Becks, Murphys.

Directions From M6, A590 then R onto A5074

Free House

Open 12-3 6-11.30

Restaurant 12-2 6-9 Av 3 course à la carte £25 Av 3 course fixed price £11.95

Accommodation s£45 d£50

AA members can call AA Hotel Booking Service on 0990 050505 to book at AA recognised hotels and B & Bs in the UK and Ireland, or through our Internet site: http://www.theaa.co.uk/hotels

DENT Cumbria

Sun Inn
DENT Map 07 SD78

Main St LA10 5QL ☎ 015396 25208

17th-century inn with original oak beams and open coal fire, situated in the centre of the village. A range of snacks is available such as deep fried Brie with cranberry sauce. Home-made main dishes typically include chicken curry, leek and mushroom pie, and vegetable lasagne. Principal beers: Dent Bitter, Kamikaze & T'Owd Tup Stout.

Directions From M6 through Sedburgh, Dent signed, 4 1/2m

Free House

Open 11-2.30 7-11 (wknds & summer 11-11, Sun 12-10.30)

Bar food 12-2 7-8.30 Av main course £4.90

Accommodation s£19.50 d£35

DOCKRAY Cumbria

The Royal Hotel
DOCKRAY Map 11 NY32

CA11 0JY ☎ 017684 82356

Royal because Mary Queen of Scots stayed here overnight, this 16th-century coaching inn is set amid Lakeland fells a mile from Ullswater. It has a friendly atmosphere with a blazing log fire in winter and a flagstone floor. House specialities include Cumberland sausage and Whitby scampi. Principal beers: Castle Eden, Boddingtons, Jennings, Others on rotation: Pedigree Old Speckled Hen.

Free House

Bar food 12-2.30 6-9 Av main course £5.75

Restaurant 12-2.30 6-9 Av 3 course à la carte £13

Accommodation s£27.50 d£55

ELTERWATER Cumbria

The Britannia Inn
ELTERWATER Map 07 NY30
LA22 9HP ☎ 015394 37210
Overlooking the village green in the unspoilt village of Elterwater in the Langdale Valley, this cosy traditional inn offers a dependable bar menu. A meal may include rainbow trout, chicken and asparagus lasagne, fillet of haddock in breadcrumbs, or home-made steak and mushroom pie.
Free House
Open 11-11
Bar food 12-2 6.30-9.30 Av main course £6.50
Accommodation s£19 d£38

ESKDALE GREEN Cumbria

Bower House Inn
ESKDALE GREEN Map 06 NY10
CA19 1TD ☎ 019467 23244
Set among the fells of the western lakeland, alongside the village cricket green, this traditional country pub offers an imaginative menu. A meal here may include roast duckling with black cherries, locally bagged pheasant with cranberries, or ostrich fillet with wild mushrooms and brandy sauce. Principal beers: Hartleys XB, Youngers Scotch, Theakstons best.
Free House
Open 11.30-2.30 5.30-11
Bar food 12-2 6.30-9.30 Av main course £5.50
Restaurant 7-10.30 Av 3 course à la carte £19.50

King George IV Inn
ESKDALE GREEN Map 06 NY10
CA19 1TS ☎ 019467 23262
In the heart of some of England's most spectacular scenery, this 'old world' pub may date back, in parts, to the Roman era. Theakston's Old Peculiar steak pie, grilled tuna with sauce Basquaise, or duck and onion pancakes may be on today's menu. Over 200 single malt whiskies also available. Principal beers: Theakston Best, Old Peculier, Cumberland Ale, Courage Directors.
Directions A590 to Greenodd, A5092 to Broughton-in-Furness then over Ulpha Fell
Free House
Open 11-3 6-11 (Sun 12-3, 7-10.30)
Bar food 12-2 6-9 Av main course £5.50
Restaurant 12-2 7-9 Av 3 course à la carte £15
Accommodation s£23 d£42

GRASMERE Cumbria

The Travellers Rest Inn
GRASMERE Map 11 NY30
LA23 9RR ☎ 015394 35604
A listed 16th-century coaching inn, with oak beams and inglenook fireplaces, surrounded by stunning views. Food ranges from sandwiches and cold platters to dishes such as moules marinière, steaks, and five-bean chilli. To finish there's apple cinnamon crumble or hot chocolate fudge cake. Principal beers: Jennings Mild, Jennings Bitter, Jennings Cumberland Ale, Sneck Lifter.
Directions From M6 take A591 to Grasmere, pub 1/2m N of Grasmere
Free House
Open 11-11 (Sun 12-10.30)
Bar food 12-3 6-9.30 Av main course £6
Accommodation s£16.95 d£33.90

HAVERTHWAITE Cumbria

Rusland Pool
HAVERTHWAITE Map 07 SD38
LA12 8AA ☎ 01229 861384
The river just 100m away gives its name to this traditional Lakeland coaching inn, which has recently been extensively refurbished. Food ranges from snacks, sandwiches and Cumbrian specialities to à la carte dishes such as salmon in a creamy white wine and herb sauce. Principal beers: Castle Eden, Flowers IPA, Boddingtons.
Directions M6 J36 take A590 towards Barrow-in-Furness
Free House
Open 11-11 (winter 11-3,6-11)
Accommodation s£30 d£30

HAWKSHEAD Cumbria

Queens Head Hotel
HAWKSHEAD Map 07 SD39
Main St LA22 0NS ☎ 015394 36271
A good choice of traditional English dishes is offered at this 16th-century black and white hotel. Seafood is a speciality, including smoked cod, halibut stuffed with salmon mousse, and crab and prawn thermidor. Also featured are local venison, pheasant and mallard. Panhagarty is just one of the vegetarian options. Principal beers: Hartleys XB, Frederics, Robinsons, Castlemaine.
Directions M6 J36 A590 to Newby Bridge. Take 2nd R, 8m to Hawkshead
Free House
Open 11-11
Bar food 12-2.30 6.15-9.30 Av main course £6.95
Restaurant 12-2.30 6.15-9.30 Av 3 course à la carte £15
Accommodation s£35 d£56

HEVERSHAM Cumbria

Blue Bell Hotel
HEVERSHAM Map 07 SD48
Princes Way LA7 7EE ☎ 015395 62018
Once the local vicarage, this hotel is full of period character. 'Light bites' include giant Yorkshire pudding with Cumberland sausage, and potato specials from around the world (with haggis, chilli and curry) as well as ploughman's and sandwiches. Typical table d'hôte dishes are steak, game pie and fresh fish.
Directions On A6 between Kendal & Milnthorpe
Free House
Open 7am-12midnight
Restaurant 12-2.30 7-9.30 Av 3 course à la carte £14 Av 5 course fixed price £18.95
Accommodation s£39.50 d£60

KENDAL Cumbria

Gateway Inn
KENDAL Map 07 SD59
Crook Rd LA8 8LX ☎ 01539 724187
Offering a warm welcome, the Gateway is so named as it is the 'gateway' to the Lake District and the Dales. It offers excellent home-cooked food, delightful views and log fires. The bar menu includes grilled gammon and scampi, and specials include roast pheasant in whisky, and leek and Stilton pie. Principal beers: Thwaites.
Directions From M6 J38 take A590/A591, follow signs for Windermere
Free House
Open 9-11
Bar food 12-2 6.30-9 Av main course £6.50
Restaurant 12-2 6.30-9 Av 3 course à la carte £15
Accommodation s£25 d£50

KIRKBY LONSDALE Cumbria

Snooty Fox Tavern
KIRKBY LONSDALE Map 07 SD67
Main St LA6 2AH ☎ 015242 71308
A listed Jacobean inn with a great atmosphere in the lovely old Westmorland town. Meals range from salads, jacket potatoes and filled baguettes to the inn's own recipe Cumberland sausage, poached turbot with cockles and clams in a Chardonnay sauce, and ragoût of Holker venison in a crisp pastry case. Principal beers: Timothy Taylors Landlord, Hartleys XB, Theakstons Best Bitter.
Directions M6 J36 take A65 tavern 6m
Free House
Open 11-11
Bar food 12-2.30 6.30-10 Av main course £5.95
Restaurant 12-2.30 6.30-10 Av 3 course à la carte £14
Accommodation s£30 d£46

The Sun Inn
KIRKBY LONSDALE Map 07 SD67
Market St LA6 2AU ☎ 015242 71965
Traditional pub food prepared from fresh produce is served in the bar at this 16th-century inn. The restaurant, 'Mad Carews' (from J Milton Hayes' well known poem) offers an extensive menu of dishes including steak, kidney and red wine pudding, Mongolian Surf 'n' Turf, vegetarian crêpe and Himalayan lamb.

contd.

Principal beers: Black Sheep, Dent, No 3, Boddingtons.

Directions From M6 J36 take A65
Free House
Open 11-11 (Sun 12-10.30)
Bar food 11-2 6-10 Av main course £5.25
Restaurant 7-10 Av 3 course à la carte £16
Accommodation s£22 d£44

Whoop Hall Inn
KIRKBY LONSDALE Map 07 SD67
Burrow with Burrow LA6 2HP
☎ 015242 71284
The ghost of a murdered coachman is a relic of this coaching inn's history, as are the oak beams and log fires. The restaurant, on four levels, offers a good choice, including half a roast duckling on an orange and lime reduction, and baked red mullet with tomato and basil cream sauce. Principal beers: Theakstons, Marstons Pedigree, Wadworths 6X, Boddingtons.
Free House
Open 7-12
Bar food 11.45-2.15 6-10 Av main course £5.50
Restaurant 11.45-2.15 6-10 Av 3 course à la carte £12
Accommodation s£49.50 d£65

LAZONBY Cumbria

Joiners Arms
LAZONBY Map 12 NY53
Townfoot CA10 1BL ☎ 01768 898728
18th-century village inn, formerly a farmhouse and barn, close to the River Eden with fine Pennine views. A selection of bar snacks and light meals is available. Main course menu includes home-made dishes such as steak and kidney pie, chicken and mushroom pie, and lasagne. Mushroom Stroganoff for vegetarians. Principal beers: Draught Bass, Draught Stones, Tennents, Worthington.
Directions Take A6 N to Plumpton, R to Lazonby
Free House
Open 12-3.30 6.30-11.30
Bar food 12-2 6.30-8.30 Av main course £5.25
Accommodation s£20 d£36

LITTLE LANGDALE Cumbria

Three Shires Inn
LITTLE LANGDALE Map 07 NY30
LA22 9NZ ☎ 015394 37215
19th-century slate-built Lakeland inn, situated at the meeting point of the old counties of Cumberland, Westmoreland and Lancashire. Dinner menu regulars are grey mullet grilled with chermoula and couscous, served with tomato and coriander sauce, and salmon with steamed leeks and ginger in an orange butter sauce. Principal beers: Websters Yorkshire, Ruddles County, Black Sheep, John Smiths Smooth.

Directions follow signs to Windermere, then Ambleside, from A593 3m W of Ambleside take small rd to R signed The Langdales
Free House
Bar food 12-2 6.30-9 Av main course £5.75
Restaurant 6.30-8.30 Av 3 course à la carte £11.25 Av 4 course fixed price £17.95
Accommodation s£25 d£50

MELMERBY Cumbria

The Shepherds Inn
MELMERBY Map 12 NY63
CA10 1HF ☎ 01768 881217
Built of local Lazonby sandstone, this 18th-century pub faces the village green at the foot of Hartside Pass, and has good

Pennine views. The home prepared food caters to all tastes, with dishes such as shepherd's pie, venison and Roquefort crumble and vegetable biryani. Principal beers: Jennings, Cumberland, Holts Traditional, Black Sheep Riggwelter.

Directions On A686 NE of Penrith
Free House
Open 10.30-11 (Sun 12-3) 6-11 (Sun 7-10.30)
Bar food 10.30-2.30 6-9.45 Av main course £6.50
Restaurant 10.30-2.30 6-9.45 Av 3 course à la carte £12.50

NEAR SAWREY Cumbria

Tower Banks Hotel
NEAR SAWREY Map 07 SD39
LA22 0LF ☎ 015394 36334
Featured in the Tale of Jemima Puddleduck, this is the pub next door to Beatrix Potter's house. Its beamed bar has high-backed settles on a rough slate floor and a log fire in winter. Home cooked dishes include Lakeland game pie, Esthwaite trout, and steaks from the grill. Principal beers: Theakstons Bitter, XB, Old Peculier.
Directions On B5285 SW of Windermere
Free House
Open 11-3 6-11
Bar food 12-2 6.30-9 Av main course £5
Restaurant 6.30-9
Accommodation s£33 d£45

NETHER WASDALE Cumbria

The Screes Hotel
NETHER WASDALE Map 06 NY10
CA20 1ET ☎ 019467 26262
Attracting walkers, climbers and townsfolk, this early 19th-century inn is set amid spectacular mountain scenery. Traditional and local dishes appear alongside an interesting selection of vegetarian meals. The range includes local rainbow trout, Cumberland sausage with black pudding and Mexican sweet potato galettes. Principal beers: Yates, Jennings, Theakston.
Directions E of A595 between Whitehaven & Ravenglass
Free House
Open 12-3 6-11
Bar food 6.30-9 Av main course £5
Accommodation s£25 d£40

OUTGATE Cumbria

Outgate Inn
OUTGATE Map 07 SD39
LA22 0NQ ☎ 015394 36413
Formerly a toll house, this 18th-century pub is situated between Lakes Windermere and Coniston. The specials menu offers chicken in red wine sauce, pork chops with apple and stuffing, as well as pies like chicken, ham and mushroom, and game. Well known for its traditional jazz on a Friday night. Principal beers: Hartleys XB, Robinsons Best Bitter, Fredricks.
Directions From M6, A684 to Kendal, A591 to Plumgarths, then B5284 to Outgate
Hartleys
Open 11-3 6-11
Bar food 12-2 6-9 Av main course £5.95
Accommodation d£25

RAVENSTONEDALE Cumbria

Black Swan Hotel
RAVENSTONEDALE Map 07 NY70
CA17 4NG ☎ 015396 23204
Built of Lakeland stone at the turn of the century, this comfortable hotel is in an old Westmorland village setting. Jack Thornley's award-winning black pudding comes grilled with a mild mustard sauce, followed perhaps by locally farmed

contd.

rainbow trout with fresh herbs and white wine. Principal beers: Jennings, Youngers, Mitchells, Black Sheep.
Directions M6 J38 take A685 E towards Brough
Free House
Open 8.30-11
Bar food 12-2 7-9.30 Av main course £6
Accommodation s£40 d£70

The Fat Lamb Country Inn
RAVENSTONEDALE Map 07 NY70
Crossbank CA17 4LL
☎ 015396 23242
Built in the mid 1600s as a farmworker's cottage, then extended to become a farm plus coaching stop and inn, the property has, this century, been variously derelict, a garage, a transport café and, since the mid 1970s, a country inn. Dishes range from cider baked ham to Cantonese chicken. Principal beers: Mitchells Original Bitter.
Directions On A683 between Sedburgh and Kirkby Stephen
Free House
Open 12-3.30 6-11.30
Bar food 12-2 6-9 Av main course £6
Restaurant 12-2 6-9 Av 3 course à la carte £14 Av 5 course fixed price £17
Accommodation s£32 d£56

SCALES Cumbria

White Horse Inn
SCALES Map 11 NY32
CA12 4SY ☎ 017687 79241
Built around 1650 as a farmhouse, this inn is situated on the lower slopes of Blencathra. Typical dishes are grilled black pudding with malt whisky and Cumberland mustard sauce; Borrowdale trout with capers, lemon and parsley sauce, and sticky toffee pudding served with cream or ice cream. Principal beers: Hesket Newmarket Blencathra, Jennings Best.
Directions Off A66 between Keswick & Penrith
Free House
Open 12-2.30 6.30-10.30
Bar food 12-2 6.45-9 Av main course £7.50

SEATHWAITE Cumbria

Newfield Inn
SEATHWAITE Map 07 SD29
LA20 6ED ☎ 01229 716208
Unspoilt sixteenth-century coaching inn in Wordsworth's favourite valley, a favourite of walkers, climbers and just plain strollers. Homely food comes in generous portions and takes in potted shrimps, soups, cold home-cooked ham, steak pie, Cumberland sausages, and Lancashire hotpot. Principal beers: Theakstons Best, XB, Old Peculier, Marstons Pedigree.

Directions A590 toward Barrow, then R onto A5092, A595, follow for 1m, R at Duddon Bridge, 6m to Seathwaite
Free House
Open 11-3 6-11.30 (Wknds 11-11.30)
Bar food 12-3 6-10 Av main course £4.95
Restaurant 12-3 6-10 Av 3 course à la carte £8.95

SEATOLLER Cumbria

The Yew Tree Country Restaurant
SEATOLLER Map 11 NY21
CA12 5XN ☎ 01768 777634
Originally two miners' cottages, dating from 1628, this inn retains many original features, complemented by displays of memorabilia. Local produce figures prominently, including duckling and pike from

Derwentwater, black pudding, and Cumberland sausage. Yew Tree apple cake and sticky toffee pudding are among the satisfying sweets. Principal beers: Jennings.
Directions M6 J40 A66 to Keswick. B5289.Restaurant 7m at foot of Honister Pass
Open 12-5 6.30-9.30
Bar food 12-2.30 6.30-9.30 Av main course £7.50
Restaurant 12-2.30 6.30-9.30 Av 3 course à la carte £15

THIRLSPOT Cumbria

The Kings Head
THIRLSPOT Map 11 NY31
CA12 4TN ☎ 017687 72393
Many attractive architectural features have been retained at this 17th-century former coaching inn, including oak beams, inglenooks, oak panelling and flagstone floors. The menu offers cold snacks as well as trout pâté, beefsteak and kidney pie, Thai green curry, and vegetable brochette. Principal beers: Theakstons XB, Jennings Bitter.
Directions From M6 take A66 to Keswick then A591, pub 4m S of Keswick
Free House
Open 11-11 (Sun 11-10.30)
Bar food 12-3 6-9.30 Av main course £6
Restaurant 12-3 7-9 Av 3 course à la carte £16.95 Av 4 course fixed price £16.95
Accommodation s£18.95 d£38

TROUTBECK Cumbria

Mortal Man Hotel
TROUTBECK Map 07 NY40
LA23 1PL ☎ 01539 433193
Tucked in the hamlet of Troutbeck beneath the fells and commanding wonderful views, this 300 year old inn acquired its name from the legendary giant buried in the hotel's foundations. A range of well presented dishes - roast lamb served with a redcurrant jelly tartlet - includes vegetarian specials. Principal beers: Theakston Best, Sally Birketts Ale, John Smiths, Guinness.
Directions 2 1/2m N of jct between A591 & A592, L at Troutbeck sign the R at T jct, Hotel 800yrds on R
Free House
Open 12-2.50 5.50-11.20
Bar food 12-1.50 6.30-9 Av main course £5.75
Restaurant 1-2 7.30-8 Av 5 course fixed price £21.50
Accommodation s£55 d£90

Queens Head Hotel
TROUTBECK Map 07 NY40
LA23 1PW ☎ 015394 32174
An Elizabethan pub in the Lake District countryside, with stone flagged floors, oak beams and a four-poster bar. The imaginative starters include game bortsch, and duck with parsnip chutney and spiced kumquats. Typical main dishes are roast venison with apricots, and lentil and pistachio nut loaf for vegetarians. Principal beers: Lancaster Bomber, Boddingtons, Tetleys, Stella.
Directions From M6 J36 take A590, A591 to Winderemere then N to Troutbeck
Free House
Open 11-11
Bar food 12-2 6.30-9 Av main course £8
Restaurant 6.30-9 Av 3 course à la carte £15
Accommodation s£40 d£60

ULVERSTON Cumbria

Royal Oak
ULVERSTON Map 07 SD27
Spark Bridge LA12 8BS
☎ 01229 861006
An early 19th-century inn with a large disused bobbin mill to the rear, situated in the Lake District National Park. Dishes range from filled rolls and beefburgers to steaks and Cumberland sausage from the grill, with other options such as home-made salmon and prawn pie and tortellini ricotta. Principal beers: Tetley, Boddingtons, Wadworths 6X.
Directions From Ulverston take A590 N.Village off A5092
Free House

contd.

Open 11-3 5.30-11
Bar food 12-2.30 6-9.30 Av main course £6.50

WASDALE HEAD Cumbria

Wasdale Head Inn
WASDALE HEAD Map 11 NY10
CA20 1EV ☎ 019467 26229
Located in spectacular and unspoilt Cumbrian mountain country, this inn was the birthplace of British climbing and is still the forward base of the Wasdale Mountain Rescue Team. Walkers are welcome, a full and varied bar menu is available, and beer festivals are regular events. Principal beers: Jennings, Yates, Wasdale, Black Sheep.
Free House
Open 11-11
Bar food 11-2.30 6-9.30 Av main course £5.50
Restaurant 7-9 Av 3 course à la carte £15.50 Av 3 course fixed price £15.50
Accommodation s£29 d£58

Co Durham

BARNARD CASTLE Co Durham

The Morritt Arms Hotel
BARNARD CASTLE Map 12 NZ01
Greta Bridge DU2 9SE
☎ 01833 627232
Traditional coaching inn hospitality is offered at this 17th-century hostelry, and the Dickens Bar is renowned for its 50-year-old mural of Pickwickian characters. Dishes include a vegetarian gnocchi Romana, char-grilled tuna steak with vegetables confit, and quick-fried medallions of beef with spring onions, ginger and black bean sauce. Principal beers: Landlord, Theakston, Tetley.
Directions 10m from A1/A66 Scotch Corner roundabout
Free House
Open Open all day
Bar food 12-3 6-9.30 Av main course £5.95
Restaurant 12-2 7-9.30 Av 3 course à la carte £16.95 Av 3 course fixed price £15.95
Accommodation s£45 d£70

COTHERSTONE Co Durham

The Fox and Hounds
COTHERSTONE Map 12 NZ01
DL12 9PF ☎ 01833 650241
Overlooking the village green, this 18th-century coaching inn is not more than a few yards from the River Tees. Diners can choose from a menu which may include tournedos Rossini, rack of Teesdale lamb, Cumberland sausage Yorkshire pudding, or braised beef in Guinness. Principal beers: Hambleton, White Boar, Caffreys.
Directions From A66, turn onto B6277, Cotherstone signposted
Free House
Open 11-3 6-11.30
Bar food 11-3 6-11.30 Av main course £6
Restaurant 11.30-3 6-11.30 Av 3 course à la carte £20
Accommodation s£37 d£50

DURHAM Co Durham

The Three Horse Shoes Inn
DURHAM Map 12 NZ24
'Running Waters', Sherburn House
DH1 2SR ☎ 0191 3720286
A comfortable old country inn, which prides itself on its food and well stocked cellar. Starters include a seafood platter, paté and garlic mushrooms, while main courses offer a range of salads and steaks, and dishes such as gammon and pineapple, steak and kidney pie, or scampi with tartare sauce.
Directions A177, turn R onto B-road, then R onto A181, inn 1/2 on R
Free House
Open 11.30-2.30 6.30-11
Bar food 11.30-1.45 6.30-10.45 Av main course £4.50
Restaurant 11.30-1.45 6.30-10.45 Av 3 course à la carte £7 Av 4 course fixed price £6.25
Accommodation s£30 d£36

ELWICK Co Durham

The McOrville Inn
ELWICK Map 08 NZ43
34 The Green TS27 3EF
☎ 01429 273344
Noted for its friendly atmosphere, 'The Mac' is situated overlooking the green in a pretty village setting. Traditional home-cooked food is served in generous portions, ranging from burgers, platters and pies in the bar to chops, steaks and giant cod in

the restaurant, with specials such as Thai curry. Principal beers: Castle Eden Ale, Black Sheep, Heineken, Stella Artois.

Directions 1/4m from A19
Whitbread
Open 11-3 5.30-11
Bar food 12-2 5.30-8.30 Av main course £4.50
Restaurant 5.30-8.30 Av 3 course à la carte £12

MIDDLETON IN TEESDALE Co Durham

The Teesdale Hotel

MIDDLETON IN TEESDALE Map 12 NY92

Market Square DL12 0QG ☎ 01833 640264

In the heart of the High Pennines this 17th-century coaching inn has been tastefully modernised, yet retains much traditional charm. A full menu may offer spaghetti Milanese, spinach noodles Napolitaine, pork and capsicum chilli, or fillet of trout with breadcrumbs and almonds. Principal beers: Burtons, Guinness, Caulders Cream.
Free House
Restaurant 12-2 7.30-8.30 Av 4 course fixed price £19.95
Accommodation s£38.50 d£50

ROMALDKIRK Co Durham

Rose and Crown

ROMALDKIRK Map 12 NY92

DL12 9EB ☎ 01883 650213

Built in 1733, this typical old coaching inn sits on the Green next to the church. Home-made soup and Greenland prawns appear among the starters, followed perhaps by steak and kidney pie, or char-grilled chicken breast with tomato sauce and fresh pasta. Steamed puddings and trifle are among the traditional desserts. Principal beers: Theakstons Best, Marstons Pedigree.

Directions 6m NW from Barnard Castle on the B6277
Free House
Open 11.30-3 5.30-11
Bar food 12-1.30 6.30-9.30
Restaurant 12-1.30 7.30-9
Accommodation s£58 d£80

SEDGEFIELD Co Durham

The Dun Cow Inn & Restaurant

SEDGEFIELD Map 08 MZ32

43 Front St TS21 3AT
☎ 01740 620894 620895

In the centre of the village by the church, this historic inn serves food in both bars and the beamed restaurant. The bar menu includes jacket potatoes, hot filled baguettes, and dishes such as chicken curry, while the restaurant offers roast Northumbrian lamb, steaks, and pan-fried breast of wood pigeon. Principal beers: Scottish & Newcastle, Becks, Theakstons.
Directions A689 towards Teesdale, L at 1st roundabout into village, R down main st. 150yrds on L
Free House
Open 11-3 6-11
Bar food 12-2 6.30-10
Restaurant 12-2 6.30-10
Accommodation s£25 d£40

Greater Manchester

ASHTON-UNDER-LYNE Greater Manchester

The Station

ASHTON-UNDER-LYNE Map 07 SJ99

2 Warrington St OL6 6XB
☎ 0161 3306776 3437778

Built in 1845 to serve the then new railway, the Station has a collection of 'railwayana' and hosts three or four beer festivals a year. Typical menu includes seafood pie, Lancashire hot pot,

contd.

asparagus and Stilton quiche, and beef and Guinness stew. Principal beers: Boddingtons, Marstons Pedigree.
Directions A627
Free House
Open 11.30-11 (Sat 11.30-3, 7-11, Sun 12-2, 7-10.30)

BAMFORD Greater Manchester

Egerton Arms
BAMFORD Map 07 SD81
Ashworth Rd OL11 5UP
☎ 01706 46183
Known locally as the Chapel House and reputedly over five centuries old. Ask to hear the tale of Margaret, the friendly ghost, while perusing a menu of wholesome, traditional fare with some continental and Asian dishes such as Karachi kidneys, pork Madagascar or pasta al tonno. Principal beers: Websters, Theakstons.
Directions Bamford on B6222
Free House
Open 12-3 6-10.30 (Sun 12-9)
Bar food 12-2.30 6-9 Av main course £4.50
Restaurant 12-6 6-10.30 Av 3 course à la carte £15 Av 3 course fixed price £12.95

DELPH Greater Manchester

Green Ash Hotel
DELPH Map 07 SO90
New Tame OL3 5TS ☎ 01457 871035
There's quite a history to this listed stone building. It dates from 1800 and was a Co-op from 1888 to 1954. Restored from dereliction is was converted into a hotel in 1988. Food ranges between carvery lunches, a French-style à la carte and an international bistro selection. Principal beers: Tetley,McGuiness,Bass.
Directions Just off A670 NE of Oldham
Free House
Restaurant 12.30-2.30 7-10 Av 3 course à la carte £20 Av 4 course fixed price £15.95
Accommodation s£20 d£39.50

DIDSBURY Greater Manchester

The Woodstock Tavern
DIDSBURY Map 07 SJ89
139 Barlow Moor Rd M20 2DY
☎ 0161 4453317
Woodstock is a large Victorian house converted into a tavern four years ago. The menu ranges from traditional to more exotic fare, with an emphasis on fresh fish, spicy foods and vegetarian dishes. Examples are char-grilled wild boar steak, seafood gumbo, and chilli rellenos on Mexican rice. Principal beers: Staropramen, Worthingston, Bass, Grolsch.
Directions From end of dual carriageway turn R at traffic lights) 0.5m on R
Bass
Open 12-11 (Sun 12-10.30)
Bar food 12-8.30 12-8.30 Av main course £4.50

DIGGLE Greater Manchester

The Diggle Hotel
DIGGLE Map 07 SE00
Stationhouses OL3 5JZ
☎ 01457 872741
This family run free house in a picturesque hamlet, surrounded by lovely views, features beamed ceilings and a cosy, friendly atmosphere. The home-made menu caters for every appetite from a light snack, Chef's soup of the day, to 'Jaw's , a 'whopping' battered haddock to satisfy the really hungry. Principal beers: Boddingtons, Oldham Bitter, Flowers, Chesters Mild.
Directions off the A670 between Oldham & Huddersfield
Free House
Open 12-3 5-11
Bar food 12-2.15 5-10 Av main course £4.60
Accommodation s£25 d£35

MANCHESTER Greater Manchester

Dukes 92
MANCHESTER Map 07 SJ89
14 Castle St, Castlefield M3 4LZ
☎ 0161 8398646
Converted from old stables, this stylish canal-side pub is by the 'Dukes Lock', the 92nd on the Rochdale canal (hence the name). It offers a snack menu with over 50 European cheeses and 10 patés served with fresh granary bread. Many of the cheeses and two of the patés are vegetarian. Principal beers: Hop Garden, Timothy Taylor Landlord, Boddingtons Bitter.
Directions Town centre
Free House
Open 11.30-11

Mash & Air
MANCHESTER Map 07 SJ89
40 Chorlton St M1 3HW
☎ 0161 6616161
Two eating experiences are on offer here: Mash, a brasserie, and Air, an à la carte restaurant. 'Mash' is the first stage in the brewing process, which is a feature of the complex. The 'Mash' menu offers tomato risotto fritters and ravioli of seared salmon, while 'Air' includes terrine of char-grilled vegetables, and Orkney scallops. Principal beers: Own brew.
Directions City centre
Free House
Open 12-12 (Mon-Wed) 12-1am (Thu-Sat/Sun last orders 10.30)
Bar food 12-12 12-12 Av main course £7
Restaurant 12-3 6-11 Av 3 course à la carte £25

The White Lion
MANCHESTER Map 07 SJ89
43 Liverpool Rd, Castlefield M3 4NQ
☎ 0161 8327373
One of the oldest licensed premises in Manchester, the White Lion is adjacent to Castlefield's historic roman fort and the Granada Studios – watch out for television celebrities enjoying a pint. The menu covers light lunches to main courses such as mushroom Stroganoff. There is live jazz on some evenings.
Free House
Open 11-11
Bar food 12-10 6-10 Av main course £4.50

MOSSLEY Greater Manchester

Woodern Tavern
MOSSLEY Map 07 SD90
Manchester Rd OL5 9AY
☎ 01457 833133
The Woodend has open fires and is said to be haunted (there are many tales apparently!). Try the Woodend Sandwich, a slice of topside with fried onions and mushrooms, topped with melted cheddar, and served with chips. Other dishes are steak and kidney pie, chilli con carne, and cheese and broccoli bake. Principal beers: Marstons.
Free House
Open 12-11
Bar food 12-2 5.30-8.30 Av main course £3.95
Restaurant 12-2 5.30-8.30 Av 3 course à la carte £10

OLDHAM Greater Manchester

The Roebuck Inn
OLDHAM Map 07 SD90
Brighton Rd, Strinesdale OL4 3RB
☎ 0161 624 7819
Situated at the edge of Saddleworth Moor, this inn dates back to the 18th-century with a name derived from the reddish colour of the brook which runs underneath it. Bar snacks and a selection of steak meals are available, including tournedos Rossini, with mushroom Stroganoff for vegetarians. Principal beers: Oldham Brewery, Boddingtons Gold, Boddingtons.
Directions From Oldham take A62 then A672 towards Ripponden. 1m turn R at petrol station into Turf Pit Lane. Pub 1m.
Free House
Open 12-3 6-12
Bar food 12-3 6-10 Av main course £5
Restaurant 12-3 6-10 Av 3 course à la carte £12

The White Hart Inn
OLDHAM Map 07 SD90
Stock Port Rd, Lydgate OL4 4JJ
☎ 01457 872566
Priding itself on its quality food, wine and service, this 200-year-old inn offers both informal brasserie meals and fine dining. Bread is freshly baked on the premises and dishes range from local sausage of chicken and black pudding to fillet of seabass and salmon with lemon grass and bean sprouts. Principal beers: JW Lees, Webster Green Label, IPA Flowers, Boddingtons.
Directions From Manchester, A62 to Oldham, R onto bypass, A669 to Lees, Inn 2-3m after Grotton
Free House
Open 12-12
Bar food 12-2.30 6-9.30 Av main course £9.50
Restaurant 12-2.30 7-9.30 Av 3 course à la carte £23 Av 3 course fixed price £23
Accommodation s£50 d£55

AA members can call AA Hotel Booking Service on 0990 050505 to book at AA recognised hotels and B & Bs in the UK and Ireland, or through our Internet site: http://www.theaa.co.uk/hotels

Lancashire

BELMONT Lancashire

Black Dog
BELMONT Map 07 SD61
2/4 Church St BL7 8AB
☎ 01204 811218
A typical moorland village pub, dating from 1750, with its own courthouse with the original seats still in situ. Dishes range from home-made pizzas to fillet of red salmon in lobster sauce, or chicken tikka masala to venison steak in red wine sauce. Principal beers: Joseph Holt.
Free House
Open 12-4 7-11
Bar food 12-2 7-9 Av main course £4
Accommodation s£29.50 d£38

BILSBORROW Lancashire

Owd Nell's Tavern
BILSBORROW Map 07 SD53
Guy's Thatched Hamlet, Canal Side PR3 0RS ☎ 01995 640010
A flagged-floored, thatched, canal-side tavern offering a wide range of popular home-made fare. The jocular menu includes chip butties, spicy buffalo wings with (hot) dead parrot dip, Morecambe Bay potted shrimps, beef burgers, steak and kidney pudding, and barbecued chicken, plus a 'don't dessert me' chocoholic cheesecake. Principal beers: Thwaites, Chesters, Jennings, Bass.
Free House
Open 7.30-11 (Mon-Sat) 8-10.30 (Sun)
Bar food 11-4 4-11 Av main course £5
Restaurant 12-2.30 5.30-11 Av 3 course à la carte £12

BLACKBURN Lancashire

Millstone Hotel
BLACKBURN Map 07 SD62
Church Ln, Mellor BB2 7JR
☎ 01254 813333
There's quite a history to this 17th-century former farm and ale house, situated next to the village church. The diverse modern menu offers dishes as diverse as lamb balti and bangers and mash; and puddings ranging from Grand Marnier chocolate mousse to home-made sticky toffee pudding. Principal beers: Thwaites Bitter, Mild, Premium Smooth, Guinness.
Free House
Open 12-2 7-11 (Sun 7-10.30)
Bar food 12-2 7-9
Restaurant 12-2 7-9.30 Av 3 course fixed price £21
Accommodation s£49 d£58

BLACKO Lancashire

Moorcock Inn
BLACKO Map 07 SD84
Gisburn Rd BB9 6NF
☎ 01282 614186
The Moorcock is an old moorland inn and former farmhouse, with log fires providing a warm welcome in winter. 'Old fashioned English cooking', with some continental dishes is offered in the bar and restaurant, such as gammon steak with eggs or pineapple and lasagne Bolognese. Principal beers: Daniel Thwaites Bitter and Mild, Carling, Carlsberg.
Free House
Open 12-2.30 6-10
Bar food 12-2 6.30-10 Av main course £5
Restaurant 12-2 6.30-10
Accommodation s£15 d£30

CLITHEROE Lancashire

Assheton Arms
CLITHEROE Map 07 SO74
Downham BB7 4BJ
☎ 01200 441227
Beams, a large stone fireplace and traditional decor characterise this 17th-century pub. The food is cooked to order and seafood specialities are always available. The menu offers a wide choice from a ploughman's lunch to poached salmon with prawn and cucumber sauce or beef oriental with ginger and spring

onions. Principal beers: Boddingtons bitter, Flowers Original.
Whitbread
Open 12-3 7-11
Bar food 12-3 7-11 Av main course £7

DARWEN Lancashire

Old Rosins Inn
DARWEN Map 07 SD62
Treacle Row, Pickup Bank, Hoddlesden BB3 3QD ☎ 01254 771264
A country inn with panoramic views of the West Pennines, Old Rosins is only 15 minutes' drive from several major towns. Traditional home-made fare is served, including chicken and ham pie, freshly battered cod, and beef cooked in Old Peculier. Principal beers: Old Peculier, Flowers, Martons, Boddingtons.
Free House
Open 11.25-11.30
Restaurant 7-10 Av 3 course à la carte £16 Av 4 course fixed price £14.95
Accommodation s£39.50 d£49.50

FENCE Lancashire

The Forest Inn
FENCE Map 07 SD83
Cuckstool Ln BB12 9PA
☎ 01282 613641
Former farmhouse situated in Cuckstool Lane, so-called because of the ducking stool used there during the witch trials. The blackboard menu offers a daily choice of specials. Main courses typically include Indonesian chicken satay, Scottish salmon, and baked stuffed mushrooms and tomatoes with pine nut pesto and shallot confit. Principal beers: Theakstons, XB, Mild,Worthington.
Directions From M65 J13 take A6068 towards Padiham. Turn L after 1.5m onto B6248. Pub 300m on R
Free House
Open 12-11 (Sun 12-10.30)
Bar food 12-2.30 5.30-9.30
Restaurant 12-2.30 5.30-9.30

GALGATE Lancashire

The Stork Hotel
GALGATE Map 07 SD45
Conder Green LA2 0AN
☎ 01524 751234
Situated on the River Conder, the Stork has been a public house, under various names, since the mid-17th century. The menu ranges from traditional pub fare such as toasties and baked potatoes, to quail with apricot and Stilton stuffing, baked monkfish steak, and crocodile in lime, coriander, and vermouth sauce. Principal beers: Boddingtons, Tetleys, Carlsberg.
Directions M6 J33 take A6 north. At Galgate turn L & next L to Conder Green
Free House
Open 11-11 (Sun 12-10.30)
Bar food 12-2.30 6.30-9 Av main course £5
Accommodation s£22.50 d£36

GOOSNARGH Lancashire

Ye Horns Inn
GOOSNARGH Map 07 SD53
Horns Ln PR3 2FJ ☎ 01772 865230
The character of this coaching inn, which dates from 1782, has hardly changed over the years. Its location is rural, two miles from the nearest village, and it has a unique bar that customers can 'sit behind'. Traditional English dishes are served including roast duckling and sticky toffee pudding. Principal beers: Tetley Bitter, Boddingtons Bitter.
Directions From M6 J32 take A6 N.At traffic lights turn R onto B5269.In Goosnargh follow Inn signs
Free House
Open 12-3 6.30-11
Bar food 12-2 7-9.30 Av main course £6.50
Restaurant 12-2 7-9.30 Av 3 course à la carte £12 Av 5 course fixed price £15.50
Accommodation s£45 d£70

HESKIN GREEN Lancashire

Farmers Arms
HESKIN GREEN Map 07 SD51
85 Wood Ln PR7 5NP
☎ 01257 451276
Rumoured to be haunted by the ghost of a young boxer, killed during a match held in the attic above the stables, this pretty country inn offers a wide range of food, from salads and sandwiches to steaks and fresh fish dishes. Principal beers: Boddingtons, Castle Eden, Flowers, Speckled Hen.
Directions on the B5250 between the M6 and Eccleston
Free House
Open 12-11.30

LANCASTER Lancashire

Farmhouse Tavern
LANCASTER Map 07 SD46
Morecambe Rd LA1 5TB
☎ 01524 69255
At this homely farmhouse with historic connections, reputed to boast a tunnel leading to Lancaster Castle, Stephen and Diane Hunt offer a friendly atmosphere and plenty of activities for children. Good selection of straightforward fare is offered with traditional roasts on Sundays. Principal beers: Boddingtons, Guinness, Heineken, Stella.
Free House
Open 11-10 (Sun 12-10.30)
Accommodation s£37 d£49

MERECLOUGH Lancashire

Kettledrum Inn & Restaurant
MERECLOUGH Map 07 SD83
302 Red Lees Rd BB10 4RG
☎ 01282 424591
Named after the 1861 Derby winner (who won £160 for the Pope!), this country inn and restaurant offers fine views of the Pendle Hills. Today's menu may feature 'Dracula's Nightmare' - mushrooms in garlic, poached Speyside salmon, lamb cutlets, Highlander's game pie, or spinach and ricotta cannelloni. Principal beers: John Smiths, Theakstons, Tetleys, Masseys.
Directions from Burnley town centre, past Burnley FC, 2 1/2m, 1st pub on L
Free House
Open 11.30-3 5.30-11 (Summer & Sun 11.30-11)
Bar food 12-2.30 6-9.30
Restaurant 12-2.30 6-9.30 Av 3 course à la carte £11.50

PARBOLD Lancashire

The Eagle & Child
PARBOLD Map 07 SD41
Maltkiln Ln, Bisham Green L40 3SG
☎ 01257 462297
Situated on the village green, this brick-built early 18th-century inn is furnished with antiques and large oak tables. The best local ingredients are used in a variety of dishes, such as steak in real ale pie, char-grilled chicken fillet, and roundels of monkfish with red pesto and pasta. Principal beers: Coachhouse Gunpowder Mild, Thwaites, Tim Taylors Landlord, Flowers.
Bisham Green
Open 12-3 5.30-11.30
Bar food 12-2 5.30-8.30 Av main course £7
Restaurant 12-2 5.30-8.30 Av 3 course à la carte £11

RIBCHESTER Lancashire

The White Bull
RIBCHESTER Map 07 SD63
Church St PR3 3XP ☎ 01254 878303
A listed building, older than its date stone of 1707, incorporating four Roman pillars from the Temple of Minerva. Food comprises a good choice of grills, steaks, seasonal salads and hot platters - the latter ranging from Principal beers: Flowers IPA, Boddingtons Mild, Boddingtons Bitter, Theakstons.
Whitbread
Open 11.30-3 6.30-11
Bar food 11.30-2 6.30-9.30 Av main course £5.50
Restaurant 11.30-2 6.30-9.30 Av 3 course à la carte £11

SHUTTLEWORTH Lancashire

The Fishermans Retreat
SHUTTLEWORTH Map 07 SD81
Twine Valley Park, Riding Head Ln, Turn-cum-Shuttleworth BL0 0HH
☎ 01706 825314
Family run for everyone's enjoyment, this down to earth establishment was built with stone from surrounding derelict mills. It is set in 30 acres on the West Pennine fringe, surrounded by trout lakes and running water. A wide variety of home-made meals is offered, including Twine Valley rainbow trout. Principal beers: Ruddles Best bitter, Ruddles County, John Smiths.
Directions On A56 N of Bury
Courage
Open 12-11

SLAIDBURN Lancashire

Hark to Bounty Inn
SLAIDBURN Map 07 SD75
BB7 3EP ☎ 01200 446246
Dating back to the 13th-century, this inn boasts its own court room. The story behind the name relates to the noise made by the local squire's favourite dog c1875. The menu offers traditional

favourites such as Cumberland sausage with apple sauce alongside some more adventurous dishes. Principal beers: Old Peculier, Theakstons Bitter, Mild, Becks.
Scottish & Newcastle
Open 11-11
Bar food 12-2 6.30-9 Av main course £5.75
Restaurant 12-2 6.30-9 Av 4 course fixed price £8.95
Accommodation s£24.75 d£49.50

WADDINGTON Lancashire

Lower Buck Inn
WADDINGTON Map 07 SD74
Church Rd BB7 3HU ☎ 01200 428705
The heart of the Ribble Valley is home to this small 18th century traditional country pub. A typical menu includes seafood platter, plaice stuffed with prawns, trout almonde, and a selection of sandwiches, omelettes, and jacket potatoes. The staff will also cook any meal requested with 24 hours prior notice. Principal beers: Timothy Taylor BB & Landlord.
Directions A59 signpost Waddington
Free House
Open 11-11 (Mon-Wed 11-3, Sun 12-10.25)
Bar food 12-3 6.30-10 Av main course £5
Restaurant 12-2.55 6.30-10 Av 3 course à la carte £12.50
Accommodation s£17.50 d£35

WHALLEY Lancashire

Freemasons Arms
WHALLEY Map 07 SD73
8 Vicarage Fold, Wiswell BB7 9DF
☎ 01254 822218
Originally three cottages, the building and interior of the pub remain largely unchanged, characterised by antique furniture, wooden beams and brass and copperware. The food is freshly cooked and offers a good choice of specials, fresh fish and meat dishes, including home-made steak and kidney plate pie, and seafood au gratin. Principal beers: Jennings beers, Belhaven mild, Carlsberg Export, Guinness.
Free House
Open 12-11
Bar food 12-3 6.30-11 Av main course £6.50
Restaurant 12-3 6.30-11 Av 3 course à la carte £14.75

WHITEWELL Lancashire

The Inn At Whitewell
WHITEWELL Map 07 SD64
Forest of Bowland BB7 3AT
☎ 01200 448222
An authentically old fashioned inn, with antiques and open fires, set by the River Hodder with dramatic views down the valley to the fells beyond. Classical British cooking from fresh ingredients results in dishes such as roast guinea fowl with a delicate lime gravy, and the best market fresh fish. Principal beers: Bentleys Bitter, Marstons Pedigree, Boddingtons, Stella Artois.
Free House
Open 7-12
Bar food 12-2 7.30-9.30 Av main course £7
Restaurant 7.30-9.30 Av 3 course à la carte £20
Accommodation s£49.50 d£63

WREA GREEN Lancashire

The Grapes Hotel
WREA GREEN Map 07 SD33
Station Rd PR4 2PH ☎ 01772 682927
The Grapes is the only pub in Wrea Green, which was voted Best Kept Village in Lancashire 1996. A selection from the Henry's Table menu may include butterfly chicken, lamb rogan josh, bangers and mash, plaice Neptune, or spinach and ricotta tortellini. Principal beers: Theakstons, Boddingtons.
Directions From M55 J3 follow signs for Kirkham then Wrea Green
Greenalls
Open 11-11
Bar food 12-2.30 5.30-10 Av main course £4.50
Restaurant 12-2.30 5.30-10 Av 3 course à la carte £10.50 Av 3 course fixed price £10.95

Merseyside

BARNSTON Merseyside

Fox and Hounds
BARNSTON Map 07 SJ28
Barnston Rd L61 1BW ☎ 0151 6487685
An original 20s-built pub, with a traditional bar and coal fires, enjoying a good local trade. Favourites, such as home-made soup, lasagne, quiche and

contd.

coronation chicken, are always available, other dishes - perhaps glazed supreme of salmon or Somerset pork chop - depend on the creative mood of the cook. Principal beers: Gillespies, Websters, Ruddles, Theakstons.
Free House
Open 11-11
Bar food 12-2 Av main course £5.25

LIVERPOOL Merseyside

Everyman Bistro
LIVERPOOL Map 07 SJ39
9 Hope St L1 9BH ☎ 0151 7089545
Beneath the Everyman theatre, this bistro is a popular city meeting place for all ages and backgrounds. Counter service offers salads, snacks, pizza, quiches and a selection of daily-changing specials from Italian meatballs to vegetarian and vegan dishes with home-made patisserie for pudding. Principal beers: Cains, Boddingtons, Stella Artois, Hoegaarden.
Directions Town centre. Bistro in basement of Everyman Theatre.
Open 10-midnight
Bar food 10-2 Av main course £3.50
Restaurant 12-12 12-12 Av 3 course à la carte £7.50

Northumberland

ALLENDALE Northumberland

Kings Head Hotel
ALLENDALE Map 12 NY85
Market Place NE47 9BD
☎ 01434 683681
Dating from 1776, the King's Head is the oldest inn in Allendale, situated in the centre of the North Dales village. The menu offers some interesting dishes including Northumbrian stottie cheese pizza (a hearty local delicacy), a feast of a mixed grill, and a good vegetarian selection, plus blackboard specials. Principal beers: Jennings Cumberland, Taylor Landlord, Theakstons Best Bitter.
Directions From Hexham take B6305/B6304/B6295
Free House
Open 11-11 (Sun 12-10.30)
Bar food 12-3.30 6.30-9.30 Av main course £4.95
Accommodation s£25 d£42

ALLENHEADS Northumberland

The Allenheads Inn
ALLENHEADS Map 12 NY84
NE47 9HJ ☎ 01434 685200
An eccentric and entertaining pub crammed full with an unbelievable amount of antiques and memorabilia. It was built in 1770 and is located high in the hills in a small Pennine village. Bar food includes traditional pies, lasagne, cod, and chilli, with several vegetarian options. Principal beers: Tetleys, Kilkenny, Calders.
Directions From Hexham take B6305 , then B6295 to Allenheads
Free House
Open 11-2.30 (Except Tue lunch in Winter) 7-11
Bar food 11-2 7-10 Av main course £4.50
Restaurant 7-9.30 Av 3 course à la carte £10
Accommodation s£25 d£43

ALNWICK Northumberland

Masons Arms
ALNWICK Map 12 NU11
Stamford, Rennington NE66 3RX
☎ 01665 577275
Family-run 18th-century coaching inn on the 'Great North Road', in the village of Alnwick, which is famous for its castle and

traditional character. A meal here may include Northumbrian game casserole, lentil and mushroom cannelloni, or a selection of steaks. Principal beers: Ruddles, Boddingtons, Theakstons.
Directions 3 1/2m from A1 on B1340
Free House
Open 12-2 6.30-11
Bar food 12-2 7-9 Av main course £6
Restaurant 12-2 7-9 Av 3 course fixed price £10
Accommodation d£24.50

BAMBURGH Northumberland

Victoria Hotel

BAMBURGH Map 12 NU13
Front St NE69 7BP ☎ 01668 214431
A recently refurbished Victorian hotel with a modern brasserie, situated on the Northumbrian coastline in a quiet village overlooking the village green and castle. Dishes include steak and kidney pudding and salmon and fennel fishcakes, followed perhaps by glazed lemon tart or bread and butter pudding. Principal beers: Theakstons Best, Ruddles, John Smiths, McEwans.
Directions Bamburgh approx 20m N of Alnwick
Free House
Open 10-11
Restaurant 8am-10pm 6-10
Accommodation s£30

BERWICK-UPON-TWEED Northumberland

Canty's Brig Riverside Bar & Bistro

BERWICK-UPON-TWEED Map 12 NT95
Paxton TD15 1SY ☎ 01289 386255
Canty's sits by the river Whiteadder on the Scotland-England border, and free trout fishing is available for customers. There is also a family room and a special play area for children. Canty's special seafood grill, baked Eyemouth sole, or Stilton and vegetable strudel may be on the menu. Principal beers: Broughton Brewery, Guinness, Carlsberg.
Directions 1m off Berwick bypass (A1) on B6461
Open 11.30-3 5.30-11.30
Bar food 12-3 6.30-9.30 Av main course £4.95
Restaurant 12-3 6.30-9.30 Av 3 course à la carte £15

The Rob Roy

BERWICK-UPON-TWEED Map 12 NT95
Dock Rd, Tweedmouth TD15 2BQ
☎ 01289 306428
There is a cosy, rustic atmosphere at this stone-built pub. The bar has a salmon fishing theme, appropriately enough, as seafood is the speciality of both the bar and restaurant, where lobster, oysters, crab, monkfish and salmon are served. Meat options, such as grilled border lamb, are also available. Principal beers: Tennants, Guinness.

Free House
Open 11.30-2.30 7-11
Bar food 12-2.30 7-9 Av main course £6.50
Restaurant 12-2 7-11.45 Av 3 course à la carte £20
Accommodation s£23 d£39

BLANCHLAND Northumberland

Lord Crewe Arms
BLANCHLAND Map 12 NY95
DH8 9SP ☎ 01434 675251
Thought to be one of the oldest inns in England in one of the prettiest villages. The Crypt Bar menu ranges through soup and prawn cocktail to smoked salmon salad, and wild boar and pheasant pie, with vegetarian dishes such as nut Wellington. There is also a formal restaurant. Principal beers: Vaux Samson, Double Daxin, Wards.
Directions Off A68 NW of Consett take B6278 then B6306
Free House
Open 11-3 7-11.30
Bar food 12-2 7-9 Av main course £5.50
Restaurant 7-9.15 Av 3 course à la carte £26
Accommodation s£80 d£110

CARTERWAY HEADS Northumberland

The Manor House Inn
CARTERWAY HEADS Map 12 NZ05
DH8 9LX ☎ 01207 255268
Converted 18th-century farmhouse, almost 1,000 feet above sea level on the edge of the North Pennines. Walkers and dogs are welcome, while children can expect an "amazing level of tolerance". The bar menu may offer monkfish, scallop and leek fettucine, roast venison steak, or spiced pork casserole. Principal beers: Big Lamp, Butterknowle.
Directions A69 W from Newcastle, L onto A68 then S for 8m. Inn is on L
Free House
Open 11-3 6-11
Bar food 12-2.30 7-9.30 Av main course £8
Restaurant 12-2.30 7-9.30 Av 3 course à la carte £14
Accommodation s£23 d£39.50

CHATTON Northumberland

The Percy Arms Hotel
CHATTON Map 12 NU02
Main Rd NE66 5PS ☎ 01668 215244
Set in the heart of rural Northumberland and originally built as a shooting lodge, the Percy Arms has been a pub since 1873. Game and vegetable pie, Grenada gammon, Aberdeen Angus steaks, or Norwegian prawn salad with Marie Rose sauce may be on the menu today. Principal beers: Theakstons,McEwans.
Directions From Alnwick take A1 north, then B6348 to Chatton
Free House
Open 11-3 6-11
Bar food 12-1.30 6.30-9.30 Av main course £6
Restaurant 6.30-9.30 Av 3 course à la carte £13
Accommodation s£15 d£20

CORBRIDGE Northumberland

The Angel Inn
CORBRIDGE Map 12 NY96
Main St NE45 5LA ☎ 01434 632119
Local produce is a feature of the food at this 17th-century coaching inn, freshly prepared and cooked to order. Dishes include fillet of Cheviot lamb on a red wine glaze garnished with minted pears, and fillet of Tynedale salmon wrapped in spinach with a blue cheese gratin. Principal beers: Theakstons BB, XB, Beamish, John Smiths.
Scottish & Newcastle
Open 7.15-8.45
Bar food 12-2.15 5.30-8.45 Av main course £5.95
Restaurant 12-2.15 5.30-8.45 Av 3 course à la carte £18.95 Av course fixed price £14.95
Accommodation s£42 d£64

DUNSTAN Northumberland

Cottage Inn
DUNSTAN Map 12 NU21
NE66 3SZ ☎ 01665 576658
An 18th-century building with a walled garden, once part of the Craster estate, situated just a few minutes from the sea. English and local dishes feature on the menus, with plenty of fresh fish and vegetarian options. Dishes include game, port and oyster pie and a fisherman's platter. Principal beers: Ruddles, Theakston, Guinness, Carlsberg.
Directions 6m W of A1
Free House
Open 11-3 6-11
Bar food 12-3 6-10.15 Av main course £5.25
Restaurant 12-3 7-10.15 Av 3 course à la carte £14

ETAL Northumberland

Black Bull
ETAL Map 012 NT93
TD12 4TL ☎ 01890 820200
Over 300-years-old and the only thatched pub in Northumberland. Situated by the Cheviot Hills with just a short walk to the River Till. Lunchtime menu typically offers liver sausage and bacon casserole, and chicken Chasseur; while evening dishes include breast of duckling marinated with honey, soy sauce and ginger. Principal beers: Lorimers Scotch, Lambtons, Thorne, Guinness.
Directions 10m N of Wooler R off A697, L at Jct for 1m then L into Etal.
Vaux
Open 11-11
Bar food 11.30-3 6.30-9.30 Av main course £6
Restaurant 6.30-9.30 Av 3 course à la carte £14

GREAT WHITTINGTON Northumberland

Queens Head Inn & Restaurant
GREAT WHITTINGTON Map 12 NZ07
NE19 2HP ☎ 01434 672267
Former coaching inn dating from early 1600s. Bar scenes for the BBC drama *When The Boat Comes In* were filmed here. Imaginative starters include mandarin chicken livers in a golden box, and avocado with Stilton mousse. Poultry dishes include guinea fowl with apricots, and duck in chocolate and raspberry vinegar sauce. Principal beers: Furstenburg, Durham Magus, Queens Head Bitter, Hambleton Bitter, Courage Directors.
Directions Off A68 & B6318 W of Newcastle upon Tyne
Free House
Open 12-3 6-11
Bar food 12-2.30 6.30-9.30 Av main course £5.95
Restaurant 12-2.30 6.30-9.30 Av 3 course à la carte £20 Av 3 course fixed price £13.95

HALTWHISTLE Northumberland

Milecastle Inn
HALTWHISTLE Map 12 NY76
Military Rd NE49 9NN
☎ 01434 321372 320682
A mere 500 metres from Hadrian's Wall, this slate-roofed stone inn dates back to the early 17th century. There is an extensive wine list and full bar and restaurant menus which may include chevreau and rosemary sausages with gooseberry sauce, wild boar and duckling pie, or pan fried trout fillet. Principal beers: Tetley, Black Sheep, Butterknowle, Hexhamshire.
Directions Leave A69 at Haltwhistle, pub at junction with B6318
Free House
Open 12-3 6-11
Bar food 12-2 6.30-9 Av main course £5.75
Restaurant 12-2 7-9 Av 3 course à la carte £15.95 Av 3 course fixed price £15.95

HAYDON BRIDGE Northumberland

The General Havelock Inn
HAYDON BRIDGE Map 12 NY86
Ratcliffe Rd NE47 6ER
☎ 01434 684376
Built as a private house in 1840, but licensed since 1890, this pub is in a riverside location with a terrace to take full advantage of the view. The food is all home-made from soups to puddings. Typical dishes are seafood Mornay and breast of chicken with tarragon. Principal beers: Tetley Bitter, Cask.
Directions On A69, 7m west of Hexham
Free House
Open 11-2.30 7-11
Bar food 12.00-1.30 7.30-9.00 Av main course £5
Restaurant 12.00-2.00 7.00-11.00 Av 4 course fixed price £19.50

HEXHAM Northumberland

Dipton Mill Inn
HEXHAM Map 12 NY96
Dipton Mill Rd NE46 1YA
☎ 01434 606577
Once a farm and water mill, this inn is a true local where town meets country. A pretty stream runs through

contd.

the garden from where there are pleasant walks. On Sundays in mid-August, the pub hosts a slug show! Home-made food includes sandwiches, salads and specials like chicken in sherry. Principal beers: Hexhamshire Shire Bitter, Devil's Water, & Whapweasel.
Directions A695 from Newcastle-U-T
Free House
Open 12-2.30 6-11 (Sun 12-4.30, 7-10.30)
Bar food 12-2.30 6.30-8.30

LONGFRAMLINGTON Northumberland

Granby Inn
LONGFRAMLINGTON Map 12 NU10
NE65 8DP ☎ 01665 570228
A 200-year old coaching inn that lies at the heart of Northumbria, the Granby is a family-run business which has retained much of its original character. Diners here may sample entrecôte Bordelaise, rump au poivre, lobster thermidor, or wheat and walnut casserole. Principal beers: Guinness, Stones, Worthington, Carling.
Directions 11m N of Morpeth on the A697
Free House
Open 11-3 6-11
Bar food 11-2 6-9.30 Av main course £5.50
Restaurant 12-2 7-9.30 Av 3 course à la carte £15
Accommodation s£29.50 d£54

AA members can call AA Hotel Booking Service on 0990 050505 to book at AA recognised hotels and B & Bs in the UK and Ireland, or through our Internet site: http://www.theaa.co.uk/hotels

LOW NEWTON BY THE SEA Northumberland

The Ship
LOW NEWTON BY THE SEA Map 12 NU22
NE66 3EL ☎ 01665 576262
Sitting in the corner of a quadrangle that leads directly onto the beach, the Ship is the only pub in the small fishing village of Low Newton. In summer the bay is busy with yachts and boats. A basic bar menu includes locally renowned crab sandwiches, toasties, and home-made apple pie. Principal beers: Exhibition, Scotch, Theakston, Ruddles.
Directions NW from A1 at Alnwick
Free House
Open 11-11 (Nov-Easter 11-3, 7-11)

MATFEN Northumberland

The Black Bull
MATFEN Map 12 NZ01
NE20 0RP ☎ 01661 886330
The picturesque Northumberland village of Matfen is the location for this leaf-covered inn. Full à la carte and bar menus are available. A meal may include monkfish à l'Américaine, tournedos Rossini, Northumbrian game pie, casserole of pheasant Basquaise, or Cumberland sausage. Principal beers: Scottish & Newcastle.
Directions Leave A69 at Corbridge, join B6318. 2m N sign to Matfen
Free House
Open 11-3 6-11
Bar food 12-2 6.30-9.30 Av main course £5
Restaurant 12-2 7-9.30
Accommodation s£32.50 d£55

NEWTON ON THE MOOR Northumberland

Cook and Barker Inn
NEWTON ON THE MOOR Map 12 NU10
NE65 9JY ☎ 01665 575234
With splendid views of the Northumberland coast, the restaurant area of this country inn was once a 17th-century smithy. The à la carte menu offers seafood, game, Oriental, steak and vegetarian dishes, such as monkfish with vermouth butter sauce, and roast venison with poached white peach and claret sauce. Principal beers: Theakstons BB and XB, Ruddles, Director, John Smiths.
Directions 0.5m from A1 S of Alnwick
Free House
Open 11-3 6-11 (Sun 6-10.30)
Bar food 12-2 6-8 Av main course £5.50
Restaurant 12-2 7-9 Av 3 course à la carte £24 Av 4 course fixed price £3200
Accommodation s£35 d£65

ROWFOOT Northumberland

The Wallace Arms
ROWFOOT Map 12 NY66
NE49 0JF ☎ 01434 321872
One mile from Featherstone Castle, this country pub, built in 1856, stands in a rural setting. It is a good area for walkers, and is the start point of the South Tyne Trail. Baked rainbow trout in a jacket, beef and ale pie, and pork chop in an almond and cider sauce may be part of the menu. Principal beers: Hexhamshire Bitter & Whapweasel, Newcastle.
Free House
Bar food 12-2 7-9 Av main course £5
Restaurant 12-2 7-9 Av 3 course à la carte £10

SEAHOUSES Northumberland

The Olde Ship Hotel
SEAHOUSES Map 12 NU23
NE68 7RD ☎ 01665 720200
There is a large collection of nautical memorabilia at this hotel, which overlooks the harbour. Traditional dishes are offered in both the bar and restaurant, including fresh crab mayonnaise, fisherman's pie or beef stovies, and clootie dumpling, a local fruit pudding steamed in a cloth and served with custard.
Directions Off A1 on B1340 signposted 'coastal route'
Free House
Open 11-3 6-11
Bar food 12-2 7-8.30 Av main course £4.75
Restaurant 12-2 7-8.30 Av 3 course à la carte £8.50 Av 4 course fixed price £12.50
Accommodation s£30 d£60

STANNERSBURN Northumberland

The Pheasant
STANNERSBURN Map 12 NY78
NE48 1DD ☎ 01434 240382
Over 375 years old, this traditional Northumbrian inn has beamed ceilings, exposed stone walls and open fires. It is located in a hamlet of 12 houses with fell and valley views. Food ranges from snacks to full meals such as home-made soup, trout with prawn filling, and pecan pie. Principal beers: Courage, Tetley, Carlsberg.
Directions From A69 take A6079, then B6320 to Bellingham.Cross bridge & turn onto C200. 8m to Keilder Water
Free House
Open 11-3 (Sun 12-3) 6-11 (Sun 7-10.30)
Bar food 12-2.30 7-9 Av main course £5.95
Restaurant 12-2.30 7-9 Av 3 course à la carte £15
Accommodation s£25 d£50

WARDEN Northumberland

The Boatside Inn
WARDEN Map 12 NY96
NE46 4SQ ☎ 01434 602233
A recently refurbished pub situated close to the River Tyne in the heart of Roman wall country. Bar food includes open sandwiches, steak and ale pie and fresh cod and chips. The restaurant offers grills, vegetarian dishes and specialities

contd.

such as Northumbrian lamb casserole with leek dumplings. Principal beers: Theakstons, Gillespies, McEwans Scotch.
Directions Just off A69 west of Hexham, follow signs to Warden Newborough & Fourstones
Free House
Open 11-3 5.30-11
Bar food 12-2.30 7-10 Av main course £5.25
Restaurant 12-2.30 7-10 Av 3 course à la carte £15

WARENFORD Northumberland

Warenford Lodge
WARENFORD Map 12 NY78
NE70 7HY ☎ 01668 213453
Stincotto - Italian shank of pork roasted with wine and herbs, rabbit Victoriana, Basque pipérade baked with egg, or North country supper of trout may be part of an eclectic menu at this solid stone pub situated in farmland close to the Northumberland coast. Principal beers: McEwans Scotch, Theakstons, Carlsberg.
Directions 100yds E of A1,N of Alnwick
Free House
Open 12-2 7-11
Bar food 12-1.30 7-9.30 Av main course £6.50
Restaurant 12-1.30 7-9.30 Av 3 course à la carte £15

Tyne & Wear

WHITLEY BAY Tyne & Wear

The Waterford Arms
WHITLEY BAY Map 12 NZ37
Collywell Bay Rd, Seaton Sluice
NE26 4QZ ☎ 0191 2370450 2965287
The building dates back to 1899 and is situated close to the small local fishing harbour, overlooking the North Sea. Splendid beaches and sand dunes are within easy reach. Seafood dishes are the speciality, such as halibut in prawn and lobster sauce, and salmon in crab and champagne sauce. Principal beers: Waggledance, Wards Bitter, Samson, Lorimers Scotch, Lambtons.
Directions FromA1 N of Newcastle take A19 at Seaton Burn then follow signs for A190 to Seaton Sluice
Vaux
Open 11-2 5-10.50 (Summer open all day)
Restaurant 11-2 5-10 Av 3 course à la carte £12.45
Accommodation s£25 d£25

Yorkshire, East Riding of

BEVERLEY Yorkshire, East Riding of

White Horse Inn
BEVERLEY Map 08 TA03
22 Hengate HU17 8BP ☎ 01482 861973
Commonly known as 'Nellies', after a previous landlady, this pub is thought to date from around 1585. Offers a wide range of bar snacks and light lunches. The specials board typically features home-made curries and quiches, mushroom Stroganoff, and chicken Chasseur. Principal beers: Old Brewery Bitter, Dark Mild, Extra Stout, Sovereign Bitter.
Directions A1079 from Hull to A1174 into Beverley
Samuel Smith
Open 11-11 (Sun 10.30-12)
Bar food 12-2 Av main course £3.95

BRANDESBURTON Yorkshire, East Riding of

The Dacre Arms
BRANDESBURTON Map 08 TA14
Main St YO25 8RL ☎ 01964 542392
Since the 16th century, a pub has always stood on this site, when it was once the most important posting station in the East Riding. Specialities include beefsteak and ale pie, pork scaloppine, and Southern fried chicken. There are also grills, Yorkshire puddings and vegetarian dishes available. Principal beers: John Smiths, Smooth, Tetleys, Old Peculier.
Free House
Open 11.30-2.30 6-11 (Sat-Sun, BHs all day, Fri 11.30-2.30,5.30-11)
Bar food 12-2 6-10.30 Av main course £5
Restaurant 7-9.30 Av 3 course à la carte £12

BREIGHTON Yorkshire, East Riding of

Ye Olde Poachers Inne
BREIGHTON Map
YO8 7DH ☎ 01757 288849
The building is over 400-years-old, complete with medieval rest and armour decorating the walls. Medieval theme nights are another of its attractions. The menu includes a range of char-grilled steaks and seafood dishes, including smoked salmon cornets, and giant green lipped mussels from New Zealand. Principal beers: Marstons Pedigree, Marstons, Murphys, Old Speckled Hen.
Free House
Open 11.30-3 6-11
Accommodation s£29.50 d£39.50

DRIFFIELD Yorkshire, East Riding of

The Bell
DRIFFIELD Map 08 TA05
Market Place YO25 7AN
☎ 01377 256661
Grade II listed building with banqueting facilities, an oak-panelled bar with over 350 whiskies, and its own leisure centre with pool, jacuzzi and sauna. Typical menu includes chicken Chasseur, poached salmon fillet in Hollandaise sauce, lamb cutlet in herb crust with Cumberland sauce, and grilled sirloin steak. Principal beers: Stones Trad, Hambleton Ales, Malton.
Directions Town centre
Free House
Open 10-11
Bar food 12-1.30 7-10 Av main course £5
Restaurant 7-9.30 Av 3 course à la carte £18
Accommodation s£58 d£78

FLAMBOROUGH Yorkshire, East Riding of

The Seabirds Inn
FLAMBOROUGH Map 08 TA27
Tower St YO15 1PD
☎ 01262 850242
A cheery traditional pub with many items of interest on display, a lot of them relating to ships and shipping - the village juts out to sea with coastline on three sides. Naturally, in a fishing village, there is an emphasis on seafood, and all meals are freshly cooked to order. Principal beers: John Smiths Cask, Boddingtons, Stella, Fosters.
Directions On B1255 E of Bridlington
Free House
Open 11-3 7-11
Bar food 11.30-2 7-9 Av main course £5
Restaurant 11.30-2 7-9 Av 3 course à la carte £11

HUGGATE Yorkshire, East Riding of

The Wolds Inn
HUGGATE Map 08 SE85
YO4 2YH ☎ 01377 288217
Village coaching inn built in the 16th-century. A wide range of snacks is available. Special starters include imperial dim sum with hoi sin sauce, deep fried camembert with cranberry sauce, and salted duck breast with plum sauce. Turkey cooked in cider and garlic is a main course option. Principal beers: John Smiths, Joshua Tetley, Theakstons.
Directions S 0f A166 between York & Driffield
Free House
Open 12-2.30 6.45-11
Bar food 12-2.30 7-9.30 Av main course £4.50
Restaurant 12-2.30 7-11.30 Av 3 course à la carte £13 Av 3 course fixed price £7.95
Accommodation s£22.50 d£35

HULL Yorkshire, East Riding of

The Minerva Hotel
HULL Map 08 TA02
Nelson St HU1 1XE ☎ 01482 326909
Built in 1830 on land reclaimed from the River Humber, the hotel sits right on the river's edge, providing great views of passing ships. There's a micro brewery on the premises, and most of the food is also home made. Specialities are steak and ale pie and huge haddock. Principal beers: Pilot's Pride, Tetley, Carlsberg.
Allied Domecq
Open 11-11

contd.

Bar food 12-2 6-9 Av main course £4.50
Restaurant 12-2 6-9 Av 3 course à la carte £8.25

LOW CATTON Yorkshire, East Riding of

The Gold Cup Inn
LOW CATTON Map 08 ST75
YO4 1EA ☎ 01759 371354
Traditional whitewashed inn near the River Derwent. The restaurant was used for the TV presentation of Catherine Cookson's *The Cinder Path.* Typical main course dishes are halibut and prawn florons, and braised oxtail. Vegetarian dishes include haricot beans with apple and cider, and crisp lentil patties with tomato and onion sauce. Principal beers: Tetley, John Smiths.
Directions 1m S of A166 or 1m N of A1079, E of York
Free House
Open 12-3 (Sat-Sun 12-11)
Bar food 12-3 6-10.30 Av main course £5
Restaurant 6-10.30

LUND Yorkshire, East Riding of

Wellington Inn
LUND Map 08 SE94
19 The Green YO25 9TE
☎ 01377 217294
Mid-19th-century village green pub. The bar snacks menu is displayed on the blackboard. In the restaurant, starters include home-made game terrine, and double baked goats cheese soufflé. Main courses on offer include Barbary duck breast with apricot and blackcurrant stuffing. There is an impressive wine list, too. Principal beers: Bateman Mild, Timothy Taylors Landlord, Black Sheep best bitter, John Smiths.
Directions On B1284 NE of Beverley
Free House
Open 12-3 7-11
Bar food 12-2 Av main course £5.50
Restaurant 12-2 7-10 Av 3 course à la carte £17.50

NORTH DALTON Yorkshire, East Riding of

Star Inn
NORTH DALTON Map 08 SE95
Warter Rd YO25 9UX ☎ 01377 217688
Right next to the village pond, the Star is an 18th-century coaching inn in an idyllic setting. Enjoy the Yorkshire hospitality, open fires and old wooden beams as well as the comprehensive menu. Try swordfish steak, mushroom Stroganoff or roast sirloin of beef. There is a separate lunch menu. Principal beers: John Smiths, Fosters, Becks.
Directions A614 from Driffield, then B1246
Free House
Open 11-3 6-11
Bar food 12-2 7-9.30 Av main course £6.25
Restaurant 12-3 7-9.30 Av 3 course à la carte £12
Accommodation s£35 d£44.50

SKIDBY Yorkshire, East Riding of

Half Moon Inn
SKIDBY Map 08 TA03
16 Main St HU16 5TG
☎ 01482 843403
Don't pass this quaint village pub, a popular walkers' watering hole, without sampling the 'champion' Yorkshire puddings offered with a variety of fillings, including vegetarian. There is a large play area for children and a hitching rail for hungry riders. Principal beers: John Smiths, Theakstons, Beamish Red Chestnut Mild, Guinness.
Directions Between Willerby & Beverley on A164, approx 4m S of Beverley
Scottish & Newcastle
Open open all day

Yorkshire, North

ACASTER MALBIS Yorkshire, North

The Ship Inn
ACASTER MALBIS Map 08 SE54
Moor End YO2 1XB
☎ 01904 705609 703888
Once a haunt of Cromwell's soldiers, who commandeered the house opposite as an armoury, this coaching house dates back to the 17th century. A meal here might feature rainbow trout with almonds, mushroom and

sweet pepper Stroganoff, or roast gammon with cloves and a honey and mustard crust. Principal beers: Tetleys, Timothy Taylor Landlord.
Free House
Open 11.30-11
Bar food 12-2.30 6.30-9.30 Av main course £4.95
Accommodation s£28.50 d£36.50

AKEBAR Yorkshire, North

The Friar's Head
AKEBAR Map 07 NZ19
Akebar Park DL8 5LY
☎ 01677 450201 450591
An old stone building, associated with the local abbey, with beams and log fires. The south aspect is covered with a large conservatory, full of plants and vines, facing Wensleydale farmland. Imaginative dishes, including lunchtime snacks, include kleftiko, a Cypriot lamb dish, fresh seafood tagliatelle, and Thai chicken. Principal beers: John Smith, Theakston, Black Sheep.
Directions From A1 take A684 W toward Leyburn, 1m from Patrick Brompton, pub in Akebar Pk on L
Free House
Open 10.30-3 6-12
Bar food 10.30-3 6-12 Av main course £7
Restaurant 10.30-3 6-12 Av 3 course à la carte £14

APPLETREEWICK Yorkshire, North

The Craven Arms
APPLETREEWICK Map 07 SE06
BD23 6DA ☎ 01756 720270
A traditional Dales pub, surrounded by beautiful views, with log fires and an open Yorkshire range. There is a comprehensive selection of bar food, from sandwiches and basket meals to grilled steak. Dishes might include mixed vegetable pancake, curry, lasagne, fried fish and home-made steak and kidney pie. Principal beers: Black Sheep, Tetley, Theakston Best, XB.
Directions From Skipton take A59 towards Harrogate, B6160 N. Village signd on R.(Pub just outside village)
Free House
Open 11.30-3 6.30-11
Bar food 12-2 7-9.30 Av main course £5

ASENBY Yorkshire, North

Crab & lobster
ASENBY Map 08 SE37
YO7 3QL ☎ 01645 577286
A 17th-century thatched pub set in six acres of lovely gardens. Modern British food is served, including lots of fish. Typical dishes are crab risotto with mustard and coriander, smoked haddock fishcake with parsley sauce, and roast lamb rump with curried cous-cous and aubergine. Principal beers: Black Sheep, Timothy Taylor, Theakston XB, John Smiths.
Directions From A1(M) junc take A168 towards Thirsk
Free House
Open 11.30-3 6.30-11
Bar food 11.30-3 6.30-11 Av main course £9
Restaurant 11.30-3 6.30-11 Av 3 course à la carte £25 Av 2 course fixed price £11.50

ASKRIGG Yorkshire, North

Kings Arms Hotel
ASKRIGG Map 07 SD99
Market Place DL8 3HQ
☎ 01969 650258
Well known as the Drovers Arms in the BBC filming of *All Creatures Great and*

contd.

Northern England

Small, this Dales pub was built as a manor house in 1760, becoming a coaching inn during the early 1800s. Food is cooked to order and ranges from local fare to continental and oriental dishes. Principal beers: Dent Bitter, Yorkshire Bitter, Youngers, Theakston XB.
Directions N off A684 between Hawes & Leyburn
Free House
Open 11-3 (Sun 12-3/Sat 11-5) 6.30-11 (Sun 7-10.30)
Bar food 12-3 6.30-11 Av main course £6
Restaurant 12-3 7-12 Av 3 course à la carte £15 Av 5 course fixed price £25
Accommodation s£50 d£79

BAINBRIDGE Yorkshire, North

Rose & Crown Hotel
BAINBRIDGE Map 07 SD99
DL8 3EE ☎ 01969 650225
Catering for the needs of wayfarers for over 500 years, this traditional Dales hotel is situated at the head of the village overlooking the green. The Forest Horn is still blown each evening from Holyrood to Shrovetide. English fare ranges from Wensleydale cheese sandwich to grilled sirloin steak. Principal beers: Youngers Scotch Bitter, Websters Yorkshire Bitter, John Smiths Smooth, Guinness.
Directions On A684 between Hawes & Leyburn
Free House
Open 11-11 (Sun 12-10.30)
Bar food 12-2 6-9.30 Av main course £4.95
Restaurant 12-2 6-9.30 Av 3 course à la carte £9.95
Accommodation s£30 d£48

BILBROUGH Yorkshire, North

The Three Hares Inn & Restaurant
BILBROUGH Map 08 SE54
Main St YO2 3PH ☎ 01937 832128
A dining pub, with the atmosphere of a country inn, offering imaginative food and sensibly priced wines. The restaurant used to be the village smithy and the furnace is still visible. Here the food is more stylish than in the bar, but fresh local produce is used throughout. Principal beers: Timothy Taylors Landlord, Black Sheep, Marstons Pedigree, Fullers London Pride.
Directions Off A64(York/Leeds rd)
Free House
Open 12-2.30 7-11 (Sun 7-10)
Bar food 12-2 7-9.30 Av main course £6.95
Restaurant 12-2 7-9.30 Av 3 course à la carte £19.50

BOROUGHBRIDGE Yorkshire, North

The Black Bull Inn
BOROUGHBRIDGE Map 08 SE36
6 St James St YO5 9AR ☎ 01423 322413
A listed 13th-century building retaining some original oak timbers and an inglenook fireplace. Everything is home made, with dishes such as beef stewed in stout, steaks, spaghetti pizzaiola, and chicken stuffed with Cheddar and sage. Tempting desserts include tart tatin and sticky toffee pudding. Principal beers: Black Sheep, John Smiths.
Free House
Open 11-11.30 (Sun 12-11)
Bar food 12-2.30 7-9.30 Av main course £4.80
Restaurant 12-2.30 7-9.30 Av 3 course à la carte £15 Av 4 course fixed price £10.95
Accommodation s£32 d£38

BREARTON Yorkshire, North

Malt Shovel Inn
BREARTON Map 08 SE36
HG3 3BX ☎ 01423 862929
Built in 1525, this pub is the oldest building in the hamlet of Brearton. Low, heavily beamed ceilings and a fine example of a 16th-century oak partition wall. A blackboard menu operates and typically includes steak and ale pie, venison braised in red wine, and goats cheese and leek tart. Principal beers: Daleside Nightjar, Old Mill bitter, Durham Magus, Black Sheep Riggwelter.

Directions From A61(Ripon/Harrogate) take B6165 towards Knaresborough. Turn at Brearton - 1.5m.
Free House
Open 12-3 6.45-11
Bar food 12-2 7-9 Av main course £5.50

BROUGHTON Yorkshire, North

Bull Inn
BROUGHTON Map 07 SD95
BD23 3AE ☎ 01756 792065
Resting on the edge of the Yorkshire Dales at the front of Broughton Hall, yet accessibly on the main A59, a friendly welcome awaits at this newly refurbished real country pub. Romany mushrooms could be an appetiser with Cumberland sausage to follow. There's a Junior menu for children. Principal beers: Jennings Bitter, Old Smoothie, Theakstons, Stella Artois.
Directions on A59 4m from Skipton from M6
Jennings Brothers
Open 11-11
Bar food 12-10 Av main course £6

BUCKDEN Yorkshire, North

The Buck Inn
BUCKDEN Map 07 SD97
BD23 5JA ☎ 01756 760228
A Georgian coaching inn set in the heart of the Yorkshire Dales National Park. English/French cuisine is served, beginning perhaps with a slice of warm seafood tart, followed by pan-fried calves' liver set on bubble and squeak. Desserts include traditional crêpes Suzette. Principal beers: Theakstons.
Directions From Skipton take B6265, then B6160
Free House
Open 8am-11pm
Bar food 12-2 6.30-9 Av main course £8.95
Restaurant 6.30-9 Av 3 course à la carte £22.95 Av 4 course fixed price £22.95
Accommodation s£31 d£62

BURNSALL Yorkshire, North

The Red Lion
BURNSALL Map 07 SE06
By the Bridge BD23 6BU
☎ 01756 720204
16th-century ferrymen's inn with riverside views, surrounded by fells and moorland. Bar menu offers a selection of local Yorkshire cheeses served with home-made chutney and relishes. Main course dishes include steamed salmon with asparagus Mussolini and Hollandaise sauce, and fillet of lamb with rosemary jus and wild mushroom ravioli. Principal beers: BlackSheep, Theakstons, Tetley.
Directions From Skipton take A59 east take B6160 towardsBolton Abbey, Burnsall 7m
Free House
Open 8 12 (Sun closes 10.30)
Bar food 12-2.30 6-9.30 Av main course £8.50
Restaurant 12-2.45 7-9.30 Av 3 course à la carte £21.50 Av 4 course fixed price £21.50
Accommodation s£39.50 d£79

CARLTON Yorkshire, North

Foresters Arms
CARLTON Map 07 SE08
DL8 4BB ☎ 01969 640272
17th-century coaching inn with a stream running through the back field. The burial mound to the rear of the pub dates from the Plague. Main dishes include sautéed duckling with lemon and thyme stuffing and claret jus, and braised lamb with pearl barley and Madeira sauce. Principal beers: John Smiths, Theakstons, Tetleys.
Directions S of Leyburn off A684 or A6108
Free House
Open 12-3 (Not Mons) 6.30-11
Bar food 12-2 7-9
Restaurant 12-2 7-9.30 Av 3 course à la carte £26
Accommodation s£35 d£60

CARTHORPE Yorkshire, North

The Fox & Hounds
CARTHORPE Map 08 SE38
DL8 2LG ☎ 01845 567433
Small family-run pub formerly the village smithy. Now features a modernised L-shaped bar and high-ceilinged restaurant. Blackboard options include salmon fillet with ginger and spring onions and halibut steak with grain mustard sauce. Not forgetting the home-made duck liver pâté in port jelly. Principal beers:

contd.

Theakstons, John Smiths.
Directions Off A1
Free House
Open 12-2.30 7-11
Bar food 12-2.30 7-11 Av main course £8
Restaurant 12-2.30 7-11 Av 3 course à la carte £16

CLAPHAM Yorkshire, North

New Inn
CLAPHAM Map 07 SD76
LA2 8HH ☎ 015242 51203
18th-century Dales coaching inn situated near Clapham Beck and a waterfall. Bar menu offers a selection of snacks, light meals and blackboard specials. A la carte main courses include fillet steak tournedos Rossini, gammon steak with hot Cumberland sauce, and poached salmon with a whole grain mustard sauce. Principal beers: Fullbeck Bitter, Dent Bitter, Black Sheep, Theakston XB.
Directions On A65 in Yorkshire Dale National Park
Free House
Bar food 12-2 7-9 Av main course £5
Restaurant 7-8 Av 3 course à la carte £15
Accommodation s£40 d£59

COXWOLD Yorkshire, North

The Fauconberg Arms
COXWOLD Map 08 SE57
Main St YO6 4AD ☎ 01347 868214
In a Doomsday Book recorded village, this historic 17th-century inn is named after the family to whom Henry VIII gave the village and estate. In an old world setting, sample food prepared by the landlady: roulade of oak smoked sea trout, duck sausage with Calvados and onion gravy. Principal beers: Theakstons, Tetley, John Smith.
Directions Take A19 from York, 2m turn left, signposted alternative route for caravans/heavy vehicles. 5m to village.
Free House
Open 11-3 6-11
Bar food 12-2 7-9 Av main course £5.95
Restaurant 12-2 7-9 Av 3 course à la carte £11
Accommodation s£24 d£40

DACRE BANKS Yorkshire, North

The Royal Oak Inn
DACRE BANKS Map 07 SE16
HE3 4EN ☎ 01423 780200
18th-century Dales village inn with views of the River Nidd. A typical menu includes mussel and onion soup, Wensleydale ploughman's, rabbit, ham, mushroom and onion pie, and local Nidderdale trout poached with tarragon, butter and dry white wine. There are also regular speciality theme dinner party menus. Principal beers: Daleside, Black Sheep, John Smiths.
Directions From A59(Harrogate/ Skipton) take B6451 towards Pateley Bridge
Free House
Open 12-2.30 7-11
Bar food 12-2 7-9 Av main course £6
Restaurant 12-2 7-9 Av 3 course à la carte £10.50

DANBY Yorkshire, North

Duke of Wellington Inn
DANBY Map 08 NZ70
YO21 2LY ☎ 01287 660351
A country inn built in 1732. Said to have acquired its name when the Duke of Wellington used it as a staging post and recruiting centre. The menu includes steaks, seafood dishes and home-made cottage pie, with vegetarian options like mushroom and nut fettucine, and Stilton, celery and walnut quiche. Principal beers: Smiths Magnet, Camerons Strongarm, Ruddles, Speckled Hen.
Directions From A171 between Guisborough & Whitby take rd signed 'Danby & Moors Centre'
Free House
Open 11-3 7-11.30
Bar food 12-2 7-9.30 Av main course £5.75
Restaurant 12-2.30 7-9.30 Av 3 course à la carte £12
Accommodation s£20 d£40

EAST WITTON Yorkshire, North

The Blue Lion
EAST WITTON Map 07 SE18
DL8 4SN ☎ 01969 624273
Built by the Marquis of Aylesbury in the

18th century, this village pub has remained relatively untouched by the 20th, and is ideal for those visiting the Yorkshire Dales. A meal here may include roasted wood pigeon with peas and ham, jugged hare, or a Thai-styled seafood selection. Principal beers: Black Sheep, Theakstons, John Smiths.
Free House
Open 11-11
Bar food 12-2.15 7-9.30 Av main course £10
Restaurant 12-2.15 7-9.30 Av 3 course à la carte £19.95

EGTON BRIDGE Yorkshire, North

Horseshoe Hotel
EGTON BRIDGE Map 08 NZ80
YO21 1XE ☎ 01947 895245
Grade II listed pub on the banks of the River Esk. A wide range of bar snacks and light meals available. Main course dishes range from sirloin of local beef with Stilton sauce, and garlic chicken, to bacon chops with peach sauce, and fillet of duck with plum and port sauce. Principal beers: Theakstons.
Directions From Whitby take A171 towards Middlesborough Village signed in 5m
Free House
Open 11.30-3.30 6.30-11
Bar food 12-2 7-9 Av main course £6
Restaurant 12-2 7-9 Av 3 course à la carte £15
Accommodation s£26 d£38

ELSLACK Yorkshire, North

The Tempest Arms
ELSLACK Map 07 SD94
BD23 3AY ☎ 01282 842450
An old-style country pub, with a stream at the bottom of the garden, in a small village leading to the moors. There's a choice of fresh fish, sirloin steak, roast duck, and dishes such as tagliatelle blush, with strips of smoked salmon and a sauce of cream, herbs and sun-dried tomatoes. Principal beers: Jennings.
Directions From Skipton take A59 towards Gisburn.Village signed on L
Jennings Brothers
Open 11-11
Bar food 12-2.15 6-9.30 Av main course £6
Restaurant 12-2.15 6-9.30 Av 3 course à la carte £18
Accommodation s£47.50 d£59.50

ESCRICK Yorkshire, North

Black Bull Inn
ESCRICK Map 08 SE64
Main St YO4 6JP ☎ 01904 728245
A 19th-century village pub serving the local community and tourists alike, with a welcoming fire in winter. A good selection of value for money food is offered, including hot baguettes, cold platters, steak and kidney pie, grills, traditional fish and chips and mushroom Stroganoff. Principal beers: Tetley, John Smiths.
Directions On A19 (York to Selby rd)
Free House
Open 11-3 5.30-11
Bar food 12-3 6-10 Av main course £5
Restaurant 12-3 6-10 Av 3 course à la carte £12

FERRENSBY Yorkshire, North

The General Tarleton Inn
FERRENSBY Map 08 SE36
Boroughbridge Rd HG5 0QB
☎ 01423 340284
18th-century inn named after British officer who fought in the war against the American colonies, and then became MP for Liverpool. Fishing, shooting and golf available in the area. Typical menu includes confit of duck and Toulouse sausage, grilled calves liver and bacon, and Lancashire hot pot. Principal beers: Black Sheep, Tetleys, Carlsberg.
Free House
Open 12-3 6-11
Bar food 12-2 6-9.30 Av main course £7
Restaurant 12-2 7-9.30 Av 3 course à la carte £20
Accommodation s£47.50 d£47.50

GOATHLAND Yorkshire, North

Mallyan Spout
GOATHLAND Map 08 NZ80
The Common YO22 5AN
☎ 01947 896486
Named after the famous waterfall behind the hotel, this family-run establishment

contd.

is situated in open moors on the edge of a beautiful village. The menus offer fresh fish from nearby Whitby, home-cured beef and gravadlax, and man-sized Yorkshire pudding with steak and kidney casserole. Principal beers: Malton Double Chance, Theakstons Best Bitter.
Directions Off A169 (Whitby/Pickering rd)
Free House
Open 11-11
Bar food 12-2 6-9 Av main course £4.50
Restaurant 12-1.30 7-9 Av 3 course à la carte £19.50 Av 3 course fixed price £19.50
Accommodation s£45 d£65

HAROME Yorkshire, North

The Star Inn
HAROME Map 08 SE68
YO6 5JE ☎ 01439 770397
A 14th-century thatched pub with some parts dating from the 9th century. The 'Mouseman of Kilburn' furniture adorns the bar - indeed it was the first bar he put in. The same fine food is offered throughout and everything is home-made, from the bread to the chocolates with coffee. Principal beers: Black Sheep Special, John Smiths, Theakstons Best Bitter.
Directions From Helmsley take A170 towards Kirkbymoorside.0.5m turn R for Harome
Free House
Open 11-3 6.30-11
Bar food 12-2 7-9.30 Av main course £10
Restaurant 12-2 7-9.30 Av 3 course à la carte £20 Av 3 course fixed price £20

HAWES Yorkshire, North

Board Hotel
HAWES Map 07 SD88
Market Place DL8 3RD ☎ 01969 667223
Traditional Dales pub where a range of home-made pies feature on the menu, such as Yorkshire trencher, game pie, Cumberland chicken pie, Portuguese fish pie, and a cheese and vegetable pie for vegetarians. Local rainbow trout is also available. Principal beers: Yorkshire bitter, Black Sheep bitter, Websters, Pedigree bitter.
Directions M6 J37 - A684 east
Free House
Open 11-11
Bar food 11-2 6.30-9.30 Av main course £4.50
Restaurant 11-4 7-9.30 Av 3 course à la carte £8 Av 3 course fixed price £7.50
Accommodation d£38

HETTON Yorkshire, North

Angel Inn
HETTON Map 07 SD95
BD23 6LT ☎ 01756 730263
An old Yorkshire Dales pub with lots of beams, open fires and nooks and crannies. There is a good variety of dishes, all freshly cooked, such as terrine of Tuscan vegetables with tapénade crostini, char-grilled breast of local wood pigeon, and Hetton Mess, supplemented by daily specials. Principal beers: Tetleys Bitter, Black Sheep Bitter & Special.

Directions A59 to Grassington via B2165, L at Rylstone for Hetton
Free House
Open 12-2.30 6-10.30
Bar food 12-2.30 6-10 Av main course £8.50
Restaurant 12-2 6-10 Av 3 course à la carte £26 Av 3 course fixed price £26.50

HOVINGHAM Yorkshire, North

The Worsley Arms Hotel
HOVINGHAM Map 08 SE67
YO6 4LA ☎ 01653 628234
Built in 1841 by Sir William Worsley on the edge of the North Yorkshire Moors. Food is served in The Restaurant or in the Cricketers Bistro, which has an inventive approach to traditional dishes, such as char-grilled rib steak with roast plum tomatoes, and fishcakes with rosemary cream. Principal beers: John Smiths, Theakstons, Double Chance, Milton Brewery.
Directions A64 from York towards Scarborough into Norton then onto B1257
Free House
Open 12-2.30 6-11
Bar food 12-3 6-11 Av main course £9
Restaurant 12-3 7-10 Av 3 course à la carte £25 Av 4 course fixed price £23.50
Accommodation s£55 d£70

HUBBERHOLME Yorkshire, North

The George Inn
HUBBERHOLME Map 07 SD97
BD23 5JE ☎ 01756 760223
18th-century Dales pub with stone flagged floors and wide-beamed ceilings. Writer, JB Priestley's favourite pub. Typical dishes are turkey and mushroom pie, lamb and apricot pie, spinach and mushroom lasagne, and breast of chicken stuffed with Boursin cheese and poached in a white wine and cream sauce. Principal beers: Theakston.
Directions At Buckden on B61609 take turn to Hubberholme
Free House
Open 11.30-3 6.30-11
Bar food 12-2 6.30-8.45 Av main course £6.50
Accommodation s£25 d£38

KETTLEWELL Yorkshire, North

Racehorses Hotel
KETTLEWELL Map 07 SD97
BD23 5QZ ☎ 01756 760233
Small 18th-century inn situated between the River Wharfe and Park Gill Beck. Bar meals range from Kilnsey trout with toasted almonds, to poached Scottish salmon, and Arbroath smokies. Restaurant dishes include sirloin steak with Madeira sauce, and Gressingham duck with orange and cranberry sauce. Principal beers: Theakstons Best, Black Bull, John Smiths, Fosters.
Directions From Skipton take B6265, after 6m continue on B6160 toward Kettlewell, hotel over 2nd bridge on L
Free House
Open 11-11
Bar food 12-2 6.30-9 Av main course £7.50
Restaurant 6.30-9 Av 3 course à la carte £17
Accommodation s£22

KIRKBYMOORSIDE Yorkshire, North

George & Dragon Hotel
KIRKBYMOORSIDE Map 08 SE68
Market Place YO6 6AA ☎ 01751 433334
An atmosphere of civilised calm pervades in this charming 17th-century coaching inn, where you can relax by the open fire and read the papers. The menu covers a blend of traditional and modern English cooking, including venison sausages, rabbit casserole, Whitby crabcakes and roasted sweet peppers. Principal beers: Timothy Taylors Landlord,Black Sheep Bitter,Theakstons Best Bitter.
Directions Just off A170 between Scarborough & Thirsk
Free House
Open 10-3 6-11
Bar food 12-3 6-11 Av main course £7.90
Restaurant 12-2.15 6.30-9.15 Av 3 course à la carte £17
Accommodation s£49 d£79

KIRKHAM Yorkshire, North

Stone Trough Inn
KIRKHAM Map 08 SE76
Kirkham Abbey YO6 7JS
☎ 01653 618713
Opt for home-made baking or à la carte at this characterful inn, opposite Kirkham Abbey and with views of the River Derwent. Fresh Whitby haddock is deep fried in golden crispy batter, seafood pie is a potato and cheese topped fishy feast. Principal beers: Tetley, Taylors Landlord, Jennings Cumberland, Old Peculiar.

contd.

Directions 1 1/2m off A64, between York & Malton
Free House
Open 12-2 6-11
Bar food 12-2.30 6-11 Av main course £5.95

LEYBURN Yorkshire, North

Sandpiper Inn
LEYBURN Map 07 SE19
Market Place DL8 5AT ☎ 01969 622206
Built in the 17th century, the Sandpiper was originally a nursery garden and flower shop, and has been a pub for only 30 years. Garden is outstanding. Typical menu includes chicken curry, grilled gammon with Swaledale cheese, and Cumberland sausage. Principal beers: Dent Bitter, Black Sheep, Theakstons, John Smiths.

Directions From A1 take A684 to Leyburn
Free House
Open 11-2.30 6.30-11
Bar food 12-2 7-9 Av main course £5.25
Restaurant 12-2 7-9 Av 3 course à la carte £14.50
Accommodation s£25 d£40

LINTON Yorkshire, North

The Fountaine Inn
LINTON Map 07 SD96
BD23 5HJ ☎ 01756 752210
A 16th-century inn located in the Yorkshire Dales National Park on the banks of the River Beck, the Fountaine has been voted the prettiest pub in England. The bar menu may feature Linton Lample pie, lamb, ham and apple, panfried Whitby haddock, or loin of pork with apple sauce. Principal beers: Black Sheep, Theakstons.

Directions From Skipton take B6162 8m turn R for Linton
Free House
Open 11.30-2.30 7-10.30 (Open all day in summer)
Bar food 12-2.30 6.30/7-7 Av main course £6.45

MOULTON Yorkshire, North

Black Bull Inn
MOULTON Map 08 NZ20
Dl10 6QJ ☎ 01325 377289
A pub converted into a panelled seafood restaurant, conservatory and private dining rooms, one of which is a 1932 Pullman carriage called The Brighton Belle. A wide range of bar snacks is available, while main course meals include lobster in rich brandy and cream sauce, and chateaubriand béarnaise. Principal beers: Theakstons, John Smiths, Guinness, Carlsberg.
Directions 1m S of Scotch Corner off A1
Free House
Open 12-2.30 6-10.30
Bar food 12-2.30 Av main course £5
Restaurant 12-2.30 6-10.30 Av 3 course à la carte £25 Av 3 course fixed price £14.95

MUKER Yorkshire, North

The Farmers Arms
MUKER Map 07 SE16
DL11 6QG ☎ 01748 886297
Village Dales pub with stone flagged floor, pine settles and open fire. Snacks, toasties, baps and salads, plus a main course menu which includes home-made curries and sweet and sour turkey, and breaded trout. For vegetarians there's a home-made potato, cheese and leek bake. Principal beers: Butterknowle, Old Peculiar, Theakstons, XB.
Directions From Richmond take A6108 towards Leyburn, turn R onto B6270
Free House
Open 11-3 (Open longer hours in summer) 7-11 (Sun 7-10.30)
Bar food 12-2.30 7-9 Av main course £4.75

AA members can call AA Hotel Booking Service on 0990 050505 to book at AA recognised hotels and B & Bs in the UK and Ireland, or through our Internet site: http://www.theaa.co.uk/hotels

OSMOTHERLEY Yorkshire, North

Three Tuns Inn
OSMOTHERLEY Map 08 SE49
South End DL6 3BN ☎ 01609 883301
450-year-old building situated on the Yorkshire Moors near Lyke Lake. Main course dishes range from local pork with sage and apricot sauce, fresh sea bass with lemon butter, and halibut steak topped with prawns and cheese, to roast lamb with fresh strawberry and mint sauce. Principal beers: Theakstons Bitter, XB, Old Peculier, Beamish Stout.
Directions Off A19
Free House
Open 11.45-3.30 6.45-11
Bar food 11.45-3.30 6.45-11 Av main course £6.50
Restaurant 11.45-3.30 6.45-11 Av 3 course à la carte £12.50
Accommodation s£47.50 d£60

PATELEY BRIDGE Yorkshire, North

The Sportmans Arms Hotel
PATELEY BRIDGE Map 07 SE16
Wath-in-Nidderdale HG3 5PP
☎ 01423 711306
17th-century hotel within easy reach of Gouthwaite Reservoir and its abundant birdlife. Bar menu offers local seafood dishes such as Nidderdale trout with bacon and capers. Typical restaurant dishes include baked avocado with Chaumes and Stilton, and feuilleté of lobster in an orange and white wine sauce. Principal beers: Youngers, Theakstons, John Smiths, Guinness.
Directions From A1 take A59 towards Skipton then B6451 & B6165
Free House
Open 12-2.30 6.30-11
Bar food 12-2.30 7-9.30 Av main course £8.50
Restaurant 12-2 7-9.30 Av 3 course à la carte £21 Av 4 course fixed price £21
Accommodation s£40 d£60

PICKERING Yorkshire, North

The White Swan
PICKERING Map 08 SE88
Market Place YO18 7AA
☎ 01751 472288
16th-century coaching inn once used as a smugglers' safe house. Lunchtime bar menu offers green Thai chicken curry, and Whitby fishcakes with pesto mayonnaise and sautéed apples. Restaurant dishes include char-grilled venison haunch with wild berry jus, and seared salmon fillet with Provençale cream and braised butter beans. Principal beers: Black Sheep Best, Black Sheep Special, Malton Brewery Double Chance.
Directions Town centre
Free House
Open 11-11 (Tue-Fri closed 3-5.30) 12-10.30 (Sun closed 3-7)
Bar food 12-2.30 7-9.30 Av main course £5.50
Restaurant 12.30-2.30 7.30-9.30 Av 3 course à la carte £18 Av 2 course fixed price £7.95
Accommodation s£45 d£70

PICKHILL Yorkshire, North

Nags Head Country Inn
PICKHILL Map 08 SE38
YO7 4JG ☎ 01845 567391 567570
The Nag's Head has been run by the same management for a quarter of a century, and can cater for business conferences of up to 34 people. The menu may include fillet of beef Wellington, grilled duck breast with plum sauce, or smoked haddock and prawn kedgeree. Principal beers: Hambleton Bitter, Theakston Black Bull, Theakston Old Peculier, Tetley Bitter.
Directions 1.25m E of A1(4m N of A1/A61 junction).W of Thirsk
Free House
Open 11-11
Bar food 12-2
Restaurant 12-2 7-9.30
Accommodation s£36 d£50

RAMSGILL Yorkshire, North

The Yorke Arms
RAMSGILL Map 07 SE17
HG3 5RL ☎ 01423 755243
Former coaching inn which was converted into a hotel in the late 19th-century, situated near Ramsgill Beck, a tributary of the River Nidd. Typical bar specials include pear, Stilton and walnut quiche, baked whole trout filled with spinach, and griddled venison cooked in port wine and sultana sauce. Principal beers: Gillespies, Coors lager, McEwans, Theakstons.

contd.

Directions From A61 N of Harrogate take B6165 to Pateley Bridge. Follow signs for Ramsgill
Free House
Open 11-11 (Sun 12-10.30)
Bar food 12-2 7-9 Av main course £6
Restaurant 12-2 7-9 Av 3 course à la carte £18 Av 4 course fixed price £19.25
Accommodation s£40 d£65

RIPLEY Yorkshire, North

The Boars Head Hotel
RIPLEY Map 08 SE26
Ripley Castle Estate HG3 3AY
☎ 01423 771888
A listed building in the centre of one of the few remaining model estate villages, completely rebuilt in the 1830s by Sir William Amcotts Ingilby, eccentric and MP. Dishes are internationally influenced, including seared pheasant breast on deep-fried lemon cabbage, and timbale of wild mushrooms, spinach and pinenuts with sauce vierge. Principal beers: Timothy Taylor, Theakstons, Bass, Guinness.
Directions 3m N of Harrogate on A61
Free House
Open 11-3 5-11
Bar food 12-2 6.30-10 Av main course £7.95
Restaurant 12-2 7-9.30 Av 3 course fixed price £27.50
Accommodation s£85 d£98

ROSEDALE ABBEY Yorkshire, North

The Milburn Arms Hotel
ROSEDALE ABBEY Map 08 SE79
YO18 8RA ☎ 01751 417312
Awarded two AA Rosettes for its fine cuisine, the Priory Restaurant has an appropriate setting in this charming 16th century hotel. The cellar holds more than fifty selected wines. Menu may offer pan-fried chicken's liver with red shallots, sautéed king scallops with asparagus, and desserts such as glazed lemon tart. Principal beers: Bass, Stones, Black Sheep, Caffreys.
Directions A170 W from Pickering 3m, L at sign to Rosedale then 7m
Bass
Open 11-11
Bar food 12-3 6.30-10.30 Av main course £8.50
Restaurant 12-3.30 7-11.30 Av 3 course à la carte £25
Accommodation s£39.50 d£64

White Horse Farm Hotel
ROSEDALE ABBEY Map 08 SE79
YO18 8SE ☎ 01751 417239
Established as a tap room in the 18th century, this former farm has become, with sympathetic alterations, a two-star hotel and country pub, serving real ale and over 30 malt whiskies. Traditional food including plenty of game is served, with occasional surprises like kangaroo brioche. Principal beers: Theakstons Best, OP & XB, John Smiths Best, Tetleys Best.
Directions A64 from York, onto A169 then A170, exit at Wrelton, then 7m
Free House
Open 12-2.30 6.30-11
Bar food 12-2 6.30-9.30 Av main course £7.95
Restaurant 12-1.30 7-8.45 Av 3 course fixed price £16
Accommodation s£40 d£60

SAWLEY Yorkshire, North

The Sawley Arms
SAWLEY Map 08 SE26
HG4 3EO ☎ 01765 620642
Set in a beautiful, prize winning garden close to historic Fountains Abbey, enjoy cosy beamed, antique filled surroundings at this pub, a favourite of the late 'James Herriot'. Relish excellent traditional dishes like smoked Lidderdale trout with horseradish Chantilly, home-made steak pie and delicious puddings, served on china and cut glass. Principal beers: Theakstons, Youngers.
Directions From A1 take B6265 towards Pateley Bridge. Village on L.
Free House
Open 11.30-3 6.30-10.30
Bar food 12-2 7-9 Av main course £6
Restaurant 12-2 7-9 Av 3 course à la carte £17

SCAWTON Yorkshire, North

The Hare Inn
SCAWTON Map 08 SE58
YO7 2HG ☎ 01845 597289
800-year-old building set in the North Yorkshire Moors National Park. Mentioned in the Domesday Book. Past famous visitors include Richard III, Cromwell and the novelist James Herriott. The main course menu offers Shanghai beef curry, plus home-made game and rabbit pies, with a peanut Stroganoff for vegetarians. Principal beers: North Yorkshire, Theakstons, John Smiths.
Free House
Open 12-3 7-11
Bar food 12-2 7-9 Av main course £6

SETTLE Yorkshire, North

Golden Lion Hotel
SETTLE Map 07 SD89
Duke St BD24 9DU ☎ 01729 822203
Built around 1640 as a coaching inn and retaining original features such as a grand sweeping staircase into the bar lounge, and an inglenook fireplace. Bar menu offers a good selection of snacks and pasta dishes. Main course dishes include roasted duck with a kiwi fruit and plum sauce. Principal beers: Daniel Thwaites Traditional, Chairmans.
Directions On A65 in town centre
Daniel Thwaites
Open 11-11 (Sun 12-10.30)
Bar food 12-2.30 6-10 Av main course £5.50
Restaurant 12-2.30 6-10 Av 3 course à la carte £10.50
Accommodation s£22.50 d£45

SINNINGTON Yorkshire, North

Fox & Hounds Country Inn
SINNINGTON Map 08 SE78
YO6 6SQ ☎ 01751 431577
A listed 18th-century coaching inn, with a mounting step still by the door, in a pretty village on the edge of the North York Moors. Bar food includes cod and chips, and roast lamb, while the restaurant might have black pudding fritters, grilled brill and apple and raspberry crumble. Principal beers: Camerons Bitter, Marstons Pedigree, Camerons Ruby Red.
Directions Just off main A170 Thirsk to Scarborough Rd
Free House
Open 11-11 (Sun 10.30-12)
Bar food 12-2.30 6.30-9.30 Av main course £7
Restaurant 12-2.30 6.30-9.30 Av 3 course à la carte £19
Accommodation s£34 d£50

STARBOTTON Yorkshire, North

Fox & Hounds Inn
STARBOTTON Map 07 SD97
BD23 5HY ☎ 01756 760269
400-year-old building set in the Yorkshire Dales. The bar has a large stone fireplace, oak beams and flagstone floor. Alongside traditional bar fare, the main course offers dishes such as turkey and coriander burgers, Moroccan style lamb, chick pea and vegetable curry, and parsnip, chestnut and tomato crumble. Principal beers: Black Sheep, Theakstons.
Free House
Open 11.30-3 6.30-11
Bar food 12-2 7-9 Av main course £6.50
Accommodation d£44

SUTTON-ON-THE-FOREST Yorkshire, North

Rose & Crown
SUTTON-ON-THE-FOREST Map 08 SE56
Main St YO6 1DP ☎ 01347 810351
Situated at the heart of a pretty village, this is an 'eating pub' with a regular drinking clientele. Interesting snacks, available at lunchtime only, include hot bacon and Gruyère muffins. The full menu might offer salmon fishcake, boudin blanc sausage on a rösti, and bread and butter pudding. Principal beers: Beamish Red, Theakstons.
Directions On B1363 N of York
Free House
Open 11-2.30 6-11
Restaurant 11-2.30 6-11

TERRINGTON Yorkshire, North

Bay Horse Inn
TERRINGTON Map 08 SE67
YO6 4PP ☎ 01653 648416
A grade II listed building set in the Howardian Hills near Castle Howard. A wide selection of starters and main courses on the menu, including Scottish smoked salmon, game pie and spiced lemon chicken. Vegetarian dishes include Hazelnut and vegetable loaf, and asparagus, cream and mushroom

pancake. Principal beers: Youngers and Theakstons.
Free House
Open 12-3 6.30-11
Bar food 12-2 7-9 Av main course £6.50
Restaurant 12-2 7-9 Av 3 course à la carte £11.50

THORNTON WATLASS Yorkshire, North

The Buck Inn
THORNTON WATLASS Map 08 SE28
HG4 4AN ☎ 01677 422461
Country inn next to the village cricket green. The pub wall serves as one of the boundaries. Typical main course dishes are beef and beer curry, pork chop casseroled in sage, mushroom and apple, spicy duck in a honey and soy sauce, and bean and baby sweetcorn casserole. Principal beers: Black Sheep, Theakston, John Smiths, Tetleys.
Directions From A1 at Leeming Bar take A684 to Bedale, then B6268. Village 2m on R
Free House
Open 11-2.30 6-11 (Sat open all day) (Sun 12-10.30)
Bar food 12-2 6.30-9.30 Av main course £5.75
Restaurant 12-2 6.30-9.30 Av 3 course à la carte £12 Av 3 course fixed price £8.95
Accommodation s£30 d£44

THRESHFIELD Yorkshire, North

The Old Hall Inn
THRESHFIELD Map 07 SD96
BD23 5HB ☎ 01756 752441
Situated at the heart of the Yorkshire Dales, this village green inn dates back to the 1700s. Lunchtimes provide a selection of local Dale sausages, seafood and vegetarian meals. Evenings typically feature pheasant and bramble pie with suet pastry crust, and pork fillet with garlic mash and caramelised shallots. Principal beers: Timothy Taylors.
Free House
Open 11.30-3 6-11
Bar food 12-2 6.15-9.30 Av main course £6.25
Restaurant 12-2 6.15-9.30 Av 3 course à la carte £13.50

WASS Yorkshire, North

Wombwell Arms
WASS Map 08 SE57
YO6 4BE ☎ 01347 868280
Originally used as a grainstore during the early 17th-century, this small pub is divided into four areas each one with its own character. Said to be haunted. Lunchtime bar snacks available, plus light lunches which include smoked salmon and scrambled eggs, baked aubergine, and local venison sausages. Principal beers: Black Sheep bitter, Timothy Taylor Landlord, Guinness, Carlsberg lager.
Free House
Open 12-2.30 7-11 (Sun 7-10.30)
Bar food 12-2 7-9
Accommodation s£27.50 d£49

WEST BURTON Yorkshire, North

Fox & Hounds
WEST BURTON Map 07 SE08
DL8 4JY ☎ 01969 663279
A 200-year-old coaching inn overlooking the village green, close to the heart of Wensleydale. Main courses include locally produced West Burton sausages, home-made tipsy beef pie and Barbary duck breast with orange and sherry sauce. Vegetarian meals, such as home-made Stilton and broccoli quiche, are also available. Principal beers: Black Sheep, Websters, John Smiths.
Free House
Open 11-3 6.30-11
Bar food 11-2 6.30-8.45 Av main course £5

Restaurant 6.30-8.45 Av 3 course à la carte £12 Av 3 course fixed price £11.50
Accommodation s£30 d£40

WEST WITTON Yorkshire, North

The Wensleydale Heifer Inn
WEST WITTON Map 07 SE08
DL8 4LS ☎ 01969 622322
17th-century coaching inn situated in the Yorkshire Dales National Park, which is well known as James Herriot country. Both the bistro and restaurant have a strong seafood bias and a meal may include cullen skink (smoked fish soup), roast monkfish, or shellfish samosas. Principal beers: Theakstons, John Smiths, Stella Artois.
Free House
Open 10-11 (all day)
Bar food 12-2 6.30-9 Av main course £6.50
Restaurant 12-2 7-9 Av 3 course à la carte £13.95 Av 4 course fixed price £22.50
Accommodation s£54 d£70

WHITBY Yorkshire, North

The Magpie Café
WHITBY Map 08 NZ81
14 Pier Rd YO21 3PU ☎ 01947 602058
Housed in a distinctive black and white building overlooking the harbour in the historic port of Whitby. There is an impressive range of seafood specialities, including dishes with locally caught crab and lobster. Vegetarian meals are also available, plus a choice of over 30 home-made desserts and cakes.
Free House
Open 11.30-9 (Sun-Thu in Winter 11.30-6.30)

WIGGLESWORTH Yorkshire, North

The Plough Inn
WIGGLESWORTH Map 07 SD85
BD23 4RJ ☎ 01729 840243
Situated deep in the countryside with views of Pen-y-Ghent and Inglesborough, the Plough was built in 1725 as a farmhouse and developed as a coaching inn (the farming was dropped c1939). The hotel now offers bar meals, a conservatory restaurant, and a bistro-cum-American diner. Principal beers: Tetleys, Boddingtons.
Directions A65 from Leeds then B6478 to Wigglesworth
Free House
Open 9-2.30 7-11
Bar food 12-2 7-10 Av main course £5.50
Restaurant 12-2 7-10 Av 3 course à la carte £16.50 Av 3 course fixed price £16.50
Accommodation s£22.50 d£29.50

YORK Yorkshire, North

Betty's Café Tea Rooms
YORK Map 08 SE65
6-8 St Helens Square YO1 2QP
☎ 01904 659142
Established by Swiss confectioner Frederick Belmont who travelled on the maiden voyage of the Queen Mary liner. The café's interior design is based on the liner's. An impressive menu offers a wide selection of sandwiches, rolls, toasts, tea breads, scones, desserts and ice creams. Alsace wines are a house speciality. Principal beers: Sam Smiths, Black Sheep, Theakstons.
Open 9-9

contd.

Yorkshire, South

PENISTONE Yorkshire, South

Cubley Hall
PENISTONE Map 08 SE20
Mortimer Rd, Cubely S30 6AW
☎ 01226 766086
Country pub and restaurant well situated for a number of local bridle paths. Typical house specials include Oriental style pork steak with stir fry soy sauce and exotic vegetables, home-made meat and potato pie, and turkey, ham and leek pie topped with cranberry and rosemary pastry crust. Principal beers: Tetleys, Burton Ale, Marstons Pedigree.
Free House
Bar food 11.30-9.30 11.30-9.30 Av main course £5.95
Restaurant 7-late Av 3 course à la carte £16 Av 4 course fixed price £13.95
Accommodation s£56.50 d£66.50

WENTWORTH Yorkshire, South

Rockingham Arms
WENTWORTH Map 08 SK39
8 Main St S62 7TL ☎ 01226 742075
A typical village pub serving traditional beer in a convivial atmosphere. Outside, there is a large orchard beer garden overlooking the pub's bowling green. Dishes from the daily special board include tandoori chicken, Yorkshire pudding filled with Old Peculiar casserole, and vegetable crumble. Principal beers: Theakstons, John Smiths, Fosters, Kronenbourg.
Directions M1 J36 to Hoyland Common then B6090
Scottish & Newcastle
Open 11-11 (Sun 12-10.30)
Bar food 12-2.30 5-9 Av main course £4.75

Yorkshire, West

CLIFTON Yorkshire, West

Black Horse Inn
CLIFTON Map 07 SE12
HD6 4HJ ☎ 01484 713862
'Old World' inn, - partly listed because of internal beams, - which was once a meeting place for the Luddites. Today's menu may feature Dover sole Meunière, pork fillet schnitzel, chicken Chasseur, roast beef and Yorkshire pudding, or Cornette Washington. Principal beers: Whitbread Trophy, Boddingtons, Castle Eden, Taylors Landlord.
Directions N of Brighouse
Whitbread
Open 11-3 5.30-11 (Sun 12-3, 5.30-10.30)
Bar food 12-2.30 5.30-9.30 Av main course £5
Restaurant 12-2.15 5.30-9.30 Av 3 course à la carte £13 Av 3 course fixed price £11.95
Accommodation s£24 d£36

DEWSBURY Yorkshire, West

West Riding Licensed Refreshment Rooms
DEWSBURY Map 08 SE22
Dewsbury Railway Station, Wellington Rd WF13 1HF ☎ 01924 459193
Converted 18th-century railway station building on the Trans-Pennine route. Daily blackboard specials include a range of meat, fish, vegetarian and vegan meals, such as Alaskan fishcakes, walnut escalopes, lamb pasticcio and carrot roulade with water cress filling. An always changing selection of real ales is also available.

Principal beers: Batemans Dark, Mild, XB, XXXB.
Open 11-11 (Sun 12-10.30)
Bar food 12-4 Av main course £3.25

HAREWOOD Yorkshire, West

Harewood Arms Hotel

HAREWOOD Map 08 SE34
Harrogate Rd LS17 9LH
☎ 01132 886566

A country house hotel, recently refurbished, situated opposite Harewood House. Home-cooked English fare is served in both the bar and restaurant. Bar meals include some interesting platters, with paté, cheese, fruit and pickles, and some more sustaining dishes such as beef casserole or fish pie. Principal beers: Old Brewery Bitter, Sovereign Bitter, Ayingerbrau lager.
Directions On A61 S of Harrogate
Samuel Smith
Open 8-11
Restaurant 12-1..45 7-10 Av 3 course à la carte £15.95 Av 4 course fixed price £15.95
Accommodation s£455 d£60

HAWORTH Yorkshire, West

The Old White Lion Hotel

HAWORTH Map 07 SE03
Main St BD22 8DU
☎ 44(01535) 642313

The Rev Patrick Brontë, father of the renowned literary family, was a regular at this 300-year-old coaching inn. The bar menu serves both snacks and substantial meals, including roast beef and Yorkshire pudding. The restaurant offers a wide choice, with chef's specials such as chicken Italia and seafood crêpe. Principal beers: Wilsons, Websters, Theakstons, John Smiths.
Directions Centre of village adjoining Tourist Info Centre
Free House
Open 11-3 6-11
Bar food 11.30-2.30 6.30-9.30 Av main course £5
Restaurant 7-9.30 Av 3 course à la carte £14 Av 3 course fixed price £12

HALIFAX Yorkshire, West

The Rock Inn Hotel

HALIFAX Map 07 SE02
HX4 9BS ☎ 01422 379721

A wayside inn situated in a tranquil valley midway between Halifax and Huddersfield. East meets west in Churchill's Restaurant, with its British, French and Italian dishes set against Japanese, Chinese and Thai specialities. Toasties, burgers and popular hot meals feature on the bar menu. Principal beers: Theakstons, Black Sheep, Caffreys, John Smiths Smooth.
Directions From M62 J24 follow signs for Blackley & Holywell Green
Free House
Open 11-11
Accommodation s£45 d£59

HORBURY Yorkshire, West

Quarry Inn

HORBURY Map 08 SE21
70 Quarry Hill Rd WE4 5NE
☎ 01924 272523

Built in the latter part of the 19th-century with four cottages attached. House specials change daily and typically include chicken balti, fisherman's pie, and vegetable lasagne for vegetarians. Other main dishes include sirloin steak, Scottish haddock and chicken stir fry with a home-made piquant sauce. Principal beers: Marstons Pedigree, John Smiths, Tennants, Fosters.
Directions On the A642 approx 2.5m from Wakefield
Marstons
Open 11-3 5.30-11
Bar food 12-2 5.30-8.30 Av main course £4.50
Restaurant 12-2 5.30-8.30 Av 3 course à la carte £9
Accommodation s£20 d£25

LEDSHAM Yorkshire, West

The Chequers Inn
LEDSHAM Map 08 SE42
Claypit Ln LS25 5LP ☎ 01977 683135
Village estate setting. This pub is closed on Sundays because the lady of the manor was offended by the drunken farm workers back in 1836. Among the house specials are home-made steak and mushroom pie, beef Stroganoff, fresh dressed crab with lemon mayonnaise, and Stilton and celery quiche. Principal beers: Youngers Scotch, Theakston Best, John Smiths.
Directions between A1 & A656 above Castleford
Free House
Open 11-5 5.30-11 (Sat 11-11)
Bar food 12-2.15 6.30-9.15 Av main course £5.95

LEEDS Yorkshire, West

Whitelocks
LEEDS Map 08 SE23
Turks Head Yard, Briggate LS1 6HB
☎ 0113 2453950
First opened as a bar in 1715 by the Whitelock family who held the licence for 90 years. Bar meals range from steak grills, and roast lamb with redcurrant jelly, to salmon steak with Hollandaise sauce, and Whitelocks seafood pie in a creamy fish sauce. Principal beers: IPA, No 3, 80/-, Theakstons Bitter.
Directions Next to Marks & Spencer in Briggate,Leeds
Scottish & Newcastle
Open 11-11 (Sun 12-10.30)
Bar food 12-8 12-8 Av main course £2.25
Restaurant 12-2.30 5.30-8 Av 3 course à la carte £10

MELTHAM Yorkshire, West

Will's O' Nat's
MELTHAM Map 07 SE11
Blackmoorfoot Rd HD7 3PS
☎ 01484 850078
The name means 'William son of Nathaniel' - dating from a time when many people in a small community shared the same surname. It is a friendly pub with comfortable seating and old photographs adorning the walls. The cooking is predominantly English with an emphasis on vegetarian and fish dishes. Principal beers: Old Mill, Tetley.
Directions A62 from Huddersfield then off B6107 towards Holmfirth
Free House
Open 11-3 (Sun 12-3:30) 6-11 (Sun 7-10.30)
Bar food 11/12-2 6/6.30-9.30/10 Av main course £4.60
Restaurant 11/12-2 6/6.30-9.30/10

NEWALL Yorkshire, West

The Spite
NEWALL Map 07 SE14
LS21 2EY ☎ 01943 463063
Traditional village pub which boasts a legend of feuding landlords, a vast collection of framed bank notes, and a friendly fox known as 'The Clifton Poacher'. Today's specials board may feature dim sum with soya and oyster sauce, Cumberland sausage with apple sauce, or 'old fashioned meat and potato pie'. Principal beers: John Smiths Smooth, Websters Yorkshire Bitter.
Scottish Courage
Open 11.30-3 6-11 (Sun 12-2, 7-10.30)
Bar food 12-2 7-8.45 Av main course £5.50
Restaurant 12-2 7-8.45

POOL Yorkshire, West

The White Hart
POOL Map 08 SE24
Main St LS21 1LH ☎ 0113 2843011
Situated at the centre of the village, this building was originally a farmhouse, dating from the 18th century and licensed around 1825. Great British food is served, such as bangers and mash, cod and chips and beef and ale pie. Lighter lunches include soup and sandwiches. Principal beers: Stones, Bass, Worthingtons.
Directions From M1 J47 follow signs for airport.Then A658.Village 3m
Bass
Open 11-11 (Sun 12-10.30)

RIPPONDEN Yorkshire, West

Old Bridge Inn
RIPPONDEN Map 07 SE01
Priest Ln HX6 4DL ☎ 01422 822595
Restored, 14th-century inn situated in narrow cobbled lane close to a stream and the Packhorse Bridge. Typical examples from the blackboard menu

include pheasant pie, chicken, broccoli and Stilton pie, Penne pasta with creamed salmon and leeks, and potted smoked trout with lime butter and horseradish. Principal beers: Timothy Taylors Landlord, Black Sheep, Ryburn
Directions 5m from Halifax in village centre by church
Free House
Open 11.30-11
Bar food 12-2 6.30-10 Av main course £4.50
Restaurant 7.30-9.30 Av 3 course à la carte £22.50

RODLEY Yorkshire, West

Olive Tree
RODLEY Map 08 SE23
'Oaklands', 55 Rodley Ln LS13 1NG
☎ 0113 2569283
A Greek restaurant in an imposing Edwardian building, formerly the residence of the local mill owner. Starters comprise dips, seafood, stuffed vegetables, filo pastries and meatballs. Main courses include swordfish, kalamari, chicken souvlaki, steaks and vegetarian moussaka. Principal beers: Carlsberg, John Smiths.
Directions At junction of A6120 & A657
Free House
Open 12-2 6-11
Restaurant 12-2 6-11 Av 3 course à la carte £18 Av 3 course fixed price £11.95

ROYDHOUSE Yorkshire, West

The Three Acres Inn
ROYDHOUSE Map 08 SE21
HD8 8LR ☎ 01484 602606
Turn of the century coaching inn situated in the Pennine countryside south of Huddersfield. Main meals include terrine of duck breast and belly pork with spiced pears and onion focaccia, grilled venison steak with spiced red cabbage and beetroot jus and, to follow, pancotta with poached fruits in Grappa. Principal beers: Mansfield Bitter, Timothy Taylors Landlord, Old Speckled Hen, Riding Bitter.
Directions From Huddersfield take A629 then B6116,take L turn for village
Free House
Open 12-3 7-11
Bar food 12-2 7-9.45 Av main course £7.95
Restaurant 12-2 7-9.45 Av 3 course à la carte £20
Accommodation s£30 d£50

SHELF Yorkshire, West

Duke of York
SHELF Map 07 SE12
West St, Stone Chair HX3 7LN
☎ 01422 202056
There's a vast array of brassware and jugs at this 17th-century former coaching inn, and the atmosphere is lively. Traditional pub food is served, including a range of snacks, grills, chicken specialities, Indian dishes and vegetarian options. Daily specials include a large list of fresh fish. Principal beers: Taylors Best, Taylors Landlord, Whitbread Trophy, Boddingtons.
Directions M62 J25 to Brighouse.Take A644 N.Inn 500yds on R after Stone Chair r'about
Whitbread
Open 11-12 (Sun 12-11)
Bar food 12-2 5-9 Av main course £8
Accommodation s£28 d£38

THORNTON Yorkshire, West

Ring O'Bells
THORNTON Map 07 SE03
212 Hilltop Rd BD13 3QL
☎ 01274 832296
A 19th-century building converted from a chapel and two cottages high in the Pennines. The chapel bells called the congregation to worship - hence the pub's name. There's an imaginative menu, supplemented by daily specials, offering pies, steaks, fresh fish and vegetarian dishes. Principal beers: Websters, John Smiths, Theakstons, Black Sheep.

contd.

Directions From M62 take A58 for 5m, turn R at Xroads onto A644, after 4 1/2m follow signs for Denholme, on to Well Head rd into Hilltop rd
Free House
Bar food 12-2 5.30-9.30 Av main course £6.50
Restaurant 12-2 7-9.30 Av 3 course à la carte £12 Av 2 course fixed price £6.50

WIDDOP Yorkshire, West

Pack Horse Inn
WIDDOP Map 07 SD93
HX7 7AT ☎ 01422 842803
Dating from the 1600s, this former farmhouse is in a remote moorland area, 300 yards off the Pennine Way and half a mile from Hardcastle Crags. Quality and quantity are both evident in the pub food, with dishes ranging from sandwiches and salads to fresh fish and steak au poivre. Principal beers: Thwaites, Theakstons, IPA.
Directions Off A646 & A6033
Free House
Open 12-3 7-11
Bar food 12-2 7-10 Av main course £5.50
Accommodation s£20 d£28

Scotland

Beyond and between great Scottish cities lies some of Britain's most romantic and superlative scenery, which includes its highest mountain, deepest lake, largest trees and most remote terrain.

• Aberdeen City • Aberdeenshire •
• Angus • Argyll & Bute •
• City of Edinburgh •
• City of Glasgow •
• Dumfries & Galloway •
• Dundee City • East Lothian •
• Falkirk • Fife • Highlands • Moray •
• Perth & Kinross • Renfrewshire •
• Scottish Borders • South Ayrshire •
• Stirling • Western Isles •

Aberdeen City

ABERDEEN Aberdeen City

Prince of Wales
ABERDEEN Map 15 NJ90
7 St Nicholas AB10 1HF
☎ 01224 640597
The pub dates from 1850 and has the longest bar in the city at 60 feet. It has a reputation for good value, and the home-cooked food might include steak pie, breaded haddock and macaroni cheese. Other options are freshly made baguettes and baked potatoes with various fillings. Principal beers: Tennents lager.
Directions city centre
Free House
Open 11-12
Bar food 11.30-2.30 Av main course £3.70

Aberdeenshire

KINCARDINE O'NEIL Aberdeenshire

Gordon Arms Hotel
KINCARDINE O'NEIL Map 15 NO59
North Deeside Rd AB34 5AA
☎ 01339 884236
A granite-built coaching inn dating from around 1820, which retains much of its period character. All meals are prepared on the premises using fresh local ingredients, and the traditional high teas are particularly family orientated. A separate vegetarian menu is also available. Principal beers: McEwans, Export, Carlsberg, Heineken.
Free House
Open 11.30-11 (Mon-Wed) 11.30-12 (Thurs-Sun)
Bar food 12-2 5-9 Av main course £4.75
Restaurant 12-2 5-9 Av 3 course à la carte £8.50
Accommodation s£16 d£20

MARYCULTER Aberdeenshire

Old Mill Inn
MARYCULTER Map 15 NO89
South Deeside Rd AB12 5FX
☎ 01224 733212
A 200-year-old mill, with original timbers and beams, set on the banks of the River Dee, only 10 minutes from Aberdeen city centre. There's an interesting selection of dishes ranging from steak and kidney pie to grilled halibut and banana with a mango chutney cream and raspberries. Principal beers: Tennants, Special, Guinness.
Directions 5m W of Aberdeen on B9077
Free House
Open 11-11 (Sun-Thurs) 11-12 (Fri-Sat)
Bar food 12-2 5.30-9.30 Av main course £7.50
Restaurant 12-2 5.30-9.30 Av 3 course à la carte £15.50
Accommodation s£30 d£40

NETHERLEY Aberdeenshire

Lairhillock Inn and Restaurant
NETHERLEY Map 15 NO89
AB39 3QS ☎ 01569 730001
A former coaching inn, the oldest part of which was originally a farmhouse, set in its own 50 acres on Royal Deeside. A signature dish of the restaurant, which is in a converted byre, is rack of lamb with glazed shallots, bacon julienne, rosemary gravy and hot mint jelly. Principal beers: Flowers, Boddingtons, Export.
Directions From Aberdeen take A90 then B9077 for Durris then B979
Free House
Open 11-2.30 5-11
Bar food 12-2 6-9.30
Restaurant 12-2 7-11 Av 3 course à la carte £27.95 Av 3 course fixed price £27.95
Accommodation s£65

OLDMELDRUM Aberdeenshire

The Redgarth
OLDMELDRUM Map 15 NJ18
Kirk Brae AB51 0DJ ☎ 01651 872353
There are magnificent views of Bannachie and the surrounding countryside from this friendly establishment. Cask conditioned ales from all over the UK are served in the lounge bar, along with a range of snacks, and there is a varied menu of home-cooked dishes using fresh local produce. Principal beers: Redgarth Ale, Tennants, Caffreys, Guinness.
Directions On A947
Free House
Open 11-2.45 5-11
Bar food 12-2 5-9 Av main course £4.75
Restaurant 12-2 5-9 Av 3 course à la carte £12
Accommodation s£40 d£50

STONEHAVEN Aberdeenshire

Marine Hotel
STONEHAVEN Map 15 NO88
9/10 Shorehead AB39 2JY
☎ 01569 762155
Built 100 years ago, this four-storey hotel is situated in a fishing village overlooking the harbour. Not surprisingly, seafood figures prominently, alongside steak sizzlers, chilli and burgers, with favourite sweets such as sticky toffee pudding and death by chocolate. Snacks are also served in the bar.
Directions 15m south of Aberdeen on A90
Free House
Open 11-12
Bar food 12-2 5-10 Av main course £6
Restaurant 12-2 5-10 Av 3 course à la carte £12 Av 3 course fixed price £6
Accommodation s£27.50 d£40

Angus

GLENISLA Angus

The Glenisla Hotel
GLENISLA Map 15 NO26
PH11 8PH ☎ 01575 582223
17th-century coaching inn situated in the Valley of Glenisla, not far from the ruins of Forter Castle. Lunchtime meals include casserole of Glenisla pheasant cooked in cider, and Perthshire ham with parsley sauce. Supper menu features casseroled venison with fruits of the forest, and grilled duck with ginger wine sauce. Principal beers: Boddingtons, Theakstons, McEwans.

Directions On B951
Free House
Open 11-2.30 5.30-11 (July-Oct open all day)
Bar food 12-2.30 6.30-21 Av main course £11
Restaurant 12-2.30 6.30-9 Av 3 course à la carte £16 Av 3 course fixed price £10
Accommodation s£35 d£60

Argyll & Bute

ARDENTINNY Argyll & Bute

Ardentinny Hotel
ARDENTINNY Map 10 NS18
Loch Long PA23 8TR
☎ 01369 810209
A 1720 droving inn with turret staircase, situated beside Loch Long. Bar menu features beef olives in a red wine and onion gravy, and skippers macaroni. Restaurant dishes include Barbary duck breast with light and sweet beetroot sauce, leek and potato crumble, and local salmon with cucumber and ginger spaghetti. Principal beers: McEwans, Miller, XB.

contd.

Free House
Bar food 12-3 6-9.30 Av main course £6.95
Restaurant 7-9.30 Av 3 course à la carte £24 Av 4 course fixed price £24
Accommodation s£36 d£68

ARDFERN Argyll & Bute

The Galley of Lorne Inn
ARDFERN Map 10 NM80
PA31 8QH ☎ 01852 500284
A former droving inn situated on the shores of Loch Craignish, where seals can often be seen, and a wide variety of sea birds. There are two restaurants, which were once the stable-yard of the inn. Local seafood, game and char-grilled steaks are features of the menus. Principal beers: McEwans Export, Millers Export Lager, Theakstons, Guinness.
Directions 25 S of Oban. A816 then B8002
Free House
Open 12-11
Bar food 12-2 6.30-9 Av main course £5
Restaurant 6.30-9.30 Av 3 course à la carte £13
Accommodation s£28.50 d£33.50

CAIRNBAAN Argyll & Bute

Cairnbaan Hotel & Restaurant
CAIRNBAAN Map 10 NR89
PA31 8SJ ☎ 01546 603668
Originally a coaching inn, the hotel was built towards the end of the 18th-century in response to the construction of the Crinan Canal. Main dishes include casserole of West Highland lamb cooked with yoghurt and apricots, smoked haddock and salmon Boulangère, and mushroom Stroganoff flamed in brandy with soured cream. Principal beers: Bass, Deuchars IPA, Caffreys, Tennents Velvet.
Directions From Glasgow Airport take A82/A83 to lochilphead,then A816 to Cairnbaan
Free House
Open 11-11
Bar food 12-2 7-9 Av main course £8
Restaurant 7-9 Av 3 course à la carte £20
Accommodation s£45 d£65

CLACHAN-SEIL Argyll & Bute

Tigh an Truish Inn
CLACHAN-SEIL Map 10 NM71
PA34 4QZ ☎ 01852 300242
Originally a drover's inn this small, homely pub's name refers to the Isle of Seil residents' custom of changing from kilts to trousers before going to the mainland. No such dress code is needed now to enjoy home made fare with a wealth of fresh seafood in season. Principal beers: Youngers No.3, Guinness, Murphys, Fosters.
Directions 14m S of Oban, take A816, 12m turn off B844 toward Atlantic Bridge
Free House
Open 11-2.30 5-11.30 (summer 11-11.30)
Bar food 12-2.15 6-8.30 Av main course £5.50
Accommodation d£40

DERVAIG Argyll & Bute

See **Mull, Isle of**

DUNOON Argyll & Bute

Coylet Inn
DUNOON Map 10 NS17
Loch Eck PA23 8SG ☎ 01369 840426
18th-century coaching inn on the shore of Loch Eck, used for BBC ghost story starring Emma Thompson. Said to be haunted. Bar snacks, seafood starters and Scottish beef steaks are regulars. Daily blackboard might include warm duck salad with home-

made orange marmalade, or local venison sausage. Principal beers: McEwans, Guinness.
Free House
Open 11-2.30 5-12
Bar food 12.30-2 7-9.30 Av main course £5
Restaurant 12.30-2 7-9.30 Av 3 course à la carte £15
Accommodation s£19.50 d£39

KILBERRY Argyll & Bute

Kilberry Inn
KILBERRY Map 10 NR17
PA29 6YD ☎ 01880 770223
Converted post office croft with white stone walls and red tin roof. All of the meals are home-made and displayed on the blackboard menu. Main course dishes range from rump steak and kidney pie, and local salmon fish pie salad, to Scotch beef in red wine and topped with Stilton. Principal beers: Scottish and Newcastle, Greenmantle Ales (bottled).
Directions From Lochgilphead take A83 south. Take B8024 signposted Kilberry
Free House
Open 11-2.30 5-11
Bar food 12.15-2 6.30-9 Av main course £7.50
Restaurant 12.15-2 6.30-9 Av 3 course à la carte £25
Accommodation s£36.50 d£63

KILNINVER Argyll & Bute

Scottish Salmon Centre
KILNINVER Map 10 NM82
PA34 4QS ☎ 01852 316202
Bar and restaurant that is part of an exhibition centre which takes as its theme the life of the salmon, "one of Scotland's greatest ambassadors." Obviously, salmon features heavily on a menu that may also include steamed Scottish mussels, butterfly chicken breast, Langoustine prawns, or sirloin steak in whisky and mustard sauce. Principal beers: Budweiser, Tennents, McEwans.
Directions 6m S of Oban on A816
Free House
Open 10-10
Restaurant 12-2.30 6-10 Av 3 course à la carte £20

MULL, ISLE OF Argyll & Bute

The Old Byre Heritage Centre
DERVAIG Map 13 NM45
PA75 6QR ☎ 01688 400229
Previously a cowshed and a chocolate factory, this licensed tearoom is part of a museum that explores the history, flora and wildlife of Mull. Typical menu includes vegetable quiche, vegetable and lentil soup, a selection of filled rolls, and the Mull speciality - Clootie Dumpling. Principal beers: Tennents, McEwan.
Directions on the B8073 from Tobermory
Open 10.30-6.30

OBAN Argyll & Bute

The Barn
OBAN Map 10 NM83
Cologin, Lerags PA34 4SE
☎ 01631 564618
A 200-year-old converted byre, three miles from Oban in a private glen, with its own large duck pond. Good-value home-cooked food is served, including snacks, seafood (Friday night's speciality), game casserole and mushroom moussaka. Cranachan and apple pie are among the traditional puddings. Principal beers: Calders 70/-, Guinness, Lowenbrau, Tetleys.
Open 11-1
Bar food 12-2.30 6-9 Av main course £5.75

TAYNUILT Argyll & Bute

Polfearn Hotel
TAYNUILT Map 10 NN03
PA35 1JT ☎ 01866 822251
A traditional granite villa near the River Awe. Once the home of Colonel Campbell-Preston, a celebrated former Colditz POW. The extensive bar menu contains many seafood dishes, including the house speciality, Loch Etive mussels cooked in wine, onions and parsley. Game and vegetarian dishes are also available. Principal beers: McEwans, Beamish, Guinness.
Free House
Open 11-3 5.30-11
Bar food 12-3 5.30-9 Av main course £7
Restaurant 7-7.30 Av 3 course à la carte £18 Av 5 course fixed price £18
Accommodation s£25 d£40

TAYVALLICH Argyll & Bute

Tayvallich Inn
TAYVALLICH Map 10 NR78
PA31 8PL ☎ 01546 870282
Situated on the shores of Loch Sween in a superb natural anchorage, this small inn features the freshest of local scallops, mussels, oysters, crab and lobster. Dishes on offer include Tayvallich seafood symphony, steamed chicken with puy lentils and red pepper sauce, and prime sirloin steak. Principal beers: Alloa 70/-, 80/-, Carlsberg, Kilkenny.
Directions From Lochgilphead take A816 then B841/B8025
Free House
Open 11-2.30 (11-12 June-Oct) 6-11
Bar food 12-2 6-8.30 Av main course £6
Restaurant 7-9 Av 3 course à la carte £25

City of Edinburgh

EDINBURGH City of Edinburgh

The Tattler
EDINBURGH Map 11 NT27
23 Commercial St EH6 6JA
☎ 0131 554 9999
A comfortable Victorian pub in the Port of Leith offering 'a friendly pint by the fire, a tasty snack in the bar or dinner in the restaurant'. Local fish is a speciality of the modern Scottish menu, including fresh mussels and seared salmon suprême, along with steaks and Auld Reekie ham. Principal beers: Burton, Tetley, Carlsberg.
Directions 5 mins from city centre in Port of Leith
Free House
Open 9-1
Bar food 12-2.30 6-10 Av main course £5.50
Restaurant 12-2.30 6-10 Av 3 course à la carte £15

RATHO City of Edinburgh

The Bridge Inn
RATHO Map 11 NT17
27 Baird Rd EH28 8RA
☎ 0131 3331320 3331251
Originally built in 1750, the Bridge Inn has served travellers on the Union Canal through good times and bad. The current landlord was instrumental in re-opening the canal in the 1970s. A meal here may include Ratho haggis fillet steak, venison casserole, roast duckling, or Newhaven haddock fillet. Principal beers: Belhaven.
Directions From Newbridge roundabout A89/A8 follow signs for Ratho
Free House
Open 12-11 (Mon-Thu) (Fri,Sat 12-12) (Sun 12.30-11)
Bar food 12-9 12-9 Av main course £5.75
Restaurant 12-2 6.30-9 Av 3 course à a carte £20

SOUTH QUEENSFERRY City of Edinburgh

Hawes Inn

SOUTH QUEENSFERRY Map 11 NT17

Newmalls Rd EH30 9TA

☎ 0131 3311990

Robert Louis Stevenson stayed here in 1886 while he wrote Kidnapped, and Sir Walter Scott mentioned it in The Antiquary. Overlooking the magnificent Forth Railway Bridge, it has an old world charm. The menu features haggis, neaps and tatties and Man of Glen mussels as well as steaks and fish dishes. There is live blues and jazz on Mondays. Principal beers: Calders 70/-, Calders Cream, Arrows 80/-, Beachers IPA.

Directions A90 from Edinburgh

Free House

Open 7-12

Restaurant 12-2 6.30-10 Av 3 course à la carte £25 Av 3 course fixed price £23.95

Accommodation s£34 d£55

City of Glasgow

GLASGOW City of Glasgow

Buttery

GLASGOW Map 11 NS56

652 Argyle St G3 8UF ☎ 0141 221 8188

Close to the heart of Glasgow this Victorian pub offers a varied menu, which may feature toasted tomato bread with salmon and spinach and saffron cream, Buttery Scottish steak sandwich with wild mushrooms, grilled sole with seaweed, baked pineapple with curried vegetables, or aubergine and tomato gateau. Principal beers: Calders 80/-, Carlsberg Export lager.

Directions Town centre

Free House

Open 12-2.30 6-10.30

Bar food 12-2.30

Restaurant 12-2.30 7-10.30 Av 3 course fixed price £14.85

Rab's Ha

GLASGOW Map 11 NS56

53 Hutchieson St G1 1SH

☎ 0141 5531545

Named after a renowned Glaswegian glutton, this friendly establishment comprises a cellar restaurant, ground floor bar and first floor hotel, all in a listed building. There is a good choice of bar food, and restaurant dishes include traditional haggis, salmon with sorrel and vermouth, and blueberry and oatmeal crumble. Principal beers: McEwans 70/-, 80/-, Guinness, Murphys.

Directions City centre

Free House

Open 10-12

Restaurant 5.30-10.30 Av 3 course à la carte £16

Accommodation s£35 d£45

Ubiquitous Chip

GLASGOW Map 11 NS56

12 Ashton Ln, Off Byres Rd G12 8SJ

☎ 0141 3345007

Described as a 'genuine heavy drinking Scottish pub', the eating is done 'Upstairs at the Chip', where dishes are based on fresh local foods. There's vegetarian haggis with neeps and tatties, silverside beef with rich gravy, roasted chicken leg stuffed with skirlie, and baked salmon marinated in honey, tamari and ginger. Principal beers: Furstenberg lager, Caledonian 80/-, Caledonian IPA.

Free House

Open 11-11 (Sun-Thurs) 11-12 (Fri-Sat)

Dumfries & Galloway

ISLE OF WHITHORN Dumfries & Galloway

The Steam Packet Inn

ISLE OF WHITHORN Map 11 NX43

Harbour Row DG8 8HZ

☎ 01988 500334

A busy family-run hotel with a relaxed atmosphere and an emphasis on good value food and drink. The bar has a distinctly nautical flavour and is a focus for the yachting and fishing fraternity. Dishes range from haggis and chips to fresh lobster or chicken with Cinzano beurre blanc. Principal beers: Theakstons XB, McEwans, Caffreys, Harp.

Directions From Newton Stewart take A714,then A746 to Whithorn, then Isle of Whithorn

Free House

Open 11-11

Bar food 12-2 7-9.30 Av main course £4.50

Restaurant 7-9.30 Av 3 course à la carte £13.50 Av 3 course fixed price £13.50

Accommodation s£22.50 d£22.50

KIRKCUDBRIGHT Dumfries & Galloway

The Royal Hotel
KIRKCUDBRIGHT Map 11 NX65
St Cuthbert St DG6 4DY
☎ 01557 331213
The Pheasant Carvery & Grill is the place for food at this traditional hotel. An interesting and varied menu covers world-wide dishes such as Cajun mushrooms, hot mozzarella melt, Galloway sauce steak, chicken chimichanga and deep-fried ice cream. At weekends the carvery offers two roasted local joints. Principal beers: Tennants, Caffreys, Youngers, Sulwath Criffel real ale.
Directions Off A75 into Kirkcudbright on A711
Free House
Open 10.30-12
Bar food 12-2.30 6-9 Av main course £4.25
Restaurant 12-2.30 7-9 Av 3 course à la carte £7.95
Accommodation s£19 d£38

MINNIGAFF Dumfries & Galloway

Creebridge House Hotel
MINNIGAFF Map 10 NX46
DG8 6NP ☎ 01671 402121
The 18th-century former home of the Earls of Galloway achieves a real country pub feel. There's a choice between flamboyant Scottish bistro cooking in the bar and brasserie, or traditional Scottish/French cuisine in the Garden Restaurant, all dishes using quality local produce. Principal beers: Orkney Dark Island, Tetley Bitter, Calders.
Directions From A75 into Newton Stewart, turn right over river bridge, hotel 200yds on left.
Free House
Open 12-2.30 6-11.30
Bar food 12-2 6-9 Av main course £6.95
Restaurant 7-8.30 Av 3 course à la carte £22 Av 4 course fixed price £22
Accommodation s£42 d£54

MOFFAT Dumfries & Galloway

Black Bull Inn
MOFFAT Map 11 NT00
Churchgate DG10 9EG
☎ 01683 220206
The main building of this hotel dates from the 16th-century and was used by Graham of Claverhouse as his headquarters. Scottish bard Robert Burns was a frequent visitor circa 1790. A varied menu includes traditional Scottish fare such as Moffat ram pie, Devil's beef tub pie, Rabbie's roast and haggis. Principal beers: McEwans, Theakstons.
Free House
Open 11-11
Bar food 11-2.15 5-9.15 Av main course £4.55
Restaurant 11.30-2.15 5-9.30 Av 3 course à la carte £8 Av 3 course fixed price £7
Accommodation s£20 d£29

NEW ABBEY Dumfries & Galloway

Criffel Inn
NEW ABBEY Map 11 NX96
2 The Square DG2 8BX
☎ 01387 850305
A small 19th-century country inn, this friendly establishment is situated in a village built around Sweetheart Abbey. Scottish home fare includes the traditional high tea and specials might include lamb gigot in tomato and red pepper sauce or cottage pie. Over a 100 whiskies are stocked. Principal beers: Belhaven, Tennents, Guinness.
Directions From Gretna Green take A75 to Dumfries, A710 S to New Abbey
Free House
Open 12-2.30 5.30-11
Bar food 12-2 5-8 Av main course £9
Restaurant 12-2 5-8 Av 3 course à la carte £10
Accommodation s£22 d£22

Dundee City

BROUGHTY FERRY Dundee City

Fisherman's Tavern
BROUGHTY FERRY Map 12 NO43
10-14 Fort St DD5 2AD
☎ 01382 775941
Listed 16th-century fisherman's cottage, converted into a pub in 1857. Situated on the north side of the Tay Estuary. A wide selection of starters, snacks and light meals are available. Main meals include steak and Guinness pie, goujons of chicken, fisherman's pie, and vegetarian nut roast. Principal beers: Belhaven 80/-, St. Andrews, Maclays 80/-
Free House
Open 11-1 (Sun 12.30 -12)

Bar food 11.30-2.30 3-7 Av main course £4.50
Accommodation s£17 d£34

DUNDEE Dundee City

Mercantile Bar

DUNDEE Map 11 NO43
100/108 Commercial St DD1 2AG
☎ 01382 225500
Busy town centre pub with upstairs restaurant. Bar snacks include filled baked potatoes and salads. Main course dishes feature chicken in a spicy American sauce, chicken balti, lamb in mushroom sauce and, for vegetarians, there is a mushroom Biriyani. A wide selection of malt whiskies is available. Principal beers: Tartan Special, Draft Miller, McEwans 80/- & 70/-, Tennents lager.
Directions Town centre
Free House
Open 10-11 (Sun 12-10.30, Thu-Sat 10-12)

East Lothian

EAST LINTON East Lothian

Drovers Inn

EAST LINTON Map 12 NT57
5 Bridge St ☎ 0162086 0298
At this characterful old railway inn set in a picturesque village, relax to 20s-style background music in the downstairs bar while enjoying wholesome Drovers' lamb hot pot. Try the house speciality, char-grilled suckling pig cooked Spanish style with honey and ginger glaze, in the antique furnished restaurant. Principal beers: Belhaven, Carlsberg.
Directions Off A1 5m past Haddington, follow rd under railway bridge, then L.
Free House
Open 11-2.30 5-11 (Sun 12.30-11)
Bar food 11.30-2 5-10 Av main course £6
Restaurant 11.30-2 6-9.30 Av 3 course à la carte £20.25

Falkirk

CASTLECARY Falkirk

Castlecary House Hotel

CASTLECARY Map 11 NS77
Main St G68 0HD ☎ 01324 840233
Main building is a 19th-century coaching inn. A la carte menu offers escargots in mustard batter, and pasta

and courgette stew. A wide range of steak dishes is also available. Main dishes include sea bass with Provençale herb crust, poached in Vermouth, and pheasant with ginger and whisky sauce. Principal beers: Tennants, Special and Velvet, Guinness, Caffreys.
Directions Off A80 N of Cumbernauld
Free House
Open 6.45-11.30 (Sun, Mon-Wed) 6.45-12 (Thur-Sat)
Bar food 12-2 6-9 Av main course £4
Restaurant 12-2 7-10 Av 3 course à la carte £15 Av 3 course fixed price £15
Accommodation s£15 d£45

Fife

ANSTRUTHER Fife

The Dreel Tavern

ANSTRUTHER Map 12 NO50
16 High St KY10 3DL
☎ 01333 310727
There's plenty of atmosphere to this 16th-century coaching inn with its oak beams and coal fire. The menu offers ploughman's, fish or steak pie, burgers, baked potatoes and fried chicken, with daily specials such as haddock Mornay and roast beef with Yorkshire pudding. Principal beers: Arrol's 80/-, Orkney Dark Island, Calders.
Free House
Open 11am-12 midnight
Bar food 12-2 6.15-9.15 Av main course £4.95
Restaurant 12-2 6.15-9.15

Scotland

ELIE Fife

The Ship Inn
ELIE Map 12 NO40
KY9 1DT ☎ 01333 330246
A traveller's hostelry since 1838, the Ship is only feet away from the beach of Elie Bay where annual cricket and rugby matches are held. A regularly varied menu may offer sole fillets princess, beef steak pie, tuna and peach salad, or seafood crepes. Principal beers: Bellhaven, Theakstons Best, Tartan Special.
Directions Follow A915 & A917 to Elie.Follow signs from High St to Watersport Centre to the Toft.
Free House
Open 12-11 (Sun 11-12.30)
Accommodation s£30 d£25

FALKLAND Fife

Kind Kyttock's Kitchen
FALKLAND Map 11 NO20
Cross Wynd KY15 7BE
☎ 01337 857477
An informal country tea room in a listed building amidst the 18th-century architectural splendour of Falkland. Lunchtime offerings include Scotch broth with home-made wholemeal bread, pizzas, salads and sandwiches. The freshly baked scones, cakes and puddings are a real treat.
Directions A92 N from Glenrothes and take A912
Open 10.30-5.30
Restaurant 12-5.30 Av 3 course à la carte £9

KIRKCALDY Fife

Hoffmans
KIRKCALDY Map 11 NT29
435 High St KY1 2SG ☎ 01592 204584
The pub is built to a Dutch design, to acknowledge the business brought to the town by Dutch sailors in the last century. The food is cooked on the premises from fresh produce, and typical dishes include gravlax with Arran mustard dressing, and roast loin of pork with Calvados sauce. Principal beers: Scottish and Newcastle, Export, Lager, Guinness.
Directions Town centre
Free House
Open 11-12mid
Bar food 12-2 7-9.30 Av main course £4.50
Restaurant 12-2 7-9.30 Av 3 course fixed price £9.95

LOWER LARGO Fife

Crusoe Hotel
LOWER LARGO Map 11 NO40
2 Main St KY8 6BT ☎ 01333 320759
Lower Largo is the birthplace of Alexander Selkirk, whose adventures were immortalised by Daniel Defoe in Robinson Crusoe, hence the name. The hotel is at the harbour's edge, and on the Fife coastal walk. Food ranges from bar snacks to full restaurant meals, including flambé dishes. Principal beers: McEwans, Dry Blackthorn, Becks, Miller.
Directions A92 to Kirkcaldy East, A915 to Lundin Links, then R to Lower Largo
Free House
Open 11-12 (Sun 12.30-12)
Bar food 12-2.30 5-7 Av main course £4.85
Restaurant 12-2.30 7-9.45 Av 3 course à la carte £22.50 Av 3 course fixed price £15
Accommodation s£53 d£65.50

MARKINCH Fife

Town House Hotel
MARKINCH Map 11 NO20
1 High St KY7 6DQ ☎ 01592 758459
Numerous awards have been won for the cooking at this family-run hotel. Dishes might include Chinese-style sweet and sour chicken, balti curry, rib-eye steak and herb-crusted fillet of salmon. The menu is supplemented by daily specials including haggis and clootie dumpling. Principal beers: Calders 80/-, Skol lager.
Directions Off A92(Dundee/Kirkcaldy rd) Hotel opp. rail station
Free House
Open 12-2 6.15-11
Restaurant 12-2 6.15-9 Av 3 course à la carte £10.95
Accommodation s£25 d£40

ST MONANS Fife

The Cabin
ST MONANS Map 12 NO50
16 West End KY10 2BX
☎ 01333 730327
There is a 20ft well at the Cabin with pure water reputed to have healing properties. The harbourside bar and restaurant has lots of wood, brass and antique-style furnishings, plus a sunny terrace for outdoor dining. Naturally, seafood is a feature, along with home-made brown bread, pickles, sauces and puddings. Principal beers: Belhaven, St Andrews.
Free House
Open 11-9.30 (Easter-Oct) 11-8 (Nov-New Year)
Bar food 12-2.30 5-9.30 Av main course £6
Restaurant 12-2.30 6-9.30 Av 3 course à la carte £16

Highland

ALTNAHARRA Highland

Altnaharra Hotel
ALTNAHARRA Map 14 NC53
IV27 4UE ☎ 01549 411222
Remote Highland hotel also known as the Sportsmans Retreat since it is in an area which has been famous for salmon and trout angling since the early 1800s. Main course dishes range from Scottish herring in oatmeal, and lobster Monegasque, to roast grouse, and mustard rabbit with spiced peaches. Principal beers: McEwans, Miller.
Directions A9 to Bonar Bridge, A336 to Lairg & Tongue
Free House
Bar food 12-2.30 Av main course £7.50
Restaurant 7-9 Av 3 course à la carte £22 Av 4 course fixed price £22
Accommodation s£51 d£102

APPLECROSS Highland

Applecross Inn
APPLECROSS Map 13 NG74
Shore St IV54 8LR ☎ 01520 744262
Approached by the 'pass of the cattle', one of the fastest rising roads in Britain, the Applecross is ideally situated for walkers, anglers, bird watchers, and rock climbers. The menu may feature haggis flambé with Drambuie, oysters, squat lobster, Stornoway black pudding, or venison casserole. Dining room small so pre-booking advised. Principal beers: McEwans, Export, Strongbow, Gillespies Stout.
Directions From Lochcarron to Kishorn then turn L onto unclassifed rd to Applacross over the 'Bealach Na Ba'
Free House
Open Mar-Nov 11-11, Nov-Mar, Mon-Thur 11.30-2.30, 5-10, Fri-Sun 11.30-11.30.
Bar food 11.30am-9pm same-same Av main course £5.95
Restaurant 6.30-8.30 Av 3 course à la carte £17.50 Av 3 course fixed price £17.50
Accommodation s£22.50 d£45

ARDVASAR Highland

Ardvasar Hotel
ARDVASAR Map 13 NG60
IV45 8RS ☎ 01471 844223
Overlooking the breath-taking Sound of Sleat and the mountainous wilderness of Knoydart this traditional white-washed Scottish island hotel is ideal for a relaxing, peaceful holiday. A typical menu includes baked shoulder of lamb with leeks, roast cod steak, fresh Skye salmon mousse, and fresh local crab. Principal beers: Export, Guinness, Caffreys.
Free House
Open 11-11
Bar food 12-2 5-7 Av main course £10
Restaurant 7.30-8.30 Av 3 course à la carte £25
Accommodation s£40 d£70

AVIEMORE Highland

The Old Bridge Inn
AVIEMORE Map 14 NH81
Dalfaber Rd PH22 1PU
☎ 01479 811137
A haven for walkers, riders and skiers, this traditional Highland inn nestles

contd.

beside the River Spey. Specialities include open sandwiches with Spey salmon and roast beef, and char-grill dishes such as suprême of chicken or devilled double loin lamb chop, served with salad and baked potatoes. Principal beers: Carlsberg lager, Guinness, Murphys.
Free House
Open 11-9 (Sun-Wed) 11-12 (Thur-Sat)
Bar food 12-2 6-9 Av main course £5.75
Restaurant 12-2.30 6-10 Av 2 course fixed price £15

CARRBRIDGE Highland

Dalrachney Lodge Hotel
CARRBRIDGE Map 14 NH92
PH23 3AT ☎ 01479 841252
In its own 16 acre grounds on the banks of the Dulnain River affording beautiful views of the Cairngorms, this cosy, friendly, former shooting lodge offers wholesome dishes using the best Scottish produce. Enjoy poached Speyside salmon with a broccoli sauce or an Angus steak with Macallan and chicken liver. Principal beers: McEwans.
Directions A9 onto A938 for 1 1/2m, through village, pub on R
Free House
Open 12-2 5.30-11
Bar food 12-2 5.30-9.30 Av main course £5
Restaurant 12-2 6.30-9 Av 3 course à la carte £17 Av 5 course fixed price £25
Accommodation s£30 d£55

CAWDOR Highland

Cawdor Tavern
CAWDOR Map 14 NH85
The Lane IV22 5XP ☎ 01667 404777
The original workshop to the castle, in the conservation village of Cawdor, this pub has a traditional atmosphere with oak panelling and an open log fire. The home cooked Taste of Scotland fare might include breast of chicken filled with haggis and served with a Drambuie and mushroom cream sauce. Principal beers: Burton, Carlsberg, Calders.
Free House
Open 11-3 5-11
Bar food 12-2 5.30-9 Av main course £5.95
Restaurant 12-2 5.30-9 Av 3 course à la carte £11

CONTIN Highland

Achilty Hotel
CONTIN Map 14 NH45
IV14 9EG ☎ 01997 421355
A 300-year-old coaching inn with a bar and restaurant created from the old farm steadings. Bric-a-brac and old farming implements are set against beams and stone walls. A wide range of traditional dishes with Scottish flavours is offered, including lamb Dunvegin and venison Macduff. Principal beers: McEwans Export, Theakstons XB.
Directions On A835
Free House
Open 11-midnight (Sat 11-11.30,Sun 12.30-11)
Bar food 12-2.30 5.30-9.30
Restaurant 5.30-9.30 Av 3 course à la carte £15
Accommodation s£22.50 d£22.50

DORES Highland

Dores Inn
DORES Map 14 NH53
South Loch Ness IV1 2TR
☎ 01463 751203
On the shores of Loch Ness, The Dores Inn is ideal for those who want to take in the beauty of the area, or perhaps scan the waters for bigger fish! Haggis, neeps and tatties, trout in almond crumb, or pasta carbonara could be on today's menu. Principal beers: Calders, Carlsberg, Guinness, Blackthorn.
Directions On B862 SW of Inverness
Free House
Open 11-11 (Sun 12.30-11)
Bar food 12-2 6-8.30

DORNOCH Highland

Mallin House Hotel
DORNOCH Map 14 NH78
Church St W25 3LP ☎ 01862 810335
Modern hotel within easy reach of the sea. Bar food includes an interesting selection of soups and broths such as the seafood creel broth. Local lobster is also available, and venison marinated in red

wine in a sauce of apricots, walnuts and hazelnuts all soaked in Madeira wine. Principal beers: John Smiths, Theakstons, Murphy, Carlsberg.
Free House
Open 11-11
Bar food 12-2 6.30-9 Av main course £6.95

FORT AUGUSTUS Highland

The Lock Inn
FORT AUGUSTUS Map 14 NH30
Canalside PH32 4AU
☎ 01320 366302
A former bank and post office, this 150-year-old building, with stone walls and oak beams, is right on the banks of the Caledonian Canal. The village is surrounded by mountains at the south end of Loch Ness. Traditional Scottish fare is served, featuring fresh seafood, game and steaks. Principal beers: McEwans, Miller.
Directions On the banks of Caledonian Canal in Fort Augustus
Free House
Open 11-1 (Sun 12.30-11)
Bar food 12-3 6-9 Av main course £5
Restaurant 6-10 Av 3 course à la carte £18

GARVE Highland

Inchbae Lodge Hotel
GARVE Map 14 NH36
N23 2PH ☎ 01997 455269
19th-century hunting lodge situated on the banks of the River Blackwater. Haggis is served traditionally with neeps and tatties. A vegetarian haggis is also provided. Seafood dishes include West Coast mussels and local smoked salmon. Wood pigeon is braised in red wine and Marsala with bacon, mushroom, celery and shallots. Principal beers: Belhaven Best, McEwans, Murphys, Tennants.
Directions On A835 midway between Inverness & Ullapool. Hotel 6m N of Garve
Free House
Open 11-2.30 5-10.30
Bar food 12-2 5-8.30 Av main course £6

Restaurant 7-8 Av 4 course fixed price £21
Accommodation s£37 d£64

GLENELG Highland

Glenelg Inn
GLENELG Map 14 NG81
IV40 8JR ☎ 01599 522273
Renovated 200-year-old inn overlooking the atmospheric Isle of Skye. Its palindromic Gaelic name means 'The Glen of Hunting'. Local oysters, mussels, prawns, wild salmon and venison are a prominent part of the menu. In the evenings, the bar area comes alive with the sound of traditional Scottish folk music. Principal beers: S and N Beers.
Directions From Shiel Bridge (A87) take unclassified road to Glenelg
Free House
Bar food 12.30-2 7.30-9 Av main course £5

ISLE ORNSAY Highland

Hotel Eilean Iarmain
ISLE ORNSAY Map 13 NG71
IV43 8QR ☎ 01471 833332
Visitors must go 'over the sea tae Skye' to this 19th-century inn. Sea views are spectacular, as are the wildlife and nearby castles. The one rosette restaurant offers a menu which may feature scallops and monktails in saffron sauce, quails eggs with spinach and mushrooms, or beef fillet with onion and Stilton. Principal beers: McEwans lager, McEwans export, Murphys, McEwans.

contd.

Directions From Skye Bridge take A87 then A851 S
Free House
Open 12-12
Bar food 12-2.30 6.30-9.30 Av main course £5.95
Restaurant 12-2 7.30-9 Av 3 course à la carte £28 Av 4 course fixed price £28
Accommodation s£60 d£90

KYLESKU Highland

Kylesku Hotel
KYLESKU Map 14 NC23
IV27 4HW ☎ 01971 502231
Waterside location with splendid views across the Loch. Said to be haunted by the Ghost of Glencoul. Bar meals range from venison terrine, and chicken tikka, to mussels in garlic and lobster sauce. Main dishes include grilled local salmon, and supreme of chicken with tarragon sauce. Principal beers: John Smiths, Theakstons, Murphys, Carlsberg.
Directions On A894 N of Unapool
Free House
Open 11-11
Bar food 12-2 6.30-9 Av main course £6.95
Restaurant 12-2 6.30-9 Av 3 course à la carte £18

LYBSTER Highland

The Portland Arms Hotel
LYBSTER Map 15 ND23
KW3 6BS ☎ 01593 721208
Built in the early 1800s as a staging post on the New Parliamentary Road. Dinner menu offers starters like Coronation chicken with bananas, pineapple and light curry mayonnaise. Steak dishes are available such as peppered sirloin with brandy and cream sauce. Haggis with whisky cream and onion sauce is also served. Principal beers: Guinness, Caffreys, Tennants.
Directions Off A99 south of Wick
Free House
Open 11-2.30 5-11
Bar food 11.30-2.30 7-9 Av main course £5.95
Accommodation s£38.50 d£58.50

PLOCKTON Highland

Creag-nan-Darach Hotel
PLOCKTON Map 14 NG83
Innes St IV52 8TW ☎ 01599 544222
Situated a mere 100 yards from the sea front. Its Gaelic name means 'Hill of the Oaks'. The BBC series Hamish Macbeth was filmed in the village. Daily choices available on the blackboard menu. Main courses typically feature moules Marinière, home-made chicken and ham pie, and locally caught langoustine. Principal beers: Lowenbrau, Calders, Guinness.
Directions On A87 to Kyle of Lochalsh take turn at Balmacara. Plockton 7m N.
Free House
Open 11-01 11-12
Bar food 12-2.30 5.30-9.30 Av main course £6.50
Restaurant 12-2.30 5.30-9.30 Av 3 course à la carte £15 Av 3 course fixed price £15
Accommodation s£26 d£44

The Plockton Hotel
PLOCKTON Map 14 NG83
Harbour St IV52 8TN ☎ 01599 544274
Village inn situated on the shore overlooking Loch Carrow. Offers a good selection of bar snacks and starters including haggis with whisky and cream. Main course dishes feature herring in oatmeal, local venison in wine, herbs, redcurrant jelly and juniper beans, and ham Jamaican, topped with dark rum & Demerara sugar. Principal beers: Tennants, Caffreys.
Directions On A87 to Kyle of Lochalsh take turn at Balmacara.Plockton 7m N.
Free House

Open 11-12 (Weekdays) 11-12.30 (Weekends)
Bar food 12-2.30 6-9
Accommodation s£25 d£27.50

ULLAPOOL Highland

The Argyll Hotel
ULLAPOOL Map 14 NH19
Argyll St IV26 2UB ☎ 01854 612422
Traditional Scottish food using local produce is offered at this small family owned hotel. Dishes include steak Argyll, prime Scotch beef topped with a whisky, onion and cream sauce, and a seafood platter of the best local catch of the day. Alternatives might be Thai chicken curry or Highland venison. Principal beers: Orkney Dark Island, Tennants.
Free House
Open 11-11.30
Bar food 12.30-2.30 5.30-9 Av main course £6
Accommodation d£17.50

The Ceilidh Place
ULLAPOOL Map 14 NH19
14 West Argyle St N26 2TY
☎ 01854 612103
A former boatshed overlooking Lochbroom, the Ceilidh Place runs a busy programme of arts events, and has its own bookshop. Vegetarian and seafood dishes figure prominently, and typical dishes might be a ratatouille crêpe glazed with mozzarella, or monkfish and prawn tails in a thermidor sauce. Principal beers: Orkney, Gillespies. Belhaven, Tennants, Guinness.
Free House
Open 11-11
Bar food 11-10 7-9.30 Av main course £4
Restaurant 7-9.30 Av 3 course à la carte £16
Accommodation s£45 d£90

Morefield Hotel & Mariners Restaurant
ULLAPOOL Map 14 NH19
North Rd FV26 2TQ ☎ 01854 612161
Owned by a former commercial scallop diver, local seafood is of course the speciality, especially shellfish. Aberdeen Angus beef and chicken dishes also get a look in. Dishes range from natural oysters to halibut steak flambéed in Pernod, served with julienne of leek in a

creamy piquant sauce. Principal beers: Belhaven, Tennants, Caffreys, Guinness.
Free House
Open 11-2.30 5-11
Bar food 2 5.30-9.30 Av main course £6
Restaurant 6.30-9.30 Av 3 course à la carte £15
Accommodation s£30 d£45

Moray

FOCHABERS Moray

Gordon Arms Hotel
FOCHABERS Map 15 NJ35
80 High St W32 7DH
☎ 01343 820508
Set beside the River Spey, this 200 year old coaching inn retains its original charm. A full range of fare from snacks to à la carte in the restaurant features some local dishes such as cullen skink or salmon, alongside staple favourites such as lasagne or jacket potatoes.
Free House
Open 11-11
Bar food 12-2.30 5-9.30 Av main course £5
Restaurant 12-2.30 5-9.30 Av 3 course à la carte £14.25
Accommodation s£40 d£60

Perth & Kinross

ABERFELDY Perth & Kinross

Ailean Chraggan Hotel
ABERFELDY Map 14 NN84
Weem PH15 2LD ☎ 01887 820346
Ailean Chraggan is gaelic for the plain beneath the rocks, and the hotel overlooks the Tay Valley to the hills beyond. Seasonal local produce is used wherever possible; look out for Loch Etive prawns and mussels, Tay salmon,

contd.

and popular casseroles, such as venison in red wine. Principal beers: Gillespies Stout, Tartan Special, Carlsberg Export.
Free House
Open 11-11
Bar food 12-2 6.30-9.30 Av main course £8
Restaurant 12-2 6.30-9.30
Accommodation s£30 d£60

ALMONDBANK Perth & Kinross

Almondbank Inn
ALMONDBANK Map 11 NO02
31 Main St PH1 3NJ
☎ 01738 583242
Situated on the banks of the River Almond, and offering a range of steak dishes including sirloin with rich port wine sauce, and sirloin with brandy and green and black peppercorn cream sauce. Chicken is served with home-made Mexican barbecue sauce, or with home-made white wine and mushroom sauce. Principal beers: Green Mantle Real Ale, Guinness, Tennants.
Directions Take A85 from Perth to Crieff for 3 miles
Free House
Open 11-11
Bar food 12-2.15 5-8.30 Av main course £4.75
Restaurant 12-2.15 5-8.30

CLEISH Perth & Kinross

Nivingston House
CLEISH Map 11 NT09
KY13 7LS ☎ 01577 850216
Situated at the foot of the Cleish Hills, parts of this hotel date back to 1725. The bar lunch menu includes Scottish smoked salmon and venison burgers, while in the restaurant typical fare includes scotch sirloin steak, lamb gigot chop, and wild duck breast with cranberry and port sauce. Principal beers: Calders, Carlsberg lager.
Free House
Open 12-2.30 6-11
Bar food 12-2.30 Av main course £5.50
Restaurant 12-2.30 Av 3 course à la carte £15.25 Av 3 course fixed price £25
Accommodation s£77.50 d£99.50

COMRIE Perth & Kinross

The Granary
COMRIE Map 11 NN72
Drummond St PH6 2DW
☎ 01764 670838
Comrie is a conservation village set in beautiful countryside. The Granary Coffee Room is traditional in style specialising in home baking and home-made preserves and ice cream. Wholesome soups and open sandwich salad platters are served with home-made bread, and there's a good choice of teas and coffees.
Directions 25m W of Perth on A85
Free House
Open 10-5
Restaurant 10-5 Av 3 course à la carte £7

Tullybannocher Farm Food Bar
COMRIE Map 11 NN72
PH6 2JY ☎ 01764 670827
In a plain wooden building but in a fine setting of rolling lawns with a view of Strathearn's hills, this restaurant offers Scottish baking, fresh salads and home cooking. Try the pork pâté with oatcakes, haddock fillet with prawns and mushrooms and traditional clootie dumpling. Principal beers: Tennents, Caledonian, Becks, Guinness.
Directions On A85, 1/4m W of Comrie
Bar food 10.30 10.30

GLENDEVON Perth & Kinross

Tormaukin Hotel
GLENDEVON Map 11 NN90
FK14 7JY ☎ 01259 781252
The Tormaukin, which is old Scots for 'hill of the mountain hare', was originally a drovers' inn. It dates from 1720 and retains its exposed stonework, beams and open fires. Fresh local produce is cooked to order providing a good choice of both traditional and international dishes. Principal beers: Harviestons, Burtons, Carlsberg, Guinness.
Directions On A823 between Gleneagles & Yelts o'Muckhart
Free House
Open 11-11
Bar food 12-2 5.30-9.30 Av main course £7

Restaurant 6.30-9.30 Av 3 course à la carte £22
Accommodation s£24.75 d£40

KILLIECRANKIE Perth & Kinross

The Killiecrankie Hotel
KILLIECRANKIE Map 14 NN96
PH16 5LG ☎ 01796 473220
Originally built as a country manse, the hotel is just five minutes from the site of the Battle of Killiecrankie, where a soldier leapt an 18-foot gorge to escape pursuing Highlanders. The restaurant menu offers an interesting mix, and bar food ranges from ploughman's to grilled herring in oatmeal. Principal beers: Calders and Carlsberg.
Directions Off A9 between Pitlochry & Blair Atholl
Free House
Open 11-2.30 6-11
Bar food 12.30-2 6.30-9.30 Av main course £7
Restaurant 7-8.30 Av course fixed price £28

KINNESSWOOD Perth & Kinross

Lomond Country Inn
KINNESSWOOD Map 11 NN10
KY13 7HN ☎ 01592 840253
Built on the slopes of the Lomond Hills, overlooking Loch Leven, this country inn is perfect for golfers, walkers and anglers. Also nearby are Loch Leven Castle and Vane Farm RSPB Reserve. Typical menu includes breast of Barbary duck, deep-fried Pittenweem haddock, and roast lamb with wine and mint. Principal beers: Draught Bass, Jennings.
Free House
Open 11-11
Bar food 12-3 6-10 Av main course £5.50
Restaurant 12-3 6-10 Av 3 course à la carte £15 Av 2 course fixed price £10
Accommodation s£35 d£59

KINROSS Perth & Kinross

The Muirs Inn Kinross
KINROSS Map 11 NO10
49 Muirs KY13 7AU ☎ 01577 862270
On the edge of Kinross, a historic market town, this traditional Scottish country inn specialises in home-cooked fare. The range is enormous: a Taste of Scotland menu, a Taste of the World menu (a different country each week), bar bites menu, and a High Tea menu.
Free House
Open 11-3 5-11 (Sat 11-11.45, Sun 12-11)

Bar food 12-3 5-11 Av main course £4
Restaurant 12-3 5-11 Av 3 course à la carte £10 Av 4 course fixed price £12.50
Accommodation s£39.50 d£29.50

MOULIN Perth & Kinross

Moulin Hotel
MOULIN Map 14 NN95
11-13 Kirkmichael Rd PH16 5EN
☎ 01796 472196
300-year-old coaching inn, situated at Pitlochry which is commonly known as the gateway to the Highlands. The dinner menu offers haggis with onion cream, casserole of Straun pheasant with mustard and ale of Atholl, and Tay salmon wrapped in lemon sole with white wine, prawn and cucumber sauce. Principal beers: Moulin Brewery (in house), Light, Braveheart, S&N.

Directions From A9 at Pitlochry take A924. Moulin 0.75m
Free House
Open 11-11 (Sun-Thur) 11-11.45 (Fri-Sat)
Restaurant 12-2.30 6-9 Av 3 course à la carte £16 Av 0 course fixed price £13
Accommodation s£30 d£40

Scotland

Renfrewshire

HOUSTON Renfrewshire

Fox & Hounds
HOUSTON Map 10 NS46
South St PA6 7EL ☎ 01505 612448
One of the coaching inns on the west coast route, the Fox & Hounds has plenty of old world charm. The menu offers a choice from the char-grill - chops, steak and chicken - and there's a varied selection of other dishes, including haggis, roast venison and fish braised in white wine with herbs. Principal beers: Tennents.
Directions M8 - Glasgow Airport. A737- Houston
Free House
Open 11-12
Bar food 12.30-2.30 5.30-10 Av main course £6
Restaurant 12.30-2.30 5.30-10 Av 3 course à la carte £16

Scottish Borders

EDDLESTON Scottish Borders

Horse Shoe Inn
EDDLESTON Map 11 NT24
EH45 8QP ☎ 01721 730225 730306
Surrounded by border hills and beautiful countryside this village pub was once a blacksmith's forge and coach stop. Poached fillet of salmon, trio of lamb cutlets, chateaubriand, tournedos Rossini, or steak and ale pie could turn up on the menu. Principal beers: Tennents, Broughton ales.
Free House
Open 8am-12 midnight
Bar food 12.30-3 6-9.30 Av main course £4.95
Restaurant 12.30-3 6-9.30 Av 3 course à la carte £12.50
Accommodation s£20 d£20

INNERLEITHEN Scottish Borders

Traquair Arms Hotel
INNERLEITHEN Map 11 NT33
Traquair Rd EH44 6PD
☎ 01896 830229
A comfortable family-run inn, dating from the 19th-century, with traditional furnishings, open fires and a relaxed atmosphere. Contemporary 'Taste of Scotland' dishes are offered in the bar and restaurant, including Finnan Savoury, a house original comprising smoked haddock, onions, Ayrshire cheddar and double cream. Principal beers: Traquair Bear Ale, Greenmantle, Calders.
Directions 6m E of Peebles on A72. Hotel 100metres from junc with B709
Free House
Open 7am-12
Restaurant 7-9 Av 3 course à la carte £14
Accommodation s£42 d£52

JEDBURGH Scottish Borders

The Pheasant Lounge Bar
JEDBURGH Map 12 NT62
61/63 High St TD8 6DQ
☎ 01835 862708
A family-run lounge bar and restaurant, the Pheasant is situated at the north end of the High Street and has a distinctive red sandstone front. There is one menu, regardless of where you sit, supplemented by blackboard specials, including liver and onions, curries, spaghetti Bolognese and traditional roasts. Principal beers: Scottish Brewers, Youngers, Murphys.
Directions Town centre
Free House
Bar food 12-2.30 6-9.30 Av main course £5
Restaurant 12-2.30 6-9.30 Av 3 course à la carte £10

MELROSE Scottish Borders

Burts Hotel
MELROSE Map 12 NT53
Market Square TD6 9PN
☎ 01896 822285
Comfortable, family-run market-town hotel where warm hospitality and good food are taken seriously. The bar offers the likes of simple steaks, ploughmans, and salmon fish cakes, whilst the imaginative restaurant menu takes in seared West Coast scallops with black

pudding and a Traquair Ale beurre blanc. Principal beers: Belhaven, Sandy Hunters, Marstons Pedigree, Carlsberg.
Free House
Open 11-2.30 5-11
Bar food 12-2 6-9.30 Av main course £5.80
Restaurant 12-2 7-9 Av 3 course à la carte £24.75 Av 3 course fixed price £24.75
Accommodation s£46 d£82

ST BOSWELLS Scottish Borders

Buccleuch Arms Hotel
ST BOSWELLS Map 12 NT53
The Green TD6 0EW ☎ 01835 822243
Traditional Scottish pub grub in the bar and Taste of Scotland dishes in the restaurant are offered at this 16th-century inn. A typical meal might comprise smoked trout mousse with lemon and dill mayonnaise; grilled loin of Border lamb stuffed with haggis and coated with Madeira sauce, and sticky toffee pudding. Principal beers: Calders, Greenmantle, Murphys, Carlsberg.
Free House
Accommodation s£35 d£60

SELKIRK Scottish Borders

Tibbie Shiels Inn
SELKIRK Map 12 NT42
St Mary's Loch TD7 5NE
☎ 01750 42231
Historic coaching inn on the shore of St Mary's Loch, named after Isabella (Tibbie) Shiel, the wife of Lord Napier's mole catcher. Robert Louis Stevenson and Gladstone were among the famous visitors. Bar meals include a selection of vegetarian specials. Seafood, game and steak dishes are available in the restaurant. Principal beers: Broughton, Belhaven, Guinness, Tennants.
Directions From Moffat take A708. Inn is 14m on R
Free House
Open 11-11
Bar food 12.30-2.30 6.30-8.30 Av main course £4.75
Restaurant 6.30-8.30 Av 3 course à la carte £13.50

SWINTON Scottish Borders

Wheatsheaf Hotel
SWINTON Map 12 NT84
Main St TD11 3JJ ☎ 01890 860257
Traditional Scottish country inn overlooking village green. Close to the River Tweed and many historic houses in the Scottish Borders. The varied menu includes locally smoked Tweed salmon, grilled goats cheese with apple chutney, and roast Gressingham duckling glazed with Tweedside honey in a Grand Marnier liqueur sauce. Principal beers: Greenmantle, Boddingtons.
Directions On A6112 Coldstream/Duns road
Free House
Open 11-2.15 6-11
Bar food 12-2.15 6.30-9.30 Av main course £5.50
Restaurant 12-2.15 6.30-9.30 Av 3 course à la carte £15
Accommodation s£32 d£52

TUSHIELAW INN Scottish Borders

Tushielaw Inn
TUSHIELAW INN Map 11 NT31
7D7 5HT ☎ 01750 62205
A 19th-century coaching inn with an idyllic location on the banks of Ettrick Water. Traditional home-made fare is offered along with inventive specials, such as creamy smoked haddock crumble, and baked chicken breast with tomato and basil sauce topped with Brie. Principal beers: Broughton Best, McEwans, Tennants.
Directions At junction of B709 & B711 (W of Hawich)
Free House
Open 12-2.30 6-11
Bar food 12-2.30 6-11 Av main course £5.25
Restaurant 12-2.30 6-11 Av 3 course à la carte £14
Accommodation s£17.10 d£22.50

TWEEDSMUIR Scottish Borders

The Crook Inn
TWEEDSMUIR Map 11 NT12
ML12 6QN ☎ 01899 880272
Reputed to be Scotland's oldest coaching inn, dating from 1604, the Crook was the first overnight stop on

contd.

the Edinburgh to London route, and Robbie Burns wrote his Willie Wastle poem in the bar. Dishes range from 'honey lemon pickled kippers' to lamb chops with gooseberry and mint sauce. Principal beers: Green mantle, McEwans, Guinness.

Free House

Open 8am-12mid

Bar food 12-9.30 12-9.30 Av main course £5.50

Restaurant 12-9.30 12-9.30

Accommodation s£36 d£2

South Ayrshire

SYMINGTON South Ayrshire

Wheatsheaf Inn

SYMINGTON Map 10 NS33

Main St KA1 5QB ☎ 01563 830307

17th-century village inn converted from an old farmhouse which still has its original walls and fires. Main seafood courses include monkfish tails in shrimp and Cognac cream and halibut steak in Mornay sauce, while typical meat dishes are tenderloin of pork in Calvados and mushroom and grilled Ayrshire ham steak. Principal beers: Belhaven.

Belhaven

Open 11-12

Stirling

BRIG O'TURK Stirling

The Byre Inn

BRIG O'TURK Map 11 NN50

FK17 8HT ☎ 01877 376292

An atmospheric Victorian building - a converted stone cow byre - with traditional Scottish music, a log fire and old local photographs. Home cooking is served in generous helpings, with dishes such as Cajun spiced salmon gâteau, and roast venison with port and redcurrant sauce. Principal beers: Maclays - Wallace, Thistle, Guinness.

Free House

Open 12-3 6-11

Bar food 12.30-2.30 6.30-9 Av main course £5.50

Restaurant 12.3-2.30 6.30-11 Av 3 course à la carte £23

DRYMEN Stirling

Clachan Inn

DRYMEN Map 11 NS48

2 Main St G63 0BG ☎ 01360 660824

Oldest registered inn in Scotland and once owned by Rob Roy's sister. The starters include chef's hickory smooth pâté. Among the many speciality items in Steak Corner are sirloin Balmoral, blackeyed sirloin and Clannachan fillet, which is steak stuffed with Borders haggis with whisky cream. Principal beers: Guinness.

Free House

Open 11-12

Bar food 12-4 6-10 Av main course £4.50

Restaurant 12-4 6-10 Av 3 course à la carte £12

STRATHBLANE Stirling

Kirkhouse Inn

STRATHBLANE Map 11 NT57

Glasgow Rd GG3 9AA ☎ 01360 770621

This friendly local, at the foot of the Campsie Hills, dates back to the 17th century. Interesting dishes add a twist to tradition; haggis rolled in oatmeal with whisky cream sauce in the lounge bar or kidneys with wild mushrooms and tournedos of Scottish fillet Principal beers: Tennents, McEwans, Maclays.

Directions From M8 take A81 thru Beardsen & Milngavie then on for 4 or 5m

Free House

Open 11-11 (weekends 11-12)

Bar food 12-2.30 6-9.30 Av main course £7

Restaurant 12-2.30 7-9.30 Av 4 course fixed price £18.95

Accommodation s£30 d£50

Western Isles

LOCHBOISDALE Western Isles

Polochar Inn

LOCHBOISDALE Map 13 NF71

Polochar H58 5TT ☎ 01878 700215

Remote inn with fine sea views, taking its name from the ancient standing stone nearby. Bonnie Prince Charlie is said to have visited after landing at Eriskay. Bar menu includes haggis with clapshot, while the carte specialises in Aberdeen Angus steak

dishes and local seafood. Principal beers: Tennants, Caffreys.
Directions From Lochboisdale travel W & take B888. Hotel at end of road
Free House
Open Mon-Wed 11-11, Thu-Fri 11-1am, Sat 11-11.30, Sun 12.30-11
Bar food 12.30-2.30 6.30-9.30 Av main course £5
Restaurant 12.30-2.30 6.30-9.30 Av 3 course à la carte £20

Whisky maturing in bonded warehouse, Glengoyne Distillery, Scotland

Central London

KEY TO PUB LOCATIONS

Each pub in London has a map reference, eg C2. The letter 'C' refers to the grid square located at the bottom of the map. The figure '2' refers to the grid square located at the left hand edge of the map. For example, where these two intersect, Buckingham Palace can be found.

Due to the scale of the map, only a rough guide to the location of a pub can be given. A more detailed map will be necessary to be precise.

Greater London

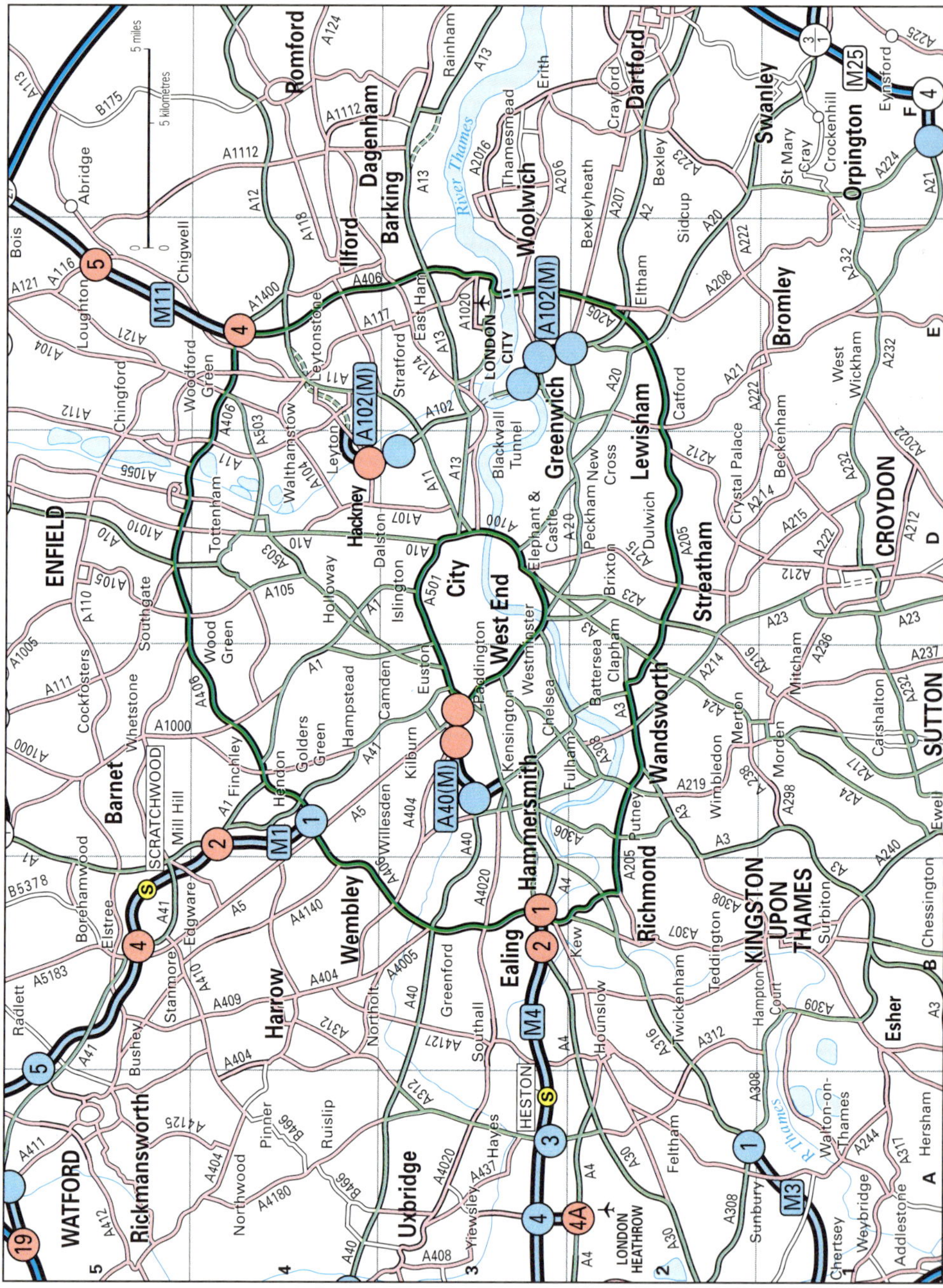

KEY TO ATLAS

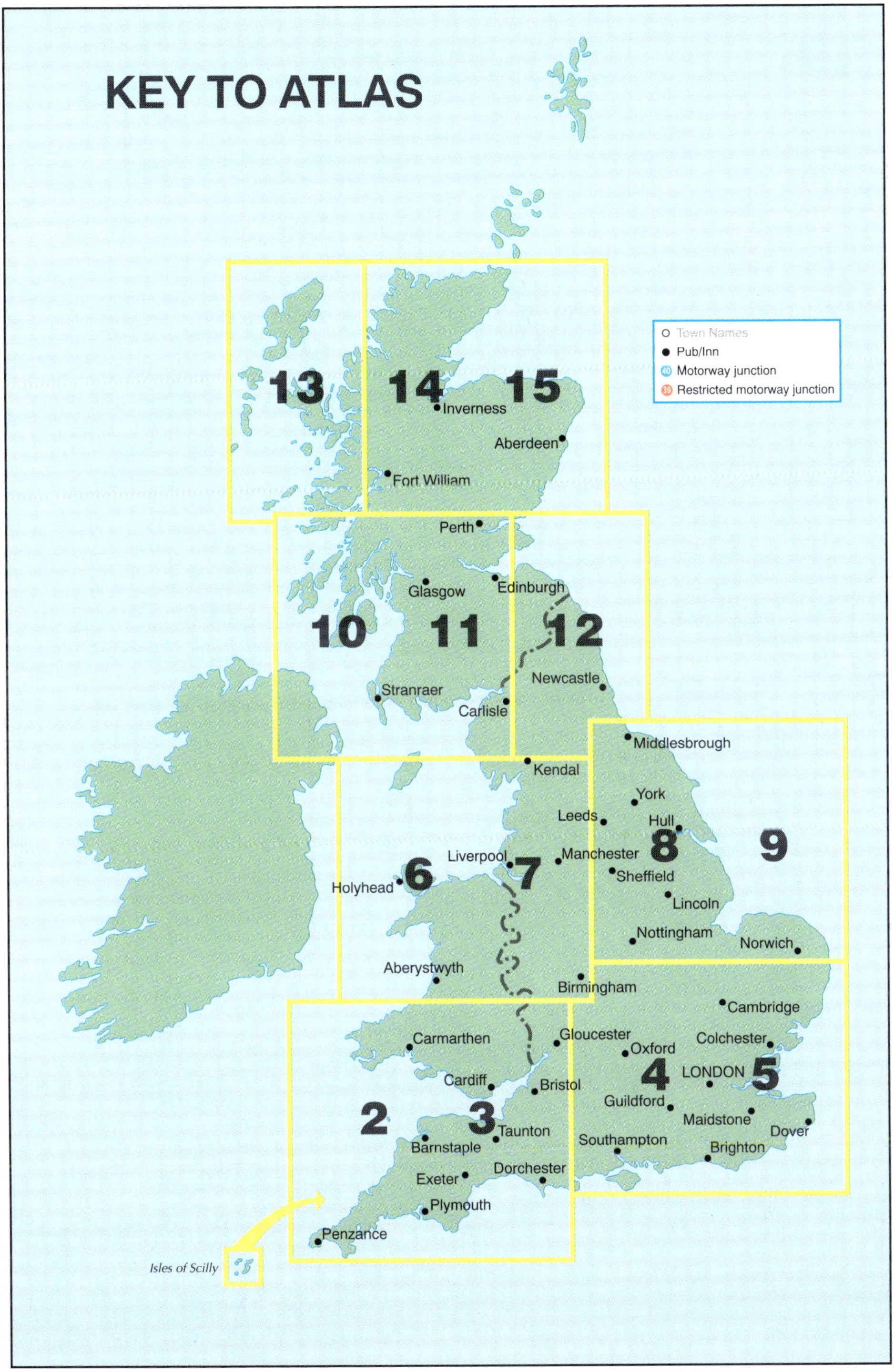
Town Names
Pub/Inn
Motorway junction
Restricted motorway junction
13
14
15
Inverness
Aberdeen
Fort William
Perth
Glasgow
Edinburgh
10
11
12
Stranraer
Newcastle
Carlisle
Middlesbrough
Kendal
York
Leeds
Hull
Liverpool
Manchester
8
9
Holyhead
6
7
Sheffield
Lincoln
Nottingham
Norwich
Aberystwyth
Birmingham
Cambridge
Carmarthen
Gloucester
Oxford
Colchester
Cardiff
4
LONDON
5
Bristol
2
3
Guildford
Maidstone
Taunton
Dover
Barnstaple
Southampton
Brighton
Exeter
Dorchester
Plymouth
Penzance
Isles of Scilly

2
SM
SN
SW
SS
SX
Llwyndafydd
Nevern
Cilgerran
Strumble Head
Porthgain
Letterston
Rosebush
Abergo
PEMBROKESHIRE
CARMART
Ramsey Island
Wolf's Castle
Pont-ar-gothi
St Brides Bay
Broad Haven
Haverfordwest
St Clears
Landshipping
Skomer Island
Milford Haven
Amroth
Skokholm Island
Carew
Pembroke Dock
Lamphey
LLANELLI
Stackpole
Caldey Island
Carmarthen Bay
Reynoldston
Town Names
Pub/Inn
BLAE G Blaenau Gwent
BRDGND Bridgend
MYR TD Merthyr Tydfil
NEWPT Newport
RHONDD Rhondda Cynon Taff
TORFN Torfaen
V GLAM Vale of Glamorgan
Zelah
ST AUSTELL
St Agnes
Mithian
Mevagissey
Portreath
St Ewe
Redruth
Truro
Lundy
Portloe
Philleigh
Veryan
Mylor Bridge
St Mawes
Ludgvan
Penzance
St Just
Wendron
Constantine
Helston
Mousehole
Helford Passage
Porthleven
Land's End
Lamorna
Gunwalloe
Gweek
Helford
Mount's Bay
Lizard Point
Barnsta
Hartland Point
Umb
Morwenstow
Okeham
Boscastle
Land's End
Trebarwith
Launceston
Port Gaverne
Altarum
Isles of Scilly
Tresco
St Marys
Trevose Head
CORNWALL
Bodmin Moor
Horsebridge
Peter
Chapel Amble
Buckland
Egloshayle
Monachorum
St Mawgan
Metherell
Dunmere
Bodmin
Bere Ferrers
Lostwithiel
Pillaton
Lanlivery
Lerryn
Saltash
ST AUSTELL
Par
Pelynt
Fowey
Kingsand
SEE INSET
Dodman Point
A487
A486
A484
A485
A478
A40
A4076
A477
A48
A30
A3075
A390
A3078
A39
A3083
A388
A386
A3072
A395
A38
A392
A391
A387

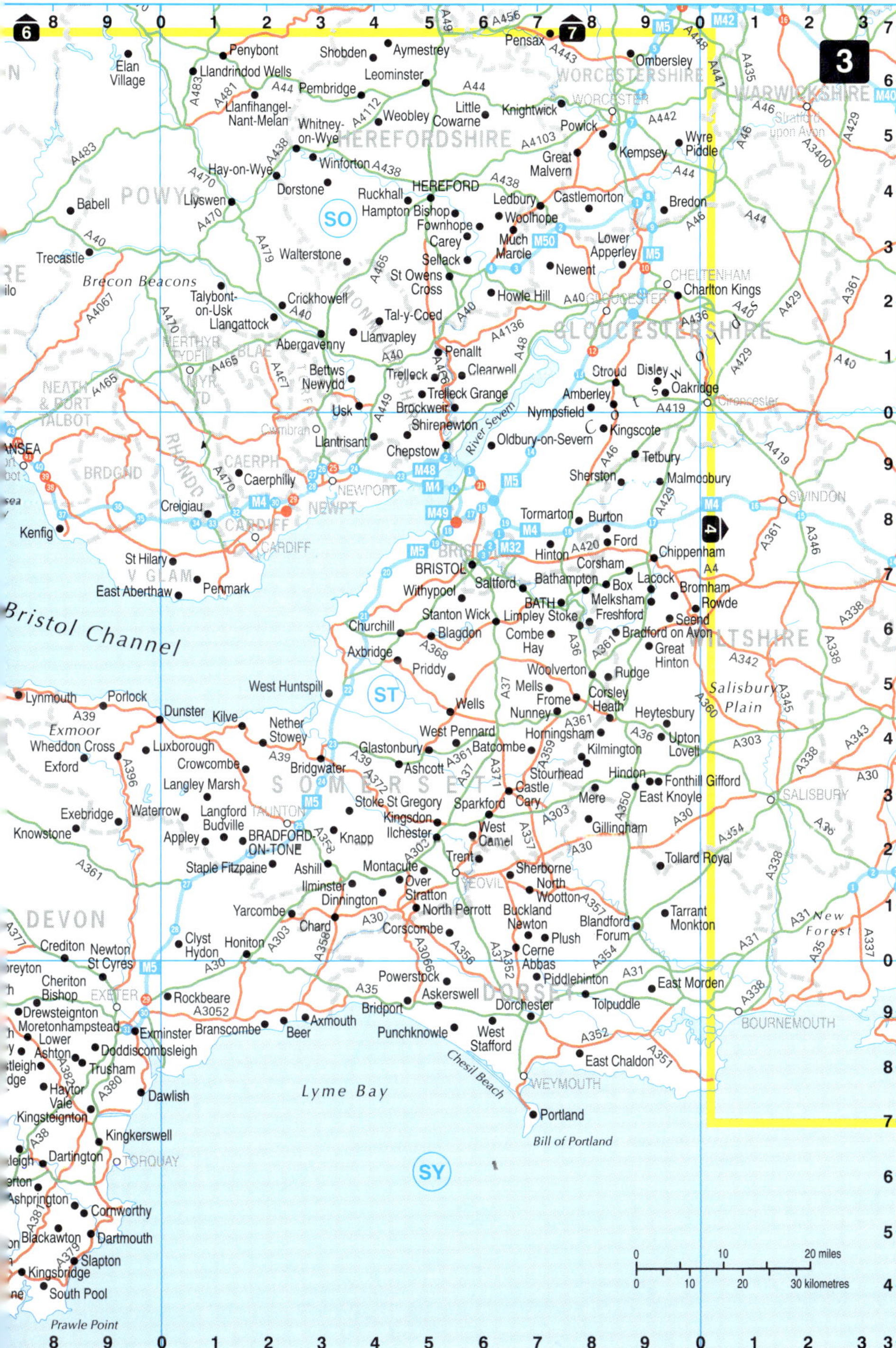

3
6
7
4
Penybont
Llandrindod Wells
Elan Village
Llanfihangel-Nant-Melan
Shobden
Aymestrey
Leominster
Pembridge
Weobley
Little Cowarne
Whitney-on-Wye
Winforton
Hay-on-Wye
Dorstone
Llyswen
Babell
POWYS
HEREFORDSHIRE
Ruckhall
HEREFORD
Hampton Bishop
Fownhope
Carey
Sellack
St Owens Cross
Walterstone
Trecastle
Brecon Beacons
Talybont-on-Usk
Llangattock
Crickhowell
Abergavenny
Tal-y-Coed
Llanvapley
Penallt
Trelleck
Clearwell
Trelleck Grange
Bettws Newydd
Usk
Brockweir
Shirenewton
Llantrisant
Chepstow
River Severn
Oldbury-on-Severn
Pensax
Ombersley
WORCESTERSHIRE
WORCESTER
Knightwick
Powick
Kempsey
Great Malvern
Wyre Piddle
Ledbury
Woolhope
Much Marcle
Castlemorton
Bredon
Lower Apperley
Newent
Howle Hill
CHELTENHAM
Charlton Kings
GLOUCESTER
GLOUCESTERSHIRE
Stroud
Disley
Oakridge
Amberley
Nympsfield
Kingscote
Cirencester
Tetbury
Sherston
Malmesbury
WARWICKSHIRE
Stratford upon Avon
SWINDON
NEATH & PORT TALBOT
SWANSEA
BRIDGEND
CAERPHILLY
Caerphilly
RHONDDA
NEWPORT
Creigiau
CARDIFF
Kenfig
St Hilary
V GLAM
Penmark
East Aberthaw
MERTHYR TYDFIL
Cwmbran
Bristol Channel
Tormarton
Burton
Ford
Hinton
Chippenham
BRISTOL
Corsham
Saltford
Bathampton
Box
Lacock
Bromham
Rowde
Withypool
BATH
Melksham
Limpley Stoke
Freshford
Seend
Stanton Wick
Churchill
Blagdon
Combe Hay
Bradford on Avon
Great Hinton
WILTSHIRE
Axbridge
Priddy
Woolverton
Rudge
Salisbury Plain
West Huntspill
Wells
Mells
Frome
Corsley Heath
Nunney
Heytesbury
Lynmouth
Porlock
Dunster
Kilve
Nether Stowey
Exmoor
Wheddon Cross
Luxborough
West Pennard
Horningsham
Upton Lovell
Glastonbury
Batcombe
Kilmington
Exford
Crowcombe
Bridgwater
Ashcott
Stourhead
Hindon
Fonthill Gifford
Langley Marsh
SOMERSET
Castle Cary
Mere
East Knoyle
SALISBURY
Exebridge
Waterrow
Langford Budville
TAUNTON
Stoke St Gregory
Sparkford
Kingsdon
Gillingham
Knowstone
Appley
BRADFORD-ON-TONE
Knapp
Ilchester
West Camel
Tollard Royal
Staple Fitzpaine
Ashill
Montacute
Trent
Sherborne
YEOVIL
Ilminster
Over Stratton
North Wootton
Dinnington
Yarcombe
North Perrott
Buckland Newton
Tarrant Monkton
DEVON
Chard
Corscombe
Blandford Forum
Plush
New Forest
Crediton
Newton St Cyres
Clyst Hydon
Honiton
Cerne Abbas
Cheriton Bishop
EXETER
Powerstock
Piddlehinton
East Morden
Rockbeare
Askerswell
DORSET
Drewsteignton
Bridport
Dorchester
Tolpuddle
Moretonhampstead
Exminster
Branscombe
Beer
Axmouth
BOURNEMOUTH
Lower Ashton
Doddiscombsleigh
Punchknowle
West Stafford
Trusham
Haytor Vale
East Chaldon
Chesil Beach
WEYMOUTH
Dawlish
Lyme Bay
Kingsteignton
Portland
Bill of Portland
Kingkerswell
Dartington
TORQUAY
Ashprington
Cornworthy
Blackawton
Dartmouth
Slapton
Kingsbridge
South Pool
Prawle Point
SO
ST
SY
M4
M5
M32
M48
M49
M50
M40
M42
A44
A38
A30
A303
A350
A36
A37
A39
A40
A46
A429
A419
A420
A361
A338
A354
A35
0 10 20 miles
0 10 20 30 kilometres

For continuation pages refer to numbered arrows

NORFOLK
Stow Bardolph
Bawburgh
NORWICH
Hethersett
GREAT YARMOUTH
Thompson
Mundford
Brandon Creek
Toft Monks
LOWESTOFT
Beccles
Thetford
St Peter South Elmham
Bressingham
Ely
Rickinghall
Southwold
Blyford
Walberswick
Bardwell
Icklingham
Thornham Magna
Laxfield
Dunwich
Reach
Risby
BURY ST EDMUNDS
SUFFOLK
Saxtead Green
Eastbridge
Horningsea
Cotton
Brandeston
Fen Ditton
CAMBRIDGE
Lidgate
Horringer
Rattlesden
Framsden
Snape
Aldeburgh
Rede
Hartest
Cockfield
Orford
Hindlesham
Lavenham
Chelsworth
Melton
Orford Ness
Duxford
Hinxton
Lindsey
Kersey
Hadleigh
IPSWICH
Great Chishill
Great Yeldham
Stoke-by-Nayland
Levington
Wendens Ambo
Honey Tye
Arkesden
Castle Hedingham
Nayland
Higham
Holbrook
Erwarton
Blackmore End
Dedham
Rickling Green
Gosfield
Harwich
Little Dunmow
Langham
COLCHESTER
The Naze
Feering
Wivenhoe
Little Canfield
Young's End
High Easter
ESSEX
Great Braxted
Wickham Bishops
CLACTON-ON-SEA
Little Waltham
CHELMSFORD
Tillingham
Sample
North Fambridge
Stock
Burnham-on-Crouch
Foulness Island
Basildon
SOUTHEND-ON-SEA
Horndon on the Hill
Leigh-on-Sea
R Thames
Tilbury
Cliffe
Sheerness
Isle of Sheppey
MARGATE
Eynsford
Boyden Gate
Burham
Wrotham
Faversham
Hernhill
Fordwich
Borough Green
Ightham
Newnham
Selling
CANTERBURY
Chillenden
Ivy Hatch
MAIDSTONE
Ringlestone
Chilham
Shipbourne
Linton
Lenham
Hadlow
KENT
Pluckley
Brabourne
Speldhurst
Smarden
ASHFORD
TUNBRIDGE WELLS
Biddenden
Hartfield
Goudhurst
Iden Green
Withyham
Folkestone
CHANNEL TUNNEL TERMINAL
Mayfield
Strait of Dover
Black Boys
Old Heathfield
Ewhurst Green
Chiddingly
Warbleton
Dungeness
Gun Hill
Cowbeech
Upper Dicker
HASTINGS
Berwick
Arlington
West Firle
Alciston
Litlington
EASTBOURNE
Exceat
Beachy Head
TL
TM
TQ
TR
TV
1 North Moreton
2 South Moreton
3 Dorchester-on-Thames
4 Brightwell Baldwin
5 Bolter End
6 Fawley
7 Great Missenden
8 Cholesbury
9 Middle Barton
10 Upper Oddington
11 Bledington
12 Painters Forstal
13 Eastling
Town Names
Pub/Inn
0 10 20 miles
0 10 20 30 kilometres

For continuation pages refer to numbered arrows

7
12
8
4
3
North York Moors
Yorkshire Dales
THE PENNINES
NORTH YORKSHIRE
LANCASHIRE
GREATER MANCHESTER
WEST YORKSHIRE
SOUTH YORKSHIRE
CHESHIRE
DERBYSHIRE
NOTTINGHAMSHIRE
STAFFORDSHIRE
SHROPSHIRE
WEST MIDLANDS
LEICESTERSHIRE
WREXHAM
FLINTS
Peak District
SD
SE
SJ
SK
SO
SP
Ambleside
Troutbeck
Outgate
Hawkshead
Near Sawrey
Kendal
Crosthwaite
Haverthwaite
Heversham
Canal Foot
Cartmel
Beetham
Casterton
Barbon
Dent
Kirkby Lonsdale
Clapham
MORECAMBE
LANCASTER
Galgate
Ravenstonedale
Muker
Bainbridge
Askrigg
Hawes
Leyburn
Akebar
West Witton
East Witton
West Burton
Carlton
Hubberholme
Buckden
Starbotton
Kettlewell
Ramsgill
Pateley Bridge
Settle
Threshfield
Burnsall
Linton
Hetton
Appletreewick
Dacre Banks
Wigglesworth
Slaidburn
Whitewell
Waddington
Clitheroe
Broughton
Elslack
Blacko
Newall
Harrogate
Ripon
Thirsk
Northallerton
Scotch Corner
Malton
YORK
Selby
LEEDS
Goole
Pontefract
Wakefield
Dewsbury
Barnsley
DONCASTER
Bilsborrow
Goosnargh
Fence
Haworth
Whalley
Ribchester
Widdop
Thornton
Wrea Green
PRESTON
Blackburn
Mereclough
Shelf
Halifax
Clifton
Darwen
Shuttleworth
Ripponden
Huddersfield
Heskin Green
Belmont
Bamford
Bury
Meltham
Parbold
Delph
Diggle
Oldham
Mossley
Ashton-under-Lyne
MANCHESTER
Bootle
St Helens
LIVERPOOL
Didsbury
Warrington
Broomedge
Penketh
Birchvale
Hayfield
Hope
SHEFFIELD
Barnston
Runcorn
Prestbury
Pott Shrigley
Castleton
Over Peover
Bollington
Tideswell
Litton
Northwich
Wildboarclough
Little Longstone
CHESTER
Swettenham
Little Budworth
Eaton
Wincle
Warmingham
Smallwood
Handley
Burwardsley
CREWE
Butterton
Marford
Broxton
Barthomley
Tissington
Tushingham cum Grindley
Wybunbury
Ashbourne
Malpas
STOKE-ON-TRENT
Burleydam
Whitchurch
Hanmer
Cresswell
NOTTINGHAM
DERBY
Wem
Hodnet
Norbury Junction
Abbots Bromley
STAFFORD
Burton upon Trent
LOUGHBOROUGH
Nesscliffe
Yoxall
SHREWSBURY
TELFORD
Madeley
Coalport
Norton
Minsterley
LEICESTER
Oakham
Much Wenlock
Morville
WOLVERHAMPTON
Picklescott
Bridgnorth
Heathton
West Bromwich
Nuneaton
Netherton
BIRMINGHAM
Munslow
Stourbridge
Hopton Wafers
COVENTRY
Llanfair Waterdine
Ludlow
Bewdley
M6
M55
M65
M61
M66
M62
M58
M60
M63
M56
M53
M621
M1
M18
M180
M181
A1(M)
M54
M42
M5
M69
M45
M6
A685
A683
A684
A6108
A59
A65
A682
A6068
A629
A640
A628
A57
A616
A623
A6
A56
A556
A54
A53
A523
A515
A50
A52
A516
A564
A38
A51
A518
A519
A34
A41
A49
A442
A458
A5
A528
A495
A525
A483
A570
A565
A458
A4117
A4113
A448
A449
A45
A452
A444
A46
A14
A4304
A427
A47
A607
A606
A6003
A447
A42
A453
A60
A617
A6097
A614
A631
A620
A619
A618
A156
A159
A161
A635
A638
A63
A163
A64
A170
A167
A168
A172
A169
A61
A658
A58
A590
A591
A5087
A533
A534
A500
A441
A4
A488
A489

For continuation pages refer to numbered arrows

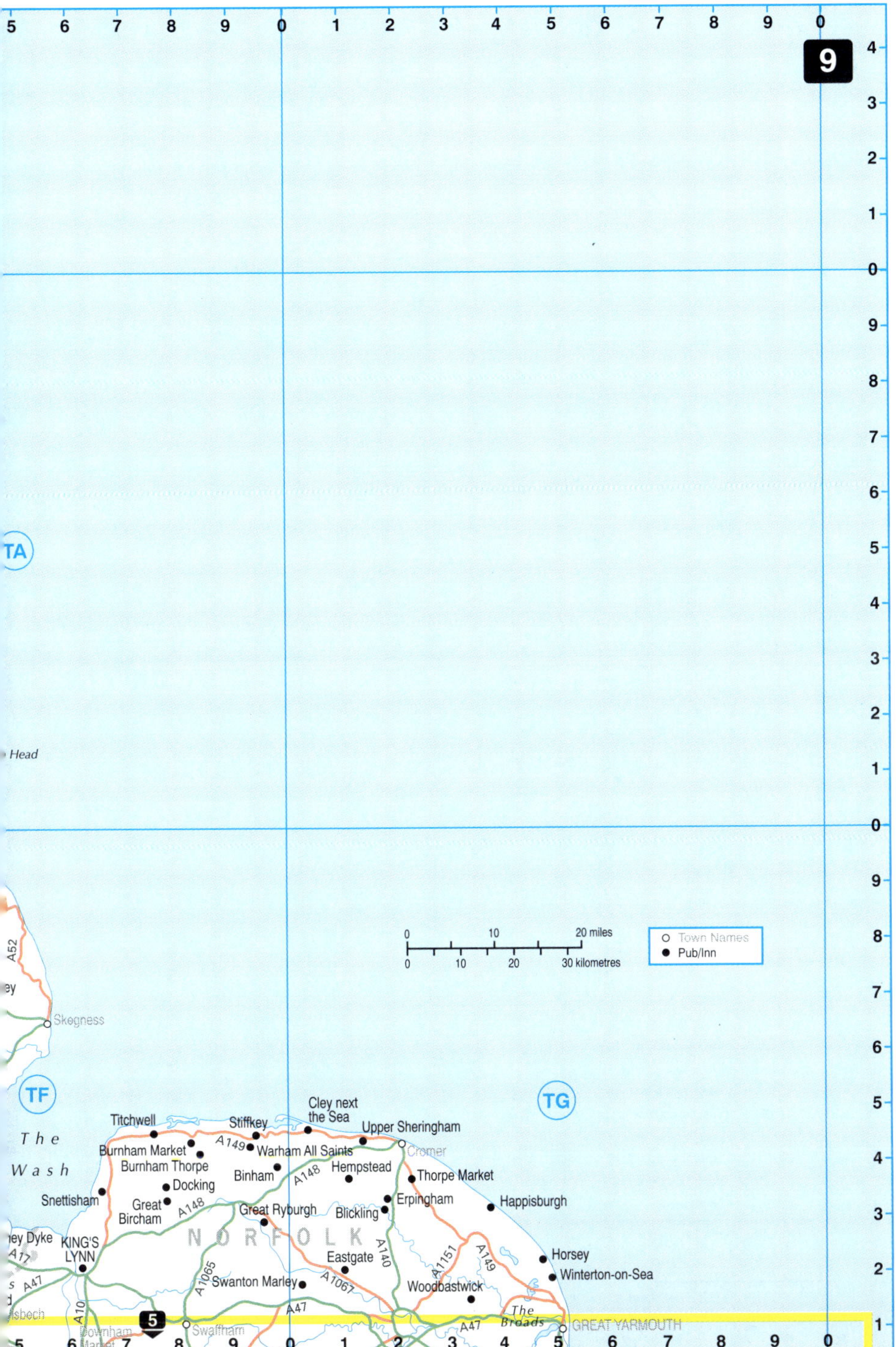

9
TA
TF
TG
Head
Skegness
The Wash
Titchwell
Stiffkey
Cley next the Sea
Upper Sheringham
Cromer
Burnham Market
Burnham Thorpe
Warham All Saints
Binham
Hempstead
Thorpe Market
Docking
Snettisham
Great Bircham
Erpingham
Happisburgh
Great Ryburgh
Blickling
KING'S LYNN
NORFOLK
Eastgate
Horsey
Winterton-on-Sea
Swanton Marley
Woodbastwick
The Broads
GREAT YARMOUTH
Swaffham
Downham Market
A52
A149
A148
A1065
A1067
A140
A1151
A47
A10
A17
0 10 20 miles
0 10 20 30 kilometres
Town Names
Pub/Inn
5

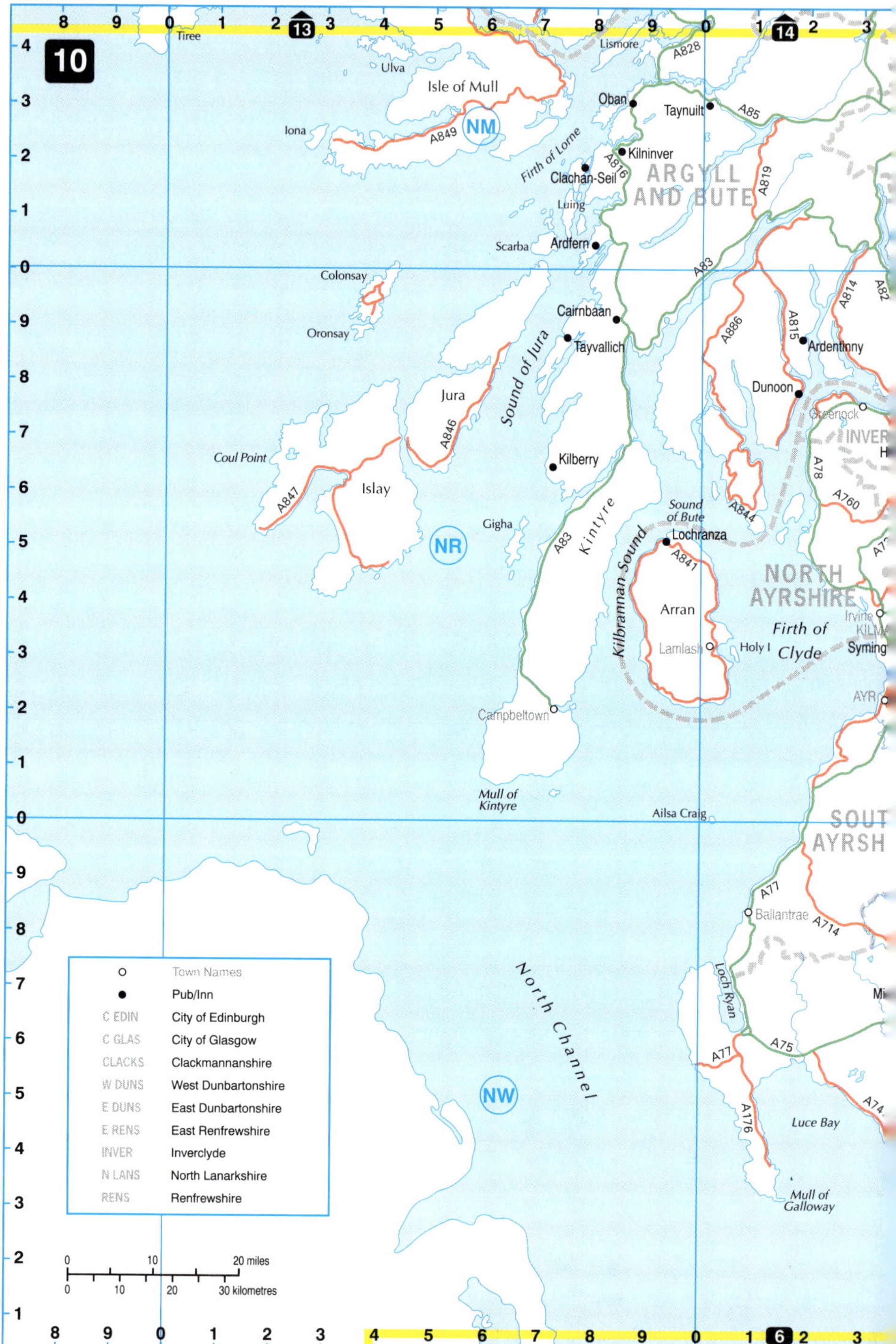

For continuation pages refer to numbered arrows

11
15
12
7
PERTH AND KINROSS
DUNDEE CITY
Arbroath
DUNDEE
Almondbank
PERTH
Firth of Tay
Comrie
St Andrews Bay
St Andrews
NO
Glendevon
Falkland
FIFE
Fife Ness
Kinross
Kinnesswood
Lower Largo
NORTH
SEA
Markinch
Isle of May
Cleish
CLACKS
STIRLING
Kirkcaldy
Firth of Forth
FALKIRK
South Queensferry
Dunbar
Castlecary
EDINBURGH
WEST
LOTHIAN
EAST
LOTHIAN
St Abb's Head
C EDIN
Ratho
MIDLOTHIAN
Lammermuir Hills
COW
N LANS
East Kilbride
Eddleston
NT
Berwick-upon-Tweed
Holy Island
SOUTH
LANARKSHIRE
Uplands
Coldstream
Galashiels
Innerleithen
BORDERS (SCOTTISH)
Tweedsmuir
Jedburgh
The Cheviot Hills
Tushielaw Inn
Hawick
Alnwick
Moffat
Southern
Otterburn
DUMFRIES AND GALLOWAY
NORTHUMBERLAND
Morpeth
Dumfries
New Abbey
Corbridge
Hexham
CARLISLE
Kirkcudbright
NY
Consett
Abbey Head
Solway Firth
Blencogo
Bassenthwaite
DURHAM
WORKINGTON
Penrith
Scales
Dockray
CUMBRIA
Thirlspot
North Head
Buttermere
Seatoller
Lake District
Wasdale Head
Grasmere
A827
A826
A822
A94
A92
A90
A85
A914
A91
A915
A917
A84
A9
A823
M90
A92
A91
A811
M9
M80
A1
A198
M9
M73
M8
A71
A8
A1107
A70
A702
A706
A68
A73
A726
A703
A7
A6105
A701
A697
A6112
M74
A721
A71
A698
A72
A8089
A1
A73
A702
A70
A708
A701
A74(M)
A68
A697
A74
A6088
A1
A701
A702
A76
A68
A696
A712
A709
A74(M)
A713
A711
A75
A69
A695
A68
A710
A75
A689
A689
A6
A691
A596
A595
A686
A689
M6
A66
A66
A68
A5086
A591
A66
A688
A595
A66
6
7
8
9
0
1
2
3
4
5
6
7
8
9
0
1

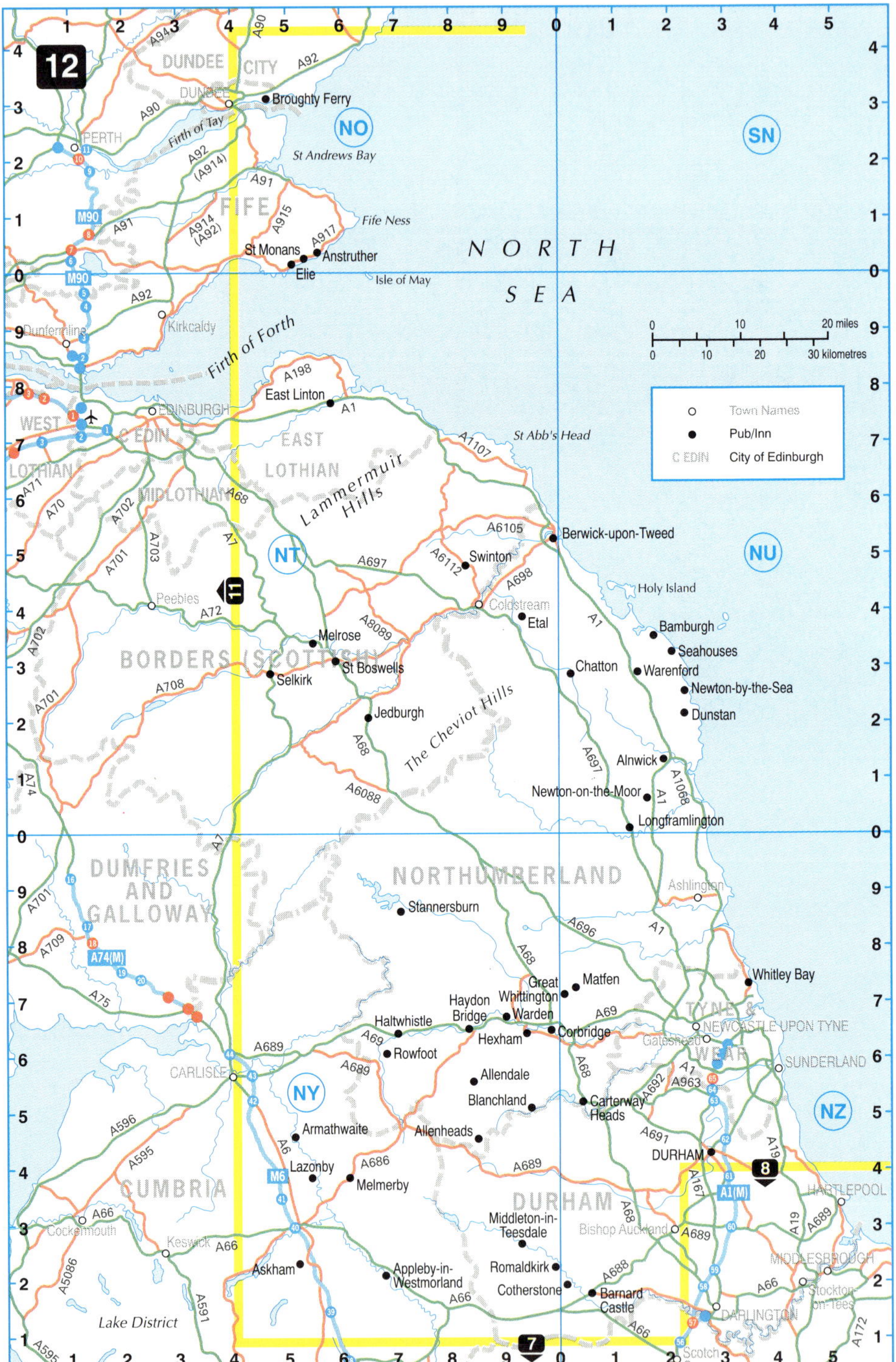

For continuation pages refer to numbered arrows

13
0 10 20 miles
0 10 20 30 kilometres
Town Names
Pub/Inn
NA
NB
NF
NG
NL
NM
Rudha Rhoshanais
(Butt of Lewis)
A857
Tolsta Head
Gallan Head
Broad Bay
Steornabhagh
(Stornoway)
A858
Eye Peninsula
Point of Stoer
The Minch
Outer Hebrides
Scarp
A859
Isle of Lewis
WESTERN ISLES
Summer Isles
Tairbeart
(Tarbert)
Greenstone Point
Toe Head
Shiant Islands
Rudha Reidh
Pabbay
Sound of Harris
Harris
Uibhist a Tuath
(North Uist)
Gairloch
A832
14
Loch nam Madadh
(Lochmaddy)
A867
The Little Minch
Dunvegan Head
A87 (A856)
Sound of Raasay
Rona
Inner Sound
Beinn na Faoghla
(Benbecula)
A896
A890
Applecross
Raasay
Uibhist a Deas
(South Uist)
Rudha Hallagro
A863
A865
Scalpay
Sconser
Kyle of Lochalsh
Dornie
Isle of Skye
A87
(A850)
Loch Baghasdail
(Lochboisdale)
Isleornsay
Sound of Barra
Eriskay
Cuillin
A851
Canna
A87
Barra
A888
Ardvasar
Sound of Sleat
Sound
Rum
Mallaig
Eigg
Inner Hebrides
A830
Mingulay
Muck
Sound of Arisaig
Coll
A861
A884
Loch Linnhe
Dervaig
Sound of Mull
Tiree
10

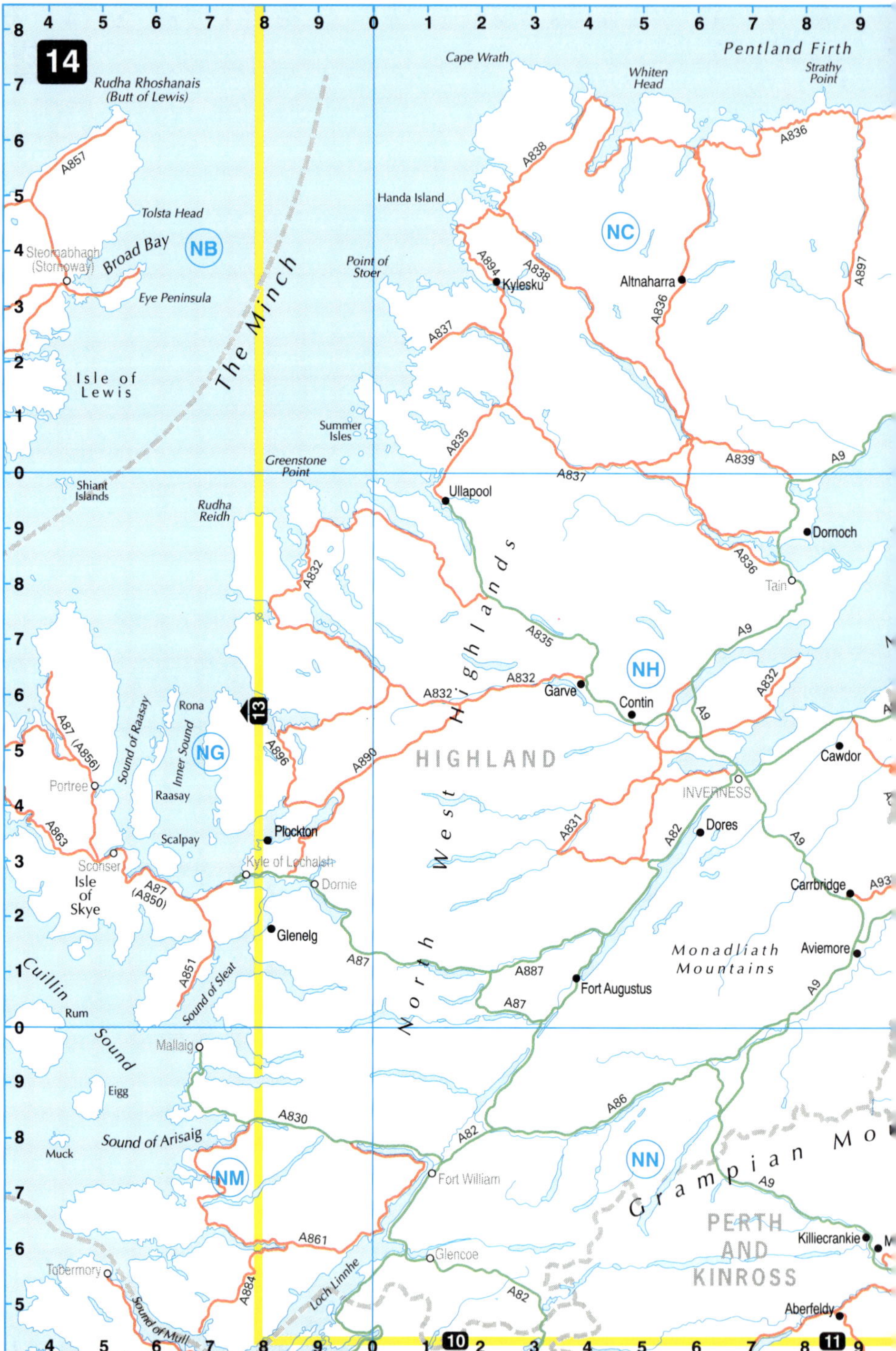

For continuation pages refer to numbered arrows

15
Island of Stroma
Duncansby Head
John O'Groats
A836
Noss Head
A9
A99 (A9)
Lybster
ND
Fraserburgh
A98
A95
Fochabers
A941
NJ
A97
A950
Peterhead
NK
A947
A952
(A92)
A90 (A952)
Huntly
A920
A96
A941
Glenlivet
A97
A920
A90 (A92)
ABERDEENSHIRE
A939
A944
A939
A97
Oldmeldrum
ABERDEEN CITY
A944
ABERDEEN
A93
A980
A93
Kincardine O'Neil
Maryculter
Netherley
A90
A957
Stonehaven
A92
Town Names
Pub/Inn
0
10
20 miles
0
10
20
30 kilometres
NO
Glenisla
ANGUS
A90
A935
A926
A932
Forfar
Lunan Bay
A933
A90
12
Arbroath

Index

A

B

C

D

E

H

S

T

U

V

W

Y

Reader's Recommendations

If you have recently eaten well at a pub or restaurant that is not included in this guide, we should be interested to hear about it. Please send this form to Head of Guidebooks, Editorial Department, AA Publishing, Fanum House, Basingstoke RG21 2EA.

Recommendations, and/or any adverse comments will be carefully considered, but the AA cannot guarantee to act on them nor to enter into correspondence about them. Complaints are best brought to the attention to the management of the pub or restaurant at the time, so that they can be dealt with promptly and, it is hoped, to the satisfaction of both parties.

Your name and address

....

....

....

....

....

....

Name and address of the establishment

....

....

....

....

....

Did you have a bar snack or full meal?

....

Did you eat at lunchtime or in the evening?

....

Approximate cost of a main course bar snack? *(if applicable)*

....

Approximate cost a meal for two £ *(if applicable)*

(continued over)

Style of cooking: eg Pub food/English/French/Italian/Thai/Indian/Chinese/ Other (please specify)

....

....

....

Comments

....

Reader's Recommendations

If you have recently eaten well at a pub or restaurant that is not included in this guide, we should be interested to hear about it. Please send this form to Head of Guidebooks, Editorial Department, AA Publishing, Fanum House, Basingstoke RG21 2EA.

Recommendations, and/or any adverse comments will be carefully considered, but the AA cannot guarantee to act on them nor to enter into correspondence about them. Complaints are best brought to the attention to the management of the pub or restaurant at the time, so that they can be dealt with promptly and, it is hoped, to the satisfaction of both parties.

Your name and address

....

....

....

....

....

....

Name and address of the establishment

....

....

....

....

....

Did you have a bar snack or full meal?

....

Did you eat at lunchtime or in the evening?

....

Approximate cost of a main course bar snack? *(if applicable)*

....

Approximate cost a meal for two £ *(if applicable)*

(continued over)

Style of cooking: eg Pub food/English/French/Italian/Thai/Indian/Chinese/ Other (please specify)

Comments